READER'S DIGEST

ON THE ROAD USA

Reader's Digest

The Reader's Digest Association, Inc.
Pleasantville, New York / Montreal

ON THE ROAD USA

Project Editor	Carroll C. Calkins
Project Art Editor	Gilbert L. Nielsen
Art Editor	Perri DeFino
Project Coordinator	Don Earnest
Associate Editors	Noreen B. Church, Diana Marsh (Copy Desk), Thomas A. Ranieri
Assistant Editor	D. Diefendorf
Project Research Editor	Hildegard Anderson
Research Editors	Shirley Miller, Maymay Quey Lin
Art Associate	Morris Karol
Associate Picture Editor	Richard Pasqual
Project Secretary	Jason Peterson

Contributors

Editor	Margaret Perry
Writers	Shelley Aspaklaria, Robert Brown, David Caras, Laura Dearborn, Diane Hall, Signe Hammer, Guy Henle, Archie Hobson, John Kiely, Anne Lubell, Susan Macovsky, Mona Malone, Richard Marshall, Barbara Rogan, Tim Snider, Richard Sudhalter, Robert Thurston, Carol Weeg, Joseph Wilkinson, Elaine Williams, Donald Young
Copy Editor	Harriett Bachman
Researchers	Mary Hart, Nathalie Laguerre, Mary Lyn Maiscott, Raissa Silverman, Kelly Tasker
Art Associates	Joseph Dyas, Bruce McKillip
Picture Researcher	Marian Paone
Indexer	Sydney Wolfe Cohen

Reader's Digest General Books

Editor in Chief	John A. Pope, Jr.
Managing Editor	Jane Polley
Art Director	David Trooper
Group Editors	Norman B. Mack, Susan J. Wernert, Joseph L. Gardner (International), Joel Musler (Art)
Chief of Research	Monica Borrowman
Copy Chief	Edward W. Atkinson
Picture Editor	Robert J. Woodward
Rights and Permissions	Pat Colomban
Head Librarian	Jo Manning

How to use this volume

This volume contains two books. The first half is the North–South book, covering interstates that run north to south and have odd numbers. The second half is the East–West book, covering interstates that run east to west and have even numbers.

The map on the next two pages shows all the North–South routes and refers you to detailed maps on which numbered brackets indicate segments of each interstate. Maps for the East–West interstates are located in the middle of this volume.

When you turn to any two-page section in the North–South book, you'll see a green line along the outer side of each page. It represents the segment of interstate covered on those two pages. The boxed exit numbers on the lines are keyed to descriptions of the points of interest. The small numbers between the exit boxes indicate the distance (to the nearest mile) between exits. The total number of miles covered by a two-page section is shown at the bottom of each page. Where interstates intersect, you'll find cross-references to the appropriate North–South or East–West section. How to use the East–West book is described in the middle of this volume.

When going south, leaf through the first half of this volume from front to back. When going north, leaf through from back to front. When there are two exit numbers for one destination, the first exit is for drivers headed south; the second, for drivers headed north.

Most entries describe such sites as parks, museums, and natural wonders. But cities are included when they are on or near an interstate. A city's highlights are mentioned; for maps and further information, contact the tourist bureau that's listed. Virtually all the attractions are 30 minutes or less from the interstate exit. And when some spectacular destination—like Mt. Rainier—is within reasonable reach, we have included it in a box entitled "If You Have Some Extra Time."

We have made every effort to provide accurate information. Our driver-reporters visited each site; our researchers contacted each place to double-check their reports. But you may still encounter surprises. A site may change the dates it's open, adopt a new admission policy—or close altogether. Exit numbers also change, and some interstate segments, scheduled to be completed by our publication date, may not be finished. But the detailed maps in the front and middle of this volume and the mileage between exits shown on the interstate lines should help keep you oriented. We trust that any inconvenience will be more than compensated for by the hundreds of suggestions for restful and rewarding things to see and do within easy range of the interstates.   —*The Editors*

About the directions and other information

Mileage at the beginning of an entry is rounded to the nearest half-mile; no mileage is given for a drive of 5 minutes or less. Driving time is approximate and may vary with conditions. In a city entry, mileage and time (to the tourist bureau) appear when the city is not on the interstate. In directions the word *Route* (abbreviated Rte., as in Rte. 101) is used for all numbered noninterstate highways and roads—U.S., state, and local. At the end of an entry, the dates given are inclusive; thus Mon.–Fri. and May–Sept., mean Monday *through* Friday and May *through* September. If admission fees are not mentioned, they are not required. Symbols (below) appear when relevant.

 Picnicking Camping Trailers Hiking Swimming Fishing Wheelchairs

North–South Interstates

MAP EXPLANATION

Featured Interstate Highways

Other Interstate Highways

Divided Highways

Principal Highways

Connecting Highways

SCALE IN MILES AND KILOMETERS

ONE INCH 190 MILES
0 25 50 100 150

ONE INCH 304 KILOMETERS
0 50 100 150 240

•———— 35 ————• Mileage between dots.

✪ Capital Cities

HIGHWAY MARKERS

🔟 Interstate 🔟 U.S. 🍁 Trans-Canada

🔟 State and Provincial ② Mexico Federal

© 1988 H. M. Gousha
Box 49006 • San Jose, CA 95161-9006
Simon & Schuster Inc.

M-12-WJ-1227-S

Map page I

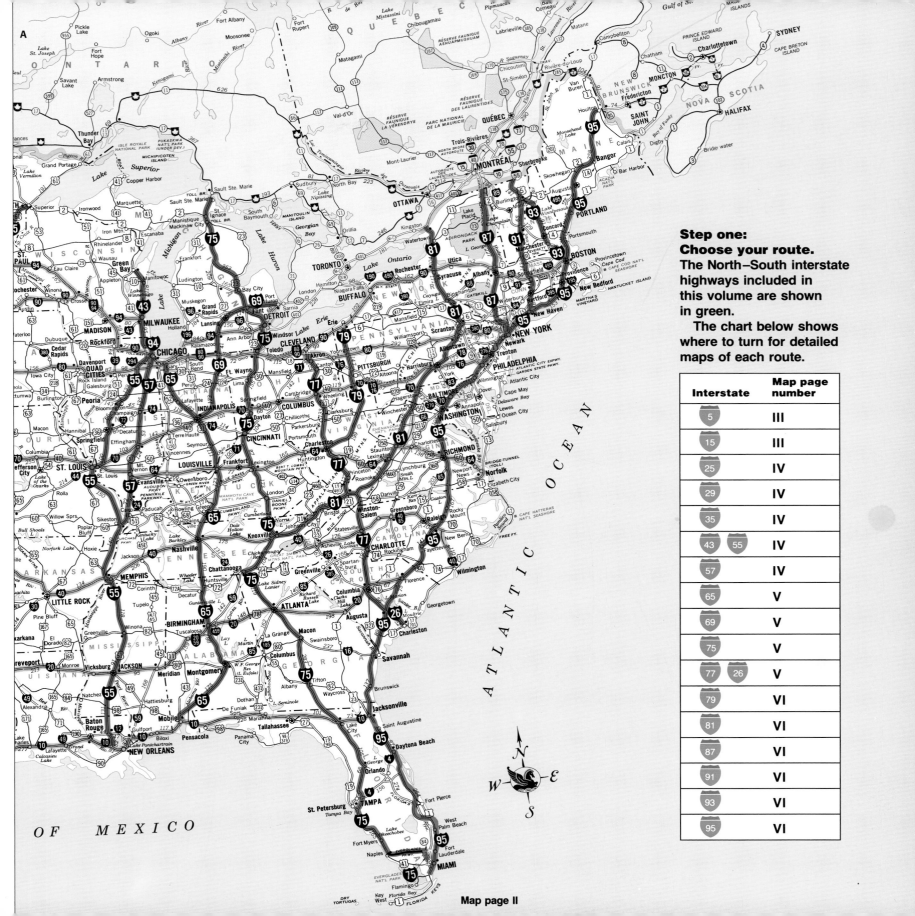

Step one:
Choose your route.
The North–South interstate highways included in this volume are shown in green.

The chart below shows where to turn for detailed maps of each route.

Interstate	Map page number
5	III
15	III
25	IV
29	IV
35	IV
43 55	IV
57	IV
65	V
69	V
75	V
77 26	V
79	VI
81	VI
87	VI
91	VI
93	VI
95	VI

Map page II

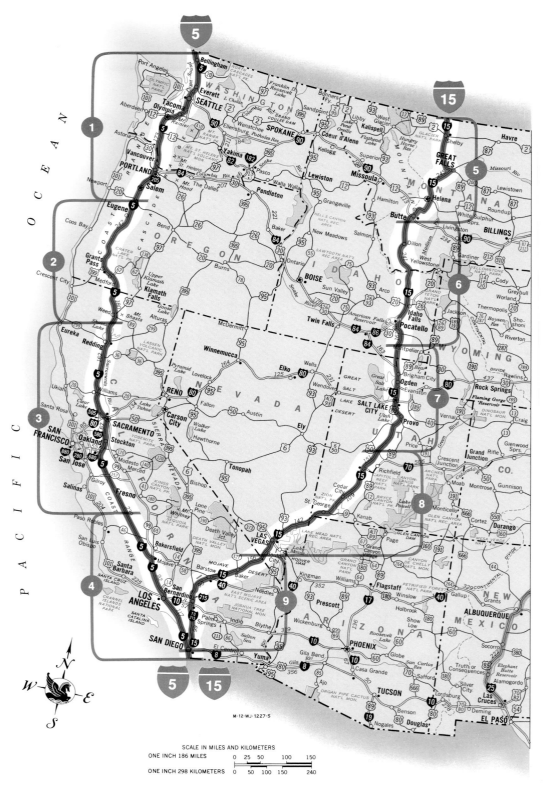

Step two:
Choose a section of the route. Each interstate has been divided into segments indicated by numbered red brackets.

Each number represents a two-page section in the book. Turn to the appropriate numbered section to find the points of interest (and exit numbers) on the bracketed stretch of highway you plan to drive.

The interstates highlighted below are included on map pages III and IV. The others are on map pages V and VI.

SCALE IN MILES AND KILOMETERS

ONE INCH 186 MILES   0   25   50   100   150

ONE INCH 298 KILOMETERS   0   50   100   150   240

M-12-WJ-1227-S

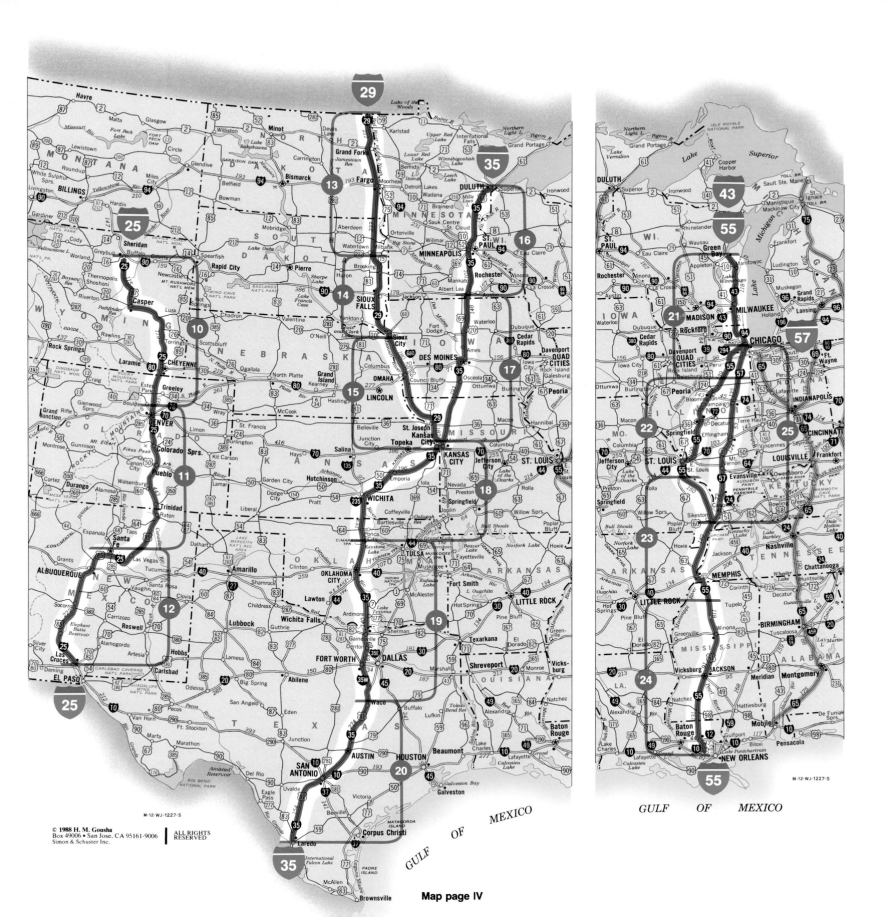

M-12-WJ-1227-S

M-12-WJ-1227-S

Map page IV

GULF OF MEXICO

GULF OF MEXICO

Step two:
Choose a section of the route. Each interstate has been divided into segments indicated by numbered red brackets.

Each number represents a two-page section in the book. Turn to the appropriate numbered section to find the points of interest (and exit numbers) on the bracketed stretch of highway you plan to drive.

The interstates highlighted below are included on map pages V and VI. The others are on map pages III and IV.

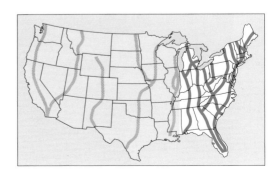

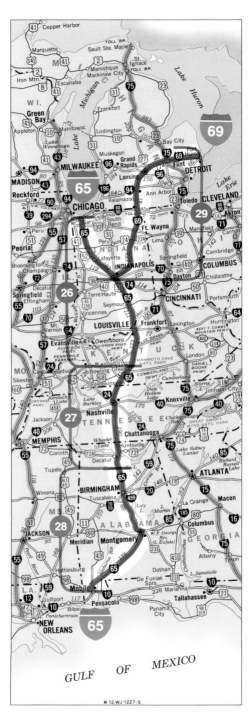

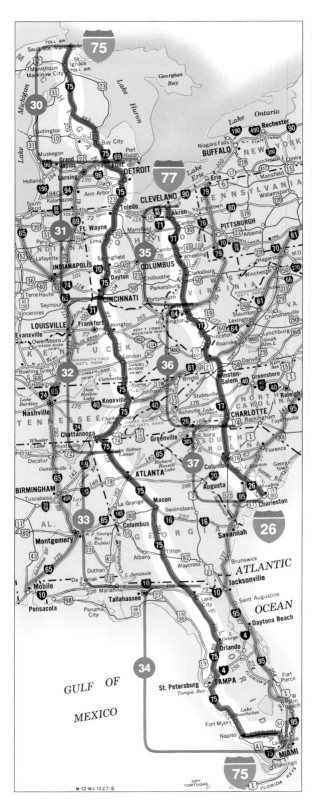

SCALE IN MILES AND KILOMETERS

ONE INCH 186 MILES   0   25   50   100   150

ONE INCH 298 KILOMETERS   0   50   100   150   240

M-12-WJ-1227-S

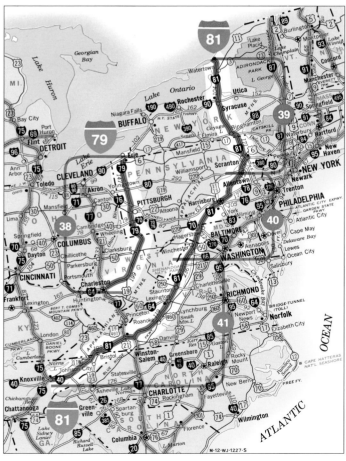

SCALE IN MILES AND KILOMETERS
ONE INCH 151 MILES
ONE INCH 243 KILOMETERS

0 25 50 100
0 50 100 161

M-12-WJ-1227-

M-12-WJ-1227-S

Map page VI

CANADA
U.S.A.
WA

276

23

253

2

250

18

231

42

189

23

90 166

See
E–W book,
sec. 1.

39

127

16

111

6

276 Peace Arch State Park

2 min. Follow signs. The imposing masonry arch, with one support in each country, commemorates the lasting peace between Canada and the United States. It was built by volunteer labor from each country, and children donated the first funds for the creation of the surrounding park with its fine views of Semiahmoo Bay. Broad lawns spread across the border, and formal flower beds provide bright accents of color. *Open year-round.*

276. *A graceful monument in a tranquil setting celebrates a peaceful border.*

253 Bellingham, WA 98227

Visitors/Convention Bureau, 904 Potter St. (206) 671-3990. More than 25 parks affirm this community's appreciation of its beaches, lakes, and woodlands. The splendor of the San Juan Islands can be viewed from a hilltop arboretum, and island cruises and whale-watching trips are offered by the local marina. Handsome brick buildings memorialize the 1890's lumber boom. The Whatcom Museum of History and Art is a fine example of Victorian architecture.

250 Chuckanut Drive
231

Exit 250: south on Rte. 11. Exit 231: north on Rte. 11. This scenic route (allow 35 minutes to drive its 21 miles) adds about 30 minutes to the time it would take on the interstate—if you don't stop. But be forewarned: there are some tempting trails, overlooks, and picnic areas

along the way. At the northern end this curving drive hugs forested cliffs that provide spectacular views of the San Juan Islands across the Bellingham, Chuckanut, and Samish bays. Watch, too, for the distinctive red bark of the broad-leaved Pacific madrones among the lush green of the conifers. At the southern end the drive straightens and runs through fertile farmlands, where barns, in various interesting stages of collapse, may foretell the future of the handsome new and old farm buildings still standing.

189 Boeing 747/767 Division Assembly Plant Tour

4 mi./7 min. West on Rte. 526. The plant, an 11-story structure covering 62 acres, is by volume one of the largest buildings in the world. Boeing 747's and 767's are assembled here, and eight of each can be accommodated at the same time. The tour begins with a slide show of the company history and a 6-minute film on the assembly of a 767, then goes on to the viewing balcony, from which you can see the work under way. On the flight line you'll get a close look at the gigantic, gleaming finished products. *Open Mon.–Fri. Children under 12 not admitted.*

166 Seattle, WA 98101

Convention and Visitors Bureau, 1815 7th Ave. (206) 447-4200. Here on seven hills, almost surrounded by water, is one of America's most dramatic settings for a city. The Space Needle in Seattle Center provides stunning views of Puget Sound, Lake Washington, and (weather permitting) the distant Olympic Range, Cascade Range, and the majesty of Mt. Rainier. Downtown attractions include the waterfront, Pioneer Square, and Pike Place Market, where the display of fresh fruits and vegetables has become an art form.

111 Tolmie State Park

5 mi./10 min. West on Marvin Rd. Unlikely as it may seem, the main attractions here are snorkeling and scuba diving around the wooden barges submerged to create an artificial reef to attract fish and other sea life.

The white buoys offshore mark the barges' location. There is good fishing for flounder and ling cod. At low tide you can also dig for butter, horse, and razor clams. For land-oriented visitors there is an interesting hour-long walk through the forest of some 30 species of trees—mostly firs, maples, and alders. *Open daily Apr.–Sept.; Wed.–Sun. Oct.–Mar.*

105 Olympia, WA 98507

Visitor Convention Bureau, 1000 Plum St. (206) 357-3370. The chief business here is government, as evidenced by the beautifully landscaped grounds and the massive masonry dome of the capitol dominating the skyline. A few blocks to the south is the State Capital Museum, where the state's Indian heritage and pioneer past are memorialized. Priest Point Park, the public market, and the waterfront are other popular destinations.

166. *The Space Needle features an observation deck and revolving restaurants.*

77 Rainbow Falls State Park

16 mi./20 min. West on Rte. 6. The peaceful stillness of this wooded parkland is punctuated by the song of the small cascade that gives the park its name. The waters spill over a wide shoulder of projecting rock, sometimes forming a colorful rainbow in the morning sun.

Swimming, fishing, boating, and hiking through the forest of towering trees entice visitors, who share the woodland with elks, deer, and raccoons. Ducks and gray herons often gather in the river here. A swinging footbridge and several log cabins contribute to the peaceful rustic setting. *Open year-round.*

49 Mount St. Helens National Monument Visitor Center

5 mi./10 min. East on Rte. 504. The mysteries of the Mt. St. Helens cataclysmic eruption that changed the Pacific Northwest skyline in the spring of 1980 are graphically explained at this center, where you can walk through a model of a volcano and look down into a simulated magma chamber. A seismograph constantly monitors the real mountain's activity.

Situated on the shores of scenic Silver Lake, the center is about 60 miles from the mountain, which can be seen on clear days.

A short nature trail follows the lakeshore, where bald eagles, ducks, great blue herons, and other water birds congregate, especially in the mornings and evenings. *Open daily except Thanksgiving Day and Christmas.*

299 Portland, OR 97204

Convention and Visitors Association, 26 SW Salmon St. (503) 222-2223. The favored flowers in the City of Roses are at their best in Washington Park from mid-May to late November. Here, too, is a superb Japanese garden, a forestry center, a museum of science and industry, and some inviting picnic areas. The zoo is famous for its Asian elephants. Other attractions include a unique block-wide landscaped water fountain, a magnificent mansion, museums of Oregon's history and art, and a museum of advertising.

278 Champoeg State Park

6 mi./10 min. West on Ehlen Rd.; bear right on Champoeg Rd. Although the town of Champoeg was washed away by the raging waters of the Willamette in 1861, the site is still of historic significance. For it was here that American settlers on the West Coast formed their first provisional government. Exhibits and films recall this event and the lives of local Indians, explorers, and trappers as well. This beautiful 600-acre park with a spacious rolling landscape of shady lawns and forested campsites is a pleasant place to relax. There are also playfields, and cycling and fishing are popular. Sheep from the neighboring farms often graze on the park grounds. *Open year-round. Admission charged weekends Memorial Day–Labor Day.*

253 Salem, OR 97301

Convention and Visitors Association, 1313 Mill St. SE. (503) 581-4325. The gilded statue of the pioneer standing atop the capitol pays tribute to those who first cleared the wilderness in the Oregon country. By the mid-1800's churches and homes were established, and some interesting examples of these, along with a woolen mill, are maintained in Mission Mill Village. Nearby are the Bush House and the Deepwood Estate, which reveal the taste for beauty and elegance that developed in the 19th century. And historic buildings grace the Willamette University campus.

248 Enchanted Forest Theme Park

3 min. East on Delaney, right on Enchanted Way; follow signs. Among the storybook favorites encountered in three dimensions in this amusement park are Snow White and the Seven Dwarfs, Humpty-Dumpty, the Three Bears, and Alice in Wonderland. There's a slide that goes down through the Old Lady's Shoe, and a bobsled ride on Ice Mountain. Pathways through the pleasant wooded site lead to a haunted house, a castle, a gingerbread house, and a mining town. Children of a certain age are indeed likely to be enchanted. *Open mid-Mar.–Sept. Admission charged.*

Section **1** (366 miles)

See map page III.

If You Have Some Extra Time:

Mount Rainier National Park

127 *60 mi./75 min.* Should you happen to be on the road when "the mountain is out," as they say in Washington, you will see how Mt. Rainier dominates the skyline and why this dormant volcano has become a major point of reference from the shores of Puget Sound to central Washington.

If you would like to experience the mountain up close, allow about 2 hours to get from the interstate to the visitor center at Paradise. A stop at the Kautz Creek Mudflow, just inside the entrance to the park, is of ecological interest. In 1947 a great swatch of forest was devastated, and the road was buried under 20 feet of mud and debris. Here you can see how the forest is regenerating itself.

At the Longmire Visitor Center the mountain looms even larger against the sky but is still at a distance. It is not until you drive the 10-mile stretch of zigzag road to the aptly named Paradise Visitor Center that the full impact of Mt. Rainier hits you. From here you'll have a stunning panoramic view of evergreen forests, alpine meadows, glacier fields, and the ice-capped 14,410-foot summit rising grandly above it all.

From Paradise you can walk the trails, where in summer more than 30 kinds of wildflowers light up the landscape. You may also glimpse mountain goats, deer, marmots, and birds of many kinds. *How to get there: Exit 127, south on Rte. 7 to Elbe; follow signs on Rte. 706 to park entrance. Open year-round. Admission charged.*

216 Linn County Historical Museum, Brownsville

4 min. East on Rte. 228, left on Main St., right on Park Ave. Linn County, which originally extended to the Rocky Mountains and south to California, has lost a little in size; but, as evidenced by the museum and historic houses here, a lively sense of the past is retained. It's not surprising that the museum, in a turn-of-the-century bungalow-style depot, with four railroad cars, a circus train, and a caboose, has a large collection of railroadiana. A prairie schooner that brought some early settlers to the Brownsville area establishes the pioneer presence, and the period settings of replicas of a barbershop, a millinery salon, a general store, a bank, and a telephone switchboard recall the mid-19th century. The nearby Moyer House, built in 1881, can be toured on request. A self-guiding walking tour covers other historic buildings. *Open Tues.–Sat., P.M. Sun., and holidays May–Sept.; Thurs.–Sat. and P.M. Sun. except holidays Oct.–Apr. Admission free but donations encouraged.* 🚐 ♿

119. *The Bengal tiger's cool appraisal encourages the use of a telephoto lens.*

199 / 195 Armitage State Park

Exit 199: 4 mi./7 min. West on Van Duyn Rd., left on Coberg Rd. Exit 195: 3.5 mi./7 min. West on Belt Line Rd., right on Coberg Rd. This small and well-kept park is on the McKenzie River, a favorite of fishermen and boaters. There's picnicking in the shade of the redwoods, maples, and firs, recreation areas on the spacious lawns, and hiking along the 1½-mile winding trail that follows the edge of the river. The McKenzie joins the Willamette, another famous Oregon river, about 2 miles downstream from here. *Open year-round. Admission charged on weekends and holidays.* 🪑 🚶 🎣 ♿

194 Eugene, OR 97401

Convention and Visitors Bureau, 305 W. 7th Ave. (800) 452-3670; (800) 547-5445 outside OR. The pleasant tree-shaded campus of the University of Oregon is an attraction in itself, and the Museum of Art has an extensive collection of Oriental art. Also on campus is the Museum of Natural History. The city's pioneer and Victorian eras are represented in the Lane County Historical Museum. Rhododendrons are featured in Hendricks Park, while Owens Municipal Park is noted for its roses.

119 Wildlife Safari, Winston

5 mi./8 min. West on Rte. 42, right on Lookingglass Rd. to Safari Rd.; follow signs. There are about 100 species, some threatened or endangered, among the 600 animals and birds that roam freely in this spacious and attractive setting. The 2½-mile self-guiding auto route leads through the Asian section, which has Bengal tigers, yaks, and deer, along with rheas, emus, and other unusual birds. The African area includes hippo ponds, the world's largest antelope, lions, and Cape buffaloes. Zebras, elephants, cheetahs, wildebeests, Bactrian camels, and rhinos are among the other exotic animals you may also see at close range. At the Safari Village you'll find a petting zoo for children, as well as animal shows and elephant rides. *Open year-round. Admission charged.* 🪑 🚐 🚶 ♿

76 Wolf Creek Tavern

2 min. West from exit. The route that I-5 follows between Portland and Sacramento is much like that of the original stagecoach road in the 1860's. The trip took 6 days then, and some 60 stage stops along the way supplied a change of horses as well as food and lodging for passengers. The Wolf Creek Tavern has provided virtually continuous service for more than 100 years. It is an operating restaurant and hostelry, but a self-guiding tour of the premises is encouraged. In the ladies' parlor, the men's sitting room, and the main staircase, all beautifully restored, one can savor an intimate sense of a bygone era. *Open daily except first 2 weeks in Jan.* 🪑 ♿

61. *Kayaks and the large tour boat are dwarfed by Hellgate's rocky ramparts.*

61 Hellgate Canyon and Indian Mary Park

9.5 mi./25 min. West on Merlin-Galice Rd. to Hellgate Overlook. Two adjacent sites—Hellgate Canyon and Indian Mary Park—reveal contrasting aspects of the scenic Rogue River. At Hellgate, where it rushes through the rocky narrows, the river is popular with white-water boatmen and rafters, whom you may see in action. At the park the river widens, slows its pace, and becomes inviting to fishermen and swimmers. The perspective from water level dramatizes the canyon's formations of folded rock, sheer cliffs, and forested slopes. In the shady recesses of the park, the native trees and shrubs have been agreeably supplemented with species from many other states and nations. *Open year-round.*
🪑 ⛺ 🚐 🚶 🏊 🎣

<table>
<tr><td>40</td></tr>
<tr><td>27</td></tr>
</table>

Jacksonville National Historic Landmark

Exit 40: 11.5 mi./15 min. South on Old Stage Rd. Exit 27: 6 mi./15 min. West on Barnett Rd., right on Riverside Ave., left on Main St. (Rte. 238); follow signs. During the gold boom in the mid-19th century, Jacksonville survived fire, flood, and epidemic. But when the gold began to run out and the railroad bypassed the town, it went into decline. In recent years more than 80 buildings, dating from the 1850's up to 1916, have been restored and refurbished, and the town has become a national historic landmark.

The handsome courthouse, from about 1883, houses a museum, and there's a bank in the impressive U.S. Hotel, built in 1880. Pioneer Village (admission charged), north of town, features such early-day necessities as a smokehouse, a country schoolhouse, a saloon, and Applegate Valley's first store and post office. The large collection of horse-drawn vehicles includes a hearse, a stagecoach, and several covered wagons. *Open year-round.*

19 Lithia Park, Ashland

Exit 19: 3 mi./10 min. Right on Valley View Rd., left on Rte. 99 to Ashland; follow signs. Exit 11: 5 mi./10 min. North on Rte. 99 to Ashland; follow signs. The 100-acre Lithia Park takes its name from the area's naturally carbonated mineral water (you can taste it in the park's fountain). Created in 1893 as a hub of culture and entertainment, the park, now an outstanding example of American landscape architecture, is the scene of evening band concerts, ballet performances, and silent films in its open-air theater.

Quiet forest paths follow Ashland Creek through the park, which is located in a canyon at the base of Mt. Ashland. Lithia Park also has a Japanese garden, duck ponds, tennis courts, and a formal rose garden. An excellent booklet describes more than 90 kinds of shrubs and trees, including towering silver maples, Russian olives, and a wide variety of Japanese maples, found on the Woodland Trail. This tranquil place can excite the senses and calm the spirit. *Open year-round.*

CMS. *Just beyond the forested ridge the interstate cuts a swath between Siskiyou Lake in the foreground and Mt. Shasta's majestic profile in the distance.*

CY Siskiyou County Museum, Yreka

Central Yreka exit. 3 min. West to Main St.; follow signs. Most of the essential tools, equipment, materials, firearms, and miscellaneous goods required to survive (and prosper) in the early days of the county are thoughtfully displayed in this excellent museum, a replica of an 1854 ranch hotel.

Prehistoric times are represented by marine fossils and mastodon bones. There are early Indian artifacts, as well as those of the Chinese, who came to this area in the mid-1850's, when gold was discovered. The country store, the blacksmith's shop, and the millinery and music shops are much as they were in pioneer days. A separate building houses the museum's collection of vintage horse-drawn vehicles. *Open Mon.–Sat., P.M. Sun. Memorial Day–Labor Day; Tues.–Sat. rest of year.*

CMS Mount Shasta Scenic Drive

Central Mt. Shasta exit. 5 min. East on Lake St., left on Pine St., right on W. Alma St., left on Everitt Memorial Hwy. The 14-mile roadway through the Shasta-Trinity National Forest takes you up the mountain to the 7,750-foot level, past outstanding views of sweeping valleys and purple mountain peaks. At the roadway's end Mt. Shasta seems close enough to touch.

If you wish to extend your stay, pitch a tent at either McBride Springs or Panther Meadows campground. Hiking trails leading to the mountain's 14,162-foot summit begin where the scenic drive stops. *Open year-round up to Bunny Flat (12 mi.); last 2 mi. closed in winter because of snow.*

CAS Castle Crags State Park

Castella exit. 2 min. West from exit. Formed some 170 million to 225 million years ago as granite became heated and forced its way up through the earth's surface, these jagged mountain peaks, carved by glaciers, soar to a height of some 6,000 feet. A 2-mile drive from the park's entrance will take you to an overlook for a spectacular panorama of these and other mountain peaks etched against the skyline.

Camping, picnicking, swimming, hiking, and trout fishing are especially delightful in this thickly forested park, where the fragrance of the evergreen trees fills the crystal-clear air. *Open daily except during heavy snows.*

61

21

40

13

27

8

19

8

11

OR
CA

32

CY

35

CMS

10

CAS

38

5

5

CV

5

CR

31

RB

30

O/C

42

ROUTE
20

58

See
E–W book,
sec. 17.

80

J

CV Shasta Dam and Lake

Central Valley–Shasta Dam exit: 6 mi./20 min. West on Rte. 151. With a spillway three times higher than Niagara Falls and two-thirds of a mile across, the dam was built between 1938 and 1949 to store surplus winter runoff for summer irrigation and for flood control in the Sacramento and San Joaquin valleys. It traps the waters of the McCloud, Pit, and Sacramento rivers, forming Lake Shasta—one of the nation's most diversified recreation areas—and creating one of California's largest power plants. The dam's visitor center has an observation theater overlooking the spillway.

With marinas, hiking trails, a camping and picnic area, superb fishing sites, and some 345 houseboats available for rent, the lake is a magnet for vacationers seeking active refreshment as well as relaxation. *Open year-round.*

CR Shasta State Historic Park

Central Redding Hwy. exit: 8 mi./15 min. West on Rte. 299. During California's 1850 gold rush, when all roads north of San Francisco stopped at Shasta City, a boomtown that shipped out as much as $100,000 in gold each week, it became known as the Queen City of the North. Its prosperity lasted approximately 18 years, until a new north-south stage route, and later the railroad, bypassed it. The city's ruins, now preserved in this park, evoke life in the region during the mid-1800's. The museum, formerly the county courthouse, has the original jail cells and contains a fine collection of artifacts, books, and art related to California. A tree-shaded picnic area is popular with visitors. *Open daily except Thanksgiving Day, Christmas, and New Year's Day. Admission charged.*

RB William B. Ide Adobe State Historic Park

Red Bluff/N. Main St. exit: 5 min. South on N. Main St., left on Adobe Rd. Red Bluff/S. Main St. exit: 4 mi./10 min. North on S. Main St., right on Adobe Rd. William B. Ide was a leader of the Bear Flag Rebellion, an 1846 revolt by American settlers in California against their Mexican rulers. Ide built his adobe house overlooking the scenic Sacramento River around 1850 and established a ferry that became an important link on the California-Oregon Trail. He also served the county as a judge and, on one occasion, as court clerk, prosecutor, and defense attorney—on the same case. In the well-restored house a wide range of period household items and farm tools is on display. The park provides a pleasant picnic spot, and you can fish for trout and salmon. *Open year-round.*

O/C Bidwell Mansion State Historic Park, Chico

Orland/Chico exit: 21 mi./30 min. East on Rte. 32 to Chico, left on Sacramento Ave., right on the Esplanade. The charm and elegance of another era are recalled in this parklike estate. In 1865 John Bidwell, farmer, statesman, and humanitarian, started to build his three-story, 26-room mansion on the 22,000-acre Rancho Arroyo Chico in order to successfully woo and win the socially prominent, idealistic Annie Ellicott Kennedy of Washington, D.C. The shaded lawns, the footbridge over Arroyo Creek, and groves of towering oaks and sycamores invite strolling. *Open daily except Thanksgiving Day, Christmas, and New Year's Day. Admission charged.*

ROUTE 20 Colusa – Sacramento River State Recreation Area

9 mi./15 min. East on Rte. 20. Despite its humble origins (it was once a city dump), this 63-acre park with a half-mile sandy beach, junglelike river forest, and boat-mooring facilities, now appeals to anglers, picnickers, campers, boaters, and sunbathers. A looped trail leads from the day-use area to the forest and beach. The Sacramento River offers good fishing, including king salmon, steelhead, sturgeon, catfish, and striped bass. A variety of birds inhabit the recreation area. *Open year-round. Admission charged.*

J Sacramento, CA 95814

J St. exit: Convention & Visitors Bureau, 1421 K St. (916) 442-5542. The gold rush that made this city a boomtown and the state capital is memorialized in the Old Sacramento Historic District and Sutter's Fort State Historic Park. The fort—the first restored in the U.S.A.—has many original shops and historic artifacts. An Indian museum in the park features the handiwork of those who found their way to this region without the lure of gold. The Crocker Art Museum, with its opulent Victorian gallery, features old masters' drawings, Oriental art objects, contemporary paintings, and photographs. Car and rail buffs will enjoy the California Towe Ford Museum and the California State Historic Railroad Museum.

CV. *Snowmelt from Mt. Shasta and adjacent peaks contributes to the waters of the lake.*

If You Have Some Extra Time: Yosemite National Park

ROUTE 140 **91 mi./2 hr.** As you enter the stone corridor of the Yosemite Valley, you are sure to be overwhelmed by the magnificence of the granite domes, vertical cliffs, sculptured spires, and dazzling waterfalls. Elsewhere in the park—as if this were not enough—there are alpine meadows, limpid lakes, creeks and rivers, and scores of mountain peaks. Three superb stands of sequoia trees, including the Mariposa Grove, with its 2,700-year-old Grizzly Giant soaring up to a height of 209 feet, provide awe-inspiring views for both you and your camera. Of the six major waterfalls in the park, Bridalveil, with its gossamer veil, is the loveliest, and Yosemite, with its three-part cascade, is the most dramatic, especially during the heavy runoff in May. In spring, wildflowers carpet the meadows, and in fall the park blazes with colorful foliage.

Stop off at the visitor center for the slide program and information about the very impressive range of plants, birds, and animals to be found in the park. Trail maps available there show the many options for exploration.

The road to Glacier Point—open from Memorial Day, or earlier if plows can get through, until the first heavy snow in November—leads to a breathtaking panorama of the valley and the peaks of the Sierra Nevada. From this perspective the scale of these mountains is made dramatically clear. The entire range, about 400 miles long and 50 to 80 miles wide, is a single block of granite. In this context the valley that seems so overwhelming when you are on its floor is no more than a minor crack in that incredible mass of rock. *How to get there: Rte. 140 exit, east on Rte. 140 to park entrance. Open year-round. Admission charged.*

EM Micke Grove Park and Zoo, Lodi

Eight Mile Rd. exit: 7 mi./11 min. East on Eight Mile Rd., left on Micke Grove Rd. At this attractive and varied 65-acre park, you'll find a museum with an extensive collection of farming tools and equipment; a zoo featuring the bald eagle and the rare snow leopard; a nature trail with signs noting the effect of agriculture on land and wildlife; an amusement park with a small merry-go-round and a miniature train ride; indoor and outdoor picnic areas; and a Japanese garden designed by the onetime superintendent of the Imperial Palace Garden in Tokyo. *Park open year-round; zoo open daily except Christmas; museum open P.M. Wed.–Sun. except Thanksgiving Day, Christmas Eve, Christmas, and New Year's Day. Admission charged.* 🍴🚶🏊

J. *The leisurely pace of the past can be enjoyed in Sacramento's Historic District.*

ROUTE 120 Caswell Memorial State Park

13 mi./16 min. East on Rte. 120, right on Manteca Rd., left on W. Ripon Rd., right on Austin Rd. A hundred years ago, the riverbanks and plains of the Central Valley were dominated by towering oak trees native only to California. A 138-acre slice of that magnificent hardwood forest is preserved at this park, which contains some "weeping oaks" that are 100 feet tall and 6 feet in diameter. Throughout the park you'll spot rabbits, foxes, and muskrats, and in the nearby Stanislaus River there are bluegill, bass, catfish, sturgeon, buffalo carp, and salmon. The history of the area is recounted in a shelter at the head of the Oak Forest Nature Trail. *Open year-round. Admission charged.* 🍴⛺🚐🚶🏊🎣

ROUTE 152 San Luis Reservoir State Recreation Area

6 mi./10 min. West on Rte. 152. These three man-made lakes, which cover more than 16,000 acres, are a welcome sight for travelers. Swimming, boating, and water-skiing are the main activities. Fishermen find this is a good spot for striped bass, bluegill, and crappie. Perched on a knoll at the end of a massive earth-filled dam is the Romero Visitors' Center, run by the California Department of Water Resources. It provides a sweeping view of the dam, the San Luis

Reservoir, and the mountains beyond. One exhibit tells the story of the California State Water Project, which, together with the Central Valley Project, is one of the world's largest public works enterprises. *Park open year-round; visitor center open daily except Thanksgiving Day, Christmas, and New Year's Day. Admission charged for park.* 🍴⛺🚐🏊🎣♿

COA R. C. Baker Memorial Museum, Coalinga

Coalinga exit: 11 mi./13 min. West on Jayne Ave., left on Elm Ave. This charming museum tells the story of oil and coal discovery in a small western boomtown during the days of the wild frontier. Coalinga's Spanish-sounding name is actually a contraction of Coaling Station A, a rail coal-loading site around which the town grew. The museum, named for the man whose oil tool company once occupied the building, displays an amazing assortment of items. A sampling of things you'll see might include 300 pieces of barbed wire; the jaw, teeth, and tusks of a fossilized elephant; a prehistoric snail; an Arabian saddle; an early telephone booth; old Christmas cards; a pair of beaded moccasins; oilfield equipment; period clothing and furniture; and photos of the damage inflicted upon Coalinga by a major earthquake in 1983. *Open Mon.–Sat. and P.M. Sun. except holidays.*

STO — Tule Elk State Reserve

Stockdale Hwy. exit: 5 min. West on Stockdale Hwy., left on Morris Rd., right on Station Rd. Enormous herds of tule elk that once roamed California were reduced almost to extinction by hunters and by the conversion of marshland to farmland in the 19th century. This grassland reserve now shelters 32 of the rare animals. Visitors can view the elk, some with impressive racks of antlers, from a tree-shaded picnic area. The animals congregate at two nearby watering holes rimmed with marsh plants, where they come to wallow in the water and cool off—one of their favorite activities. *Open year-round.*

STO — Kern County Museum, Bakersfield

Stockdale Hwy. exit: 20 mi./28 min. East on Stockdale Hwy., left on Chester Ave. The county's pioneer life is vividly displayed here in more than 50 buildings, including a rough-hewn log cabin, a one-room schoolhouse with a potbellied stove, a dentist's office with an early X-ray machine, a ranch house and cook wagon, and a train depot with telegraphic equipment. The museum features Indian artifacts, dioramas of animals and birds native to the area, historical photographs, and exhibits of trade tools. At the nearby Lori Brock Children's Museum (a separate entity with the same hours) youngsters can take part in various hands-on educational experiences. *Both museums open daily except Thanksgiving Day, Christmas, and New Year's Day. Admission charged.*

FT — Fort Tejon State Historical Park

Ft. Tejon exit: 1 min. West from exit; follow signs. Territorial expansion and the discovery of gold in the 1850's called for army troops to patrol the frontier. The assignment went to the 1st Dragoons, who dressed somewhat like French Legionnaires. Visitors can inspect their sparsely furnished barracks, the officers' residence, and the cramped orderlies' quarters. A tree-shaded brook borders the museum, which provides a graphic representation of life in the army, the ways of the Indians in the area, and the story of the Camel Corps, led by Lt. Edward F. Beale. *Open daily except Thanksgiving Day, Christmas, and New Year's Day. Admission charged.*

MAG — Six Flags Magic Mountain, Valencia

Magic Mountain Pkwy. exit: 1 min. Follow signs. From a breathtaking stand-up roller coaster ride to shooting the rapids in a raft, this theme park has plenty of excitement. Several rides loop above the park, and flowers, trees, and blossoming vines line the walkways. Looney Tunes characters stroll about, and children can ride a pirate ship or spin in a birdcage in Bugs Bunny World. There are games, a petting zoo, performing dolphins and sea lions, and demonstrations of crafts. *Open daily late May–mid-Sept.; weekends and school holidays, mid-Sept.–late May except Christmas. Admission charged.*

PAS — Los Angeles, CA 90071

I-10 *Pasadena Frwy. exit (south): Visitor Information Center, 505 S. Flower St., Level B. (213) 689-8822.* The maze of freeways in and around L.A. can frustrate even the most unflappable driver, but a little aggravation is a small price to pay for this vast city's considerable charms. Mulholland Drive in the Hollywood Hills or the 27-story City Hall Tower downtown provide spectacular views of the city. Hollywood Boulevard has changed since the old days, but Mann's Chinese Theater is a plush reminder of the glamour that was. For a look at modern-day moviemaking, take the Universal Studios tour. If you prefer still pictures, sample the outstanding collections at the Los Angeles County Museum of Art. Griffith Park, the largest municipal park in the country, has over 4,000 hilly acres to explore. The Los Angeles Zoo has 2,500 animals, and the 165-acre Descanso Gardens boasts an astonishing variety of blossoming plants.

ROUTE 710 — The Queen Mary and the Spruce Goose, Long Beach

17 mi./21 min. South on Rte. 710. Now permanently berthed at Long Beach, the *Queen Mary* was among the grandest of the great ocean liners. The lifestyles of the privileged who crossed the Atlantic on it are reflected in its opulent art deco ballrooms, staterooms, and promenade deck. Displays also recall its troop-carrying days during World War II. On the lower decks you can see one of the ship's engine rooms and a large collection of intricately crafted models of ships, including many famous ones. The other major attraction here is now called by its nickname. The *Spruce Goose*, an enormous wooden airplane with a 320-foot wingspan, was a pet project of the eccentric millionaire Howard Hughes. Flown only once, the white aircraft now sits dramatically over a mirrorlike reflecting pool, with its roomy cargo bay, flight deck, and cockpit open for viewing. Also here is a village of shops and restaurants. *Open year-round. Admission charged.*

HAR — Disneyland, Anaheim

Harbor Blvd. exit: 5 min. Follow signs. "The greatest piece of design in the United States" is how a noted designer once described Disneyland. This 76-acre theme park may also be one of the America's

HAR. *Who better than Disney could create a working replica of a riverboat?*

greatest pieces of enchantment. You can shake hands with the Seven Dwarfs, take a jungle cruise down a murky lagoon, see swashbuckling pirates in action, sip a soda at an old-fashioned turn-of-the-century ice cream parlor, and pose for snapshots with Mickey Mouse, Donald Duck, and other Disney characters. Horse-drawn buggies and sleek monorails provide transportation to the seven theme areas: Adventureland, Frontierland, Fantasyland, Tomorrowland, New Orleans Square, Bear Country, and Main Street U.S.A.—all perfectly maintained and spotlessly clean. *Open year-round. Admission charged.* ♿

74. *Fountains and gardens echo the mission's unpretentious style and charm.*

ROUTE 74 — Mission San Juan Capistrano

2 min. West on Rte. 74; follow signs. Although best known for the swallows that return each March 19, this charming mission is worth a visit any time of year. The ruins of the old stone church built in 1797 by Father Junípero Serra are adorned with great vines of bougainvillea. Still standing is his long rectangular chapel with elaborate murals and an extravagant baroque altar. The bells of Capistrano hang in wall arches next to the church, and the surrounding courtyards are graced with fountains and planted with lilies and palms. Stone vats for tallow making, a smelter, and dyeing, weaving, and candlemaking shops reflect the villagelike atmosphere of an early California mission. *Open year-round. Admission charged.*

ROUTE 78 — Lawrence Welk Museum, Escondido

20 mi./30 min. East on Rte. 78, left on I-15, right on Deer Springs Rd.; follow signs. Sidewalks paved with musical instrument shapes lead to this museum in a theater lobby in a luxurious retirement community named for the popular bandleader. A recreation of the Welk bandstand and stage set dominates a room lit with crystal chandeliers. Welk's long career is chronicled in photos, letters, gold records, and awards, including the ballroom-dancing years from the 1920's through the 1950's. You'll see his first accordion and scenes from his television show. *Open year-round.* ♿

CV — Torrey Pines State Reserve

Carmel Valley Rd. exit: 3 mi./8 min. West on Carmel Valley Rd., left on N. Torrey Pines Rd.; follow signs. This beautiful, rugged coastal reserve is named for the rare Torrey pines that grow on the hilltops. It rises from a long, sandy beach and a series of canyons to a clifftop plateau. The canyons are densely covered with succulents, laurel sumac, and sage, and are veined with sandy footpaths. From Red Butte, with its needle-sharp rock formations, you can watch for migrating whales from December through March and enjoy magnifi-

CV. *Contorted shapes of the Torrey pines reveal the unremitting power of the wind.*

cent ocean views any time of year. Two trails lead down to the beach. Swimming is permitted, but be careful: rip currents are present, and the waves can be rough. The adobe visitor center serves as a living museum and the starting point for ranger-guided nature walks. *Open year-round. Admission charged.* 🏕 🚶 🐾 ♿

ROUTE 209 — Cabrillo National Monument, San Diego

10 mi./20 min. South on Rte. 209; follow signs. Juan Rodríguez Cabrillo was the first European to explore this section of the Pacific Coast, and it was this windswept finger of land that greeted him when he sailed into the harbor here. Today, at this park named in his honor, he wouldn't recognize the view to the east: a panorama of ocean freighters against a backdrop of San Diego's white skyscrapers. But to the west is the vast unchanged Pacific, where whale watching is now popular from late December to mid-March. Exhibits in the visitor center concentrate on the peninsula's natural features and Indian artifacts as well as Spanish explorers. There is also a restored lighthouse; and a 2-mile round-trip nature trail, edged by chaparral, runs alongside the harbor. *Open year-round.* 🚶 ♿

ROUTE 163 — San Diego Zoo

5 min. North on Rte. 163; continue on Richmond St.; follow signs. With a population of 3,200, representing some 800 species from around the world, this fine zoo is a veritable United Nations of the animal kingdom. If you have time, take the 40-minute guided bus tour for orientation, then return to your favorite spots on foot or by means of outdoor escalators and moving walkways. You'll see Australian koalas, highland gorillas, miniature deer, giant anteaters, Mongolian wild horses, and the world's largest collection of parrots and parrotlike birds. The children's zoo, scaled to four-year-olds, features a nursery where baby mammals are bottle-fed, bathed, and diapered. There are elephant and camel rides, animal shows, an overhead Skyfari, "behind the scenes" group tours, and special facilities for the disabled. *Open year-round. Admission charged.* 🏕 🚶 ♿

22

HAR

35

ROUTE 74

30

ROUTE 78

16

CV

9 — See E–W book, sec. 56.

ROUTE 209 — 3 — 8

ROUTE 163 — See N–S book, sec. 9.

15

End I-5

If You Have Some Extra Time: Glacier National Park

363 **90 mi./2 hr.** The name is exactly appropriate. Not only are glaciers a dominant aspect of the park today; they and their predecessors over millions of years are its creators. The irresistible force of moving ice sculpted the cliffs, spires, and ridges, shaped the slopes where forests thrive, and leveled the land for the prairies and meadows. Some 50 remaining glaciers still feed more than 200 lakes and 1,450 miles of streams and rivers.

The St. Mary Visitor Center at the east entrance has explanatory exhibits and information about the many interesting varieties of flora and fauna to be found here.

The Going-to-the-Sun Road, the park's only east-west crossing, is open from about June to mid-November. If you have time for it, this 50-mile drive is one of the most spectacular in the country. At least try to take the first 5 miles to the parking turnoff, from which Triple Divide Peak is visible to the southeast. The runoff flows to three oceans: the Arctic, the Pacific, and the Atlantic.

About 13 miles farther west, at Logan Pass, the road crosses the Continental Divide. From the visitor center here there's a 3-mile round-trip self-guiding nature trail and boardwalk across brooks and meadows to an unforgettable view overlooking Hidden Lake. This reserve of more than a million acres is worthy of an extended visit. There are some 15 inviting campgrounds to stay in and many miles of trails for hiking and horseback riding. But even a brief encounter with such a magnificent wilderness is better than none at all. *How to get there: Exit 363, west from Shelby on Rte. 2, then right on Rte. 89 to the eastern park entrance. Open year-round, but eastern roads are usually closed owing to heavy snow mid-Nov.–mid-Apr. Admission charged.*

358 Williamson Park

4 min. East from exit, right on Marias Valley Rd.; follow signs. Nestled in the scenic Marias River Canyon and shaded by stands of cottonwoods, this beautiful little park is a popular picnic spot. Hikers enjoy exploring the canyon walls, and there is a playground for children. A local hillside serves as an informal rifle range, no doubt to the consternation of the large deer population. The river can be a busy place with its swimmers, boaters, and anglers (catfish, northern pike, and walleye are the most frequent catches). Since only primitive camping is permitted, this bucolic riverside park is ideal for those who want to get away from it all. *Open Apr.–Sept. Admission charged.*

280 Charles M. Russell Museum and Studio, Great Falls

5 min. East on Central Ave. W. (becomes 1st Ave. N.), left on 13th St. N. The Old West is preserved in Charles Russell's paintings, which depict scenes from the lives of the Plains Indians and the American cowboy. Born in 1864, Russell was one of the most important and prolific of the western painters, producing over 4,500 works. This outstanding cultural complex includes Russell's log cabin studio, with his easel and brushes, clay figurines, and the Indian, Mexican, and cowboy guns and artifacts that appear in his paintings. A museum houses 7,500 works by Russell and his contemporaries, a Browning firearm collection, and Edward Curtis's Indian photographs. The artist's restored house, built around 1900, may be viewed only in the summertime. *Open daily May–Sept.; Tues.–Sun. Oct.–Apr. except Thanksgiving Day, Christmas, New Year's Day, and Easter. Admission charged.*

280 Giant Springs State Park, Great Falls

9 mi./20 min. East on Central Ave. W. (becomes 1st Ave. N.), left on 15th St., right on River Dr. The centerpiece of this beautiful 100-acre riverside park is Giant Springs—one of the world's largest, discharging 134,000 gallons of water per minute. It was discovered by Meriwether Lewis during his portage around the Great Falls in 1805. Plaques tell of Lewis and Clark's portage and the dangers they faced from storms and grizzly bears. Today the major pastimes are picnicking, hiking, and casting in the Missouri for trout. The springs' constant 52° F temperature and its pure water make it ideal for growing trout. A self-guiding tour of the fish hatchery includes audio programs about fish production, growth, and management. *Open year-round.*

270 Ulm Pishkun State Monument

7 mi./20 min. West on access road; follow signs. This high, sheer cliff jutting up from 50 to 80 feet above the prairie was used as early as A.D. 500 by primitive hunters. At the *pishkun*—an Indian word for a cliff or corral where they killed buffalo—large herds were stampeded over the cliff to their deaths. The carcasses provided food for the winter, hides for clothing and shelter, and bones for tools. The jump was abandoned after the mid-1800's, when buffaloes became scarce. Today you'll see the centuries-old piles of bones and tepee rings from Indian encampments. Signs explain the history of the buffalo jump and the daily life of prairie dogs, which have a sizable town here near the picnic area. *Open daily mid-Apr.–mid-Oct.*

209 | Gates of the Mountains

5 min. East on access road. While exploring the Missouri River in the summer of 1805, Meriwether Lewis referred to this canyon that the river flows through as the Gateway to the Rocky Mountains and noted that some of the cliffs appeared to be on the verge of tumbling over on him. Cruise boats have been plying the waters of the canyon for more than a century, and today it appears much the same as it did in Lewis's day—a rugged land of limestone bluffs crumpled and folded by the earth's inner pressure, punctuated by caves, and etched with ancient Indian petroglyphs.

The cruises provide an excellent opportunity to see wildlife. Rocky Mountain goats inhabit the cliffs, and bighorn sheep visit salt licks at the river's edge. More than 100 species of birds have been sighted. The cruise boat stops at the Meriwether Campground—the very spot where the Lewis party made camp. You can stay here and explore the backcountry for a few hours, or a few days, and catch a later boat back. *Cruises daily Memorial Day–Labor Day. Fee charged.*

209. *The drama of the cliffs that Lewis saw is now somewhat muted by the trees.*

192 | Norwest Bank Helena Museum of Gold

5 min. West on Rte. 12, left on Last Chance Gulch St. What better place for a gold museum than in a bank? Henry Elling, the bank's first president, came here in 1898 with his collection of gold nuggets. The collection has grown over the years to include samples from 18 Montana gulches and from California and Alaska. Gold in many of its native forms is on display here—from pumpkin seed and sheet gold to flakes and gold in quartz. Of some 700 nuggets, the largest, from Alaska, has a troy weight of 46 ounces. "Character" nuggets, sculpted by nature into unusual shapes, are valued by collectors, and the museum has a fine assortment of them, including cowboy boots, buffalo skulls, and Jimmy Durante. A collection of prized gold coins includes $4 "Stellas," with a mid-1980's value of $1,500 each; Lewis and Clark commemorative dollars, minted in 1904–05; and a mid-19th-century octagonal $50 piece, which is also known as a California slug. *Open Mon.–Fri. except holidays.*

192 | Frontier Town

19 mi./25 min. West on Rte. 12. Frontier Town was created by the late John Quigley. In the 1940's he selected a 20-acre site atop the 6,320-foot-high MacDonald Pass and, working mostly by himself for some 30 years, built this town of logs and rocks. You'll see a frontier fort, a jail, a bank, a general store, a chapel, and other buildings furnished with antiques. The complex contains 46 rooms, 54 log doors, and more than 260 tons of stonework. Quigley also made wood carvings and log furniture, hewing a bar top from a 50-foot-long Douglas fir log. The 75-mile view of the Helena Valley and distant mountains is spectacular. *Open daily Apr.–Oct. Admission charged.*

164 | Elkhorn

19.5 mi./30 min. South on Rte. 69, left on Elkhorn Rd.; follow signs. Off the beaten track but worth the visit, this old mine site is the genuine article, and it presents some colorful opportunities for photographers. Elkhorn was a late-19th-century boom-town, with a peak population of about 2,500. The Elkhorn Mine produced some 9 million ounces of silver, 8,500 ounces of gold, and 4 million pounds of lead. Today, along with 30 or 40 timeworn buildings, there are still mine tailings, equipment rusting in the forests, and abandoned shafts in this privately owned ghost town nestled amid mountains and thick fir forests. Trailheads lead into the surrounding Deerlodge National Forest, where rugged mountain hiking, camping, trout fishing, snowmobiling, and cross-country skiing are popular. *Open year-round.*

126 / 124 | Copper King Mansion, Butte

5 min. Exit 126: east on I-115, left on Montana St., left on Granite St. Exit 124: north on Montana St., left on Granite St. This luxurious 32-room mansion is an outstanding example of Victorian architecture. It was built in the 1880's by William Andrews Clark, a U.S. senator and a multimillionaire entrepreneur with interests in real estate, banking, and oil as well as copper companies. The opulently furnished home has frescoed ceilings, Tiffany glass windows, hand-carved woodwork, ornate chandeliers, and an organ with 825 pipes. On the 1½-hour guided tour, you'll see fine examples of period art and glassware, dolls, toys, and women's fashions. *Open year-round. Admission charged.*

64 / 63 | Beaverhead County Museum, Dillon

Exit 64: 2 min. South on Montana St. Exit 63: 4 min. North on Atlantic St., left on Bannack St. This county was the site of Montana's first gold rush. Later on, ranching, timber, farming, and the mining of other minerals became the linchpins of the economy. In this large structure the county's diverse and colorful past is reflected in exhibits that include Indian artifacts, boomtown memorabilia, branding irons and farming implements, gold and mining paraphernalia, weapons from both world wars, and collections of china, crystal, glass, silver, and watches. Several mounted animals are excellent examples of taxidermy. *Open daily May–Aug.; P.M. Mon.–Fri. Sept.–Apr.*

209

17

192

28

164

38

See E–W book, sec. 2.

90

126

2

124

90

64

1

63

4

15

59. *The three R's were dispensed here, sometimes to the tune of a hickory stick.*

59 Bannack State Park

25 mi./30 min. West on Rte. 278, left on access road; follow signs. This park has a surprising main attraction—a ghost town. Bannack, which was Montana's first territorial capital, sprang up in 1862 when gold was discovered in Grasshopper Creek. In addition to saloons, dance halls, and stores, the town had two hotels, a billiard parlor, a Chinese restaurant, and a Masonic temple with public school. A self-guiding tour covers some two dozen sites, and the visitor center has exhibits on Bannack's past. *Open year-round.*

44 Clark Canyon Reservoir

3 min. West on Rte. 324. Some 10 miles long and 3 miles wide, this extensive lake created by damming the Red Rock River is popular for outdoor activities of all kinds. A sandy shore close to several campgrounds draws bathers and picnickers, and fishermen from boat and shore angle for trout and ling cod, known to grow rapidly in these waters. Hunting for waterfowl is an attraction in fall, while ice fishing and snowmobiling are popular pastimes in the winter. A monument on the north shore marks the site where Lewis and Clark camped and traded with Indians when they changed from boats to horses to continue exploring the vast new territories that America had acquired in the West. *Open year-round.*

44. *Light snow and thin ice add a wintry dimension to a Montana March morning.*

172 U.S. Sheep Experiment Station

2 min. East on access road; follow signs. Five thousand to 10,000 sheep, depending on the season, are kept here, some in corrals, others on the range pastures of the station. Jointly run by the U.S. Department of Agriculture and the University of Idaho College of Agriculture, this research facility is not well known, despite its excellent facilities for visitors. A guided tour includes lambing pens, shelters, and displays of different breeds of sheep. Depending on the season, you may see lambs being born (2,500 each year), sheep sheared, or guard dog and predator-control experiments. *Open Mon.–Fri. except holidays.*

143 Beaver Dick Recreation Area

15 mi./20 min. East on Rte. 33. This small wayside park is named after "Beaver Dick" Leigh, an English-born mountain man who married a Shoshone Indian woman and lived in this area until 1899. He was well known as a guide, outfitter, and picturesque character. The park adjoins the Henry Fork of the Snake River, where anglers like to try for trout and whitefish. A spacious lawn, a covered picnic shelter, and a children's playground make it an appealing spot for a family outing.

Three miles to the west are the Menan Buttes, two glassy cones of lava rising 800 feet above the plain. A roadside marker explains how they were formed. *Open daily Apr.–Oct.*

118 Idaho Falls of the Snake River

2 min. East on Broadway, left on Memorial Dr. Here in the heart of Idaho Falls, the magnificent waterfalls of the Snake River are surrounded by the picturesque buildings of the city and the lush greenery of nearby parks. The watery spectacle combines natural cascades with a 1,500-foot-wide man-made dam, which diverts water from the river to irrigate 7,000 acres of land. Adjacent to the falls, the east and west banks of the river have picnic tables, playgrounds, and signboards that explain the hydroelectric projects and the history of the dam. Several parks, including one on an island, provide opportunities for swimming, boating, trout fishing, jogging, and sunbathing. *Open year-round.* 禾 🚣 🐟

118 Bonneville Museum, Idaho Falls

3 min. East on Broadway. The passing parade of history in eastern Idaho has included Indians, trappers, prospectors, pioneers, farmers, and ranchers. This museum in a former public library in Idaho Falls chronicles them all with artifacts, interpretive panels, photographs, and other memorabilia. Displays cover the history of Idaho Falls, gold panning, harvesting Idaho potatoes, ranching, and atomic energy. There is also a complete kitchen from Idaho Falls' early days and mounted specimens of local wildlife. *Open Mon.–Sat. Admission free but donations encouraged.*

118 Tautphaus Park, Idaho Falls

5 min. East on Broadway, right on Yellowstone Hwy., left on 17th St., right on Rollendet St. Eighty acres of lawns and large stands of pine and cottonwood in this pleasant city park provide an ideal setting for a stroll, a picnic, a cookout on a grill, or a game on one of the spacious playfields. For children, an amusement park offers swings, an arcade, pitch-and-putt golf, a Ferris wheel, and other diversions. Everyone will enjoy the park's zoo, which houses ostriches, trumpeter swans, goats, elk, deer, zebras, llamas, and other inhabitants. *Park open year-round; zoo open daily June–Aug., weekends only Sept.–Oct. Admission charged for zoo.* 禾 ♿

93 Bingham County Historical Museum, Blackfoot

2 mi./7 min. East on Bergner Ave. (Judicial St.) into Blackfoot, left on N. Shilling St. Built in 1905 by a prominent merchant, this 15-room lava-rock and lumber house was once the center of Blackfoot's social life. Today it houses a remarkably varied assortment of antiques and Idaho memorabilia. Some of the items are expected: guns and ammunition from the black-powder days, red velvet-upholstered furniture, Indian relics, and a 13-star American flag. But you'll also find a rocker handmade by Mor-

mon leader Brigham Young, a hand-carved English piano, a hand-loomed Liberty rug that tells the story of America in pictures, an unusually fine doll collection, 200 miniature kerosene lamps and lanterns, a Quaker afghan rug, and equipment from the local mental hospital, including its first electric shock machine. *Open P.M. Wed.– Fri. Feb.–Nov. except holidays.*

69 67 Bannock County Historical Museum, Pocatello

Exit 69: 2 mi./10 min. West on Clark St., left on 1st Ave., then right on Center St. Exit 67: 3 mi./10 min. North on S. 5th St., left on Benton St., right on Garfield St. In the days before the railroad, the Shoshone Indians lived here on 1.3 million acres, including the land on which the city of Pocatello now stands. The strongest aspect of this small museum is its depiction of two implacable rivals: the established Indian tribes and the irresistible iron horse that ultimately uprooted them. The Indian photo archive is particularly poignant, recording a people determined and proud yet defenseless against the inevitable. Beadwork and leatherwork can be seen here, as well as samples of Indian food and its preparation. Railroad memorabilia include wheels, wrenches, oilcans, uniforms, and hundreds of photos. *Open P.M. Tues.–Sat. except holidays.*

67 Ross Park, Pocatello

3 min. North on S. 5th St., left on Fredregill Rd., left on S. 2nd St. A choice of pleasures is offered on this rolling, tree-shaded site. On the lower level are the baseball fields, playgrounds, a swimming pool, and a band shell where concerts are given on Sunday evenings in the summer.

Pleasureland Amusement Park, located on the slopes, offers a variety of booths and rides and a zoo with such permanent residents as buffaloes, grizzly bears, sandhill cranes, swans, and golden eagles. During the summer animals from other zoos in the area are occasional visitors.

A full-scale replica of Old Fort Hall, a trading post established in 1834, sits on the bluff above the zoo. It served the early fur traders and was a well-known landmark on

the Oregon Trail. Log cabins, a blacksmith's shop, covered wagons, and Indian tepees recall the history of the fort. *Open daily June–mid-Sept.; Tues.–Sat. Apr.– May. Admission charged.* 禾 🚶 🚣 ♿

47 Lava Hot Springs Foundation

11 mi./15 min. East on Rte. 30. Geologists estimate that the springs have been at a level 110° F for 50 million years, evidence of the region's continuing volcanic history. A self-supporting state agency operates hot mineral pools (masseurs available) and, on the other side of town, two large swimming pools, one of them Olympic size with a 33-foot-high diving board. The waters— non-

47. The surrounding dry hills make the town swimming pools even more inviting.

sulfurous, odor-free, and soothing—draw more than 250,000 visitors yearly for pleasure and for treatment of arthritis and other ailments. It's a resort surrounded by parks, tennis courts, golf courses, and the trout-rich Portneuf River, which is enjoyed by anglers year-round. Also worth a look are the sunken flower gardens, planted on the lava terraces of an extinct volcano and in fullest bloom from August to October. *Open year-round.* 禾 ⛺ 🚐 🚶 🚣 🐟 ♿

15

17

ID
UT

50

84

See
E–W book,
sec. 16.

364

14

360

14

19

327

3

325

17

17 Weston Canyon

15 mi./30 min. Southeast on Rte. 36. The rugged rock formations in this scenic 1½-mile-long canyon stand out in remarkable contrast to the rolling stretches of scrub brush, sage, maple, and cedar in the surrounding Caribou National Forest. Even though there are no marked trails, you can enjoy the scenery on short hikes, and Weston Canyon Reservoir offers a tempting selection of largemouth bass, perch, and trout. In winter, snowmobiling and ice fishing are popular. *Open year-round.*

364 Box Elder Tabernacle, Brigham City

5 min. East on Rte. 91, left on Main St. Built on a site selected by Brigham Young himself, this imposing 1,200-seat Mormon landmark is as much a work of art as a historic building. The structure, which still bears Brigham City's original name, was started in the 1860's and then rebuilt in 1896–97 after a fire left only the stone walls standing. Gothic in design, it is a masterpiece of fine workmanship, with arched windows and doors, slender buttresses with graceful pinnacles, and a majestic steeple. Inside there are some fine examples of inlaid and carved woodworking and decorative painting techniques. *Tours daily May–Oct.*

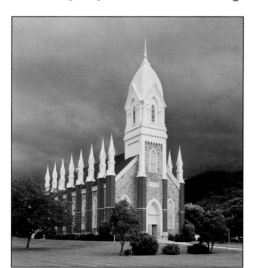

364. *Heavenly aspirations are impressively symbolized by the dramatic spires.*

360 Willard Bay State Park

1 min. West from exit. A scant quarter-mile from the interstate, this park bustles with boaters, swimmers, and fishermen taking advantage of a 9,900-acre man-made lake. The freshwater lake, which has marinas at both its north and south ends, was reclaimed from the salt marshes of the Great Salt Lake. On the land, Russian olive, elm, and poplar trees shade camping areas. The park is a haven for birds, and more than 200 species have been sighted. Many can be spotted in the early morning along the lake's dike. The sign at Exit 354 leads to the park's older, less interesting southern section. *North marina open year-round; south marina open daily Apr.–Oct. Admission charged.*

346 Ogden, UT 84401

Golden Spike Empire, 2501 Wall Ave. (801) 399-8288; (800) 255-8824 outside UT. In the railroad era, towns in which the steam trains stopped were likely to prosper. Ogden's Mediterranean-style station is an imposing monument to the commercial impact of the iron horse. It is now the centerpiece of the 25th Street Historic District, where commercial buildings of bygone days have been converted to modern use. Among the displays in the station are model railroads, classic cars, a gem collection, firearms, and a gunsmith's shop.

Ft. Buenaventura State Park, a reconstruction of a fort established by pioneer Miles Goodyear, recalls the life and times of the mountain men. Visitors with a scientific bent will enjoy the local planetarium and the Natural Science Museum.

327 / 325 Lagoon Amusement Park and Pioneer Village

Exit 327: 3 min. South on Lagoon Dr.; follow signs. Exit 325: 3 min. North on Lagoon Dr.; follow signs. In this 100-year-old amusement park, you'll find everything from traditional arcade games to a merry-go-round with real hand-carved animals, Dracula's Castle, gardens and fountains, and an opera house that features Broadway musicals. Rides include bumper cars, a Tilt-A-Whirl, and an 85-foot-high double-loop roller coaster called the Fire Dragon. Pioneer Village, with century-old buildings brought from various parts of Utah, contains a jail, a two-story log cabin, a Pony Express station, and a narrow-gauge railroad. Guns, dolls, carriages, and Ute Indian beadwork are among the items on display. *Open daily Memorial Day–Labor Day; weekends only Apr.–May and Sept. Admission charged.*

310 Salt Lake City, UT 84101

Convention & Visitors Bureau, 180 S. West Temple. (801) 521-2822; (800) 831-4332 outside UT. No other city in America owes so much to one group of people. Since its founding in 1847 by Brigham Young, who told his hardy band of followers: "This is the place," Salt Lake City has been largely the creation of the Mormons (members of the Church of Jesus Christ of Latter-day Saints). The city is built around Temple Square, where the dominant structure is the Temple, with its six Gothic spires. The Temple is closed to the public. But visitors are welcome at the impressive, acoustically excellent Tabernacle, where the world-famous choir can be heard Sunday mornings and Thursday nights, and public organ recitals are given weekdays at noon and at 4 P.M. on Saturdays and Sundays.

The state capitol, the Pioneer Memorial Museum, and the Council Hall draw tourists to Capitol Hill. In Pioneer Trail State Park there are some interesting renovated historic buildings; other attractions include the State Arboretum and Liberty Park.

301 Bingham Canyon Mine

14 mi./20 min. West on Rte. 48; follow signs. The world's first open-pit copper mine, and America's largest man-made excavation, is an awesome 2½ miles across and half a mile deep. From the visitor center on the mine's rim, you can see drilling, blasting, and loading, as well as electric shovels that lift 55 tons at a scoop into trucks as big as houses. A pamphlet explains how 12 pounds of copper are produced from 1 ton of ore. An audio program explains the day-to-day operation of the mine. *Open daily mid-Apr.–Oct.*

The cave system is known for its profusion of helictites that grow up, down, and even sideways—seemingly defying gravity. The main feature of the largest cave is a 2-ton stalagmite called the Great Heart of Timpanogos. Other cave areas such as the Cavern of Sleep, Father Time, and the Jewel Box also contain stalactite, stalagmite, and flowstone formations. The 3-hour tour begins with a 1½-mile hike to the cave entrance at an elevation of 6,730 feet. Programs given at the visitor center explain the ecology of this beautiful canyon, the evolution of the caves, and the history of the area. *Open daily except Thanksgiving Day, Christmas, and New Year's Day; cave tours mid-May–mid-Oct. Admission charged.*

275. Few of the many falls of the same name so clearly fulfill the description.

287 — Timpanogos Cave National Monument

10 mi./20 min. East on Rte. 92. Three caverns connected by a man-made tunnel are the centerpiece of this 250-acre park on the rugged slopes of the Wasatch Mountains.

275 — Bridal Veil Falls

8 mi./20 min. East on Rte. 189. The world's steepest passenger tram ascends 1,228 feet, at a 45° angle, to the summit of Cascade Mountain. The glass-bottomed car provides breathtaking views of the falls as you glide above them. At the mountaintop a quarter-mile trail reaches the head of the spring-fed falls, where the water begins its tumultuous 600-foot cascade. Another trail offers scenic views of the Utah Valley to the west. If you are leery of steep rides, you might like to know that there's never been an accident here in more than a million passenger-miles. *Open daily mid-May–mid-Oct. Admission charged.*

268 — Utah Lake State Park

5 min. West on Center St.; follow signs. This freshwater lake, a feeding ground for ducks and geese, covers 96,900 acres. Fishermen come for the walleyed pike, bass, catfish, bluegill, and trout. Docks, ramps, and beaches provide full access to warm-weather boating and swimming. An outdoor ice rink is popular with skaters in winter. Hikers can stretch their legs on a trail that starts in the park and follows a stream for 45 miles up a nearby canyon. *Open year-round. Admission charged.*

266 — Provo, UT 84601

Convention and Visitor Bureau, 899 S. University Ave. (801) 374-8687. Brigham Young University, founded here in 1875, has become a cultural and educational center for the community as well as the students. The art gallery, the fine arts center, with its unusual collection of music and old instruments, the planetarium, a life-science museum, and the Museum of Peoples and Cultures are among the most interesting university facilities open to the public.

Utah in the mid-1800's is recalled in the Pioneer Museum collections of art and artifacts and in the McCurdy Historical Doll Museum's display of more than 3,000 dolls in theme settings.

202 — Yuba State Park

5 min. East on access road; follow signs. A scenic landscape is the backdrop for the various attractions at an unusual jade-green lake, which is the largest of several reservoirs along the Sevier River and owes its color to a high concentration of minerals. You'll find many inviting places to picnic, camp, or just contemplate the diverse scenery. Boat ramps at Yuba Dam and at Painted Rocks provide access to water sports and fishing along both sides of this 22-mile reservoir. During the cold winter months the park is popular with snowmobilers and hardy anglers who fish through the ice for perch, northern pike, and catfish. *Open year-round. Admission charged.*

266. With surrounding mountains and tree-filled streets, nature stakes a claim in Provo.

80
310
80
9
See E–W book, sec. 18.
301
14
287
12
275
7
268
2
266
202
64
39
15

167 | 163 | Territorial Statehouse State Park, Fillmore

Exit 167: 3 min. South on Rte. 99 to Capitol Ave. Exit 163: 3 min. North on Rte. 99 to Capitol Ave. The oldest surviving government building in Utah was commissioned by Brigham Young and designed by the architect of Salt Lake's Mormon Temple. But the full plan for a cruciform-shaped building with a central Moorish dome was abandoned when the territorial legislature moved to Salt Lake City. Today the structure is a museum housing 19th-century room settings, tools, antique clothing, quilts, weapons, musical instruments, household objects, and a large collection of Paiute Indian relics. *Open year-round. Admission charged.*

I-70 | Fremont Indian State Park

16 mi./25 min. East on I-70. Mule deer, kit foxes, coyotes, and marmots now roam the red rocks and sage wilderness of Clear Creek Canyon, where Indians of the Fremont culture lived from A.D. 500 to 1400. The visitor center contains interpretive exhibits and some of the rich lode of Indian artifacts unearthed here, but the real adventure lies in exploring the canyon. You'll see petroglyphs along the quarter-mile Art Rock Trail; the more rugged Discovery and Overlook trails provide fascinating insights into the Fremonts' use of natural resources. A concessionaire offers both horse-and-wagon and horseback-riding trips into the backcountry. Clear Creek's sparkling waters are favored by fishermen. *Open year-round. Admission charged.*

112 | 109 | Old Beaver County Courthouse Museum, Beaver

Exit 112: 5 min. South on Rte. 160, left on Center St. Exit 109: 5 min. North on Rte. 160, right on Center St. In the mid-1800's, Brigham Young sent a group of Mormons to settle the wilderness that is now Beaver County. Many of the county's current residents are descended from these pioneers, whose sturdy stone buildings still survive—in fact, more than 115 are listed in *The National Register of Historic Places.* Prominent among them is the Old Beaver County Courthouse, which now houses a museum where the area's pioneers are remembered. This brick structure of about 1877, with a charming clock tower, rests on a massive foundation of volcanic rock. *Open P.M. Tues.–Sat. Memorial Day–Labor Day.*

59 | Iron Mission State Park

3 min. East on Rte. 56, left on Rte. 91. Horse-drawn vehicles are the focus of this park, which features a bullet-scarred stagecoach from Butch Cassidy's territory and wagons of all uses and descriptions culled from all over Utah. The site is named for the Mormon mission that in 1851 joined a group of British miners in their quest for iron ore. The beginning of the iron industry in the area is commemorated by a diorama in the park museum. *Open daily except Thanksgiving Day, Christmas, and New Year's Day. Admission charged.*

59 | Cedar Breaks National Monument

24 mi./30 min. East on Rte. 56, right on Rte. 91, left on Rte. 14, left on Rte. 148. Cedar Breaks is a 3-mile-long natural amphitheater that cuts 2,000 feet deep into the side of the Markagunt Plateau. Tiered layers of red, yellow, and violet in the rock of the Wasatch Formation, accented by the deep green of pine, juniper, and fir, create a series of dramatic compositions. The high country atop the plateau is known for its ancient bristlecone pines, which grow to be thousands of years old, golden aspen groves, spruce forests, and seasonal extravaganzas of wildflowers. You can view all this splendor from overlooks along a 5-mile scenic drive. *Open late May–late Oct. Admission charged.*

40 | Kolob Canyons of Zion National Park

1 min. East from exit. Zion National Park proper is a vast and justly popular place, but one of its most dramatic areas is also one of the least visited: the Finger Canyons of northern Zion Park (also called the Kolob Canyons, from a Mormon term). Just beyond the visitor center a 5-mile spur road winds upward through Taylor Creek Canyon, Lee Pass, and Timber Creek Canyon. Turnoffs, scenic picnic spots, and well-marked trails afford beautiful vistas of the red Navajo sandstone monoliths that tower over deep, narrow box canyons. Hikers who venture on a challenging 6-mile walk will see majestic Kolob Arch, firmly

75. *Contrasting blue skies accentuate the red of Elephant Rock's ancient sandstone.*

buttressed by 700-foot-high red sandstone cliffs; its 310-foot span makes it possibly the longest freestanding arch in the world. *Open year-round but may be inaccessible in winter.* 🛏 🚶 ♿

6 Snow Canyon State Park

7 mi./15 min. North on Rte. 18; follow signs. Named for a pair of prominent pioneer brothers, Lorenzo and Erastus Snow, this 6,500-acre park contains two distinct lava flows, one from 3 million years ago and the other from 1,000 years. The pristine sand dunes and stratified red sandstone cliffs up to 750 feet tall may look familiar: they have appeared in several Hollywood westerns. Here, too, you'll see lava caves, Indian petroglyphs, natural ponds that once served as Indian watering holes, yuccas and Joshua trees, and the occasional coyote, mule deer, owl, or blue jay. *Open year-round. Admission charged.* 🛏 ⛺ 🚐 🚶 ♿

6 Historic Jacob Hamblin Home, Santa Clara

7 mi./15 min. North on Rte. 18, left on Sunset Blvd. (becomes Santa Clara Dr.). Jacob Hamblin was a passionate convert to Mormonism, and he was a remarkable man in many ways. Confirmed in 1854 by Brigham Young as a missionary to the Indians, he expanded his role to become a peacemaker among the Paiute, Navajo, and Hopi tribes and between the Indians and white settlers. In 1870 he advised a government team surveying the Grand Canyon. Somehow he found time to marry four women, father 24 offspring, and adopt several Indian children. His 1863 sandstone house is now restored and maintained by the Mormons, whose guides convey a vivid sense of pioneer life. *Open daily except Thanksgiving Day and Christmas.*

75 Valley of Fire State Park

15 mi./25 min. East on Rte. 169. The colorful rock sculptures of Nevada's oldest state park define a remarkable landscape distinct from the rest of the Mojave Desert. Established in 1935, the park was named for its predominantly red rocks, though vis-

itors might well imagine that the name derives from noontime temperatures of up to 120° F. In the summer it's best to visit in the early morning hours, when the wind-carved rocks glow red, lavender, and gold and shadows accentuate the textures and convoluted shapes of the hardened sand dunes from the Jurassic period. That's also when the park's animal inhabitants—coyotes, jackrabbits, kit foxes, lizards, snakes, and the rare desert tortoise—are astir. A signed trail leads past 1,000-year-old petroglyphs (carved by Anasazi Indians) to a natural rock basin. There are numerous other scenic trails, overlooks, and gravel roads. The air-conditioned visitor center has interpretive geological and historic exhibits. *Park open year-round but may be inaccessible after rainstorms; visitor center open daily except Christmas and New Year's Day.* 🛏 ⛺ 🚐 🏊 ♿

33 Red Rock Canyon Recreation Lands

15 mi./25 min. West on Rte. 160, right on Rte. 159; follow signs. Rarely are thrust fault lines as clearly delineated as those of the 65-million-year-old Keystone Thrust Fault, where gray limestone has pushed up and over the younger red Aztec sandstone. A 13-mile loop drive provides stunning roadside vistas and access to a variety of short trails into the canyons. It's only a short walk to Lost Creek, site of a perpetual spring and a seasonal waterfall, and 2 miles round-trip to a ruined homestead in Pine Creek Canyon. If you hike, carry water and beware of flash floods. Wild burros, descendents of pack animals abandoned by prospectors, thrive in this arid environment. *Open year-round but may be inaccessible in winter.* 🛏 🚶 ♿

27 Clark County Southern Nevada Museum, Henderson

17 mi./22 min. Northeast on Rte. 146, right on Boulder Hwy., left on Museum Dr. A new exhibition hall houses the main collection of this local historical museum. Artifacts are placed in context by a time line that traces human habitation in the area back 10,000 years, from the prehistoric hunters of mammoths and great bison, through the Anasazi and Southern Paiute

If You Have Some Extra Time:

Hoover Dam

27 **33 mi./45 min.** This great arc of concrete set in the rocky narrows of Black Canyon is a spectacular expression of mankind's determination to control a raging river. In 1928 Congress approved a project to dam the Colorado River to generate electricity, control flooding, and distribute water for agricultural, industrial, and domestic use. When the dam was finished in 1935, the impounded water created Lake Meade, an inland sea 110 miles long with more than 800 miles of shoreline.

The elegant proportions of the dam in its rugged setting are a remarkable synthesis of natural and man-made beauty. The structure, 660 feet thick at the bottom, 45 feet thick at the top, and 1,244 feet across, is a national historic landmark. Guided tours penetrate deep into the heart of the monolith, and one can feel the throb of the mighty turbines and generators that link the dam to thousands of southwestern households. *How to get there: Exit 27, northeast on Rte. 146 (Lake Meade Dr.), right on Rte. 93 (Boulder Hwy.) to dam. Open year-round. Admission charged.*

people, to the early Mormon settlers. In addition, the museum's Heritage Street features a restored 1912 California-style bungalow, a mining-town cottage, a 1931 train depot, a replica of a frontier printshop, and other historic structures. Outdoor exhibits include a ghost town and a Paiute camp. *Open daily except Christmas, New Year's Day, and possibly other holidays. Admission charged.* 🛏 🚶 ♿

UT
AZ

AZ
NV

91

75

42

33

6

27

NV
CA

48

15

15

CR

3

GT

9

40

BAR

See
E—W book.
sec. 36.

32

PAL

20

ROUTE
138

24

See
E—W book,
sec. 48.

10

ROUTE
60

CR—GT. *Not fancy, but silver worth millions came up through shafts like this.*

CR GT Calico Ghost Town

4 mi./5 min. Calico Rd. exit: North on Calico Rd.; follow signs. Ghost Town Rd. exit: North on Ghost Town Rd.; follow signs. Perched on a ridge above the undulating Mojave Desert, this town is named for the multicolored rocks that enriched silver miners during the 1880's. The town virtually died after the price of silver dropped in 1896, but today it bustles with activity. You can tour a silver mine, ride on an ore train, camp out in the canyon below the town, or picnic in the desert. At the reconstructed firehouse you can inspect a handsome old-time pump wagon trimmed with gleaming brass appointments. Modern shops are located nearby in the period buildings. *Open daily except Christmas. Admission charged.*

BAR California Desert Information Center, Barstow

Barstow Rd. exit: 2 min. North on Barstow Rd. Whether you are about to cross the great Mojave Desert or have already done so, a stop here will enhance your appreciation of the region and its plant and animal life. Noteworthy among the displays are preserved specimens of desert rattlers (surprisingly small in size) and other creatures to watch out for when exploring on foot. Should you plan to venture onto desert roads in a four-wheel-drive vehicle, the center will provide you with a detailed map of the Mojave. On view part of the year is the Old Woman meteorite, the second largest ever found in the United States (the remainder of the year the Smithsonian has the real meteorite, while the center displays a replica). Weighing over 6,000 pounds, it was discovered in 1975 in the Old Woman Mountains in the eastern Mojave. Across the street from the center is a park with picnic tables. *Open daily except Christmas and New Year's Day.*

PAL Roy Rogers—Dale Evans Museum, Victorville

Palmdale Rd. exit: 5 min. West on Palmdale Rd., right on Kentwood Blvd., right on Civic Dr. The corridors of this museum are lined with nostalgic family photos and memorabilia portraying Roy Rogers and his wife and costar, Dale Evans, from childhood through their long entertainment careers. Rogers's favorite horse, Trigger, has been mounted in a lifelike rearing position, wearing the saddle used in all Roy Rogers movies. Nearby stands Dale's buckskin gelding, Buttermilk. The museum displays costumes, parade saddles, and movie props. One of Rogers's cars, a yellow convertible, and his big-game trophies, shown in dioramas of African and Alaskan wildlife, take you beyond the cowboy image; so do the honors awarded the couple for humanitarian and professional work. *Open daily except Thanksgiving Day and Christmas. Admission charged.*

ROUTE 138 Silverwood Lake State Recreation Area

12 mi./20 min. East on Rte. 138; follow signs. At the southern edge of the Mojave Desert, you'd hardly anticipate such a dramatic and refreshing change of scene. This park, tucked away in the San Bernardino National Forest, has a remarkably beautiful setting. Lush green mountains rise sharply from a shimmering sapphire lake, which offers a variety of water sports; and its sprawling, 13-mile shoreline harbors a number of inviting picnic spots, including three reachable only by boat. There are miles of paths for hiking and biking. Miller Canyon is a more secluded area, where bears are commonly seen.

The drive to the park is rewarding in itself. Although steep and curvy in stretches, Route 138 offers spacious views of the lake and mountains. *Open year-round. Admission charged.*

ROUTE 60 The Mission Inn, Riverside

12 mi./20 min. East on Rte. 60, right on Rte. 91, right at 7th St. exit. A national historic landmark, the Mission Inn is steeped in Old World charm. The block-long building is an enchanting blend of baroque Spanish and Moorish architectural motifs—towers, a dome, scalloped arches, carved pillars, and a cloistered garden. Although it resembles an old Spanish mission, the inn was built in the 20th century for hotel owner Frank Miller over a 30-year period. Miller wanted it to be part hotel, part museum, and he filled it with Spanish, Mexican, and Oriental art and antiques. Many famous people have visited Mission Inn, including several U. S. presidents. Among the highlights seen on a guided tour is the exquisite St. Francis Chapel, which is adorned with Louis Comfort Tiffany stained-glass windows. *Open year-round. Admission charged for tours.*

ROUTE 60 Prado Regional Park

14 mi./20 min. West on Rte. 60, left on Euclid Avenue. This quiet, lovely oasis is a soothing place in which to unwind. The park's 1,200 acres of gently rolling terrain are carpeted with manicured lawns kept

emerald-green by sprinklers. Ducks and swans glide on the tranquil 56-acre lake, and neat blacktop lanes wind around to picnic spots, shaded pavilions, ballfields, and camping areas. Groves of eucalyptus and the hazy outline of mountains accentuate the beauty. Riding trails encircle the park, and horses can be rented. The park is next to a national wildlife refuge and is visited by cranes, herons, and other waterfowl. *Open daily except Christmas. Admission charged.*

ROUTE 74 — Lake Elsinore State Park

5 min. West on Rte. 74. Fronting on a large, beautiful lake rimmed with mountains, this California park is ideal for families. The spacious sandy beach is studded with young palms and has pleasant picnic facilities. Rowboats and water bikes are rented, and anglers can try for bass, catfish, bluegill, carp, and crappie. The tree-shaded camping areas are inviting, and young children will enjoy the playground facilities and wading area. *Open year-round. Admission charged.*

PAL — Pala Mission

Pala Road exit: 6.5 mi./12 min. East on Pala Rd. (Rte. 76), left on Rte. 16. Located on the Pala Indian Reservation, this is the only *asistencia*, or sub-mission, in California that has continuously ministered to the Indian people since its founding. The Pala Mission, established by Franciscan friars in 1815, is operated today by Comboni missionaries from Italy. The restored chapel, with its white walls, beamed ceiling, and tile roof, is moving in its simplicity. Indian designs with religious symbols are painted on the interior walls. The original bells in the cemetery-garden bell tower still ring out reassuringly to the villagers. A small museum contains church items and Indian artifacts. *Open Tues.–Sun. Admission free but donations encouraged.*

DS — Lawrence Welk Museum, Escondido

Deer Springs Rd. exit: 5 min. East on Deer Springs Rd.; follow signs. In a luxurious retirement community named for the popular bandleader, sidewalks paved with musical instrument shapes lead to this theater lobby and museum. A re-creation of the Welk bandstand and stage set dominates a room lit by crystal chandeliers. Photographs, letters, gold records, and many awards chronicle Welk's long career, including the ballroom-dancing years from the 1920's to the 1950's. You'll see his first accordion and scenes from broadcasts of his television shows. *Open year-round.*

FR — Mission Basilica San Diego de Alcala

Friars Road exit: 5 min. East on Friars Rd., right on Rancho Mission Rd., left on San Diego Mission Rd. Known as the Mother of Missions, this was the first of the early California missions and was built by Father Junípero Serra in 1769. The mission's tall white walls enclose an inner sanctuary of gardens and candle-lit shrines. A *campanario* with bells in its arches stands guard at the church's main entrance. Inside, the decor is surprisingly simple: a red tile floor, exposed beams, and a rough-hewn wooden altar. The cavelike rooms where the friars lived are equally stark, but

FR. White walls, red tile, and green plants add charm to a place of the spirit.

the religious vestments and vessels on display are richly ornate. Other exhibits detail the mission's history and, amid the hibiscus and other tropical plants, give color to the main courtyard. In the mission garden there is a wishing well reputed to bring answers to prayers. *Open year-round. Admission charged.*

I-8 — San Diego Zoo

8 mi./15 min. West on I-8, left on Rte. 163 to Park Blvd. exit; follow signs. With a population of 3,200, representing some 800 species from around the world, this fine zoo is a veritable United Nations of the animal kingdom. If you have time, take the 40-minute guided bus tour for orientation, then return to your favorite spots on foot or via outdoor moving walkways and escalators. You will see highland gorillas, Australian koalas, miniature deer, giant anteaters, Mongolian wild horses, and the world's largest collection of parrots and parrotlike birds. The children's zoo is scaled to four-year-olds and features a nursery where baby mammals are bottle-fed, bathed, and diapered. You'll also find elephant and camel rides, animal shows, behind-the-scenes group tours, and special facilities for the handicapped. *Open year-round. Admission charged.*

I-8 — Cabrillo National Monument

15 mi./30 min. West on I-8, left on Rte. 209; follow signs. Juan Rodríguez Cabrillo was the first European to explore this section of the Pacific Coast, and it was this wind-swept finger of land that greeted him when he sailed into the harbor here. Today, at the park named in his honor, he wouldn't recognize the view to the east: a panorama of ocean freighters against a backdrop of San Diego's white skyscrapers. But to the west is the vast unchanged Pacific, where whale-watching is now popular from late December to mid-March. Exhibits in the visitor center concentrate on the peninsula's natural features, local Indian artifacts, and Spanish explorers. There is also a restored lighthouse; and a nature trail, edged by chaparral, runs along the harbor. *Open year-round.*

28

ROUTE 74

27

PAL

16

DS

26

FR   See E–W book sec. 56.

1

I-8   8

See N–S book, sec. 4.

5

End I-15

90

I-90

299

See E–W
book,
sec. 3.

2

117

182

42

140

29

111

I-90 | Fort Phil Kearny National Historic Site

15 mi./20 min. North on I-90 to Exit 44, northwest on Rte. 193; follow signs. Constructed in 1866 in violation of the U.S. treaty with the Sioux nation, Ft. Kearny was held under continual siege by Chief Red Cloud and his warriors until it was abandoned in 1868 and was later destroyed by fire. Today the visitor center displays an outline of the fort and the barracks, along with reproductions of army weapons and bows and arrows. Information panels in an adjacent cabin tell the dramatic story of the Wyoming Indian wars and the Bozeman Trail, and describe life on the reservation and frontier. *Open daily June–mid-Oct.*

299 | Jim Gatchell Memorial Museum, Buffalo

5 min. West on Rte. 16; follow signs. Pioneer druggist Jim Gatchell, who dealt frequently with the Indians of the Sioux and Cheyenne tribes, amassed a large collection of their artifacts. Treasures include headdresses, beadwork, and arrowheads. Also on display are guns and shell casings believed to have been used at the Battle of the Little Bighorn, rifles and spent cartridges from the fabled Johnson County shooting war, ore and fossil samples, and the switchboard of the Occidental Hotel, an inn immortalized by Owen Wister's *The Virginian*, a best-selling 1902 novel about a cowhand. *Open daily June–Labor Day. Admission free but donations encouraged.*

182 | Edness Kimball Wilkins State Park

4 min. North on Rte. 253 (Hat Six Rd.), right on Rte. 20/26. These 315 acres near the old Oregon Trail, where the North Platte River reflects the aged cottonwoods along its edges, seem far removed from the busy world. Plans for the park include nature trails, shaded bicycle paths, a riding trail, and additional picnicking areas. The park contains four river-fed ponds that provide pleasant swimming and canoeing in warm weather and ice skating in winter. During the summer members of the Audubon Society often come to bird-watch. *Open year-round.*

140 | Wyoming Pioneer Memorial Museum, Douglas

4 min. East on exit road, right on W. Center St. Almost every object that has ever been used, found, or lost in the West seems to be on display at this remarkably complete museum. Winchesters, six-shooters, Indian arrowheads and spearpoints, tomahawks and war clubs, fossils, furniture, buffalo skulls, branding irons, carriages, cars, swords, and saddlebags—the collection is almost overwhelming. Among the priceless objects are a bugle from Custer's last battle and a hand-made water canteen used by mountain man Jim Bridger at Ft. Laramie. The more artistic displays feature ladies' ornate silk fans and fine glassware and crystal. *Open Mon.–Fri. and P.M. weekends Memorial Day–Oct.; Mon.–Fri. Nov.–Memorial Day except Thanksgiving Day, Christmas, and New Year's Day.*

140 | Fort Fetterman State Historic Site

8 mi./12 min. North on Rte. 93. Soldiers considered duty at this Wyoming outpost a hardship. Pounded mercilessly by savage winter gales, the North Platte River valley was a barren place where fresh produce was a rarity, female companionship all but unknown, and desertion a regular occurrence. Yet the post survived from 1867 until 1882 as a major staging point for supplies and military operations against the Plains Indians. Today's restoration includes the officers' quarters—which house a small museum displaying uniforms and insignia, Indian regalia, and swords and firearms—and the ordnance shed, used now to display farm and military wagons. The fort overlooks scenic rolling hills. *Open daily Memorial Day–Labor Day.*

111 | Glendo State Park

5 min. East into Glendo; follow signs. This park, one of Wyoming's largest, entices vacationers who come to enjoy the idyllic setting, with its rock outcroppings, pine-shaded hills, and lake with 78 miles of shoreline and sandy beaches. Campers can pitch tents anywhere in the park's 10,197 acres, and there's plenty of room for hiking. Boating, water- and jet-skiing, swimming, and fishing are also popular here. *Open year-round.*

92 | Oregon Trail Ruts–Register Cliff State Sites, Guernsey

16 mi./20 min. East on Rte. 26, right on Wyoming St. In the 1800's thousands of Mormons, cattlemen, sheep farmers, and gold seekers followed the Oregon Trail. As

140. *Modern transportation has reduced travel time, but the horizon remains unchanged.*

If You Have Some Extra Time: Rocky Mountain National Park

257A
257B **35 mi./50 min.** The awe-inspiring scale of this aptly named park in northern Colorado, with more than 100 rugged rocky peaks rising above 10,000 feet, is impressively portrayed in a large relief map at the headquarters building at Beaver Meadows, where you can also see a movie that gives a colorful overview of the highlights.

To see the most spectacular scenery, as well as some of the native animals, take Trail Ridge Road, the nation's highest continuous paved highway, which winds along up to 12,183 feet and crosses the Continental Divide. For about 11 miles the road traverses an area of treeless tundra comparable to that of the Arctic Circle. A walk on Tundra Nature Trail allows close-up inspection of the grass, lichens, and dwarf wildflowers, with long views of the rolling expanse of alpine landscape.

Farview Curve Overlook, a few miles west of the Continental Divide, provides a splendid view and a turnaround for the drive back to Estes Park. You can also continue downhill past Lake Granby to Route 40 and then south to I-70, a distance of about 75 miles.

Trail Ridge Road is closed in winter, from late October until Memorial Day, but the trails and roads open year-round at lower levels reveal other attractions in the park. Just below the tree line, the spruces, firs, and pines are stunted by the ferocious cold and wind; lower down they grow tall and straight, and on the drier slopes lodgepole pines predominate. Lower still are the ponderosa pines, and where these have burned off, quaking aspens thrive, showing their shimmering gold foliage in fall. *How to get there: Exit 257A and Exit 257B, west on Rte. 34. Admission charged.*

their wagons lumbered westward, the iron rims cut ruts—many from 4 to 6 feet deep—in this sandstone ridge. At nearby Register Cliff many of these wagon trains, attracted by the camping sites and available water, stopped to rest. The settlers carved their names, dates, hometowns, and destinations in the soft sandstone, leaving a poignant record that still evokes the courage and spirit of these hardy pioneers.

Today, fishermen come to try their luck in the nearby North Platte River, where rainbow and brown trout abound. *Open year-round, weather permitting.*

9 | Cheyenne, WY 82001

Chamber of Commerce, 301 W. 16th St. (307) 638-3388. The phrase "Cheyenne to Deadwood 1876" is still visible on the side of a weather-beaten stagecoach at the Cheyenne Frontier Days Old West Museum, where more than 30 horse-drawn vehicles colorfully recall the days before the automobile. Also shown are an ambulance, a hearse, and sightseeing coaches, along with fancy saddles, rodeo memorabilia, and exhibits on the advent of the railroad and the decline of the Plains Indian tribes.

In Lions Park the solar-heated Cheyenne Botanic Gardens and a lake for swimming, boating, and fishing are especially popular with visitors.

The focus of the Wyoming State Museum is the state's history and frontier life. The museum's exhibits recall the days of the Shoshone and Arapaho Indians, cowboys, pioneer women, and mountain men. Indian beadwork, guns owned by Buffalo Bill Cody, and a diorama of an 1880's cattle roundup are among the highlights.

269 | Lory State Park

15 mi./27 min. West on Rte. 14, right on Rte. 287, left on Rte. 28. This 2,600-acre park lies at the very gateway to the Rockies. From sheltered coves at Horsetooth Reservoir the land sweeps dramatically upward through hogback ridges to Ranger Peak at 7,015 feet. Prairie grass gives way to mountain shrubs and then to stands of ponderosa pine. Some 25 miles of trails offer hikers choices ranging from easy to challenging. From Arthur's Rock, which can be reached by trail, there's a sweeping view of Fort Collins. *Open year-round. Admission charged.*

257B
257A | Centennial Village, Greeley

18 mi./25 min. Exit 257B: east on Rte. 34, left on 14th Ave., left on A St. Exit 257A: proceed as above. This museum village, opened in 1976 to mark the state's 100th birthday and the nation's

200th, offers a view of life between 1860 and the 1920's. Two adobe structures remained comfortable in the height of summer, while the Swedish-American farm dwelling allayed winter doldrums with a dazzling white interior. Carpenter House has a potbellied stove and tea-leaf china. At Stevens House a pump organ and parlor piano evoke gracious turn-of-the-century living. Other sites include a church, a newspaper office, a firehouse, a carriage house, a blacksmith's shop, and a schoolhouse with ink-stained desks. *Open Mon.–Fri. and P.M. weekends Memorial Day–Labor Day; Tues.–Sat. mid-Apr.–Memorial Day and Labor Day–mid-Oct.*

240 | Longmont Museum

7 mi./10 min. West on Rte. 119, right on Kimbark St. Several exhibits here trace the history of Longmont and the surrounding St. Vrain Valley. The classic Americana on display range from prospector's pans to a high-wheeler or "penny-farthing" bicycle, and from turn-of-the-century washing machines to a jukebox from the early 1960's. The space exhibit celebrates local astronaut Vance Brand with memorabilia from his life in Longmont and from his 1975 Apollo-Soyuz mission. *Open Mon.–Sat. except holidays. Admission free but donations encouraged.*

19

92

83

See E–W book, sec. 19.

9

80

WY

CO

37

269

12

257B 0

257A 0

257B

17

240

See E–W book, sec. 27.

70

30

25

210

54

156B

6

150B

8

142

1

141

3

138

37

101

7

94

210. *As the nearby Rockies recede at night, a man-made range of buildings comes to light.*

210 | Denver, CO 80202

Convention & Visitors Bureau, 225 W. Colfax Ave. (303) 892-1112. There is a wealth of museums, parks, and shopping areas in the Mile High City. The Denver Art Museum, covered with a million reflecting tiles, houses a superb Indian collection, with many Mesoamerican pieces. Nearby is the U.S. Mint, where you can watch money being stamped. Among the stately old mansions on Capitol Hill is the popular Molly Brown House, former home of the feisty and "unsinkable" heroine of the *Titanic*. The flavor of Denver's past has been preserved in Larimer Square, with its restored shops, restaurants, arcades, and gaslights. There are some 4,000 acres of parks within the city, one of which, City Park, contains the Denver Museum of Natural History, with its planetarium, and the Denver Zoo.

156B / 150B | United States Air Force Academy

Exit 156B: 2 min. West on access road. Exit 150B: 2 min. West on access road. Situated just north of Colorado Springs, the nation's youngest service academy (founded in 1954) occupies 18,000 acres of rolling, grassy high prairie, at an elevation of 7,200 feet, with the Rocky Mountains rising dramatically in the background. A map available at the gatehouses leads you on a 14-mile self-guiding auto tour. The famous Cadet Chapel, with its 17 aluminum spires and aircraft-related interior, is a short walk from the visitor center; guided tours are given every half-hour in summer. The chapel's terrace affords an extensive view of the parade ground and other buildings. *Open year-round.* ♿

142 | Colorado Springs, CO 80903

Convention & Visitors Bureau, 104 S. Cascade Ave., Suite 104. (719) 635-7506; (800) 888-4748 outside CO. From almost anywhere in town, the Rocky Mountains are a scenic presence, Pikes Peak in particular. The early history of this fast-growing city of resorts and high-tech industries is recalled at the Pioneers' Museum. The Fine Arts Center features works by American artists, and the Pro Rodeo Hall of Champions and the Museum of the American Cowboy pay tribute to these western skills. Specialists enjoy the comprehensive displays at the American Numismatic Association. Pikes Peak Ghost Town and the Garden of the Gods are, respectively, interesting man-made and natural attractions.

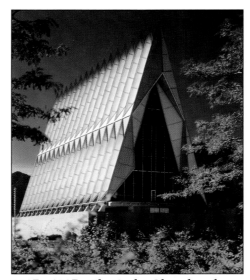

156B–150B. *The Cadet Chapel evokes aspirations of flight as well as spirit.*

141 | Garden of the Gods, Colorado Springs

5 mi./9 min. West on Rte. 24; follow signs. This spectacular array of ancient rock outcrops owes its name to a mid-19th-century visitor who, when his companion proclaimed the area suitable for a beer garden, replied that it was more fitting as a "garden of the gods." Fortunately, his vision prevailed, and the 1,300-acre park, which is now a registered natural landmark, has remained unspoiled. The area is unique for its oddly shaped red and white sandstone formations with names like the Kissing Camels, the Three Graces, and the Sleeping Indian. Jutting as high as 300 feet above the ground, these rocks date back some 250 million years or more, when they were sloughed off by the emerging Rocky Mountains. *Open year-round.* 🧺 🚶 ♿

141 | Cave of the Winds

6 mi./10 min. West on Rte. 24. Discovered in 1880, this dramatic series of underground caverns in the Front Range of the Rocky Mountains was formed by the rushing waters of an inland sea some 500 million years ago. The guided tour, which covers nearly a mile in 45 minutes, takes you through 21 chambers with such fanciful names as Canopy Hall and Oriental Garden. The cave is surprisingly non-claustrophobic, since it is well lighted and in general the ceilings are high. Man-made paths make walking easy, but there are a few short steep stairways. *Open daily except Christmas. Admission charged.* 🧺

141 | Mount Manitou Incline, Manitou Springs

6.5 mi./20 min. West on Rte. 24, left on Rte. 24 (business), left on Ruxton Ave. If you don't have time for the 3-hour round-trip on the popular Pikes Peak cog railway, this ride in a cable car up an adjoining summit offers an inviting alternative. Starting from a station just across from the Pikes Peak depot, the mile-long incline rises some 2,200 feet into the Pike National Forest. At the top there are panoramic views of Manitou Springs and Colorado Springs, as well the hiking trail that climbs Pike's Peak. *Open May–Sept. Fare charged.* 🧺 🚶

141. *Nature's work, left, in the Garden of the Gods looks like a Giacometti.*

138 Will Rogers Shrine of the Sun, Colorado Springs

7 mi./20 min. West on Lake Ave., left on Lake Circle, left on Walnut Ave.; bear right on Miranda Rd., right on Cheyenne Mountain Blvd.; continue on Cheyenne Mountain Zoo Rd. A winding road that begins in the Cheyenne Mountain Zoo takes you to a mountaintop memorial to one of America's best-known humorists. After Rogers was killed in a 1935 plane crash, Spencer Penrose, the monument's benefactor, dedicated the site, with its 80-foot stone tower, to his good friend. The shrine affords views of the Plains to the east, Pikes Peak to the west, and Colorado Springs below. The extensive zoo boasts a major collection of animals, including a large giraffe herd. *Open year-round. Admission charged.* 🜉 ♿

101 / 94 The Greenway and Nature Center of Pueblo

Exit 101: 7 mi./8 min. West on Rte. 50, left on Pueblo Blvd. (Rte. 45), right on W. 11th St. Exit 94: 6 mi./10 min. West on Pueblo Blvd. (Rte. 45), left on W. 11th St. Some 20 miles of an inviting trail stretch along the banks of the Arkansas and Fountain rivers in this unique urban park, called the Greenway, set in a lush cotton-wood canyon. On the east the trail leads to the Pueblo City Park (see below); to the west it connects with the full-facility Pueblo State Recreation Area. The Nature Center shows some examples of this semiarid region's flora and fauna. At the Raptor Center, injured birds of prey receive loving care. *Greenway open year-round; Nature Center and Raptor Center open daily except Thanksgiving Day, Christmas, and New Year's Day.* 🜉 ♣ 🐟 ♿

101 / 94 Pueblo Zoo and City Park

Exit 101: 6 mi./8 min. West on Rte. 50, left on Pueblo Blvd. (Rte. 45), left on Goodnight Ave. Exit 94: 5 mi./9 min. West on Pueblo Blvd. (Rte. 45), right on Goodnight Ave. The centerpiece of this attractive city park is a charming zoo. In a barnyardlike petting zoo, roosters and rambunctious African pygmy goats run loose, and penned donkeys, sheep, and pigs can be petted. The zoo's other residents include antelopes, monkeys, deer, camels, zebras, prairie dogs, and a small herd of bison. The park also has a pool, free tennis courts, and an amusement minipark with half a dozen or so children's rides. *Zoo and park open year-round; pool open Memorial Day–late Aug.; amusement area open Memorial Day–Labor Day. Admission charged.* 🜉 ♣

13B Baca House and Bloom House, Trinidad

3 min. East on Main St. Although these two beautifully restored and authentically refurbished houses are next to each other, there are striking differences. The unpretentious two-story house once owned by Don Felipe Baca, a sheep rancher, has thick adobe walls. The whitewashed interior gives a bright, airy feel. By contrast, the three-story brick mansion built for cattleman and banker Frank Bloom a decade later has wrought-iron railings capping its wraparound porch and mansard roof. The interior is a profusion of Victorian-era patterns and furniture. The Pioneer Museum, in the Baca servants' quarters, displays memorabilia from Trinidad's frontier days. *Open Mon.–Sat. and P.M. Sun. Memorial Day–Labor Day. Admission charged.*

452 Sugarite Canyon State Park

6 mi./9 min. East on Rte. 72, left on Rte. 526. Near the famed skiing area, this pleasant wooded canyon is one of New Mexico's newest state parks. It was once the home of prosperous coal mines, and their tailings can still be seen on the surrounding cliffs. But nature has reclaimed the canyon, filling it with pines, cottonwoods, and scrub oaks. The park's centerpiece is 120-acre Lake Maloya, which extends across the state line into a Colorado wilderness area. It is popular with local anglers, who come to try for rainbow trout. *Open year-round. Admission charged.* 🜉 ⛺ 🚐 ♣ 🐟 ♿

366 Fort Union National Monument

7 mi./ 10 min. West on Rte. 477. Built near the juncture of two branches of the Santa Fe Trail, Ft. Union played a vital role in the nation's westward expansion. Beginning in 1851, it was a way station for Missouri entrepreneurs who opened up trade in the Mexican land that later became the U.S. Territory of New Mexico. The fort was abandoned in 1891, when the railroad replaced wagon travel. Today you can see some of the remains—the stone foundations of the enlisted men's and officers' quarters, the crumbling adobe walls of the quartermaster depot, and the remnants of brick chimneys. *Open daily except Christmas and New Year's Day. Admission charged Memorial Day–Labor Day.* 🜉 ♣

366. *Crumbling symbols of the old West: adobe walls and handmade wheels.*

81

13B

19

CO

NM

452

86

366

59

25

See
E–W book,
sec. 37.

307 Pecos National Monument

299 *Exit 307: 4 mi./8 min. North on Rte. 63. Exit 299: 8 mi./12 min. East on Rte. 50, right on Rte. 63.* The 1¼-mile-long trail that winds among these rock- and grass-covered mounds provides only a suggestion of the Indian settlement that once thrived on this valley ridge in the Sangre de Cristo Mountains. In the mid-1400's the Pecos Pueblo, with its four- and five-story dwellings, was home to some 2,000 Pecos Indians, whose strategic location became a center of trade with the buffalo-hunting Plains Indians to the north and the Indian farmers of the Rio Grande to the south. Visitors can climb down wooden ladders into two restored kivas (circular underground ceremonial rooms). The visitor center, with its displays of Pecos pottery, tools and jewelry, and a film about the pueblo's past, reconstructs the colorful history of the people who once lived here. *Open daily except Christmas and New Year's Day. Admission charged.* ⊼ ♿

284 Santa Fe, NM 87501

Convention and Visitors Bureau, 201 W. Marcy St. (505) 984-6760; (800) 528-5369 outside NM. The charm of Santa Fe is derived from its Spanish and Indian past. The adobe Palace of Governors, built in 1610 and said to be the oldest public building in the United States, is now a major repository of southwestern history. The San Miguel Mission, one of the oldest churches in America, was also built in the early 1600's. During the Pueblo uprising of 1680, which drove the Spaniards back to El Paso, the mission was destroyed, but in 1710 it was completely reconstructed. Both structures have managed to retain their original Spanish flavor, despite the many years of conflict that finally ended in 1846 when the U.S. Army raised the American flag and took Santa Fe without resistance.

The Wheelwright Museum has outstanding collections of Indian art. Ethnic crafts from around the world are superbly displayed in the Museum of International Folk Art. The downtown area invites walking, but at an elevation of 7,000 feet, Santa Fe requires a visitor to take it easy at first.

307–299. *Ladder leads to a ceremonial chamber. Mission ruins are in background.*

234 Sandia Peak Aerial Tramway, Albuquerque

6 mi./10 min. East on Tramway Rd.; follow signs. One of the world's longest aerial tramways carries riders on a trip of 2.7 miles, from Sandia Peak's desert base, over canyons and dense forests, to its verdant top. During the 15-minute ride, which covers a vertical rise of 3,800 feet, you may spot mule deer below and golden eagles circling overhead. From Sandia Peak, part of the Cibola National Forest, you can enjoy a view of more than 11,000 square miles. You'll also find hiking trails and areas for rock climbing and hang gliding. In winter the tram serves as a ski lift, giving access to 25 miles of trails. *Open daily Memorial Day–Labor Day; Thurs.–Tues. and P.M. Wed. Labor Day–Memorial Day. Admission charged.* ⊼ 🚶 ♿

225 Albuquerque, NM 87103

Convention & Visitors Bureau, 305 Romero St. NW. (505) 243-3696; (800) 284-2282 outside NM. The Spanish influence is pleasantly recalled in the Old Town area, with its plaza and the San Felipe de Neri church (1706). The handsome architecture on the University of New Mexico campus has been influenced by the Indian pueb-

los. Anthropology, geology, and the arts are featured in the city's excellent museums. One of the most intriguing is the New Mexico Museum of Natural History. Here you can step into a volcano or an Ice Age cave and admire a model of a flying quetzalcoatlus with its wingspan of 40 feet. World War II correspondent Ernie Pyle's home is open to the public. The Indian Pueblo Cultural Center details the culture and history of the peoples of New Mexico.

222 National Atomic Museum, Albuquerque

6 mi./10 min. East on Gibson Blvd., right on Wyoming Blvd. A B-52 bomber used in the last atmospheric nuclear tests, a 280-mm. atomic cannon, and futuristic-looking surface-to-air missiles occupy the grounds outside this museum, which focuses on nuclear weaponry. Exhibits and films illustrate the history of the first atom bomb and include full-size models of its first two designs. Also featured are planes and missiles created to carry atomic weapons, the development of the hydrogen bomb, advances in weapons technology, and safety and testing. Peaceful uses of nuclear technology for medicine, agriculture, and industry are also demonstrated. *Open daily except Thanksgiving Day, Christmas, New Year's Day, and Easter.* ♿

175 Salinas National Monument, Abó Pueblo Unit

30 mi./35 min. East on Rte. 60, north on Rte. 513. Built by Tompiro Indians before A.D. 1200, Abó grew into one of the largest Pueblo Indian communities in the pre-Spanish Southwest, but was abandoned in the 1670's as a result of disease, drought, and warfare. Today a self-guiding tour tells visitors of the rise and fall of the Pueblo Indian people here. Native religion is represented by the round, partly subterranean spiritual centers called kivas. They form an architectural and cultural contrast to the excavated ruins of the San Gregorio de Abó mission church. The mission's thin sandstone buttressed walls, 40 feet high in places, loom over mounds that cover the sites of houses and other structures of the pueblo. *Open daily except Christmas and New Year's Day. Admission charged.* ♿

150 / 147 — San Miguel Mission, Socorro

4 min. Exit 150: south on Loop I-25 (business; Rte. 60), right on Otero St.; follow signs. Exit 147: north on Loop I-25 (business; Rte. 60), left on Otero St.; follow signs. The town of Socorro reportedly was named for the aid ("succor") that Piro Indians were said to have given to Spanish explorers. A wall from the original San Miguel Mission, begun by the Spanish in 1598, is incorporated with the present adobe church, constructed between 1615 and 1626. The chapel wing completed the building in 1853. The interior has hand-carved ceiling beams and pews. You can see other artifacts in the church office. The twin bell towers present a dramatic night-sky silhouette. *Open year-round.*

139 / 124 — Bosque del Apache National Wildlife Refuge

Exit 139: 9 mi./15 min. East on Rte. 380, right on Rte. 85. Exit 124: 10 mi./15 min. East on gravel road, left on Rte. 85. Greater sandhill cranes, once in danger of extinction, leap and dance in remarkable displays that can be viewed from the sanctuary's 15-mile loop road. You may also spot a very rare whooping crane, with an 8-foot wingspan, or an endangered bald eagle. Great blue herons are common, as are many shorebirds and songbirds, mule deer, and coyotes. The visitor center has a station for observing wildlife as well as exhibits on natural history. *Refuge open year-round; visitor center open daily Oct.–Mar.; Mon.–Fri. Apr.–Sept. except Christmas and New Year's Day. Admission charged.*

83 — Elephant Butte Lake State Park

4 mi./6 min. East on Rte. 52. With 36,733 acres of water and 45,000 of land, the park offers a variety of recreational opportunities: camping, picnicking, sailing, water-skiing (there's a ski jump), and swimming from sandy beaches; fishermen come for catfish, trout, pike, crappie, and black, white, and striped bass. The place called Damsite at the southern end of the lake affords an impressive view of Elephant Butte, the neck of an ancient volcano that is said to resemble an elephant's head rising from the water. A colorful marina rents boats, water skis, and fishing gear. The hiking trails lead past picnic sites shaded by cottonwoods. *Open year-round. Admission charged.*

139–124. *Snow geese find conditions at the Bosque del Apache Refuge to their liking.*

76 — Geronimo Springs Museum, Truth or Consequences

3.5 mi./8 min. East on Broadway, left on Pershing St., left on Main St. The soothing 110° F mineral water that bubbles beside this museum attracted Indians long before Geronimo Springs became a spa for white settlers. The museum contains murals of the Indian, the Spanish, the Mexican, and the Anglo cultures, and exhibits of ranching and mining activities. Why the town's name was changed in 1950 from Hot Springs to Truth or Consequences, the title of a radio (and later TV) show, is also explained. *Open Mon.–Sat. and P.M. Sun. except holidays. Admission charged.*

19 — Fort Selden State Monument

2 min. West on access road. Set on the banks of the Rio Grande, this fort was established in 1865 to protect settlers from Apaches. The troops also escorted travelers along the Jornada del Muerto ("Journey of Death") desert trail to the north. Exhibits in the visitor center contain uniforms, including the plumed hats and Prussian-style coats of the Buffalo soldiers, a renowned black cavalry unit. The remains of the walls are marked with signs. *Open daily except holidays. Admission charged.*

3 / I-10 — La Mesilla Historic Village

Exit 3: 3 mi./8 min. West on University Ave., right on Rte. 28; follow signs. Exit I-10: 4 mi./16 min. West on I-10 to Exit 140, south on Rte. 28; follow signs. This quaint Spanish-style village was Mexican until 1854, when the Gadsden Purchase was signed and the American flag was raised in its plaza. The town's history includes a period of Confederate occupation, a trial of Billy the Kid, and harassment by Geronimo. The mission-style church of San Albino dominates the plaza, and restored adobe buildings house restaurants, gift shops, and art galleries. The Gadsden Museum contains a collection of the folk wood carvings of saints and other religious figures known as *santos. Village open year-round; museum open daily except Thanksgiving Day, Christmas, and Easter. Admission charged for museum.*

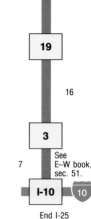

3
147
8
139
15
124
41
83
7
76
57
19
16
3
See E–W book, sec. 51.
7
I-10 10
End I-25

80

138

39

100

35

 215 **Pembina State Historic Site**

2 min. East on Stutsman St. Built in 1797 by the Northwest Fur Company, Ft. Pembina was the first European settlement in North Dakota. With the building of Ft. Daer in 1812, this region became more military in character. Though picnic sites and playgrounds have long ago replaced Ft. Daer, the area's history is recalled by a visit to the Pembina State Museum. Here one can almost hear the ringing shots of firing practice and the haggling of fur-clad traders. *Museum open P.M. Fri.–Mon. Memorial Day–Labor Day.*

138 **Grand Forks County Historical Society**

4 mi./9 min. East on 32nd Ave. S, left on Belmont Rd. Built in 1879, this log cabin was the birthplace of wheat king Thomas Campbell, Jr., noted for industrializing his farm. At the turn of the century a huge wing was added, creating the structure known as Campbell House, now used as a museum. Pioneer furnishings and utensils in the cabin contrast with the elegance of ostrich feathers and opera hats in the newer addition. Local history is further recalled in a number of other buildings, including Myra House, a carriage house, a post office, and a schoolhouse. *Museum open year-round; buildings open P.M. daily mid-May–mid-Oct. Admission charged.*

100 **KTHI TV Tower, Blanchard**

12 mi./14 min. West on Alt. Rte. 200, right on Rte. 18. The 2,063-foot television station KTHI tower, built in 1963, was the world's tallest structure until a tower about 58 feet higher was built in Poland. The KTHI tower can send signals across a 100-mile radius, almost twice the distance of most other towers. Although the tower is stabilized by 27 guy wires, the top sways as much as 10 feet in gusty winds. In 1986 this engineering marvel was considered to be in excellent condition by structural engineers, and there have been no accidents since construction began more than 30 years ago. There are no tours, but visitors are invited to drive to the base of the tower, look up, and be amazed. *Open year-round.*

65 **Bonanzaville, U.S.A., West Fargo**

63 *Exit 65: 4 mi./9 min. West on Rte. 10. Exit 63: 4.5 mi./6 min. West on I-94 to Exit 85, east on Rte. 10.* Bonanzaville, U.S.A., is a regional museum complex of almost 50 buildings. An aircraft museum, a railroad depot, a collection of dolls, a fire station, and a barn with live animals are some of the attractions. Among the dwellings, you'll find a reproduction of a sod house, log cabins, and early homes, including one that was owned by D. H. Houston, who devised an early type of roll

65–63. *In the 1920's the operator would say "Number, please" and connect the lines.*

film and a folding camera. The Red River and Northern Plains Regional Museum (headquarters for Bonanzaville) displays collections of military items, toys, models of ships and cars, musical instruments, and one of the most comprehensive American Indian exhibits in this area. *Museum and buildings open Mon.–Fri. and P.M. Sat.–Sun. late May–late Oct.; museum open Tues.–Fri. late Oct.–late May except Thanksgiving Day, Christmas, and New Year's Day. Admission charged.*

63 **Plains Art Museum, Moorhead**

6 mi./9 min. East on I-94 to Exit 1, north on Rte. 75, left on Main Ave. A Sioux baby bonnet trimmed with dentalia shells, a dance bustle made of feathers and tin, and Ojibwa dance caps of porcupine quills and deer hair are examples of the excellent Native American art in this museum. The collection also includes the work of American impressionist Mary Cassatt, as well as painters Jerry Ott and Luis Jimenez. Many of the items sold in the museum shop were made by area artists and craftsmen. *Open Tues.–Sat. and P.M. Sun. except Thanksgiving Day, Christmas, and New Year's Day. Admission free but donations encouraged.*

37 **Fort Abercrombie State Historic Site**

7 mi./9 min. East on Rte. 4, right on Rte. 81. Disgruntled over the withholding of goods promised by treaty, the Sioux Indians besieged this fort for nearly 6 weeks in 1862. Military personnel and the settlers who sought protection fended off Indian attacks with 12-pound howitzers until reinforcements arrived and the attacks ceased. The stronghold became a stop for expeditions and frontier-bound pioneers until it was abandoned in 1877. The museum near the fort holds an assortment of local artifacts gleaned from attics, basements, parlors, and private collections. There's an interesting miscellany of portraits of pioneers, painted Norwegian food chests, stone hammers, foot warmers, waffle irons, and a model of the fort. *Fort open year-round; museum open daily June–Aug.; Thurs.–Mon. last 2 weeks in May and first 2 weeks in Sept. Admission charged for museum.*

207. *The setting sun adds an aura of mystery to the angular lines of Blue Cloud Abbey.*

23 | Chahinkapa Park, Wahpeton

12 mi./17 min. East on Rte. 13, left on 1st St. Located between the Bois de Sioux River and the Bois de Sioux golf course (its 18 holes lie in two states), this large and appealing city park has facilities for biking, tennis, basketball, swimming, and horseshoes. There are also picnic areas, playgrounds, and a free campground (3-day limit). Chahinkapa Zoo houses bobcats, mountain lions, Scandinavian blue foxes, eagles, peacocks, exotic waterfowl, a miniature horse, and a moose. At Grandpa's Little Zoo, small children can pet the sheep, goats, rabbits, ducks, and donkeys. *Open year-round.*

23 | Richland County Historical Museum, Wahpeton

12 mi./17 min. East on Rte. 13, left on 2nd St. The 2,000-page, 508-pound visitors' book with space for 760,000 signatures is the first of the many distinctive items encountered in this museum. The collection of Indian artifacts was assembled by Esther Horne, the great-great-granddaughter of Sacajawea, the Shoshone woman guide who accompanied Lewis and Clark on their famous expedition in 1804–06. The collection includes Sioux dolls, birch-bark boxes, ceremonial clubs, a buffalo-bone breastplate, and various articles of leather clothing with excellent beadwork. A reproduced 1887 claim shack and period rooms feature 19th-century furniture. Exhibits of clothing contain horsehide mittens, elegant hats, fans, baby clothes, and dresses. A collection of World War I memorabilia, farm equipment, and farm-related photographs, and an assortment of miscellaneous items are also displayed. *Open P.M. Fri.– Sun. May–Nov. except Thanksgiving Day.*

232 | Roy Lake State Park

23 mi./30 min. West on Rte. 10; follow signs. Artifacts found here reveal that this was the site of a pre-Columbian Indian village, thought to have been the most northerly settlement of a culture that prevailed in the area from A.D. 900 to 1300. The park's two sections, east and west, border the lake, where crystal-clear glacial waters nurture an abundance of perch, bullheads, bluegills, walleyes, and largemouth bass. The park has hiking trails, a beach for swimming and sunning, campgrounds, and a ramp for launching boats. Cabins occupy the tip of the western section. Winter sports enthusiasts can enjoy the trails for cross-country skiing and snowmobiling. *Open year-round. Admission charged May–Sept.*

213 | Hartford Beach State Park

18 mi./20 min. East on Rte. 15. The 22,400 acres of Big Stone Lake are the headwaters of the Minnesota River, on the border between Minnesota and South Dakota. In the late 19th and early 20th centuries, pleasure steamers cruised its waters, and hotels catered to vacationers. Wooded bluffs on the lake, their heights topped with prairie and meadow, provide scenic panoramas of Big Stone Island, a nature preserve that can be reached only by boat in summer or across the ice in winter. *Open year-round. Admission charged.*

207 | Blue Cloud Abbey

10 mi./15 min. East on Rte. 12. Located on a hill above the Whetstone Valley prairie, this community of 50 or so Benedictine monks welcomes visitors seeking prayer, peace of mind, or simple relaxation. The complex of modern-looking stone buildings was constructed by the monks themselves in the 1950's and 1960's. Also to be found here is the American Indian Culture Research Center, which coordinates the monks' service activities among Indian communities and displays such items as a ceremonial pipe and a model of a burial scaffold. The abbey itself features a glowing stained-glass window and a fine mural depicting the monks' work among the Indians. *Open year-round.*

177 | Kampeska Heritage Museum, Watertown

4 mi./8 min. West on Rte. 212, right on Maple St. The museum occupies the main floor, basement, and mezzanine of the former public library, a handsome building with classical columns and ornate woodwork. The exhibits detail the cultural history of Codington County (the first white settlers arrived in the 1870's) and include a series of period rooms furnished in the styles favored locally early in the 20th century. A bank interior with handsome oak and marble furnishings, a well-provisioned general store, and a telephone switchboard also recall the early days in South Dakota. *Open P.M. Tues.–Sun. June–Aug.; P.M. Tues.–Sat. Sept.–May.*

26

37

15

23

ND
SD
44

232

19

213

6

207

30

177

37

140

132

109

I-90

79

8

23

25

5

See
E—W book,
sec. 4.

90

140 | Oakwood Lakes State Park

12 mi./15 min. West on Rte. 30; follow signs. Eight glacial lakes, 3,000 acres of sparkling blue formed during the last ice age, are set amid the lush meadows and woodland that were once, according to legend, an Indian tribal meeting place. Later it became the haunt of trappers and farmers, as evidenced by the Mortimer Cabin, which was built by a fur trader in 1867–70. The structure is furnished crudely, as it might have been when first occupied. In a meadow now reverting to prairie land are Indian mounds. To the south the site of a onetime fort is marked by a solitary log cabin. On Scout Island (actually a peninsula) the ¾-mile Tetonkaha Trail loops through marsh, scrubland, and stands of cottonwoods—favored by bald eagles for roosting and nesting—willows, and bur oaks. From the southern tip of the nature trail you can enjoy some unusually fine lake views. *Open year-round. Admission charged.*

132 | McCrory Gardens, Brookings

2 min. West on Rte. 14, right on 20th St. These 70 acres of ornamental gardens, which are maintained by the South Dakota State University Horticulture-Forestry Department, are a delightful resource for those planning their own landscaping. The numerous varieties of annuals, perennials, dwarf conifers, vines, and roses, some of them especially hybridized to withstand the rigors of the South Dakota climate, are all carefully labeled. There are test beds of 140 varieties of Kentucky bluegrasses and perennial ryegrasses. An adjoining arboretum has a good collection of ornamental shrubs and trees. *Open year-round.*

132 | State Agricultural Heritage Museum, Brookings

6 min. West on Rte. 14, right on Medary Ave.; follow signs. A colorful account of agriculture on the plains of South Dakota from the 1860's to the present is displayed here. Noteworthy exhibits include a claim shanty built in 1882—20 years after the Homestead Act went into effect—its walls still covered with the original newspaper liners, and a magnificently restored 1915 Case steam-traction engine, resplendent in black, red, and green. Collections of historical photographs and posters bring the past to life; and remarkable exhibits honor the state's leading agronomists and pioneer breeders of hybrid corn, rust-free wheat, and fruit trees hardy enough to withstand the winters here. A small heritage garden contains an impressive living museum of South Dakota's native grasses and staple crops. *Open Mon.–Sat. and P.M. Sun.*

109 | Lake Herman State Park

19 mi./25 min. West on Rte. 34. The campground and picnic areas of this 176-acre peninsula park overlook beautiful Lake Herman and are shaded by stands of native oak. The site was frequented by Indians, and occasionally an arrowhead can be found along the trail. The peninsula's first white settler, Herman Luce, lived here, and the log cabin he built in 1871 still stands. There's good hiking, cycling, and cross-country skiing on the nearly 50 miles of trails, and fishing for walleye is popular. Along the Luce Trail, which circles the 15-acre pond at the center of the park, hikers can see hackberry and box elder trees, wild roses, cotoneasters, and Virginia creeper. More than 200 species of birds have been observed in the area. *Open year-round. Admission charged.*

109 | Prairie Village

22 mi./30 min. West on Rte. 34; follow signs. To wander through this collection of more than 40 buildings brought from the surrounding area, and now restored, is to come as close as possible to life as it was on the prairie in the late 1800's.

The depot, country store, blacksmith's shop, schoolhouse, dentist's office, barbershop, church, saloon, and jail were staples of most small communities, and the hotel and opera house were not uncommon. Characteristic of the prairie are the claim shanty, the sod house, and a plot of plants and grasses that once grew here. Without water from the windmill, the trademark structure here, life would not have been possible. There's a fine old carousel, locomotive and popcorn wagon—all originally steam-driven—and a number of antique tractors and threshing machines. *Open daily May–Sept. Admission charged.*

I-90 | Buffalo Ridge

5 mi./8 min. West on I-90 to Exit 390; follow signs. The buffalo are still at home on the range, although they don't roam as widely as they did in days gone by. Here, alongside Interstate 90, a herd of 40 to 50 bison graze on their 160-acre preserve.

140. *Cottonwoods add golden hues to the skyline and waters of Oakwood Lake.*

109. *All the needs, from shirts to seeds, could be fulfilled at the country store.*

The man-made attraction is a reproduction of a 19th-century western cow town. It has a blacksmith's shop, a gunsmith's shop, an opera house, a stagecoach office, and the all-important jail, among other displays. Models in many of the exhibits will speak contemporary dialogue when activated by a push button. *Open year-round. Admission charged.*

79 Sherman Park, Sioux Falls

5 mi./6 min. East on 12th St., right on Kiwanis Ave. The park, with meadows, ballfields, tennis courts, a skating rink, a children's playground, and shady picnic grounds, lies on the banks of the Big Sioux River. At the northern end is the U.S.S. *South Dakota* Battleship Memorial, a full-size concrete plan of the warship, and a museum of memorabilia. The rest of the park is devoted to the Great Plains Zoo, where a collection of some 300 animals from all parts of the world ranges from the elegantly aloof snow leopard to the appealing Sicilian donkey. The Delbridge Museum of Natural History at the zoo features mounted animals in lifelike dioramas. One exhibit shows what the world looks like to the animals. *Open daily except Christmas. Admission charged.*

38 Union County State Park

5 min. East on Rte. 15, right on Rte. 1C. The park includes the slopes of a glacial moraine and a mixture of woodlands, old meadows reverting to scrub, and prairies. From Parkview Hill, one of the highest points in southeastern South Dakota, there are sweeping views of the area. The Arboretum Trail wanders through plantings of many types of trees that can survive in this climate—for example, the smoke tree, the white poplar, the ponderosa pine, the honeysuckle, and the Kentucky coffee tree. In the fall the trees put on a colorful display and provide berries and seeds for birds and small mammals. *Open year-round but may be inaccessible in winter.*

26 Shrine to Music Museum, Vermillion

8 mi./10 min. West on Rte. 50, left on Pine St., right on Clark St. The delights of this remarkably complete music museum range from violins by the great instrument makers at Cremona—Stradivari, Guarneri, and the Amati family—to sinuously beautiful wood and ivory lutes and such ingenious creations as the "spittoon with bell-ringer and electric igniter" made by Stanley Fritts for his Korn Kobblers band. Other special

treasures include European and American keyboard instruments, many of them masterpieces of the cabinetmaker's art, various Italian stringed instruments, nonwestern curiosities, including trumpets made from human leg bones, folk instruments, and a glittering assortment of American band instruments. *Open Mon.–Sat. and P.M. Sun. except Thanksgiving Day, Christmas, and New Year's Day. Admission free but donations encouraged.*

150 Stone State Park

5 mi./8 min. Northwest on Rte. 12. This 1,100-acre park is on the crest and valleys of a loess bluff, one of nature's wonders. Loess is a type of wind-blown soil or loam found mainly in China, the U.S.A., and a few places in Europe. A ridge-top road affords splendid views of the Missouri Valley and heavily wooded hills. Numerous bridle, hiking, cross-country skiing, and snowmobile trails crisscross this unusual terrain once held sacred by the Indians. The self-guiding Carolyn Benne Nature Trail winds through lush wooded-valley vegetation and crosses marshlands and prairies. An informative pamphlet describing the plants on this trail is available. *Open year-round. Admission charged.*

NEB Sioux City Public Museum

Nebraska St. exit: 3 mi./9 min. North on Nebraska St., right on 29th St. Built of pink-colored Sioux Falls quartzite in the early 1890's, the Peirce Mansion first changed hands when the original owner lost his fortune and raffled off the house for $1 a chance. Since then, the mansion has had more than nine different owners and for a while served as a dormitory for student nurses before it became a public museum in 1961. Rooms display pioneer materials, ranging from antique needlework to a furnished log cabin interior, and depict the natural history of the area through displays of birds, animals, fish, and minerals. A number of Indian artifacts are also on display. *Open Mon.–Sat. and P.M. Sun. except holidays. Admission free but donations encouraged.*

112 Lewis and Clark State Park

2 min. West on Rte. 175. Named for Meriwether Lewis and William Clark, the first white men to lead an exploratory expedition to the Pacific Northwest, this 286-acre park is located on a horseshoe-shaped lake formed by the Missouri River. Lewis and Clark spent several days here in 1804 observing the plants and animals. Today you can easily do the same on the nature trails. Along with other varieties of plants and animals, you'll see jack pines, diamond willows, wild roses, coyotes, white-tailed deer, and possibly the elusive mink. The adjacent Blue Lake, covering 983 acres, offers a variety of water activities, including swimming, water-skiing, boating, and fishing. A replica of the keelboat that was used on the 1804 expedition sits on the lakeshore. *Open year-round. Admission charged.*

75 Harrison County Historical Village

5 mi./9 min. East on Rte. 30. The 10 buildings in this complex provide an appealing view of the past in this area of western Iowa. An 1870 tricycle, 100-year-old light bulbs, antique wedding gowns, and a 1540 Spanish pike are among the various articles presented in the main building. The Jail exhibits the first police radio used in the county, the Medical Building displays an early X-ray machine and medicine bottles, and the Chapel has antique Bibles, including a New Testament written in Cherokee. Other buildings display early-day items such as a hickory-frame bicycle, an 1830 McCormick reaper, a 12-pound buffalo gun, and an unusual combination high chair/baby carriage. *Open Tues.–Sat. and P.M. Sun. May–Sept. Admission charged.*

57 | 3 The Historic General Dodge House, Council Bluffs

Exit 57: 3 mi./5 min. South on Rte. 192, left on 9th Ave., left on 3rd St. Exit 3: 3 mi./10 min. North on 6th St., right on 5th Ave., right on 3rd St. This three-story Victorian mansion, built in 1869 by Gen. Grenville Dodge, befits the man who once surveyed some 60,000 miles of track and who later presided over 16 railroad companies. The house is elegantly detailed throughout. In the dining room, where two graceful silver tea services are displayed, the general was host to five U.S. presidents and other luminaries. On the ground floor you'll see front and back parlors with fine lace curtains, Austrian crystal chandeliers and pier mirrors at each end. A child's bedroom houses an appealing exhibit of period toys and baby clothes as well as a four-story dollhouse furnished in detail. The third-floor ballroom holds a square rosewood grand piano, a pump organ, and a large music box. *Open Tues.–Sat. and P.M. Sun. except Jan. Admission charged.*

54 Omaha, NE 68183

Convention & Visitors Bureau, 1819 Farnam St., Suite 1200. (402) 444-4660. There's much more to Nebraska's largest city than the well-known grain and livestock business. It is also rich in parks and museums. The Joslyn Art Museum, an impressive art deco building clad in pink marble, houses fine regional and international collections. A replica of President Lincoln's funeral car, along with other railroad memorabilia, is on view at the Union Pacific Historical Museum. The Great Plains Black Museum features rare photos and displays on black American history, and the Omaha Children's Museum has a variety of hands-on exhibits. Gerald Ford was born here, and his birth site includes exhibits, gardens, and a model of the original house. The Old Market, a shopping area that was once a fruit and vegetable market, has a number of interesting shops, pubs, galleries, restaurants, and boutiques. The famous Boys Town offers self-guiding and conducted tours of its campus.

10 Waubonsie State Park

6 mi. /8 min. East on Rte. 2, right on Rte. 239. The striking terrain of this spectacular park (named for an Indian chief) is made up of glacial sediment deposited by the wind. The dramatic landscape, with yucca and other dry-land plants, seems to have been magically transported from semiarid areas farther west of these midwestern plains. The geological formations—called loess hills—can be found only here in Iowa, in Missouri, and in China. A striking feature of the topography is the delicately terraced "cat steps" on the western side of the steep, narrow ridges. Other areas of the park are less spectacular, but they are invitingly bright with flowers in spring and colorful foliage in fall. *Open year-round. Admission charged.*

84 Big Lake State Park

9 mi./12 min. West on Rte. 118, left on Rte. 111. At 615 acres, this is the largest natural lake in Missouri. It is an oxbow lake thought to have been left behind when the meandering Missouri River carved a more direct route downstream. It is now the habitat of beavers and other river creatures, as well as waterfowl attracted to the shallow water and lush marshlands. Pelicans, great blue herons, and in winter, bald eagles are among the more interesting species to be seen here. The lake is deep enough for boating and water-skiing; yet it is shallow enough to offer excellent fishing for catfish, carp, crappie, bass, and bluegill. *Open year-round.*

46 St. Joseph, MO 64502

Chamber of Commerce, 7th and Felix Sts. (816) 232-4461. This pleasant city has a variety of museums and historical attractions, many of which are within an easy walk of one another. At the Pony Express Museum you'll see how the mail was carried to California for a brief period before the age of the telegraph. The Patee House Museum, once the Pony Express headquarters, now has communications displays, an old train, and a restored city street from the 1800's. Excellent exhibits on American Indians and the history of the West are housed in the St. Joseph Museum, and the Albrecht Art Museum has formal gardens and displays of American art from the past three centuries. Hundreds of antique dolls and toys reside in the city's Doll Museum, and at the Jesse James Home you can visit this famous outlaw's last place of refuge. If you find the outdoors more appealing, there are 1,550 lovely acres of city parks that invite exploration.

Road signs (left margin): 112, 37, 75, 18, 57, 3, 54, 5, 3, 39, 10

See E–W book, sec. 21.

IA / MO

20 Pirtle's Weston Vineyards Winery

12 mi./15 min. West on Rte. 92, right on Rte. 45. For those who don't believe that wine is made in Missouri, there's Pirtle's. This establishment produces eight wines made from grapes, an apple wine, and mead, made from honey and described by the owner as man's oldest type of wine. All of these can be tasted and purchased in the upstairs portion of the winery, which was once a Lutheran church. Built in 1867, the brick church now has stained-glass windows made by the vintner and containing the winery's wild rose motif. The cellars, with a capacity of 20,000 gallons, occupy the church's ground floor (this area is not open to the public). *Open Mon.–Sat. and P.M. Sun. except holidays.*

I-70 Kansas City, MO 64107

Convention & Visitors Bureau, 1100 Main St., Suite 2550. (816) 221-5242; (800) 523-5953 outside MO. It may come as a surprise, but this beautifully planned city has more miles of boulevards than Paris and,

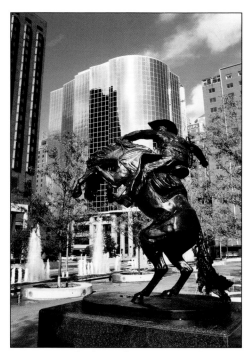

I-70. *In a sleek modern setting, "Bronco Buster" recalls Kansas City's rugged past.*

like Rome, has many beautiful fountains. Its shopping centers, too, are noted for their appealing ambience. The Country Club Plaza, which spreads over 55 acres, is known for its architectural echoes of Seville, Spain, as well as for its shops; Crown Center is an 85-acre city within a city; and at Westport Square some handsome Victorian structures have been turned into shops and restaurants. Among the museums here are the unique Miniature Museum and the Nelson-Atkins Museum of Art, noted for the range of its holdings and special emphasis on works from China and India. Swope Park, which contains the Kansas City Zoo and other attractions, is one of the largest municipal parks in the nation.

I-70. *This modest home was called the Summer White House from 1945 to 1953.*

I-70 Independence, MO 64050

Truman Home Ticket and Information Center, 223 N. Main St. (816) 254-9929. As might be expected, "the man from Independence," our 33rd president, is well remembered here. There is in fact a Harry S Truman Historic District, a walking tour of which begins at the Truman home (the Summer White House) and winds through a well-preserved neighborhood of brick sidewalks and stately homes. Elsewhere in the city is the Truman Library and Museum, which has a reproduction of his White House office among other exhibits. The restored office and courtroom where Truman began his career is located in the Independence Square Courthouse. There's

also a 35-minute audiovisual presentation. Other historic places include the 19-acre Bingham-Waggoner Estate and the Vaile Mansion, a classic example of Victorian architectural exuberance.

I-70 Agricultural Hall of Fame and National Center

18 mi./30 min. West on I-70 to Exit 224, north on Rte. 7; follow signs. An important aspect of Americana is recalled here in this major national institution that is dedicated to American farmers. In the Hall of Rural Living, displays re-create the parlor, sewing room, kitchen, and other elements of the country home of an imaginary grandmother. Her laundry room has manual and early electric washers, and her "back-porch yard" overflows with canning equipment and glassware. In Ye Ol' Town, scenes of rural life include a general store, a telephone exchange, a dentist's office, and a wheelwright's shop. Also noteworthy are the Museum of Farming, a vast warehouse filled with farm equipment, the National Farmers Memorial, with massive bronze-relief panels depicting farmers past, present, and future, and Farm Town U.S.A., which includes a 100-year-old railroad station, a blacksmith's shop, and a restored one-room schoolhouse. *Open daily Apr.–Nov. Admission charged.* ♿

I-70 Wyandotte County Historical Society and Museum

21 mi./30 min. West on I-70 to Exit 224, north on Rte. 7; follow signs. History here in the heart of the Central Plains starts with the Indians, most notably the Wyandots, an educated people who emigrated from Ohio in 1843 and built a town complete with church, school, and council house. The exhibits in this museum trace life in the region from those days until well into this century. Other displays concentrate on local industries. Transportation is a popular theme, with memorabilia from the railroads and riverboats, which caused this strategically located crossroads to boom, and from the various streetcars that once plied the streets of nearby Kansas City, Kansas. A 1903 steam-driven fire truck is also on display. *Open Tues.–Sun. late Feb.–late Dec. except Thanksgiving Day.*

51

84

38

46

26

20

23

See N–S book, sec. 18.

🛣 35

See E–W book, sec. 29.

🛣 35 🛣 70   I-70   🛣 70

End I-29

256

235

214

180

131

256 | The Depot, Duluth

1 min. Continue on Michigan St. Duluth's splendid old Union Depot has been transformed into a series of museums, galleries, and a theater. At ground level is Depot Square, a complex of turn-of-the-century shops and the Lake Superior Museum of Transportation. Minnesota's first railway engine, the 1861 brown and yellow *William Crooks*, is resplendent with sparkling steel and brass fixtures and a green boiler. On Level 2 there are displays about early settlers as well as excellent collections of costumes, dolls, and glass. Level 3 features the Heritage Room, with exhibits ranging from Victorian furniture to tin bathtubs, and Level 4 has the Sieur Dulhut Room, which documents the culture of the native Ojibwas and offers a gallery of paintings of Indian life by Eastman Johnson. *Open daily except Thanksgiving Day, Christmas Eve, Christmas Day, New Year's Day, and Easter. Admission charged.* ♿

235 | Jay Cooke State Park

6 mi./8 min. East on Rte. 210. The St. Louis River has cut a deep gorge through the rugged terrain here, where the dramatic sound of rushing water contrasts with the stately serenity of the hardwood forest. Beginning near the nature center, the Carlton

Trail traverses an enchanting landscape that includes a swinging bridge, tilted slabs of rock sliced by waterfalls, isolated pools, and birch-covered islands in midstream. Oldenburg Point, an overlook on the more elevated Ogantz Trail, affords a scenic view of the river valley. Other trails penetrate the forested interior. Altogether, there are some 50 miles of trails in the park. *Open year-round. Admission charged.*

214 | Moose Lake State Recreation Area

1 min. East on Rte. 137. Echo Lake, edged with meadows, marshland, and woods, attracts anglers who try for bass, pike, or panfish. To the north of the lake lie about a thousand acres of pleasant rolling terrain that was once farmland. Today it is planted with pine and spruce to supplement the stands of mature aspen, birch, and maple. One hiking trail follows the edge of the lake, and three others extend into the wooded slopes. *Open year-round. Admission charged.*

180 | Kanabec History Center, Mora

19 mi./24 min. West on Rte. 23. Located in a 30-acre park on the Snake River, this museum preserves the history and portrays the lives of the early settlers of Minnesota's

heartland. Exhibits include an abundant assortment of homemade furnishings, such as cabinets, cupboards, and tables; early household and agricultural equipment; manuscripts; and photographs. On the grounds you will find a 1904 schoolhouse and an 1899 log structure, along with early farm machinery. Seasonal highlights include quilt shows, craft demonstrations, workshops, and art exhibits. The history center's library has genealogical listings and other family historical data, which are available to the public for research. *Open Mon.–Sat. and P.M. Sun. and holidays. Admission charged.*

131 | Carlos Avery Wildlife Area

5.5 mi./9 min. West on Rte. 18. The meadows and marshland of this beautiful, unspoiled wildlife preserve are traversed by sandy roads that may present a challenge in winter and spring to vehicles designed for more civilized surfaces. Nevertheless, the reeds and cattails that alternate with tracts of oak, birch, and aspen create an interesting environment for appreciative observers of nature. Certain parts of the area, which have been designated as wildlife sanctuaries, are not open to the public. *Open year-round.* ♿

17C | Minneapolis—St. Paul, MN 55402

Convention & Visitors Association, 15 S. 5th St. (612) 348-4313; (800) 445-7412 outside MN. In summer the parks and waterways clearly dominate the activity here near the headwaters of the Mississippi River. Less obvious are the ways Minnesotans use to cope with the cold. In the dead of winter the enclosed skyways can make you forget you are this far north. Nicollet Mall is a focal point in Minneapolis. Its famed Guthrie Theater and Walker Art Center beckon, there's an excellent zoo, and the Grain Exchange offers a look at the operations of a grain market. Across the river in St. Paul you can visit the state capitol, the Science Museum of Minnesota, the opulent Victorian mansion of territorial governor Alexander Ramsey, and if you choose to forsake the comfort of the skyways in late January, the Winter Carnival.

235. *These jagged rocks have long resisted the smoothing action of the St. Louis River.*

21

21

34

49

I-35 West   I-35 East

3B   Valleyfair, Shakopee

9 mi./15 min. Southwest on Rte. 13 and Rte. 101, right on Valley Park Dr. Thrilling rides with such exhilarating names as Looping Starship, High Roller, Corkscrew, and Flying Trapeze entice the adventurous to this 65-acre amusement park. A six-story movie theater with a gigantic screen offers excitement similar to that of the rides, and six theatrical programs throughout the park feature live entertainment. *Open mid-May–Labor Day; weekends only in Sept. Admission charged.*

92   Minnesota Zoo, Apple Valley

3 min. South on Cedar Ave.; follow signs. Almost everything about this zoo is exemplary: the grounds are clean and well landscaped, displays are nicely labeled and described, and the animals live in appropriate environments. Five different trails explore a variety of habitats. The Ocean Trail has crabs, clown fish, and sea anemones; the cry of tropical birds echoing from cliffs can be heard on the Tropics Trail; the Minnesota Trail shows animals native to the region; the Northern Trail has hardy outdoor animals; and the Discovery Trail permits close encounters with a number of domestic and exotic animals. *Open daily except Christmas. Admission charged.*

56   Sakatah Lake State Park

13 mi./20 min. West on Rte. 60. This state park lies on the south shore of Sakatah Lake. The lake, actually a widening of the Cannon River, was created when massive blocks of ice were left behind by retreating glaciers at the end of the Ice Age—some 11,000 years ago. The river is a natural ecological boundary between Minnesota's "big woods" country to the north and the oak barrens to the south. The rolling terrain of the park is wooded with bur oaks, white oaks, walnut trees, and other hardwoods; and it is traversed by a section of the 42-mile Sakatah Singing Hills State Trail. This multiple-use trail, which follows the right-of-way of an abandoned railway line, is suitable for bicycling. *Open year-round. Admission charged.*

92. *Cool cat. A Siberian tiger, obviously comfortable in the snows of Minnesota.*

40   The Village of Yesteryear, Owatonna

3 mi./7 min. East on Rte. 14/218, left on Rte. 6 (Austin Rd.). The centerpiece of this fine historical village in southern Minnesota is Dunnell House, built in 1868–69 and featuring a "widow's walk" cupola modeled after examples in Maine. The house has some unusual antiques, including hand-painted Bavarian china, a decanter once used by President Lincoln, and a variety of antique hats, lace blouses, and dresses. Victorian toys and baby carriages are displayed in the basement. On the grounds are eight other historical buildings, including St. Wenceslaus Church, built in 1876 by Bohemian Catholics in the former town of Saco. *Open P.M. Wed. and weekends mid-May–mid-Sept. Admission charged.*

13   Freeborn County Museum and Village, Albert Lea

5 min. West on I-90 to Exit 158, south on Bridge Ave.; follow signs. Twelve historic buildings are preserved here in southern Minnesota, along with a variety of exhibits that tell the story of this county's early days. The main exhibition hall displays pioneer articles ranging from trunks and baby clothes to a Swedish harp. There's also a well-equipped kitchen, a comfortable parlor, an elegant millinery shop, Indian artifacts, antique bottles, a mammoth

tusk from a local gravel pit, and much more. The Red Barn houses a fully equipped train depot, a barbershop, bank, jail, firehouse, tractors, steam engines, agricultural equipment, and automobiles.

Elsewhere in the village is the first log house in Freeborn County (built in 1853), a rural schoolhouse, a hardware store, a collection of millstones, a genteel parsonage, a cobbler's shop, an 1870's church, and a general store that stocks everything from hatpins to horse collars. *Open P.M. Tues.–Sun. June–Aug.; P.M. Sun. May and Sept.–Oct. Admission charged.*

11   Helmer Myre State Park

3 min. East on Rte. 46, right on Rte. 38. The sweet smell of tall-grass prairie and the shining expanse of Albert Lea Lake (2,600 acres) are the most immediate attractions of this park in southern Minnesota. The terrain reflects the park's glacial past and varies from prairie to oak savanna, marsh, forest, and esker. The park is well known for its waterfowl and shorebirds, and more than 450 varieties of wildflowers grow here. Hikers will find several well-maintained trails, and canoe rentals are available. An interpretive center on Big Island features an outstanding collection of Indian artifacts. *Open year-round. Admission charged.*

27

17C

94

See E–W book, sec. 12.

14   39

3B

92

I-35 West   I-35 East

35   32

56

16

40

27

See E–W book, sec. 5.

13   90

2

11

MN

IA

21

35

35

208

14

194

29

165

54

ROUTE 30

24

I-235 80

See E–W book, sec. 21.

15

80 I-235

4

68

12

208   Rice Lake State Park

10 mi./15 min. West on Rte. A38, right on Rte. R74. The park lies on small but attractive Rice Lake, which has an irregular wooded shoreline. A trail for hikers and horseback riders follows the shore; there is also a stone picnic shelter and a place from which to launch canoes. *Open year-round. Admission charged.*

194   Kinney Pioneer Museum

2 min. East on Rte. 18. The museum's comprehensive displays reveal what the old days were like in north-central Iowa. Military collections span the Civil War and World War I, and several period rooms exhibit such local furnishings as the 1878 cradle used for the first child born to settlers in nearby Clear Lake, and a grand piano brought by oxcart from Dubuque. There are good displays of looms, sewing machines, and radios and cameras (including a World War II Japanese gun camera). Antique dolls, music boxes, an apple press, a telephone switchboard, several working models of steam engines, horse-drawn vehicles, vintage automobiles, and a broom maker actually assembling brooms all add to the museum's period atmosphere.

On the grounds you can see a furnished log cabin, a blacksmith's shop, a one-room schoolhouse dating from 1921, and a caboose from the Milwaukee Railroad that's full of related memorabilia: a book of yellowing Iowa Central waybills from 1904, old photographs, telegrams, and overalls. *Open P.M. Wed.–Fri. and Sun., May–Sept. Admission charged.*

165   Beeds Lake State Park

8 mi./11 min. East on Rte. 3; follow signs. A trail winds around the wooded shore of the unusually lovely man-made lake in this park, and a 600-foot dike provides an enticing sandy swimming beach. The dam itself has a high stone spillway, and in the spring a wide pool forms at the bottom of the bubbling waterfall. The park is also an animal and bird refuge. Overall, the gentle and attractive terrain makes an appealing change from the farm country that surrounds the park. *Open year-round. Admission charged.*

ROUTE 30   Ledges State Park

21 mi./30 min. West on Rte. 30, left on Rte. 17; follow signs. This park is a wild area that gets its unusual name from the sand-

stone cliffs on Pease Creek, a miniature canyonland in the woods that can be seen from a loop road. (In wet weather the creek may overflow, closing the road.) Several trails wind up and down the park's ravines and ridges, and overlooks (especially the aptly named Inspiration Point) provide some spectacular vistas of the floodplain of the Des Moines River. On the Riverside Floodplain Trail you'll find an observation area in a region of wetlands prairie, and for bird-watchers there's a wildfowl blind on Lost Lake along the Ledges Nature Trail. On the Wildlife Loop Trail you can see exhibits of several native animals in their natural environment. *Open year-round. Admission charged.*

I-235   Des Moines, IA 50309

I-235   *Convention & Visitors Bureau, 309 Court Ave., Suite 300. (800) 451-2625.* Across from the gold-domed capitol, the Iowa State Historical Building provides an introduction to the history and prehistory of the region. The governor's house, Terrace Hill, is a superb example of a mid-19th-century mansion, which is now opulently furnished as it was in the 1870's. Salisbury House is a 42-room replica of King's House in Salisbury, England. The interior spaces contain furnishings in the Tudor style and are highlighted by the rich colors of Oriental rugs and stained-glass windows. Modern tastes in art and architecture are displayed in the Des Moines Art Center. Visitors can ride a train through the grounds of the Blank Park Zoo.

68   Walnut Woods State Park

5 min. East on Rte. 5; follow signs. Here on the bank of the Raccoon River is one of the largest surviving natural stands of black walnut trees in North America. These majestic specimens tower over a stone lodge set on manicured lawns, lending the park an impressive manorial character. Picnickers appreciate the tree-shaded grounds beside the river, while fishermen concentrate mostly on catching catfish. Both walking trails and bridle paths invite further exploration of the park. *Open year-round. Admission charged.*

208. *This pair of Canada geese created their nest from the available building supplies.*

56. *This is the view of one hot-air balloon in flight as seen from another.*

56 National Balloon Museum, Indianola

15 mi./17 min. East on Rte. 92, left on Rte. 65/69 (N. Jefferson St.). Indianola is proud of its position as host of a national race of some 200 balloons, usually held for ten days from late July to early August. This museum is an offshoot of that event. Its collection illustrates the colorful history of ballooning as depicted on pewter and china plates, commemorative medals, postage stamps, and enamel lapel badges representing specific balloons as well as in historical photographs, prints, and paintings. Samples of balloon fabrics and gas cylinders and a World War II training basket are also on display. A new building has been designed with an interior spacious enough to accommodate an inflated balloon. *Open Mon.–Fri., by appointment on weekends (515) 961-8415, except holidays.*

56 Madison County Museum and Historical Complex, Winterset

11 mi./21 min. West on Rte. 92, left on Rte. P71 (1st St.), right on W. Summit St., left on S. 2nd Ave. Set atop a hill in the town of Winterset, this museum commands a view of present-day Madison County, and its large collection illuminates the region's past. Among many other objects you can see dolls, tin toys, musical instruments, local advertising items, clocks, clothing, medical and dental equipment, household utensils, Indian artifacts, portraits, farm equipment, quilts, fossils, and—if you can imagine it—a collection of some 7,500 pencils and ballpoint pens.

Outside the main building are three authentic log structures: a blacksmith's shop, an 1850's schoolhouse, and a log house that later became the Pleasant View Post Office. *Open daily mid-May–mid-Oct. Admission charged.*

4 Nine Eagles State Park, Davis City

10 mi./12 min. East on Rte. 69, right on Rte. J66. Miles of hiking and equestrian trails wind over the 1,100 acres of ridged and heavily wooded terrain in the park. A sandy swimming beach provides access to the beautifully clear waters of Nine Eagles Lake. The park's notable fauna include white-tailed deer, pheasants, wild turkeys, and a variety of migratory aquatic birds. Anglers can test their mettle against the bass, bluegill, crappie, and channel catfish in the lake. *Open year-round. Admission charged.*

92 Lake Paho Wildlife Area

23 mi./30 min. East on Rte. 136. The lake comes as a relief to the eye amid the vast green and yellow checkerboard of this rich farm country. Paho (from the Indian word meaning "first") was the first lake constructed by Missouri's Department of Conservation; and it is first and foremost a place for fishermen, who try for catfish, crappie, bluegill, walleye, and largemouth bass. Bow-and-arrow fishing is permitted in season. You can rent boats for fishing. A number of fish-rearing ponds adjoin the lake; the 8- to 10-inch fingerlings are used to stock lakes in all parts of the state. Bird-watchers will delight in the resident flock of huge Canada geese, as well as the migratory birds seen in spring and fall. *Open year-round.*

48 Wallace State Park

3 min. South on Rte. 69, left on Rte. 121. This is a small park (500 acres), but its terrain is surprisingly wild and heavily wooded. Several hiking trails crisscross the land, allowing visitors to explore the valleys and ridges formed when streams cut through the glacial loess that underlies the rolling landscape of this part of northwestern Missouri. Deer Creek winds through the park, its banks shaded by majestic sycamores. (Some historians claim that a Mormon trail once crossed the creek.)

Six-acre Lake Allaman lies in a natural clearing near the park's center. It has sandy swimming beaches, and it is also popular with anglers, who seek bluegill, largemouth bass, and channel catfish. A trail traces most of its perimeter. Bird-watching is another popular activity here. *Open year-round.*

26 Watkins Woolen Mill State Historic Site, Lawson

7 mi./16 min. East on Rte. 92, left on Rte. RA. These 475 acres, once part of Waltus Watkins's 19th-century plantation, represent an early and very successful example of an enterprise that integrated both farming and industry. The site's main attraction is Watkins Mill—the only 19th-century woolen mill in America that still has all its original machinery, from carding and spinning to weaving and finishing equipment. During the Civil War the mill turned out blankets and cloth that were purchased by both the Union and the Confederacy.

Watkins's brick home, an example of Greek revival architecture, is furnished to reflect the taste of the 1870's. Restored outbuildings include a summer kitchen and the octagonal Franklin School.

The Watkins Mill State Park grounds are mostly wooded, providing a pleasant contrast to the surrounding farmland. A paved biking and hiking trail traces Williams Creek Lake, which fishermen appreciate for its bass, catfish, and sunfish. You can picnic in the historic area near the mill or beside the lake. *Park open year-round; mill open daily except Thanksgiving Day, Christmas, New Year's Day, and Easter. Admission charged.*

See E–W book, sec. 29.

I-70 Independence, MO 64050

Truman Home Ticket and Information Center, 223 N. Main St. (816) 254-9929. The man from Independence, our 33rd president, is well remembered here. There is a Harry S Truman Historic District, a walking tour of which begins at the Truman home (the Summer White House) and winds through a neighborhood of brick sidewalks and stately homes. The restored office and courtroom where Truman began his career is in the Independence Square Courthouse. Other historic places include the 19-acre Bingham-Waggoner Estate and the Vaile Mansion, a classic example of Victorian architectural exuberance.

2C Kansas City, MO 64107

Convention & Visitors Bureau, 1100 Main St., Suite 2550. (816) 221-5242; (800) 523-5953 outside MO. It may come as a surprise, but this beautifully planned city has more miles of boulevards than Paris and, like Rome, has many beautiful fountains. Its shopping centers are noted for their appealing ambience. The Country Club Plaza has architectural echoes of Seville, Spain; Crown Center is an 85-acre city within a city; and at Westport Square some handsome Victorian structures have been converted into shops and restaurants. Among the museums here are the unique Miniature Museum and the Nelson-Atkins Museum of Art, noted for the range of its holdings and an emphasis on works from China and India. Swope Park, with the Kansas City Zoo and other attractions, is one of the nation's largest municipal parks.

I-70 Agricultural Hall of Fame and National Center

18 mi./30 min. West on I-70 to Exit 224, north on Rte. 7; follow signs. An important aspect of Americana is recalled in a national institution dedicated to farmers. In the Hall of Rural Living, displays re-create the parlor, sewing room, and kitchen of the country home of an imaginary grandmother. Her "back-porch yard" overflows with canning equipment. The scenes of rural life in Ye Ol' Town include a general store, a telephone exchange, and a wheelwright's shop. Also noteworthy are the Museum of Farming, a warehouse filled with farm equipment, the National Farmers Memorial, which displays bronze-relief panels, and Farm Town U.S.A., with a 100-year-old railroad station and a restored one-room schoolhouse. *Open daily Apr.–Nov. Admission charged.* ♿

2C. *"The Scout" and his horse overlook a scene that was unimaginable in their time.*

I-70 Wyandotte County Historical Society and Museum

21 mi./30 min. West on I-70 to Exit 224, north on Rte. 7; follow signs. History here in the heart of the Central Plains starts with the Indians, most notably the Wyandots, an educated people who emigrated from Ohio in 1843 and built a town complete with church, school, and council house. These Huron people gave their name to the county that today contains Kansas City, Kansas. The exhibits in this museum trace life in the region from those days until well into this century. Other displays concentrate on local industries. Transportation is a popular theme, with memorabilia from the railroads and riverboats, which caused this strategic crossroads to boom, and from the streetcars that once plied Kansas City's streets. A 1903 steam-driven fire truck is also on display. *Open Tues.–Sun. late Feb.–late Dec. except Thanksgiving Day.*

187 / 183 Old Depot Museum, Ottawa

5 min. Exit 187: west on Rte. 68, left on Rte. 59 (Main St.), right on Tecumseh St. Exit 183: north on Rte. 59 (Main St.), left on Tecumseh St. The depot-stationhouse that shelters this local historical collection was built in the late 1800's by the Santa Fe Railroad. Spacious rooms—from a typical schoolroom and a Victorian parlor to a general store and a dentist's office—re-create everyday life in 19th-century Kansas. Other displays are devoted to regional military and transportation history. *Open P.M. Sun. May–Sept.*

155 Melvern State Park

11 mi./17 min. North on Rte. 75, left on Rte. 278. Pleasantly located on the northern shore of 6,900-acre Melvern Lake, this well-developed park is popular for camping, fishing, boating, water-skiing, swimming, and horseback riding. One of the park's most attractive features is a 395-acre tract of virgin tallgrass prairie, providing 20th-century vacationers with a glimpse of what the land looked like centuries ago, when vast herds of bison roamed across present-day Kansas. *Open year-round. Admission charged.* ⛺ ▲ 🚐 🚶 🐎 🐟 ♿

187–183. *This reproduced parlor depicts the engaging clutter of Victorian decor.*

130 | Emporia Gazette Building

5 min. South on Rte. 99, left on 12th St., right on Merchant St. This is a working newspaper office, and though formal tours are offered by appointment only, unofficial tours given by well-informed staff members can usually be arranged through the receptionist in the lobby. The *Gazette*, a stronghold of liberal Republicanism, was once the domain of William Allen White, the paper's longtime editor (1895–1944) and the confidant of presidents (including both of the Roosevelts). A display room showcases White's books and other memorabilia, and his small office, used since the turn of the century, can be seen. The newsroom also retains its old-fashioned ambience despite the contemporary computer terminals used by reporters. *Open Mon.– Fri. and A.M. Sat. except holidays.*

71 | Butler County Historical Museum, El Dorado

5 min. East on Rte. 54 (Central Ave.). The colorful history of this south-central region of Kansas from the era of the Wichita Indi-

ans, through Old West cattle drives, to the discovery of oil in 1915, is captured in this excellent museum. El Dorado became a boomtown during the era of frenzied oil drilling, and the town remains prosperous to this day. The rambling outdoor exhibit area, which includes a full-size oil derrick, is as engaging as the artifacts and historical exhibits housed inside. A shaded picnic area and playground are near the museum. *Open Tues.–Sat. except holidays.* ♿🚻

49 | Wichita, KS 67202

Convention & Visitors Bureau, 100 S. Main St. (316) 265-2800. Although it's the largest city in Kansas and a major producer of petroleum and aircraft, the days of the buffalo, cowboys, and cattle drivers are not forgotten in Wichita. The Native American presence is thoughtfully represented in the Indian Center Museum. At Old Cowtown Museum some 30 buildings on 17 acres authentically re-create a frontier town in the days when Wichita was a stopping place on the Chisholm Trail.

A fascinating cross section of life in Victorian times can be seen at the Wichita–Sedgwick County Historical Museum, in a Romanesque revival extravaganza known as the Palace of the Plains, which was built in 1892. Several other interests may be pursued at the Omnisphere and Science Center, the innovative Children's Museum, a beautiful botanic garden, and the city's excellent zoo. For art lovers there's the Wichita Art Museum, and on the Wichita State University campus you can see a superb collection of outdoor sculptures and explore the Ulrich Museum.

33 / 19 | Bartlett Arboretum

Exit 33: 10.5 mi./16 min. West on Rte. 53, left on Rte. 81, left on Rte. 55. Exit 19: 16 mi./20 min. West on Rte. 160, right on Rte. 81, right on Rte. 55. This fragrant oasis is a refreshing contrast to the surrounding flat grasslands of south-central Kansas. Its 20 acres of flowers, ornamental trees, and colorful shrubs can be seen from the shaded walkways that follow the edges of the still waters of the lagoon. Some 25,000 tulips bloom in the spring and thou-

sands of chrysanthemums in the fall. But this arboretum is still lovely, and much less crowded, when the flowers have finished blooming. *Open daily Apr.–mid-Nov. Admission charged.*

214 | Pioneer Woman Statue and Museum, Ponca City

18 mi./30 min. East on Rte. 60, left on Rte. 60 (business), left on Rte. 77, right on Lake Rd. This memorial to the courage and fortitude of pioneer womanhood stands appropriately on one of the last parcels of land to be homesteaded in Oklahoma. The 17-foot bronze statue depicts a youthful, undaunted pioneer woman striding alongside her young son. Commissioned by oil magnate and onetime Oklahoma governor E. W. Marland, it was dedicated in 1930. The adjacent museum, which was built about 30 years later, has in its collection a variety of appliances, furnishings, clothing, and other pioneer trappings that show what daily life was like for those who settled and tamed the Oklahoma prairie around the turn of the century. *Museum open Wed.–Sat. and P.M. Sun. except Christmas; statue accessible year-round.* ♿

214. *"Pioneer Woman" and son stride purposefully (and forever) westward.*

35

186

29

157

29

See
E–W book,
sec. 39.

40 | **I-40** | **40**

20

108

57

51

4

47

16

31A

7

24

186   Cherokee Strip Museum

1 min. East on Rte. 64. On Sept. 16, 1893, more than 100,000 people waited for the gunshot that signaled the start of a race to claim a free piece of this flat cinnamon-colored land. The museum illustrates the hard life of the homesteaders by featuring re-creations of a 19th-century doctor's office, a general store, and a pioneer kitchen. Paintings by local artists, Oto-Missouri beadwork, and other Indian artwork represent the territory's inhabitants before 1893. A one-room schoolhouse, a sorghum mill, a jail, a horse-drawn threshing machine, and an enclosure with two white-tailed deer occupy the tree-shaded grounds of the museum. *Open Tues.–Fri. and P.M.. Sat.–Sun. except holidays.*   ⊼

157   Oklahoma Territorial Museum, Guthrie

2 mi./6 min. West on Rte. 33, left on Ash St., left on Oklahoma St. This spacious museum incorporates the Carnegie Library, where the first state governor was inaugurated in 1907 during Guthrie's brief reign

157. *The pump organ still evokes the charm of family music-making at home.*

as Oklahoma's capital. The Pfeiffer Memorial Building, also part of the museum, contains displays of pioneer life. New exhibits portray the wild land rush during which the Oklahoma Territory was settled by white pioneers in 1889. Another gallery houses a windmill, and there are stagecoaches, phaetons, and other horse-drawn vehicles. You'll even find examples of

pump organs and other musical instruments that somehow found their way to the raw frontier. A large collection of cowboy and Indian portraits also includes a portrait of Lon Chaney, who got his start in show business as a stagehand at a Guthrie music hall. *Open Tues.–Fri. and P.M. Sat.–Sun. except holidays.*   ♿

157   State Capital Publishing Museum, Guthrie

2 mi./8 min. West on Rte. 33, left on 2nd St.; follow signs. The fiery editorials of the daily newspaper published in this four-story Victorian building were one reason why officials moved the state capital from Guthrie to Oklahoma City in 1910; a year later the *State Capital* failed. But the building was used for publishing until the 1970's; in 1982 it was converted into a museum. Some aspects of a turn-of-the-century newspaper plant are evoked by a Victorian sales office with a beautifully restored teller's cage and an exhibit of antique typewriters. The pressroom is filled with inky old printshop machinery, including Linotypes and a battery of platen and cylinder presses. *Open Tues.–Sat. and P.M. Sun. except holidays.*

I-40   Oklahoma City, OK 73102

Convention and Tourism Bureau, 4 Santa Fe Plaza. (405) 278-8912. The highlights in this large city, more than 600 square miles in area, are widespread and varied. The National Cowboy Hall of Fame and Western Heritage Center attracts those interested in western lore and artifacts, and the National Softball Hall of Fame appeals to sandlot ballplayers of all ages. The state capitol is unique in that there are producing oil wells on its grounds. Nearby, the State Museum presents the major events in the colorful history of the Indian Territory and Oklahoma. Kirkpatrick Center is a large museum complex featuring African, Oriental, and American Indian art, as well as photography, science, and aerospace displays, a planetarium, and gardens. Oklahoma City's enormous zoo has some 4,000 animals in addition to the Aquaticus, which features dolphin and sea lion shows and varied displays of aquatic life.

108   Little River State Park, Clear Bay Area, Norman

17 mi./20 min. East on Rte. 9; follow signs. Oak-covered hills surround Lake Thunderbird, a popular spot for swimming, sailing, sailboarding, and water-skiing (skis and boats are rented at Calypso Cove). Fishermen try for crappie, bass, and catfish, and a stable in the park offers horseback riding and hayrides. If you hike along the trail, you may see a "rock rose," a reddish-brown rose-shaped cluster of sandy barite crystals sometimes found on sandstone outcroppings. After long weathering, the "roses" become detached and fall down onto the sandy soil. *Open year-round. Admission charged.*   ⊼ ▲ ⛺ 🚶 🎣 ♿

51   Turner Falls Park, Davis

47

5 min. Exit 51: south on Rte. 77. Exit 47: north on Rte. 77. Where Honey Creek plunges 77 feet over limestone ledges and through holes dissolved in the canyon walls, it forms the largest waterfall in Oklahoma. The creek's two natural pools below the falls, one with a sandy beach, have helped swimmers escape the summertime heat since 1868. Visitors can hike steep trails to caves, a natural limestone arch, and fortresslike rock formations near the falls, or take a 1½-mile trip on a miniature train. The woodlands of oak, sycamore, and eastern red cedar are home to white-tailed deer, raccoons, opossums, and a variety of birds. *Open year-round. Admission charged.*   ⊼ ▲ ⛺ 🚶 🎣 🐟

31A   Eliza Cruce Hall Doll Museum, Ardmore

5 min. East on Rte. 199, left on E St. to Ardmore Public Library. This delightful assortment of more than 300 rare and unusual dolls was assembled from many countries by Eliza Cruce Hall of Ardmore. Among the entrancing figures in the display are "court dolls" of carved wood that belonged to Marie Antoinette, an English Queen Anne doll (circa 1728), wood and leather English peddler dolls, dolls made in 1860 to model the latest fashions, and a pair of George and Martha Washington bisque dolls by Emma Clear. Other items include character dolls, miniatures, china dolls, Bye-Lo babies, Kabuki dancers, wax dolls, and toys from around the world. The collection will appeal as much to adults as to children. *Open Mon.–Sat.* ♿

24 Lake Murray State Park

4 min. East on Rte. 77S (scenic). The clear waters of Lake Murray, in Oklahoma's largest park, have made it a favorite site for water sports. Abundant bulrushes, cattails, and other vegetation at the lake provide a habitat for the sizable fish population that draws herons and bald eagles as well as anglers. On land you can play tennis or golf, ride horses or bicycles, or go hiking through forests of oak, ash, elm, red cedar, and hickory. The unique Tucker Tower, a fortresslike museum and nature center set atop a 25-foot rock cliff, features displays of local fossils, minerals, and artifacts. *Park open year-round; tower open Wed.–Mon. mid-May–mid-Sept.; Wed.–Sun. mid-Sept.–mid-May.* 🍴 ⛺ 🏕 🏃 🦆 🎣 ♿

496B Leonard Park–Frank Buck Memorial Zoo, Gainesville

1 min. Southwest on Rte. 51. Aristocratic-looking Chilean flamingos wade through a shallow pool, acrobatic monkeys cavort in their cages, and peacocks fan their multicolored feathers as they roam freely around the grounds. Named for a Gainesville native who captured and trained wild animals, the Frank Buck Zoo displays animals in ways that permit remarkably close viewing. One of the most popular residents is Gerry, an elephant who survived a Texas flash flood by holding her trunk above the water for 24 hours when her body was pinned between a building and a tree. Verdant Leonard Park features the area's first jail and a Civil War veterans' monument that recounts the grim story of local lynchings. *Open year-round.* 🍴 🦆 ♿

428D Dallas, TX 75202

Convention & Visitors Bureau, 400 S. Houston St. (lobby of Union Station). (214) 746-6700. Highlights of life in Dallas include the Neiman-Marcus store, the Cotton Bowl, banking, business, glass-walled skyscrapers, and the $50 million Dallas

428D. *A dazzling Dallas skyline brightens the prairie for miles around.*

Museum of Art. At Fair Park the old and the new are combined with a steam train museum, a science museum, and an aquarium. In Old City Park a bit of 19th-century Dallas is preserved. There's a famous zoo and some unusual museums, such as the Biblical Arts Center and the Telephone Pioneer Museum. Although they recall a time of national trauma, the John F. Kennedy Memorial Plaza and the Texas School Book Depository attract many visitors.

54A Fort Worth, TX 76109

54B *Convention and Visitors Bureau, 123 E. Exchange Ave. (817) 624-4741.* Although a large modern city, Fort Worth has not forgotten the Texas of song and story. Activities at the Stockyards Historical District on the north side of the city include cattle trading and shopping for rodeo gear and western wear. The city also boasts three world-famous art museums: the Kimbell, which displays works ranging from pre-Columbian times to the present; the Amon Carter, which has a fine collection of sculpture, photographs, and paintings featuring the American West; and the Modern Art Museum of Fort Worth, noted for its 20th-century art. The Museum of Science and History offers imaginative exhibits of interest to children as well as adults. The city center is enhanced by the terraced Water Gardens.

ROUTE 67 Cleburne State Recreation Area

23 mi./35 min. Southwest on Rte. 67, left on Park Rd. 21. In the midst of rolling and flat grazing land, this tranquil 1,068-acre park provides a beautiful wooded oasis. The deer, quail, and raccoons that made this a favorite Indian hunting ground are still abundant, and many bird varieties can be observed. The park's 110-acre lake, backed up behind an earthen dam, is filled with clear water that comes from underground springs, and it invites swimming, boating, and fishing. *Open year-round. Admission charged.* 🍴 ⛺ 🏕 🏃 🦆 🎣

368A Lake Whitney State Recreation Area

19 mi./30 min. West on Rte. 22, right on Rte. FM933, left on Rte. FM1244. An attractive lake extending for 45 miles along the Brazos River was an added benefit of a dam built to control flooding and produce power. This 1,000-acre park lets the visitor take full advantage of the lake, which has an excellent swimming beach and is a popular spot for fishing. The park's flat grasslands and occasional clumps of hardwoods provide protection for a variety of wildlife, including deer, raccoons, opossums, armadillos, and many kinds of birds. In spring the plains are carpeted with brightly colored wildflowers. *Open year-round. Admission charged.* 🍴 ⛺ 🏕 🦆 🎣

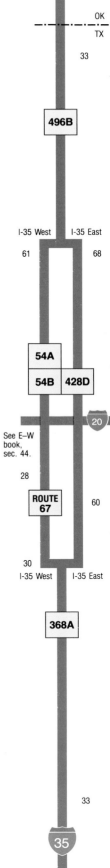

OK
TX

33

496B

I-35 West   I-35 East
61   68

54A

54B   428D

20

See E–W book, sec. 44.

28

ROUTE 67   60

30
I-35 West   I-35 East

368A

33

35

335B

41

294A

35

259

26

233A

18

215

9

206

15

191

16

335B Texas Ranger Hall of Fame and Museum, Waco

1 min. East from exit. Often outnumbered but rarely outfought, the Texas Rangers have become an American legend. They were established by Stephen Austin in 1823, when Texas was still part of Mexico, to protect American settlers. Fittingly, this museum, dedicated to commemorating the exploits of these colorful lawmen, has one of the finest and largest collections of Old West memorabilia to be seen in Texas. The gun collection is especially notable, including many used by famous people (such as Billy the Kid and Buffalo Bill) or involved at historic incidents (the shoot-out that killed Bonnie and Clyde). Ft. Fisher Park, which surrounds the museum, has more than 100 campsites and fishing piers on the Brazos River. *Park open year-round; museum open daily except Thanksgiving Day, Christmas, and New Year's Day. Admission charged.*

294A Belton Lake

5 mi./15 min. West on Rte. 190 (business), right on Rte. 317, left on Rte. 439. Backed up behind an earthen dam, this lake, built and run by the U.S. Army Corps of Engineers, extends for some 26 miles along the valleys of the Leon River and Cowhouse Creek. The lake's main purpose is to prevent flooding and to supply water, but the 13 parks along its southern and eastern shorelines also offer more than 225 campsites and access to the water for water-skiing, sailing, and fishing. Although there are no lifeguards and only one developed beach, swimming is permitted at many sites. Check at the headquarters building for maps and information on the parks. *Open year-round.*

259 Inner Space Cavern

1 min. West from exit. On your way to or from the cavern, which extends under the interstate, you'll pass directly over it. Discovered in 1963, the cavern contains some magnificent examples of stalactites, stalagmites, and flowstone as well as the smaller, much rarer helictites, which grow in all directions and produce beautiful, delicate shapes. Also found here are the remains of a number of Ice Age animals, including the woolly mammoth, saber-toothed tiger, and other extinct species. A guided tour of the cavern takes about an hour, and its natural wonders have been enhanced by sound and light shows. *Open daily Memorial Day–Labor Day; Wed.–Sun. rest of year except 2 weeks during Christmas holidays. Admission charged.*

233A Austin, TX 78704

Convention & Visitors Bureau, 400BS. 1st St. (512) 478-0098. When Mirabeau Lamar, who later served as president of the Republic of Texas, camped with some buffalo hunters here on the Colorado River in 1838, he reportedly suggested that this would be a good place for the capital of the new republic—which it became. The current state capitol building—in true Texas style—is taller than the U.S. Capitol in Washington. The river, called Town Lake where it runs through the city, is still a major attraction, and Zilker Park, with access to the lake, has canoe rentals. The park is noted for its azaleas, roses, oriental garden, miniature train ride, and the Texas-size spring-fed swimming pool.

In the Texas Memorial Museum you'll see reconstructed dinosaurs, Indian artifacts, dioramas, and a large gun collection.

215 / 206 Pioneer Town, Wimberley

Exit 215: 21 mi./35 min. West on Rte. 150, left on Rte. 3237, right on Rte. 12; follow signs. Exit 206: 18 mi./25 min. West on Rte. 12; follow signs. With its boardwalks and false-front pawnshop and saloon, this replica of a late 19th-century Texas town looks like a set for a western movie. The buildings include a general store, opera house, livery stable, assay office, log chapel, and—more surprising—a house built from soda bottles. Two museums house an interesting collection of western art, including many bronzes by the noted artist Frederic Remington. A half-scale version of an 1870's steam train offers a 15-minute ride through the surrounding countryside. *Open Thurs.–Tues. Memorial Day–3rd week of Aug.; Sat. and P.M. Sun. Sept.–Nov., Mar.–May.*

206 Aquarena Springs, San Marcos

5 min. West on Aquarena Springs Dr. In this large, interesting amusement park, the emphasis is on water. Boats with glass bottoms glide over crystalline waters, giving wonderful views of fish and plant life, an archeological site, and even the bubbling springs that feed the lake. A half-hour show features swimmers performing underwater ballet and comedy acts. An especially popular performer is Ralph the Swimming Pig, who dives in and paddles across the water. Other attractions include a trained-bird show, an aerial cable car, a 300-foot tower with observation deck, gardens, and a frontier town. *Open daily except Christmas. Admission charged.*

233A. *The capitol's dome still proudly holds its own on Austin's growing skyline.*

191. *The flotilla of sailboats attests to the size and popularity of Canyon Lake.*

191 Canyon Lake

16 mi./20 min. West on Rte. 306. Several parks border on this 13,000-acre lake, built and maintained by the U.S. Army Corps of Engineers to control the devastating flooding that once plagued this area. Together they offer some 600 campsites and a full range of other facilities with an emphasis on water sports, fishing, and boating. Each park has its own character. On the north shore scuba divers prefer to go to North Park, while Jacobs Creek Park attracts sailboarders and sailors, and Canyon and Potters Creek parks appeal to families. On the south shore fishermen seem most at home at Cranes Mill Park, while younger people gather at Comal Park. *Open year-round.*

175 Natural Bridge Caverns

8 mi./10 min. West on Natural Bridge Caverns Rd. A 60-foot-wide natural limestone bridge provides a fitting entrance to this extraordinary complex of caverns discovered by four college students in 1960. The exceptionally well preserved calcite formations have a striking range of colors. Shapes vary from regular pointed stalactites and rounded stalagmites to those that resemble chandeliers, mushrooms, forests, and almost transparent draperies; and water dripping throughout continues to change the formations. The largest chamber is 350 feet long and 100 feet wide. Guided tours that pass through half a mile of these subterra-

nean wonders are given every half hour and take an hour and a quarter. *Open daily except Thanksgiving Day, Christmas, and New Year's Day. Admission charged.*

158B San Antonio, TX 78205

Visitor Information Center, 317 Alamo Plaza. (512) 299-8155. The Alamo is, of course, the major historical treasure of this city. The second best known attraction is the Paseo del Rio—a below-street-level string of sidewalk cafés, clubs, hotels, and artisans' shops that line the banks of the meandering San Antonio River. A good spot for an overview is the top of the 750-foot-high Tower of the Americas. Be sure to visit the San Antonio Museum of Art and the Witte Museum's displays of anthropology, history, and natural science. The 1749 Spanish Governor's Palace and the Alamo's four sister missions further reveal the city's historic heritage.

158B. *The Alamo: fabled in song and story and a frequently photographed site.*

1A Nuevo Santander Museum Complex, Laredo

2 mi./10 min. West on Washington St. to Laredo Junior College; follow signs. This campus museum is housed in three build-

ings that were once part of Ft. McIntosh. Built around the turn of the century, the main structure was formerly the post's chapel and now displays traveling exhibits that highlight the influence of diverse cultures on local history and art. The 19th-century guardhouse is devoted to military history, while a former warehouse contains implements and vehicles once used on area ranches and farms, as well as displays depicting daily life in these local settings. Guides give tours of the museum and some of the other army post buildings that remain here. *Open Mon.–Thurs., A.M. Fri., and P.M. Sun.*

SU Museum of the Republic of the Rio Grande, Laredo

Santa Ursula Ave. exit: 1 mi./10 min. South on Santa Ursula Ave., right on Zaragoza St. In 1840 three of Mexico's northern states rebelled against the central government and formed the Republic of the Rio Grande. The republic lasted less than a year, but it left behind a legacy that is commemorated in this simple stone and adobe building that was once its capitol. The three original rooms are furnished in period style, while the larger front room, added in 1861, has traveling exhibits of artistic, cultural, historical, and scientific interest. While here, also visit St. Augustine Church and other historic structures around and near the plaza. *Open Tues.–Sun. except holidays and one week in Apr.*

SU El Mercado, Laredo

Santa Ursula Ave. exit: 5 min. South on Santa Ursula Ave., right on Hidalgo St. Laredo's city hall, from its inception in 1883, was intended to house more than the machinery of municipal government. Until 1930 it also accommodated a theater and a market hall. In 1985 the city government moved its offices out and renovators moved in, transforming the space into El Mercado—exclusively a marketplace.

El Mercado is alive with the color and the flavor of this border region, with a range of merchandise that runs the gamut from inexpensive souvenirs and T-shirts to fine hand-wrought jewelry and exquisitely embroidered garments. *Open year-round.*

175

17

158B

10

See
E–W book,
sec. 52.

157

1A

0

SU

TX
U.S.A.

End I-35   MEXICO

172. *Beaupre Place (also the Cotton House) reveals a yearning for elegance.*

ROUTE 172 | Heritage Hill State Park, Green Bay

5 mi./6 min. West on Rte. 172, right on Webster Ave.; follow signs. Overlooking the Fox River, this 48-acre park commemorates the settlement and development of northeastern Wisconsin. The pioneer section includes a replica of one of the state's first Catholic churches (a bark-covered chapel built in 1672), a 1762 fur trader's cabin, and a replica of the first courthouse. The small-town area has a village green, a blacksmith's shop, a general store, and two distinguished houses: Tank Cottage, one of Wisconsin's oldest remaining structures (late 1700's), and Beaupre Place, a Greek revival house from the 1840's. Two original buildings from Ft. Howard, the hospital and the company barracks kitchen, form part of the military heritage area. Nearby is the farm heritage area, featuring a Belgian-style farmstead. *Open daily May–mid-Nov. Admission charged.* ⛩

ROUTE 172 | The National Railroad Museum, Green Bay

6 mi./9 min. West on Rte. 172, right on Ashland Ave., right on Cormier Ave. A British locomotive, cars that served in General Eisenhower's World War II staff train,

a 1910 engine used to explain how steam locomotives work, and 75 pieces of equipment ranging from one of the smallest engines ever made to the Union Pacific *Big Boy*, America's largest steam locomotive, are among the highlights of this extensive collection. In mid-1989 the museum expects to open a new building, which will feature permanent exhibits on railroading and an audiovisual presentation on the role of the railroad in American history. The admission includes a 20-minute ride on an 1890's Barney and Smith coach. *Open daily May–mid-Oct. Admission charged.*

48 | Kohler-Andrae State Parks, Sheboygan

5 min. East on Rte. V, right on Rte. KK, left on Old Park Rd. Here you'll find two idyllic lakeshore parks with wide sandy beaches, dunes, stands of birches, pines, and aspens, and wild roses that come almost to the water's edge. The Sanderling Nature Center provides an introduction to the ecology of the dunes, and a well-signed trail along the dunes identifies the local flora. *Parks open year-round; nature center open Memorial Day–Labor Day. Admission charged.* ⛩ ▲ 🚐 🚶 🏊 🎣

17 | Cedar Creek Settlement, Cedarburg

5 mi./10 min. West on Rte. C, right on Rte. 57 (becomes Washington Ave., Rte. 143). Beside the grassy banks of Cedar Creek stands a pioneer stone building that was once the Wittenberg Woolen Mill. Below the massive tamarack beams of the old mill, a community of craftspeople and others manufacture and sell their wares. The largest establishment is the Stone Mill Winery, located in the old cellars. Tours begin at a small wine museum—which has a collection of spigots, cooper's tools, corks, and wine labels—and end with wine tasting. A blacksmith's shop with a high ceiling, hooded furnace, and a clutter of tools turns out traditional iron products, and on the second floor of the mill you can see a working potter. Other shops sell handmade toys, antiques, clothes, stencils, gourmet goods, candles, grapevine wreaths, and Christmas ornaments. *Open Mon.–Sat. and P.M. Sun. except holidays.*

1S | Milwaukee, WI 53202

Convention & Visitors Bureau, 756 N. Milwaukee St. (414) 273-7222; (800) 291-0903 outside WI. There's still beer in Milwaukee, and three breweries offer tours, but the city has many other attractions. The arts are well represented by the vast Milwaukee Art Museum; Villa Terrace, an Italian Renaissance-style home with displays of antique furniture and decorative arts; and the extensive collection of the Charles Allis Art Museum in a resplendent Tudor-style mansion. No less interesting is the Milwaukee Public Museum, with its environmental dioramas, dinosaur skeletons, and Indian artifacts among other displays. Mitchell Park boasts a noted horticultural conservatory; and the zoo, a few miles west of downtown, is one of the country's best.

1S. *Dolphins at the zoo dance to entertain their audience of other mammals.*

326 | Cliffside County Park, Sturtevant

9 mi./15 min. East on 7 Mile Rd., right on Michna Rd.; follow signs. The park has two distinct areas: one includes the campground, a baseball diamond, and tennis courts; the other, lying behind the children's playground, is an area of woods, rough meadowland, and cliff-top paths. At the first fork in the trail, bear left to cross a meadow leading to the cliffs, or walk through the woods. The loop to the lake is a walk of 30 to 45 minutes; there are good views, but the cliff overlooking the lake is steep and crumbly, and there's no beach access. *Open daily mid-Apr.–mid-Oct.* ⛩ ▲ 🚐 🚶

333 Racine Zoological Gardens

11 mi./15 min. East on Rte. 20, left on Rte. 32 to Goold St.; follow signs. Situated on the shores of Lake Michigan, this 28-acre zoo has an interesting variety of animals. Wolves and birds of prey make their home in a wooded area near a lake. Nearby, rhesus monkeys and Barbary sheep dwell on a rocky island in a smaller lake, and penguins, pelicans, and other waterbirds have their own watery domains as well. Camels, elephants, kangaroos, deer, and a beautiful white tiger with blue eyes can also be seen here. *Open year-round.*

ROUTE 41 / ROUTE 173 Illinois Beach State Park (Southern Unit), Zion

Rte. 41 exit: 11 mi./15 min. South on Rte. 41, left on Wadsworth Rd. Rte. 173 exit: 8 mi./10 min. East on Rte. 173 (Rosecrans Rd.), right on Rte. 41; proceed as above. This extensive state park on Lake Michigan is divided into northern and southern units. But first-time visitors are encouraged to head for the southern unit. The long beach here is covered with fine sugarlike sand and acres of dunes—the state's only dunes. Beachcombers love to collect the large smooth rocks shaped and polished by the elements. Nature trails wind through a rapidly changing landscape of wetlands, prairie, oak forest, and dunes. *Open year-round.*

41–173. *Echoes of impressionism resound in the reeds and reflections of Dead River.*

OH Chicago, IL 60611

E. Ohio St. exit: Tourism Council, 163 E. Pearson St. (312) 280-5740. This great cosmopolitan metropolis, ideally situated on the southwestern shore of Lake Michigan, boasts a number of world-class attractions. The Art Institute is known for its wide-ranging permanent collection and creative special exhibitions. The Terra Museum, opened in 1987, has a superlative collection of American art; the John G. Shedd Aquarium, the world's largest such indoor facility, with more than 200 tanks, displays some 1,000 wonders of the deep. For an intimate sense of the city, take the El (the elevated railroad) around the Loop; and for a breathtaking overview of the city and lake, try the observation area on the 103rd floor of the Sears Tower, at this writing the tallest building in the world.

250A / 250B Pilcher Park, Joliet

7 mi./10 min. Exit 250A: East on I-80, left on Rte. 30, right on Gougar Rd. Exit 250B: Proceed as above. Situated along the banks of a creek, the wooded park offers upland hikes, ski and bike trails, picnic areas, and an interpretive nature center that has displays of native plants, birds, and mammals. Programs matched to the seasons include maple sugaring, birdwatching, fishing contests, ski races, and

OH. *From the perspective of Sears Tower, other skyscrapers seem rather earthbound.*

pond and woodland study trips. One of the various walks is a quarter-mile self-guiding trail marked with informative story boards. Also featured are an artesian well with mineral water, a greenhouse, and a paved trail for the blind and handicapped. *Open year-round.*

240 Goose Lake Prairie State Natural Area, Morris

7 mi./12 min. West on Pine Bluff Lorenzo Rd., right on Jugtown Rd. More than 1,500 acres of wild prairie, one of the largest remaining tracts in the United States, demonstrate what the Midwest was like before barns, crops, towns, and highways changed the landscape of the Plains forever. The visitor center has displays that explain the prairie, the plants, and wildlife that live there, and the impact of man on its ecology.

From the center the 1½-mile Tallgrass Nature Trail leads through a section of prairie grass amid seasonal wildflowers and past potholes and marshland. Prairies like the one preserved here once covered almost three-quarters of Illinois. A trail-guide pamphlet identifies the native plants and the geology of the area. The park provides the welcome sense of openness and solitude that characterizes this unique environment. *Open daily except Christmas and New Year's Day.*

18

WI

IL

ROUTE 41

ROUTE 173

2

47

See E–W book, sec. 6.

90

OH

90 94

55

46

See E–W book, sec. 23.

250A

250B

80

10

240

4

55

236

236 Kankakee River State Park

22 mi./25 min. East on Rte. 113, left on Warner Bridge Rd. The many moods of the Kankakee as it changes with the seasons are revealed in the 11 miles of parkland and riverbank and a dramatic canyon watercourse. Whether the river is a spring-time torrent or a placid hot-summer stream, the park offers activities that range from angling to ski touring. Hiking and riding trails meander through the wild forest, prairie, sand dunes, and along the river-banks. Picnic areas and campgrounds are found throughout the park. A favorite feature is Rock Creek Canyon, where a waterfall tumbles through the deep limestone gorge. Canoes and horses are available for rent. *Open daily except Christmas and New Year's Day.*

167 Moraine View State Recreation Area

20 mi./30 min. South on Veterans Pkwy., left on Rte. 9, right on Le Roy-Lexington Rd.; follow signs. In the midst of a rolling prairie landscape, this attractive park surrounds a wooded lake. A scenic drive wanders through varied terrain, going past campsite, picnic, and visitor center facilities. A choice of trails provides opportunities for different activities according to the season. Winter ice fishing and ski touring can become angling and canoeing in July along the more than 5 miles of shoreline. As you stroll along the half-mile Tanglewood Nature Trail, you will find signposts that indicate the glacial ancestry of the various woodland, marsh, prairie, and pond life here. *Open daily except Christmas and New Year's Day.*

157 Miller Park and Zoo, Bloomington

2 mi./10 min. North on Veterans Pkwy., left on Morris Ave. Bird cries of the tropics and the bellow of sea lions are an added aspect of this city park that is set in pleasant tree-studded meadows. There is a lake for swimming and paddleboats, an outdoor theater, tennis courts, miniature golf, and a bandstand. In the small well-managed zoo you'll find snow leopards, Indian lions, and tigers from Sumatra in outside cages, as well as a refreshing pool for the sea lions. A skylit room, with trees and two waterfalls, suggests a tropical rain forest where rare birds fly. The petting zoo has farmyard animals, a llama, and a deer. *Open year-round. Admission charged.*

123 Railsplitter State Park

2 min. East on Rte. 55 (business). This park on the southern outskirts of Lincoln is a quiet and restful place for a picnic, even though it wraps around a state prison. You can glimpse the Lincoln Correctional Center through the trees just after entering the park. Nevertheless, the focus of the 751-acre preserve named for Abraham Lincoln is Salt Creek, with good waters for fishing for bass, bluegill, catfish, carp, and sunfish. There are outdoor stoves beside the creek, and small shelters and running-water outlets throughout the grounds. *Open daily except Christmas and New Year's Day.*

98B 92A Lincoln Home National Historic Site, Springfield

Exit 98B: 3 mi./10 min. West on Clear Lake Ave. and Jefferson St., left on 9th St. Exit 92A: 4 mi./15 min. North on I-55 Loop; continue on S. 6th St., right on Myrtle St., right on 9th St. Abraham Lincoln was 35, recently married, and a partner in a local law firm when he bought this 5-year-old clapboard house in Springfield in 1844. It was his home for 17 years, the only one he ever owned, and three of his four sons were born here. It was in the formal front parlor, where the best furniture was kept—and where the children were not allowed—that he was formally notified of his nomination for the presidency in 1860. Period flavor pre-dominates. There are in all some 65 furnishings that belonged to the family, including Lincoln's lap desk and shaving mirror. The exteriors of other homes along the broad, tree-shaded streets of the 12-acre historic site are being restored. *Open daily except Thanksgiving Day, Christmas, and New Year's Day.*

88 Lincoln Memorial Garden and Nature Center

5 min. East on E. Lake Dr.; follow signs. It was the belief of landscape architect Jens Jensen, who designed this 77-acre woodland garden in the 1930's as a living memorial to Abraham Lincoln, that "art springs from native soil." He proved the concept here, with nature trails that wind for 5 miles among indigenous flowers and trees and beautifully balanced patches of woodland and open spaces. The circular seats of eight "council rings" of local stone encour-

98B–92A. *It is not surprising that Lincoln chose such a simple, straightforward house.*

age discussion and quiet companionship. Perhaps the most striking aspect is that all this, including idyllic Lake Springfield, Shadbush Lane, Witch Hazel Trail, Dogwood Lane, and other walks are man-made but seem to be part of nature's grand design. *Open year-round.*

60 Beaver Dam State Park

20.5 mi./25 min. West on Rte. 108 to Carlinville; follow signs. Although beavers made the original lake, local fishermen a century ago doubled its depth with dams at both ends. Since then the placid waters and pristine shoreline have endeared the lake to those who come for largemouth bass, sunfish, bluegill, and channel catfish. Most important, it's a quiet place, 737 acres of oak and hickory forests, campgrounds, a shady picnic area, and leafy hiking trails. A small lakeside stand sells bait and tackle and rents boats from April through October; no boats with gasoline engines are allowed. Nothing disturbs the serenity of trees, sky, and water. The only sounds to be heard are those of nature in this domain of raccoons, foxes, songbirds, and wild turkeys. *Open year-round.*

11 Cahokia Mounds State Historic Site, Collinsville

5 mi./10 min. South on Rte. 157, right on Collinsville Rd. From A.D. 900 to 1250 a mighty society flourished here. Cahokia, a major town built by the people of the Mississippian Indian culture, had 20,000 to 40,000 inhabitants who farmed the surrounding land and traded with peoples as far away as the Atlantic and Gulf coasts. They also labored for centuries to build these impressive earthworks, adding the dirt a basketful at a time. The 100-foot-high Monks Mound, the largest of the 60 surviving mounds here, was the site of a temple that was also the leader's residence. A few of the mounds were burial sites, but most were bases for the homes of the elite or for ceremonial buildings. Woodhenge, a giant circle of cedar posts, was a sun calendar that determined the changing seasons. A museum offers exhibits. *Open daily except Thanksgiving Day, Christmas, and New Year's Day.*

ARCH St. Louis, MO 63102

Arch/Downtown exit: Convention and Visitors Commission, 10 S. Broadway. (314) 421-1023; (800) 247-9791 outside MO. The three spans across the Mississippi here dramatize the role of St. Louis as a jumping-off place to the West, and the magnificent 630-foot Gateway Arch commemorates the days of the wagon trains, when the only river crossings were by water. From the top of the arch one can contemplate the vast reaches so full of promise and danger in the days of the pioneers, an era graphically interpreted in the Museum of Westward Expansion located beneath the arch.

An excellent zoo has more than 2,500 animals and a miniature railroad to provide an easy introduction. Featured in the 79-acre botanical garden is the domed Climatron greenhouse and the largest Japanese garden in the United States.

ARCH. *The pioneers it celebrates could only be astounded by the Gateway Arch.*

207 196 Six Flags Over Mid-America

Exit 207: 30 mi./35 min. West on I-44. Exit 196: 21 mi./30 min. West on I-270, left on I-44. The grassy, well-tended grounds of this amusement park house attractions with French, Spanish, and English themes. You'll find lots of rides that elicit screams of delighted excitement—shooting the rapids on Thunder River or plunging on the Screamin' Eagle roller coaster. There are gentler rides as well for those who want something less daring. Between the rides you can enjoy a variety of

207–196. *The reality and fantasy of rabbit and friend capture the park's essence.*

musicals, special performances, and changing shows. Guest services include public lockers, a first aid station, wheelchairs, rental strollers, and a free kennel. *Open daily late May–late Aug.; weekends mid-Apr.–mid-May and early Sept.–mid-Oct. Admission charged.*

ROUTE M Sandy Creek Covered Bridge

13 mi./20 min. West on Rte. M, left on Rte. 21, left on Goldman Rd., right on Lemay Ferry Rd. To cross this bridge in 1880, it cost 3 cents per foot passenger, 25 cents per carriage drawn by two or more horses, and 37 cents per stage wagon—considerable sums in those days. The 74½-foot span, which is 18 feet wide, still has half its original timbers and is one of only four of its kind remaining in Missouri. Covered to protect the underlying wood structure, the bridge is supported by a Howe truss reinforced by iron rods. Barn-building techniques were used in constructing these bridges; thus their familiar appearance may have made it easier for draft animals to enter. An informative display explains the technology of covered bridges. Shade trees and a sparkling stream make this an ideal spot for a picnic. *Open year-round.*

6

92A
4

88

28

60

49

See E–W book, sec. 29.

70

See E–W book, sec. 33.

11

12

64

IL
MO

70

ARCH
2

207

11

196

11

ROUTE M

8

55

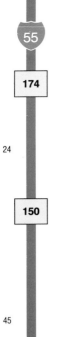
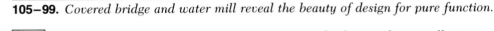

105–99. *Covered bridge and water mill reveal the beauty of design for pure function.*

174 Washington State Park

23 mi./35 min. Southwest on Rte. 67, right on Rte. 110, left on Rte. 21, right on Rte. 104. Indians of the Middle-Mississippian culture once carved their ceremonial symbols on limestone outcroppings here. Today informative displays interpret these petroglyphs, now sheltered by lean-tos to protect them from further erosion by the elements. The park's inviting hiking trails, where the rare collared lizard is occasionally spotted, wind through limestone glades and bluffs that tower above the Big River. The park has a fine range of visitor facilities, and swimming, fishing, canoeing, and tubing are permitted on the river. *Open year-round.*

150 Historic Ste. Genevieve

6 mi./15 min. East on Rte. 32 (becomes Center Dr., then 4th St.), right on Merchant St. The 18th-century French heritage of this Missouri town is evident in a number of historic houses built between 1770, when Ste. Genevieve was a part of upper Louisiana, claimed by France, and 1820. The French Creole-style Amoureaux House, with its *poteaux-en-terre* ("posts-in-ground") foundation and long 10-post porch, once belonged to a French noble-man. On display inside are collections of cast-iron toys and antique dolls. Among other historic houses are the Guibourd-Valle House, with graceful period furnishings and hand-hewn oak beams, and the authentically restored Bolduc House, with 18th-century gardens and frontier kitchen. *Information Center open daily except Easter, Thanksgiving Day, and Dec. 25–Jan. 2. Admission charged to sites.*

105 Trail of Tears State Park

11 mi./15 min. North on Rte. 61, right on Rte. 177. Spectacular cliffs and vistas distinguish this park, which was named for the tragic forced migration of some 13,000 Cherokees from their ancestral lands in the Southeast to western reservations in 1838–39. When about one-third of the Indians died en route of disease, exposure, and starvation, the migration became known as the Trail of Tears. The main hiking trail, some 10 miles long, stretches through some rugged areas, including the 180-foot-high limestone bluffs that overlook the Mississippi River. Hikers, equestrians, and botanists may see the cucumber magnolias, spicebushes, and Indian pinks, as well as deer or the rare bald eagle. A lakeside beach is a pleasant place for a picnic. *Open year-round.*

105 / 99 Bollinger Mill State Historic Site, Burfordville

Exit 105: 10 mi./20 min. South on Rte. 61, right on Rte. 72, left on Rte. 34; follow signs. Exit 99: 11 mi./22 min. North on Rte. 61, left on Rte. 72; proceed as above. This old mill and a nearby covered bridge, located on the tree-shaded banks of the Whitewater River, make an idyllic scene that is irresistible to both picnickers and photographers. The original mill, constructed of wood about 1800, was partially burned down by Union soldiers during the Civil War and later rebuilt of brick and stone. The mill functioned until 1953, and it can still be made to run. *Open Mon.–Sat. and P.M. Sun. except holidays. Fee charged for guided tour of mill.*

96 Rose Display Garden, Cape Girardeau

3.5 mi./10 min. East on Rte. K (William St.), left on West End Blvd., left on Broadway, right on Perry Ave. Of particular interest to rose growers, this garden set in the northwest corner of Capaha Park boasts more than 200 plantings of outstanding species and varieties. Visitors may admire examples of grandiflora, floribunda, shrub, and hybrid tea roses, among others. Breeders submit roses for various tests for scent, color, hardiness, and disease resistance. The garden is administered by the Council of Garden Clubs. *Open year-round.*

96 The Glenn House, Cape Girardeau

4.5 mi./10 min. East on Rte. K (William St.), right on Spanish St. Local architect Edwin Branch Deane built this Victorian house for his daughter Lulu and her husband in 1883. The interior, much of it still original, includes some intriguing touches: lamps that run on both electricity and kerosene, radiators with plate warmers, and green silk moiré wallpaper. One of the bedrooms evokes life on the river with nautical memorabilia and a model riverboat. The bathroom has a pink marble sink, original lead plumbing, an overhead-tank toilet, and a collection of antique shaving mugs. *Open P.M. Wed.–Sat. Apr.–Dec. except holidays. Admission charged.*

49 / 44 Hunter-Dawson State Historic Site, New Madrid

Exit 49: 3.5 mi./10 min. South on Rte. 61, left on Rte. U. Exit 44: 5 mi./15 min. North on Rte. 61, right on Rte. U. This gracious home, surrounded by some of the state's oldest trees, was begun by local merchant and sawmill owner William Hunter in the late 1850's and completed by his wife after his death. The building, with its white clapboard siding, green shutters, and long rear porches, is a blend of the Greek revival and Italianate styles typical of the antebellum period in Missouri. The 15 rooms contain furnishings from 1860 to 1880, including portraits of Hunter and his wife. *Open Mon.–Sat. and P.M. Sun. Admission charged.*　⊼

44 / 34 Hampson Museum State Park

Exit 44: 7 mi./10 min. South on Rte. 181, left on Rte. 61; follow signs. Exit 34: 7 mi./10 min. East on Rte. 118, left on Rte. 61; follow signs. The Nodenas were farm-based Indians who lived in this part of Arkansas from about A.D. 1350 to 1700. The museum exhibits weapons, ornaments, and objects they used for hunting and games. The clay they mixed for ceremonial and utilitarian vessels was fortified with shells. One rare "head pot," with incised lines that may represent tattooing, scarification, or skin painting, was used for ceremonial purposes. The displays, which explain the Nodenas' trade networks, their methods of hunting and agriculture, and other aspects of their lives, are laid out with a clear and concise commentary. *Open Tues.–Sat. Admission charged.*　⊼ ♿

12 Memphis, TN 38103

Visitors Information Center, 207 Beale St. (901) 526-4880. King Cotton still plays a major role in the city's economy, Beale Street and W. C. Handy are appropriately memorialized, and a riverboat still plies the mighty Mississippi; but probably the best-known attraction is Graceland, home of Elvis Presley, the King of Rock and Roll. Tours are so popular that reservations are suggested. Call (901) 332-3322; or (800) 238-2000 from out of state.

The river that brought life to Memphis is honored at Mud Island by a scale model of the Mississippi from Cairo, Illinois, to New Orleans and the Gulf of Mexico, as well as by displays on the waterway's history. The Memphis Pink Palace Museum and Planetarium features exhibits on natural history, pioneer life, and the Civil War. The National Ornamental Metal Museum has a working blacksmith on the premises. For nature lovers there is a zoo with an aquarium and a botanic garden. The Victorian Village has some 18 landmarked buildings in styles that include late Gothic revival.

280 Arkabutla Lake

11 mi./16 min. West on Rte. 304, left on Rte. 301 to dam. Well stocked with crappie and catfish, Arkabutla Lake is especially inviting for anglers, but its 34,000 acres of water surface allow plenty of room for water-skiing, swimming, and sailing as well. The lake, named for an Indian chief who allegedly lived here long ago, was created in 1942 by damming the Coldwater River. The area has campgrounds, boat ramps, swimming beaches, nature trails, and a picnic ground shaded by sweet gums and oaks. *Open year-round; field office open Mon.–Fri.*　⊼ ▲ ⊞ 🚶 🏊 🎣 ♿

252 John W. Kyle State Park

9 mi./15 min. East on Rte. 315. Chickasaw Indians traded and hunted in this area before settlers began arriving in the 1830's. These days the park is noted for its nature trails and a pine-shaded picnic ground. Sardis Lake is well known for its catfish, crappie, and bass, and boats are available for rent. The campgrounds are supplemented by fully furnished cabins as well as tennis courts and a swimming pool. *Open year-round.*　⊼ ▲ ⊞ 🚶 🏊 🎣 ♿

243A Rowan Oak, Oxford

23 mi./28 min. East on Rte. 6, left on Lamar Ave., left on Old Taylor Rd. This columned white frame house, set among cedar and magnolia trees, was built in 1844 by a local planter, Robert Sheegog. It was spared when the town of Oxford was razed by Northern troops in 1864. In 1930 the house was bought and restored by the world-famous southern novelist William Faulkner, who occupied it until his death in 1962. It is now maintained by the University of Mississippi to preserve the memory of Faulkner. The rooms contain such treasures as portraits, paintings, a Japanese doll, and a Chickering piano. In Faulkner's office you can see an outline and notes for *A Fable* that he sketched on the walls. Outside are barns, stables, and other outbuildings. *Open Mon.–Fri., A.M. Sat. and P.M. Sun. except Christmas, New Year's Day, and university staff holidays.*

243A. *Lighted interior at dusk could serve as a reminder of Faulkner's brilliance.*

MO
AR

44

10

34

34

See E–W book, sec. 40.

40

40

AR
TN

12

TN
MS

24

280

28

252

9

243A

16

55

227

206

21

21

185

35

150

17

133

35

98B

20

See
E–W book,
sec. 45.

227 George Payne Cossar State Park

4 mi./6 min. East on Rte. 32, left on access road. Situated on a peninsula on huge Lake Enid, this state park is a favorite with fishermen and campers. Facilities include playgrounds, boat and bike rentals, a nature trail, picnic areas, a swimming pool, a lodge, and a locally famous restaurant. The park's hardwood forest is especially beautiful in the fall. *Open year-round. Admission charged.*

206 Historic Old Grenada

4 min. Southeast on Rte. 7. Once Choctaw Indian land, this area in the early 1830's had developed into the two politically rivalrous towns of Pittsburg and Tullahoma, which were divided only by a surveyor's line now known as Line Street. On July 4, 1836, a symbolic marriage ceremony was performed (accompanied by a barbecue), and the two towns were united under the name Grenada. Majestic oaks shade the streets of the historic district, where dozens of lovely old homes built in the early to the mid-19th century recall Mississippi's antebellum past. Most of these buildings are located on Margin and Main streets. The Whitaker Manse, whose columns were brought from New Orleans, is one of the most beautifully restored homes in the state, and Townes House, with its elegant columns and balconies, was the headquarters for Jefferson Davis in 1861.

206 Hugh White State Park

10 mi./15 min. East on Rte. 8; follow signs. Named for a former Mississippi governor, the park is situated around 64,000-acre Grenada Lake, which was created by a dam along the Yalobusha River. The lake offers some of the area's best fishing—for crappie and striped bass—as well as boating, water-skiing, and swimming from a sandy beach. There are tennis courts, a marina, boat-launching facilities, bikes and boats for rent, and overnight accommodations that range from 20 full-service cabins to primitive campsites in a secluded area overlooking the lake. *Open year-round. Admission charged.*

185 Florewood River Plantation State Park

30 mi./50 min. West on Rte. 82 through Greenwood, left on access road. The invention of the cotton gin in 1793 increased fiftyfold the speed with which cotton bolls could be separated from their seeds. By the mid-1850's King Cotton accounted for more than half of all U.S. exports, and plantations such as Florewood flourished in the fertile Delta region of western Mississippi.

The 28 buildings on this 100-acre site are copies of the 19th-century structures typical in the area. Costumed interpreters (on duty March to December) portray a planter, a mistress of the house, a candlemaker, and other workers. At the Cotton Museum you will see artifacts that explain the history of cotton and its impact in the Old South. In the fall you can pick a few bolls of cotton and try to imagine what it was like to pick cotton from dawn to dusk. *Open Tues.– Sat. and P.M. Sun. except Thanksgiving Day, Christmas, and New Year's Day. Admission charged.*

185. *This humble plant led to vast fortunes—and promoted the evils of slavery.*

150 Holmes County State Park

2 min. East on access road. Favored by campers, this park has a variety of accommodations that range from tent sites to air-conditioned cabins overlooking a lake. One of the two lakes in the park is for fishing (bass, catfish, and bream), and the other is for paddleboating and swimming (from a sandy beach). Among other facilities, the

park provides a skating rink, an archery range, a rustic lodge, and a 4-mile nature trail that winds through groves of white and red oak, dogwood, cedar, and loblolly pine. Its nearness to the interstate highway makes the park a convenient place to stop for a quick and quiet picnic. *Open daily except Christmas. Admission charged.*

133 Casey Jones Railroad Museum State Park, Vaughan

2 min. East on access road. On April 30, 1900, engineer Jonathan Luther "Casey" Jones, at the throttle of the *Cannonball Express*, was running behind schedule. Racing to make up time, he was unable to stop at a warning signal, rammed into the rear of a freight train near Vaughan, and was killed. A legend was born when a friend of Jones's, engine wiper Wallace Saunders, composed "The Ballad of Casey Jones," and the song was picked up and elaborated on by vaudevillians. The bell from Casey's engine and a rail that Union soldiers heated and twisted into a "Sherman's necktie" are among the artifacts exhibited at this former depot, located a few hundred yards from the site of Casey's wreck. Railroad memorabilia and historical displays chronicle the Illinois Central Railroad's past, and a 1923 locomotive is displayed on the grounds. *Open Tues.–Sat. except Thanksgiving Day, Christmas, and New Year's Day. Admission charged.*

98B Jackson, MS 39216

Visitor Information Center, 1180 Lakeland Dr. (601) 960-1800. Jackson's importance as a state capital and rail center brought destruction during the Civil War, but it has also helped to make this the state's leading city today; and the sense of local history is still strong. The mansion where 40 state governors have lived, which briefly served as headquarters for Union general Ulysses S. Grant, is furnished with excellent period pieces. The State Historical Museum in the Old State Capitol features dioramas illustrating the history of the state; the Museum of Natural Science also uses dioramas. The homes of two former mayors are of interest: The Oaks, an antebellum wood-

98B. *Great dynasties were built on the simple, ingenious cotton gin.*

frame cottage hand-hewn in 1846, and the Manship House, a charming Gothic revival structure built about 10 years later. The history and culture of blacks in Mississippi is featured in the Smith-Robertson Museum and Cultural Center.

98B | Mississippi Agriculture and Forestry Museum, Jackson

3 min. East on Lakeland Dr. Life-size tableaux, complete with sound effects and voices, show vivid re-creations of loggers in action, workers hauling cotton bales, and life in a sharecropper's cottage. Themes include logging days, the "rail age," and the "era of roads." Exhibits explain cotton processing, the impact of electricity, and the economics of farm life.

Also here is the National Agricultural Aviation Museum, which focuses on the fight against the boll weevil, featuring crop-dusting planes along with strange boll-weevil catchers of pre-spraying days.

At the Fortenberry-Parkman Farm across the street, you can talk to workers about rural life in the South in the early 20th century. *Open Tues.–Sat. and P.M. Sun. except Thanksgiving Day, Christmas, and New Year's Day. Admission charged.*

13 | Percy Quin State Park

5 min. West on Rte. 48. Spread along the shores of Lake Tangipahoa, this beautifully landscaped park features an arboretum of flowering shrubs. During the summertime there's also swimming at a wide sandy beach, pedal boats and canoes for rent, and observation decks overlooking the water shaded by tall loblolly pines. Fishing is also popular. Eight miles of marked trails lead through the park, one of which passes a beaver dam, where these busy builders are occasionally seen. The Liberty White Railroad's red caboose serves as a reminder of another era. *Open year-round. Admission charged.*

I-12 | Fairview-Riverside State Park

25 mi./30 min. East on I-12 to Exit 57, south on Rte. 1077, left on Rte. 22. A fine old two-story white house with a handsome galleried veranda greets visitors at the entrance to this 98-acre park. A wood boardwalk on the Tchefuncta River winds among cypresses thickly hung with Spanish moss. Egrets ascend from branches reflected in the murky water, and the surface of the river is rippled by alligators on the prowl. Water-skiing is popular upstream, and fishermen come to the park for the abundance of bluegill, bass, perch, and catfish. *Open year-round. Admission charged.*

I-10 | New Orleans, LA 70112

26 mi./35 min. Tourist & Convention Commission, 1520 Sugar Bowl Dr. (504) 566-5011. The music, food, architecture, history, and ambience have made New Orleans one of America's most celebrated cities. Jackson Square is a good place to start a walking tour of the French Quarter, the city's best-known area. On the square you'll see the beautiful St. Louis Cathedral and the superb wrought-iron balconies of the Pontalba Apartments. At the nearby French Market you'll find outdoor cafés and eye-catching displays of produce. At night the sound of music—blues, ragtime, Cajun zydeco, country, and of course New Orleans jazz—emanates from clubs and bars that line the length of Bourbon Street.

The St. Charles streetcar still clangs and rattles through the Garden District, an area of large live oaks and handsome antebellum houses that also rewards strolling. To experience the majesty of the Mississippi River, which loops dramatically around the city, try the free ferry or one of the cruises.

I-10. *The tried and true sounds of early jazz can still be savored in the French Quarter.*

85

13

MS
LA

49

I-12

30

See E–W book, sec. 53.

I-10   10

End I-55

See
E-W book,
sec. 13.

See
E-W book,
sec. 23.

See
E-W book,
sec. 29.

I-94 — Chicago, IL 60611

Tourism Council, 163 E. Pearson St. (312) 280-5740. This metropolis, beautifully situated on the southwestern shore of Lake Michigan, boasts a number of world-class attractions. The Art Institute is known for a wide-ranging permanent collection as well as creative special exhibitions. The Terra Museum, opened in 1987, has a superlative collection of American art; the John G. Shedd Aquarium, the world's largest such indoor facility, with more than 200 tanks, displays some 1,000 wonders of the deep. For an intimate sense of the city, take the El (the elevated railroad) around the Loop; and for a breathtaking overview there's the observation area on the 103rd floor of the Sears Tower, at this writing the tallest building in the world.

237 — Champaign County Historical Museum

3 mi./10 min. East on I-74 to Champaign, right on Prospect Ave., left on University Ave. This handsomely crafted turn-of-the-century house, on a street with many others of that period, is a museum in itself. The superb detail of the woodwork and cabinetry is done in the arts and crafts style, an American reaction against the over-ornate decor imported from Europe. The rooms, with their furnishings and samples of period dress, portray the lifestyle of the well-to-do in this era and in this neighborhood. *Open daily except Aug. and Jan. Admission charged.*

237 — Lake of the Woods County Park

4 min. West on I-74 to Exit 172, right on Rte. 47. The rolling, lightly wooded hills of the park, with nature trails and a 26-acre lake for swimming and boating (rentals available), are an inviting contrast to the surrounding farmland. There's also a golf course, an early American museum, and a botanical garden. The museum features some 3,000 items that illustrate the ingenuity and hard work required to wrest a living from the land in the days of the pioneers. The botanical garden presents plants native to the prairie, dye plants, herbs, roses, and a conservatory with a collection of tropical plants. From the brick bell tower there's an interesting view of the landscape. *Open year-round. Vehicle charge May–Sept.*

203 — Rockome Gardens

6 mi./12 min. West on Rte. 133; follow signs. Here in the heart of Illinois Amish country is a commercialized tourist attraction that is nonetheless engagingly eclectic and eccentric. Brightly colored barns and buildings adorned with the obligatory hex signs contrast with the more authentic blacksmith's shop and machine shed. In a class by themselves are the memorable walls, fences, and fanciful forms made of chunks of rock set in concrete and the house built of Fresca bottles. In season craft shows, festivals, and auctions are scheduled every weekend. *Open daily May–Oct. Admission charged.*

190 — Fox Ridge State Park

15 mi./30 min. East on Rte. 16 through Charleston, right on Rte. 130. Hills, valleys, and woods come as a welcome surprise here on a plain that seems boundless. This oasis was not made accessible without the obvious labor of building boardwalks, bridges across steep little gorges, and steps up the hillsides for fine views of the forest canopy and the Embarras (pronounced Am-braw) River below. Be advised that the trails are on the arduous side, although there is one short trail for the handicapped. Free fishing boats suggest an outing on secluded 18-acre Ridge Lake, perhaps to try for largemouth bass or channel catfish. *Open daily except Christmas and New Year's Day.*

203. *On back roads in the Amish country horse-and-buggy days still prevail.*

127 — Ingram's Pioneer Log Cabin Village, Kinmundy

3 mi./12 min. East to Rte. 37, left on Rte. 37, left on Monroe St.; follow signs. Log cabins are tangible reminders of the dogged resourcefulness of our pioneer forebears. Trees had to be felled, cut to length, squared, and notched with hand tools, and the foundations, fireplaces, and chimneys laid with stones dug and hauled from the fields. The cabins here—several homes, a general store, a cobbler's shop, a preacher's home, an apothecary shop, and an inn— were built between 1818 and 1860 and are furnished with spinning wheels, cradles, rope beds, chests, quilts, and other period pieces. The handwritten family records posted outside confirm their authenticity. The crafts people in period dress demonstrating early-day skills further define the meaning of self-reliance. *Open daily mid-Apr.–mid-Nov. Admission charged.*

116 — William Jennings Bryan Museum, Salem

2 mi./10 min. East on Rte. 50 to Rte. 37 (S. Broadway) in Salem, right to museum. Bryan, a former congressman, secretary of state, and three-time presidential nominee, was born in this simple frame house, where he lived for his first seven years. He was a renowned orator, and his style is demonstrated here in a recording of his celebrated cross of gold speech. Here, too, are his baby clothes, his Spanish-American War uniform, and political buttons and ribbons. The modest objects by which he is remembered are in poignant contrast with his accomplishments. *Open Fri.–Wed. except Thanksgiving Day, Christmas, and New Year's Day.*

95 — Mitchell Museum, Mount Vernon

2 mi./10 min. East on Rte. 15 (becomes Broadway), left on 27th St., right on Richview Rd. The striking, windowless white

1. *Stands of bald cypress and tupelo gum have established themselves in scenic Horseshoe Lake, where the Mississippi flowed before changing course in its rush to the sea.*

marble museum building, surrounded by an elegantly proportioned colonnade, is on the parklike grounds of Cedarhurst, the 80-acre estate of the late John and Eleanor Mitchell. The structure embodies their dream of providing an art center for this part of Illinois. The exhibits here include shows circulating nationally as well as works by local residents. The judiciously eclectic Mitchell collection of paintings, drawings, and sculpture, displayed in an administration building nearby, has works by Eakins, Sargent, Andrew Wyeth, and other 19th- and 20th-century masters. The attractive wooded grounds contain a lake and two nature trails. *Open P.M. Tues.–Sun. except holidays.*

77 **Wayne Fitzgerrell State Park**

5 min. West on Rte. 154, across first part of causeway over Rend Lake. As many as 2 million people per year seek recreation here, but the 19,000-acre Rend Lake and 21,000 adjacent acres of public land are sufficient to accommodate them. Stop at the visitor center for orientation and suggestions for your visit. Boating, hiking, swimming, and fishing are popular, and there's a wildlife refuge with a viewing platform. During the tourist season interpretive programs are sponsored. *Park open year-round; visitor center open Apr.–Oct.*

40 **Ferne Clyffe State Park**

7 mi./15 min. East on road to Goreville, right on Rte. 37. The series of bluffs, rocky gorges, waterfalls, and shelter rocks that flank the varied trails make hiking here a pleasure. Campsites on Deer Ridge catch a welcome cool breeze in summer. The Cherokees hunted here in 1838–39 while traveling west to a new reservation. The lake is stocked with bluegill and bass. *Open year-round except Christmas and New Year's Day.*

1 **Horseshoe Lake Conservation Area**

12 mi./15 min. North on Rte. 3; follow signs. An enchanting landscape surprisingly reminiscent of swamplands in the Deep South survives here in an oxbow lake formed by a meander of the Mississippi River. Bald cypress, swamp cottonwood, and tupelo gum trees growing in the shallow lake and along its edges are reflected in its dark, still water—except for the

places where green algae lie as flat and dense as the baize on a billiard table. Plants and animals typical of a southern swamp flourish here. A spillway stabilized the lake, which is now less susceptible to flooding. Some bald eagles and upwards of 150,000 Canada geese winter at the lake. *Open year-round.*

1 **Magnolia Manor, Cairo**

3 mi./10 min. Southeast on Rte. 3 to Cairo, right on 28th St. to Washington Ave. Cairo resident Charles Galigher supplied flour to Union troops during the Civil War, profited handsomely, and in 1872 completed this 14-room red brick Victorian house. Great magnolia trees stand in front of the manor, and an ornamental fountain plays in the garden. In 1880 Galigher's friend, President Ulysses S. Grant, attended a glittering reception here and stayed overnight. The Cairo Historical Association, established in 1952, made the restoration of the mansion its first priority. Some furnishings, including Grant's bed, are original, and some antiques have been donated. A cupola atop the fourth story provides a view of the Ohio and Mississippi rivers. *Open year-round. Admission charged.*

1. *Ornamental excess is a surprising element of the stern Victorian era.*

63

127

11

116

21

64

95

64

18

See E–W book, sec. 33.

77

37

40

39

1

IL

MO

See N–S book, sec. 23.

55

End I-57

90

80 84

See E–W book, sec. 6 for I-90; sec. 23 for I-80; sec. 13 for I-94.

259

6

253

75

178

64

See E–W book, sec. 30.

114

70

46

68

259 Indiana Dunes National Lakeshore

20 mi./25 min. East on I-94 to Exit 22B, east on Rte. 20, left on Mineral Springs Rd. These 1,800 acres of woodland trails and 3 miles of beach dominated by towering lakefront dunes evince an almost lyrical delicacy in an obviously industrial environment. A number of plants are relics of the colder climates that existed here at the end of the Ice Age, leaving a remarkable diversity of vegetation: arctic bearberry, together with prickly-pear cacti and northern jack pines, shares dune slopes with southern dogwoods. Although the dunes are large (Mt. Tom rises more than 190 feet) and are anchored against the wind by marram grass, sand cherry, cottonwoods, and other native plants, they are susceptible to erosion. *Open year-round.*

253 Wilbur H. Cummings Museum of Electronics, Valparaiso

17 mi./25 min. East on Rte. 30, left on Rte. 2, left on Lincoln Way. Electronic technology changes so quickly that yesterday's marvel soon becomes today's antique. This museum has electronic devices from the period of Edison and Marconi to the present, knowing that its latest state-of-the-art exhibits will soon be obsolescent. Among the highlights are a 1950's Seeburg jukebox that plays 78-r.p.m. records, Admiral Byrd's transmitter from a South Pole expedition, one of the first pinball machines, and radios by Atwater-Kent, Crosley, Philco, and other noted manufacturers. The museum is on the campus of Valparaiso Technical Institute. *Open year-round.*

178 Tippecanoe Battlefield

5 mi./17 min. North on Rte. 43, right on Rte. 225; follow signs. In 1811, Gen. William Henry Harrison, who was to become the ninth president of the United States some 30 years later, led his troops to victory over the Indian Confederacy at Tippecanoe Creek in what is now north Indiana. Fortunately, Harrison faced The Prophet rather than his brother, the formidable Tecumseh. The Prophet had convinced his followers that the white man's musket balls would pass through them harmlessly. This led to ill-advised bravado and defeat for the Indians, with relatively few losses for the whites. Indians had inhabited this area for a period of more than 2,000 years. But this battle put the region firmly in the hands of the other side; and in the War of 1812, Harrison finally ended the Indian threat to the old Northwest Territory by defeating Tecumseh himself at the Battle of the Thames. *Open daily except Thanksgiving Day, Christmas, and New Year's Day. Admission charged.*

178. *The size of the battlefield monument almost overwhelms the victorious general.*

114 Indianapolis, IN 46225

Convention & Visitors Association, 1 Hoosier Dome, Suite 100. (317) 639-4282. Nearly everyone knows that in May, Indianapolis boasts one of the world's largest sports events, the Indy 500. But there are also other attractions worthy of note. Consider, for example, the Indianapolis Museum of Art, the Indiana State Museum, and the Children's Museum, one of the largest and most varied of its kind. You can visit the home of James Whitcomb Riley and the 16-room Victorian mansion of Benjamin Harrison. There's a new zoo and three large parks. Festival Market Place in old Union Station has shops and restaurants, while City Market offers fresh produce and restaurants. And even if it isn't May, the Speedway is worth a visit. The Hall of Fame Museum displays antique and classic cars and more than 32 speedsters that have won the race since it began in 1911; and you can get the feel of the "Brickyard" on a minibus ride around the circuit.

68 Brown County State Park

14 mi./25 min. West on Rte. 46. This park's 15,543 hilly acres of pine, spruce, locust, and walnut trees, most of them planted by the Civilian Conservation Corps in the 1930's, are a change of scene from the miles of surrounding farmland. Impressive vistas in the park, Indiana's largest, can be seen from the 26 miles of bridle paths and 11 miles of hiking trails; a self-guiding nature trail is available, and there is fishing as well as a variety of other recreational activities at the lodge. The nature center in the park is equipped with a bird-watching station and a snake exhibit. *Open year-round.*

33 Hardy Lake State Recreation Area

9 mi./15 min. East on Rte. 256; follow signs. Hardy Lake was created in 1970, when Quick Creek was dammed as a water conservation project. Today anglers gravitate to the lake's southern section, which is well stocked with largemouth bass, crappie, and channel catfish. Launching ramps scattered around the lake and a marina with boats for rent (May–October) attract water-skiers and boat-racers. The beach is equipped with a bathhouse, rest rooms, and food concessions. A hookup campground with rest rooms, showers, and drinking fountains is a short walk through the woods from the lake. Primitive camping is available at water's edge. *Open year-round. Admission charged Apr.–mid-Sept.*

114. *Engineers and ironworkers cooperated to create the classic City Market in 1886.*

ROUTE 62 **Howard Steamboat Museum, Jeffersonville**

5 min. East on Rte. 62, right on Spring St., left on Market St. Overlooking the Ohio River, this 22-room mansion was built in 1894 by Edmunds Howard, whose family-owned shipyard produced some of the world's most elegant steamboats. The same superb craftsmanship of the Howard vessels was also lavished on this luxurious Victorian home. The hand-carved wooden archways, 36 chandeliers, and a grand stair-

62. *The steamboat models are as carefully crafted as were the originals.*

case are all modeled on ones originally designed for steamboats. Also on display are scale models of famous boats, the neo-Louis XV–style furniture, a $35,000 brass bed, a 9-foot-wide pilot's wheel, and related memorabilia. *Open Tues.–Sun. except holidays. Admission charged.*

JEF **Louisville, KY 40202**

MAB

Jefferson St. exit; Muhammad Ali Blvd. exit. Visitors Information Center, 400 S. 1st St. (502) 584-2121. Since Churchill Downs is a primary attraction here, the grounds are open out of racing season; and at the Kentucky Derby Museum at the Downs, various media are employed to give the feel of Derby Week. For those with a little time to spend, the *Belle of Louisville*, an honest-to-goodness stern-wheeler, cruises the Ohio River in a style that travelers were once accustomed to. The J. B. Speed Art Museum, next to the University of Louisville, has contemporary and traditional art in a handsome neoclassical building; and the Museum of History and Science features natural history, aerospace exhibits, and hands-on learning. Old Louisville (Victorian houses), Butchertown (a German neighborhood), and Portland (French and Irish) are among the lovingly restored city districts.

94 **Schmidt's Coca-Cola Museum, Elizabethtown**

6 mi./12 min. West on Rte. 62, right on Ring Rd., left on Rte. 31W. Located in a bottling plant run by the Schmidt family since the turn of the century, this museum celebrates some 100 years of Coca-Cola with countless examples of advertising and memorabilia. After passing by a pool of Japanese carp in the lobby and a gallery demonstrating the latest high-speed bottling techniques, the visitor enters an area with an astonishingly large collection of trademark-emblazoned items: glasses, toys, clocks, fans, trays, cards, ashtrays, and dispensers. An especially nostalgic touch is the 1893 soda fountain with a marble and onyx counter, elaborate mirrors, and Tiffany lamps. *Open Mon.–Fri. except holidays. Admission charged.*

91 **Abraham Lincoln Birthplace National Historic Site**

81 *Exit 91: 13 mi./18 min. South on Rte. 61. Exit 81: 12 mi./20 min. East on Rte. 84, right on Rte. 61.* The first two years of Lincoln's life were spent at the Sinking Spring farm, where the legendary one-room log cabin with dirt floor is now preserved within a dignified memorial building reached by a flight of 56 steps (one for each year of Lincoln's life). The visitor center displays the Lincoln family Bible, and the nearby limestone spring for which the farm was named is speckled with shiny coins, like a wishing well. *Open daily except Christmas.*

53 **Kentucky Action Park, Cave City**

5 min. West on Rte. 70. Don't worry—on the Alpine Slide you can control your own speed as you ride down the steep quarter-mile chute from the hilltop to a meadow below. Other attractions include go-carts and bumper boats; and on the chair lift ride up to the Alpine Slide, you'll enjoy some beautiful views of the valley. In the glassware store, artisans can be seen shaping glass into animals, stagecoaches, galleons, and other designs. *Open daily Memorial Day–Labor Day; weekends only Easter–Memorial Day and Labor Day–Oct. Admission charged.*

35

33 | 33

ROUTE 62

2 | IN / KY

0 | 64

JEF | See E–W book, sec. 33.

MAB

42

94

3

91

10

81

28

53

31

65

22 The Hobson House, Bowling Green

4 mi./14 min. West on Scottsville Rd. (becomes Broadway, then 12th St.), right on State St., left on Main St.; follow signs. This handsome Italianate mansion overlooking the Barren River owes its survival to the fraternal sentiments of two officers on opposite sides of the Civil War. Union colonel Atwood Hobson built the three-story brick mansion; his friend, Confederate general Simon Bolivar Buckner, spared the partially built house when his forces occupied Bowling Green from September 1861 to February 1862. Now fully restored as a living museum, the house contains many choice period pieces from Kentucky and environs, including a charming rococo Louis XV–style bed from Louisiana. An elegant central hall leads to double parlors with frescoed ceilings. *Open Tues.–Sun. Admission charged.*

92 The Hermitage

I-40 *Exit 92: 8 mi./20 min. East on Old Hickory Blvd.; follow signs. Exit I-40: 16 mi./25 min. East on I-40 to Exit 221, north on Rte. 45; follow signs.* Andrew Jackson—war hero, Tennessee gentleman, and the seventh president of the United States—is fittingly remembered at this 625-acre historic site, where two of his homes have been faithfully restored. The "early Hermitage" is a simple log cabin in which Jackson lived happily with his wife, Rachel, from 1804 to 1819. The Hermitage, their second home, is a gracious mansion with wide verandas and Doric columns. Most of the furnishings belonged to the Jackson family, including the crystal, the fine banquet table, mirrors, and a number of impressive family portraits. *Open daily except Thanksgiving Day and Christmas. Admission charged.*

90 Opryland U.S.A., Nashville

80 *Exit 90: 5.5 mi./8 min. South on Rte. 155 (Briley Pkwy.); follow signs. Exit 80: 12 mi./20 min. East on I-440 to Exit 53, left on Rte. 24, right on I-40 to Exit 215, north on Rte. 155 (Briley Pkwy.); follow signs.* This 120-acre stage show and park complex combines the Grand Ole Opry, the legendary country music showcase, with numerous other attractions. The amusement park rides, some with names based upon musical themes—from "The Old Mill Scream" to the "Rock n' Roller Coaster"—appeal to both adults and children. Also part of Opryland are the Roy Acuff Museum, which has a fine collection of memorabilia from country music's early days, and the *General Jackson*, a paddlewheel showboat that offers both day and night cruises. *Open daily Memorial Day–Labor Day; weekends Mar.–May and Sept.–Oct. Admission charged.*

85 Nashville, TN 37213

Tourist Information Center, James Robertson Pkwy. (615) 242-5606. The city's renown as the headquarters of country music tends to obscure the many other rewarding aspects of this gracious state capital. Tribute is paid to antiquity in the splendid Greek revival capitol and in the Parthenon, an exact-size replica of the ancient temple containing a museum and a gallery. Exhibits in the Tennessee State Museum depict life from prehistoric times through the Civil War, and at Fort Nashborough cabins, stockaded walls, and artifacts recall pioneer days. The Country Music Hall of Fame and other museums celebrate Nashville's musical heritage.

65 Carnton Mansion, Franklin

4 mi./10 min. West on Rte. 96, left on Mack Hatcher Memorial Bypass, right on Rte. 431, left on Carnton Lane. Randal McGavock, at one time mayor of Nashville, built this imposing three-story brick house in 1826 and probably planned it to take advantage of the prevailing breeze—it can sweep past the columns of the south-facing front porch, through the central hall, and up the grand staircase to freshen the upper rooms. The mansion's sparse but elegant furnishings include family portraits and parlor and dining room settings. *Open Mon.–Sat. and P.M. Sun. Apr.–Dec.; Mon.–Fri. Jan.–Mar. Admission charged.*

65 The Carter House, Franklin

4 mi./10 min. West on Rte. 96; follow signs. The pockmarks and bullet holes on the house and smokehouse here recall the Bat-

340. *The latest developments in rocketry soon become historic artifacts of engineering.*

tle of Franklin, one of the bloodiest engagements of the Civil War. On November 30, 1864, Confederate general John B. Hood launched a desperate attack against the Union forces that were entrenched around the house and its outbuildings. Among the more than 1,700 Confederate fatalities was Capt. Theodrick "Tod" Carter, whose father and sisters found him mortally wounded less than 200 yards from the family home. The visitor center has a small museum and auditorium. The modest but handsome house, with hand-poured glass windows and Doric columns, is furnished with original family and period pieces. *Open Mon.–Sat. and P.M. Sun. except holidays. Admission charged.* 🏕♿

46 President James K. Polk Ancestral Home, Columbia

10 mi./20 min. West on Rte. 99, left on Rte. 315 (becomes N. Garden St.), right on W. 7th St. This unpretentious two-story brick house, built by President James K. Polk's father in 1816, was the Tennessee home of the 11th president of the United States for only 6 years, between his college days and his marriage. The contents of the building, however, represent Polk's entire career. Among the paintings is a series showing Polk as a young lawyer and at both the beginning and end of his presidency. Several pieces of White House china, silver, and crystal are on display, and an Inauguration ball gown worn by Sarah Polk, along with the ornate fan given to her for that occasion, are also exhibited. *Open daily Mon.–Thurs. and P.M. Sun. except Thanksgiving Day, Christmas Eve, Christmas, and New Year's Day. Admission charged.*

340 Mooresville Historic Town

1 min. East on Rte. 20/Alt. 72. Like Rip Van Winkle, this charming and well-preserved hamlet seems to have slumbered for many years. And since it has not been featured as a tourist attraction, it retains a good measure of grace and dignity. Incorporated in 1818, Mooresville is one year older than the state of Alabama itself. The streets, lined by venerable shade trees and virtually free of cars, retain their 19th-century serenity. It takes 15 or 20 minutes to stroll through the village and admire the fine old federal-style houses, all inhabited and immaculately maintained. You might start at the circa-1840 post office, which is constructed of poplar and still has its original post office boxes; and you can also pay a visit to the Mooresville Brick Church, built in 1839 for Robert Donnel, one of the founding fathers of the Cumberland Presbyterian Church. 🚶

340 Point Mallard Park, Decatur

10 mi./20 min. West on Rte. 20/Alt. 72, left on Rte. 31, left on 8th St. SE. Pleasantly situated on a wooded peninsula across the Tennessee River from a national wildlife refuge, this 750-acre park is a swimmer's paradise. As bathers bob on floats in the churning waters of the turbine-driven wave pool (America's first), they look like strangely contented survivors of a shipwreck. Three serpentine water slides, a sandy river beach, and a huge swimming pool round out the aquatic fun. You can also sample an 18-hole golf course, minigolf, tennis, a hiking trail, playing fields, and in winter, an outdoor ice-skating rink. *Open year-round.* 🏕⛺🚐🚶🏊🎣

340 The Space and Rocket Center, Huntsville

15 mi./20 min. East on Rte. 20/Alt. 72; follow signs. You can ride in a simulated space shuttle, spin in a centrifuge, or amble through a space station; or you can explore the Lunar Lander, walk alongside a *Saturn V* rocket displayed in stages, and watch Space Camp trainees practice their zero-gravity skills. In any case you'll be impressed at the courage it takes to sit on top of a rocket filled with thousands of gallons of volatile fuel and about to be launched for the moon. *Open daily except Christmas. Admission charged.*

318 / 310 Hurricane Creek Park

Exit 318: 4 min. South on Rte. 31. Exit 310: 5 min. East on Rte. 157, left on Rte. 31. This deep Appalachian gorge surrounded by trails and tunnels is an intriguing place to explore. William Rodgers, an air force major, spotted it from a jet plane in 1958, and upon his retirement he bought the land, developed it, and opened the rugged canyon to the public in 1963. Steep trails of varying degrees of difficulty descend through narrow rock fissures to a creek spanned by a rope bridge. The most challenging route leads to Twilite Tunnel, a dark and winding 600-foot passage up through the mountain. The gorge is laced with hickory, pine, and mountain laurel. *Open year-round.* 🏕🚶

308 Ave Maria Grotto

5 mi./12 min. East on Rte. 278; follow signs. This unique garden of architectural miniatures is the result of one man's loving labor. During the almost 70 years that Brother Joseph Zoettl lived in the Benedictine Abbey of St. Bernard, he created more than 125 scaled-down reproductions of shrines and famous buildings. You'll see the city of Jerusalem, the Lourdes Basilica, the Hanging Gardens of Babylon, a fanciful Temple of the Fairies, and the elaborate 27-foot-high Ave Maria Grotto. Amazing for both sheer quantity and accuracy (Brother Joseph saw only two of the originals, basing most of his constructions on research and photos), these highly detailed works were made with a variety of ordinary found and donated materials, such as floats from Irish fishing nets, cold cream jars, marbles, and for the dome of St. Peter's Basilica in Rome, an old birdcage. *Open year-round. Admission charged.*

308. *St. Peter's Basilica is the centerpiece in the grotto's Roman group.*

65
308
24
284
24
See E–W book, sec. 46.
20
260
1
259B
13
246
34
212
7
205
24
181
8
173
1
172

308 Clarkson Covered Bridge, Cullman

8 mi./15 min. West on Rte. 278; follow signs. Doves like to roost in the rafters beneath this circa-1904 covered truss bridge, supported by four massive stone piers. With a span of 275 feet, it is one of the largest structures of its kind in Alabama. Retired, restored, and inscribed in *The National Register of Historic Places*, the bridge provides a charming focal point for the adjacent small park. As you stroll across, notice the shadows that are cast by the latticelike construction. A short nature trail and picnic area are idyllically set amid tall trees beside the creek. *Open daily Memorial Day–Labor Day.*

284 Rickwood Caverns State Park

4 mi./10 min. West on Rte. 160, right on access road. Your descent into this cool, eerie labyrinth takes you back some 260 million years. The shells and marine fossils embedded in the walls verify that this was once below the ocean. At the lowest level lies an underground lake, where blind fish swim through dark waters. The 102 steps leading out of the caverns may be difficult for some. In addition to the usual camping facilities, the park has an Olympic-size swimming pool, and a narrow-gauge train circles it. *Open daily June–Labor Day; weekends March–May and Sept.–Oct. Admission charged.*

260 / 259B Birmingham, AL 35203

Convention & Visitors Bureau, 2027 1st Ave. N. (205) 252-9825. The character of the city as viewed from the base of Vulcan's statue on Red Mountain is dramatically different from the smokestack industry image that originally inspired the 55-foot cast-iron monument. Alabama's largest city now boasts an excellent museum of fine arts, the Southern Museum of Flight, a children's museum, and the unique Red Mountain Museum, where a deep cut into the mountain for a highway provides close-up observation that reveals some 150 million years of layers of sedimentation and fossils from ancient seas. At the Birmingham Botanical Gardens there's a conservatory of rare plants and a charming Japanese garden; the excellent zoo is nearby. Arlington Antebellum Home, a handsome Greek revival house, has extensive gardens and interesting collections of furniture and decorative art. The early days of the iron industry are recalled in the reconstructed Sloss Furnaces, which are now a walk-through museum.

246 Oak Mountain State Park

5 min. Follow signs. Opportunities for recreation here in Alabama's largest state park—nearly 10,000 acres set in a deep, wooded Appalachian valley—range from canoeing, fishing, swimming, and tennis to BMX bike riding and rugged mountain hiking. Those interested in waterside pursuits have three lakes to choose from, and there are some 30 miles of hiking trails. For the adventurous, a twisting and unimproved mountain road leads to a parking lot and the half-mile walk to scenic Peavine Falls. *Open year-round. Admission charged.*

212 Lay Dam Generating Plant Tour

10 mi./15 min. North on Rte. 145, right on Rte. 55; follow signs. Here is a rare opportunity to descend into the heart of a mammoth hydroelectric dam and to see how running water is transformed into megavolts of electricity. The tour begins 40 feet below the top of the dam in the central generating area, where 85-foot-high turbines are situated in each of the 26 gates of the dam. In the control room, walls of gauges and meters monitor every function of the plant's machinery. The observation deck looks across Lay Lake to a wooded valley where a receding line of towers transmits the boon of light and power to distant places. *Open year-round. For tour call (205) 755-4520.*

205 Confederate Memorial Park

9 mi./15 min. South on Rtes. 31 and 143. This park was established to commemorate the Confederate veterans who, long after the fighting had ceased, were left destitute and without federal pensions. To help these victims of circumstance, Jefferson Manley Falkner Soldiers Home opened its doors in 1902. Civil War memorabilia and photos and accounts of the home's occupants are displayed in the visitor center–museum. On two hillsides overlooking the park, cemeteries contain the graves of more than 200 veterans, 15 Confederate wives, and the tomb of an unknown soldier. Most of the headstones date from 1912 to 1936. *Open year-round. Admission free but donations encouraged.*

181 / 173 Jasmine Hill Gardens, Montgomery

Exit 181: 17 mi./23 min. East on Rte. 14, right on Rte. 231, left on Jasmine Hill Rd. Exit 173: 18 mi./22 min. East on North Blvd., left on Rte. 231, right on Jasmine Hill Rd. Added to the seasonal color of the lovely trees, shrubs, and flowers in this 17-acre garden is the constant refreshing sense of fun and fantasy provided by more than 30 originals and reproductions of classic Greek sculpture. The Greek gods, nymphs, animals, athletes, and heroes are charmingly displayed throughout the grounds. A replica of the ruins of Hera's Temple surrounds a reflecting pool, where water lilies bloom and goldfish glide under Hera's steady gaze. Terra-cotta dogs guard stone pathways lined with roses and honeysuckle, and ivy-shaded arbors lead to romantic pavilions and some secluded stone benches. *Open Tues.–Sun. and Mon. holidays except Thanksgiving Day, Christmas, and New Year's Day. Admission charged.*

172 Montgomery, AL 36104

Chamber of Commerce, 41 Commerce St. (205) 834-5200. Montgomery bears witness to two of the South's most momentous events. Near the state capitol is the official residence used by Jefferson Davis as president of the Confederacy. It is now a Confederate museum. Nearby is the Dexter Avenue King Memorial Baptist Church, where the Reverend Dr. Martin Luther King, Jr., advocated nonviolent protests as a way of ending racial segregation. The Old South lives again in the 27 homes and buildings of the Old North Hull Street His-

172. *Cozy bedroom in the Jefferson Davis house. Note the flip side of the quilt.*

toric District, and at the Teague House and the Rice-Semple-Haardt House. For a restful interlude there's an excursion cruise on the *General Richard Montgomery*, an Alabama River paddle wheeler.

130 Sherling Lake Park

4 mi./7 min. North on Rte. 185, left on Rte. 263. When William Bartram, the well-known naturalist, passed through this site in 1775 on his exploration of the Southeast, he probably admired the many giant umbrella magnolias that still grace this tranquil place. A wide boulevard leads to a jade-green lakeshore where manicured lawns separate Sherling Lake from the surrounding dense woodland. You can circle the lake on a 2-mile-long boardwalk with handsome bridges and observe the many bird species attracted to the shore by strategically placed feeders. *Open year-round.*

57 Claude D. Kelley State Park

9 mi./12 min. North on Rte. 21; follow signs. A paved road leads through secluded pine woods to the Little River, where a dam has created a small lake. The knee-deep water near the dam is favored by children for wading. More adventurous swimmers will find the reddish waters of the river refreshing on summer days. Anglers will enjoy casting off from atop the dam. A short distance from the lake area, shaded picnic tables, barbecues, and a playground enhance this pleasant park, whose tranquillity is protected by the Little River State Forest across the road. *Open year-round.*

31 Historic Blakeley State Park

16 mi./20 min. South on Rte. 225. This wooded 3,800-acre park memorializes the last great battle of the Civil War, where fighting continued for hours on April 9, 1865, after General Lee had surrendered in Virginia. Self-guiding maps of the Blakeley park and battleground are available from the park ranger. One trail traverses woodland atop some well-preserved Confederate breastworks; near the beaver pond, a bucolic picnic and cane-pole fishing spot, you can see the incongruously peaceful remains of a gun emplacement. The park sponsors an annual reenactment of the South's heroic last stand in early April.

Another trail leads to the 1,000-year-old Jury Oak, which early 19th-century settlers reportedly used as a courthouse. The judge sat in a fork among the lower branches while the defendant stood below. And if the verdict was guilty, the Hanging Tree was just a few steps away. *Open daily except Christmas. Admission charged.*

1 Mobile, AL 36602

Chamber of Commerce, 451 Government St. (205) 433-6951. In this charming city one feels the essence of the Old South: the magnolias, live oaks, crape myrtles, camellias, and azaleas in abundance and scores of gracious antebellum houses. The five historic districts and the neighborhoods adjoining them constitute a veritable museum of architectural styles—from federal to Victorian—including Oakleigh, a classic of southern design, and the Richards–D.A.R. House, adorned with ornate lace ironwork. Other highlights include the City Museum and a reconstructed French fort. In Battleship U.S.S. *Alabama* Memorial Park, you can board the World War II battleship as well as a submarine and see a B-52 bomber and other aircraft of the era.

I-10 Bellingrath Gardens and Home, Theodore

15 mi./20 min. West on I-10, left on Rte. 90, left on Bellingrath Rd. Floral exuberance and abundance characterize these 65 acres of gardens, created in the midst of a semi-tropical jungle along a river. One of the first delights along the walking tour is the Oriental-American garden. Here a wooden teahouse sits between a carp stream and a placid lake, where swans glide against a backdrop of weeping Yoshima cherry trees. Near the imposing brick house are brilliant beds of perennials. The wheel-shaped rose garden—where roses bloom in every shade from lemon-yellow to deep scarlet—is an inviting source of color and fragrance for 9 months of the year. In the fall one of the world's largest outdoor displays of chrysanthemums—some 80,000 plants—brightens the landscape. A conservatory houses orchids and other exotic plants.

Antique furnishings and objets d'art are displayed in the former Walter D. Bellingrath home, and the nearby Boehm Gallery houses more than 230 of the famed porcelain sculptures created by Edward Marshall Boehm. *Open year-round. Admission charged for garden and home.*

I-10. *Azaleas add a splash of color to the subtle palette of the Japanese garden.*

42

130

73

57

26

31

34

1   See E–W
     book,
     sec. 54.
2
I-10   10

End I-65

69

CANADA

U.S.A.
MI

94 | **I-94**

See
E–W book,
sec. 14.

61

137

75

See
N–S book,
sec. 30.

47

90

15

**ROUTE
27B**

44

See
E–W book,
sec. 14.

94 | **38**

2

36

39

MI
IN

80 90

154

See E–W book,
sec. 23 for I-80;
sec. 7 for I-90.

90–27B. *One property of static electricity is the creation of instant hairdos.*

I-94 | Lakeport State Park

8 mi./11 min. East on I-94, north on Pine Grove Ave. (becomes Rte. 25). The south (FDR) unit of this lakeside park has pleasant picnic grounds shaded by tall oaks, maples, and pines, as well as a fine swimming beach that looks out on ships making their way to or from Port Huron, Detroit, or Windsor. The north unit, located a mile farther along Route 25, is a spacious campground set in open and wooded terrain. The north unit also has access to a beach on Lake Huron. *Open year-round. Admission charged.*

137 | Crossroads Village and Huckleberry Railroad, Flint

8 mi./11 min. North on I-475 to Exit 11, east on Carpenter Rd., left on Bray Rd.; follow signs. The village re-creates a Genesee County community of the 1870's, with costumed interpreters playing the parts of local characters. Old-style mills grind corn and turn logs into lumber, and an old Baldwin steam locomotive takes visitors on a 45-minute scenic tour of the village. *Open daily Memorial Day–Labor Day, P.M. Fri.–Sun. in Dec. Admission charged.*

90 | ROUTE 27B | Impression 5, Lansing

Exit 90: 7 mi./12 min. South on Rte. 127 to Grand River Ave. exit; continue on Howard St., right on Michigan Ave., left on Museum Dr. Rte. 27 (business) exit: 7 mi./15 min. Northeast on Rte. 27 (business; becomes I-496), north on Larch St., left on Michigan Ave., left on Museum Dr. This imaginative science museum offers excellent hands-on demonstrations that make it fun to learn about the sciences of physics, chemistry, electronics, biology, and computing. Visitors of all ages can take a sensitivity test, play with molecules and fiber optics, experiment with integrated circuits, look through stereoscopic microscopes, or produce computer artwork on a "flatbed plotter-digitizer." *Open Mon.–Sat. and P.M. Sun. except Memorial Day, Thanksgiving Day, Christmas Eve, Christmas, New Year's Day, and Easter. Admission charged.*

38 | Binder Park Zoo

11.5 mi./14 min. West on I-94 to Exit 100, south on Beadle Lake Rd.; follow signs. Set in the woodland of Binder Park, the zoo provides naturalistic environments for many of its animals. A boardwalk through a pinewoods overlooks the exhibit areas, where Formosan sika deer reside; bison, peacocks, and prairie dogs can also be seen; and llamas, Sicilian donkeys, ponies, and a yak can be fed and petted at the petting zoo. A variety of waterbirds inhabit the zoo's pond, and around its edge are enclosures for gibbons, eagles, emus, and wallabies. *Open daily late Apr.–late Oct. Admission charged.*

36 | Honolulu House, Marshall

5 min. East on I-94 (business loop); follow signs. This curious home, modeled on the executive mansion in Honolulu, was built in 1860 by Judge Abner Pratt, a former U.S. consul in the Sandwich (Hawaiian) Islands, who strove to create the exotic atmosphere of the Pacific islands in Michigan. The two-story house has a broad veranda and an observation tower that is reached from the central hall by a spiral staircase; the rooms have 15-foot ceilings, and the murals—wreaths of tropical plants mixed with lilies, cattails, and classic cupids—have been restored to their appearance in 1885, when a new owner remodeled the house and had the original murals embellished. The furnishings are from the mid- to the late 19th century. *Open P.M. daily late May–Oct. Admission charged.*

154 | Pokagon State Park

2 min. West on Rte. 727. This park, named for Potawatomi chief Pokagon, has year-round appeal. In winter the thrill seekers head for the 1,780-foot refrigerated toboggan slide, where they can streak down and over hills at 45 miles per hour. The slide is open from Thanksgiving to March, and the toboggans, rented by the hour, can hold up to four passengers. Other attractions in this

36. *Over 4,000 miles from the original, but the architectural mix retains its charm.*

vast area include trails for hikers and cross-country skiers (rentals available), ice fishing, ice skating, sledding, and year-round camping. In summer, visitors come to fish, boat, and swim from Lake James's wide and sandy beaches. *Open year-round. Admission charged.* 🏕 ⛺ 🚐 🚶 🏊 🎣 ♿

129 Auburn Cord Duesenberg Museum

2 mi./6 min. East on Rte. 8; follow signs. This exceptionally fine collection of classic cars enshrined in the art deco Auburn Automobile Company showroom elegantly illustrates the golden age of automotive design. The display includes a silver and black 265-h.p. Duesenberg, a scarlet and chrome Cord, a 1937 black and chrome Cord Sportsman, a Stutz Bearcat, early Auburn sedans, a racing Bugatti, a Ferrari, and an Aston Martin. *Open daily except Thanksgiving Day, Christmas, and New Year's Day. Admission charged.*

111A 102 Historic Fort Wayne

Exit 111A: 3 mi./15 min. South on Rte. 27, left on Superior St., then left on Barr St. Exit 102: 10 mi./30 min. East on Jefferson Blvd., left on Rte. 27, left on Superior St., right on Barr St. A reconstructed fort of stout log and mud-chinked walls with formidable blockhouses recalls Ft. Wayne's role as an important frontier outpost in the early 19th century. The fort's colorful history is illustrated with weaponry, tools, and documents from the warring Indians, English, French, and the newly established Americans. *Open daily mid-Apr.–Labor Day; Tues.–Sun. early Sept.–late Oct. Admission charged.* 🏕 ♿

86 78 Huntington Lake

8 mi./15 min. Exit 86: west on Rte. 224, left on Rte. 5. Exit 78: north on Rte. 5. The 8,322-acre Huntington Reservoir property, which once belonged to the Miami Indians, offers a variety of recreational opportunities, from model-airplane flying to camping in a mature forest of oak and shagbark hickory on a steep bluff over the water. A beach, a boat ramp, and attractive picnic areas and shelters are located

129. *Auburns still rank high among the all-time classics of automobile design.*

along the shore. The narrow lake is stocked with channel catfish, walleye, bass, bluegill, and crappie, and there is small game and waterfowl hunting in season. *Open year-round. Admission charged Memorial Day–Labor Day.* 🏕 ⛺ 🚐 🚶 🏊 🎣

41 Ball Corporation Museum, Muncie

11 mi./20 min. East on Rte. 332, right on Wheeling Ave. (becomes High St.). The Ball brothers' ventures in containers of every kind, from wooden egg barrels in the late 1800's to Pepsi-Cola cans, are chronicled in an exhibit in the reception area of the Ball Corporation headquarters. Glass preserving jars of all shapes, sizes, and hues are displayed, including one filled with elderberry syrup put up in 1888. *Open Mon.–Fri. except holidays.*

34 26 Mounds State Park

Exit 34: 3 mi./10 min. West on Rte. 32; follow signs. Exit 26: 5 mi./15 min. North on Rte. 9, right on Rte. 232. The fate of the ancient Adena and Hopewell Indians who built these burial and ceremonial mounds and earthworks is unknown. At one time there were 11 mounds

here, but today only three are recognizable. Replicas of the tools these Indians used are displayed in the mid-19th-century Bronnenberg House. Trails for horseback riding, hiking, and cross-country skiing pass the mounds and earthworks. *Open year-round. Admission charged.* 🏕 ⛺ 🚐 🚶 🏊 🎣 ♿

5 Conner Prairie, Noblesville

4 mi./8 min. West on 116th St., right on Allisonville Rd.; follow signs. Visitors are encouraged to take part in the activities of this convincingly reconstructed early-19th-century village. Interpreters dressed in period clothing play the parts of people from the era. Townspeople exchange gossip at the inn, the teacher gives an Old World history lesson in the schoolhouse, and costumed weavers, potters, carpenters, a blacksmith, and a physician discuss and demonstrate their work in houses and shops. The most noteworthy of the 39 buildings here are the Museum Center, which features an audiovisual presentation, and the Conner Mansion, built in 1823. *Open Tues.–Sat. and P.M. Sun. May–Oct.; Wed.–Sat. and P.M. Sun. Apr. and Nov. except Thanksgiving Day and Easter. Admission charged.* 🏕 ♿

I-465 Indianapolis, IN 46225

Convention & Visitors Association, 1 Hoosier Dome, Suite 100. (317) 639-4282. Nearly everyone knows that in May, Indianapolis boasts one of the world's largest sports events, the Indy 500. But there are also other attractions worthy of note. Consider, for example, the Indianapolis Museum of Art, the Indiana State Museum, and the Children's Museum, one of the largest and most varied of its kind. There's a new zoo and three large parks. In Union Station in the heart of downtown, Festival Market Place, with its many shops and restaurants, attracts crowds. And even if it isn't May, the Speedway is worth a visit. The Hall of Fame Museum displays antique and classic cars and more than 32 speedsters that have won the race since it began in 1911; and you can get the feel of the "Brickyard" on a minibus ride around the circuit.

25

129

18

111A

9

102

16

86

8

78

87

41

7

34

8

26

21

5

5

I-465 65 70

End I-69

See E–W book, sec. 30 for I-70; N–S book, sec. 26 for I-65.

To reach I-70 or I-65 go south on I-465.

339. *The palisaded fort is an accurate reconstruction of a British outpost.*

394 Soo Locks, Sault Sainte Marie

2 mi./7 min. East on Easterday Ave., left on Rte. 75 (business), left on Portage Ave. More than 20 vessels per day pass through the Soo Locks —from small pleasure boats to 1,000-foot-long giant freighters carrying more than 70,000 tons of cargo. The oldest of the four locks dates back to 1914, while the newest and biggest was completed in 1968. A hydroelectric power plant at nearby St. Marys Rapids provides power for the locks, and the surplus is sold by a private company for homes and businesses in Sault Sainte Marie. Comprehensive displays at the information center describe the history of the locks and their importance. *Open daily mid-May–mid-Nov.*

386 Brimley State Park

11 mi./14 min. West on Rte. 28, right on Rte. 221, right at T-junction; follow signs. This attractive little park looks out across Brimley Bay to Lake Superior. The lake narrows here as it approaches the St. Marys River (which connects it with Lake Huron), and from the park you can see 1,000-foot-long freighters on their way to and from the Soo Locks. *Open year-round. Admission charged.*

339 Colonial Michilimackinac State Historic Park

2 min. Headed south: north on Louvingny St., right on Huron St. Headed north: north on Nicolet St. Ft. Michilimackinac, built here about 1715 by the French and occupied by the British from 1761 to 1781, has been reconstructed on its original site, re-creating with great authenticity the spirit and character of the settlement's early days. Within the fort's walls are a powder magazine, the commanding officer's house, and merchants' quarters stocked with pelts, barrels, and trade goods. The adjacent Mackinac Maritime Park displays maritime artifacts from ships and boats that once plied these waters, including the hull of an 1891 steam yacht. At the old Mackinac Point lighthouse a museum features exhibits on the maritime history of the Straits of Mackinac. *Open daily mid-May–mid-Oct. Admission charged.*

282 Call of the Wild, Gaylord

4 min. East on Rte. 75 (business), right on S. Wisconsin Ave. This wildlife museum has numerous bird and animal specimens, ranging from a polar bear to cougars, realistically mounted in dioramas representing their natural habitats. Most are shown in some characteristic pose or activity (the beavers, for example, are gnawing on aspens beside their dam), and often birds and animals that share an environment are grouped together. In many cases, recordings of the creatures' voices can be heard. An ingenious system of mirrors allows you to see some scenes and animals in different seasons. *Open daily except Thanksgiving Day, Christmas, and New Year's Day. Admission charged.*

259 Hartwick Pines State Park

4 min. North on Rte. 93. The glory of the park is a 49-acre forest of majestic virgin pines more than 140 feet tall, a remnant of the days when vast tracts of Michigan were densely covered by primeval forests. A visitor center and museum recall the lumberjacks, lumber barons, and pulp mills of Michigan's so-called White Pine Era from 1840 to 1910. Those roistering days are brought vividly to life by the authentic lumber camp, with a bunkhouse, a store, a blacksmith's and a carpenter's shop, and the foreman's cabin. Logging equipment and a steam-operated sawmill are also on display. The 2-mile Mertz Grade Nature Trail follows the track of a railroad that once carried lumber to mills in Grayling, and the AuSable River Foot Trail cuts through forest and clearing to skirt the East Branch of the AuSable River. *Park open year-round; exhibit buildings open Apr.–Oct. Admission charged.*

239 South Higgins Lake State Park

7 mi./9 min. West on Rte. 103, left on Rte. 100. More than 1,000 acres of woods and lake here include some well-developed facilities for camping and picnicking, a boat basin, a long sandy beach, and a nature trail animated by gulls and black squirrels. Fringed with birch and evergreen trees, the crystalline lake has distant views of woods and hills on its far shores. Just across the road from the park is the 700-acre Marl Lake area, a smaller lake with a much wilder environment (no camping permitted), with trails through the woods along the lake's perimeter. *Open year-round. Admisson charged.*

190   Gladwin City Park

23 mi./26 min. West on Rte. 61, left on City Park St. Set in the midst of central Michigan country, which is known for its abundant lakes and rivers, Gladwin is a pleasant little town in which to stop and relax—and it is made all the more pleasant by this lovely city park along the Cedar River. The recreational facilities here are unusually complete: camping and picnic grounds are supplemented by tennis courts, a ballfield, and a playground for children; river swimmers enjoy a sandy beach; and a riverside path makes for scenic strolling. *Park open year-round; camping permitted Apr.–Nov.*

168   Tobico Marsh

5.5 mi./7 min. East on Beaver Rd., left on N. Euclid Rd. The varied habitat provided by woods, the wetlands of Tobico Lagoon, and dry uplands make this 1,700-acre refuge, about half a mile from Bay City State Park's entrance, a bird-watcher's paradise. Trails wind among rare flowers and shrubs to the water's edge, and two 30-foot-high observation towers afford treetop views of the lagoon and the more than 60 species of water birds that come by the thousands during spring and fall migrations. To enter the refuge, get the gate key from the park manager or the nearby Jennison Nature Center. *Open year-round.*

162A   Historical Museum of Bay County, Bay City

3 mi./6 min. East on Rte. 25, right on Washington Ave. The museum occupies the old Michigan National Guard Armory building, a severe but handsome structure that dates from 1909—just 10 years before the museum itself was founded. Today, the collections contain some 60,000 artifacts, representing all aspects of life in Bay County. A chronological history of Bay County is depicted in a planned history maze, with displays portraying Indian life and early industries, such as mining and shipping. *For hours call (517) 893-5733.*

149B   Saginaw-Tokushima Friendship Gardens

4 mi./9 min. West on Rte. 46, right on Rte. 13 (Washington Ave.). In 1970 the sister cities of Saginaw, Michigan, and Tokushima, Japan, marked their friendship by creating these traditional Japanese gardens. Greeted by a beautiful antique stone lantern, visitors proceed along a garden path to a charming bridge of ancient design that crosses a stream beside a tranquil lake. The Japanese Cultural Center and Tea House, one of the few fully authentic Japanese tea houses in America, is a true international joint effort. Americans built the foundation, external walls, and roof while Japanese craftsmen finished the interior, with its ceiling of handwoven cedar strips, walls made of a light brown mud-plaster, and

cedar-frame shoji screens with rice paper. Visitors may participate in a traditional Japanese tea ceremony. *Gardens open Tues.– Sun. Memorial Day–Labor Day; tea house open P.M. Tues.–Sun. Memorial Day–Labor Day; gardens and tea house open P.M. Wed.–Sun. Labor Day–Memorial Day. Admission charged.*

149B   Shiawasee National Wildlife Refuge, Saginaw

12 mi./20 min. West on Rte. 46, left on Rte. 13, right on Curtis Rd. From September to November, as many as 25,000 Canada geese and 50,000 ducks visit this refuge on their fall migration, lured here by thousands of acres of wetlands and 1,500 acres that are sharecropped for the birds' benefit. There are some 5 miles of hiking trails that cross farmland, shallow pools of water, and green-tree impoundments (areas annually flooded by a system of dikes to provide the birds with access to new sources of food). Another 5 miles of trails in the northern section of the park (west on Route 46, south on Center Road, left on Stroebel Road) explores mostly hardwood forests and bottomland. Bald eagles have begun to nest here, and white-tailed deer are common. *Open year-round.*

125 / 111   Crossroads Village and Huckleberry Railroad, Flint

Exit 125: 6 mi./10 min. East on I-475 to Exit 11, east on Carpenter Rd., left on Bray Rd.; follow signs. Exit 111: 13 mi./15 min. North on I-475 to Exit 11, east on Carpenter Rd.; proceed as above. The village re-creates a Genesee County community of the 1870's, with costumed interpreters playing the parts of the miller, doctor, apothecary, printer, sawyer, and other local characters. Old-style mills grind corn and turn logs into lumber, and an old Baldwin steam locomotive takes visitors on a 45-minute scenic tour through the village and along Mott Lake on the Huckleberry Railroad. Special events take place in summer, ranging from antique auto and hot-air balloon shows to festivals. During December the village becomes a wonderland of colored lights. *Open daily Memorial Day–Labor Day, P.M. Fri.–Sun. in Dec. Admission charged.*

168. *A Canada goose escorts goslings on the algae-tinted waters of Tobico Lagoon.*

Section **30** (295 miles)
See map page V.

239

49

190

22

168

6

162A

13

149B

24

125

14

69

111   See N–S book, sec. 29.

10

75

75
101
20
81
31
See
E–W book,
sec. 14.
94
50
9
41
47
MI
OH
I-280
7
201B
8
80 90
See E–W
book,
sec. 24.
for I-80;
sec. 7
for I-90.
37
193
156

101 Seven Lakes State Park, Fenton

4 mi./8 min. West on Grange Hall Rd., right on Fish Lake Rd. This unusually lovely park has varied landscapes, scenic views, and six lakes of different sizes. The largest has a gravel beach, and its irregular shoreline embraces numerous small bays and inlets. Foot trails wind along the shores of three lakes and through meadows dotted with wildflowers. The rich avian life includes ring-necked pheasants and downy woodpeckers. *Open year-round. Admission charged.*

81 Bald Mountain Recreation Area, Lake Orion

6 mi./8 min. North on Rte. 24, right on Greenshield Rd. The wild scenery here is crisscrossed by several hiking trails; and there are three lakes, one of which (Upper Trout Lake) has a broad, sandy swimming beach. The park is known for the abundance of its wildflowers, which flourish in habitats ranging from young woodlands to rough meadows and bottomlands. The less developed north unit of the park can be reached by continuing north on Route 24 and following signs. *Open year-round. Admission charged.*

50 Detroit, MI 48226

Convention and Visitors Bureau, 2 E. Jefferson Ave. (313) 567-1170. Although best known for its automobiles, Detroit still keeps an antique electric trolley system in service, along with an ultramodern elevated people mover, which provides an interesting perspective of the city. To take a tour of the auto plants always requires some advance planning. But the industry is powerfully represented in Diego Rivera's great frescoes of the city in the Detroit Institute of Arts, which in addition has exceptionally well-rounded collections from every major period.

The city also offers such varied attractions as the bustling open-air Eastern Market, with its vast displays of flowers and vegetables, two zoos, a children's museum, a family amusement park, and a freshwater aquarium. You can also take a tour of a Motown recording studio.

41 Henry Ford Museum and Greenfield Village, Dearborn

8 mi./12 min. North on Rte. 39 (Southfield Hwy.), left on Oakwood Blvd. The scope, variety, and quality of one of the nation's largest museum complexes are extraordinary. The exhibits represent most of the aspects of America's cultural and technological history. In the extensive Henry Ford Museum you will see George Washington's campaign chest and the rocking chair Abraham Lincoln was sitting in when he was assassinated; the 600-ton Allegheny locomotive, one of the largest coal-burning engines ever built; and steam engines as big as houses. The adjoining Greenfield Village, spread over 81 acres, has most of the amenities, and all of the charm, of a small 19th-century town. You'll find tree-lined streets and historic buildings brought here from their original sites—the Wright brothers' cycle shop, Henry Ford's birthplace, and Thomas Edison's laboratory complex from Menlo Park, New Jersey, among others. *Museum open daily except Thanksgiving Day and Christmas; village interiors open daily except early Jan.–mid-Mar. Admission charged for each.*

156. *Prices—and styles—have changed but the barber pole remains the same.*

I-280 / 201B Toledo, OH 43604

Office of Tourism & Conventions, 218 Huron St. (419) 243-8191. This major Great Lakes port is a city of iron and coal, where bicycle and wagon shops gave way to auto parts makers and a thriving glass industry. The Toledo Museum of Art has magnificent glass displays, as well as extensive collections in many periods of painting and sculpture. The Portside Festival Marketplace, on the waterfront, is a lively and likely focus for a visit.

193 Fort Meigs State Memorial

4 mi./10 min. South on Rte. 20, right on Rte. 65; follow signs. Built on a bluff above the rapids of the Maumee River, Ft. Meigs played a key role in America's victory in the War of 1812. It was built in February 1813, and in May survived a siege and bombardment by the British Army; in July the British were repulsed again, and this failure paved the way for their defeat in the Battle of Lake Erie. The present fort is a reconstruction of the original; three of the seven blockhouses contain exhibits about the war and about the construction of forts. *Open Wed.–Sat., P.M. Sun and holidays late May–early Sept.; Sat. and P.M. Sun. early Sept.–late Oct. Admission charged.*

156 Ghost Town

6 mi./15 min. South on Rte. 15/68; continue on Rte. 68; follow signs. The quaint houses, stores, and other buildings here, some original and some faithfully reproduced, are so full of authentic memorabilia from pioneer days that they almost give visitors the impression that their occupants might return at any moment. A row of businesses in this homey town includes the Noah's Ark Emporium, a Chinese laundry, a barbershop, an undertaker, and other establishments, all fully equipped with 19th-century goods and utensils and peopled by mannequins. In the middle of town a replica of an original Drake oil derrick stands next to a 25-foot covered bridge, one of the shortest in Ohio. *Open Tues.–Sun. Memorial Day–Labor Day; weekends only in Sept. Admission charged.*

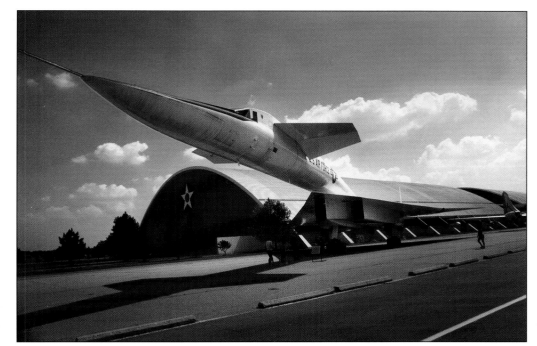

58–54C. *The Valkyrie is an experimental bomber with dramatic implications of speed.*

you will see almost 200 planes and missiles on display. They span the history of aviation from the Wright brothers' kitelike 1909 Military Flyer to a charred and battered Apollo capsule that circled the moon. *Open daily except Christmas.* ⊼ ♿

53A Dayton, OH 45402

Convention & Visitors Bureau, Chamber Plaza, 5th and Main Sts. (513) 226-8248 or (800) 221-8234; (800) 221-8235 outside OH. This river city, settled in 1796, seems to have invention in the air. The cash register, the electric starter, and the pull-tab tin-can top all were devised by Daytonians. But the best-known local wizards were Orville and Wilbur Wright. One of their first planes is among the attractions in Carillon Park. Also to be seen there are relics of canals, railroads, and airways.

Dayton is also the home of the last Wright bicycle shop, as well as the print-shop where the brothers published the work of the black poet Paul Laurence Dunbar, whose home is now a museum. Other highlights: the National Aviation Hall of Fame and the baroque collections in the Dayton Art Institute.

1F Cincinnati, OH 45202

1E *Convention and Visitors Bureau, 300 W. 6th St. (513) 621-2142.* In the downtown section of this city, which was a starting place for settlers heading west on the Ohio River, a modern 16-block skywalk now connects department stores, specialty shops, and restaurants. The Cincinnati Art Museum's galleries—numbering more than a hundred—offer works from all major cultures and periods. The Taft Museum, in a federal-style house, displays porcelains, enamels, and paintings by European masters.

The Museum of Natural History features a large, realistic cave and exhibits related to prehistoric Indians and primitive cultures. The outstanding zoo has more than 1,200 species and is especially noted for its gorillas and white tigers.

Across the river, in Covington, Kentucky, the Riverside Historic District recalls the early days in the area.

---

125 Railroad Exhibit, Lima

5 min. West on Rte. 309/117 (Bellefontaine Ave.), right on Shawnee St.; follow signs. A massive steam locomotive built in 1949 was the last one constructed at the Lima Locomotive Works (originally called the Lima Machine Company), which had been manufacturing steam engines since 1878. Painted black with white-rimmed wheels, *Nickel Plate No. 779* is a marvel of brute power intricately harnessed by a network of pipes, cylinders, and valves. The cab of the engine, several coaches—including a luxurious private Pullman car—a red caboose, an outfitted depot–ticket office, and an old signal standard add to this nostalgic memorial to the days of steam power. *Open year-round.* ⊼

111 Neil Armstrong Air and Space Museum, Wapakoneta

2 min. West on Wapak-Fisher Rd.; follow signs. This futuristic winged structure set on a hillside is dedicated to Ohioan Neil Armstrong, the first man to walk on the moon. The Infinity Room illustrates the vastness of space with endlessly receding perpectives in a mirrored cubicle and an Astro-Theater dealing with space life. Another area chronicles the history of flight and the part played by other Ohioans, most notably the Wright brothers. From their embryonic flight at Kitty Hawk, it is indeed a giant leap to the *Gemini 8* spacecraft, which has been cut away to show the cramped interior conditions and the complicated array of dials and switches that the pilot had to master. *Open daily Mar.–Nov. Admission charged.* ♿

58 United States Air Force Museum, Dayton

54C *Exit 58: 6 mi./15 min. East on Needmore Rd. (becomes Harshman Rd.), right on Springfield St. Exit 54C: 5 mi./10 min. East on Rte. 4, right on Harshman Rd.; proceed as above.* "Where eagles rest" is the motto of this museum with an impressive array of military aircraft and related displays. Fighter biplanes from World War I still look sleek and deadly. Messerschmitts, Spitfires, and Mustangs from World War II nestle under the wings of Flying Fortresses and Liberators. In the museum's main hangar and nearby annex

125

14

111

53

See E–W book, sec. 30.

70

58

4

54C

1

53A

52

1F

0

1E

OH

KY

19

75

60

See
E–W book,
sec. 34.

64

115

11 64

104

9

95

19

76

38

13

38

25

KY
· — · — · —
TN

175 Big Bone Lick State Park

8 mi./15 min. West on Rte. 338; follow signs. The coming of the Ice Age drove huge herds of prehistoric mammals southward. Drawn to this marsh for the mineral deposits of its sulfur springs, many woolly mammoths, mastodons, enormous ground sloths, peccaries, and polar bears were fatally mired in the soft ground. Their bones, once so plentiful that early explorers used them to pitch tents, are now gone—but not forgotten. Two life-size models of the extinct mammals are on display side by side along the 1-mile self-guiding trail. A small museum, tennis courts, and a pool are additional enticements to visit this scenic spot. *Open year-round.*

115 Lexington, KY 40507

104 *Convention & Visitors Bureau, 430 W. Vine St. (606) 233-1221.* For all the publicity about horses here in the bluegrass country, it's not necessary to be an equestrian to enjoy a visit. There are historic houses of note, two inviting university campuses, and some interesting renovated shopping areas. In the Georgian-style Mary Todd Lincoln House, you can see furnishings similar to the ones that were here when the future First Lady lived in the structure as a girl. While the Todd House has an engaging charm, the Hunt-Morgan House, with its 19th-century furnishings and woodwork, is a study in restrained elegance of the federal style. Ashland, the handsome estate of the famous statesman Henry Clay, lies on the outskirts of town. The Italianate house, surrounded by lawns and woodlands, also has an attractive formal garden. The University of Kentucky campus offers an art museum and a mile-long "Tree Trail" through the area.

95 Fort Boonesborough State Park

6 mi./10 min. Northeast on Rte. 627, right on Rte. 388. In 1775 Daniel Boone had just established this vital frontier post on the banks of the Kentucky River when his daughter was captured by Indians. With a few companions Boone set off after the marauders and, against all odds, recovered

the girl. On a hill close to its original site, Boone's fort has been lovingly reconstructed, from its log walls and blockhouses to the pioneer lifestyle itself. You'll see blacksmiths, toymakers, weavers, and spinners at work. You can also swim in the river or fish for perch, catfish, and bass. *Park open year-round; fort open daily Apr.–Sept.; Wed.–Sun. Sept.–Oct. Admission charged to fort.*

76 Churchill Weavers, Berea

2.5 mi./7 min. Northeast on Rte. 25, right on Rte. 1016; follow signs. The ancient art of handweaving is practiced to perfection by the skilled Churchill Weavers. The founder, Carroll Churchill, designed a fly shuttle loom—which is used here—when he and his wife were missionaries in India. In 1922 the Churchills started a local cottage industry to provide employment in impoverished Appalachia. A self-guiding tour of this now-thriving business begins with the finished blankets and accessories in the gift shop, then goes through tagging, inspection, and mending areas to the actual loom room, where weavers produce original designs. *Loomhouse open Mon.–Fri.; gift shop open Mon.–Sat. and P.M. Sun. except Christmas and New Year's Day.*

38 Levi Jackson Wilderness Road State Park

4 mi./10 min. East on Rte. 192, right on Rte. 25, left on Rte. 1006. During the late 18th century an estimated 200,000 pioneers surged westward across the Appalachians along the Wilderness Road, part of which was originally known as Boone's Trace, which passes through this fascinating park. The hardships of the journey are memorialized by a profusion of roadside graves and a small cemetery in which some 20 members of the McNitt Party, who were massacred by Indians in 1786, lie buried. The Mountain Life Museum consists of seven original relocated log cabins, including a two-room schoolhouse, a blacksmith's shop, and an 1880's Methodist church. Period furnishings, a collection of Indian artifacts, and examples of pioneer utensils bring a bygone era vividly to life. *Open year-round.*

25. *A carpet of moss and subtle rainbows puts this falls in a class by itself.*

25 Cumberland Falls State Resort Park

15 mi./30 min. Southwest on Rte. 25W; continue west on Rte. 90. In 1780 Zachariah Green led a party of hunters down the uncharted waters of the Cumberland River in what is now Kentucky. His poplar boat meandered gently between wooded bluffs until it rounded a curve and suddenly came upon a 68-foot drop in the river. Scrambling for safety, the hunters abandoned their craft. Cumberland Falls is now a popular resort favored by honeymooners for its wonderfully romantic cascade and frequent rainbows, or on a moonlit night, lovely "moonbows" in the falls' mist. *Open year-round.*

122 Museum of Appalachia

3 min. Northeast on Rte. 61. The atmosphere of an Appalachian mountain village-museum stems from the authenticity of each detail. A lifetime's labor of love by owner and operator John Rice Irwin, this living museum began as one log cabin and grew to a 65-acre village of more than 30 buildings. Some 250,000 period artifacts illustrate every aspect of the lives led by the resourceful mountain folk, who either made what they needed or did without. The 10,000-square-foot barn-museum is home to cooper's, carpenter's, and leather shops and displays of folk art, musical instruments, early agricultural tools, Appalachian basketry, textiles, and rifle making. You'll also see a log church, a loomhouse, a gristmill, an iron jail, an underground dairy, and a dirt-floor cabin. *Open daily except Christmas. Admission charged.*

122 81 American Museum of Science and Energy, Oak Ridge

Exit 122: 15 mi./ 25 min. Southwest on Rte. 61; follow signs. Exit 81: 20 mi./25 min. Northwest on Rte. 321, right on Rte. 95. The secret life of Oak Ridge, Tennessee, helped to change the course of world history. An important part of the Manhattan Project in World War II, it produced the uranium required for the first atom bomb. Oak Ridge has remained in the forefront of nuclear research and production ever since that time. The museum's purpose is to inform the visitor of contemporary energy requirements and the methods of energy generation as well as the history of energy use in the United States and alternatives for the future. The exhibits are dynamic, inviting participation wherever possible. Models demonstrate the basic principles of science. *Open daily except Thanksgiving Day, Christmas, and New Year's Day.*

I-275 I-40 Knoxville, TN 37902

Convention and Visitors Bureau, 500 Henley St. (615) 523-2316. The colorful time of year in Knoxville is mid-April, when the dogwoods are in bloom; but the city's historic houses, the museums, and the excellent zoo are reasons enough for a visit any time of year.

Early colonial days are recalled at the Gen. James White Fort with its stockade. The territorial era (1790–96) is represented by the handsome home of the then governor, William Blount. The Armstrong-Lockett House, built in 1834, has notable collections of old silver and furniture, and the Civil War era is recalled at Confederate Memorial Hall. The Knoxville Museum of Art, which is located on the 1982 World's Fair site, features a popular display of period rooms re-created in miniature.

49 McMinn County Living Heritage Museum, Athens

5 mi./10 min. East on Rte. 30, right on Jackson St., left on Robeson St. A visit to this charming museum is akin to rummaging through the attic of an entire community. The large collection is housed in the Old College Building, a porticoed mid-19th-century red brick edifice that is now part of the Tennessee Wesleyan College campus. Displays cover the region's heritage from the era of the Cherokee nation to the 1930's. Quaint surprises among the exhibits include a once-elegant single-seater phaeton, a handmade doll with chicken feathers for hair, and 17th-century African trade beads. The quilt collection is a highlight. *Open Tues.–Fri. and P.M. weekends except holidays. Admission charged.*

I-24 Chattanooga, TN 37402

Convention and Visitors Bureau, 1001 Market St. (800) 338-3999; (800) 322-3344 outside TN. Towering majestically over the city, Lookout Mountain offers an interesting variety of attractions in itself. A steep-incline railway runs to the summit, where on a clear day the rocky lookout that gave Chattanooga its Cherokee name provides a view of several states. Rock City Gardens, also at the top, features intriguing rock formations and trails that lead to spectacular vistas. If you take an elevator deep within the mountain, you can see 145-foot-high Ruby Falls and some spectacular caverns. Significant Civil War battles are commemorated at Cravens House and at Confederama, both located at Lookout Mountain.

In the city proper, a railroad museum and the Chattanooga Choo-Choo center celebrate a bygone era and offer rides in vintage-style cars. The Hunter Museum of Art, overlooking the Tennessee River, has a fine collection of American paintings, and the Houston Museum presents American and European antiques and decorative arts.

141 Chickamauga–Chattanooga National Military Park

7.5 mi./15 min. West on Rte. 2, left on Rte. 27. Dedicated in 1895, this was the first national military park in the U.S. It was established not only to commemorate the 34,000 men who were casualties at Chickamauga—either killed, missing in action, or wounded—during the Civil War, but as a place to study what occurred from a historical and military perspective. The grounds look much as they did in the autumn of 1863, when more than 120,000 troops were engaged in a widespread bloody conflict, the objective of which was to control Chattanooga (the North proved victorious). A row of Civil War–era cannons greets you at the visitor center. Inside, there are displays illustrating the battles as well as a fine collection of firearms dating from 1690 to 1917. *Open daily except Christmas.*

I-24. *The cannon is a reminder that it was not always peaceful on Lookout Mountain.*

64

122

15

I-275

4

I-40 40

See E–W book, sec. 41.

20

40

81

32

49

59

I-24 TN

GA

141

33

75

75

131

29

124

13

116

21

PT

INT

20

See E–W
book,
sec. 46.

92

42

67

26

58

10

53

131 New Echota State Historic Site

3 min. Northeast on Rte. 225; follow signs. In 1825 the Cherokee nation established its capital, New Echota. The tribe adopted a republican form of government, developed a written form of their language, and adapted in other ways to the white man's world. But in 1838–39 they were forced by the government to leave their land and move to Oklahoma, traveling on what became known as the Trail of Tears. New Echota fell into disuse and all but vanished, but it was partially restored in the 1950's. Today five structures represent the onetime capital of the Cherokees: the Supreme Court Building, a tavern, a typical Cherokee cabin, the house of Samuel Worcester (a missionary who devoted his life to the Cherokees), and the tiny printing office where the bilingual *Cherokee Phoenix* was published. *Open Tues.–Sat. and P.M. Sun. except Thanksgiving Day and Christmas. Admission charged.*

124 Etowah Mounds State Historic Site, Cartersville

5 mi./15 min. West on Rte. 113 to Cartersville, left on Etowah Dr.; continue on Indian Mounds Rd. These ceremonial earthen mounds are located on a 54-acre site along the banks of the Etowah River, which between about A.D. 1000 and 1500 provided

124. *Marble mortuary figures of striking sculptural power found at Etowah.*

water, nourishment, protection, and transportation for a thriving community of Indians. The mounds served as temples and tombs, and also provided the foundation for the priest-chief's home. Three flat-topped mounds remain, along with the vestiges of a moat that encircled the town in a protective arc from the riverbank. The largest mound, at 63 feet, may have served as an observatory. This site has been partially excavated, and some of the most outstanding archeological finds are displayed in a museum at the visitor center. *Open Tues.–Sat. and P.M. Sun. except Thanksgiving Day and Christmas.*

116 Kennesaw Mountain National Battlefield Park

5 mi./12 min. Southwest on Barrett Pkwy., right on Rte. 41 (Cobb Pkwy.), left on Old Rte. 41; follow signs. The Battle of Kennesaw Mountain in June 1864, part of Sherman's campaign against Atlanta, was one of a series of bloody engagements in which the Confederate forces fought to save the vital railroad and manufacturing center. The Southerners managed to repel Union attacks and hold their position for about 2 weeks, but ultimately had to retreat.

The road to the top of the mountain leads to a line of gun emplacements complete with cannons. The site affords a view for miles in all directions, including the skyline of Atlanta. It is easy to understand why the Confederates thought their position was exceptionally strong. A self-guiding auto tour and miles of hiking trails lead to key battle positions and interpretive exhibits. *Open daily except Christmas and New Year's Day.*

PT / INT Atlanta, GA 30303

Peachtree Street exit. International Blvd. exit. Convention & Visitors Bureau, 233 Peachtree St., Suite 2000. (404) 521-6600. As this bustling modern metropolis continues to grow, the essence of the Old South becomes more difficult to find. One place to look is the Tullie Smith House Restoration, an 1840's farmhouse with outbuildings, herb gardens, and craft demonstrations. On the same site is the Swan House, a 20th-century Palladian-style

structure with a formal garden. The Civil War Battle of Atlanta, depicted in the circular painted cyclorama at Grant Park, has sound and light effects and is viewed from a revolving platform. The High Museum of Art, a handsome modern building on Peachtree Street, has an excellent collection of European and American art.

The birthplace and the tomb of Nobel Prize winner Martin Luther King, Jr., are honored in a two-block national historic site. Other famous Georgians are commemorated in the Capitol's Hall of Fame.

92 Six Flags Over Georgia

13.5 mi./20 min. West on I-20 to Exit 13; follow signs. At this attractive and well-landscaped theme park just west of Atlanta, the first thing you are likely to hear are the screams of anguished delight coming from riders on such aptly named attractions as Mindbender (a loop-the-loop), Free Fall (a 10-story drop), and Great Gasp (a parachute drop). Water rides take visitors over rapids and falls and down log chutes, but there are plenty of gentler rides as well, including an 1820's-style train that circles the entire park. Other attractions to be enjoyed are performances by divers, acrobats, and musicians. *Open daily June–Aug.; weekends only mid-Mar.–May and Sept.–Oct. Admission charged.*

67 Indian Springs State Park

14 mi./20 min. East on Rte. 16, right on Rte. 23, right on Rte. 42. Creek Indians told white traders of this mineral spring, with alleged healing properties, and by the 1820's it was being enjoyed by all. But in 1825, William McIntosh, a Creek chief (with a Scottish father), signed a treaty exchanging land in southwestern Georgia for acreage west of the Mississippi—plus a cash bonus for himself. Fellow tribesmen, angered by the unauthorized treaty and the apparent bribe, murdered McIntosh. A later treaty gave whites the land, and resorts were soon developed. The spring is still here, and there's a historical museum, a miniature golf course, and a 105-acre lake for swimming, fishing, and pedal boats. *Open year-round.*

92. *Passengers on the Thunder River rapids ride can expect a dousing of white water.*

| 58 | **Museum of Arts and Sciences, Macon** |

| 52 | *Exit 58: 10 mi./15 min. South on I-475 to Exit 4, left on Rte. 41 (becomes Forsyth Rd.). Exit 52: West on Rte. 41 (Forsyth Rd.).* The galleries in this museum feature changing exhibits of work by established international, national, and local artists. The impressive permanent collection has items ranging from sculpture to abstract drawings, minerals, handwoven rugs, and African handiwork. In the science wing the main attraction is the 40-million-year-old whale fossil. The Science Hall features changing science displays, with hands-on exhibits. The petting zoo includes goats, sheep, and other animals. Also located here is the Mark Smith Planetarium, which offers educational programs along with a variety of popular entertainment. *Open daily except holidays. Admission charged.* ⊼ ⚲ ♿

| 53 | **Ocmulgee National Monument, Macon** |

5 min. East on I-16 to Exit 4, north on Martin Luther King Blvd., right on Rte. 80, right on Emery Hwy. Archeological excavations begun in 1933 have revealed that an ancient people lived in this area for more than 10,000 years. Huge earthen mounds, some up to 60 feet tall, were built between A.D. 900 and 1100 by people of the Mississippian culture. Known today as the People of the Naked Plateau, they were skilled farmers with a sophisticated social hierarchy and some knowledge of astronomy. The mounds were used for burials and other purposes not fully understood. An earth lodge has been reconstructed. *Open daily except Christmas and New Year's Day. Admission charged.* ⊼ ⚲ ⇝ ♿

| 44 | **John Cranshaw's One-Horse Farm and Gardens, Kathleen** |

14 mi./20 min. East on Rte. 96, right on Rte. 41, left on Sandefur Rd. What began in 1950 with a gift of a dozen daylilies has grown into a 5-acre garden of more than 700 varieties. This is now a commercial nursery, and Cranshaw's lilies, many of which are varieties John Cranshaw himself developed, are in demand from as far away as New Zealand. The lilies are at their best in May and June. Peacocks roam the property. *Open year-round.* ⊼ ♿

| 33 | **Georgia Veterans Memorial State Park** |

10 mi./13 min. West on Rte. 280. This 1,327-acre park pays tribute to veterans of every U.S. conflict from the French and Indian War to the Vietnam War. Among the many varied relics on display in the visitor center are U.S. cavalry saddlebags, a Civil War cannon, a German spiked helmet, and an M-6 survival weapon (a combination rifle and shotgun). Outdoors you'll see a collection of armored vehicles and artillery pieces, including a 155-mm howitzer, the B-29 bomber used for photographic work during the first atomic bomb mission, and a heavy Patton tank used in the Korean War. Nearby, Lake Blackshear provides a peaceful contrast, as well as some of the state's best largemouth bass fishing. Model-airplane flying is a very popular activity. *Open year-round.* ⊼ ⛺ 🚐 ⇝ ⇝ ♿

| 20 | **Georgia Agrirama, Tifton** |

2 min. West on 8th St. As you tour the 95 acres and see the buildings that make up the state of Georgia's official museum of agriculture, you'll get a firsthand impression of what life was like on various farms and rural towns in the post–Civil War South. Survival hinged on self-sufficiency, and reminders of that fact are provided by the log farmhouse with rope-sprung beds, the water-driven gristmill, and the wood-burning turpentine distillery, believed to be the last of its kind still operating in the South. Basic skills, such as quilting and soap making, are explained and demonstrated by guides in period costumes. You'll see a sugarcane mill, a smokehouse, a blacksmith's shop, and a restored railroad depot. *Open daily except Thanksgiving Day, Christmas, and three days prior to Christmas. Admission charged.* ⊼ ♿

| 4 | **The Barber-Pittman House, Valdosta** |

4 mi./10 min. East on Rte. 84, left on Ashley St. An eye for detail will find much to admire in this carefully restored neoclassical home, built in 1915 for E. R. Barber, one of the founders of Valdosta's Coca-Cola Bottling Works. The building's handsome exterior provides a hint of the intricate treasures that you'll find inside. Beyond the marble steps, tiled porch, and six Ionic columns that support the front porch lie such ornate surprises as a handsome fanlight over the door, brass light fixtures, a uniquely designed sheet music cabinet, a dining room illuminated by 60 bulbs set in concentric rectangular ceiling beams, and one of the earliest central vacuum-cleaning systems. Although it now houses the county's chamber of commerce, it also contains 52 pieces of original family furniture. *Open Mon.–Fri. except holidays.*

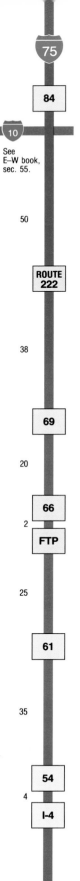

See
E–W book,
sec. 55.

84 | Stephen Foster State Folk Culture Center

5 mi./10 min. East on Rte. 136, left on Rte. 41. The familiar strains of "Old Folks at Home," "Oh, Susanna," and other Stephen Foster melodies ring out from the carillon tower. While listening, the visitor can peruse the composer's scores and manuscripts, see a piano he composed on, and admire the instruments and costumes of the minstrel bands that played such an important role in popularizing his music.

In the visitor center ingeniously mechanized dioramas depict the themes of his famous songs: horses run in the "Camptown Races," steamboats ply the Suwannee River, and cowboys gather around to hear "Oh, Susanna." Traditional crafts are represented by Seminole baskets, Cuban cigars, and artifacts from local turpentine camps. Headphones bring you the music of the region, played on banjos, by steel bands, and by a Latin dance band. *Open year-round. Admission charged.*

ROUTE 222 | Devil's Millhopper State Geological Site

5 mi./7 min. East on Rte. 222, left on 43rd Ave., left on Rte. 232. The cool interior of this vast sinkhole, 120 feet deep and 500 feet in diameter, contains plant and animal species not normally found this far south. Formed when the roof of a cavern collapsed millennia ago, the sinkhole has yielded fossils of sharks' teeth and bones of extinct land animals. Interpretive plaques along a staircase to the bottom of the giant depression explain various aspects of this phenomenon. To early settlers who named it, the sinkhole must have conjured up visions of a satanic grain grinder. *Open year-round. Admission charged.*

69 | Florida's Silver Springs

9 mi./17 min. East on Rte. 40. From glass-bottomed boats on the crystal-clear water of 17 artesian springs, you can see fish, alligators, snakes, and the bottom of the river some 80 feet below. Shows at the Reptile Institute feature rattlesnakes, boa constrictors, and a performer who wrestles with an alligator. For children the petting zoo presents deer and other approachable animals. The automobiles in the antique and classic car collection include a 1914 Overland Speedster and a model of the never-produced 1955 Gaylord. *Open year-round. Admission charged.*

66 | Lake Griffin State Recreation Area

17 mi./24 min. East on Rte. 44, left on Rte. 27. The live-oak hammock here on typical central Florida sandhills adjoins a marsh filled with water lilies, water lettuce, and water hyacinths. The length of Dead River, connecting the marsh with Lake Griffin, can be paddled in a canoe in about an hour. Denizens of this watery realm include alligators, egrets, anhingas, ospreys, and the gallinule. Nature trails wind through the hammocks, and a moss-draped live oak that grows here is said to be the second oldest in the state of Florida. *Open year-round. Admission charged.*

40. *The Ringling eye for dramatic splendor is clearly revealed in the garden.*

61 | Florida's Weeki Wachee

22 mi./32 min. North on Rte. 98, left on Rte. 50, left on Rte. 19. An underwater mermaid show at this theme park presents aqua dancing, magic tricks, and a closed-circuit televised view of a 3-minute dive to a depth of 117 feet on lung power alone. Other attractions found here include a walk through an animal forest, a birds of prey show starring hawks, owls, and eagles, and a bird show featuring parrots and macaws on bikes and roller skates. The half-hour Weeki Wachee River cruise on a silent electric boat passes an orphanage where injured pelicans are cared for. A colony of raccoons frequently shows up for a handout. *Open year-round. Admission charged.*

54 | Busch Gardens, The Dark Continent, Tampa

5 mi./10 min. West on Rte. 582, left on N. McKinley Dr. Three thousand exotic animals, from Asian elephants to Bengal tigers, performing dolphins, stage shows, and rides such as the Congo River Rapids and the 360°-loop Scorpion roller coaster are featured at this theme park and zoo. A Moroccan street bazaar has snake charmers, while in Nairobi elephants bathe in a swimming hole. Through the viewing windows of the nursery you can observe some of the 1,200 animals that are born here every year. The animals in the Serengeti Plain, including zebras, camels, ostriches, crocodiles, orangutans, tigers, and giraffes, can be seen via a steam-powered train, a monorail, or an overhead skyride. *Open year-round. Admission charged.*

40 | The John and Mable Ringling Museum of Art, Sarasota

7 mi./11 min. West on University Pkwy., left on Rte. 301, right on DeSoto Rd. The treasures of this museum on the estate of the circus magnate comprise more than 10,000 objects, both ancient and modern. Its collection of baroque art is one of the finest in America. There are also works by Cranach, Van Dyck, Hals, El Greco, Reynolds, and Gainsborough. Rubens is represented by five massive canvases of "The Triumph of the Eucharist." The Circus Galleries display posters, costumes, bandwagons, and other memorabilia, and have tributes to such greats as Emmett Kelly and the Wallendas. The mansion of the Ringlings, Ca' d' Zan ("house of John" in Venetian dialect), is a whimsical interpretation of a Venetian palazzo, with touches copied from the facade of the famous Doge's Palace in Venice and the tower of the noted 1890 Madison Square Garden in New York City. *Open daily except Thanksgiving Day, Christmas, and New Year's Day.*

If You Have Some Extra Time: Walt Disney World Resort

FTP **Florida Tpk. exit: 68 mi./90 min. I-4**
I-4 **exit: 65 mi./90 min.** To walk through the turnstile is to enter a world as you would like it to be—immaculately clean, beautifully landscaped, perfectly maintained, safe, orderly, and filled with happy people. In the Magic Kingdom, you'll find an enchanting Cinderella Castle surrounded by Frontierland, Tomorrowland, Adventureland, Fantasyland, and more. Fifteen minutes away by car or monorail is Epcot Center, which is in two parts: Future World includes pavilions, exhibits, and rides with an educational or futuristic accent; and World Showcase, set around a beautiful wide lagoon, has buildings, reconstructed street scenes, shops, and restaurants representing a dozen different countries. Unlike traditional park rides, the rides at Disney World transport you into new worlds of imagination.

For a representative sample try the Magic Kingdom's Space Mountain, Pirates of the Caribbean, or The Haunted Mansion—all three can be seen in half a day. At Epcot Center you can walk into a replica of Beijing's famed Temple of Heaven, take a ride through the greenhouses of The Land pavilion, and see remarkable agricultural innovations. The Magic Eye Theater has incredible 3-D images.

Disney World can be crowded, and some attractions have long lines, but for the most part its 20,000 employees make it work like a well-oiled machine. It takes 4 full days for a visitor to feel reasonably satisfied, but even if you have only a day it will be unforgettable. *How to get there: Florida Tpk. exit, east on turnpike to Orlando; follow signs. I-4 exit, east on I-4 to Orlando; follow signs. Open year-round. Admission charged.*

37 Myakka River State Park

9 mi./12 min. East on Rte. 72. In this 28,875-acre park (including a 7,500-acre wilderness preserve) the scenic views of Lake Myakka and the Myakka River are rivaled only by the vast expanse of prairies, hammocks, and marshes. Birding is excellent, and careful observers may be rewarded with a glimpse of a bobcat at dusk or deer grazing in the pinelands or otters by the river. The park offers some 40 miles of hiking trails and informative tours by tram or airboat. You can rent bikes, boats, and canoes, but you must bring your own horses to enjoy the 12 miles of riding trails. An interpretive center features wildlife exhibits and a movie about the park. *Open year-round. Admission charged.*

16. *Are relationships being pondered?*

22 Thomas Edison Winter Home, Fort Myers

7 mi./12 min. West on Rte. 884, right on Rte. 867. In 1885, when Thomas Edison's doctors advised a Florida vacation to restore his health, the 38-year-old inventor headed south, where he not only regained his vigor (he lived to be 84) but found a second home. Today Seminole Lodge and its gardens and laboratory evoke images of the tireless American genius performing his many experiments or puttering among his flowers. Edison bulbs light the house (they burn 10 hours a day and have yet to burn out). The museum here includes examples of early motorcars as well as a large number of Edison phonographs and light bulbs. The laboratory, devoted to extracting rubber from a hybrid strain of goldenrod, remains as it was when Edison was working here. *Open Mon.–Sat. and P.M. Sun. except Thanksgiving Day and Christmas. Admission charged.*

16 Jungle Larry's African Safari Park, Naples

6.5 mi./10 min. West on Pine Ridge Rd., left on Rte. 851. This 52-acre park is a colorful mixture of circus and safari. Leopards and lions leap through blazing hoops, and enchanting macaws play basketball and ride tiny bicycles. Walk—or take the tram—along a trail through a junglelike environment where you will see tiglons (a rare cross between tiger and lion), alligators, chimpanzees, elephants, and exotic birds. A well-shaded petting zoo gives youngsters a chance to hold rabbits and other tame animals. For an insight into how wild creatures are actually tamed and taught to do tricks, stop at the Animal Training Center. *Open Tues.–Sun. May–Nov. Admission charged.*

5 Topeekeegee Yugnee Park, Hollywood

25 mi./15 min. East on Rte. 820, left on I-95 to Exit 24, left on Sheridan St., right on N. Park Rd. The name means "gathering place" in the Seminole Indian language, and this quiet park surrounded by a busy urban area still serves that purpose. People come here to relax and enjoy the wide shaded lawns, the picnic tables and grills, or to take advantage of the park's 40-acre lake and athletic facilities. There's a filtered and chlorinated swimming lagoon boasting a wide sand beach, and a nearby 50-foot-high water slide provides excitement with 700 feet of turns, drop sections, and occasional tunnels. You'll also find a volleyball net, a basketball court, and playing fields, and paddleboats, sailboats, sailboards, and canoes are available for rent. *Open year-round. Admission charged.*

77
90
See E–W
book,
sec. 7.
E9TH
2
23
See
E–W book,
sec. 23.
80
WH
25
118
11
107A
2
105B
0
105A
12
93
12

E9TH Cleveland, OH 44114

E. 9th St. exit: Convention & Visitors Bureau, 1301 E. 6th St. (216) 621-4110. The observation deck in the Terminal Tower gives the best bird's-eye introduction to the city. You can get a more intimate look on a trolley tour; and to see where some of America's great fortunes were founded, take a boat trip down the Cuyahoga River near the steel mills. You can also view the Flats entertainment district, with its waterfront restaurants and boutiques, or stroll through one of Cleveland's many parks and visit the city's renowned zoo.

Cultural attractions in the city include the Cleveland Museum of Art, the Western Reserve Historical Society, and the Cleveland Museum of Natural History, where dinosaurs, fossils, and a variety of artifacts are on display. An exhibit at the Health Education Museum imaginatively depicts the workings of the human body.

Not to be missed is the downtown Arcade, where shops and restaurants are housed in a marvelous five-level skylit cast-iron fantasy—one of the largest such structures in the world.

WH Hale Farm and Village, Bath

Wheatley Rd. exit: 5 mi./12 min. West on Wheatley Rd., left on Cleveland-Massillon Rd., left on Ira Rd., left on Oak Hill Rd. Rural life in the mid-19th century is faithfully re-created in this engaging cluster of buildings, located on what was once the Western Reserve—the land "reserved" for settlers from Connecticut. Many of the buildings were moved to this site from other areas of Ohio. The federal-style 1826 brick farmhouse of Jonathan Hale is surprisingly elegant for an owner who had to hew his farm out of a wilderness. The village comprises a saltbox house, a meetinghouse, a log schoolhouse, a law office, a smithy, and a barn. Demonstrations of spinning and weaving, smithing, glassblowing, and candlemaking evoke the life of earlier times. The farm and village lie within the 32,000-acre Cuyahoga Valley National Recreation Area. *Open Tues.–Sat. and P.M. Sun. and holidays mid-May–Oct. and Dec. Admission charged.*

118. *The quiet charm of this secluded cove is enhanced by the morning mist.*

118 Portage Lakes State Park

7 mi./15 min. West on Rte. 619, left on Rte. 93. This meandering series of pleasant lakes and ponds extends for miles through a residential section, making it difficult to find public access. Stop first at the main park office for guidance (directions above). The park's Nimisila Reservoir, ideal for boating and fishing, is known for its wall-eyed pike, muskellunge, and bass. Launching ramps are available, and some areas are set aside for speedboats and water-skiing. *Open year-round.*

WH. *Broom making is one of the old-time crafts demonstrated in the village.*

107A Pro Football Hall of Fame

2 min. East on Fulton Rd.; follow signs. In a domed rotunda with colored glass windows, 140 stars of pro football are honored, each commemorated by a life-size bronze head, a photograph of the star in action, and a rundown of his playing history. Other sections of this four-building complex contain mementos, photographs, descriptions, and videos that relate the history of the game from its 1892 beginnings to the present. There is a comprehensive display of old and new uniforms and gear and a complete set of helmets from all the major league teams. A football action movie is shown hourly. *Open daily except Christmas. Admission charged.*

105B / 105A Canton Classic Car Museum

3 mi./10 min. Exit 105B: East on W. Tuscarawas St., right on S. Market Ave. Exit 105A: East on 6th St. Some 30 carefully restored cars from the golden age of automobiling are on display here. They stand in two rows separated by a red carpet, as though they were high-ranking dignitaries—which in a way they are. Mostly pre-World War II models, they include Franklins, a McFarlan, a Holmes, a Benham, and a Kissel among such handsome familiars as Rolls-Royces, Cadillacs, Lincolns, Pierce-Arrows, Packards, and a Model T Ford with as much brightwork as a royal yacht. Early auto advertising signs, gowns, and hats can also be seen here. *Open Tues.–Sun. May–Oct.; weekends only Nov.–Apr. Admission charged.*

93 Zoar Village State Memorial

3 mi./6 min. East on Rte. 212. Taking biblical Zoar, Lot's sanctuary from destruction, as an example, a group of German separatists, searching for religious freedom, built this communal village early in the 19th century. The buildings, ranging from simple log cabins to handsome brick structures, surround the rectangular Garden of Peace. This is still a thriving community, a living memorial to a dream fulfilled. Craftsmen demonstrate the way of life and work in that earlier era, while seven museums display original artifacts and furniture. *Open Wed.–Sun. Memorial Day–Labor Day. Admission charged.* 🚶

81 Schoenbrunn Village State Memorial

4 mi./5 min. East on Rte. 39, right on Rte. 259. This village has been re-created on the site of a mission established by David Zeisberger, one of the Moravian Brethren who had come to America seeking religious freedom. The Delaware Indians invited the Moravians to settle here in 1722. Today you'll find neat rows of log cabins, a school, and a church. God's Acre, a plot of land with rough gravestones, bears witness to the relatively high rate of infant mortality in frontier days. Costumed interpreters may demonstrate early crafts. The museum, through films, audiotapes, and exhibits, depicts the lives of the missionaries and the Christian Indians. *Open Wed.–Sun. Memorial Day–Labor Day; weekends only Labor Day–Oct.* ⛟

47 Salt Fork State Park

6 mi./12 min. East on Rte. 22. In this 21,000-acre park the extensive lake is the centerpiece, with its many arms that provide areas for boats with unlimited power, no-wave zones for sailboats and other quiet craft, and sandy beaches for swimmers. There's also an 18-hole golf course, two marinas, boat rentals, and some 26 miles of bridle paths that meander through the wooded rolling hills in the park. *Open year-round.* ⛟ ⛺ 🚐 🚶 🎣 🏊 ♿

47 Degenhart Paperweight and Glass Museum, Cambridge

1 min. West on Rte. 22. Examples of fine glassmaking are on display here in a collection established by Elizabeth Degenhart, whose husband, John, founded the Crystal Art Glass Company. This impressive assortment of hand-cut glass lamps, glass puppies and owls, midwestern patterned glass, and paperweights (some used as doorstops and grave markers) provides a broad survey of the progression of taste and styles in glassmaking from the 1840's to 1900. A reproduction of Mrs. Degenhart's dining room, with its well-stocked china cabinets, reveals the quality and extent of her personal collection. *Open Mon.–Sat. and P.M. Sun. Mar.–Dec. except holidays. Admission charged.*

47. *Not for sale but a great place for shoppers to sharpen an eye for quality.*

28 Wolf Run State Park

5 min. South on Rte. 821, left on Rte. 215. This quiet park with its 220-acre lake, its attractive beach for swimming, its boat ramp, and its good reputation for bass, catfish, crappie, bluegill, and trout fishing, is also sought out by campers. A 2½-mile hiking path along the lake's western shore follows a stretch of the old Buckeye Trail.

In winter, visitors come for cross-country skiing, sledding, and ice fishing. And for those who like to arrive by air, 20 primitive campsites are located within walking distance of Nobles County Airport. *Open year-round.* ⛟ ⛺ 🚐 🚶 🎣 🏊

1 Campus Martius Museum, Marietta

3 mi./10 min. West on Rte. 7 (3rd St.), left on Washington St. Named for an ancient Roman military training camp, Campus Martius (Latin for "field of Mars") was a fortress built in the late 1700's by Revolutionary War veterans who established the first organized American settlement in the Northwest Territory at Marietta, Ohio. The museum includes the restored five-room apartment of Rufus Putnam, a leader of the settlers and a U.S. surveyor-general, as well as Hepplewhite furniture, frontier rifles, and 18th-century women's clothing. Surveying implements and a model of a flat-bottomed riverboat complement a wealth of written and pictorial materials about pioneer life in the Marietta area. A large model of the town at the time shows the extensive prehistoric earthworks left by the Adena and Hopewell peoples. *Open daily May–Sept.; Wed.–Sun. Mar.–Apr. and Oct.–Nov. except Thanksgiving Day. Admission charged.* ♿

176 Blennerhassett Island Historical Park

5 mi./15 min. West on Rte. 50, left on Rte. 68S; follow signs. A half-hour trip on a stern-wheeler ferries visitors from Point Park to this 4-mile-long island in the Ohio River near Parkersburg, West Virginia. It was settled in 1798 by Harman Blennerhassett, a wealthy Irish immigrant who built an imposing mansion here. In 1806 he joined Aaron Burr's conspiracy to form an empire in the Southwest. Both were arrested, and Virginia seized Blennerhassett's property. In 1811 the mansion burned to the ground, and the estate fell into neglect. The island, with its ancient sycamores, walnuts, and poplars, has remained undeveloped. The mansion, its three sections harmoniously joined by a curving colonnade, has been rebuilt. *Open daily May–Oct. Admission charged.* ⛟ 🚶

81

34

47

70

See E–W book, sec. 31.

19

28

27

1

OH

WV

10

176

76

77

See
E–W book,
sec. 34,
for I-64;
N–S book,
sec. 38,
for I-79.

I-64 Sunrise Museums, Charleston

3 mi./6 min. West on I-64 to Exit 58A, east on Oakwood Rd., right on MacCorkle Ave. (Rte. 61); bear right and go up C & O ramp, right on Bridge Rd., right on Myrtle Rd. The Children's Museum, housed in a former governor's stone mansion, captivates young visitors with "open us" discovery boxes of seashells and fossils, an exhibit that explains myths and legends about natural phenomena in various cultures, a dollhouse, a ray table that bends and bounces light, a 60-seat planetarium, and models of coaches and a circus wagon. The Art Museum has a outstanding collection of 17th- to 20th-century American art, together with etchings by Rembrandt and Picasso and engravings by Matisse and Dürer. *Open Tues.–Sat. and P.M. Sun. except holidays. Admission charged.*

I-64 Kanawha State Forest

9 mi./19 min. West on I-64 to Exit 58A, south on Rte. 119, left on Oakwood Rd.; follow signs. Amid these 9,250 acres of West Virginia forest, there are 17 trails ranging from a steep climb on Overlook Rock Trail to a gentle stroll along Spotted Salamander Trail (designed for the handicapped). Joggers and bikers enjoy the paved road through this wilderness of hemlock, pine, dogwood, and sycamore trees. Beside the quiet lake there are wooden seats from which to view the scenic mountain backdrop; fishermen can try for bass, catfish, and bluegill. Deer, black bears, and raccoons populate the forest. *Open year-round. Admission charged for swimmers.*

44 The Beckley Exhibition Coal Mine

4 mi./9 min. East on Rte. 3, left on Rte. 16; follow signs. The procedures, problems, and perils encountered in this turn-of-the-century hillside mine are explained by retired miners, who ride with visitors in a "man trip" car along 1,500 feet of underground rails. At the workstations, the guides demonstrate with hand tools and machinery how coal was cut, dynamited, and loaded onto carts. They explain the

44. *On the underground tour you'll get a sense of the mine worker's hard life.*

crude safety precautions of 1900, such as the use of live flame lamps to eliminate deadly methane gas. At the museum, old-time photos, early union banners, and company scrip are graphic reminders of the union's battle for better pay and safety. *Open daily May–Oct. Admission charged.*

40 Grandview State Park

13 mi./15 min. East on I-64 to Exit 129; follow signs. Impressive views of the New River are a prime attraction of this park. At North Overlook you'll see the horseshoe bend in the river where hawks nest in a rocky gorge; and from Main Overlook the river and the trains that run beside it are some 1,500 feet below. The steep hillsides, covered with mountain laurel, hemlock, dogwood, pink lady's slipper, and rhododendrons, come alive with color in the spring and summer. There is a self-guiding nature trail, and other trails lead to beautiful rock formations and tunnels in a high cliff. Hikers may see some of the turkey vultures, grouse, wild turkeys, and deer that inhabit the park. *Open year-round.*

20 Camp Creek State Forest

5 min. South on Rte. 19; follow signs. Set in the mountains of southern West Virginia, this recreation area takes its name from the well-stocked stream that offers anglers excellent trout fishing from February through May. Hunting is also permitted, the most favored quarry being wild turkeys; permits for fishing and hunting are available in the forest office. Several scenic hiking trails meander through the woods, and the picnic areas have tables and fireplaces. *Forest open year-round; picnic and camping facilities open last weekend of Apr.–last weekend of Oct.*

40. *The New River and the railroad found an easy way through the hilly terrain.*

1 Pinnacle Rock State Park

13 mi./23 min. North on Rte. 52. Hiking trails in this 245-acre park pass through stands of rhododendron, mountain laurel, dogwood, ash, and maple trees. The park's name comes from a towerlike formation of stony gap sandstone that remained standing after eons of erosion had cut away the softer surrounding material. A steep path with stone steps leads to the top of Pinnacle Rock. There, 2,700 feet above sea level, the views of several surrounding counties are spectacular, especially during the fall foliage season. The picnic tables at the base of the rock are pleasantly shaded. The nearby town of Bramwell has many historic houses. *Open year-round.*

5 Shot Tower Historical State Park

3 min. East on Rte. 69, left on Rte. 52. Thomas Jackson, an immigrant from England, built this park's fortresslike tower, with its thick limestone walls, in about 1807; it was used to make lead shot for guns. Molten lead was poured through sieves at the top and allowed to fall some 150 feet into buckets of cooling water in an underground shaft (it was believed that the fall molded the shot into its round shape).

The park has lovely shaded picnic areas. About 100 feet from the Shot Tower is the midpoint of the New River Trail, with attractions such as an access point for fishing, a historic ferry site, and beautiful views of the New River. *Open daily late May–early Sept.; weekends late Apr.–late May and early Sept.–late Oct. Admission charged for tower.*

85 Stone Mountain State Park

18 mi./23 min. West on CC Camp Rd., right on Bypass 21 (becomes Rte. 21), left on Rte. 1002, right on John P. Frank Pkwy. Native rhododendron, mountain laurel, dogwood, and southern hemlock trees provide cover for the ruffed grouse, gray and red foxes, deer, mink, and bobcats that inhabit this beautiful, remote area. In dry weather the bare, rocky dome for which the park is named draws experienced climbers. A river and several streams are stocked with

1. *Even when viewed from the air, Pinnacle Rock is an impressive phenomenon.*

trout, attracting fishermen (who must use fly rods only) as well as beavers and otters. Pileated woodpeckers and scarlet tanagers can be seen flashing by overhead. *Open year-round.*

6A The Charlotte Nature Museum

4 mi./10 min. East on Rte. 4, left on Park Rd., right on Princeton Rd., left on Sterling Rd. Children will be fascinated by this well-organized museum, where exhibits are designed to stimulate curious minds. The Live Animal Center houses owls, chipmunks, alligators, and small reptiles; and in an adjacent room visitors can pluck clams and other shellfish from a man-made tidal pool. Elsewhere the mysteries of volcanoes are explored through hands-on exhibits, and rudimentary physics is taught through play with lenses, mirrors, and lights. A self-guiding half-mile nature trail winds through mature oaks and hickories, massive sycamores, and 100-foot-high tulip trees. *Open Mon.–Sat. and P.M. Sun. except Thanksgiving Day and Christmas. Admission charged.*

6A Mint Museum, Charlotte

7 mi./16 min. East on Rte. 4, left on Randolph Rd. The outbreak of the Civil War put an end to the minting of locally mined gold in this building, designed by the influential 19th-century architect William Strickland. The building's name survived its subsequent use by various agencies and organizations, and today the Mint is a major regional museum. The eclectic collection includes decorative art such as European porcelain and pottery, Japanese prints, African objects, and outstanding examples of pre-Columbian art. Among the painters represented here are Robert Henri, Everett Shinn, and fellow members of the Ashcan school of American painting. There are also classic works by Benjamin West, John Singer Sargent, Gilbert Stuart, John Constable, Winslow Homer, Amedeo Modigliani, René Magritte, and many others. *Open Tues.–Sat. and P.M. Sun.*

6A Hezekiah Alexander Homesite 1774, Charlotte

10.5 mi./25 min. East on Rte. 4, right on Shamrock Dr. Influential planter, justice of the peace, and patriot Hezekiah Alexander completed handsome Rock House in 1774. The cozy parlor is furnished with several fine pieces, including a Jacobean chair, a Queen Anne tilt-top table, and a Chippendale secretary. In the keeping room, where the table is set with pewter, wood, and clay dishes, you'll see a small window that enabled hot food to be passed from the kitchen. The upstairs bedrooms contain a fine blanket chest, a sampler, quilts, toys, and rope-sprung beds. A special wrench was used to tighten the ropes on the beds when they began to sag; the popular expression "Sleep tight" is believed to have come from this practice.

On the grounds is an herb garden, a reconstructed two-story springhouse, and a small museum with rotating displays from a collection reflecting the history of the Piedmont region of North Carolina and of the city of Charlotte and the local county of Mecklenburg. *Open Tues.–Fri. and P.M. Sat. and Sun. except Thanksgiving Day, Christmas, and New Year's Day. Admission charged.*

5

VA
NC
45

85

79

6A

NC
SC
28

77

Glencairn Garden, Rock Hill

82B

3 mi./8 min. South on Cherry Rd., left on Charlotte Ave., left on Edgemont St. Here we have the ideal conditions for a municipal park: a convenient, accessible, intimate enclave of beauty, repose, and privacy located in the hubbub of a modern city. This tranquil garden was bequeathed to Rock Hill's citizens by the widow of a wealthy doctor who built it in 1928 and named it after his ancestral Scottish home. Follow the wide brick steps down the slope to the water lily pond, which is fed by a decorative fountain. Tall pines and oaks soar above the plantings of azaleas and dogwood. Gravel paths, with attractive views at every turn, lead through shady hollows, and the wooden seats are in all the right spots. Truly a medicine for melancholy. *Open year-round.* ♿

Landsford Canal State Park

77

12 mi./17 min. South on Rte. 21. In the early 1800's, railroads began to compete with canals for transporting heavy freight. Because of delays in development, the Landsford Canal did not start operating until 1837, and by 1839 the more efficient steam trains put it out of business. The Catawba River, however, still flows, and visitors can still walk the 2-mile towpath along its banks and let imagination picture the cargo barges as they were pulled around the rapids on their way to and from the port of Charleston.

In spring, spider lilies anchored to rock fissures and gravel along the river create a blaze of color against the white and blue of the water. A stone building once used as a lockkeeper's house is now the Canal Museum, where local memorabilia are shown, including a marker stone dated 1823, the year construction began, and bearing the names of the designer and building supervisor of the canal. *Open Thurs.–Mon.*

Lake Wateree State Park, Winnsboro

41

10 mi./13 min. East on Rte. 41, left on Rte. 21, right on River Rd. Angling is a favorite subject at Lake Wateree, one of six major lakes in the area that sponsor popular fishing tournaments. At any time of day in the combination park store and tackle shop you'll find experts ready and willing to offer advice on how to hook bass, bream, catfish, or crappie, to argue the comparative virtues of lure, spinners, and live bait, and to compare lines and poles. Nature lovers immune to the appeal of fishing take their pleasure spotting great blue herons, egrets, and ospreys along a pleasant 1½-mile nature trail. *Open year-round.*

Sesquicentennial State Park, Columbia

17

5 min. East on Two Notch Rd. Three fine trails here—a challenging 3½-mile exercise course, an easy 2-mile hiking loop, and a quarter-mile nature trail—and the pedal boats on the 30-acre lake make this a good place to stretch your legs. The nature trail, for which there's an interpretive folder, can also be informative.

This area, the Carolina Sandhills, once covered by a primeval sea, now supports a cedar bog and a forest of scrub oak and pine. Evidence of an early-day turpentine plantation can be seen in the slash marks on several of the old longleaf pines. A restored two-story log cabin, built in 1756, was moved to the park and is now an artist's studio. The name of the park is derived from the 150th anniversary of the city of Columbia, when souvenir coins were sold and the proceeds used to purchase the 1,455 acres here. *Open year-round.*

Riverbanks Zoo, Columbia

108

2 mi. South on I-126, right on Greystone Blvd. More than 700 animals inhabit this remarkable 50-acre zoo, where specimens and spectators are separated not by bars and fences, but by light, water, and other subtle barriers—conditions ideal for snapshots. Along with the expected familiar faces, you'll find such rarities as ruffed lemurs, lion-tailed macaques, Siberian tigers, golden-lion tamarins, and South American sakis. The ecosystem birdhouse, containing one of the world's finest displays of exotic birds, provides such an authentic

108. *Polar bear finds a comfortable place to nap, far from its native land.*

habitat that several species have bred in captivity for the first time. Don't miss the man-made thunderstorms that drench the tropical rain forest exhibit several times a day. *Open daily except Christmas. Admission charged.*

Lexington County Museum

111

8 mi./15 min. West on Rte. 1. This 18-building complex is rightly called a gateway to yesterday. History comes alive here—in the Oak Grove Schoolhouse; in the 1772 Corley Log House, whose single open hearth once served for cooking, light, and heat; and in the eight-room Hazelius House, where an 1891 revival meeting inspired evangelist Charlie Tillman to write the spiritual, "Give Me That Old-Time Religion." Lovers of antiques will savor the federal-style Fox House, with its locally made furniture in the style of Sheraton and Hepplewhite and a large collection of quilts. On the grounds are dairy sheds, smokehouses, ovens, rabbit hutches, beehives, herb gardens, and a horse-operated cotton gin. *Open Tues.–Sun. except July 4, Thanksgiving Day, Christmas, and New Year's Day. Admission charged.*

149 Edisto Memorial Gardens, Orangeburg

6 mi./12 min. West on Rte. 33, right on Riverside Dr. There's an affecting contrast here between the bustle of the city and the quiet beauty of this 110-acre memorial to those who died in the four American wars of the 20th century. The gardens' most colorful plants are the roses—some 10,000 in all—which are in bloom from mid-April until the frosts of November. In springtime the azaleas, dogwood, and crab apples stand out in a setting of ancient cypress and oak trees. There are also some huge pines with wisteria climbing the trunks. Winding paths, shaded lawns, and picnic shelters combine to invite strolling, reflection, and repose. *Open year-round.*

154 169 Santee State Park

Exit 154: 23 mi./30 min. North on Rte. 301 to Santee; follow signs. Exit 169: 18 mi./25 min. North on I-95 to Exit 98, west on Rte. 6; follow signs. Lake Marion, which is fed by the Santee River, is world-renowned: state records were set here with a 55-pound striped bass and a 73-pound blue catfish. Bream, crappie, and rockfish also provide good sport, and you can rent a boat and buy bait and tackle in the park. Enticements for non-fishermen include tennis, swimming, and boating. Pedal boats and bicycles are for rent, and there's a 4-mile bike path. Three nature trails invite walkers into the wooded realm of rabbits, squirrels, and birds of many kinds. The nature center provides daily summertime activities. *Park open year-round; day-use area open mid-Mar.–mid-Oct. Admission charged in summer only.*

199A Middleton Place

13 mi./21 min. West on Rte. 17A, left on Rte. 165, left on Rte. 61. A signer of the secession document that helped touch off the Civil War, Williams Middleton came home at war's end to find that except for the south flank, his handsome three-section house was a smoldering ruin. The remaining building, repaired in 1870, stands today as a memorial to an illustrious family that includes a president of the first Continental Congress, a signer of the Declaration of Independence, and a governor of South Carolina. Portraits by Thomas Sully and Benjamin West adorn the walls, and there are many superb pieces of furniture. Among the rare first editions in the library are bird prints by Audubon and Catesby. On the grounds are the nation's oldest formal landscaped gardens, circa 1741, which have the first camellias planted outdoors in America. *Open daily except holidays and 2 weeks in Jan. Admission charged.*

216A Drayton Hall

10 mi./15 min. South on Rte. 7, right on Rte. 61. When Union troops swept through Charleston in early 1865, they burned almost every plantation home on the west bank of the Ashley River. This one was spared because the owner said (inaccurately) that it was in use as a smallpox hospital. Drayton Hall stands today as a splendid tribute to the architectural design and craftsmanship of the antebellum South. Built in 1742 for John Drayton, scion of a prominent local family, it exemplifies the best in Georgian-Palladian architecture. The absence of furnishings accentuates the symmetrical proportions of the structure and the exquisite detail of its hand-carved doorways, pilasters, overmantels, and ornamental plaster. Fortunately, temptations to deface the building by installing electricity, running water, and central heating were resisted. Some of the original 18th-century interior paint still remains, although most of the rooms were repainted in the late 19th century. *Open daily except Thanksgiving Day, Christmas, and New Year's Day. Admission charged.*

221 Charleston, SC 29403

Visitor Information Center, 85 Calhoun St. (803) 722-8330. Few American cities have quite the degree of grace, charm, and civility as historic Charleston. Among the stately old homes that one can visit are the Heyward-Washington House, a federal-style mansion built in 1772 and once visited by the first president; the Nathaniel Russell and Joseph Manigault houses, fine examples of post-colonial architecture; and the Calhoun Mansion, a Victorian home noted for its furnishings and woodwork. At the Charles Towne Landing, a 664-acre state park, there is a reconstructed settlement of 1670 and a replica of a merchant ship from the period, as well as a zoo, gardens, and nature trails. From White Point Gardens there are views of the city, the harbor, and historic Ft. Sumter. A life-size replica of a Civil War submarine is featured in the Charleston Museum, the nation's oldest.

221. *Carpenters' and wood turners' skills are well displayed here at White Point Gardens.*

38

149

5

154

15

See
N–S book,
sec. 50.

169   95

30

199A

17

216A

5

221

End I-26

See
E–W book,
sec. 7.

79

12TH

90

51

34

See
E–W book,
sec. 24.

80

30

29

34

19

8

I-279

21

8

8E

0

70

See
E–W book,
sec. 31.

12TH Presque Isle State Park, Erie

12th St. W. exit: 5 min. West on W. 12th St., right on Rte. 832. Excellent exhibits at the nature center will enhance one's appreciation of this unique Pennsylvania park. The 7-mile-long sandy peninsula serves not only as a recreational area but also as a laboratory where all stages of a 600-year ecological succession exist, from fragile sandspit to a climax forest of hemlocks, oaks, and sugar maples. To the north is the expanse of Lake Erie, to the south Presque Isle Bay, in whose sheltered waters Admiral Perry's fleet was constructed for the War of 1812. Park amenities include lake and bay fishing, a marina, sandy beaches, and miles of trails. In winter, ice fishing and cross-country skiing are popular. *Park open year-round; beach open Memorial Day–Labor Day.*

12TH Erie, PA 16501

12th St. E. exit. Chamber of Commerce, 1006 State St. (814) 454-7191. Echoes of the War of 1812 still reverberate here. In September 1813, Commodore Oliver Hazard Perry won a stunning victory over the British on Lake Erie. Six of the nine ships in Perry's fleet were built in Erie, and one of them, the reconstructed flagship *Niagara*, is proudly berthed here. The strategy and details of the historic battle are depicted in the Erie Historical Museum.

The past is further recalled in the Old Custom House, built in 1839, now an art museum open to visitors. The Cashiers House, built the same year, features some fine antique furnishings. In the Dickson Tavern, the oldest surviving building in Erie, one can savor the 19th-century equivalent of a cocktail bar.

34 Maurice K. Goddard State Park

4 mi./8 min. West on Rte. 358; make first right turn; follow signs. Lake Wilhelm, an 1,860-acre reservoir created in 1972 to control flooding, is the centerpiece of this 2,658-acre Pennsylvania park. Recreational facilities include a 200-slip marina, where rowboats, pontoon boats, canoes, and fishing tackle can be rented. Fishermen try for perch, bass, walleye, and northern pike, and because of the relatively shallow waters, enjoy excellent ice fishing in winter. Hunting is permitted in designated areas of the park, where deer and waterfowl are the usual game. Several hiking trails wind around the lake, and there's a scenic drive along the southern shore. *Open daily Memorial Day–Labor Day; Mon.–Fri. Labor Day–Memorial Day.*

29 McConnell's Mill State Park

5 min. West on Rte. 422. After driving through miles of flat farmland, you will find the sudden, violent beauty of this 400-foot-deep glacial gorge, which is studded with gigantic sandstone boulders, a dramatic surprise. From the top of the gorge, where there's a park office and a picnic area, a graded trail descends to the turbulent waters of Slippery Rock Creek and the well-restored gristmill on its bank. You can walk or drive across the nearby covered bridge (circa 1874) that spans the creek and follow any number of trails through the park's challenging but rewarding terrain. Rappeling, white-water canoeing, fishing, and hunting are popular (bring your own equipment), but swimming is forbidden. *Park open year-round; gristmill open Memorial Day–Labor Day.*

19 Old Economy Village

9 mi./12 min. North on Rte. 65; follow signs. The German-born pietists known as Harmonists came to America seeking religious freedom. They founded a communal society in 1805 at Harmony, Pennsylvania, and established Economy in 1825. The community existed until the society, which believed in Christian piety, celibacy, and hard work, was dissolved in 1905. More than a dozen structures have been restored, including homes, craft shops, and an enormous Feast Hall, which now contains a small museum featuring the Harmonists' simple, straightforward furniture, a silk exhibit, and changing displays of decorative arts. The George Rapp House, the residence of the group's founder, has also been restored. Its formal garden, where walks edged with boxwood lead through several flower beds, symbolizes the group's sense of neatness and order. *Open Tues.–Sat. and P.M. Sun. except holidays.*

I-279 Pittsburgh, PA 15222

Convention & Visitors Information Center, 4 Gateway Center Plaza. (800) 255-0855; (800) 821-1888 outside PA. Like the phoenix rising from its ashes, this clean, handsome, and eminently livable city has

I-279. *Passengers in the balloons enjoy Pittsburgh's dramatic setting from on high.*

laid to rest its former image as a place of smoke and soot. For spectacular views of the Pittsburgh area, you can take a ride on either of two inclines to the top of Mt. Washington. The Allegheny and Monongahela rivers merge to form the Ohio at Point State Park, where a museum and a 1764 blockhouse impart a sense of history. Bird lovers will find the Pittsburgh Aviary filled with exotic birds in free flight. Flower lovers can stroll through acres of tropical plants in the Phipps Conservatory. Each of 21 "nationality classrooms" reflects a different ethnic group at the University of Pittsburgh's Cathedral of Learning, and the nearby Heinz Chapel has lovely stained-glass windows. Pittsburgh has many museums: you can see European art at the Frick Art Museum, sky shows at the Buhl Science Center, and art and natural history at the complex known as The Carnegie.

8 / 8E Arden Trolley Museum, Washington

Exit 8: 4 mi./7 min. West on Race Track Rd.; follow signs. Exit 8E: 3.5 mi./6 min. East on Pike St.; follow signs. In this indoor-outdoor museum trolley buffs and children of all ages can savor the pleasure of a 1-mile ride on a 1920's trolley car, fitted with polished woodwork, chrome, and brass. Twenty-five or more trolley cars, some in working order, others undergoing restoration, are exhibited in a large carbarn. The cars come from several towns in Pennsylvania and from Boston, with one veteran of New Orleans's famous Desire car line. *Open daily P.M. July 4–Labor Day; P.M. weekends only May–June and Sept.*

148 Coopers Rock State Forest

15 mi./25 min. East on Rte. 48. Great rocks extending from the edge of lofty bluffs provide a platform for spectacular views of the Cheat River and the West Virginia valley below. There are railings for safety and telescopes to use. The park was named for an escaped prisoner, a cooper by trade, who made the area his hideout. Rock climbers come here to challenge the crags, and hikers can enjoy the miles of trails that crisscross the forest, where mountain lau-

rel and rhododendron abound. For anglers there are two trout streams and a lake. The Henry Clay Iron Furnace, once a major source of pig iron, looms unattended in the woods, its overgrown stones the last reminder of this flourishing 19th-century industry and the village that grew up around it, of which there is no trace today. *Main park road open daily May–Nov.; trails open year-round.*

139 Pricketts Fort State Park

4 min. West from exit; follow signs. Built in 1774 on the banks of the Monongahela River for protection against Indian attack, the fort, with its stockade, blockhouses, and log cabins, has been completely reconstructed. Costumed staff members demonstrate pioneer tasks, including weaving and open-fire cooking as well as fiddling. In midsummer an outdoor drama, *Pricketts Fort: An American Frontier Musical*, is presented. The nearby Job Prickett House, built in 1859, represents the more comfortable lifestyle that evolved here. *Open daily mid-Apr.–Oct. Admission charged to fort. Additional charge for drama.*

110 Watters Smith Memorial State Park

7 mi./15 min. West from exit; follow signs. A replica of the log cabin built in 1796 by pioneer Watters Smith stands here, along with the original barn, blacksmith's shop, other outbuildings, and the well. Nearby, the blue and white clapboard house built in 1876 by a later member of the Smith family contains period furnishings, including a 1912 typewriter. An elegant antique wicker two-horse open sleigh is displayed in the visitor center. Hiking trails lead through the hilly landscape. *Open daily Memorial Day–Labor Day. Admission free but donations encouraged.*

79 Cedar Creek State Park

15 mi./30 min. West on Rte. 5, left on Rte. 33/119, left on Rte. 17 (Cedar Creek Rd.). A winding road leads to this secluded valley that follows the course of a creek in the steeply wooded Allegheny foothills of West Virginia. Seven hiking trails range in

79. *A rainy scene worthy of a Japanese woodcut or an impressionist painting.*

difficulty from a rugged climb up a ridge that offers impressive views of the area to a pleasant stroll between the swimming and picnic areas. Unusually tame deer can often be seen nibbling on oaks and poplars. The park has three fish ponds, stocked with different fish at different times of year. *Park open year-round; camping Apr.–mid-Oct.; recreational facilities open Memorial Day–Labor Day.*

I-77 Sunrise Museums, Charleston

22 mi./30 min. South on I-77; continue west on I-64 to Exit 58A, east on Oakwood Rd., right on MacCorkle Ave. (Rte. 61); bear right and go up C & O ramp; right on Bridge Rd., right on Myrtle Rd. Two museums make up this complex, which occupies neighboring stone mansions. The Children's Museum, housed in a former governor's home, captivates young visitors with "open us" discovery boxes of seashells and fossils, a dollhouse, a ray table that bends and bounces light, models of coaches and a circus wagon, and a 60-seat planetarium. The Art Museum, situated next door in the mansion of the governor's son, has a fine collection of 17th- to 20th-century American art. *Open Tues.–Sat. and P.M. Sun. except holidays. Admission charged.*

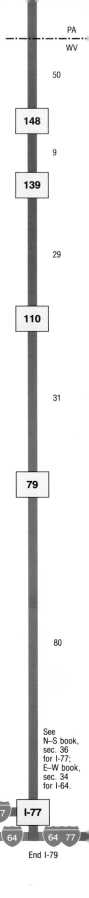

PA
WV
50
148
9
139
29
110
31
79
80
See N–S book, sec. 36 for I-77; E–W book, sec. 34 for I-64.
77 I-77
64   64 77
End I-79

50 Grass Point State Park

3 min. South on Rte. 12. This cool, breezy expanse overlooking the St. Lawrence River offers a tempting change of scene after a day at the wheel. Especially appealing are the campsites along a small bluff above the river's ship channel. At the narrow part of this very busy waterway you can see an unending stream of pleasure craft, as well as merchant ships, from around the world. Enhancing this interesting view are the many islands—both large and small—in the Thousand Islands chain.

There are picnic tables on well-tended lawns, a sandy beach at the bottom of a gentle slope, and several boat slips. A short fishing pier provides a vantage point for outwitting perch, pike, and at times, smallmouth bass. *Open mid-Apr.–mid-Sept. Admission charged.*

49 47 Agricultural Museum at Stone Mills

Exit 49: 10 mi./20 min. West on Rte. 411, left on Rte. 180. Exit 47: 11 mi./14 min. Northwest on Rte. 12, right on Rte. 180. Sponsored by the Northern New York Agricultural Historical Society, this fascinating museum is a complex of seven buildings. Exhibits of 19th-century farm equipment here include a Mehring Milker, which milked cows with a foot-operated mechanism similar to that of some early vacuum cleaners; a rare 15-foot-high horse-operated hay baler; and a seed drill with a 15-foot-long wooden box. Wall displays explain maple sugaring in the days when every farm had its "sugar bush." Across the road from the main complex, a cheese factory, built in 1897, contains old steam-powered machinery and other equipment for handling milk and making cheddar cheese, along with a display that explains the process of cheese making in this part of New York. *Open daily mid-May–Sept. Admission charged.*

45 Sackets Harbor Battlefield State Historic Site

10 mi./20 min. West on Rte. 3, right on Sulphur Springs Rd. (later called Main St.), left on Hill St. Situated on a bluff high above Black River Bay, this was the scene of two battles during the War of 1812. Today several of the buildings, including the restored Commandant's House, are open to the public. On the third weekend in July some 30,000 people come here for the annual Canadian-American 1812 Days festival, complete with parades, fireworks, and military demonstrations. The Union Hotel, built in 1817, is now a visitor center and features an exhibit that shows the way of life on the military base from 1812 to 1815. *Open Wed.–Sun. late May–mid-Oct., including holidays.*

36 Selkirk Shores State Park

Exit 36, headed south: 6 mi./15 min. Left on Rte. 2, right on Rte. 2A, right on Rte. 13, left on Rte. 3. Exit 36, headed north: 5 mi./ 10 min. Left on Rte. 13, left on Rte. 3. Set among sand dunes at the mouth of the Salmon River, the park is a favorite with fishermen, who try for the specimens here that often weigh more than 30 pounds. Other diversions include 6 miles of easy hiking trails, a bathing beach, a picnic grove, camping areas, sand-sculpting classes and softball games for children, and occasional afternoon concerts. Woodlands of pine, oak, birch, and larch have a rich undergrowth of ferns and wildflowers. *Open year-round.*

31 Oliver Stevens Blockhouse Museum, Brewerton

4 min. West on Bartell Rd., right on Rte. 11. Oliver Stevens, an early settler in the region, built a two-story blockhouse of logs and bricks in 1794 for protection from attack by the Onondaga Indians. Although the current blockhouse is a reconstruction, it is a faithful copy and highly evocative of bygone days on the frontier. An excellent collection of arrowheads traces local Indian craftsmanship from 8100 B.C. to A.D. 1100. An Owasco campsite dating back 900 years is represented by a rare clay pipe and a large stone mortar and pestle used for grinding maize. In the museum the fort's history is told with photographs, a Civil War Medal of Honor, and models of ships that once plied the local waterways. *Open June–Sept. Admission free but donations encouraged.*

18 Syracuse, NY 13202

Convention and Visitors Bureau, 100 E. Onondaga St. (315) 470-1343. In New York's fourth largest city you can visit the Everson Museum of Art, which is noted for its collections of ceramics, Oriental art, and American paintings. The Landmark Theatre, a fantasy palace built in 1928, has a richly ornate interior and is a center for plays, movies, and concerts. Other attractions in the city include the Erie Canal Museum, the Erie Canal Center, the modernized Burnet Park Zoo, and the Discovery Center of Science and Technology. A stroll on the Syracuse University campus might include stops at the Lowe Art Gallery or the huge Carrier Dome stadium. In early June some 50 huge, colorful balloons ascend to the heavens at the Hot Air Balloon Festival. And for 11 days ending on Labor Day, the Great New York State Fair offers an appealing variety of exhibits as well as many types of entertainment.

15 Lorenzo State Historic Site, Cazenovia

16 mi./22 min. South on Rte. 11, left on Rte. 20, right on Rte. 13. The beautifully proportioned federal-style mansion, built overlooking the shores of Lake Cazenovia in 1807–08 by John Lincklaen, a Dutch land developer, remained in the family for 160 years, until in 1968 it was presented to New York State. It is thought that the estate may have been named for the Florentine Medici prince. The mansion, with many original furnishings, including a copy of the desk of George Washington, an 1820's carved mahogany "plantation bed," family portraits, and fine old silver, radiates elegance and comfort. A small museum traces the history of both the family and the area and displays 19th-century vehicles. A self-guiding walking tour winds through the grounds. *Open Wed.–Sun. and Mon. holidays May–mid-Oct. Admission free but donations encouraged.*

11 The 1890 House Museum, Cortland

4 min. South on Rte. 13 (becomes Tompkins St.). Chester Franklin Wickwire, who made a fortune in copper-wire window

11. *Such opulent 19th-century luxuries as this conservatory are hardly affordable today.*

screening, fencing, and other copper products, was so impressed with the New York City mansion of James Bailey of the Barnum & Bailey Circus that he had an exact replica in reverse of that châteauesque mansion built. When completed in 1890, it featured the latest conveniences, such as central heating, indoor plumbing, and soon a few electric lights; and with its stained glass windows, cherry and oak woodwork, intricately patterned inlaid parquet floors, and handsome period furnishings, it stands today as a symbol of the height of 19th-century elegance and fashion.

The magnificent stained glass domed ceiling of the conservatory, the huge parlor fireplace, and the cozy nook beneath the stairs are classics of their kind; and the hinges, doorknobs, and latches are embossed with a woven wire design—a humble reminder of the source of the fortune that created the great house. *Open Tues.–Sun. except holidays.* &

| 4 | **Binghamton, NY 13902** |

Chamber of Commerce, 80 Exchange St. (607) 772-8860. At the Ross Park Zoo, one of the nation's oldest, you'll see beavers, otters, geese, and even a pack of wolves move about in re-created natural habitats. Children can pet the animals (not the wolves) and take a ride on a vintage carou-

sel. The Roberson Center for the Arts and Sciences has a planetarium and diverting exhibits as well as permanent art, historical, and scientific collections. Downtown Binghamton offers specialty and antique stores that both shoppers and casual strollers will find inviting. Anyone interested in architecture will be intrigued by the onion dome churches that reflect the area's Eastern European heritage.

| 60 | **Lackawanna State Park** |

3 mi./6 min. West on Rte. 524. The pleasant surroundings of this well-designed park entice visitors who come to sail, fish, and canoe on the 215-acre lake, and to swim in the 160-foot pool. A bathhouse is provided. The campsites and picnic area along the lake's western shore are shaded by oak, beech, and hemlock trees. Hiking trails wind through the park, which is home to ruffed grouse, pheasants, and other bird species, as well as deer. During the summer there are frequent hot-air balloon launchings. *Open year-round.*

| 47 | **Swetland Homestead, Wyoming** |

7 mi./16 min. North on Rte. 115, left on Rte. 315, right on Rte. 309, right on Rte. 11 (Wyoming Ave.). Built in 1797, this white

clapboard house with fluted columns at the entrance sheltered the same family for 161 years. The structure was donated to the Wyoming Historical and Geological Society in the early 1960's by the great-great-great-granddaughter of the original owner. *Open P.M. Thurs.–Sun. Memorial Day–Aug. Admission charged.*

| I-80 | **Eckley Miners' Village** |

13 mi./20 min. East on I-80 to Exit 39, right on Rte. 309, left on Freeland-Drums Hwy. to Freeland, right on Rte. 940; follow signs. Eckley is a living-history museum and hopes to maintain this status. Established in 1854 as a planned company "patch," it became home to generations of immigrant coal miners and their families. Early Victorian cottages, churches, mine buildings, and the company store stand today much as they were when shovels dug into the hillsides and daily life followed the tune of the steam whistle. More than 50 people remain, and the 58 buildings on this 100-acre site reveal the disciplined quality of life in a company town. The preserved cottages and visitor center have informative displays that tell the story of the mine patches in this anthracite region. *Visitor center open daily May–Sept., daily except holidays Oct.–Apr.; village buildings open Memorial Day–Labor Day and weekends Sept.–Oct. Admission charged.*

I-80. *For workers' houses in a company town, one plan is sufficient for all.*

11

40

4

NY

PA

49

60

30

47

22

See
E–W book,
sec. 25.

I-80   80

19

81

37 Tuscarora State Park

5 mi./10 min. East on Rte. 54; follow signs. Against a backdrop of Locust Mountain, a 96-acre lake offers swimming, fishing, and winter ice skating. Three unmarked hiking trails penetrate a virtual wilderness, where in their season deer, pheasants, ospreys, hawks, and bald eagles are likely to be sighted. The shaded picnic area offers a view of the lake through the trees. The park is for day use only, but fishermen are exempt from the rule as they pursue crappie, trout, channel cats, and walleye bass. *Open year-round.*

30 Coleman Memorial Park

9 mi./13 min. South on Rte. 72. At the turn of the century these 90 acres contained five summer mansions of the Coleman family, a successful mining and railroading clan. The land is now open to the public for daytime fun and relaxation. Six macadam tennis courts, four baseball diamonds, and a huge pool with diving boards and changing rooms offer a choice of recreation. Picnic tables are shaded by oaks, maples, pines, and sycamores, and there's stacked cordwood for the cooking fireplaces. Deer, rabbits, and many birds may be seen along an easy 2-mile trail. *Open year-round.*

28 Hershey Park, Gardens, and Chocolate World

8 mi./12 min. South on Rte. 743 to Hershey Park Dr. It started with chocolate in 1903, but today there's a theme park and zoo, 23 acres of gardens, a "Chocolate World," and a town—all named for Milton S. Hershey, the man who worked wonders with the exotic cocoa bean. When chocolate plant tours became so popular that they overwhelmed the facility, Chocolate World was set up to explain all aspects of the growing and making of Hershey's famous product. The gardens started as a rose garden but now include several other types of gardens. The theme park has 45 rides (the most popular: shooting rapids), along with live entertainment, restaurants, and shops. Although part of the park, the zoo can be visited separately. *Chocolate World open daily except winter holidays; theme park open daily Memorial Day–Labor Day, two weekends in May and Sept; zoo open daily except winter holidays; gardens open daily Apr.–Oct. Admission charged for theme park, zoo, and gardens.*

25 Harrisburg, PA 17108

Chamber of Commerce, 114 Walnut St. P.O. Box 969. (717) 232-4121. This state capital boasts an impressive Renaissance-style statehouse with a dome based on St. Peter's Basilica in Rome and a grand interior staircase copied from the Paris opera house. The nearby State Museum contains a wealth of regional artifacts from every era. The Museum of Scientific Discovery, in the business district, delivers successfully on the promise of its name. The beauty of the Susquehanna River can be enjoyed at Riverfront Park, a 5-mile stretch with a paved riverside esplanade. Some handsome 18th- and 19th-century mansions are other attractions in the Riverfront District.

17 Carlisle Barracks

3 mi./6 min. South on Rte. 11. Said to have been built by Hessian prisoners in 1777, the powder magazine now houses the Hessian Powder Magazine Museum, devoted to the history of Carlisle Barracks from the 18th to the 20th century. Exhibits include military artifacts and displays depicting life at the now defunct Carlisle Indian School, once famous for its outstanding athletes (among them the football star and Olympic decathlon and pentathlon gold medalist, Jim Thorpe). Uniforms, military awards, and photographs in the nearby Omar N. Bradley Museum present a visual biography of the distinguished high-ranking officer. In World War II he commanded more than 1.3 million men and later became a five-star general and chairman of the Joint Chiefs of Staff. *Hessian Museum open P.M. weekends May–Sept; Bradley Museum open A.M. Mon. and P.M. Wed. and Fri.*

11 Pine Grove Furnace State Park

8 mi./9 min. South on Rte. 233. This state park is named for the Pine Grove ironworkers' community that flourished here in the 1700's and 1800's. Activities include bicycling, summer and winter sports, a self-guiding walking tour of the remaining structures of the ironworkers' village, and a number of hiking trails. Deer are sometimes sighted, and birds abound. Once a stop for slaves heading north on the Underground Railroad, the ironmaster's mansion now serves as a youth hostel offering overnight shelter. In the summertime don't be surprised to see someone at the camp store

1. *The setting's quiet beauty makes it hard to imagine the carnage wrought here.*

consuming a whole half-gallon of ice cream within an hour—it's a traditional celebration for hikers who reach this, the midpoint of the 2,000-mile Appalachian Trail, which runs from Georgia to Maine. *Park open year-round; camp store open Memorial Day–Labor Day.*

6 Caledonia State Park

9 mi./12 min. East on Rte. 30, left on Rte. 233. Fine mountain country, rich in hemlocks, white pines, oaks, and rhododendrons, awaits visitors to this 1,130-acre park. The famed Appalachian Trail, which runs through the grounds, is just one of several hiking trails. The park encompasses an attractive 18-hole golf course, a summer stock playhouse, and a restaurant made up of old railroad cars—complete with a Pullman dining car and caboose kitchen. A reconstructed blacksmith's shop marks the site of the ironworks established here by Thaddeus Stevens in 1837. His outspoken abolitionist views caused Confederate troops to burn his plant to the ground in 1863. What are now children's playing fields once served as dressing stations for wounded soldiers brought from Gettysburg. *Park open year-round; campgrounds open mid-Apr.–mid-Dec.*

6A The Hager House, Hagerstown

5 min. East on Rte. 40, right on Prospect St. to City Park, right on Key St. German immigrant Jonathan Hager, for whom Hagerstown was named, completed this restored fieldstone house in 1740 on what was then the western frontier. So that his family could survive a possible Indian attack, he built the house over twin springs for a water supply and constructed walls 22 inches thick. In the basement the stone-lined pools are still filled with water, and in an adjacent fortified room narrow musket ports attest to the perils of that time and place. The interior is authentically furnished and reflects Hager's status as a fur trader and political leader. Pelts are laid across a table in the fur trading room, which also includes a mid-18th-century painted armoire and a 1777 chest painted with German designs. A separate museum building displays Hager family possessions, along with period artifacts unearthed here. *Open Tues.–Sat. and P.M. Sun. Apr.–Dec. Admission charged.*

1 Antietam National Battlefield

12 mi./15 min. East on Rte. 68, right on Rte. 65. It is remembered in history as the bloodiest single day's conflict of the Civil War. For one dreadful day in September 1862, a battle raged here through woods and cornfields that today appear much as they did then. Outnumbered more than two to one by Union forces, the Confederates inflicted more than 12,000 casualties, themselves sustaining almost 11,000—a loss they could ill afford. Although it was far from a clear-cut victory for the North, President Lincoln judged it sufficiently successful to warrant issuing his preliminary Emancipation Proclamation, which announced the abolition of slavery within the Confederacy. An excellent self-guiding auto tour provides insight into each phase of the battle. Highlights include the rebuilt Dunker Church (used as a hospital) and the 1836 Burnside Bridge, where 400 Georgia sharpshooters delayed hordes of attacking Federal troops. *Open daily except Thanksgiving Day, Christmas, and New Year's Day. Admission charged.*

80 George Washington's Office Museum, Winchester

2 mi./8 min. West on Rte. 50, right on Pleasant Valley Rd., left on Cork St. In 1755–56, during the French and Indian War, Col. George Washington is believed to have used one of the rooms in this 1748 log building as his office. Still in his early 20's, he was responsible for the construction of some 30 forts along Virginia's western frontier. This museum houses several interesting displays—including a model of Ft. Loudoun built from Washington's original plans, a photocopy of a list in his handwriting of all tools and materials used in the construction of the fort, a Brown Bess musket with bayonet, late 18th-century surveying instruments, and a large Danner compass similar to Washington's. *Open daily Apr.–Oct. Admission charged.*

If You Have Some Extra Time:

Harpers Ferry National Historical Park

12 *23 mi./30 min.* The turbulent history of this small town, at the junction of three states and two rivers, has been dictated by the strategic importance and scenic beauty of its location. People heading into the Shenandoah Valley crossed the rivers on Robert Harper's ferry. George Washington, with the eye of a strategist, saw the potential for a federal armory, and one was established in 1796. In 1859 John Brown and his abolitionist followers staged a futile attempt to capture the armory and ignite a slave revolt. Brown was captured and hanged, but the incident helped to precipitate the Civil War. During the war, the town changed hands many times and sustained damage with every battle.

The remaining 18th- and 19th-century buildings, along with the spectacular scenic beauty of the site, inspired the gradual renovation of the town and its designation as a national historical park. The visitor center in Stagecoach Inn offers exhibits and a self-guiding walking tour. Among the highlights are the quaint fire engine house where John Brown took refuge; Robert Harper's original house; the Master Armorer's House Museum; and the high rock outcrop from which Thomas Jefferson proclaimed the view to be "worth a voyage across the Atlantic." *How to get there: Exit 12, southeast on Rte. 9 to Charles Town, left on Rte. 340; follow signs.*

11

17

6

21

PA

MD

6A

5

1

MD

WV

18

12

20

WV

VA

80

48

81

81

76

34

67

41

57

1

56 64

See
E–W book,
sec. 35.

17

54

See
E–W book,
sec. 35.

64

25

50

16

49

31

42

10

39

67 Luray Caverns

13.5 mi./20 min. East on Rte. 211. These vast, spectacular caverns were first viewed by candlelight in 1878 by two men who entered by letting themselves down on ropes. Today a 1¼-mile paved path and artfully naturalistic lighting make the caverns' 64 acres accessible to all.

Over the course of millions of years the dripping of mineral-rich water has created multicolored oddities in stone that resemble everything from bath towels to rows of hanging fish to fried eggs. Highlights of the 1-hour tour include the 195-foot-deep Pluto's Chasm, a flowstone shape known as the Frozen Fountain, and a 7-million-year-old formation called the Giant California Redwood Tree. Most impressive of all is the unique Stalacpipe Organ, which produces clear tones as the stalactite formations, tuned to the music scale, are struck by electronically controlled plungers. *Open year-round. Admission charged.* 🛏

If You Have Some Extra Time: Shenandoah National Park

76 56 Exit 76: 24 mi./35 min. Exit 56: 18 mi./25 min.

This awesomely beautiful park runs along the Blue Ridge Mountains for about 100 miles. Bisecting it from north to south is the Skyline Drive, where frequent overlooks afford spectacular views of the park's valleys, streams, cliffs, and waterfalls, as well as more distant vistas of the rolling Piedmont Plateau to the east and the Shenandoah Valley to the west. The park is particularly beautiful when the azaleas are in bloom in the spring, and in the autumn when the many varieties of hardwoods are ablaze with color.

A handy system of mile-markers along the drive makes it easy to locate such highlights as Shenandoah Valley Overlook, Thornton Gap, Big Meadows, Hawksbill Gap, and the Dickey Ridge Visitor Center. Several hiking trails lead to summits, including Stony Man, whose fairly easy trail takes you to sharp, rocky cliffs that provide an unobstructed view of the valley. The park's highest peak, Hawksbill, is the target of serious hikers, and Old Rag's boulder-strewn ridge can be reached after a strenuous climb.

The park's mountain streams, such as Jeremys Run, one of the most popular, offer excellent trout fishing. Gray foxes, black bears, raccoons, and skunks make their home here, along with a wide variety of birds, the monarch butterfly, and the luna moth. *How to get there: Exit 76, east on I-66, right on Rte. 340. Exit 56, east on I-64 to Exit 19, north on Skyline Dr. Open year-round. Admission charged.*

57 Woodrow Wilson Birthplace, Staunton

2 mi./6 min. West on Rte. 250, right on Coalter St. America's 28th president was born in this Greek revival Virginia town house on December 28, 1856. Today, 12 beautifully restored rooms display a wide variety of original furnishings and family memorabilia. You'll see the Bible in which the Reverend Joseph Ruggles Wilson, a Presbyterian minister, recorded his son's birth; a period quilt; antique dolls; a rolltop desk and a typewriter desk from Wilson's study at Princeton University, where he served as president from 1902 to 1910; and two ornate brass oil lamps that he bought while he was a student at the University of Virginia. A lovely Victorian garden and a carriage house that contains Wilson's restored 1920 Pierce-Arrow presidential limousine add to the period atmosphere. A film about Wilson is shown regularly at the reception center. *Open daily Mar.–Dec.; Mon.–Sat. Jan.–Feb. except Thanksgiving Day, Christmas, and New Year's Day. Admission charged.* ♿

54 Cyrus H. McCormick Museum and Wayside

3 min. East on Rte. 606, left on Rte. 937. It's still not clear whether Cyrus McCormick invented the reaper that bears his name or simply adapted and marketed a prototype developed 20 years earlier by his father Robert. But Cyrus, now known as the father of mechanized farming, was a born entrepreneur. He expanded his horizons to the great American heartland by setting up business in Chicago and later became the millionaire founder-owner of the International Harvester Company. The blacksmith's shop in which the first reapers were built contains a replica of Cyrus's 1831 machine and models of some of his later inventions. *Open year-round.* 🛏

50 49 Natural Bridge

Exit 50: 5 min. South on Rte. 11. Exit 49: 5 min. North on Rte. 11. Natural Bridge is a single block of limestone—90 feet long, up to 150 feet wide, and 215 feet high—that straddles Cedar Creek and joins two mountains here in the

50–49. *The people in the picture help show the monumental size of the bridge.*

Blue Ridge country. The Monacan Indians named this striking natural phenomenon the Bridge of God, but geologists credit millions of years of erosion by the creek as its sculptor. On the southeast wall of the bridge are the initials G. W., carved by George Washington when he surveyed the site in 1750. It was once owned by Thomas Jefferson, who purchased it and 157 acres from George III for 20 shillings. Some of the trees are up to 1,000 years old. *Open year-round. Admission charged.* 🪑♿

42 Virginia Museum of Transportation, Roanoke

7 mi./11 min. South on I-581 to Exit 5, west on Williamson Rd., right on Salem Ave., right on 3rd St. The emphasis here is on railroading—the glamorous aspects as well as the nuts and bolts. You can stroll past locomotives and passenger cars and board a caboose on the tracks near an old freight-loading dock. Inside the museum you can browse among life-size dioramas of passenger car and sleeping car interiors, as well as photographs of passengers from a bygone era boarding trains, sitting in dining cars, and socializing in club cars. Another photo exhibit shows scenes from foundries and machine shops where trains are built.

Other modes of transportation are represented here too: there are some horse-drawn vehicles, automobiles, photographs of early local pilots, and models of spacecraft. Yet another exhibit, some 20 years in the making, shows a model circus with railroad cars, a bandwagon drawn by 40 horses, and a big top complete with elephants and trapeze artists. *Open Mon.–Sat. and P.M. Sun. except Thanksgiving Day, Christmas, and New Year's Day. Admission charged.* 🪑♿

39 Dixie Caverns

1 min. West on Rte. 460. Upon entering this cavern, you walk up into the hillside rather than down—a phenomenon shared with only a few other caverns worldwide. Discovered in 1856 by two U.S. soldiers and believed to be more than 100,000 years old, this site has several chambers; each contains bizarre formations created by continually dripping, mineral-bearing water. More than 70 weddings have been performed beneath the dome-shaped Wedding Bell. On the tour, you'll see shapes that resemble a paratrooper, a Portuguese man-of-war, and the Leaning Tower of Pisa. *Open daily except Christmas Day. Admission charged.* 🪑⛺🚐🐟♿

26 Shot Tower Historical State Park

8 mi./11 min. South on I-77 to Exit 5, east on Rte. 69, left on Rte. 52. Thomas Jackson, an immigrant from England, built this park's fortresslike tower, with thick limestone walls, in about 1807. Using lead mined in the area, it produced shot for guns. Molten lead was poured through a sieve at the top and allowed to fall some 150 feet into buckets of cooling water in an underground shaft (it was believed that the fall molded the shot into its round shape). The park has lovely shaded picnic areas. About 100 feet from the tower is the midpoint of the New River Trail, with attractions such as an access point for fishing, a historic ferry site, and beautiful views of the New River. *Open daily late May–early Sept.; weekends late Apr.–late May and early Sept.–late Oct. Admission charged for tower.* 🪑🚶🐟

16 Mount Rogers National Recreation Area

5 mi./10 min. South on Rte. 16. More than 100,000 acres of picturesque varied terrain here encompass 60 miles of the Appalachian Trail and about 300 miles of other trails, as well as the three highest mountains in Virginia. High on Whitetop Mountain (the summit can be reached by car) you can enjoy spectacular views. A herd of ponies roams freely, nibbling on mountain grasses. Some of the picnic and camping areas have excellent trout streams. *Open year-round.* 🪑⛺🚐🚶🐾🐟♿

2 Bristol Caverns

8 mi./15 min. South on I-381 (becomes Commonwealth Ave.), left on State St., right on Rte. 421. Imagine their surprise when, in 1864, settlers excavating for a root cellar discovered this wonderland of sculptured stone. The caves, however, were known to the Cherokees, who used them as a base for attacks on pioneer settlements. The caverns were first formed hundreds of millions of years ago by an underground river, and a subterranean stream still flows in the deepest parts. The rock formations are artfully lighted to accentuate their dramatic shapes and colors. *Open daily except Thanksgiving Day and Christmas. Admission charged.* 🪑

8 The Crockett Tavern Museum, Morristown

6 mi./12 min. North on Rte. 25, west on Rte. 11E; follow signs. Davy Crockett was only a boy of 10 when his parents built and ran a four-room log tavern here along one of the first roads that led west. The tavern was burned after the Civil War, but this reconstruction conveys the atmosphere of the original. The rope beds could accommodate up to six travelers, and the stone fireplace was used for cooking and heating. A loom room contains spinning wheels and other equipment for making cloth. All the furniture, the flintlock musket mounted on the wall, and the Conestoga wagon in the barn are authentic relics from the days when America was slowly pushing west. *Open Mon.–Sat. and P.M. Sun. May–Oct. Admission charged.*

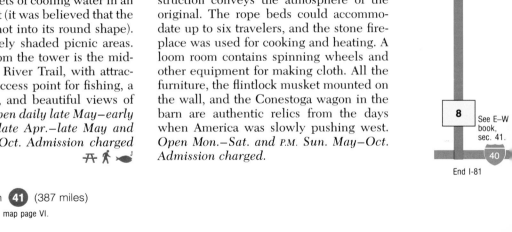

41 The Alice T. Miner Colonial Collection

3 min. East on Rte. 191, right on Rte. 9. With a discerning eye, Alice T. Miner, wife of railroad tycoon William Miner, assembled a superb collection of china, glass, pewter, silver, and fine furniture of the colonial era. A magnificent Hepplewhite sideboard, a Queen Anne tiger maple lowboy, a 1775 rope-sprung marriage bed, and a rare set of miniature 18th-century furniture used as cabinetmakers' samples stand out as antique works of art. The house, built in 1824, was later enlarged to display the collection. *Open Tues.–Sat. Feb.–Dec. Admission free but donations encouraged.*

34 Ausable Chasm

5 min. East on Rte. 9N, left on Rte. 9. If you walk the trail beside the rushing Ausable River, consider that the flat stones underfoot were worn smooth in the Cambrian period some 500 million years ago. Stratified sandstone walls flanking the river soar to dizzying heights in an endless variety of sculptural forms with names such as Pulpit Rock, Elephant's Head, and Devil's Oven. Jacob's Well is a deep hole worn into the rock by stones spun in an eddy for eons of time. At Table Rock, you board a sturdy bateau modeled on those used by French explorers and float to the landing and the bus back to the parking lot. Allow 1½ hours for the tour. *Open daily mid-May–mid-Oct. Admission charged.*

28 Fort Ticonderoga

20 mi./30 min. East on Rte. 74. Ticonderoga, commanding a strategic point on the route from Canada to the middle Colonies, was first fortified by the French, then captured by the British, who held it until May 10, 1775, when Ethan Allen and his Green Mountain Boys took it in a surprise assault. Although the fort later fell to the enemy, the Americans captured some 50 cannons, more than 2,000 pounds of lead, and a number of muskets and flints that were dragged to Boston and used against the British. The fort's history can be relived by exploring this reconstruction. The museum displays muskets, cannons, uniforms, and other period memorabilia, including General Washington's razor and corkscrew. In July and August fife-and-drum programs and cannon firings are presented by troops in period uniforms. *Open daily mid-May–mid-Oct. Admission charged.*

20 / 19 Great Escape Fun Park

Exit 20: 2 min. South on Rte. 9. Exit 19: 1½ min. North on Rte. 9. The Steamin' (some call it Screamin') Demon roller coaster does complete loop-the-loops, and the 10-minute Raging River Ride plunges thrill seekers through real rapids and waterfalls. Under the big top, gravity-defying motorcyclists, trapeze artists, and elephants strut their amazing stuff. There's a ghost town, Jungleland, and a high-diving show, plus bumper cars, Ferris wheels, scare-a-second rides, games, musical shows, gift shops, and pavilions serving food of many lands. Fantasyland, scaled for young children, offers rides on miniature trains and mechanical animals—dragons, elephants, and mice. *Open Memorial Day–Labor Day. Admission charged.*

13 / 12 Saratoga Lake

Exit 13: 6 min. South on Rte. 9, left on Rte. 9P. Exit 12: 5 min. North on Rte. 9, right on Rte. 9P. A glimpse of this woodland idyll tells the story: tranquil waters and pine vistas against a dazzling blue sky. Because most of the lakeshore is privately owned, development has been minimal—just a few well-maintained camping areas and a lone sandy beach, where the pure water makes swimming a pleasure; a float offshore has a diving board. Anglers rate the largemouth-bass fishing among the state's best, with 12-pounders no rarity. Perch, pike, and crappie abound too. *Open year-round.*

23 Albany, NY 12207

Convention and Visitors Bureau, 52 S. Pearl St. (518) 434-1217; (800) 622-8464 outside NY. Settled in the early 1600's, chartered in 1686, and declared the capital city of New York State in 1797, Albany has a rich and varied history. The Dutch presence is recalled at the Van Rensselaer family home and the Ten Broeck Mansion. The Schuyler Mansion was built for a general in the Revolution, and the New York State Museum provides insights into local history. Empire State Plaza is a monumental modern-day architectural extravaganza. Boat trips on the Hudson reveal the city's importance as a shipping center.

21 Olana State Historic Site

5 mi./8 min. East on Rte. 23B, left on Rte. 23, across Rip Van Winkle Bridge, right on Rte. 9G. The renowned landscape painter Frederick Edwin Church, eminent in the Hudson River school, built this Persian-influenced stone-and-brick villa in 1870, naming it after an ancient Turkish treasure house/fortress. He saw it as his family's refuge as well as three-dimensional art, a harmonious blend of architecture and environment. His touch is everywhere: in forest and meadow tableaux framed by the windows, in hand-stenciled decorations enlivening various rooms, but chiefly in such masterly paintings as his "Autumnal View," "Bend in the River," the brooding sunset of "The Afterglow," and the extraordinary mystery of "El Khasne, Petra," painted after he had visited that ruined city. *Grounds open year-round. Tours of house given May–Labor Day. Admission charged for house.*

21 / 20 Catskill Game Farm

Exit 21: 11 mi./20 min. East on Rte. 23B, right on Rte. 23, then left on Rte. 32. Exit 20: 11 mi./20 min. West on Rte. 212, right on Rte. 32. A half-century of dedicated conservation work has created this home for 2,000 animals and birds, including many endangered species. Stroll the compounds and see what wonders we've almost lost: the wisent, or aurochs, a rare East European bison; the llamalike South American guanaco; the barasingha, or swamp deer, from India; the long-horned scimitar oryx from the Sahara; and the blesbok, white rhino, and sable antelope from southern Africa. In the spacious bird sanctuary, crowned cranes, flamingos, cockatoos, and other avian marvels display

21. *The Persian influence is richly exemplified in the Court Hall at Olana.*

their many colors. Deer and antelope wander freely. The prairie-dog village, daily animal shows, and a sand playground appeal to youngsters. *Open daily mid-Apr.–Oct. Admission charged.*

17 | West Point Museum

16 | *Exit 17: 13 mi./25 min. East on Rte. 17, right on Rte. 9W, left on Rte. 218. Exit 16: 15 mi./30 min. East on Rte. 6, left on Rte. 293. right on Rte. 218.* The collections here date from 1777, with armament captured when the British surrendered at Saratoga. In addition to weapons, you'll find paintings, dioramas, and other works of art depicting various aspects of military life. The West Point Room, American Revolution Room, World War I and II rooms, and other galleries include information and artifacts related to all the conflicts in which America has been involved. In the Weapons Room, the escalation of warfare, from the Stone Age to the atomic era, is dramatically portrayed. *Open daily except Christmas and New Year's Day. Admission free but donations encouraged.*

16 | Bear Mountain State Park

10 mi./15 min. East on Rte. 6, right on Rte. 9W. It is ironic that these spacious hillsides, softball fields, picnic grounds, and leafy nature trails were once the proposed site of a state prison. At Trailside many outdoor displays explain the local flora, fauna, and geology; and the attractions in the nearby museum and zoo range from turtles to bears to beavers at work on a cutaway dam. An excursion boat affords a look at the full beauty of the setting, the Hudson River, and the handsome Bear Mountain Bridge. Other summer diversions include swimming, boat rentals, and fishing; winter brings ice skating and sledding. *Open year-round.*

9 | Sunnyside, Tarrytown

4 min. South on Rte. 9. "I would not exchange the cottage for any chateau in Christendom," Washington Irving wrote in 1836, after remodeling the modest 17th-century stone house he called Sunnyside. He had recently returned from 17 years abroad, where he had written "Rip Van Winkle," "The Legend of Sleepy Hollow," and other works. Every feature of the house and its 24-acre wooded grounds reflects the joy of this internationally renowned American author at living in "this dear, bright little home" overlooking the Hudson's widest sweep. The original furnishings include Irving's writing desk and, in the parlor, the rosewood piano on which his nieces accompanied his flute recitals. His dressing gown and walking stick still rest in a large bedroom armoire. *Open year-round. Admission charged.*

FDHM | The Bronx Zoo, New York Zoological Park

Fordham Rd. exit. 3 mi./12 min. East on W. Fordham Rd. and E. Fordham Rd. This 265-acre habitat ("zoo" seems so inadequate) contains one of the world's great displays of animal life. There's too much for a single visit, but you can start with Skyfari cable cars for an overview of cheetahs, giraffes, zebras, guanacos, and other African and South American mammals in natural settings, or the Bengali Express monorail for the rhinos, elephants, and tigers of Wild Asia. Special lighting in the World of Darkness permits a look at bats, owls, and other nocturnal creatures. The Holarctic Trail leads to Kodiak bears, red pandas, and snow leopards prowling the prairies and Himalayan highlands. The indoor World of Birds reproduces the lush splendors of a South American rain forest and other natural settings. There's much more here, including a children's zoo, where youngsters can be photographed holding animals. *Zoo open year-round; Children's Zoo and Wild Asia open May–Oct. Admission charged.*

9. *Decorative embellishments all but overwhelm Irving's modest cottage.*

TRI | New York, NY 10019

Triboro Bridge exit. Convention and Visitors Bureau, 2 Columbus Circle. (212) 397-8222. The crowded diversity of the city can be overwhelming, but even a short visit will be rewarding if you decide in advance what you want to see. You might choose the spectacular views from the Empire State Building or World Trade Center, or stroll on Fifth Avenue past Rockefeller Center, St. Patrick's Cathedral, and intriguing shop windows. Central Park might beckon, or Chinatown, Greenwich Village, or the South Street Seaport. For museum-goers, the choices are a challenge: will it be the Metropolitan, Whitney, Guggenheim, Frick, or Natural History? Other temptations: a boat ride in the harbor, or to the Statue of Liberty, or around the island of Manhattan. Be forewarned, however: the city is a difficult—or expensive—place to park a car.

See E–W book, sec. 9.

90

23

28

21

13

20

41

17

15

16

34

9

16

FDHM See N–S book, sec. 47.

95

TRI 5

End I-87

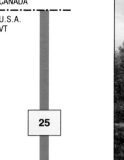

8. *Saint-Gaudens's interest in sculptural forms extended to his garden, as indicated by the subtly related shapes in the landscape that the artist helped to design.*

25 Crystal Lake State Park

3 min. North on Rte. 16. Swimmers will enjoy the sparkling clarity of aptly named Crystal Lake as well as the relative warmth of these quite shallow waters. Poplar, ash, and white pine trees shade the picnic tables along the shore. To the east Mt. Wheeler, with its base of bare granite, its wooded slopes, and its rounded summit, dominates the skyline. Canoes, sailboards, and small rafts—but not motorboats—may be launched for offshore fishing and other aquatic recreation. Likely to be crowded on weekends. *Open daily late May–mid-Sept. Admission charged.*

16 Morse Museum, Warren

17 mi./30 min. East on Rte. 25 (becomes Rte. 25C at Piermont). As a boy growing up in a small farming community, Ira Morse dreamed of hunting big game in Africa. In 1926, having established a successful shoe business, he went on the first of six safaris to the Dark Continent. Among the trophies taken by him and his son are lions, hyenas, antelope, elephant tusks, and a group of artifacts including shields, a witch doctor's rattle, a tea set made from ostrich eggs, and Masai baskets so tightly woven that they hold water. A collection of over 200 pairs of shoes from around the world represents his business interests. *Open daily mid-June–Labor Day.*

10 Quechee Gorge State Park

6 mi./8 min. North on I-89, left on Rte. 4. In the tongue of the Abnaki Indians, *quechee* (pronounced *kwee*-chee) means "a deep gorge." Aptly named, the park parallels a scenic, mile-long stretch of the Ottauquechee River, a stream flowing some 160 feet below the bridge on Rte. 4. Anglers prowl on the river's reddish-gray slate banks to try for brown and rainbow trout. Mill Pond, north of the gorge, is favored for its northern pike and bass. A softball field and horseshoe pitch are further enticements in this delightful state park.

A 1-mile hiking trail connects the pond and the river, and two more trails join the main trail to a campground, which has secluded sites under tall pines. But hikers be warned: climbing the gorge walls is ecologically as well as economically unsound; violators will incur a $500 fine. *Open daily Memorial Day–Columbus Day. Admission charged.*

8 Saint-Gaudens National Historic Site

10 mi./20 min. East on Rte. 131, left on Rte. 12A. The world-famous sculptor Augustus Saint-Gaudens bought the estate he called Aspet in 1885. The site now includes his home, studios, gardens, and a 120-acre woodland. Many of the Queen Anne and Hepplewhite pieces that grace the house are Saint-Gaudens's original furnishings, but the main attraction is the sculptor's own work—more than 100 pieces in all. They include a reduction of his famous "Lincoln the Man," a copy of the massive "Puritan," and the bronze bust of Gen. William T. Sherman. In the gardens, which the artist helped design, are the Pan Fountain and a copy of the haunting Adams memorial in Washington, D.C.

Visitors may join a tour of the house and the Little Studio, where Saint-Gaudens worked, and walk along the wooded trails to Blow-Me-Up Brook or Blow-Me-Down Pond, where the sculptor loved to go wandering. *Open daily mid-May–Oct. Admission charged.*

6 Green Mountain Railroad, Bellows Falls

4 mi./6 min. South on Rte. 5, left on Canal St., left across bridge to Depot St. Buy your ticket at the 1925 Bellows Falls brick depot, wait on one of the wooden benches, and board one of the eight coaches built between 1891 and 1931. A first-generation diesel locomotive (circa 1951) pulls the train along a right-of-way that was by turns an Indian trail, pioneer path, military road, and stagecoach route. You'll see a rocky gorge and waterfall, open farmland, two covered bridges, and unspoiled New England villages. On weekends round trips are offered: two to Chester, each taking about 2 hours, and three to Ludlow, a 4½-hour run that stops at Chester Station and Chester South. *Open daily mid-June–Oct. Train fare charged.*

2 Brattleboro Living Memorial Park

1 min. West on Rte. 9, left on Guilford St. Extension. This award-winning park situated on a series of mountain plateaus is thoughtfully designed and immaculately maintained. It offers a wealth of diversions, including a beginners' ski run (open weekends and evenings only), playing fields, several short, easy nature trails through deep woodland, a swimming pool, horseshoe and shuffleboard courts, two outdoor tennis courts, and four indoor courts that convert into a skating rink in winter. A natural amphitheater is a perfect setting for concerts. *Open year-round.*

19 Arcadia Wildlife Sanctuary, Easthampton

5 mi./13 min. West on Rte. 9, south on Rte. 10, left on Lovefield St.; follow signs. This ancient meander in the Connecticut River has filled in, creating a large marsh that supports small mammals, including muskrats and red foxes, as well as an impressive range of resident and migratory birds. Herons, wood ducks, great horned owls, northern orioles, cardinals, and bobolinks are among the scores of species you might see, if you are lucky, along the trails through fields, marshes, and woodlands and from the observation tower located beside Arcadia Marsh. The main building houses an auditorium for orientation films and lectures, a natural history library, and a gift shop. Seasonal checklists for bird-watchers are available at the main building. *Sanctuary open Tues.–Sun.; nature center open Tues.–Fri. Admission charged.*

45. *Conductor and motorman stand ready to welcome visitors for a nostalgic ride.*

3 Riverside

5 mi./9 min. East on Rte. 57, left on Rte. 159. This pleasant site beside the Connecticut River has accommodated family outings since 1840, when it was a picnic grove. Now it is a 150-acre state-of-the-art amusement park, but it still retains some charming echoes of the past.

Along with a new Ferris wheel, tall as a 15-story building, the park has a high-speed roller coaster, a loop roller coaster, and one called the Thunderbolt, which is of classic wood design. There's a brand-new water rapids/water slide and, from another era, a hand-carved carousel.

There are old-style jugglers and puppet shows and a new pavilion theater. The midway games offer both the tried-and-true dime-pitch tests of skill and the latest video extravaganzas. The section for young children includes bumper cars, a mine train ride, magic shows, and a petting zoo. On Saturdays stock-car racing is the featured attraction. *Open daily Apr.–Sept. Admission charged.*

45 The Connecticut Trolley Museum

2 min. East on Rte. 140. Along with the miracle of electricity came quiet, efficient trolleys, which provided interurban transportation during the time between the era of horsepower, produced by horses, and that of the internal combustion engine.

The trolleys were remarkable for their elegant design, as can be seen in the more than 30 examples here.

On the 3-mile ride offered, you might find yourself in the open Montreal Observation Car No. 4, with seats rising from front to back as in a theater, or a 1911 trolley from Rio de Janeiro, or perhaps in the classic 1901 open-style trolley car with etched glass panels beneath the roof. *Open daily Memorial Day–Labor Day; weekends and holidays Labor Day–Memorial Day. Fare charged for rides.*

31 Hartford, CT 06103

Visitor Information Center, The Old State House, 800 Main St. (203) 522-6766. Two of the interesting buildings are here by virtue of Hartford's being a capital city. The Old State House is a classic designed by Charles Bulfinch, and the current capitol building is a study in architectural eclecticism. Both are included, along with 21 other highlights, on the Walk, a self-guiding tour. In addition, the Mark Twain House, whose gables and Victorian verandas reflect the famous author's whimsical

31. *America's first triumphal arch was dedicated to veterans of the Civil War.*

side, contrasts with the nearby home of Harriet Beecher Stowe, a model of restrained 19th-century design.

The Museum of Connecticut History has an outstanding collection of Colt firearms, and the Wadsworth Atheneum, one of the United States' first art museums, displays an overwhelming variety of treasures. In Bushnell Park the carousel, with its superb hand-carved mounts, stands on a sweeping lawn near the Corning Fountain, which is dedicated to American Indians.

1 New Haven, CT 06510

Convention & Visitor Bureau, 900 Chapel St. (203) 787-8367. This city's classic New England green, laid out in 1638, still serves as common land and provides a setting for three handsome churches. Yale University, a major presence in the town, offers a variety of attractions. Connecticut Hall, constructed circa 1750, is the oldest building on the Yale campus. The Yale University Art Gallery has a wide-ranging and distinguished collection as does the Yale Center for British Art. The Yale University Collection of Musical Instruments presents some 850 pieces; the Peabody Museum of Natural History is noted for its exhibits in the Great Hall of Dinosaurs.

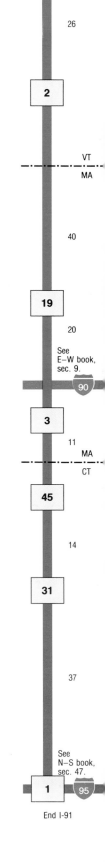

42

15

FNP2

5

FNP1

6

32

22

26

5

24

6

23

22

FNP1. *The only sign of man's handiwork is the catwalk here in nature's rocky realm.*

42 Forest Lake State Park

12 mi./20 min. North on Rte. 116; follow signs. Imposing views of 5,385-foot Mt. Monroe and 6,288-foot Mt. Washington add a special grandeur to this pleasant park. White pines, spruce, and paper birches shade the lakeside picnic area and provide a haven for downy woodpeckers, jays, and other woodland birds. In season, wildflowers add lovely splashes of color. For children there is a small playground. Although no boats may be launched from the narrow sand beach, fishing from the shore is permitted; the lake yields perch, bass, and trout. *Open daily late May–Labor Day. Admission charged.*

FNP2 Cannon Mountain Aerial Passenger Tramway

Franconia Notch Pkwy., Exit 2. 1 min. A 5-minute aerial cable car ride to the 4,200-foot summit of Cannon Mountain reveals a spectacular panorama of distant valleys and the mountains of the Franconia Range. From the tram station, walk along Rim Trail, which will take you past rocky ledges and other fine views. The best vantage

point for photographs is the summit observation tower, from which you can see five states and part of Canada.

You can go back down the mountain by tramway or take the 2-mile walking trail. *Open daily late May–late Oct., weather permitting. Admission charged.*

FNP1 The Flume

Franconia Notch Pkwy., Exit 1. 1 min. This geological wonder is the result of ancient underground volcanic pressure, the surface erosion of frost, and the rushing water of Flume Brook. The ravine's narrow gorge, 800 feet long and 12 to 20 feet wide, has mossy walls extending as high as 90 feet. Along a boardwalk you can see verdant growths of ferns, mosses, and wildflowers. Four connecting paths lead to the Flume gorge and loop back past cascades, waterfalls, and huge glacial boulders. Allow about 1½ hours to complete this 2-mile walking circuit. Or you can take a bus, which crosses one of the oldest covered bridges in New Hampshire and leaves you within a 20-minute uphill walk of the gorge. *Open daily late May–late Oct. Admission charged.*

32 Morse Museum, Warren

26

Exit 32: 17 mi./30 min. West on Rte. 112, left on Rte. 118, then right on Rte. 25C. Exit 26: 23 mi./35 min. West on Rte. 25, left on Rte. 25C. As a rural youth, Ira Morse dreamed of hunting big game in Africa. In 1926, having established a successful shoe business, he went on the first of six safaris to the Dark Continent. Among the trophies taken by him and his son are lions, hyenas, antelopes, elephant tusks, and a remarkable group of artifacts including shields, weapons, a witch doctor's rattle, a tea set made from ostrich eggs, and Masai baskets so tightly woven that they hold water. A collection of over 200 pairs of shoes from around the world recalls his business interests. *Open daily mid-June–Labor Day.*

24 Science Center of New Hampshire

5 min. East on Rte. 25, left on Rte. 113; follow signs. Beginning in a wide meadow, a ¾-mile nature trail continues on to the fringes of the forest and across a marshy place where bridges traverse small waterfalls. Along the trail you'll get a close-up

18. *The inherent beauty of well-crafted functional objects is clearly depicted in these Shaker pieces exhibited in the meetinghouse. A child's chair is in the foreground.*

look at barred owls, porcupines, raccoons, bobcats, black bears, and white-tailed deer in their wooded enclosures. The Bear Facts House, a working beehive behind glass, and a community of voles are among other exhibits. *Open daily May–Oct. Admission charged.* 🪑🚶♿

23 Endicott Rock

18 mi./24 min. East on Rte. 104, right on Rte. 3, left on Rte. 11B. In 1652 Gov. John Endicott of the Massachusetts Bay Colony carved his name, and four of his companions cut their initials, on this rock to mark the head of the Merrimack River and to set one boundary of their patent. These incisions remain clearly visible, and the rock is now protected by a granite structure (built in 1892). Nearby is an attractive public beach, with a broad expanse of sand, offering fine lake swimming. *Open year-round. Admission charged.* 🪑🏊

18 Shaker Village, Canterbury

7 mi./14 min. Follow signs. "Put your hands to work and your hearts to God" is the Shaker creed embodied in this village dating from the end of the 18th century. Their buildings, furniture, tools, and household goods all share the distinctive elegance of pure function. Among their inventions are the first flat brooms, clothespins, and the circular saw. The 90-minute guided tours help to explain the Shaker beliefs and way of life. *Open Tues.–Sat., mid-May–mid-Oct. and holiday Mondays. Admission charged for tours.* 🪑♿

15W Concord, NH 03301

Chamber of Commerce, 244 N. Main St. (603) 224-2508. In the New Hampshire Historical Society's museum you'll see a pristine model of the stagecoach that carried Concord's name throughout the West in the 1800's. Here, too, are period rooms and changing exhibits of historical interest. The Statehouse, impressively domed and porticoed, is the oldest in America in which a legislature has continuously met.

Concord's most famous citizen was President Franklin Pierce, and his restored mansion is much as it was in the 1840's, when he and his family lived there. Another beautifully restored dwelling is the Upham-Walker House.

Several examples of New England workmanship, treasured for its superb quality, are displayed at the League of New Hampshire Craftsmen.

4 The Robert Frost Farm

4 mi./8 min. East on Rte. 102, right on Bypass 28; follow signs. This 1884 clapboard house where Robert Frost and his family lived for 11 years was bought for

4. This comfortable upholstered chair was the poet's favorite place to sit and read.

him in 1900 by his grandfather, who was concerned by his seeming lack of a goal in life. Though Frost worked the land and raised some chickens, he milked his one cow late at night and again at noon to avoid early rising—to the consternation of his neighbors. In the barn, which is attached to the house, there are photographs of the family, excerpts from the poet's work, and videotapes that give additional insight into the life of the four-time Pulitzer Prize winner. A self-guiding nature trail reveals some of the environment that so influenced Frost's work. *Open daily Memorial Day–mid-Oct. Admission charged.*

44 Lowell National Historical Park and Heritage State Park

11 mi./16 min. South on I-495 to Exit 36, north on Lowell Connector to Exit 5N, right on Thorndike St., right on Dutton St. The history of this 19th-century mill town provides a fascinating overview of the Industrial Revolution. In the early 1800's Francis Cabot Lowell established a textile industry along the Merrimack River, where Pawtucket Falls could provide the power needed to drive the looms. Among the earliest workers were New England farm girls willing to conform to the strict company rules. Later on, immigrants from abroad came here to work. Excellent tours and exhibits help to explain the complex relationships among capital, waterpower, machinery, and the working people.

Across from the visitor center, the state park's museum—a former stove factory—now traces the story of waterpower in Lowell with displays and exhibits illustrating the history of the river, canal construction, machinery design, and mill architecture. On summer tours of the mills and more than 5 miles of canals, members of a living-history staff assume the roles and accents of a farm family and Irish immigrants of the era. *Open daily except Thanksgiving Day, Christmas, and New Year's Day.* 🪑♿

26 Boston, MA 02199

Convention & Visitors Bureau, Prudential Plaza. (617) 536-4100. Few places are so rewarding to explore on foot as the central section of this historic city. In a matter of a few hours one can savor the spacious tree-studded greensward of the Common, the cobbled streets and elegant homes on Beacon Hill, the maze of narrow streets in the North End, and the bustling Quincy Market. You can wander at will or take the Freedom Trail, a self-guiding walking excursion past 16 historic sites that starts at an information booth in the Common.

Among the many highlights beyond the city center itself are the Museum of Fine Arts, the charmingly idiosyncratic Isabella Stewart Gardner Museum, the Arnold Arboretum, the Franklin Park Zoo, and across the Charles River, Harvard Yard and the busy streets of Cambridge.

18

9

15W

20

4

16

NH

MA

44

25

95

See N–S book, sec. 46.

26

90

See E–W book, sec. 9.

See N–S book, sec. 46.

95

End I-93

62. *The covering to protect the timbers gives the old bridges their unique charm.*

62 | Watson Bridge

8 mi./12 min. North on Rte. 1 to Littleton, right on Carson Rd. Lush rolling farmland flanks the approach to this 190-foot covered bridge across the south branch of the Meduxnekeag River. The honest, careful workmanship shows in its heavy struts, latticed sides, and double-plank floor. Although no longer used, the bridge has been well preserved. An adjacent modern bridge now carries the traffic here. *Open year-round.*

59 | Lumberman's Museum

10 mi./15 min. West on Rte. 159. Logging is still big business in this northern region of Maine, and its colorful past is preserved here in 10 buildings. Dioramas and two life-size replicas of early logging camps (one built without nails), plus a blacksmith's shop, sawmills, a shingle machine, and a barrel-making exhibit, show how loggers lived and worked. Displays present the hand tools used in logging, including adzes and broadaxes, and the pike poles, peaveys, and swingdingles used to break up logjams in the river. There are two gigantic Lombard steam log haulers, one circa 1910, a national historic mechanical engineering landmark. You can also see more than 900 vintage photographs that document the early history of lumbering. *Open Tues.–Sun. Memorial Day–Labor Day; Mon. holidays July–Aug.; weekends early Oct. Admission charged.*

58 / 56 | Grindstone Falls

Exit 58: 16.5 mi./35 min. South on Rte. 11. Exit 56: 10 mi./24 min. West on Rte. 157, north on Rte. 11. Driving this scenic route that parallels I-95 adds about half an hour to your trip. Here in central Maine, surrounded by a seemingly endless panorama of dense forest, the Penobscot River and this small waterfall can be a welcome change from the forested landscape. Although the river drops only 2 feet, the riffle over a curious diagonal formation of slate is a refreshing sight and sound. Tall white pines shade the picnic sites. *Open year-round.*

52 / 51 | Indian Island

Exit 52: 5 min. Left on Rte. 43 to Davis Court, left over bridge. Exit 51: 4 mi./10 min. Right on Rte. 2A, left on Rte. 2. Home of the Penobscot Indians, this is one of about 200 islands that they own in the Penobscot River and its branches. The early Penobscots used an ideographic writing system similar in some ways to ancient Egyptian hieroglyphics. And when the earliest known European explorers arrived in 1524, this tribe was already part of a powerful confederacy. Today they continue to govern themselves and send a representative to the state legislature, making theirs the oldest uninterrupted government in North America. Visitors can drive through the town and explore the small museum and the craft shops, which sell moccasins and jewelry. *Open year-round.*

45A | Bangor, ME 04401

Chamber of Commerce, 519 Main St. (207) 947-0307. The 31-foot statue of Paul Bunyan, complete with ax and peavey, is a fitting memorial to the hardy loggers who worked the Maine woods in the 1800's. By 1842 Bangor was the second biggest lumber port in America. Lumber barons' mansions can be seen on a walking tour of the Broadway Historic District. The tools of the trade are on display at the Maine Forest and Logging Museum. The Bangor Historical Society's Greek revival museum features period rooms.

31 | Augusta, ME 04330

Chamber of Commerce, 1 University Dr. (207) 623-4559. The most imposing building in this city is the statehouse, rising grandly above Capitol Park. Constructed of granite from nearby Hallowell, it was designed by Charles Bulfinch, the gifted 19th-century Boston architect. The adjacent state museum is devoted to exhibits of Maine's heritage and natural history. Facing Capitol Park is the spacious home of James Blaine, a presidential nominee in 1884, which now serves as the state executive mansion. Fort Western Museum, built in 1754 to withstand Indian attacks, has rooms furnished with historical pieces.

27 | Peacock Beach State Park

3 min. South on Rte. 201. One of the few places in central Maine offering public access to the water, this park is named for the 1801 Peacock Tavern, a stagecoach inn and trading post that stands near the entrance and is now in *The National Register of Historic Places.* Pleasant Pond in the park is popular for swimming and some of the best largemouth bass fishing in central Maine. *Open daily Memorial Day–Labor Day. Admission charged.*

22 | Maine Maritime Museum, Bath

12 mi./15 min. North on Rte. 1 to Bath business district, right on Washington St. Visitors guide themselves around this restored turn-of-the-century shipyard, where apprentices still learn the trade of boat building. Dioramas of a hypothetical lobster village, a life-size 1880 cannery, and period boats lashed to an indoor wharf illustrate the history and technology of lobstering. A 142-foot Grand Banks fishing schooner can be boarded. During the summer the excursion ship *Dirigo* takes regular 40-minute trips down the Kennebec River. There's a mill and joiner's shop, a caulking shed, and a small-craft center. A new Maritime History Building, adjacent to the museum shipyard, documents more than 400 years of coastal life.

Two miles north on Washington Street, the 1844 Sewall House contains ship models, scrimshaw, navigational instruments, and a hands-on room for children. *Shipyard open late May–mid-Oct.; house open year-round. Admission charged.* 🪑♿

8 | Portland, ME 04101

Chamber of Commerce, 142 Free St. (207) 772-2811. Although they are now boutiques and restaurants, the original waterfront shops and warehouses of the Old Port Exchange still recall the age of sail, when Portland was a great port and a center for shipbuilding. The city's marine heritage is further emphasized by cruises on Casco Bay; Portland Head Light, one of the oldest lighthouses on the coast of the Atlantic that is still operating; the Portland Observatory, a 19th-century guide to navigation from which there is a spectacular view; and on a more intimate scale, the fine collection of Winslow Homer seascapes in the art museum. Other attractive echoes of Portland's past can be seen in the 18th-century Wadsworth-Longfellow House, the Tate House, and the Victoria Mansion, a 19th-century architectural extravaganza.

7 | Two Lights State Park, Cape Elizabeth

9 mi./19 min. South on Rte. 1, left on Pleasant Hill Rd., left on Spurwink Rd. (Rte. 77), right on Two Lights Rd. A dramatic coastline, where huge waves crash onto odd rock formations called fissured slat slabs, makes this 41-acre park worth a visit in any weather. Slat-block staircases lead up a scenic trail flanked by bayberry and sumac; lady's slippers, columbines, and other blossoming wildflowers add color in the summer. *Open year-round. Admission charged in summer.* 🪑🚶🐟♿

7 | Crescent Beach State Park

7 mi./11 min. South on Rte. 1, left on Pleasant Hill Rd., left on Spurwink Rd. (Rte. 77). Here a mile-long sand beach with dunes and a gentle surf lies at the edge of a typical Maine wood. White pines, larches, and oaks shelter huge leather ferns and wildflowers; visitors may catch a glimpse of red foxes, woodchucks, and deer. *Open daily Memorial Day–Labor Day. Admission charged.* 🪑🏊♿

8. *Here at Portland Head is solid evidence that the "rockbound coast of Maine" is not just a cliché. The handsome lighthouse is considered to be a classic of its kind.*

If You Have Some Extra Time:

Acadia National Park

45A *43 mi./75 min.* In this vast preserve on Mt. Desert Island you will see, among other attractions, what is arguably the most dramatic conjunction of the Atlantic and New England's granite shore. Yet the surging sea and tide pools are but part of this watery realm of lakes, coves, ponds, and an impressive fjord.

The park's crowning glory is Cadillac Mountain, a great granite mass that rises 1,530 feet above the sea. From the summit in midsummer, you and your fellow early risers can be among the first persons in the United States to watch the sun come up. When daylight arrives, there are spectacular views of the indented shore, forested hills, rock outcrops, and low-lying islands far below in the seemingly endless sea.

At the visitor center, located at the park entrance just south of Hulls Cove, you can obtain detailed maps of the scenic Park Loop Road on the island and the 150 miles of trails for biking and hiking. Horse-drawn carriages and riding horses, which are available for rent, make good use of some 40 miles of carriage roads. You will find one of the most photographed lighthouses in New England at Bass Harbor Head, overlooking Blue Hill Bay on the southern tip of the island. *How to get there: east on Rte. 395, right on Rte. 1A to Ellsworth; continue on Rte. 1 and Rte. 3 to the park. Open year-round. Admission charged.*

See
N–S book,
sec. 44.

See
E–W book,
sec. 9.

1. Fort McClary State Historic Site

7 mi./12 min. South on Rte. 236, left on Rte. 103. The first fort on the strategic heights of Kittery Point, above the Maine side of the entrance to the Piscataqua River, was built in 1715 to keep New Hampshire tax collectors from imposing heavy duties on ships from Massachusetts. The present hexagonal, 2½-story, granite and wood blockhouse, constructed about 1844 against possible attacks by the British, marks the transition from earth and timber forts to stone, as required to withstand the impact of more powerful artillery. This, the last blockhouse built in Maine, was never attacked, and it never fired a shot. Now in *The National Register of Historic Places*, it was named for Maj. Andrew McClary, who fell at Bunker Hill in 1775. *Open daily Memorial Day–Labor Day.* 🏕

7. Portsmouth, NH 03801

Chamber of Commerce, 500 Market St. (603) 436-1118. The people of Portsmouth have succeeded in preserving and reconstructing much of their cultural and architectural heritage. Rewarding evidence can be seen on a walking tour of six impressive houses, dating from 1716 to the 19th century (map and tickets available at the Chamber of Commerce). It can also be seen on a visit to Strawbery Banke, an ambitious restoration, begun in the 1950's, of a historic waterfront community. The 10-acre site accommodates some 35 buildings, mostly 18th-century houses with period furnishings, craft shops, a museum, gardens, and frequent special events.

2. Rye Harbor State Park

10 mi./20 min. East on Rte. 51, left on Rte. 1A. Known locally as Ragged Neck, this small rocky peninsula is a haven for birds and a good spot for a picnic and a swim at the adjacent mile-long sandy beach. Lobster boats attract herring gulls and terns to the nearby Isle of Shoals. Nearer shore you are likely to see egrets, blue herons, marsh hawks, snowy owls, and yellowlegs. In summer, sailboats bob in the lee of a jetty where fishermen cast for bluefish, mackerel, and a species of flounder that is known as blackback. *Open year-round. Admission charged weekends May–late June; daily, late June–Labor Day; weekends, Labor Day–Columbus Day.* 🏕

2. Hampton Beach State Park

6 mi./12 min. East on Rte. 51, right on Rte. 1A. This unspoiled, mile-long white sand beach stretching between some bluffs and the sea offers a peaceful environment for picnickers, swimmers, and surf casters. Bird enthusiasts will see sandpipers and cormorants, together with several species of gulls and terns. *Open daily Memorial Day–Labor Day. Admission charged.*

32. *The workers who brought prosperity to Lowell are memorialized here in bronze.*

58. Salisbury Beach State Reservation

4 mi./8 min. East on Rte. 110 and Rte. 1A. Campers, fishermen, swimmers, and wildlife coexist peacefully in these 520 acres of dunes. Deer, foxes, and raccoons forage among scrub pine, beach plum, and bayberry trees, while surf fishermen land striped bass, shad, bluefish, flounder, and cod along the 4-mile beach. Birders may see bald eagles, harlequin ducks, and piping plovers, a threatened species.

In the summer, programs are presented on marsh-bird identification, tide-pool life, and insect habits. First-come, first-served campsites are filled fast on holiday weekends. *Open daily Apr.–mid-Oct. Admission charged.*

54. Richard T. Crane, Jr., Memorial Reservation

12 mi./20 min. East on Rte. 133, right on Rte. 1A to Ipswich, left on Argilla Rd. In an inspiring example of sharing the wealth, the unusually fine amenities of this 1,400-acre preserve can now be enjoyed by the public. The 59-room Great House faces a half-mile swath of greensward leading to the sea and 4 miles of white sand beach. There's a sunken Italian garden, a rose garden, the Casino, and a bowling green. The natural history of Crane Beach and Castle Neck can be explored along the Pine Hollow Interpretive Trail, for which an illustrated guide is available. *Grounds open year-round; house tours four times a year. Admission charged.*

32. Lowell National Historical Park and Heritage State Park

15 mi./25 min. North on Rte. 3, right on Lowell Connector to Exit 5N, right on Thorndike St., right on Dutton St. The history of this 19th-century mill town provides a fascinating survey of the Industrial Revolution. In the early 1800's, Francis Cabot Lowell established a textile industry along the Merrimack River, where Pawtucket Falls could provide power to drive the looms. Among the earliest workers were New England farm girls willing to conform to the strict company rules. Later on, immigrants from many foreign lands came here to work. A variety of tours and exhibits explains the complex relationships that developed among capital, waterpower, machinery, and the working people.

Across from the visitor center the state park's museum was originally a stove factory. It traces the overall history of waterpower in Lowell with a number of imaginative displays and exhibits illustrating the river's history along with canal construction, mill architecture, and machinery design. The foresight and energy of these individuals whose vision turned Lowell into a thriving manufacturing center are also acknowledged. On summer tours of the canals and mills, members of a living-history staff assume the roles and accents of a farm family and Irish immigrants of the era. *Open daily except Thanksgiving Day, Christmas, and New Year's Day.*

I-93–I-90. *Historic Faneuil Hall's marketplace is a colorful accent in a busy city.*

I-93 / I-90 Boston, MA 02199

I-93 exit: 13 mi./20 min. I-90 exit: 12 mi./20 min. Convention & Visitors Bureau, Prudential Plaza (617) 536-4100. Few places are so rewarding to explore on foot as this historic city. In only a few hours one can savor the spacious tree-studded Common, the cobbled streets and elegant homes on Beacon Hill, the maze of narrow streets in the North End, and the bustling Quincy Market. You can wander at will through the city or take the Freedom Trail, a self-guiding walking excursion that starts at a booth in the Common.

Among the many highlights beyond the center of the city are the Museum of Fine Arts, the charmingly idiosyncratic Isabella Stewart Gardner Museum, the Arnold Arboretum, the Franklin Park Zoo, and across the Charles River, Harvard Yard and the busy streets of Cambridge.

7B Bristol Blake State Reservation, Norfolk

7 mi./12 min. North on Rte. 140, right on Rte. 115, left on North St. Known locally as the Stony Brook Nature Center and Wildlife Sanctuary, this 300-acre birders' paradise of woods, ponds, and marshland is partly owned by the Massachusetts Audubon Society. Among more than 150 bird species that you might see here are the American bittern, common snipe, great blue heron, and wood duck. A butterfly garden contains coreopsis, veronica, and other flowers that attract these flying jewels. A trail guide identifies plants and explains the ecology along a 1-mile walk. *Open year-round. Admission free but donations encouraged.*

6A Watson Pond State Park, Taunton

9 mi./12 min. South on I-495 to Exit 9, right on Bay St. Swimming, picnicking, and fishing are the order of the day in this attractive 14-acre park. The picnic tables are nicely dispersed beside the beach and on the rolling terrain, and some are shaded by handsome white pines. Fishermen try for the hornpout (catfish), pickerel, eels, and bass weighing as much as 7 pounds. Everyone keeps an eye out for snapping turtles, which are extremely dangerous. *Open daily Memorial Day–late Oct. Admission charged.*

21 Providence, RI 02903

Convention and Visitors Bureau, 30 Exchange Ter. (401) 274-1636. Roger Williams, who founded the town that later became Rhode Island's capital, is honored in a 4½-acre memorial park as well as a larger park just south of town. The imposing statehouse, one of the most beautiful in America, is topped by the world's second largest unsupported dome. Other attractions include the Arcade, built in 1828 (the country's oldest indoor shopping center), the Providence Athenaeum, where original Audubon illustrations can be seen, and the Rhode Island School of Design's art museum. Many of the city's landmarks on Benefit, Benevolent, and Meeting streets can be seen on tape-recorded walking tours.

5 Arcadia Management Area

5 mi./8 min. South on Rte. 102, south on Rte. 3, right on Rte. 165, left on Arcadia Rd. Miles of marked trails and dirt roads, superb fishing, and two swimming ponds are among the many attractions of this 12,000-acre area. Boats and canoes may be launched on Breakheart Pond and Wood River to pursue bass, salmon, and trout. Beach Pond has bathhouse facilities, while Browning Mill Pond offers rocky, shaded promontories for picnicking. A popular destination for hikers and backpackers is scenic Stepstone Falls. *Open June–Labor Day. Admission charged.*

90 Mystic Seaport Museum

2 min. South on Rte. 27. The artistry and resourcefulness of 19th-century New England shipbuilders as well as sailors are handsomely illustrated by the 40-odd museum buildings and the museum harbor. Along the bustling waterfront working coopers, shipsmiths, and sailmakers demonstrate the skills on which a great maritime tradition was built. Among the historic ships moored at the docks is the *Charles W. Morgan*, the last remaining whaler. In the reconstructed houses and other buildings are exhibits of scrimshaw, ship models and carved figureheads, paintings, and other marine artifacts. *Open year-round. Admission charged.*

90. *Wooden sailing ships accentuate Mystic waterfront's 19th-century ambience.*

93

See N–S book, sec. 44.

25

7B
2

6A

19

MA
RI

21

23

5

26

RI
CT

90

10

95

82 Harkness Memorial State Park, Waterford

6 mi./17 min. South on Rte. 85, right on Jefferson Ave., right on Coleman St., left on Rte. 213. The broad lawns of the former estate of the philanthropist Edward Harkness attract picnickers, while strollers enjoy wandering through the formal Italian and Oriental gardens, informal rock gardens, and the large greenhouse, which is planted with cacti, ferns, and flowers. A vine-covered pergola offers visitors welcome shade on hot days. In the 42-room stone mansion, which will be closed until May 1990 for extensive renovations, a collection of watercolors of North American birds by Rex Brasher is featured. The furnishings are few, but photos reveal the opulence of the interior in the past. Servants' quarters will also be restored during the renovations. *Grounds open year-round; buildings open Memorial Day–Labor Day. Admission charged.*

69. *The eccentric characteristics of the exterior are amply sustained on the inside.*

69 Gillette Castle State Park

18 mi./30 min. North on Rte. 9, right on Rte. 82; follow signs. The medieval-style castle was designed and built (1914–19) by William Gillette, the noted actor who portrayed Sherlock Holmes on the stage for more than 30 years. The massive fieldstone structure, with a two-story living room 50 feet long, stands on a ledge high above the Connecticut River. Gillette devised intricate, hand-carved wooden doors, handles, and locks, as well as furniture that moves on tracks. In the third-floor reproduction of Holmes's Baker Street study, all is ready for afternoon tea. The veranda offers a spectacular river view, and hiking trails follow the route of Gillette's miniature railway, long since moved to an amusement park. *Open daily Memorial Day–Columbus Day; weekends only Columbus Day–mid-Dec. Admission charged.*

51 52 The Shore Line Trolley Museum, East Haven

Exit 51: 5 min. East on Rte. 1, right on Hemingway Ave., left on River St. Exit 52: 5 min. South on High St., left on Main St., right on Hemingway Ave., left on River St. A 3-mile ride on an antique trolley is a nostalgic reminder of how pleasant and efficient transportation by electric power can be. Stops include a carbarn where trolleys are housed and restored by master craftsmen. Among the prized examples you'll see a 1920 snow sweeper from the Third Avenue Elevated Line in New York City and a superbly refurbished 1911 open car designed for beach runs. *Open daily Memorial Day–Labor Day; weekends and holidays Sept., Oct., May; non-holiday weekends Dec.; Sun., Nov., Apr. Admission charged.*

47 New Haven, CT 06510

Convention & Visitor Bureau, 900 Chapel St. (203) 787-8367. The classic New England village green, laid out in 1638, still serves as common land and provides a setting for three handsome churches. Yale University, a major presence here, provides a variety of attractions. Connecticut Hall, circa 1750, is the oldest building on the Yale campus; the Yale University Art Gallery has a wide-ranging collection; and the Yale Center for British Art has a distinguished collection in a building designed by the noted architect Louis I. Kahn. The Yale University Collection of Musical Instruments includes more than 850 pieces, and the Peabody Museum of Natural History is noted for the imaginative exhibits in the Great Hall of Dinosaurs.

18 Sherwood Island State Park

2 min. South on Sherwood Island Connector. Sweeping lawns separate two beaches—totaling 234 acres—where the gentle surf and shallow waters make swimming ideal. Linden, juniper, mugho pine, and apple trees shade the picnic area. A stone jetty gives scuba divers access to deeper water. This is a good place to fly kites, play softball, toss a Frisbee, or lounge on the observation deck of the big pavilion. *Open year-round. Admission charged.*

7 Stamford Museum and Nature Center

6 mi./20 min. Headed south: west on N. State St., right on Washington Blvd. (Rte. 137), left on High Ridge Rd., left on Scofieldtown Rd. Headed north: north on Washington Blvd.; proceed as above. The former estate of Henri Bendel, the department store founder, is now open to the public. Here you'll find a 19th-century working farm with goats, sheep, and cattle. The Tudor-style stone mansion houses a fascinating variety of natural history displays, an art gallery, and a North American Indian room. There are changing exhibits as well. The 20th century is also represented here by a planetarium (open on Sunday afternoons) and by an observatory that is equipped with a powerful telescope (open on Friday evenings). *Open year-round. Admission charged.*

19 Rye Playland

3 min. South on Playland Pkwy. From 48 rides to fireworks, musical shows, and a seaside boardwalk, this venerable amusement park—now a national historic landmark—has something for everyone. After riding the roller coaster and bumper cars, you can stroll beside oak-shaded lawns lined with games of skill or chance. Young children enjoy the pony ride, the miniature railroad, and the carousel. Older ones can work off steam at a batting cage or with pedal boats and rowboats on the man-made lake. Swimming is available at a crescent-shaped beach and in a freshwater pool. *Open Tues.–Sun. mid-May–Labor Day. Admission charged.*

New York, NY 10019

1B

1A *Convention and Visitors Bureau, 2 Columbus Circle. (212) 397-8222.* The crowded diversity of the city can be overwhelming, but even a short visit will be rewarding if you decide in advance what you want to see. You might choose the spectacular views from the Empire State Building or the World Trade Center, or stroll on Fifth Avenue past Rockefeller Center, St. Patrick's Cathedral, and intriguing shop windows. Central Park might beckon, or Chinatown, Broadway, Greenwich Village, or the South Street Seaport. For museumgoers the choices are a challenge: will it be the Metropolitan, Whitney, Frick, or Guggenheim (all close to each other)? And there's also the American Museum of Natural History to consider. Other temptations are a boat ride in the harbor to Staten Island, or to the Statue of Liberty, or around the island of Manhattan. Be forewarned, however: the city is a difficult—or expensive—place to park a car.

13 Warinanco Park, Elizabeth

2 mi./7 min. West on Rte. 439 (Bayway Ave.), left on Rahway Ave. (Rte. 27). An oasis of greenery in the midst of Elizabeth's urban sprawl, this attractive park has unusually comprehensive facilities, which serve three adjacent communities and all of Union County as well. You'll find a pond stocked with catfish and bluegill, rental rowboats and pedal boats, a 2½-mile trail for jogging or biking, and a huge indoor skating rink. Whether your game is tennis, baseball, softball, cricket, horseshoes, or Frisbee, you'll find a field to suit your needs. Nature lovers can enjoy a stroll through the colorful flower gardens set amid tall oak, elm, and American beech trees. *Open year-round.*

8 Monmouth Battlefield State Park

10 mi./14 min. East on Rte. 33. During the Battle of Monmouth on June 28, 1778, the opposing commanders, Sir Henry Clinton and George Washington, personally directed their troops. The Continental Army, rigorously trained by Baron Friedrich von Steuben at Valley Forge, inflicted heavy casualties on the British. The legend of Molly Pitcher, who carried water to American soldiers and replaced her husband on a gun crew when he fell, originated here.

The 1,520-acre park includes the restored 18th-century house of John Craig, who participated in the battle. And at the visitor center audiovisual presentations and an illuminated diorama depict the day's action. Volunteers in period uniforms reenact the battle in late June each year. For the date call (201) 462-9616. There are trails for hiking, cross-country skiing, and horseback riding. Pond fishing is for children only. *Open year-round.*

CC Philadelphia, PA 19102

Center City exit: Visitors Center, 1625 JFK Blvd. (215) 636-1666. If you plan to stop in Philadelphia, don't be in a rush. Take time to do justice to Independence National Historical Park, which includes Independence Hall along with other historic structures on Independence Square. In the park you will view the Liberty Bell, Franklin Court, Carpenters' Hall, and several handsomely restored, period-furnished 18th-century houses, among other highlights on the 42-acre site. The Philadelphia Museum of Art and the Franklin Institute Science Museum are justly renowned. The city boasts a number of other museums, dedicated to such diverse subjects as Afro-American culture, Jewish history, antique toys, Wedgwood china, fire fighting, and the art of Norman Rockwell. There's also the American Swedish Museum, a medical museum, a Civil War museum, and the Please Touch Museum for Children.

CC Pomona Hall, Camden

Center City exit: 3 mi./10 min. West on Callow Hill St., left on 6th St.; cross Benjamin Franklin Bridge; continue on I-30, right on Kaighn Ave., left on Park Blvd. The elegant simplicity of the Quaker lifestyle is revealed throughout this handsome red brick Georgian house, built in 1726 by Joseph Cooper, Jr., a friend of Benjamin Franklin's. It was enlarged in 1788 and has recently been restored. The three-story building is furnished with some exquisite 18th- and 19th-century pieces, including a Hepplewhite sideboard, a Philadelphia tea table, Windsor chairs, a Garrett clock, and a Chippendale mirror. At the large kitchen fireplace, costumed guides demonstrate open-hearth cooking. *Open Sun.–Thurs. except Aug. Admission charged.*

CC. *A young citizen respectfully admires a venerable symbol of liberty for one and all.*

See N–S book, sec. 42.

See E–W book, sec. 25.

24

32

59

Headed south: to rejoin I-95, take NJ Tpk. Exit 7A; go west on I-195 then north on I-295

Headed north: to rejoin I-95, go south on I-295; east on I-195; then north on NJ Tpk.

See E–W book, sec. 32.

36

New Jersey Turnpike

5 George Read II House and Garden

4 mi./8 min. South on Rte. 141, left on Delaware St., left on 2nd St., right on Harmony St., right on The Strand. George Read II, lawyer and son of George Read, who was a signer of the Declaration of Independence and a framer of the Constitution, built this gracious brick mansion between 1797 and 1804 on the Delaware River. The house is a prime example of the federal style, with oversize doors and windows, wood carving, fine fireplaces and plasterwork, and fanlights. The 1840's garden, with winding brick paths, boxwood, and lilies, especially brings to mind a long-vanished time of elegance and charm. *Open Tues.–Sun. Mar.–Dec.; weekends only Jan.–Feb. Admission charged.*

89 Susquehanna State Park

6 mi./10 min. West on Rte. 155, right on Rte. 161, right on Rock Run Rd. "Heaven and earth seemed never to have agreed better to frame a place for man's commodious and delightful habitation," wrote Capt. John Smith when he came here in 1608. Many followed to settle the rich valley, leaving traces that can be seen today, among them the remains of a 45-mile canal dug in the late 1700's, a 1794 gristmill, and a tollhouse for the river bridge. At Steppingstone Museum—a cluster of shops and farm buildings in the park—craftspeople demonstrate many tools and skills common in earlier eras. *Park open year-round; museum open weekends May–Sept; mill open weekends and holidays Memorial Day–Labor Day. Admission charged for museum.*

61 Baltimore, MD 21202

Office of Promotion and Tourism, 34 Market Place, Suite 310. (301) 752-8632. The American institutions honored here with museums and displays include railroads, streetcars, volunteer fire departments, the flag, and the national anthem. Baltimore's marine heritage is recalled with the U.S. frigate *Constellation*, the oldest U.S. warship still afloat, and a maritime museum; there's also a superb aquarium. The renaissance of Baltimore's inner harbor area is most notable in Harborplace, a large glass-enclosed complex of stores, markets, and restaurants. The Top of the World, which is also on the waterfront, has an observation deck from which there's a fine view of the harbor and surrounding region.

19 U.S. Naval Academy Museum, Annapolis

21 mi./25 min. East on Rte. 50, right on Rte. 70 (Rowe Blvd.), left on College Ave., right on King George St., left on Maryland Ave. The stirring story of America's naval achievements around the world is recounted with a wealth of displays in this dignified 1939 white brick building. On exhibit is the U.S.S. *Missouri's* mess table, on which the Japanese surrender was signed in 1945. Collections include model ships, commemorative coins and medals, paintings, and more than a thousand battle prints of major naval engagements. Flags include Commodore Oliver Perry's 1813 "Don't Give Up the Ship" banner.

Be sure to take the self-guiding walking tour of the historic campus, concluding with a visit to the lovely domed chapel. Also explore the adjoining town of Annapolis, which is filled with centuries-old buildings. Among those open for tours are the elegant Georgian home of Declaration of Independence signer William Paca and the colonial-era state capitol, where George Washington resigned his commission as the commander-in-chief of the Continental Army. *Open daily except Thanksgiving Day, Christmas, and New Year's Day.*

19 Washington, DC 20005

Convention & Visitors Association, 1575 I (Eye) St. NW, Suite 250. (202) 789-7000. The number of marvelous places to see here is so overwhelming that you should not begin without a plan. The three major centers are Capitol Hill, the Mall, and the White House area. The Capitol, the nation's greatest architectural monument, has evolved over 150 years to become the majestic building we see today; the interior is a vast treasure house of paintings and statuary. The Library of Congress, the Supreme Court, and the U.S. Botanic Garden are in the area.

Highlights on the Mall include the magnificent Lincoln Memorial, the Washington Monument, the National Gallery of Art, and the Smithsonian Institution, a complex of buildings that includes the Museum of Natural History, the Museum of American History, and the spectacular National Air and Space Museum. Near the White House you will see, along with the famous mansion itself, Lafayette Square, St. John's Church, the Octagon House, the Renwick Gallery, and the Corcoran Gallery, noted for its superb collection of American art.

1 Mount Vernon

Exit 1: 9 mi./20 min. South on Mt. Vernon Memorial Hwy. Exit 56: 9 mi./16 min. East on Backlick Rd., left on Rte. 1, right on Mt. Vernon Memorial Hwy. George Washington's home from 1754 until his death in 1799 is one of our

1–56. *The father of his country enjoyed a fine view of the Potomac from his front porch.*

country's most beloved shrines. The 11 meticulously restored original buildings include a smokehouse, a cookhouse, a stable, and the servants' hall. In the mansion, largely furnished with original pieces, the vibrant wall colors may come as a surprise, but they have been authenticated. Among the furnishings are a 1785 bust of the first president by Houdon and a porcelain tea service used by Martha Washington. Other highlights are the formal gardens, the tomb of Washington, and the museum. *Open year-round. Admission charged.* ♿

54 Gunston Hall

5 mi./10 min. North on Rte. 1, right on Gunston Rd.; follow signs. This is the elegant plantation mansion (circa 1755) of George Mason, one of our nation's most astute political minds. As author of the Virginia Declaration of Rights, father of the Bill of Rights, and one of the framers of the U. S. Constitution (among other notable tracts), Mason influenced many later documents in this country and abroad with his concepts of individual rights. His home reflects his intrinsic beliefs in order, balance, and proportion. It is noted for the beautiful 18th-century interior wood carvings. On the grounds you will find formal gardens, ancient boxwood—set out by Mason—a schoolhouse, a kitchen area, and a nature trail. *Open daily except Christmas. Admission charged.* ♿ 🚶 ♿

45 Fredericksburg, VA 22401

Visitor Center, 706 Caroline St. (703) 373-1776. The past is a palpable presence in this small town, which spawned heroes of the American Revolution and played a significant role in the Civil War. George Washington worked in the apothecary shop that is now a museum, and visitors may tour the house Washington bought for his mother in 1772. In the law office of his friend James Monroe you can see the desk on which the famous Monroe Doctrine was signed. Kenmore, the beautiful home of Washington's brother-in-law, has been restored, as has the Rising Sun, a popular 18th-century tavern. During the Civil War the town changed hands seven times.

45 Fredericksburg/Spotsylvania National Military Park

5 min. East on Rte. 3; follow signs. Spreading for miles on both sides of the interstate here is the greatest concentration of battlefields on the North American continent. Between December 1862 and May 1864, four savage engagements were fought in which Union attempts to crush Lee's Confederates ended in failure—at a combined cost of 100,000 casualties. It was here that Gen. Stonewall Jackson was by accident mortally wounded by his own men. To understand the sequence of the momentous events, begin at the visitor center in Fredericksburg. It requires a full day and a half to tour all the sites; there are interpretive trails to walk as well as a 100-mile auto route with numbered stops. Four historic buildings, including the Jackson Shrine, can also be visited. *Open daily except Christmas and New Year's Day.* 🚶 ♿

40 Kings Dominion

1 min. East on Rte. 30. It's five theme parks in one. Shock-Wave, the stand-up roller coaster, begins with a 95-foot drop, races in a 360° loop, and ends with a triple corkscrew—just one of the more than 40 rides here. The less intrepid can get their feet wet on one of several spectacular water rides; chime in for a sing-along; stroll, snack, and shop along International Street; mingle with Yogi Bear and pals; view some 50 species of wild animals from the Safari monorail; or look down on it all from atop a 330-foot-tall replica of the Eiffel Tower. *Open daily June–Labor Day; weekends late Mar.–May and mid-Sept.–mid-Oct. Admission charged.* 🏕 ♿

10A Richmond, VA 23219

10 *Convention and Visitors Bureau, 300 E. Main St. (804) 782-2777.* Although the imperatives of today are stylishly acknowledged at Shockoe Slip and the Sixth Street Marketplace, proud memories of the Old South are found throughout this state capital, once the Confederacy's capital. The capitol building is a handsome classic design selected by Thomas Jefferson. On Monument Ave., paved with hand-

If You Have Some Extra Time:

Colonial Williamsburg

11 **50 mi./70 min.** In this first and finest restoration of an early American town, one can come as close as is possible in the 20th century to experiencing the scope and character of colonial life in the 1700's. The main thoroughfare is the mile-long Duke of Gloucester St., which runs from the Capitol to the College of William and Mary (this country's second oldest college). Throughout this 173-acre community, shops, taverns, homes, public buildings, and a royal governor's palace are authentically restored. Wheelwrights, blacksmiths, cabinetmakers, candlemakers, bakers, bootmakers, gunsmiths, weavers, and many other shopkeepers and artisans in colonial dress explain their trades. Live sheep graze on the village green. In the blissful quiet the rhythmic clip-clop of carriage horses reinforces the illusion of a less complex and crowded time. *How to get there: east on I-64, right on Rte. 132; follow signs. Open year-round. Admission charged.*

laid brick, statues of Confederate heroes vie with stately houses for attention. Other historic highlights are St. John's Church, the Wickham-Valentine House, and the John Marshall House. Attractions of more recent vintage include the Virginia Museum of Fine Arts, the Richmond Children's Museum, the Museum of the Confederacy, and the Science Museum of Virginia, all excellent examples of their kind.

MD
VA
1
8
56
3
54
31
45
36
40
23
64
See E–W book, sec. 35
11
64
1
10A
0
10
23
95

3 | Centre Hill Museum, Petersburg

2 min. West on E. Washington St., right on N. Adams St. Several distinct architectural periods are reflected in this 1823 brick mansion. The original owner, English tobacco planter Robert Bolling, favored the federal design. His son added Greek revival features in 1850, and the third owner, Charles Davis, included colonial revival touches at the turn of the century.

Guided tours of the first and second floors are given. Early photographs of its owners and of the mansion's interior (also an exterior shot by Mathew Brady) are on display on the first floor. Spacious, beautifully appointed and maintained second-floor rooms attest to Davis's appreciation of the better things of life—including a shower stall with 13 heads. *Open daily except holidays. Admission charged.*

3 | Old Blandford Church, Petersburg

2 min. East on Wythe St., right on Crater Rd. Completed in 1735 and enlarged in 1752, this simple brick church served as a Confederate hospital during the siege of Petersburg, and some 30,000 soldiers were buried in the adjacent cemetery. In 1901 a group of local women were delegated to develop a fitting tribute. They wisely commissioned Louis Comfort Tiffany to design a set of 14 memorial windows of stained glass; as his personal contribution, Mr. Tiffany added a 15th window. This exquisite grouping, a rare American treasure, remains a luminous memorial to a tragic time. *Open daily except holidays.* ♿

3 | Petersburg National Battlefield

5 min. East on Rte. 36. Union general Ulysses S. Grant attacked Petersburg (a rail center important to the Confederates) in June 1864 and succeeded in cutting two rail lines. Gen. Robert E. Lee realized that if Petersburg fell, Richmond and the South were doomed. For 10 months the Confederate forces withstood the longest siege on American soil, but Petersburg finally fell in April 1865, forcing Lee to surrender a week later at Appomattox. Today you can explore the earthworks and battle-scarred

3. *A battlefield medical tent and table are ready to fold and move on short notice.*

terrain along a numbered auto route. History comes alive as uniformed soldiers re-enact daily life in a typical Union camp, or a fast-moving gun crew brings a cannon into action and opens fire. *Open daily except Thanksgiving Day and Christmas. Admission charged for museum.* ⛱♿

168 | Historic Halifax State Historic Site

5.5 mi./9 min. East on Rte. 903, left on Pittsylvania Ave., left on Norman St., right on Rte. 301. Founded in 1760, the river port of Halifax soon became a social and commercial center for the Roanoke Valley; it was the scene of significant political events during the American Revolution and also served as a supply depot and recruiting center during that war.

Of the remaining original buildings, the circa 1760 Owens House is the oldest; it contains several antiques of the period, including a local 1760 Halifax County corner chair. The federal-style Sally-Billy House (c. 1808) and the late 18th-century Eagle Tavern can also be seen, along with the excavated foundation of a 1762 Georgian house, which is now enclosed and protected within a museumlike structure. A museum at the visitor center displays artifacts and dioramas that document the changing fortunes of the town. *Open daily Apr.–Oct.; Tues.–Sun. Nov.–Mar.* ⛱♿

150 | Medoc Mountain State Park

11 mi./15 min. West on Rte. 44, right on Rte. 48, left on Rte. 1002. Here on the edge of the piedmont plains, a granite ridge resisted the glacial action that scoured out the lowlands to the east. A number of trails wind through the 2,300-acre park and reveal vegetation and wildlife indigenous to both ecosystems. On the 3-mile Summit Trail, loblolly and other pines are seen beside oaks and chestnuts. Pink lady's slipper, trailing arbutus, mountain laurel, and several other shrubs and flowers flourish. Among the many resident and migrating birds are red-tailed hawks, great horned owls, indigo buntings, and goldfinches. Fishermen come primarily for pickerel, bass, catfish, and gar. *Open year-round.*
⛱ ⛺ 🚐 🚶 🎣

138 | Rocky Mount Children's Museum

5 mi./10 min. East on Rte. 64 bypass, right on Rte. 64 (business), left on Beal St., left on Bryant St., left on Gay St. Live animals, dioramas of the local environment, a planetarium, and a botanical garden are combined here to help children and others gain a better understanding of science, history, and ecology. Evidence of the Tuscarora Indian presence is presented with arrowheads and other artifacts. Highlights include some of Thomas Edison's inventions and miniature horse-drawn vehicles. *Open daily mid-Mar.–mid-Oct., Mon.–Fri. mid-Oct.–mid-Mar. except holidays.* ♿

107 | Charles B. Aycock Birthplace State Historic Site

13 mi./18 min. North on Rte. 301, right on Rte. 222, right on Rte. 117, left on Rte. 1542. This modest unpainted building was the birthplace and early home of a farm boy who grew up to become a progressive and respected governor of North Carolina. The kitchen fireplace and parlor, and the barn with granary, tools, and equipment, help to illustrate life on the farm a hundred years ago. Living-history programs with the original tools and methods re-create how crops were planted and harvested, food prepared, and cloth spun and woven. *Open Tues.–Sun. Nov.–Mar.* ⛱

55 Fort Bragg, Fayetteville

40 *Exit 55: 10 mi./20 min. West on Rte. 301 (I-95 business), right on Rte. 24, left on Randolph St. Exit 40: 15 mi./30 min. North on Rte. 301 (I-95 business), left on Owens Dr. (becomes All-American Frwy.), right on Gruber Rd., left on Rte. 24, left on Randolph St.* Named after Confederate general Braxton Bragg, the post was established in 1918 to train artillery troops for World War I. In 1942 a new kind of soldier, the paratrooper, was trained here. Today the post accommodates the headquarters of the XVIII Airborne Corps, including the 82nd Airborne Division. It is also the home of the Special Forces (the Green Berets). From the visitor center a self-guiding tour passes 14 stops with signs interpreting this vast installation. A museum honors the 82nd Airborne Division; and unconventional means of war, from the Revolution onward, is the unusual theme of the JFK Special Warfare Museum. *Base open year-round; Special Warfare Museum open Tues.–Sun. except Thanksgiving Day, Christmas, and New Year's Day; Airborne Div. Museum open Tues.–Sun. except federal holidays.* ♿

193 Little Pee Dee State Park

13 mi./20 min. East on Rte. 57, left on Rte. 1722. In this park, which is named for the Pedee Indians, who once lived in this area, a 54-acre lake provides swimming in a designated area. On the half-mile nature trail through various kinds of pine and oak, bird fanciers may spot the endangered red-cockaded woodpecker and many other species. Rental boats are available. *Open daily mid-Mar.–mid-Oct., Thurs.–Mon. mid-Oct.–mid-Mar.* ⛽ ⛺ 🚐 🚶 🎣 🐟 ♿

170 Florence Air and Missile Museum

8 mi./10 min. South on Rte. 327, right on Rte. 76; follow signs. A World War II V-2 rocket, a B-26 flown by U.S. airmen in three wars, and an F-11F retired from service with the Blue Angels (the navy's precision flying team) are among the more than three dozen combat aircraft and missiles to be seen here. Exhibits trace developments in aviation and space from the beginning of U.S. air warfare in France in 1918 to the space voyages of the Apollo project and the *Challenger* tragedy. *Open year-round. Admission charged.* ♿

164 Florence Museum of Art, Science, History

4 mi./12 min. South on Rte. 52, left on Rte. 76 (W. Palmetto St.), left on Graham St. to Spruce St. A 26-room former residence in the international style houses an unusual collection that started in the 1920's with 78 pieces of Hopi Indian pottery. Over the years the museum has added Greek and Roman antiquities, textile, ceramic, and bronze items from several Chinese dynasties, African folk art, and American works of art. The South Carolina Hall of History and the museum grounds feature articles that are of particular significance in local history; these include the old town bell and the propellers from a Confederate cruiser. *Open Tues.–Sat. and P.M. Sun. except Aug. and holidays.*

164 NMPA Stock Car Hall of Fame, Darlington

8 mi./11 min. North on Rte. 52, left on Rte. 34/151. Located at the Darlington Raceway, this collection of stock cars and trophies won by the men who drove them provides an overview of life on the race track and glory at the finish line. In the museum—the dream of a famous driver, Little Joe Weatherly—you'll see record-breaking engines as well as illegal parts of cars that were found to be not "stock." Of all the displays, the most thrilling is a race simulator, where you sit in the driver's seat of a stock car and screech through two filmed laps of an actual race flashing on a screen just beyond your hood. *Open daily except Thanksgiving Day and Christmas. Admission charged.* ♿

146 Lynches River State Park

24 mi./35 min. South on Rte. 341, continue on Rte. 403, left on Rte. 541, left on Rte. 52, left on Rte. 21/147. Part of a 19th-century stagecoach route has become a 2-mile nature trail in this forest of longleaf and loblolly pines and scrub oaks where deer and raccoons may be seen. An Olympic-size swimming pool and softball field invite more active pursuits. *Open daily beginning of daylight saving time–mid-Sept., Thurs.–Mon. rest of year. Admission charged for pool.* ⛽ ⛺ 🚶 🏊 🐟 ♿

193. *Considering the relative size of the craft and the fisherman, it would seem that only catches of a modest size are to be expected in the Little Pee Dee River near the park.*

40 — See E–W book, sec. 42.

55

15

40

49

NC / SC

193

23

170

6

164

18

20 — See E–W book, sec. 47.

146

11

95

See
N–S book,
sec. 37.

135 Woods Bay State Park

12 mi./17 min. East on Rte. 378, left on Rte. 301, left on Woods Bay Rd. The park includes one of the Carolina bays, egg-shaped geologic depressions that occur on the South Atlantic coastal plain. Some of the bays are dry, but this one is flooded and supports a wide variety of wildlife and vegetation. The Mill Pond, adjoining the bay, has a nature trail through stands of oak, pine, tupelo, dogwood, sweet gum, and cypress. Warblers, ducks, herons, wood-peckers, and fish-eating anhingas inhabit the area. A cypress swamp, where alligators live, can be investigated from the safety of a boardwalk or a rented canoe. *Open Thurs.–Mon.*

135 Williams-Brice Museum/ Archives, Sumter
122

Exit 135: 16 mi./27 min. West on Rte. 378 and Rte. 76 (becomes Liberty St.), right on N. Washington St. Exit 122: 20 mi./30 min. North on Rte. 521 and Rte. 15, left on Liberty St., right on N. Washington St. More than 200 years of county history are celebrated here. In a 19th-century mansion you'll find paintings and artifacts from the Revolutionary days, including a 1796 Rembrandt Peale portrait of a local hero, Gen. Thomas Sumter, along with Confederate muskets, knives, and other trophies, as well as chandeliers, fine furniture, ornate moldings, and Oriental rugs. In the garden a log cabin, built circa 1760, reveals a more humble way of life. *Museum open Tues.–Sat. and P.M. Sun.; archives open Wed.–Sat. Admission free but donations encouraged.*

135 Swan Lake Iris Gardens, Sumter
122

Exit 135: 18 mi./29 min. West on Rte. 378 and Rte. 76, (becomes Liberty St.). Exit 122: 14 mi./26 min. North on Rte. 521 and Rte. 15, left on Liberty St. Graceful swans glide along the ebony swamp waters of a lake surrounded by colorful plantings of Japanese irises; cypress trees rise from the water, and the sweet-scented breeze rustles the leaves. Six of the world's eight swan species live here: the black Australian, mute, whooper, black-necked, coscoroba, and trumpeter. The peak flowering season is in late May, when the city of Sumter holds its annual Iris Festival; but taking a slow stroll on the sandy path beside the water in this 125-acre garden is a sensuous delight at any time of the year. *Open year-round.*

98 Santee State Park

5 min. West on Rte. 6; follow signs. The fishing in Lake Marion, which is fed by the Santee River, is world-renowned, and state records were set here with a 55-pound striped bass and a 73-pound blue catfish. Bream, crappie, and rockfish also provide good sport, and you can rent a boat and buy bait and tackle in the park. Enticements for non-fishermen include tennis, swimming, and boating. Pedal boats and bicycles are for rent, and there's a 4-mile bike path. Three nature trails invite walkers into the wooded realm of rabbits, squirrels, deer, and birds of many kinds. A nature center offers daily activities in summer. *Park open year-round; day-use area open mid-Mar.–mid-Oct. Admission charged in summer.*

98. *Some rather impressive equipment has been employed in capturing this bass.*

68 Colleton State Park

5 min. East on Rte. 61, left on Rte. 15. The Edisto River is the dominant feature in this 38-acre park. There's no swimming, but fishing is allowed. In the summer the programs for children include talks on river ecology, astronomy, reptiles, and the identification of plants. There are hiking trails beneath a dense canopy of sweet gums, live oaks, tupelo gums, and pines. Here you might see raccoons and deer. Listen for the jungle cry of the pileated wood-peckers, which nest here along with barred owls, cardinals, Carolina wrens, and jays. *Open daily Apr.–late Oct.; Thurs.–Mon., late Oct.–Mar.*

57 Tour of Historic Walterboro

4 min. South on Rte. 64 and Rte. 15 to Chamber of Commerce, 213 Jefferies Blvd. In 1784 low-country rice planters began building summer cottages here. A driving tour offers views of some 50 structures dating from the early 1800's to 1931. Look for the 1824 Glover-McLeod House with camellia gardens, carriage house, slave cabin, and stable. There are four churches and three municipal buildings open to the public, including the Old Colleton County Jail, which looks like a miniature castle, and the Colleton County Courthouse, both in *The National Register of Historic Places. Open daily except holidays.*

17 Savannah, GA 31499

Visitors Center, 301 W. Broad St. (912) 944-0456. The citizens of Savannah are justly proud of their city and their success in preserving, maintaining, and improving a remarkable heritage. The Historic Landmark District, the largest such area in the United States, includes the orderly grid of streets and squares originally laid out by Gen. James Oglethorpe in 1733. More than 1,000 historic homes grace this area and the adjacent Victorian district. Among them the visitor will find superb examples of Georgian, Regency, federal, Greek revival, Gothic revival, and Victorian architecture. Mapped tours are available for driving or walking, and bicycles can be rented.

15 Fort McAllister State Historic Park

10 mi./14 min. East on Rte. 144 and Spur Rte. 144. Ft. McAllister, a restored Confederate earthwork fort, is the centerpiece of this 1,700-acre park on the Ogeechee River. In 1863 the fort withstood a series of bombardments by Union ironclads, but in 1864 General Sherman took it from the land side, thus ending his march to the sea and causing the fall of Savannah. On a self-guiding tour you can see earthworks, a hot-shot furnace (used for heating cannonballs, which could create fires when they hit wooden ships), powder magazines, and three cannons. A museum exhibit includes a movie recounting the history of the fort. *Open year-round. Admission charged.*

10 Fort King George State Historic Site

4 mi./7 min. East on Rte. 251, right on Rte. 17, north on Rte. 99, left on McIntosh Rd. From 1721 until 1727 a small garrison of British soldiers occupied a cypress block-house that was built here to discourage the Spanish and French from colonizing the land along the Altamaha River. In addition to the site of the fort, visitors can see the locations of a large Indian village and a Spanish mission and the ruins of three sawmills. The museum recaptures the variety of events here with Indian artifacts, dioramas of daily life, and sawmill displays. *Open Tues.–Sat. Admission charged.*

6 Fort Frederica National Monument

17 mi./31 min. East on Rte. 84, left over bridge to Rte. 17. In 1736 Gen. James Oglethorpe started to build a fort on St. Simons Island to keep the Spanish from the colony he had established in Georgia. The fort, designed for the wilderness, was named for George II's only son. It briefly supported a thriving walled town, but in 1749, 7 years after the Spanish were repulsed, the garrison was disbanded. The town declined, and after a fire in 1758 it all but disappeared. An introductory film and a museum, as well as self-guiding and guided tours, help to explain the story of

95. *The oldest house has seen the flags of Spain, Britain, the U.S., and the Confederacy.*

this frontier post, now reduced to foundations and ruined barracks. *Open daily except Christmas. Admission charged.*

2 Crooked River State Park and Tabby Sugar Works

8 mi./13 min. to park, 6 mi./8 min. to sugar works. East on Rte. 40 to park signpost, east on unmarked road to second park signpost, left on Spur Rte. 40. A wooded 500-acre park along the Crooked River includes a nature trail with a boardwalk over an Indian kitchen midden. There's a swimming pool and a miniature golf course, and birders are asked to help add to an already extensive list of birds sighted in the area. Nearby is the ruin of a pre–Civil War sugar mill built of tabby—an early building material composed of lime, sand, and water. *Open year-round.*

117 Jacksonville, FL 32202

Convention & Visitors Bureau, 33 S. Hogan St. (904) 353-9736. The bend in the St. John's River here has been a crossing place and focal point since prehistoric times. Today the river can be enjoyed from either side. Jacksonville Landing, on the north side, has stores, markets, and restaurants. Riverwalk, on the opposite side, features restaurants, entertainment, and a boardwalk that is more than a mile long.

The Cummer Gallery of Art, the Jacksonville Museum of Arts and Sciences, the Jacksonville Art Museum, the Jacksonville Fire Museum, and the Lighthouse Museum provide a wealth of objects for perusal.

95 St. Augustine, FL 32084

Chamber of Commerce, 52 Castillo Dr. (904) 829-5681. When the United States purchased Florida in 1821, St. Augustine had been under Spanish rule for 2½ centuries—a legacy that is still being preserved and enhanced. The most dramatic original structure is the Castillo de San Marcos (1672–95). Although the stone fortress has been attacked and besieged, its massive walls have never been breached.

St. Augustine also boasts America's oldest house and store. The latter is a museum with a reputed 100,000 antique artifacts. In the old Spanish Quarter with its narrow streets and walled gardens there are 10 restored 18th-century houses and a blacksmith's shop that can be visited.

The Lightner Museum is remarkable for its collections of American, European, and Oriental art, cut crystal, Tiffany glass, and mechanical musical instruments.

15

38

10

19

6

26

2   GA
     FL

30

117
10

See
E–W book,
sec. 55.

37

95

5

95

93
91
92
14
91
17
88
8
86
12
84
22
79
38
71
23

93 Marineland of Florida

91 *Exit 93: 14 mi./17 min. East on Rte. 206, right on Rte. A1A. Exit 91: 17 mi./25 min. East on Rte. 100, left on Rte. A1A.* Playful otters, penguins, flamingos, and electric eels are among the entertainers at this imaginative attraction. But dolphins dominate the show as they jump through hoops, pitch balls to batters, score baskets, and even bring their books to school. Many marine species, including sharks and turtles, can be viewed and photographed through windows at two oceanariums. A nature walk, marina, boardwalk, and a seashell shop and museum are also featured here, along with an innovative play area for youngsters. *Open year-round. Admission charged.*

92 Faver-Dykes State Park

3 min. North on Rte. 1, right on Faver-Dykes Rd. This 752-acre recreation area and wilderness preserve, still unspoiled and seemingly remote, retains the tranquillity of a virgin forest. It stretches along the marshy shores of Pellicer Creek, a stream popular with fishermen, who come here to try for trout, redfish, flounder, and blue crabs. A boat ramp is provided. Several nature trails wind through stands of longleaf pines, palmettos, and live oaks, which provide shelter for deer, wild turkeys, foxes, and even bobcats, and offer shade along the marsh, inhabited by waterfowl, wading birds, and alligators. *Open year-round. Admission charged.*

88 Ormond Beach and Tomoka State Park

Beach: 5 mi./11 min. Park: 8 mi./13 min. East on Rte. 40, left on N. Beach Rd. The 400-year-old live oaks of Tomoka have witnessed the rich history of this peninsula. When the Spanish arrived here in 1605, they found a Timucuan Indian village. In 1763, when Florida became British, an indigo plantation was founded at this spot; the ruins can still be seen. Today, as nature covers the footprints of the past, visitors can enjoy camping, fishing, and boating. The brackish water of the Tomoka River yields speckled trout, sea bass, and snook.

In autumn manatees, endangered marine mammals weighing up to 2,000 pounds, come here to browse on underwater vegetation. Nearby Ormond Beach attracts both swimmers and surfers. *Open year-round. Admission charged.*

84 New Smyrna Sugar Mill Ruins State Historic Site

5 min. East on Rte. 44, right on Mission Dr. The high price of sugar, the low price of Florida land, and slave labor led New York businessmen William Depeyster and Henry Cruger to this spot in 1830, where they established a sugar plantation and mill. The mill and outbuildings were destroyed in 1835 in the first action of the Second Seminole War. The plantation and the East Coast sugar industry never recovered from the Indians' revenge for the taking of their land. Today the ruins' weathered walls and elegant arches made of coquina—a local stonelike formation of sand, shells, and corals—are all that remain. Plaques throughout the ruins describe the various steps in the demanding process of making sugar and molasses in the 19th century. *Open year-round.*

79. *These space age artifacts have a strange and compelling sculptural beauty.*

79 Kennedy Space Center

12 mi./15 min. East on Rte. 50, right on Rte. 405; follow signs to Spaceport USA. The first stop at this huge complex is Kennedy Space Center's Spaceport USA, a villagelike area that provides an introduction to the wonders of space travel. (In case you forgot your camera, you may borrow one without charge at the information center.) Guided tours include the Gallery of Spaceflight Museum and Galaxy Center, where you will see examples of space launch hardware and various films, including *The Dream Is Alive*, which re-creates the sights and sounds of spaceflight on a screen 5½ stories high. The Rocket Garden displays earlier rockets and launch vehicles.

A bus tour takes visitors to the Mercury and Gemini launch sites at Cape Canaveral Air Force Station; another tour visits Kennedy Space Center itself. *Open daily except Christmas. Admission charged for some programs.*

71 Brevard Zoo, Melbourne

2 min. East on Rte. 192. Feed for birds and mammals is available at this small but well-cared-for zoo, and the apes and monkeys, including gibbons, capuchins, and stump-tailed macaques, put on an especially good show to attract their fair share. Among the big cats to be seen are lions, a panther, a leopard, and a jaguar. The huge brown Kodiak bear dwarfs his black-furred cousin, which is also in residence here. The abundance of birds includes peafowl, which roam at large, ostrichlike rheas, African crowned cranes, and a sizable assortment of parrots and parakeets. *Open year-round. Admission charged.*

69 McLarty/Sebastian Inlet State Recreation Area

Visitor center: 16.5 mi./20 min. East on Rte. 512, right on Rte. 510, left on Rte. A1A. Some artifacts from a Spanish fleet that was wrecked in the shallows here in 1715 are displayed in the visitor center. Today the incoming breakers attract surfers; fishermen come for redfish, sharks, pompano, and bluefish, and clamming is also popular. The 576-acre recreation area,

If You Have Some Extra Time: Walt Disney World Resort

86
79
Exit 86: 41 mi./55 min. Exit 79: 38 mi./55 min. To walk through the turnstile is to enter a world as you would like it to be—immaculately clean, beautifully landscaped, perfectly maintained, safe, orderly, and filled with happy people. In the Magic Kingdom, an enchanting Cinderella Castle is surrounded by Frontierland, Tomorrowland, Adventureland, Fantasyland, and more. Fifteen minutes away by car or monorail is Epcot Center, with Future World and World Showcase. Future World has pavilions, exhibits, and rides with an educational or futuristic accent. World Showcase, situated around a beautiful wide lagoon, represents a dozen different countries with its buildings, reproduced street scenes, shops, and restaurants. Unlike traditional park rides, the rides at Disney World transport you into new worlds of imagination.

For a representative sample try the Magic Kingdom's Space Mountain, Pirates of the Caribbean, or The Haunted Mansion—all three can be seen in half a day. At Epcot Center you can walk into a replica of Beijing's famed Temple of Heaven, or take a ride through the greenhouses of The Land pavilion and see remarkable agricultural innovations. At the Magic Eye Theater three-dimensional images that are incredibly realistic leap off the screen.

Disney World can be crowded, and some attractions have long lines, but for the most part its 20,000 employees make it work like a well-oiled machine. It takes 4 days for a visitor to feel reasonably satisfied, but even if you have only a day it will be unforgettable. *How to get there: Exit 86, west on I-4 to Orlando; follow signs. Exit 79, west on Rte. 50; follow signs. Open year-round. Admission charged.*

on a long barrier island between Indian River and the Atlantic, is less than a mile across at its widest point, and includes an inlet, coves, a coastal hammock, and mangrove swamps. More than 150 bird species have been spotted here, and there are great congregations of herons. *Open year-round. Admission charged for visitor center.*

🪑 ⛺ 🚐 🏊 🎣 ♿

64 Savannas Recreation Area, Fort Pierce

5 mi./10 min. East on Rte. 712. This marshy wilderness, once a reservoir for the city surrounding it, has long been popular with fishermen. The waters contain bass, bluegills, and catfish; and flat-bottomed johnboats, pedal boats, and canoes are available for rent. The marsh provides a haven for a variety of wildlife, including alligators, which often break the surface like partially submerged logs. A petting farm, with pigs, rabbits, and other gentle animals, is popular with children. *Open year-round. Admission charged.*

🪑 ⛺ 🚐 🎣 ♿

60 59 Jonathan Dickinson State Park

Exit 60: 8 mi./15 min. East on Rte. 708, right on Rte. 1. Exit 59: 15 mi./20 min. East on Rte. 706, left on Rte. 1. The park is named for Jonathan Dickinson, a Quaker who with his wife and infant child

was shipwrecked near here in 1696. With some 10,000 acres of scrub pines, palmettos, and mangrove swamps, it stretches along the Loxahatchee River, which looks much as it did in Dickinson's day. The varied environment here supports sandhill cranes, scrub jays, bald eagles, and other woodland and marsh birds. The brackish waters of the river are home to sand sharks, snooks, sheepsheads, and manatees (an endangered species). A 9½-mile trail for backpackers leads into ever more remote territory. The Trapper Nelson Interpretive Site, which is nearby, was once the home of a colorful local recluse whose interest in plants and animals is still evident. *Open year-round. Admission charged.*

🪑 ⛺ 🚐 🚶 🐟 ♿

24 Topeekeegee Yugnee Park, Hollywood

2 min. West on Sheridan St., right on N. Park Rd. The name means "gathering place" in the Seminole Indian language, and this quiet park surrounded by a busy urban area still serves that purpose. People come here to relax and enjoy the wide shaded lawns, the picnic tables and grills, or to take advantage of the park's 40-acre lake and athletic facilities. There's a filtered and chlorinated swimming lagoon boasting a wide sand beach, and a nearby 50-foot-high water slide provides excite-

ment with 700 feet of turns, drop sections, and occasional tunnels. There's a volleyball net, a basketball court, and playing fields; paddleboats, sailboats, sailboards, and canoes are available for rent. *Open year-round. Admission charged.*

🪑 ⛺ 🚐 🏊 🎣 ♿

1 Vizcaya, Miami

3 min. Follow signs. James Deering, the cofounder of International Harvester, built this lavish villa from 1914 to 1916 as a winter residence. The name, meaning "elevated place," is from the Basque language of northern Spain, but the architecture is Italian Renaissance in style. The interior of the magnificent 34-room villa is a veritable museum. Surrounding the central courtyard are rooms resplendent with statuary, furniture, paintings, tapestries, carpets, and decorative objects in the Renaissance, baroque, rococo, and neoclassical styles.

The 28-acre grounds include a forest of hardwood hammock, a mangrove shoreline, and the studied elegance of 16th- and 17th-century Italian gardens replete with formal plantings, statuary, and water fountains. On the seaward side is the Great Stone Barge, a breakwater in the shape of a ship that created a small harbor for waterborne guests. *Open daily except Christmas. Admission charged.*

🪑 ♿

31

31

10

64

21

End I-95

EAST-WEST BOOK

When you turn to the next page, you'll find a map of the United States showing all the even-numbered East–West interstates covered in the second half of of this volume. As in the first (North–South) half of this volume, that map will guide you to more detailed maps on which numbered brackets indicate segments of each interstate. The numbers designate the two-page sections on which the suggested stopping places are described.

In this half of the volume, segments of an East–West interstate are represented by a red line running along the top of the pages. As in the North–South half, the boxed exit numbers on the line are keyed to descriptions of the points of interest. Similarly, the small numbers between the exit boxes indicate the distance (to the nearest mile) between exits. The total number of miles covered by any two-page section appears at the bottom of each page under the section number. You'll also find cross-references to other sections of this volume when interstates intersect.

When you are traveling from west to east, leaf through the site-description pages in this half of the volume from front to back. When driving west, leaf through the pages from back to front. When one destination has two exit numbers, the first exit given is for drivers headed east; the second, for drivers headed west.

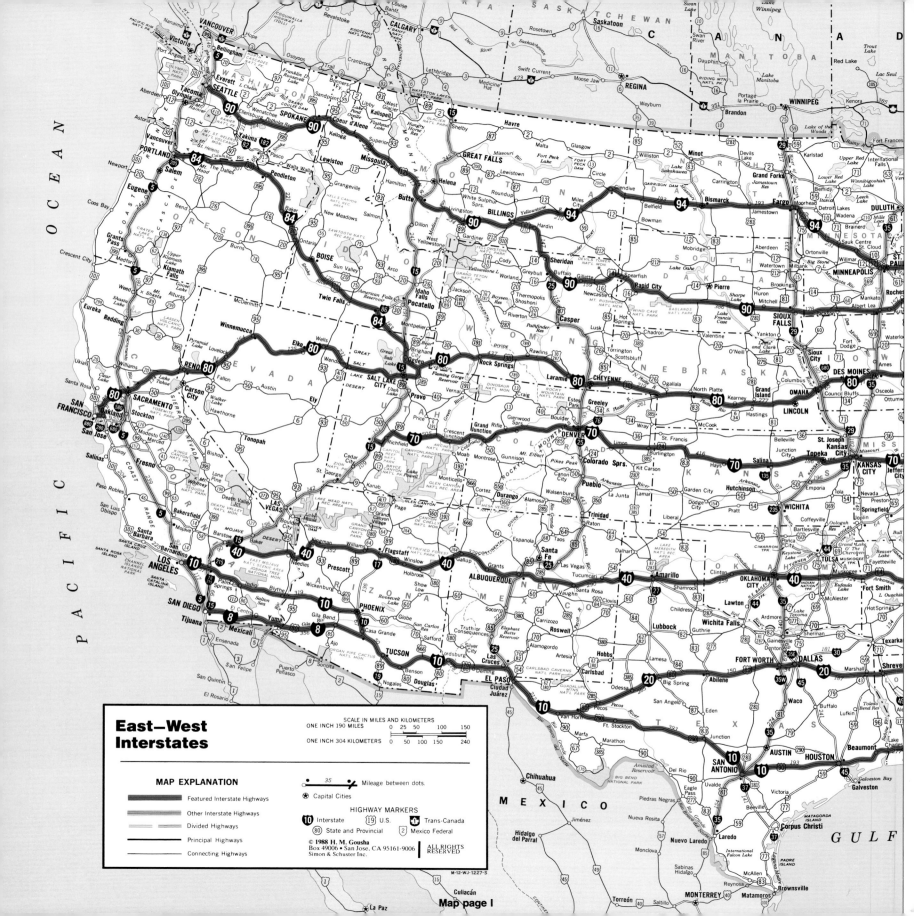

East–West Interstates

SCALE IN MILES AND KILOMETERS
ONE INCH 190 MILES 0 25 50 100 150
ONE INCH 304 KILOMETERS 0 50 100 150 240

MAP EXPLANATION

Featured Interstate Highways
Other Interstate Highways
Divided Highways
Principal Highways
Connecting Highways

·— 35 —· Mileage between dots.
✪ Capital Cities

HIGHWAY MARKERS
10 Interstate   **19** U.S.   Trans-Canada
80 State and Provincial   **2** Mexico Federal

© 1988 H. M. Gousha
Box 49006 • San Jose, CA 95161-9006
Simon & Schuster Inc.

ALL RIGHTS
RESERVED

M-12-WJ-1227-S

Map page I

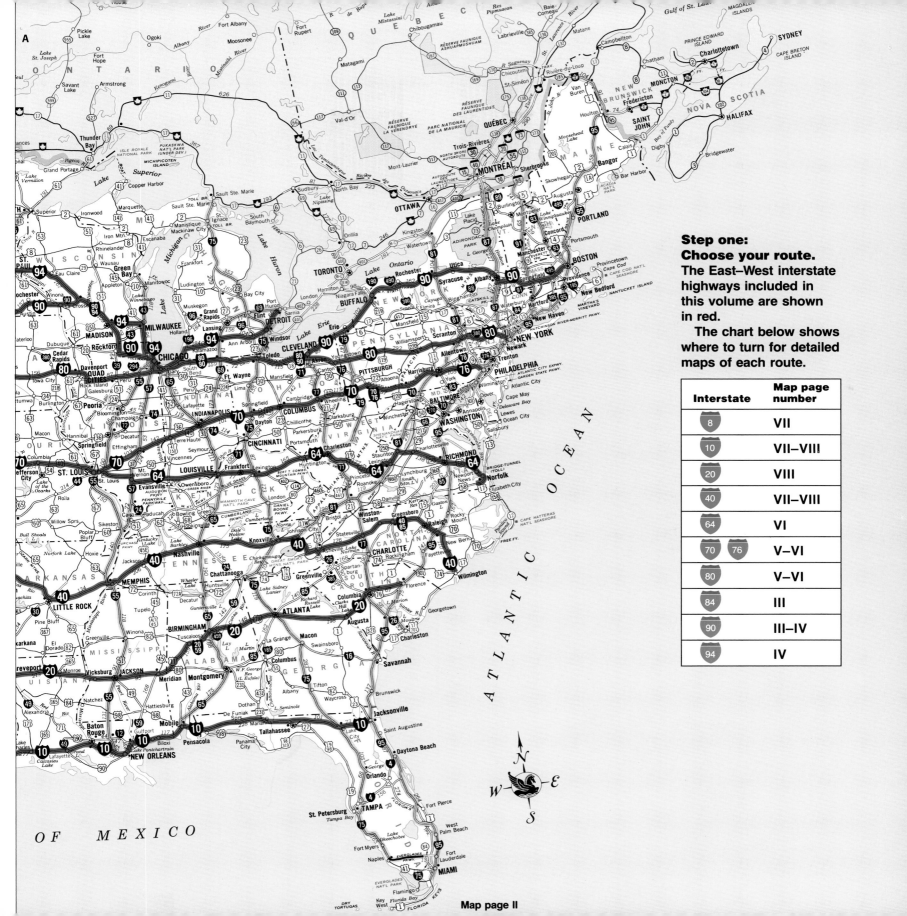

Step one:
Choose your route.
The East–West interstate highways included in this volume are shown in red.

The chart below shows where to turn for detailed maps of each route.

Interstate	Map page number
8	VII
10	VII–VIII
20	VIII
40	VII–VIII
64	VI
70 76	V–VI
80	V–VI
84	III
90	III–IV
94	IV

Step two:

Choose a section of the route. Each interstate has been divided into segments indicated by numbered red brackets.

Each number represents a two-page section in the book. Turn to the appropriate numbered section to find the points of interest (and exit numbers) on the bracketed stretch of highway you plan to drive.

The interstates highlighted at right are included on map pages III and IV. The others are on map pages V to VIII.

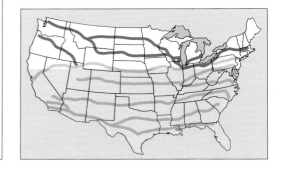

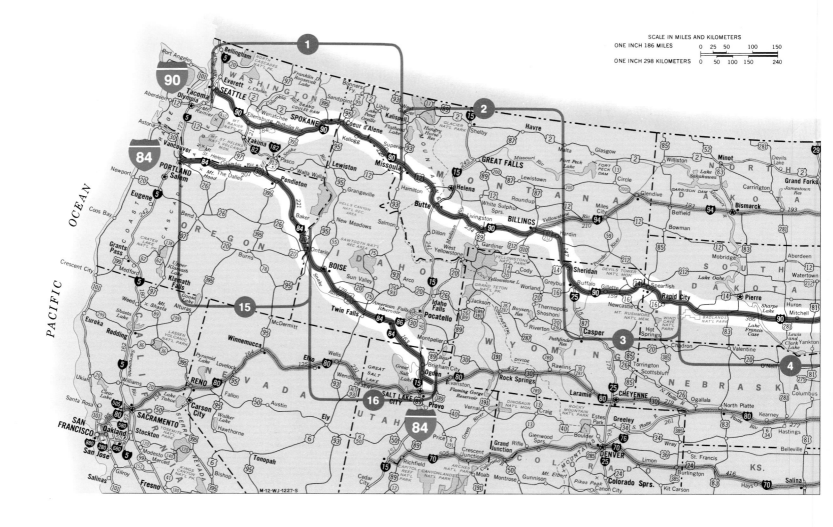

SCALE IN MILES AND KILOMETERS
ONE INCH 186 MILES 0 25 50 100 150
ONE INCH 298 KILOMETERS 0 50 100 150 240

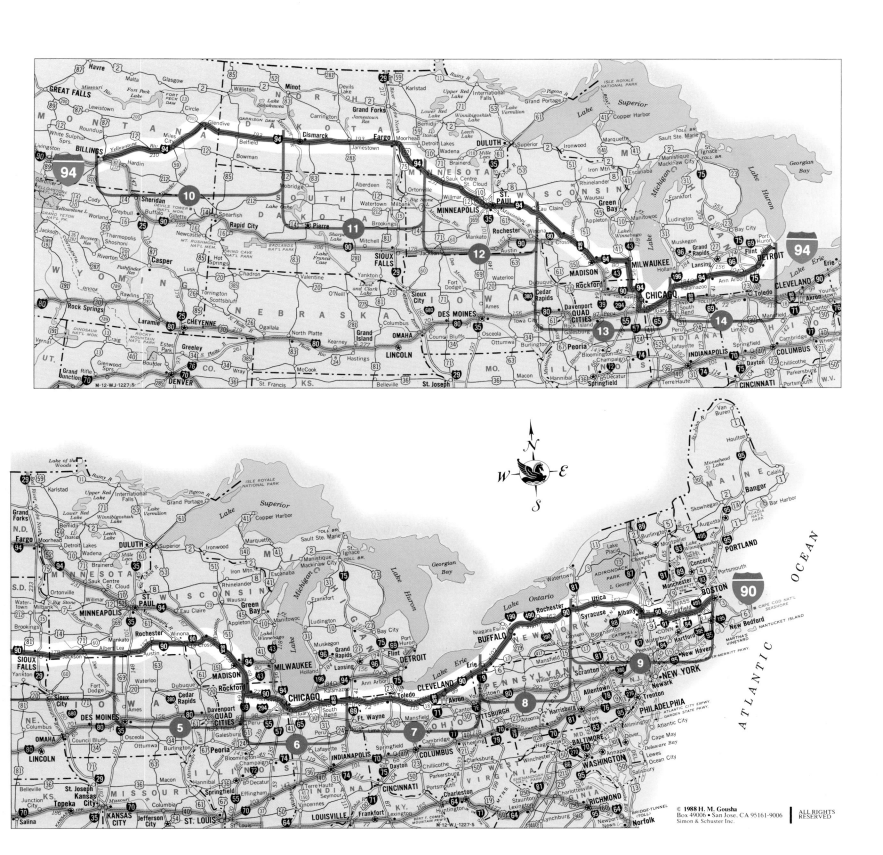

Map page IV

Step two:
Choose a section of the route.

Each interstate has been divided into segments indicated by numbered red brackets.

Each number represents a two-page section in the book. Turn to the appropriate numbered section to find the points of interest (and exit numbers) on the bracketed stretch of highway you plan to drive.

The interstates highlighted below are included on map pages V and VI. The others are on map pages III, IV, VII, and VIII.

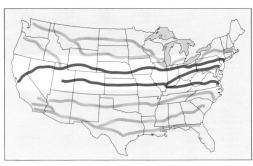

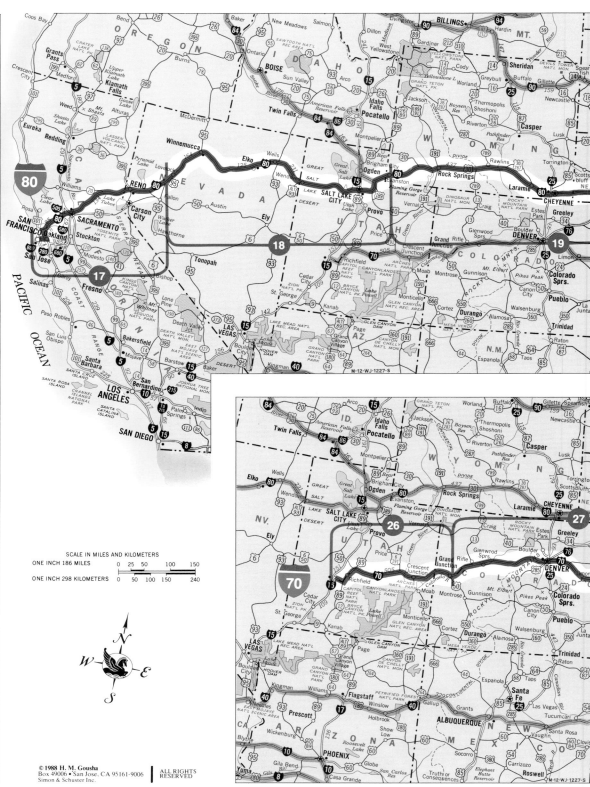

SCALE IN MILES AND KILOMETERS

ONE INCH 186 MILES   0 25 50   100   150

ONE INCH 298 KILOMETERS   0   50 100 150   240

© 1988 H. M. Gousha
Box 49006 • San Jose, CA 95161-9006
Simon & Schuster Inc.

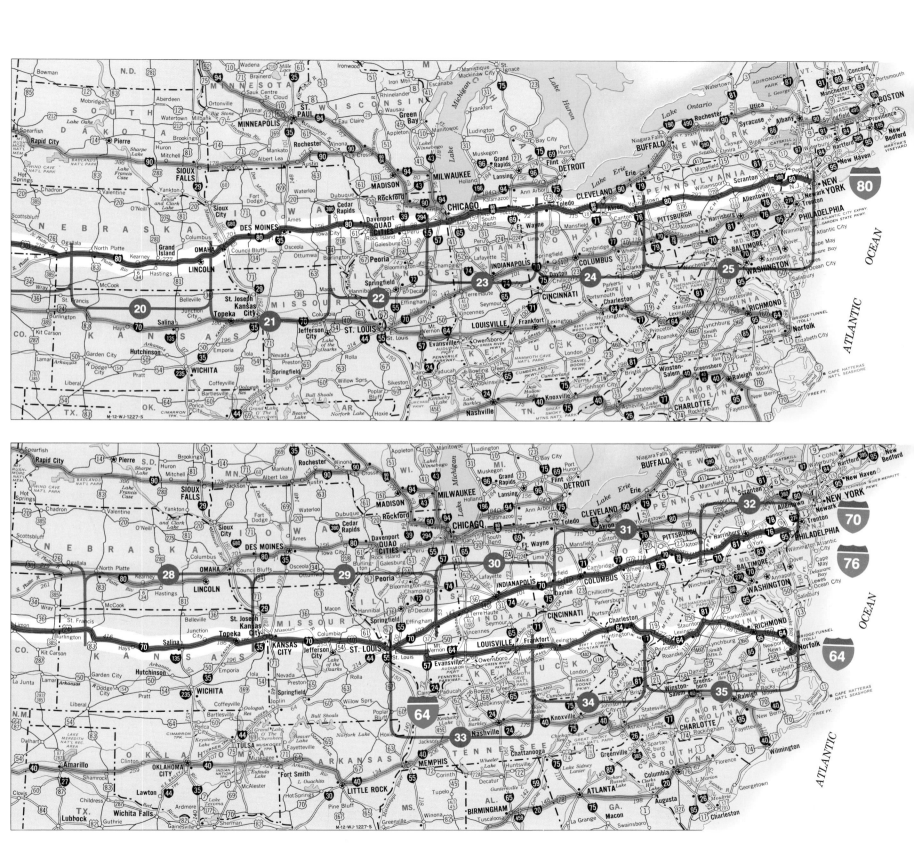

Map page VI

Step two:
Choose a section of the route.
Each interstate has been divided into segments indicated by numbered red brackets.

Each number represents a two-page section in the book. Turn to the appropriate numbered section to find the points of interest (and exit numbers) on the bracketed stretch of highway you plan to drive.

The interstates highlighted below are included on map pages VII and VIII. The others are on map pages III to VI.

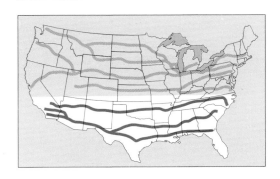

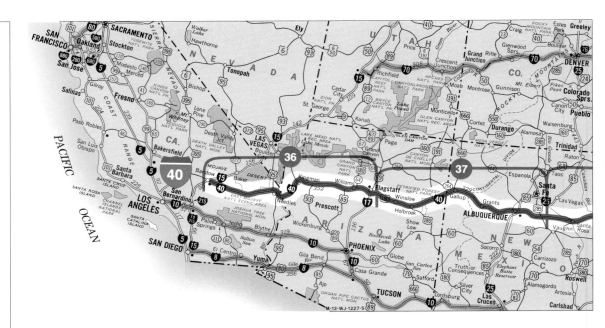

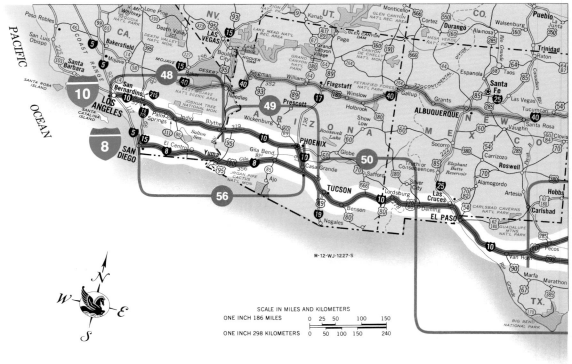

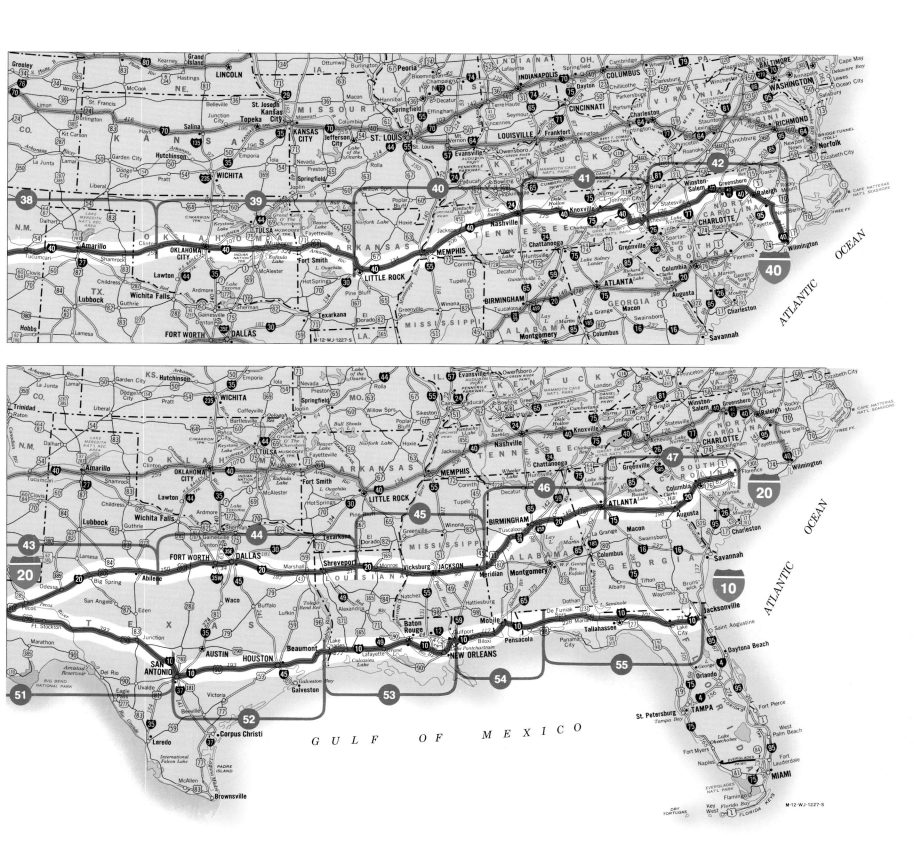

Map page VIII

4TH · Seattle, WA 98101

4th Ave. exit. Convention and Visitors Bureau, 1815 7th Ave. (206) 447-4200. Here on seven hills, almost surrounded by water, is one of America's most dramatic settings for a city. The Space Needle in Seattle Center provides stunning views of Puget Sound, Lake Washington, and (weather permitting) the distant Olympic Range, Cascade Range, and the majesty of Mt. Rainier. Downtown attractions include the waterfront, Pioneer Square, and Pike Place Market, where the display of fresh fruits and vegetables has become an art form.

31 · Snoqualmie Falls Park

5 mi./10 min. North on Rte. 202; follow signs. The falls, 110 feet higher than Niagara's Horseshoe Falls, drop from a rocky cliff into a misty pool 270 feet below. The best view of the falls is from the observation platform some 300 feet above the Snoqualmie River. A trail leads from here to the cascade's base. Other pathways in the park invite more leisurely

31. *If one were to design a waterfall (with rainbow), this could be the prototype.*

walking. Carved into the rock behind the falls is one of the country's first complete underground electric generating stations. Finished in 1898, it is a civil engineering landmark and still operating. Downstream from the falls the river offers kayaking and steelhead and trout fishing. *Open year-round.*

84 · 85 · Cle Elum Historical Society Museum

Exit 84: 5 min. East on town access road. Exit 85: 5 min. West on town access road. From 1901 to 1966 the switchboard operator's "Number, please?" was the human link in an otherwise impersonal system. The operators are gone, but the impressive switchboard, with its 1,200 terminals, is still here along with a collection of antique telephones, including an 1894 crank model encased in oak, a 1915 magneto model, and a dial phone circa 1920. Among the more recent models are a 1959 Princess, 1966 Trimline, and 1970 Touchtone. Graphic displays and replicas tell the story of Alexander Bell's influential invention. There's also a collection of old post office boxes along one wall. Other exhibits relate to Cle Elum's history as a coal-mining center. *Open daily late May–Sept., A.M. Mon.–Fri. Oct.–late May.*

115 · Olmstead Place State Park Heritage Area

5 mi./10 min. North on Main St., left on Kittitas Hwy., left on Squaw Creek Trail Rd. Sarah and Samuel Olmstead settled in this rich valley in 1875. Today their 218-acre farm is a park celebrating our pioneer farming heritage. The family's original cabin, constructed with hand-hewn cottonwood logs, has been furnished with period pieces. A later farmhouse built by the family and the granary, the wagon shed, and the red dairy barn contain household artifacts and farm equipment mostly from the 1920's to the 1940's. The leaflet for the half-mile trail along scenic Altapes Creek explains the uses of various plants in pioneer times. The trail ends at the one-room Seaton Schoolhouse, which is more than 100 years old and was moved here from a nearby meadow. *Open year-round. Buildings open P.M. Memorial Day–Labor Day.*

136 · Ginkgo Petrified Forest State Park

2 min. North on access road. About 15 million years ago upland trees were washed down into lakes and swamps here. Ancient lava flows covered the trees, and silica in the groundwater slowly turned them to stone. The petrified logs you see were exposed by erosion during the last ice age. The process is explained in an audiovisual show at the Heritage Area Interpretive Center, where exhibits also illustrate the area's natural history. The Natural Area, two miles north, features a short interpretive trail and a longer hiking trail through a prehistoric lake bed. The Wanapum Recreation Area, south of the interstate on the Columbia River, offers a swimming beach, a boat launch, and camping facilities. *Park open year-round. Interpretive center open mid-May–mid-Sept.*

176 · Adam East Museum, Moses Lake

Exit 176: 3 mi./10 min. East on Broadway, right on Balsam St. Exit 179: 5 min. North on Rte. 17; continue on Pioneer Way, left on 5th St., right on Balsam St. The impressive collection of Indian artifacts, fossils, and rocks in this small museum represents the lifework of one collector. Adam East spent over 50 years scouring the Columbia River area for items detailing the history of the Sinkiuse Indians, their prehistoric ancestors, and this land they inhabited. He deeded his collection to the city of Moses Lake, and the community built this museum. Indian arrowheads and spearpoints, saddles, beads, and war bonnets; fossil bones of mammoths, camels, and elk; petrified wood, smithsonite crystals, and memorabilia from the Civil War and World Wars I and II are among the many fascinating pieces here. *Open mid-Mar.–Oct.; P.M. only Mar.–Apr., Sept.–Oct.*

179 · Potholes State Park

17.5 mi./35 min. South on Rte. 17, right on M Southeast Rd., right on O'Sullivan Dam Rd. Fear not: the potholes for which this 1,000-acre park is named are not the kind that you encounter on roads, but rather geologic de-

179. *To judge the size of these sand dunes, note the powerboat by the island at lower right.*

pressions that formed in sand dunes during the Ice Age. In spring these craters fill up with melted snow, dotting the landscape with hundreds of little lakes. Although this park is located in the middle of the Columbia Basin desert, you'll find several surprises here, including a 20-foot-high waterfall and lakes that support rainbow trout, silver salmon, large- and smallmouth bass—and occasionally a water-skier. At the nearby Columbia National Wildlife Refuge, you may spot red-tailed hawks, eagles, great horned owls, American kestrels, white pelicans, cranes, and other birds. In winter the activities here include ice fishing, snowmobiling, and cross-country skiing. *Open year-round.*

277   The John A. Finch Arboretum, Spokane

5 min. North on Rustle St., right on Sunset Hwy.; follow signs. The quiet, parklike atmosphere of this 65-acre arboretum makes it a pleasant place for a picnic or a stroll. The setting is beautiful year-round, but there are colorful highlights from spring to fall. The Corey Rhododendron Glen (which also includes azaleas) has secluded trails along Garden Springs Creek, and is most striking in April and May. In Lilac Lane more than 75 varieties of this lovely shrub add their color and fragrance in spring. The Shrub Beds bloom from spring through summer, and in fall the Maple Section is ablaze with color. All told, there are more than 2,000 trees and shrubs in this arboretum, representing some 600 species and varieties, and most are labeled. *Open year-round.*

39   Old Mission State Park

2 min. South to Dredge Rd.; follow signs. The mission, designed by a Jesuit priest and built by Coeur d'Alene Indians in the mid-1800's, is Idaho's oldest building and has served as a way station for Indians, pioneers, soldiers, miners, and construction crews. It has been restored and still has many of the original furnishings. Adjacent to the mission is the parish house, with three rooms of primitive furnishings. It also has an altar that may be older than the church. At the visitor center you can see the personal belongings of the Jesuit missionaries and Indian artifacts, including fine bead and leather work. With the aid of a trail guide, you can visualize the former way of life in this community. *Open year-round. Admission charged.*

I-90   Coeur d'Alene District Mining Museum

Museum on I-90 (Bank St.) in Wallace. This building contains visible evidence of the rich deposits of lead, zinc, and silver that brought settlers to this region. The mining museum is dedicated to the past, present, and future of mining. Paintings and photographs interpret the life and times of the Coeur d'Alene district in the 1880's. Dioramas depict the history of mining, and there are three-dimensional exhibits of actual mine shafts, and the tools and equipment needed to exploit them. Samples of rock and ore are also displayed. There's a video show on mining, and information about a tour of the Sierra Silver-Lead Mine is available here. *Open year-round except Thanksgiving Day, Christmas, and New Year's Day. Admission charged.*

62   Burke Mining Town

7 mi./10 min. Northeast on Rte. 4. At the turn of the century Burke was a boomtown wedged in a narrow canyon where the lead, zinc, and silver mines kept it alive until after World War II (one mine kept operating until 1982). The canyon is still picturesque, and there are hiking trails to explore. A few people live in town, but it takes a vivid imagination to visualize the houses, bars, hotel, main street, and railroad that were once crowded together here. Some of the brick and concrete buildings relating to the mining operations still stand, and the foundation of the hotel can be seen. On the road to Burke the past is further recalled by former mining towns and camps with such evocative names as Mace, Yellow Dog, and Gem.

96   Aerial Fire Depot Smokejumper Center

3 min. South on Rte. 10W. Those who jump out of airplanes to fight forest fires must be considered special, and this center is where they are trained and deployed. Some 400 smokejumpers are hired for the fire season nationally, and about 100 are stationed at this U.S. Forest Service facility. The 1-hour visitor tour starts with an orientation video; then the smokejumpers show the parachute loft where they repair and pack the parachutes, and the manufacturing room where much of their special equipment is made. Training sites, air cargo, various aircraft used in firefighting, and the history of smokejumping are also seen on the tour. *Open daily June–mid-Sept.*

101 Historical Museum at Fort Missoula

7 mi./15 min. South on Reserve St., right on South Ave. This open fort—typical of those designed to encourage active patrol rather than passive defense—saw very little action against the Indians but served a number of other purposes. After the Civil War the 25th Infantry Regiment, composed of black soldiers, was headquartered here. This was also headquarters for the 25th Infantry Bicycle Corps in 1896; but despite much valiant pedaling, the bikes did not replace the horses. The 32-acre site includes the main administration building, a depot, a church, a schoolhouse, a Forest Service lookout, and other historic buildings, some of which were relocated here. Several other displays have been planned. *Open Tues.–Sat. and P.M. Sun. Memorial Day–Labor Day; P.M. Tues.–Sun. Labor Day–Memorial Day.*

184 187 Grant-Kohrs Ranch National Historic Site

3 min. Exit 184: south on I-90 (business loop); follow signs. Exit 187: north on I-90 (business loop); follow signs. This is about as close as you can come to the reality of ranch life in the Old West. Although the former 25,000 acres of open range have been reduced to 266, there are still 14 original main buildings and some 10,000 artifacts that belonged to the Grant and Kohrs families. Johnny Grant established a trading post here in the 1850's, built a fine house—a two-story log building—in the 1860's, and sold the spread to Conrad Kohrs in 1866. Kohrs and his wife, Augusta, added a brick wing. The ranch became a national historic site in 1972. A guided tour of the house and a self-guiding tour of horse stalls, bunkhouses, and other outbuildings gives a close-up view of a ranch at the turn of the century. *Open year-round. Admission charged.*

208 Historic City Hall Cultural Center, Anaconda

9 mi./10 min. West on Rte. 1 (becomes Commercial St.). The emphasis here at the former city hall is on the empire of Marcus Daly, a famous copper king, and the Anaconda Minerals Company. The permanent exhibits include panels, done by a local artist, describing the process of smelting of copper from the 1880's to the 1980's. There's also a turn-of-the-century pharmacy, with medicines, cosmetics, and advertising posters. On a rotating basis the museum offers information on Indians, trappers, homesteaders, miners, and other residents whose weapons, clothing, tools, furnishings, and photographs are on display. The Arts Center also mounts changing exhibits. *Open Tues.–Sat. and P.M. Sun. July–Sept. Admission free but donations encouraged.*

124 126 Copper King Mansion, Butte

5 min. Exit 124: east on I-115, left on Montana St., left on Granite St. Exit 126: north on Montana St., left on Granite St. This luxurious 32-room mansion is an outstanding example of Victorian architecture. It was built in the 1880's by William Andrews Clark, a U.S. senator and a multimillionaire entrepreneur with interests in real estate, banking, and oil as well as copper. So vast was his wealth that the quarter of a million dollars he paid for the house represented about half a day's earnings. The opulently furnished home has frescoed ceilings, Tiffany glass windows, and hand-carved woodwork. On the guided tour you'll also see period art and glassware, dolls, toys, and women's fashions. *Open year-round. Admission charged.*

256 274 Lewis and Clark Caverns State Park

Exit 256: 11 mi./25 min. Southeast on Rte. 2. Exit 274: 20 mi./35 min. Southwest on Rte. 287/2. These limestone caverns in the foothills of the Tobacco Root Mountains resulted from millions of years of rock uplifting and faulting and eons of water seepage. As the limestone dissolved, large underground rooms were created, along with an assortment of drip formations—stalactites and stalagmites, delicate stone draperies, tiny helictites, pencil-thin soda straws, and strange shapes that remind you of such objects as an elephant's trunk, Santa Claus, a Chinese pagoda, and Freddie the Frog. A self-guiding nature trail winds through the marvelous mountainous countryside. *Open daily May–Sept. Admission charged for tour.*

306 Museum of the Rockies, Bozeman

3 mi./10 min. South on N. 7th Ave., left on Main St., right on Willson St., right on Kagy Blvd. The amazing variety of material displayed in this museum, which is part of Montana State University, creates a graphic record of the northern Rockies: dinosaur fossils (including a huge *Triceratops* skull, nests of eggs, and baby dinosaur skeletons), beadwork and leatherwork of the Sioux, Flathead, and Blackfoot Indian tribes, and artifacts representing 19th-century Montana history.

510. *Markers show where Colonel Custer and the last of his 7th Cavalry fell in battle.*

Paintings and bronzes by Western artists are exhibited along with photographs of historic figures, including Sitting Bull, Chief Rain-in-the-Face, and Buffalo Bill Cody. A planetarium and a 100-year-old homestead are the latest additions to the museum. *Open daily except Thanksgiving Day, Christmas, and New Year's Day. Admission charged.* ♿

333 Livingston Depot Center Museum

5 min. North on Rte. 89 (business). Built in 1902, with a curving colonnade along the tracks, terrazzo walls, mosaic trim, and terra-cotta tiles, this impressive Italian Renaissance–style railroad station served as the gateway to Yellowstone National Park and as a major rail center until 1979. An exhibit titled "Yellowstone Days" traces the region's early history, with bronzes and paintings by such chroniclers of the West as Charles M. Russell and Frederic Remington. An assortment of memorabilia that once belonged to Buffalo Bill Cody is also shown. *Open daily May–mid-Oct. Admission charged.* ⛱♿

377 Prairie Dog Town State Monument

2 min. South from exit; follow signs. Black-tailed prairie dogs, members of the ground squirrel family, live in "neighborhoods": a series of burrows, called towns, that they defend against intruders, including other prairie dogs in the same town. Several sharp barks, a signal of danger, send the creatures scampering underground through the conical burrow entrances. Predators include golden eagles and badgers. Signboards describe the animals' complex social system and the arrangement of their "rooms." *Open year-round.*

446 Oscar's Dreamland Amusement Park, Billings

5 min. West on S. Frontage Rd., left on Shiloh Rd. Farm machinery is Oscar Cooke's special passion. At the Yesteryear Museum his intriguing collection of 300 antique restored tractors, 40 steam engines, 100 threshing machines, and untold numbers of combines and freight wagons is housed in three enormous buildings that cover some 2 acres. Other unex-pected treasures include some 19th-century hearses, a 1917 Liberty truck, road-building machines, an early airplane, and a 110-h.p. 1906 Best steam truck that pulled six 10-ton ore wagons at a time.

At the amusement park you can ride a restored railroad, and for a glimpse of pioneer life, stroll along a restored Main Street with fully appointed homes and stores and a jail. *Open daily May–Labor Day.* ⛱

450 Peter Yegen, Jr., Yellowstone County Museum, Billings

4 mi./10 min. North on 27th St. to airport; loop through terminal to museum. An 1893 log cabin houses a major portion of this museum, where the collections range from prehistoric times to the days of the homesteaders. The cabin's living room, dominated by a huge stone fireplace and furnished in 19th-century style, evokes life in pioneer-era Montana. Collections in four additional rooms comprise Indian clothing and artifacts, military uniforms, peace pipes, dueling pistols and six-shooters, wagons, and branding irons. Dioramas interpret the age of dinosaurs and cave people and depict the legend of Sacrifice Cliff (Indian braves riding off the top to their death). *Open Mon.–Fri. and P.M. Sun. except holidays.*

510 Custer Battlefield National Monument

2 min. East on Rte. 212. On the slopes of a ridge above the Little Bighorn River, markers show where Lt. Col. George Armstrong Custer and 51 of his men fell in battle against the Sioux and Cheyenne nations in 1876. To the south and east are the vast plains of sagebrush and prairie grass of southeastern Montana, where the rest of Custer's 210 troops died. At the visitor center, dioramas of the battlefield and biographical portraits of the protagonists—Custer, Maj. Marcus Reno, Capt. Frederick Benteen, and chiefs Sitting Bull, Gall, and Two Moon—explain the reasons for the conflict and its outcome. One of Custer's buckskin suits, his Colt revolver, Chief Sitting Bull's beaded bag, and other belongings are displayed. Guided tours of the battlefield are available in the summer. *Open year-round. Admission charged.* 🚶♿

If You Have Some Extra Time:

Yellowstone National Park

333 *53 mi./75 min.* Just 5 miles from the north entrance in Gardiner, Montana, is Mammoth Hot Springs, a travertine fantasy of flat terraces and rounded forms shaped by the flow of mineral-laden water—a fitting introduction to the marvels of America's first national park. In some 3,500 square miles of wilderness, you'll find vast forests, grassy meadows, streams, and lakes. The Grand Canyon of the rushing Yellowstone River has a waterfall almost twice as high as Niagara's Horseshoe Falls. A forest of petrified trees, an obsidian cliff, and 1,000 miles of hiking trails add to the park's majesty.

The most famous of the dramatic geysers is Old Faithful, which earned its name by erupting at regular intervals. In recent years the average has been 70 to 73 minutes. You have seen the pictures, but nothing can prepare you for the event itself. Near the appointed time—posted for each eruption—there can be wisps of steam and spurts of water to announce the impending phenomenon. Then, with a roar, comes the heart-stopping surge of boiling water shooting up as high as 180 feet.

On the 142-mile Grand Loop Road, you may see moose, elk, deer, bison, and bighorn sheep. Be careful with animals; this is their territory, and we are intruders. *How to get there: south on Rte. 89 to Gardiner (only entrance open year-round). Admission charged.*

23 | Trail End Historic Center, Sheridan

4 min. West on 5th St., left on Clarendon Ave. This luxurious home was built in about 1910 by John Kendricks, who became governor of Wyoming in 1914 and was elected to the U.S. Senate two years later. The house, which then cost $165,000 to build and furnish, is in the Flemish style (new to these parts at the time), with curved gables, a red tile roof, and walls and chimneys of pale brick.

The furnishings and woodwork are superb, from the piano-finish mahogany, the huge Kurdistan rug, and the French brocade wall panels in the coffered drawing room to the library's quarter-sawn oak paneling with antique English finish. On the third floor a ballroom with a musicians' loft, a dance floor of Maryland maple, and a beamed ceiling seems ready for festivities. *Open daily Memorial Day–Labor Day; limited hours Labor Day–Memorial Day.*

23 / 33 | Bradford Brinton Memorial

Exit 23: 6 mi./10 min. South on Rte. 87, right on Rte. 335; follow signs. Exit 33: 13.5 mi./17 min. West on Rte. 342, right on Rte. 87, left on Rte. 335; follow signs. This part of Wyoming is prime cattle country; and the Quarter Circle A Ranch, built in 1892 and bought by Bradford Brinton as a summer home in 1923, is an authentic reminder of a way of life enjoyed by the more prosperous landowners in northern Wyoming. The ranch-style house retains its fine original furnishings and Brinton's outstanding collection of western art (Indian crafts, as well as paintings and bronzes by Charles Russell, Frederic Remington, Frank Johnson, and Edward Borein). The grounds are nicely maintained, and there are lovely views of the Bighorn Mountains' front range. *Open daily mid-May–Labor Day.*

44 | Fort Phil Kearny National Historic Site

5 min. Northwest on Rte. 193; follow signs. Constructed in 1866 in violation of a treaty with the Sioux nation, Ft. Kearny was held under continual siege by Chief Red Cloud and his warriors until it was abandoned in 1868 (it was later destroyed by fire). Today the visitor center displays an outline of the fort and the barracks, along with reproductions of army weapons and bows and arrows. Panels in an adjacent cabin tell the dramatic story of the Wyoming Indian wars and the Bozeman Trail, and describe reservation and frontier life. *Open daily June–mid-Oct.*

153–185. *The irresistible force of an ancient volcano is documented in stone.*

56 / 58 | Jim Gatchell Memorial Museum, Buffalo

5 min. Exit 56: west on Rte. 16; follow signs. Exit 58: proceed as above. Pioneer druggist Jim Gatchell, in dealing with the Indians of the Sioux and Cheyenne tribes, amassed a large collection of their artifacts. The treasures include guns and shell casings believed to have been used during the massacre of Custer's troops at the Little Bighorn and the switchboard of the Occidental Hotel, an inn immortalized by Owen Wister in his best-selling 1902 novel, *The Virginian. Open daily June–Labor Day.*

132 | The Wyodak Mine

3 min. South from exit, right on Rte. 51. When the coal supplies here are exhausted some 30 years from now, the land will be returned to range, since there is continuous reclamation in progress. In the meantime, Wyodak mines 3 million tons of coal per year and puts nearly two-thirds of it on a conveyor belt that runs under the highway to America's largest air-cooled condensing power plant, just across the road. Visitors see both old and new mining equipment, including 120-ton-capacity coal-haulers. Free bus tours of this and other area mines are available at most local motels. For reservations for the power plant tour, call (307) 686-1248. *Mine and power plant open Mon.–Fri. June–Aug.*

153 / 185 | Devils Tower National Monument

Exit 153: 29 mi./35 min. Northeast on Rte. 14, left on Rte. 24, left on Rte. 110. Exit 185: 28 mi./35 min. Northwest on Rte. 14, right on Rte. 24, left on Rte. 110. The neck of a 60-million-year-old volcano towers imperiously more than 860 feet above its base. It's a magnificent monolith with an aura of mystery and menace. The Indians, believing that the claws of a celestial bear had fluted its walls, called the tower Bear Lodge. These days you're likely to see rock climbers inching their way to the summit, a teardrop-shaped plateau where hawks soar and chipmunks scamper through the sagebrush and buffalo grass. A trail skirts the tower's base. *Open year-round. Admission charged.*

12 | D. C. Booth Historic Fish Hatchery, Spearfish

4 min. West on Jackson Blvd., left on Canyon St. Before D. C. Booth founded the fish hatchery here in 1899, there were no trout in the streams of the Black Hills. The original hatchery building now houses the National Fish Culture Hall of Fame and an informative museum that commemorates Booth's work and the early years of the National Fish Hatcheries. Among the memorabilia, you'll see photographs of the early railroad fish cars and old equipment that Booth and others used in their fish-culture activities. Rainbow trout abound in the hatchery ponds. Visitors will enjoy feeding the fish, and anglers will want to try their luck at adjacent Spearfish Creek, a high-quality trout stream. *Museum open daily late May–late Sept.; grounds open year-round. Admission charged.*

30 Bear Butte State Park

9 mi./14 min. East on Rte. 34, left on Rte. 79. The peak of 4,426-foot-high Bear Butte looms above the plain like an outrider, and Indians still make pilgrimages to it as a sacred mountain. It's a place of great beauty and mystery, and when clouds swirl about its peak it looks so somber and brooding that one can easily understand its importance in Indian culture. Geologically, it is called a laccolith—a place where molten rock has raised the land's surface without breaking through, similiar to a volcano that did not erupt. Buffalo graze on the mountain's slopes, and at its foot lies Bear Butte Lake, where there is camping and picnicking. A visitor center records the butte's history. *Open year-round.*

30 Broken Boot Gold Mine, Deadwood

13 mi./18 min. West on Rte. 14A. This mine, which received its name when a miner's old boot was unearthed in a pile of debris, was opened in 1878, and by the time it closed in 1904 it had produced gold worth $1.5 million in turn-of-the-century dollars. The tour (the only underground mine tour in the Black Hills region still open to the public) takes you down the "main drift," a tunnel that runs into the hill horizontally for nearly 300 yards and into the house-size "stopes," the chambers from which the ore was removed. With the aid of searchlights, you can still see pockets of gold ore in the walls. *Open daily May–Sept. Admission charged.*

46 Black Hills Petrified Forest

4 min. East from exit; follow signs. A guided tour takes you along the crest of Piedmont Butte, where numerous petrified trunks of cypress and primitive palm trees lie where they fell, or where the earth millions of years ago moved them. Some actually still stand upright, and many are half buried in a matrix of sandstone. The museum displays samples of petrified wood and provides a detailed account of Black Hills geology as well as the process of petrifaction, the gradual conversion of organic matter into stone, or a stonelike substance. *Open daily mid-May–mid-Sept. Admission charged.*

57 Sioux Indian and Pioneer Museums, Rapid City

4 min. South on I-190 (becomes West Blvd.). Two fine museums occupy the same stone building in Halley Park. The Sioux Indian Museum displays the arts and crafts of the Sioux and other North American Indians: quillwork, beadwork, carvings, paintings on hide, featherwork, musical instruments, and costumes. The Pioneer Museum, which complements the Indian Museum, chronicles the history of the Black Hills region from the time of the first fur traders, with historic photographs, tools, and other memorabilia of trappers and prospectors, as well as some fine antiques and clothing. *Both museums open Mon.–Sat. and P.M. Sun. June–Sept; Tues.–Sat. and P.M. Sun. Oct.–May except Thanksgiving Day, Christmas, and New Year's Day. Pioneer Museum closed Jan.*

57 Mount Rushmore National Memorial, Keystone

21 mi./30 min. South on I-190, east on Quincy St., right on Mt. Rushmore Rd. (Rte. 16), left on Rte. 16A. The surprise here is how natural the granite faces of Washington, Jefferson, Lincoln, and Theodore Roosevelt appear as they gaze out from their mountain fortress. They seem to belong here—as they belong to the history of our country. Far below at the visitor center, there's a viewing terrace and information on how the carving was done. The sculptor, Gutzon Borglum, began his blasting and drilling in 1927 and didn't finish his monumental labor until 1941, just short of his 74th birthday. His studio, down a steep hill from the visitor center, contains a large model of the memorial, photographs of the work at various stages, and a display of sculptor's tools. *Open year-round.*

57. *Our 1st, 3rd, 26th, and 16th chief executives are memorialized here for the ages.*

131. *This fantasyland is even more astounding seen in its setting of surrounding prairie.*

110 | Wall Drug Store

2 min. Exit north; follow signs. This famous drugstore-café-shopping complex began as a humble small-town drugstore in 1931 and took off when Ted and Dorothy Hustead began to lure travelers with signs promising free ice water. These days the dramatically expanded store is still owned by the Hustead family and patronized by up to 20,000 people per day in summer. Besides the famous ice water, drugstore, and café, visitors will find shops that sell western goods, a traveler's chapel, "clothed wild animals," and the jackalope, a stuffed jackrabbit with antelopelike horns. One of the signs advertising the store says it's "like a museum—see it free." *Open daily mid-Mar.–Nov.; Mon.–Sat. Dec.–mid-Mar. except holidays.*

131 | Badlands National Park

9 mi./15 min. South on Rte. 240. Some of this country's strangest and most spectacular landscapes can be seen in this part of South Dakota, where the earth has been laid bare by eons of rain and wind, and the ancient strata of mud, rock, and ash have been carved into jagged ruins, mesas, and pinnacles. In late summer golden prairie grass tops the mesas, and lone plants cling to life in the cracked mud of valley floors. There are many overlooks along the Scenic Loop Road, and the short Door Trail (accessible to the handicapped) leads to miniature ravines and spikes embedded with nodules of pink rock. The Cliff Shelf Nature Trail passes gnarled junipers where magpies nest and a pool where cattails grow. The Cedar Pass Visitor Center gives an account of the geological and natural history of the park. *Open year-round. Admission charged.*

152 | Badlands Petrified Gardens

1 min. South on access road. Sixty million years ago an inland sea covered western South Dakota. Logs sank into the muddy seabed and eventually became petrified. Now an extensive collection of these stone tree remnants can be seen in the gardens here, their ancient bark, roots, and wormholes clearly visible. The museum has an excellent collection of minerals and fossils, including rare specimens of petrified wood. *Open daily May–late Oct. Admission charged.*

192 | Pioneer Auto Museum and Antique Town, Murdo

1 min. North from exit; follow signs. About three dozen buildings, spread over more than 10 acres, house a variety of nostalgic displays, including exhibits of minerals, gems, and toys. A fine collection of more than 200 antique automobiles features an early camper (the Motor Palace Camp Car) and a 1909 Auburn, used on the roadless prairie to locate land for homesteaders. You can also see a train depot and telegraph office, a church, a blacksmith's shop, a bank, and a barbershop. *Open daily except Thanksgiving Day, Christmas, New Year's Day, and Easter. Admission charged.*

260 | Old West Museum

1 min. East on I-90 (business loop). Here you will find an overwhelming variety of curiosities, antiques, and Old West Americana. Vintage radios, pocket knives, sausage stuffers, antique cars, clocks, Indian artifacts, musical instruments, 200 dolls, and 120 tractor seats are included, as well as an ivory-handled 1876 Colt Peacemaker pistol with cattle brands on the barrel and a pair of buffalo-head spurs. The Old Time Main Street has a number of shops and offices, including a general store with a hard-to-come-by package of Pfeiffer's Florentine Hair Promoter. Another building houses an 80-foot-long model steam train and a governess buggy attached to a stuffed zebra. *Open daily Apr.–Oct. Admission charged.*

332 | Mitchell Corn Palace

2.5 mi./6 min. North on Rte. 37, left on Rte. 38, right on Sanborn St., left on E. 1st Ave., left on N. Main St. The Moorish-style exterior of the spectacular Corn Palace is decorated from top to bottom with murals made from multicolored corncobs, sorghum, wheat, rye, and native grasses. The designs change yearly, and new ones are completed before the Corn Palace Week celebration in late September. Permanent corn murals decorate the auditorium, where entertainment is presented. *Open daily Memorial Day–Labor Day, Mon.–Fri. Labor Day–Memorial Day except Thanksgiving Day, Christmas, and New Year's Day.*

I-29 — Sherman Park, Sioux Falls

4.5 mi./8 min. South on I-29 to Exit 79, east on 12th St., right on Kiwanis Ave. The park, with meadows, ballfields, tennis courts, a skating rink, a children's playground, and shady picnic grounds, lies on the banks of the Big Sioux River. At the northern end is the U.S.S. *South Dakota* Battleship Memorial, a full-size concrete plan of the warship, and a museum of memorabilia. The Great Plains Zoo in the park has some 300 animals, ranging from the elegantly aloof snow leopard to the appealing Sicilian donkey. The Delbridge Museum of Natural History shows mounted animals in lifelike dioramas. *Open daily except Christmas. Admission charged.*

12 — Blue Mounds State Park

5 mi./8 min. North on Rte. 75. This is a place of great beauty, named for the large purple outcrops of Sioux quartzite in cliffs that rise suddenly from the fertile plain, as if to exalt and preserve the wild prairie that crowns them. To the north are two lakes with picnic and swimming areas, and a tract of fenced prairie where bison graze. Trails cross the prairie and follow the edge of the cliffs, where oak trees and wild roses grow, and prickly pear sprouts in cracks in the lichened quartzite. *Open year-round. Admission charged.*

332. *The Corn Palace: an uncommon tribute to common crops that are cultivated here.*

42 — Nobles County Pioneer Village, Worthington

4 min. Southeast on Rte. 266, left on Rte. 35 (Oxford St.), left on Rowe Ave.; follow signs. This museum-village complex presents a remarkably complete panorama of the region's history, and of the tools and institutions that shaped it. The Agricultural Building includes tools and equipment, from wire fencing to tractors, that turned the prairie into farmland, and the Transportation Building contains a wide selection of antique buggies, sleighs, and other vehicles. A restored train depot has a display of period railroad cars. Other establishments—the blacksmith's shop, firehouse, town hall, newspaper office, lawyer's office, saloon, hospital—are here too, as well as a photo shop, with its big scrapbooks of old-fashioned postcards. A farmhouse, built in Worthington around 1880, is furnished with careful fidelity to the period, and so are the two-room parsonage and the old Lutheran church nearby. *Open Mon.–Sat. and P.M. Sun. May–Sept. Admission charged.*

64 — Kilen Woods State Park

12 mi./15 min. North on Rte. 86, right on Rte. 24. The park lies on the west bank of the Des Moines River in a landscape that comprises prairie, wooded ravines, and steep hillsides. From the sturdy observation tower there's a pleasant view of the river and the uplands. Trails crisscross prairie, oak savanna, woods, and floodplain, and a nature center provides a detailed account of the native birds, animals, trees, flowers, and grasses that make the park a wildlife oasis within the surrounding farmland. *Open year-round. Admission charged.*

102 — Pioneer Museum, Fairmont

5 min. South on Rte. 15, right on Blue Earth Ave. The museum is the headquarters of the Martin County Historical Society, which since 1929 has been gathering pioneer and other memorabilia of early life in the area. Exhibits include the furnished interior of an 1890 home, ladies' old-fashioned gowns, a one-room schoolhouse, military relics, and tools and equipment used in local trades, professions, industries, and home life. *Open P.M. Tues.–Fri. and Mon. evenings May–Sept. Admission free but donations encouraged.*

12. *The fragile beauty of prickly-pear flowers is a refreshing surprise in hot, dry places.*

119 — James B. Wakefield House Museum, Blue Earth

5 min. South on Rte. 169, right on E. 6th St. The museum occupies a two-story brick home built in 1868 by James B. Wakefield, who founded Blue Earth City and also served as a lieutenant governor of Minnesota. His office is preserved on the ground floor, along with memorabilia about Wakefield and his friend Henry Constans, who founded the Constans Hotel (at the corner of 5th and Main streets). On the second floor are such relics of local history as a kettle that belonged to the first white settler, a rolling pin made in 1867 from a tree that stood near the courthouse, and an 1865 christening dress. *Open P.M. Mon.–Sat. Admission free but donations encouraged.*

158 Freeborn County Museum and Historical Village, Albert Lea

3 min. South on Bridge Ave.; follow signs. Twelve historic buildings are preserved here in southern Minnesota, along with a variety of exhibits that tell the story of Freeborn County's early days. The main exhibition hall displays pioneer articles ranging from trunks and baby clothes to a Swedish harp. There's also a well-equipped kitchen, a comfortable parlor, an elegant millinery shop, Indian artifacts, antique bottles, a mammoth tusk from a local gravel pit, and much more. The Red Barn houses a fully equipped train depot, a barbershop, a bank, a photo studio, a jail, a firehouse, tractors, steam engines, agricultural equipment, and automobiles. Elsewhere in the historical village is the first log house built in Freeborn County (1853), a rural schoolhouse, a hardware store, a cobbler's shop, an 1870's church, and a general store that stocks everything from hatpins to horse collars. *Open P.M. Tues.–Sun. June–Aug.; P.M. Sun. May and Sept.–Oct. Admission charged.*

I-35 Helmer Myre State Park

5 min. South on I-35 to Exit 11, east on Rte. 46, right on Rte. 38. The sweet smell of tall-grass prairie and the shining expanse of Albert Lea Lake (2,600 acres) are the most immediate attractions in the park. The terrain reflects its glacial past and varies from prairie to oak savanna, marsh, forest, and esker (rock and sand deposits left by glacial streams). The park is well known for its waterfowl and shorebirds, and it has more than 450 kinds of wildflowers. There are several trails, and canoes are rented. An interpretive center on Big Island has an outstanding collection of Indian artifacts. The nearby town of Albert Lea also has many excellent parks. *Open year-round. Admission charged.*

175 Mower County Historical Center, Austin

5 min. East on West Oakland Ave., right on Rte. 105 (12th St.). This complex of museums and historic buildings presents highlights of regional history and aspects of daily life in southern Minnesota since the first settlers ar-

rived. The Indian Museum has an excellent collection of artifacts, and there is an 1862 log cabin and an 1870 rural school. The Pioneer, Rural Life, and Hormel museums illustrate the area's early settlement and later prosperity: here are surveyor's instruments, farm tools, a loon-feather cape, and George Hormel's first (1890's) meat-packing establishment. The Rahilly Museum displays a 1910 eight-seater omnibus, the Railroad Museum shows a Baldwin locomotive, and the Communications Museum specializes in telephone equipment. The Headquarters Building (1856) contains old-time county miscellany, including a general store and the county's recruiting station from the Civil War. In the Fireman's Museum a 1926 chain-driven pumper and fire-fighting badges and patches from all over the world are displayed. *Open P.M. daily, June–Aug.*

252 Julius C. Wilkie Steamboat Center, Winona

9 mi./14 min. North on Rte. 43, left on Homer Rd. (becomes Mankato Ave.), left on Sarnia St., right on Main St. This full-size replica of a paddle wheeler rests in a dry dock in Levee Park beside the Mississippi River. It features a steamboat museum with model paddleboats, photographs, steamboat prints by Currier and Ives, relics of the original *Wilkie*, bills of lading, and other mementos of the steamboat era. Perhaps the most interesting items are the manuscripts, books, and other memorabilia of Robert Fulton, father of the commercial paddleboat and a canal engineer who built early models of submarines and torpedoes. The rest of the *Wilkie*, from the pilothouse to the lavish Grand Salon, gives a vivid impression of what the old riverboats were like in their heyday. While here, try the walking tour of Winona's many turn-of-the-century structures. *Open daily May–Oct. Admission charged.*

3A Hixon House, La Crosse

4.5 mi./11 min. South on Rte. 53 (becomes Rose St., then Copeland Ave.), left on Vine St., left on 7th St. Banker, philanthropist, and lumber mogul Gideon Hixon built this home in 1859 and furnished it according to 19th-century standards of comfort and opulence.

The woodwork is exceptional, from the hand-carved teak desk and bookcases in Hixon's study to the sliding birch doors in the parlor. Throughout the house elegant imported items capture one's attention: Wedgwood pottery from his personal collection, a screen of Chinese silk in the master bedroom, and a "Turkish nook" with an olivewood harem screen. The dining room has a handsome coffered ceiling and is furnished with Chippendale and Hepplewhite chairs. The place settings have hand-painted Limoges china. *Open P.M. daily June–Labor Day. Admission charged.*

41 The Little Red Schoolhouse, Tomah

3 min. North on Rte. 131 (Superior Ave.). In use from 1864 to 1965, this small, classic one-room schoolhouse, reminiscent of simpler times, now stands in Tomah's Gillette Park. You can see photographs of the students dating back to the early 1900's, schoolbooks from 1910 and the 1920's, a small collection of minerals, and map stencils for the children's geography lessons. *Open P.M. daily Memorial Day–Labor Day.*

87. *The sandstone, obviously vulnerable to erosion, is so porous that trees can grow.*

87 The Dells

2 min. East on Rte. 13/23. The Dells of the Wisconsin River are narrow chasms or ravines that have been carved out of sandstone cliffs (formed millions of years ago) by the relentless erosive action of water against rock after the Ice Age meltdown. The walls of the cliffs are corrugated and in places capped by overhangs and pedestals of rock. These picturesque formations can be seen if you take one of the commercial boat tours from the docks in downtown Wisconsin Dells. Boats operate from mid-April to mid-October. Two other outstanding attractions in this area are

The Stand Rock Indian Ceremonial (*5 mi./7 min. from Exit 87; east on Rte. 13/23, left on Rte. 12/16, right on Rte. A, left on Stand Rock Rd.*) offers a program of traditional North American Indian dances performed by Native Americans in a magnificent natural amphitheater. *Performance every evening mid-June–Labor Day. Admission charged.*

The Winnebago Indian Museum (*6.5 mi./10 min. from Exit 87; east on Rte. 13/23, across bridge, left on River Rd.*) displays an excellent collection of Indian clothing, ornaments, and weapons along with other artifacts. *Open daily Apr.–Dec. Admission charged.*

92 106 Mid-Continent Railway Museum, North Freedom

Exit 92: 13.5 mi./18 min. South on Rte. 12, right on Rte. 136, left on Rte. PF. Exit 106: 21 mi./28 min. West on Rte. 33, continue on Rte. 136, left on Rte. PF. A restored 1894 depot is the starting point for rides through the peaceful Baraboo River valley in an authentic steam train. Railroad equipment—including a snowplow, a boxcar, and a baggage car—is displayed in the Coach Shed, along with the 1884 D & R No. 9, one of the oldest steam locomotives used regularly in North America, and the 1925 Montana Western gas-electric car No. 3l, which preceded the diesel engine. Refreshments are served in an old Marquette & Huron line mountain car. A children's playground is adjacent to the picnic area. *Open daily mid-May–Labor Day; weekends only, Labor Day–mid-Oct. Admission charged.*

135. *A Norwegian who died for his adopted land is honored on the grounds of the capitol.*

92 106 Circus World Museum, Baraboo

Exit 92: 10 mi./15 min. South on Rte. 12; follow signs. Exit 106: 14 mi./20 min. West on Rte. 33; follow signs. The Ringling Brothers circus had its winter quarters in Baraboo until 1918. The complex of 30 buildings now serves as both an active showplace and a home for circus memorabilia. In season performances are presented daily under the big top, and an extensive museum of circus history includes automated miniatures, air calliopes, and displays commemorating various circus stars. The world's largest collection of circus wagons contains fine examples of gilding and carving. The menagerie, with its tigers, camels, hippos, and other animals, draws fascinated viewers. *Open daily early May–mid-Sept. Admission charged.*

135 Madison, WI 53703

Convention & Visitors Bureau, 121 W. Doty St. (608) 255-0701. The capitol, set on an isthmus between two lakes in the downtown area of this attractive city, is reputed to be the largest state capitol building in the United States and is open for tours. Architecture on a smaller scale is also important: Frank Lloyd Wright's Unitarian Meeting House (1949–51) is open to the public, and several other buildings designed by Wright, a Wisconsin native, can be viewed from the street. The State Historical Museum features Indian and French voyageur exhibits, while the University of Wisconsin's Elvehjem Museum of Art displays works of all periods. On the university campus you can visit an arboretum, Indian effigy mounds, and Babcock Hall, where you can get college-educated ice cream.

147 Lake Kegonsa State Park

3.5 mi./6 min. South on Rte. N, right on Koshkonong Rd.; follow signs. This park, near Madison, has more than 300 acres of woodland, prairie, and marsh, as well as an extensive shoreline on 3,209-acre Lake Kegonsa ("lake of many fish" in Winnebago, and the lake reportedly lives up to it). The White Oak nature trail loops through woods past a group of Indian mounds. Inviting mown paths wind through quiet prairie. *Open year-round. Admission charged.*

171A Milton House Museum

5 mi./7 min. North on Rte. 26. This onetime stagecoach inn and Underground Railroad station, built in 1844, was the first structure in the U.S.A. to be made from poured grout. Today the building is a lively museum of local history where one can still see the tunnel in which its builder, Joseph Goodrich, sheltered fugitive slaves. The interior of the inn, furnished with loving attention to detail, displays rope beds, period clothing, and the original guest book. On the grounds there's a buggy shed, an 1844 blacksmith's shop, and the 1837 log cabin Goodrich lived in before Milton House was built. A country store sells gifts and souvenirs. *Open daily June–Labor Day; weekends, May and Labor Day–mid-Oct. Admission charged.*

175 The Tallman Restorations, Janesville

3 mi./7 min. West on Rte. 11, right on S. Franklin St.; follow signs. Here you'll find a striking Italianate mansion considered to be one of the largest and most important mid-19th-century house museums in the Midwest. When it was built in 1855–57, this three-story residence contained many then-uncommon luxuries, including a marble sink with running water in each bedroom. The exterior is enhanced by cast-iron arches over the windows and a small cupola on the roof. The parlor where William and Emeline Tallman entertained Abraham Lincoln one weekend in

175. *The house is noted for the elegance of the proportions and decorative details.*

1859 is especially noteworthy, although the future President of the U.S. found it too formal and withdrew to the more casual family parlor. Nearby, an elegant horse barn now houses a visitor center. One of the region's earliest mansions is located on the grounds—an 1842 Greek revival house containing portraits of local citizens as well as decorative art brought to this area by pioneer families in the 19th century. *Open Tues.–Sun. June–Aug.; weekends only May and Sept.–mid-Oct. except holidays. Admission charged.*

ROUTE 20B Rockford, IL 61104

Rte. 20 (business) exit: Convention & Visitors Bureau, 220 E. State St. (800) 521-0849; (800) 423-5361 outside IL. For a pleasant introduction to Illinois' second largest city, take one of the narrated tours on a riverboat or on an old-fashioned trolley. A highlight of the trolley ride is Sinissippi Gardens Greenhouse and Lagoon, with its elegant sunken gardens, aviary, and floral clock.

A number of historic homes attest to Rockford's 19th-century heritage: the 20-room Tinker Swiss Cottage, the dwelling made of oak logs by early settler Stephen Mack, the brick home of Swedish settler John Erlander, and the Greek revival Graham Genestra House. Museum lovers will enjoy Midway Village in the Rockford Museum Center with its turn-of-the-century blacksmith's shop, jail, bank, and other town fixtures and displays. Exhibits on science topics and the state of Illinois's wildlife are housed in the Victorian mansion of the Burpee Museum of Natural History; an excellent art collection in the Rockford Art Museum invites attention; and the renowned Time Museum has some 2,500 clocks dating from ancient times to the space age.

M-H Illinois Railway Museum, Union

Marengo-Hampshire exit: 10 mi./13 min. West on Rte. 20, right on Union Rd.; follow signs. The golden age of railroading returns in all its glory at this "museum in motion." Here you'll see one of only two surviving Norfolk & Western Mallet locomotives—113 feet long and weighing 458 tons when loaded with coal and

M-H. *Enviable luxury, as enjoyed by those who could afford a private car.*

water. Also on exhibit is the oldest still operating diesel locomotive in the country, an 1859 horse-drawn streetcar, and the stainless steel *Silver Pilot.* The rolling stock includes a luxurious 1910 Pullman observation car, massive snow-sweepers with cane-bristled brushes, and a rare interurban sleeping car. Rides are available on several trains. *Open Mon.–Sat. Memorial Day–Labor Day; Sun. mid-Apr.–Oct. Admisson charged.*

ROUTE 31 Fox River Trolley Museum, South Elgin

7 mi./12 min. South on Rte. 31. The authentic clang, clang, clang of the trolley is heard here as vintage cars make their 3-mile round-trip through scenic vistas of water and trees on the Fox River Line, built in 1896. The museum's impressive collection includes the oldest working interurban trolley in America, the only surviving streetcar post office, an 1887 caboose, a 1920's elevated train from Chicago, and one of America's last streetcars—a model with rubber wheels built in 1951. *Open Sun. and holidays mid-May–Oct. and P.M. Sat. July–Labor Day. Fare charged for rides.*

OH Chicago, IL 60611

E. Ohio St. exit: Tourism Council, 163 E. Pearson St. (312) 280-5740. This great cosmopolitan metropolis, beautifully situated on the southwestern shore of Lake Michigan, boasts a number of world-class attractions. The Art Institute is known for a wide-ranging permanent collection and creative special exhibitions. The Terra Museum, opened in 1987, has a superlative collection of American art; the John G. Shedd Aquarium, the world's largest such indoor facility, with more than 200 tanks, displays some 1,000 wonders of the deep. For an intimate sense of the city, take the El (the elevated railroad) around the Loop; and for a breathtaking overview of the city and lake, try the observation area on the 103rd floor of the Sears Tower, at this writing the tallest building in the world.

1   Wolf Lake Park, Hammond

2 mi./5 min. East on Indianapolis Blvd. (Rte. 12/20), right on Calumet Ave. (Rte. 41). Despite the unpromising surroundings of highways, high-tension lines, and gas storage tanks, this 452-acre park is an obvious success, boasting a large lake, an 18-hole miniature golf course, and other recreational facilities. Canoes, paddleboats, and sailboards are rented. The annual Augustfest, held during the first week of the month, brings some 300,000 people here for entertainment, food, and carnival attractions. A fishing pier and a boat ramp entice the angler to try for walleye, northern pike, or bass. *Open daily mid-June– mid-Sept. Admission charged.*

31   Wilbur H. Cummings Museum of Electronics, Valparaiso

15 mi./25 min. South on Rte. 49, right on Rte. 130. Electronic technology changes so quickly that yesterday's marvel soon becomes today's antique. This museum has electronic devices from the period of Edison and Marconi to the present, knowing that its latest state-of-the-art exhibits will soon be obsolescent. Among the highlights are a 1950's Seeburg jukebox that plays 78-r.p.m. records, Admiral Byrd's transmitter from a South Pole expedition, one of the first pinball machines, and radios by Atwater-Kent, Crosley, Philco, and other noted manufacturers. First-generation computers and VCR's, studio TV equipment, and other outmoded wonders are displayed and ex-

plained. The museum is at Valparaiso Technical Institute; apply for free admission at the administration building. *Open year-round.*

31   Indiana Dunes National Lakeshore

8.5 mi./13 min. North on Rte. 49, right on Rte. 12. These 1,800 acres of woodland trails and 3 miles of beach dominated by towering lakefront dunes evince an almost lyrical delicacy in an obviously industrial environment. A number of plants are relics of the colder climates that existed here at the end of the Ice Age, leaving a remarkable diversity of vegetation: arctic bearberry flourishes alongside prickly-pear cacti, and northern jack pines share dune slopes with southern dogwoods. Although the dunes are large (Mt. Tom rises more than 190 feet) and are anchored against the wind by marram grass, sand cherry, cottonwoods, and other native plants, they are susceptible to erosion. A 2-mile trail leads through red oaks and sugar maples to the restored Bailly Homestead and the Chellberg Farm. *Open year-round.*

77   Fort Joseph Museum, Niles

8.5 mi./15 min. North on Rte. 33 and Rte. 31/33. This Michigan fort, built by the French in 1691, commanded a key trade route between their holdings in Canada and Louisiana. In the French and Indian War it was held by the British, then briefly by Spain.

    The documents, pictures, books, implements, and furniture in the 100,000-item museum, located in a Victorian carriage house, bring the story to vivid life. Here, too, is a large collection of Sioux and other Indian artifacts, including pictographs of chiefs Sitting Bull and Rain-in-the-Face. *Open Tues.–Sun. Admission free but donations encouraged.*

77   Studebaker National Museum, South Bend

3 mi./9 min. South on Rte. 33, left on Jefferson Blvd. In the 1850's South Bend was known as the Wheel City, because of the scores of wagonmakers living and working here. Part of that tradition was created by the Studebaker Company, which in time went from building cov-

ered wagons to producing some of the 20th century's most imaginative automobiles. You will see examples of these at Century Center (Jefferson Boulevard and St. Joseph Street). Among the highlights are Studebaker's first automobile (a 1902 electric model), the Dictator Series of the 1930's, and the bullet-nosed models of the 1950's. Dodge, Oliver, and Flanders are also well represented. And not just cars: the 1923 Indestructo cabin trunk, for example, kindles nostalgic memories of those bygone days when a trip abroad was the event of a lifetime. At the nearby Archives Center (South Street and Lafayette Boulevard), you can see more than 60 historic horse-drawn and motorized vehicles, including four presidents' carriages. *Open daily June–Aug.; Tues.–Sun. Sept.–May. Admission charged.*

77   Potato Creek State Park

24 mi./30 min. South on Rte. 33 and Rte. 31 (business) through South Bend, right on Rte. 4. Fishermen come to Worster Lake for the bass, bluegill, brown trout, crappie, and channel catfish. The 300-acre reservoir was created in 1977, when Potato Creek was dammed, and in parts of the lake the ghostly trunks of the drowned trees can still be seen. The landscape, with woodland and scrubby pasture, shows how former farmland reverts to its natural state. You can enjoy several trails, including a 3-mile bicycle trail that goes through many scenic parts. *Open year-round. Admission charged.*

121   Pigeon River State Fish and Wildlife Area

9 mi./12 min. South on Rte. 9, left on Rte. 120; follow signs. The woods, ponds, streams, and marshland in this wildlife area, which covers some 11,500 acres, are home to deer, pheasants, and waterfowl as well as pike, bluegill, perch, and of course trout. The Curtis Creek Trout-Rearing Station, which is located in the wildlife area, successfully grows some 60,000 rainbow and brown trout per year. Although not native to Indiana, fingerlings are brought here from state hatcheries, raised in six 86-foot-long raceways, and released in various streams and lakes. *Open year-round.*

156 Pokagon State Park

4 min. South on I-69 to Exit 154, right on Rte. 727. This park, named for a Potawatomi chief, has year-round appeal. In winter, thrill seekers head for the 1,780-foot refrigerated toboggan slide, where they can streak down and over hills at 45 miles per hour. The slide is open from Thanksgiving to March, and toboggans, rented by the hour, can hold up to four passengers. Other attractions in this vast area include trails for hikers and cross-country skiers (rentals available), ice fishing, ice skating, and sledding. In summer, visitors fish, boat, and swim in Lake James. *Open year-round. Admission charged.*

156. *Literally breathtaking is this toboggan run down one steep hill and up another.*

2 Harrison Lake State Park

3

Exit 2: 20 mi./30 min. North on Rte. 15, right on Rte. 20, right on Rte. 27; follow signs. Exit 3: 20 mi./30 min. North on Rte. 108, left on Rte. 20, left on Rte. 66, right on Rte. M. The soggy black soil that once earned this region the nickname the Great Black Swamp is some of Ohio's most fertile farmland. Even amid vast fields of corn, oats, and soybeans, this 350-acre park sparkles with greenery. Harrison Lake—framed by shaded picnic areas and lush meadows—provides water activities in every season and yields bluegill, crappie, and largemouth bass. In spring, vesper sparrows, brown thrashers, and yellowthroats are some of the songbirds seen here. *Open year-round.*

4 Fort Meigs State Memorial

3.5 mi./6 min. South on Rte. 20 and Rte. 25, right on Rte. 65; follow signs. Set on a bluff above the rapids of the Maumee River, Ft. Meigs played a key role in the War of 1812. It was built in February 1813, and in May survived a siege and bombardment by the British; in July they were repulsed again, paving the way for their defeat in the Battle of Lake Erie. The present fort is a reconstruction; three of the seven blockhouses contain exhibits about the war and fort design. Within the stockade are the remains of earthworks that sheltered the troops from incoming cannon fire. *Open Wed.–Sat. and P.M. Sun. and holidays late May–early Sept.; Sat. and P.M. Sun. early Sept.–late Oct. Admission charged.*

6 East Harbor State Park

15 mi./23 min. North on Rte. 53, right on Rte. 2, left on Rte. 269; follow signs. The park is Ohio's largest on Lake Erie, and one of its most popular. It lies on a limestone peninsula and embraces three sheltered harbors. One of these, Middle Harbor, is a wildlife refuge, and a trail along its southeastern shore leads to an observation blind for watching waterfowl and shorebirds. For most people, though, boating, swimming, and fishing are the park's major attractions. Winter activities include ice fishing, ice skating, sledding, and snowmobiling. *Open year-round.*

7 Firelands Museum, Norwalk

7 mi./10 min. South (marked East) on Rte. 250, right on W. Main St. (Rte. 61), left on Case Ave. The museum is named for lands in Ohio given to residents of Connecticut whose property was torched by the British during the Revolutionary War. It includes such assorted items as early maps of the district, surveyor's equipment, exceptional collections of antique firearms (including a Chinese hand-cannon dating from 1000 B.C.), prehistoric Indian artifacts, old toys and household implements, and memorabilia of the Civil War. Other items of interest range from antique clothing to a diorama of the Milan ship canal and a mammoth bass viol. The museum occupies a federal-style town house dating from 1835 and contains period furnishings. *Open Mon.–Sat. and P.M. Sun. July–Aug.; P.M. Tues.–Sun. May–June and Sept.–Oct.; P.M. Sat.–Sun. Apr. and Nov. Admission charged.*

7 Great Lakes Historical Society Museum, Vermilion

ROUTE 2

Exit 7: 25 mi./32 min. North on Rte. 250, right on Rte. 2, left on Rte. 60. Exit Rte. 2: 17 mi./25 min. West on Rte. 2, right on Rte. 60. This fascinating lakeside museum offers a colorful account of shipping on the Great Lakes. Excellent photographs of storms and wrecks serve as vivid reminders of how dangerous these waters can be, and there are models of the many kinds of ships and boats that ply the lakes. Displays of maritime equipment include compass binnacles and steering wheels, radar units, an engine room console, and a complete steam engine. A comprehensive exhibit of safety and rescue equipment includes steam whistles and foghorns, shore beacons, and the lamp from a lighthouse on northern Lake Huron, gleaming like a precious chandelier of white and ruby crystal. If you are heading west, do not take Exit 144 for I-90 and the Ohio Turnpike; instead, continue west on Rte. 2. *Open daily Apr.–Dec.; weekends only Jan.–Mar. Admission charged.*

E9TH Cleveland, OH 44114

E. 9th St. exit: Convention & Visitors Bureau, 1301 E. 6th St. (216) 621-4110. The observation deck in the Terminal Tower gives the best bird's-eye introduction to the city. You can get a more intimate look on a trolley tour; and to see where some of America's great fortunes were founded, take a boat trip down the Cuyahoga River near the steel mills. You can also shop at the boutiques of the Flats entertainment district, stroll through one of Cleveland's many parks, and visit the city's renowned zoo. The cultural attractions include the Cleveland Museum of Art, the Western Reserve Historical Society, and the Cleveland Museum of Natural History, where dinosaurs, fossils, and many artifacts are displayed. The Health Education Museum depicts the workings of the human body. Not to be missed is the downtown Arcade, where shops and restaurants are housed in a marvelous five-level skylit cast-iron fantasy.

193 Holden Arboretum, Kirtland

7 mi./15 min. South on Rte. 306, left on Kirtland-Chardon Rd., left on Sperry Rd. The 3,000-acre arboretum is a park for all seasons, but is most impressive in May and June, when azaleas, crab apples, and other flowering trees and shrubs are in their full glory. There are 20 miles of hiking trails, from which many of the special plantings can be seen. Under construction is a sensory trail for the visually handicapped that will feature the aromas and textures of plants. *Open Tues.–Sun. Admission charged.*

200 Fairport Harbor Marine Museum and Light Tower

8 mi./15 min. North on Rte. 44, right on Rte. 2, north on Rte. 535, bear left on High St. at fork. The Fairport Harbor Light, during the hundred years of its service, was both a landmark

200. *Abandoned lighthouse and Frontenac pilothouse are part of the marine museum.*

to the settlers en route to the West and an important beacon to ships plying Lake Erie. There has been a light here since 1825, and though today's lighthouse tower, built of Berea sandstone in 1871, is no longer functional, it and the handsome red brick museum next door confirm the area's maritime heritage. *Open Sat.–Sun. Memorial Day–Labor Day. Admission charged.*

218 Geneva State Park

5 mi./8 min. North on Rte. 534. Sounds of the waves and fresh breezes blowing off Lake Erie provide a welcome respite from highway noise and fumes. The major attraction is a large marina (with completion scheduled for the spring of 1989). Beside the marina is a recreation area with a swimming beach with protected bathing and a picnic area studded with silver maple trees. There are also 91 campsites within walking distance of the lake. Nature trails through woodlands, meadows, and swampland invite further pleasant pursuits. *Open year-round.*

218 Erieview Amusement Park

6 mi./10 min. North on Rte. 534, right on Rte. 531 (Lake Rd.). The 700-foot beach, the miniature railway, and the rides for children are the relaxing side of the park. For excitement there's the Wild Water Works water slide. This maze of water chutes winding down over wooden supports resembles a work of conceptual art and is recommended only for the stout of heart. *Open weekends Mother's Day–mid-June; daily mid-June–Labor Day. Admission for rides only.*

5 Presque Isle State Park, Erie
I-79

Exit 5: 8 mi./12 min. North on Rte. 832. I-79 exit: 8 mi./12 min. North on I-79, left on W. 12th St., right on Rte. 832. Excellent exhibits at the nature center will enhance one's appreciation of this unique park. The 7-mile-long sandy peninsula serves not only as a recreational area but also as a place to view all stages of a 600-year ecological development, from fragile sandspit to a

mature forest of hemlocks, oaks, and sugar maples. To the north is the expanse of Lake Erie, to the south Presque Isle Bay, where Commodore Perry's fleet was constructed for the War of 1812. Park amenities include fishing, a marina, sandy beaches with lifeguards, picnic areas, and miles of trails. In winter, ice fishing and cross-country skiing are popular. *Park open year-round. Beach open Memorial Day–Labor Day.*

I-79. *Dedicated fishermen, ever hopeful, continue their quest until the end of day.*

I-79 Erie, PA 16501

Chamber of Commerce, 1006 State St. (814) 454-7191. For all its success as a modern industrial center, echoes of the War of 1812 still reverberate here. In September 1813, Commodore Oliver Hazard Perry won a stunning victory over the British on Lake Erie. Six of the nine ships in Perry's fleet were built in Erie, and one of them, the reconstructed flagship *Niagara*, is proudly berthed here. The strategy and details of the historic battle are depicted in the Erie Historical Museum, a Romanesque revival mansion with handsome period rooms and beautifully restored Tiffany windows. A planetarium is housed in a building adjoining the museum. The past is further recalled at the Old Custom House, built in 1839, now an art museum. The Cashiers House, built the same year, features some fine antique furnishings. In the Dickson Tavern, Erie's oldest surviving building, you can savor the 19th-century equivalent of a cocktail bar.

59 **Chadwick Bay Wine Co.**

5 min. South on Rte. 60. Small vineyards have prospered on the southern shores of Lake Erie ever since Deacon Elizah Fay first planted vines here in 1824. Chadwick Bay Wine Co. is a family business that produces up to 90,000 bottles per year of various kinds, including dry Chambourcins, medium dry Chablis and Burgundy, and the sweet Cracker Ridge white and rosé. When you visit the modern but surprisingly modest-size winery building itself, you will see the whole wine-making process from the fermentation of the grapes to bottling. At the complimentary tasting counter you are invited to sample the various wines and jellies made from wine. Live entertainment is offered Saturday and Sunday afternoons. *Open daily Mon.–Sat. and P.M. Sun.*

51 **Albright-Knox Art Gallery, Buffalo**

6 mi./10 min. West on Rte. 33, right on Rte. 198; follow signs. Although this museum has a rather forbidding neoclassical facade reminiscent of a Greek temple, its collections represent all major periods. Especially strong are the holdings of modern American and European art, which include such major painters as Willem de Kooning, Robert Rauschenberg, Jean Dubuffet, Jackson Pollock, and many others. Henry Moore, George Segal, and other modern sculptors are given the space needed to show their impressive works. You'll also find a sampling of distinguished art from the pre–Christian Era through the Renaissance, the 18th and 19th centuries, French impressionists, and such 20th-century master artists as Braque, Matisse, Picasso, and Mondrian. *Open Tues.–Sun. except Thanksgiving Day, Christmas, and New Year's Day. Admisssion free but donations encouraged.*

51 **Buffalo Zoological Gardens**

5 mi./13 min. West on Rte. 33, right on Rte. 198; follow signs. There are few creatures more appealing than a baby bison, as you may discover here, and few as odd-looking as the capybara, the world's largest rodent. Here, too, you'll find a functioning prairie-dog town and other favorite animals such as lions, zebras, polar bears, elephants, gorillas, and snakes—including an anaconda. The zoo is now working on its plan to further develop natural habitats for its residents. Children might want to ride on a camel or an elephant. *Open daily except Thanksgiving Day and Christmas. Admission charged.*

50. *Dramatic promontories enhance the view from this overlook on the American side.*

50 **Niagara Falls**

20 mi./30 min. North on I-290, north on I-190 to Exit N21, west on Robert Moses Pkwy.; follow signs. Pictures and descriptions—no matter how dramatic—cannot do true justice to this magnificent creation of nature, consisting of the 130-foot American Falls in New York and the 167-foot Horseshoe Falls in Canada. Only when you see and hear billions of gallons of water plummeting down to the misty maelstroms below can the awesome power of this spectacle be fully appreciated. The falls can be seen from the top, from the observation tower, or from a boat trip on the *Maid of the Mist*, which goes right up to the base of the falls, where in the foam, spray, and constant roar you are as much a part of this unforgettable phenomenon as you could ever wish to be. *Open year-round. Admission charged Apr.–Oct.*

48A **Akron Falls Park**

12 mi./20 min. South on Rte. 77, right on Rte. 5, right on Rte. 93; follow signs. A modest but pleasant spot to rest or picnic, this 250-acre county park has tennis courts, baseball diamonds, a skating rink, and picnic areas in addition to the waterfall. A wooded path leads down from one of the parking areas through a gorge adorned with firs and dogwood to an observation platform, where one can enjoy the cool mist from the 50-foot falls. Swallows nest in the mossy recesses of the gorge's walls, which have been hollowed out by the cascading water. *Open year-round.*

47 **Victorian Doll Museum and Chili Doll Hospital, North Chili**

12 mi./20 min. East on I-490 to Exit 4, north on Rte. 259, right on Rte. 33. Linda Greenfield created this remarkable doll museum from her own childhood collection, and she has been restoring dolls in her "hospital" for some 20 years. The museum has about 1,200 dolls, dating from the 1840's to the present, and they are made of everything from china, wood, and wax to papier-mâché and felt. There are entire circuses, a Noah's Ark, Kewpie dolls, 25 years' worth of Ken and Barbie, and flappers with cigarette holders. Dolls can be left for Linda's expert ministrations at the hospital, but the workroom itself is not open to the public. A doll collector's gift shop offers a variety of dolls and accessories for purchase. *Open Tues.–Sun. except holidays and Jan. Admission charged.*

47. *A delightful assembly of dolls and related accoutrements from the Victorian era.*

47 **Rochester, NY 14604**

45 *10 mi./15 min. Convention & Visitors Bureau, 126 Andrews St. (716) 546-3070.* Set in the beautiful Genesee Valley, New York State's third largest city has attractions ranging from photography to lilacs. The International Museum of Photography, in the 50-room mansion built by George Eastman, houses the world's largest collection of photo exhibits. Eastman was founder of the Eastman Kodak Company, which offers guided tours of its facilities in summer. The Strong Museum has superb collections of Victorian furniture, miniatures, and dolls. The Rochester Museum and Science Center features natural science exhibits, Iroquois artifacts, and planetarium shows; and major art collections are displayed at the Memorial Art Gallery. If you want to stretch your legs, take a stroll on the University of Rochester campus or through adjacent Genesee Valley Park. In the third week of May you can enjoy the ethereal fragrance of 400 varieties of lilacs in Highland Park.

44 **Granger Homestead and Carriage Museum, Canandaigua**

43 *Exit 44: 7 mi./10 min. South on Rte. 332 (becomes Main St.). Exit 43: 9 mi./ 12 min. South on Rte. 21, right on Main St.* This dignified federal-style mansion was the home of Gideon Granger, a gentleman farmer, lawyer, and postmaster-general under Presidents Jefferson and Madison. Finished in 1816, the house was intended to be, in Granger's own words, "unrivaled in the nation." It features elegant woodwork, many original furnishings, a 1,400-book library, and rococo gasolier lighting fixtures. The Carriage Museum has wagons, coaches, fire-fighting vehicles, and wonderfully curvaceous sleighs. *Open daily June–Aug.; Tues.–Sat. May and Oct.; Mon.–Sat. Sept. Admission charged.*

44 **Sonnenberg Gardens and Mansion, Canandaigua**

43 *Exit 44: 8 mi./12 min. South on Rte. 332 (becomes Main St.), left on Rte. 21 (Gibson St.), left on Charlotte St. Exit 43: 7 mi./15 min. South on Rte. 21, right on Charlotte St.* These extraordinary gardens have

44–43. *Sonnenberg's rich mélange of styles gives the mansion a unique appeal.*

been acclaimed by the Smithsonian Institution as "one of the most magnificent late Victorian gardens ever created in America." The Japanese Garden contains a bronze Buddha and an exquisite teahouse. The Italian Garden, with its fleur-de-lis design, is laid out in the grand manner. Streams, waterfalls, and geysers accent the paths of the Rock Garden. Visitors can also tour 10 rooms of the Victorian mansion that was the summer home of F. F. Thompson and his wife Mary Clark Thompson, the gardens' developer. *Open daily mid-May–mid-Oct. Admission charged.*

42 **Seneca Lake State Park**

6 mi./15 min. South on Rte. 14 to Geneva, left on Rte. 5/20; follow signs. Seneca Lake is the deepest and one of the longest of the Finger Lakes, so named because in Iroquois legend they were said to be the fingerprints of the Great Spirit. Bones and artifacts from a tribe that predates the Iroquois were found during the development of this state park, which offers a 200-slip marina, a picnic area, playgrounds, and a bathhouse with hot showers. Warm, shallow water and sandy beaches invite swimmers and sunbathers, and the adventurous angler will appreciate the lake's excellent fishing and cash-prize events. *Park open year-round; marina open daily May–Oct. Admission charged daily in summer; weekends only mid-May–Memorial Day, Labor Day–Columbus Day.*

41 **Women's Rights National Historical Park, Seneca Falls**

6 mi./15 min. South on Rte. 414, left on Rte. 5/20. The first Women's Rights Convention, held in Seneca Falls in 1848, was planned by Elizabeth Cady Stanton and several friends, all of whom were dissatisfied with society's treatment of women. Mrs. Stanton, Mary Ann McClintock, and others drafted the Declaration of Sentiments, which stated that "all men and women are created equal" and called for more rights for women. This declaration was signed by 68 women and 32 men at the convention. The park, actually a historic district encompassing several blocks of Seneca Falls, has a visitor center that offers exhibits and audiovisuals, guided tours of the Stanton home, and walking tours to pertinent structures in Seneca Falls, such as the Seneca Falls Historical Society and the Wesleyan Chapel, where the first convention was held. The National Women's Hall of Fame here pays tribute to more than three dozen notable women whose accomplishments affected the mores, customs, and welfare of a nation and the aspirations of many individuals. *Open daily Apr.– Nov.; Mon.–Fri. Dec.–Mar. Admission free but donations encouraged.*

40 **Emerson Park**

10 mi./25 min. South on Rte. 34 to Auburn, left on Rte. 20, right on Rte. 38, continue on Rte. 38A. Don't be put off by the ordinary-looking kiddie rides visible from the road. There's more: the Edwardian splendor of a green-roofed 1912 garden pavilion among lawns and flower beds that carpet the hillsides to the very edge of Lake Owasco; the Merry-Go-Round Theater, which offers summer stock productions; and the longhouses and lofty tepees of a 12th-century Owasco Indian village. The village is a living illustration of the pride and elegance of prehistoric Indian life, with its advanced techniques in farming and the making of tools, clay pots, and domestic artifacts. The nearby agriculture museum has exhibits related to farming in the region from the 19th century through the 1930's. *Open daily mid-May–mid-Sept. Admission charged for some activities.*

27   19   10   13   26   20   32

39   34   32   31   30   29   27   4

39 Beaver Lake Nature Center, Baldwinsville

10 mi./15 min. Northwest on Rte. 690, west on Rte. 370, right on E. Mud Lake Rd. The 200-acre lake and the surrounding wetlands, meadows, and woods of this preserve are as unspoiled and tranquil as a remote wilderness. It is a major staging area for thousands of migrating Canada geese, a truly awe-inspiring sight in spring and fall. Eight different trails wind through a mixed environment of woodland, bog, and marsh. In spring a wonderful array of wildflowers appears, and blossoming trilliums carpet the forest floor. Guided canoe trips attract visitors in the summer, and skiing and snowmobiling are enjoyed in the winter. *Open year-round.*

34 Verona Beach State Park

7 mi./12 min. North on Rte. 13. Constructed in 1944, this 1,700-acre park has fortunately not been overdeveloped. It is an idyllic retreat shaded by oaks and locusts, with a mile-long beach sloping gently to the inviting clear waters of Lake Oneida. Other attractions in the area include boating, fishing, and observing the wildlife. Deer, an occasional eagle, and in the fall, flocks of migrating waterfowl may be seen. *Park open year-round; camping mid-Apr.–mid-Nov.*

32 Erie Canal Village

10 mi./20 min. North on Rte. 233, left on Rte. 69/49, left on Rte. 46/49. The prosperity created by the Erie Canal in the 19th century is explained in the Canal Museum and is evident in this reconstructed village of the 1840's. Among the buildings are Bennett's Tavern, a handsome three-story gabled house, a onetime stagecoach stop that now serves refreshments; a nicely furnished farmhouse where antique quilts are displayed; an 1839 church-meetinghouse; a livery stable and a blacksmith's shop; and the 1840 Crosby House, where spinning and weaving are demonstrated. A replica of a horse-drawn packet boat takes passengers along a stretch of the canal, and a half-scale replica of a coal-fired steam locomotive pulls a passenger train along the bank. A carriage museum displays a wide range of horse-drawn vehicles. *Open daily May–Sept. Admission charged.*

31 Munson-Williams-Proctor Institute, Utica

5 min. South on Genesee St. The institute's two contrasting sections—a museum of modern art and a 19th-century mansion—are joined by a sculpture grove. The museum features such 20th-century artists as Picasso, Kandinsky, Mondrian, Pollock, and Calder.

Fountain Elms, the mansion built in the 1850's by Alfred Munson, is the very essence of the Italianate style. Listed in *The National Register of Historic Places*, the house is elegantly decorated with fine furnishings. Everything from furniture to teaspoons was the best available in the mid-19th century. A room on the second floor contains collections of dolls, toys, china, silver, and glassware. The most prized display is a collection of 289 watches and table clocks, mostly from 18th- and 19th-century Europe. *Open Tues.–Sat. and P.M. Sun. except holidays.*

27 Schoharie Crossing State Historic Site, Fort Hunter

9 mi./15 min. North on Rte. 30, left on Rte. 5S to T intersection; follow signs. Because of the turbulence of Schoharie Creek, the builders of the Erie Canal elected to cross that waterway by aqueduct in 1841. Today the 7 remaining arches of the original 14, looking more like the ruins of a Roman aqueduct than relics of a great 19th-century engineering feat, bear further witness to the river's violence. A path of about a mile leads to what's left of the giant locks that lifted barges up to the aqueduct. Charts, photographs, and documents regarding the building of the canal, the locks, and the aqueduct can be seen at the visitor center. *Open Wed.–Sun. May–Oct.*

If You Have Some Extra Time: Cooperstown

30 / 29

Exit 30: 25 mi./45 min. Exit 29: 30 mi./50 min. Here you'll find a remarkable repository of Americana, with diverse collections devoted to village life, rural life, folk art, and the sport that is our national pastime.

Village Crossroads on the outskirts of Cooperstown features original structures from the region that date from 1795 to 1850: a tavern, a country store, a lawyer's office, a printshop, a doctor's office, a druggist's shop, a schoolhouse, a barn, a church, and a pioneer home.

The adjacent Farmers' Museum is housed in a handsome barn where one can see displays of the tools and equipment used in rural upstate New York from the early to the mid-19th century.

The nearby Fenimore House, built as a private residence in 1932, now houses an outstanding collection of landscape paintings and folk art.

In Cooperstown proper, the great American sport is honored at the National Baseball Hall of Fame and Museum—founded in 1939 to celebrate baseball's centennial. The three-story building contains several theme rooms, including a Great Moments Room featuring record-breaking events and a World Series Room where memorabilia from the October Classic are on display. You can gaze upon equipment used by such stars as Babe Ruth, Lou Gehrig, Joe DiMaggio, and Mickey Mantle. A computer data base provides information on most players and teams, and there's a fabulous collection of baseball cards. The National Baseball Library behind the museum shows films of memorable games. Nearby is Doubleday Field, the onetime cow pasture where the sport was born. *How to get there: Exit 30, south on Rte. 28; Exit 29, west on Rte. 55, southwest on Rte. 80.*

4   Albany, NY 12207

Convention and Visitors Bureau, 52 S. Pearl St. (518) 434-1217; (800) 622-8464 outside NY. Settled in the early 1600's, chartered in 1686, and declared the capital city of New York State in 1797, Albany has a rich and varied history. The Dutch presence is recalled at the Van Rensselaer home and the Ten Broeck Mansion. The Schuyler Mansion was built for a general in the Revolution, and the New York State Museum provides insights into local history. Empire State Plaza is a monumental modern-day architectural extravaganza.

1   Hancock Shaker Village

9.5 mi./15 min. North on Rte. 41. Founded in 1790 on a broad meadow overlooking the Berkshire Hills, this Shaker community had some 250 inhabitants at its prime in the mid-19th century. In 1960 the last three members left, and the village fell into disrepair. Several of the 18 remaining buildings are staffed with knowledgeable craftspeople. The elegantly simple and spacious Brick Dwelling contains spindle-back chairs, fitted cabinets, polished tables, and other examples of classic Shaker furniture. The imposing circular fieldstone barn—not a typical Shaker design—stabled the cattle and served as a granary and a threshing floor. *Open daily Memorial Day–Oct. Admission charged.*

2   Chesterwood, Stockbridge

7 mi./15 min. Southwest on Rte. 102, left on Rte. 183, right on Mohawk Lake Rd.; follow signs. A splendid early 20th-century house, a large-windowed studio, and a barn–sculpture gallery compose this summer retreat of sculptor Daniel Chester French, who is best known for his statues of Abraham Lincoln at the Lincoln Memorial in Washington, D. C., and the Minute Man in Concord, Massachusetts. During the summer months, French's work is displayed on the lawns and in the gardens. The setting is an idyllic unity of woods, meadows, and the surrounding Berkshire Hills. *Open daily May–Oct. Admission charged.*

9. *A pair of oxen, bearing their heavy handcrafted yoke, make a well-rehearsed left turn.*

4   Storrowton Village, West Springfield

6 mi./10 min. South on Riverdale St. (Rte. 5), right on Memorial Ave. (Rte. 147). A collection of buildings from Massachusetts and New Hampshire, dating back to the mid-18th century and staffed with "townspeople" in costumes, has been assembled around a pretty village green. An imposing meetinghouse and the sprawling 1799 Atkinson Tavern dominate the town. Notable among the restored buildings is the Phillips House (1767), distinctive for its gambrel roof and graduated clapboarding. *Open P.M. Tues.–Sun. mid-June–Labor Day. Admission charged.*

9   Old Sturbridge Village

3 min. Southwest on Rte. 20; follow signs. Life in rural 19th-century New England has been attractively re-created on 200 acres of rolling countryside dotted with woods and ponds. Among the more than 40 buildings brought from nearby farms and towns are several houses, a tiny iron-shuttered bank, a sawmill, a gristmill, and a cidermill, a schoolhouse, a printshop, a pottery shop, and a blacksmith's shop. The typical family farm comprises the house, outbuildings, cattle, and other animals. Costumed staff members demonstrate early crafts, plow the fields, and run the community's store. *Open daily Apr.–Nov.; Tues.–Sun. Dec.–Mar. except Christmas and New Year's Day. Admission charged.*

22   Boston, MA 02199

Convention & Visitors Bureau, Prudential Plaza. (617) 536-4100. Few places are so rewarding to explore on foot as this historic city. In only a few hours one can savor the spacious tree-studded Common, the cobbled streets and elegant homes on Beacon Hill, the maze of narrow streets in the North End, and the bustling restored Quincy Market with its shops, cafés, and boutiques. You can wander at will through the city, or you can take the Freedom Trail, a self-guiding walking tour, starting at a booth in the Common.

Among the many highlights beyond the center of the city are the Museum of Fine Arts, the charmingly idiosyncratic Isabella Stewart Gardner Museum, the Arnold Arboretum, the Franklin Park Zoo, and across the Charles River, Harvard Yard and the busy streets of Cambridge.

I-90 Pictograph Caves State Historic Site, Billings

9 mi./15 min. West on I-90 to Exit 452, east on Hardin Rd., right on Coburn Rd.; follow signs. Archeologists have found more than 30,000 artifacts—projectiles, weapons, bones—buried in these caves, which may have been inhabited by hunter tribes as early as 10,000 years ago. Pictograph Cave, largest of three, is named for the primitive colored pictures—only those in red are now visible—that adorn its smooth sandstone walls. Images include tepees, animals, weapons, and shield-bearing warriors. This cave may have been the burial place of at least one group of inhabitants. Ghost Cave, the second largest, yielded bison bones and skeletons of three people. Middle Cave's steep floor made it unsuitable for occupancy. The trail to the caves leads up steep hills, and several paths branch off to overlooks and interpretive signs. *Open daily mid-Apr.– mid-Oct., weather permitting.*

I-90 Peter Yegen, Jr., Yellowstone County Museum, Billings

10 mi./15 min. West on I-90 to Exit 450, north on 27th St. to airport; loop through terminal to museum. An 1893 log cabin houses a major portion of this museum, where the collections range from prehistoric times to the days of the homesteaders. The cabin's living room, dominated by a huge stone fireplace and furnished in 19th-century style, with a high-backed rocker, Tiffany lamps, and a grandfather clock, evokes life in Montana's pioneer era. Large collections in four additional rooms comprise Indian clothing and artifacts, fossils, military uniforms, slot machines, peace pipes, dueling pistols, paintings, and branding irons. You'll also see a roundup wagon used on the Crow Indian Reservation from 1893 to 1946 and, outside, a 1031 Class L-7 locomotive, the last Northern Pacific steam switch engine that operated in Billings. Dioramas interpret the age of dinosaurs and cave people and depict the legends of Sacrifice Cliff (braves on blindfolded horses galloping off the top to their deaths as a plea to the gods to end a smallpox epidemic) and the Yellowstone River Ferry (a judge saving his wife from drowning). *Open Mon.–Fri. and P.M. Sun. except holidays.*

I-90 Oscar's Dreamland Amusement Park, Billings

13 mi./25 min. West on I-90 to Exit 446, west on S. Frontage Rd., left on Shiloh Rd. Oscar Cooke's obvious passion is farm machinery. At the Yesteryear Museum his intriguing collection of 300 restored antique tractors, 40 steam engines, 100 threshing machines, and untold numbers of combines and freight wagons is housed in three enormous buildings that cover approximately 2 acres. Other unexpected treasures include a 1917 Liberty truck, 19th-century hearses, road-building machines, an early airplane, and a 110-h.p. 1906 Best steam truck that pulled six 10-ton ore wagons at a time. At the amusement park you can ride a restored railroad, a merry-go-round, or a Ferris wheel, and for a glimpse of pioneer life, stroll along a restored Main Street with fully appointed homes and stores and a jail-house with padded cells. *Open daily May– Labor Day.*

I-90. *This family of visitors helps to reveal the vast dimensions of Pictograph Cave.*

93 95 West and East Rosebud Recreation Areas, Forsyth

Exit 93 (West Area): 1 min. North on Rte. 12; follow signs. Exit 95 (East Area): 3 min. North on Main St., right on 15th Ave. Both of these recreation areas are on the Yellowstone River. At East Rosebud there is a campground, but a weir makes the river dangerous for swimming. West Rosebud has a picnic area and a small playground. Both sites offer fishing and views of the bluffs on the northern banks of the river. *Open year-round.*

135 Range Riders Museum and Memorial Hall, Miles City

3 min. Northeast on I-94 (business loop); follow signs. This exceptional collection of Old West memorabilia commemorates the life, times, and friendships of the cowboy era and recounts the history of the region after trappers, soldiers, and settlers arrived. There are major displays of fossils and Indian artifacts, guns, knives, swords, daggers and bayonets, stuffed birds and animals, horseshoes, bits and hobbles, saddles, spurs, buggies, and coaches. Period buildings—a trading post, a hotel, a jail, a smithy, a barbershop, a dress shop, and a livery stable—re-create the 1880's Main Street of Milestown, as this city was formerly called. The Pioneer Memorial Hall shows a large collection of photographs of pioneers of many nationalities who helped settle the northern Plains. *Open daily Mar.– Nov. Admission charged.*

215 Frontier Gateway Museum, Glendive

1 min. Exit north, right on Belle Prairie Rd. This museum is a repository of the region's history and a grab bag of engaging curiosities. There are fossils and mineral specimens, cowbells, Indian bows and arrows, saddlebags and war bonnets, and replicas of 16th- and 17th-century European suits of armor. Downstairs a re-created street scene—complete with a drugstore, a general store, a dress shop, printing equipment, early radios, and a taxidermy display—portrays a vanished way of life. Outdoor exhibits include another general store, a firehouse with a 1938 fire engine, a log cabin furnished as its owner left it during World War II, and the 1910 Golden Valley schoolhouse, with schoolbooks from 1898 to 1957. *Open Mon.–Sat. and P.M. Sun. June–Aug.; P.M. daily late May and early Sept. Admission free but donations encouraged.*

215 | Makoshika State Park, Glendive

3 mi./6 min. South on Merrill Ave., left on Barry St., right on Taylor Ave., left on Snyder St. The park, in eastern Montana, preserves a spectacular tract of badlands—*makoshika* is the Sioux word for "bad lands"—and high prairie. From mesa tops there are views of weathered buttes, hogback ridges, and poly-chrome valleys ornamented with capped pil-lars, fluted walls and spires, and landslides shaped like the feet of gigantic elephants. Junipers and pines dot this arid badlands area and soften the sky-wide prairie with dark green stands. Hawks, turkey vultures, mule deer, and cottontails are abundant, and in spring the prairie and desert wildflowers bring delight. Several of the park's unim-proved roads are hazardous and should not be traveled in wet weather. A detailed guide can be obtained at the park entrance for a small charge. *Open year-round.*

6 | Chateau de Mores State Historic Site

5 min. South on access road; follow signs. Here the Marquis de Mores, one of the strang-est figures ever to ride the western Plains, tried to make his home and fortune. Born in Paris, he went to the Dakota country in 1883 to raise beef and to build a castle in the wil-derness. Within three years his venture failed; he and his wife, Medora, left Dakota forever, and in 1936 the château was given to the state. Most of its original furnishings are intact: buf-falo-skin robes vie with copies of *La Vie Pari-sienne* and Medora's French watercolors to create the *mise-en-scène* of these cosmopoli-tan pioneers, and the Trophy Room preserves both Medora's black riding habit and an array of bear traps. The visitor center displays some fascinating memorabilia of the marquis and his adventures. *Open daily mid-May–mid-Sept. Admission charged.*

6–7. *Caps of resistant material on top helped shape these fantastic sculptural forms.*

6, 7 | Theodore Roosevelt National Park, South Unit

5 min. Exit 6: east on exit road to Medora; follow signs. Exit 7: west on exit road to Medora; follow signs. Some of North America's most memorable landscapes lie within the boundaries of this magnificent park. In places the banded colors of eroded valleys and tableland stretch for miles; else-where meadows of sagebrush, pale and sil-very, yield to riverbanks where cottonwoods shine golden or bright green, depending on the season. You can see bison, which lend their archaic presence to the ancient hills, and golden eagles. In the visitor center the park's geology and natural history are illustrated, and there are mementos of Teddy Roosevelt, who ranched here before he became our na-tion's 26th president. Roosevelt was a leading advocate of the national parks system. *Open year-round. Admission charged.*

12 | Patterson Lake Recreation Area

4 min. South on Rte. 10; follow signs. Man-made Patterson Lake is part of a major Mis-souri River valley flood-control project in western North Dakota. The park has 26 miles of low-banked shoreline with swaying reed beds, about 1,190 acres of water, and 1,200 acres of land with nature trails. Visitors will find both primitive and modern camping ar-eas, children's playgrounds, and horseshoe pits. *Open year-round. Admission charged.*

13 | Joachim Regional Museum, Dickinson

1 min. South on 3rd Ave. W., left on 12th St. The emphasis in this museum is on the histo-ry of the various ethnic groups that settled this part of western North Dakota, mostly immi-grants from Hungary, Germany, Czechoslova-kia, Norway, and Russia. The exhibits change annually, but they usually include colorful folk costumes, diaries, newspaper clippings, letters, books, photographs, tools, clothing, and household articles brought here by the settlers. There is a comprehensive display of Indian clothing and ornaments, as well as an authentically decorated Plains Indian tepee. The museum is named for its benefactor, Mil-ton Joachim, a local businessman. *Open daily Memorial Day–Labor Day.*

28 Sweet Briar Lake Recreation Area

1 min. North on Rte. 48. This attractive setting is enhanced by a hillock-strewn terrain, an irregular lakeshore fringed in some places with dense reed beds, willows, cottonwoods, and prairie flowers that grow freely. In a nearby arboretum, avenues of trees that prosper locally can be seen as if in a grove. They include black and green ash, box elder, black walnuts, and butternuts. You'll also find plots of such native grasses as wild rye, big bluestem, and switch grass. On the low hills to the west and south of the park, off Exit 27, is a surreal fiberglass model of a Holstein cow—said to be the largest cow statue in the world. *Open year-round.*

33 Fort Abraham Lincoln State Park

5 mi./8 min. South on Rte. 1806. This park lies at the scenic confluence of the Heart and Missouri rivers. Ft. Abraham Lincoln was established at this strategic spot in 1872 in order to protect settlers and workers building the Northern Pacific Railroad. The fort later was the departure point for Colonel Custer's campaign against the Plains Indians; it was abandoned in 1891. Also on the grounds is the site of the Slant Indian village—formerly the home of the Mandan Indians—where you'll see four reconstructed earth lodges and the Arc of the Lone Man, a ritual site commemorating the hero who saved the Mandan nation from a great flood. *Open year-round. Admission charged.*

36 Camp Hancock State Historic Site, Bismarck

3 mi./11 min. South on State St., right on Divide Ave., left on Washington St., left on Main Ave. Here you'll see the oldest building in Bismarck, and one of the oldest in North Dakota: the supply depot of a camp built in 1872 to protect the crews then building the Northern Pacific Railroad. The structure now serves as a museum where the region's history, geology, and wildlife are described with photos, documents, and memorabilia. Colonel Custer is said to have obtained supplies from this camp at various times in the 1870's. *Open P.M. Wed.–Sun. mid-May–mid-Sept.*

36 Cross Ranch Nature Preserve

42 mi./45 min. North on Rte. 83, left on Rte. 200A. This 6,200-acre park preserves the natural and cultural history of North Dakota in all its beauty and diversity. Here you'll see a native prairie and floodplain forest that have remained virtually unchanged for the past 100 years; more than 100 archeological sites, some dating back to 6,000 B.C.; and a variety of wildlife, including mule deer and eastern and western songbirds. *Open year-round.*

37 Sertoma Riverside Park, Bismarck

7 mi./15 min. South on Centennial Rd. (becomes Bismarck Expy.), right on Washington St., left on Arbor Ave.; follow signs. Situated on the banks of the Missouri River, this 98-acre park has trails leading through a wooded area. Tennis courts and playgrounds are available, and the Dakota Zoo, the chief attraction, has some 500 animals, 125 different species, including Patagonian cavies, pygmy goats, wallabies, and African porcupines. *Park open year-round; zoo open daily early May–Sept. Admission charged for zoo.*

38 Menoken Indian Village State Historic Site

4 min. East on Frontage Rd.; follow signs. This 3-acre site, discovered in 1936, marks the spot where Indians believed to have been ancestors of the Mandans lived about 1,000 years ago. Their village was protected on one side by the steep banks of a meander in Apple Creek and on the other sides by a fortified ditch. You can still see the 20-foot-wide ditch and the depressions where some 10 to 16 earth lodges once stood. *Open year-round.*

59 Frontier Village, Jamestown

4 min. North on Rte. 281, right on 17th St. SW. Located on hills overlooking Jamestown, this reconstructed prairie town preserves the spirit and style of the Old West. The buildings, moved to the village from nearby areas, include Jamestown's first rail depot, a one-room schoolhouse, a country church, a sheriff's office, a barbershop with white enamel

33. *During the annual Frontier Army Days, Custer's 7th Cavalry is actively remembered.*

36. *Tender twigs are a staple in the diet of beavers such as this one at Cross Ranch Preserve.*

chairs, a firehouse with hose carts and hand-pumpers, and a 60-ton concrete replica of an American bison, the species that once dominated the area's plains. *Open daily Memorial Day–Labor Day.*

59 Jamestown Dam Lakeside Marina

8.5 mi./15 min. North on Rte. 281, right on 3rd St. NE, left on 5th Ave. (Rte. 20). The dam on the James River has filled a deep valley here, and the shores of the lake are indented with cliffs and small coves. A sheltering island opposite the marina provides a charming spot for a peaceful picnic. Nearby, the Martin Joos Memorial Grove offers picnickers another choice, among stands of ashes and Russian olives. *Grove open year-round; marina open May–mid-Sept.*

67 Clausen Springs Recreation Complex

20.5 mi./25 min. South on Rte. 1, left on access road; follow signs. Named for three Norwegian brothers who were the first settlers in the area, this 550-acre park site dates back to the early 19th century, when French fur traders and Indians of the Pembina colony camped here while hunting beavers and buffaloes.

Indians encamped here to protest the white man's violation of their treaty rights. During the Prohibition years people came from many miles around for Saturday night dances on a floor set up in the woods. Horned owls come to nest here during February and March. *Open year-round.*

85 Bonanzaville, U.S.A., West Fargo

2 min. East on Rte. 10. Bonanzaville is a regional museum complex of almost 50 buildings, each offering a carefully researched and well-tended display from the past—an aircraft museum, a collection of dolls, a fire station, an early bathroom offering "Hot Baths 25¢ With Soap and Towel," and a barn with live animals. Dwellings include a reproduction of a sod house, log cabins, and period homes, one of them owned by D. H. Houston, who devised an early type of roll film. The Red River and Northern Plains Regional Museum contains collections of toys, model ships and cars, and a comprehensive exhibit on Indians in this area. *Museum and buildings open Mon.–Fri. and P.M. Sat.–Sun. late May–late Oct.; museum open Tues.–Fri. late Oct.–late May except Thanksgiving Day, Christmas, and New Year's Day. Admission charged.*

1 Plains Art Museum, Moorhead

5 min. North on Rte. 75, left on Main Ave. A Sioux baby bonnet trimmed with dentalia shells, a dance bustle made of feathers and tin, and Ojibwa dance caps of porcupine quills and deer hair are among many excellent examples of Indian art in this museum. The permanent collection also includes works by American impressionist Mary Cassatt as well as painters Jerry Ott and Luis Jimenez. There are changing exhibits, and many items sold here were made by area artists and craftsmen. *Open Tues.–Sat. and P.M. Sun. except Thanksgiving Day, Christmas, and New Year's Day. Admission free but donations encouraged.*

6 15 Buffalo River State Park

Exit 6: 11 mi./13 min. North on Rte. 11, right on Rte. 10. Exit 15: 13 mi./15 min. East on Rte. 10, left on Rte. 9, right on Rte. 10. This 1,240-acre park, divided by the Buffalo River, contains one of Minnesota's largest virgin prairies. Along the trails crossing the prairie are more than 250 kinds of grasses and wildflowers; some 200 species of birds and 40 species of mammals are also in residence. Prairie chickens, upland sandpipers, bobolinks, marbled godwits, northern grasshopper mice, and rare Dakota skipper butterflies may all be seen here. You might also come across bison skulls and bones from prehistoric times. *Open year-round. Admission charged.*

61 De Lagoon Park, Fergus Falls

5 min. North on Rte. 59. There are more than 1,000 lakes in Otter Tail County, which includes the town of Fergus Falls, and this park lies on the shores of one of them. The lakes were created during the Wisconsin glacier age, which ended about 10,000 years ago. Surrounded by grasslands, De Lagoon Park is a waterfowl protection area, spacious and peaceful, containing children's playgrounds and a softball complex. Nearby Pebble Lake, which is another city park, offers a golf course and trapshooting. *Open daily mid-May–Oct.*

77   Tipsinah Mounds Park

6 mi./10 min. South on Rte. 10, right on Rte. 79. Located near the southern end of Pomme de Terre Lake, where the Chippewa Indians once made their summer camp, this park takes its name from an Indian word for a turniplike plant. The lake and an adjoining river provided food for them and formed a natural barrier to the prairie fires that were apt to sweep across the Plains from the west. Evidence of human habitation on a peninsula jutting into the lake is indicated by bone and stone tools dated to 9400 B.C.. Just east of the entrance road, traces of some 40 Indian mounds dating from A.D. 1000 to 1600 can be seen. *Open daily May–Oct.*

103   Kensington Runestone Museum, Alexandria

2 mi./8 min. North on Rte. 29. The centerpiece here is a slab of gray stone with a runic inscription describing an expedition made to this area by 8 Goths and 22 Norwegians in 1362. The stone was found, so the story goes, under the roots of an aspen tree by a Minnesota farmer named Olaf Ohman in 1898. Whether it genuinely records the exploits of a Viking expedition to these parts or is a 19th-century forgery has long been the subject of vigorous debate. The museum, with its adjunct, the Fort Alexandria Agricultural Museum, also displays collections of agricultural machinery, pioneer memorabilia, and several Indian artifacts. *Open daily mid-May–Sept.; Mon.–Fri. Oct.–mid-May. Admission charged.*

103   Lake Carlos State Park

13 mi./21 min. North on Rte. 29. Glacially formed Lake Carlos is deep and clear, and its U-shaped northern shore is surrounded by the varied terrain of this beautiful 1,261-acre park. Hikers will encounter a number of different western Minnesota landscapes: marshlands, lakeshore, steep wooded hills, meadowland, and prairie as well as smaller lakes hidden in the hills. Even on a short hike the landscape can change dramatically in a matter of minutes. Those who stay near the lake may see a heron among the reeds or hear the mournful cry of a loon, the state bird of Minnesota. Anglers are attracted by the abundance of bass, crappie, walleye, and northern pike in Lake Carlos. *Open year-round. Admission charged.*

127   Sinclair Lewis Boyhood Home, Sauk Centre

5 min. North on Rte. 71, left on Sinclair Lewis Ave. The first American to win the Nobel Prize for literature spent most of his childhood in this modest but comfortable house, just a step away from the Main Street that he would immortalize in his most famous novel, the story of a small Midwestern town. The office where his father practiced medicine is preserved, along with the RCA radio that was Lewis's gift to him in 1920, the year *Main Street* was published. Other family possessions and memorabilia include Lewis's golf clubs, childhood photographs, and the blue and white washbowl and pitcher that belonged to his first wife, Grace. Behind the home is the gray carriage house where Lewis began writing, at age 15, for the local newspaper. *Open daily Memorial Day–Labor Day. Admission charged.*

167B   Stearns County Historical Center, St. Cloud

5 mi./8 min. North on Rte. 15, right on 2nd St., right on 33rd Ave.; follow signs. One of Minnesota's largest history museums has a distinctly regional yet imaginative focus. The Stearns County granite industry, for example, is documented with a realistic full-size model of a section of a granite quarry. And as the county is one of America's largest producers of dairy products, an entire gallery is devoted to family dairy farming from 1853 to the 1980's. Dioramas with flowing water and mounted specimens illustrate local natural history. You can also see a miniature replica of a circus and memorabilia of St. Cloud's ill-fated Pan Motor Company. *Open Mon.–Sat. and P.M. Sun. Memorial Day–Labor Day; Tues.–Sat. and P.M. Sun. Labor Day–Memorial Day except holidays. Admission charged.*

207   Oliver H. Kelley Farm, Elk River

14 mi./17 min. North on Rte. 101, east on Rte. 10; follow signs. In 1867 Oliver Kelley, an energetic Minnesota farmer, writer, and agriculture leader, founded the Order of the Pa-

I-35W. *Set like a glowing jewel in the St. Paul skyline is the Winter Carnival Ice Palace.*

trons of Husbandry, a fraternal organization for farmers, whose local chapters were called Granges. Eventually the Grange had almost a million members as well as some 25,000 local branches. Kelley's farm is now a national landmark, a living-history farm where one can see the land being managed as it was in the 1860's. The plowing is done by horse and oxen; the sheep and hogs belong to strains from Kelley's day, and so do the crops—for example, King Philip corn, black Norway oats, and purple rose potatoes. In the Farmstead the domestic arts of the period are demonstrated, and in the visitor center there is a fascinating display on Kelley's life and the work of the Grange. *Open Tues.–Sun. May–Oct. Admission charged.* 🛪

I-35W   Minneapolis—St. Paul, MN 55402

Convention & Visitors Association, 15 S. 5th St. (612) 348-4313; (800) 445-7412 outside MN. In summer the parks and waterways clearly dominate the activity here near the headwaters of the Mississippi River. Less obvious are the ways Minnesotans know how to cope with the cold. In the dead of winter the enclosed skyways can make you forget you are this far north. Nicollet Mall is a focal point in Minneapolis; its famed Guthrie Theater and Walker Art Center beckon. There's an excellent zoo, and the Grain Exchange offers a look at the operation of a grain market. Across the river in St. Paul you can visit the state capitol, the Science Museum of Minnesota, the opulent Victorian mansion of Territorial Governor Alexander Ramsey, and also, if you choose to forsake the comfort of the skyways in late January, the Winter Carnival.

1   The Octagon House, Hudson

4 min. North on Rte. 35 (2nd St.), right on Myrtle St. This curious, elegant building, made of stucco and clapboard with a glassed-in cupola, is one of the few examples outside New York State of the eccentric eight-sided homes that were briefly in vogue during the mid-19th century. Built in 1855, it contains period furnishings, and the kitchen is fully equipped with turn-of-the-century utensils.

1. *In addition to charm, octagonal houses were said to have beneficial attributes.*

On the upstairs floors, also furnished with loving attention to detail, there are displays of antique clothing and dolls. The old carriage house museum contains a lavish dollhouse and a re-created blacksmith's shop. Other interesting memorabilia can be seen in the garden house. *Open Tues.–Sat. and P.M. Sun. May–Oct. except July 4. Admission charged.*

24   Crystal Cave

8 mi./12 min. South on Rte. B, left on Rte. 29; follow signs. Flowstone, stalactites, and stalagmites adorn the 30 chambers of this 13,000-year-old cave. Some of the flowstone is pure white and resembles frosting on a cake; some, colored by iron oxide, looks like strips of bacon; other formations, up to 12,000 years old, resemble waterfalls frozen in time or miniature badlands. At the deepest level of the cave, chambers have been carved by whirlpools of a glacial river. Harmless bats—eastern pipistrelles and little browns—roost in the caves and hibernate in them from late October to early April. *Open daily Memorial Day–Labor Day, weekends only Apr.–May and Sept.–Oct. Admission charged.*

41   Empire in Pine Lumber Museum, Downsville

10 mi./16 min. South on Rte. 25, left on Rte. C. In the late 1800's Downsville had one of the largest sawmills in the world. Today a fine lumber museum recalls many aspects of that era. A re-created logging camp displays "shotgun bunks" with mannequins tucked under the covers, a cook's shanty, a blacksmith's shop, a large carved bed once owned by a local lumber baron, and an unusual baking cabinet. You'll also see giant saw blades and other tools of the trade. The grounds include an old jailhouse, a lumber company payroll office, and a post office, complete with leather-hinged wooden letter boxes. *Open Mon.–Sat. and P.M. Sun. May–Oct.* 🛪

65   Paul Bunyan Logging Camp, Eau Claire

4 mi./11 min. North on Rte. 37, left on Clairemont Ave., right on Menomonie St., left on Carson Park Dr. A statue of Paul Bunyan, mythical folk hero of the North Woods, stands at the entrance to this authentic logging camp, dwarfing his blue ox, Babe. The camp—with a cook's shanty, a bunkhouse, a barn, a blacksmith's shop, and an interpretive center—was built in 1934 and is a re-creation of the lumber camps that brought prosperity to this area in the late 1800's. Among the machinery displayed is a horse-powered derrick and a rutter shoe. *Camp open daily May–Labor Day; P.M. Tues.–Sun. rest of Sept.; interpretive center open year-round. Admission free but donations encouraged.* 🛪♿

65   Chippewa Valley Museum, Eau Claire

4 mi./11 min. North on Rte. 37, left on Clairemont Ave., right on Menomonie St., left on Carson Park Dr. Adjoining the Paul Bunyan Logging Camp in Carson Park, this museum has an extensive collection that includes period furnishings, Indian artifacts, antique cars, and exhibits on farming and pioneer life in the region. Located outside the museum are the 1857 Lars Anderson cabin and a one-room schoolhouse built in 1880. *Open Tues.–Sun. June–Aug.; P.M. Tues.–Sun. Sept.–May. Admission charged.* 🛪♿

143 I-90 The Little Red Schoolhouse, Tomah

Exit 143: 4 mi./6 min. South on Rte. 12 (Superior Ave.) to Gillette Park. I-90 exit: 6 mi./8 min. West on I-90 to Exit 41, north on Rte. 131 (Superior Ave.) to Gillette Park. In use from 1864 to 1965, this small, classic one-room schoolhouse now stands in a Tomah city park, a reminder of the past. You can see photographs of the students dating back to the early 1900's, schoolbooks from 1910 and the 1920's, a small collection of minerals, and map stencils for the children's geography lessons. *Open P.M. daily Memorial Day–Labor Day.*

87 The Dells

2 min. East on Rte. 13/23. The Dells of the Wisconsin River are narrow chasms or ravines that have been carved out of sandstone cliffs (formed millions of years ago) by the relentless erosive action of water against rock after the Ice Age meltdown. The walls of the cliffs are corrugated and in places capped by overhangs and pedestals of rock. These picturesque formations can be seen if you take one of the commercial boat tours from the docks in downtown Wisconsin Dells. Boats operate from mid-April to mid-October. Two other outstanding attractions in this area are

The Stand Rock Indian Ceremonial (*5 mi./7 min. from Exit 87; east on Rte. 13/23, left on Rte. 12/16, right on Rte. A, left on Stand Rock Rd.*) offers a program of traditional Indian dances in a magnificent natural amphitheater. *Performance every evening mid-June–Labor Day. Admission charged.*

The Winnebago Indian Museum (*6.5 mi./10 min. from Exit 87; east on Rte. 13/23, across bridge, left on River Rd.*) displays a fine collection of Indian clothing, weapons, ornaments, and other artifacts. *Open daily Apr.–Dec. Admission charged.*

92 106 Circus World Museum, Baraboo

Exit 92: 10 mi./15 min. South on Rte. 12 to Baraboo; follow signs. Exit 106: 14 mi./20 min. West on Rte. 33; follow signs. The Ringling Brothers circus had its winter

92–106. Circus wagons provided a worthy challenge to the wood-carver's skill.

quarters in Baraboo until 1918. The complex of 30 buildings now serves as both an active showplace and a home for circus memorabilia. A circus parade and live performances under the big top are presented daily, and a museum of circus history includes automated miniatures, air calliopes, a merry-go-round, a trolley ride, and displays commemorating various circus stars. The world's largest collection of circus wagons contains fine examples of gilding and carving. The P. T. Barnum sideshow and the menagerie, with its tigers, camels, hippos, and other performing animals, draw fascinated viewers. *Open daily early May–mid-Sept. Admission charged.*

135 Madison, WI 53703

Convention & Visitors Bureau, 121 W. Doty St. (608) 255-0701. The capitol in the downtown area of this attractive city, set on an isthmus between two lakes, is reputed to be the largest state capitol in the United States

and is open for tours. Architecture on a smaller scale is also important here. Frank Lloyd Wright's Unitarian Meeting House (1949–51) is open to the public, and other buildings designed by Wright, a Wisconsin native, can be viewed from the street. The State Historical Museum features Indian and French voyageur exhibits. On the University of Wisconsin campus you can visit an arboretum, Indian effigy mounds, and Babcock Hall, where you'll find college-educated ice cream.

I-90 Lake Kegonsa State Park

6 mi./15 min. South on I-90 to Exit 147; continue on Rte. N, right on Koshkonong Rd.; follow signs. This attractive park, near Madison, has more than 300 acres of woodland, prairie, and marsh, as well as an extensive shoreline on 3,209-acre Lake Kegonsa. The White Oak nature trail loops through woods past Indian mounds. Inviting mown paths wind through quiet prairie. *Open year-round. Admission charged.*

310B Milwaukee, WI 53202

Convention & Visitors Bureau, 756 N. Milwaukee St. (414) 273-7222; (800) 231-0903 outside WI. There's still beer in Milwaukee, and three breweries offer tours, but the city has much more to offer. The arts are well represented by the vast Milwaukee Art Museum; Villa Terrace, an Italian Renaissance-style home with displays of antique furniture and decorative arts; and the extensive collection of the Charles Allis Art Museum, housed in a resplendent Tudor-style mansion.

No less interesting is the Milwaukee Public Museum, with its environmental dioramas, dinosaur skeletons, and Indian artifacts, among other displays. Mitchell Park boasts a noted horticultural conservatory; and the zoo, a few miles west of downtown, is one of the best such institutions in the country.

326 Cliffside County Park

9 mi./15 min. East on 7 Mile Rd., right on Michna Rd.; follow signs. The park has two distinct areas: one includes the campground, a

| WI | IL | | | | See N–S book,
sec. 21 for I-55;
sec. 25 for I-57. | | IL | IN | See
N–S book,
sec. 26. | | | See E–W book,
sec. 23 for I-80;
sec. 6 for I-90. | | IN | MI | |

7   18   2   48   90   50   65   90   40   25

333   **ROUTE 41** **ROUTE 173**   **OH**   **22**   **16**   **94**

See E–W book, sec. 6.   90   55   57   80   80   90

baseball diamond, and tennis courts; and the other, lying behind the children's playground, is an area of woods, rough meadowland, and cliff-top paths. At the first fork in the trail, bear left to cross a meadow (bright with asters and goldenrod in the fall) leading to the cliffs, or walk through the woods. The loop to the lake is a walk of 30 to 45 minutes; there are good views, but the cliff overlooking the lake is steep and crumbly, with no beach access. *Open daily mid-Apr.–mid-Oct.*

333 Racine Zoological Gardens

11 mi./15 min. East on Rte. 20, left on Rte. 32 to Goold St.; follow signs. Situated on the shores of Lake Michigan, this 28-acre zoo has an interesting variety of animals. Wolves and birds of prey make their home in a wooded area near a lake. Nearby, rhesus monkeys and Barbary sheep dwell on a rocky island in a smaller lake, and penguins, otters, pelicans, and other waterbirds have their own watery domains as well. Camels, elephants, kangaroos, deer, and a beautiful white tiger with blue eyes are among the other inhabitants in this zoo. *Open year-round.*

ROUTE 41 **ROUTE 173** Illinois Beach State Park (Southern Unit), Zion

Rte. 41 exit: 11 mi./15 min. South on Rte. 41, left on Wadsworth Rd. Rte. 173 exit: 8 mi./10 min. East on Rte. 173 (Rosecrans Rd.), right on Rte. 41; proceed as above. One of the most popular state parks in the country, this extensive recreation facility on Lake Michigan is divided into northern and southern units. But first-time visitors are encouraged to head for the southern unit. The long beach there is covered with fine sugarlike sand and acres of dunes. Beachcombers love to collect the large smooth rocks shaped and polished by the elements. Nature trails wind through a rapidly changing landscape of wetlands, prairie, open oak forest, and dunes. *Open year-round.*

OH Chicago, IL 60611

E. Ohio St. exit: Tourism Council, 163 E. Pearson St. (312) 280-5740. This cosmopolitan metropolis, beautifully situated on the southwestern shore of Lake Michigan, boasts a number of world-class attractions. The Art Institute is known for a wide-ranging permanent collection and creative special exhibitions. The Terra Museum, opened in 1987, has a superlative collection of American art; the John G. Shedd Aquarium, the world's largest such indoor facility, with more than 200 tanks, displays some 1,000 wonders of the deep. For an intimate sense of the city, take the El (the elevated railroad) around the Loop; and for a breathtaking overview there's the observation area on the 103rd floor of the Sears Tower, at this writing the world's tallest building.

22 Indiana Dunes National Lakeshore

5 min. East on Rte. 20, left on Mineral Springs Rd. These 1,800 acres of woodland trails and 3 miles of beach dominated by towering lakefront dunes evince an almost lyrical delicacy in an obviously industrial environment. A number of plants are relics of the colder climates that existed here at the end of the Ice Age, leaving a remarkable diversity of vegetation: arctic bearberry alongside prickly-pear cacti, and northern jack pines share dune slopes with southern dogwoods. Although the dunes are large (one named Mt. Tom rises more than 190 feet) and are anchored against the wind by marram grass, sand cherry, cottonwoods, and other native plants, they are susceptible to erosion. A 2-mile trail leads through red oaks and sugar maples to the restored Bailly Homestead and the Chellberg Farm. *Open year-round.*

16 Warren Dunes State Park

5 min. South on Red Arrow Hwy. Awesome sand dunes more then 200 feet high provide majestic views of Lake Michigan and attract hang gliders from far away. The dunes overlook several miles of white sand beach, and behind them lie hundreds of acres of unspoiled woods intersected by trails and a winding stream. The park, delightful in all seasons, is adorned with drifts of blooming wildflowers in spring and colorful foliage in fall; sledding, tobogganing, and cross-country skiing are popular winter activities. The park has almost 200 campsites and a number of pleasant picnic areas. *Open year-round. Admission charged.*

310B. *Domes in Mitchell Park house environmental plantings. Cannas grow in the foreground.*

78. *Curtiss Warhawk and Chance Vought Corsair, distinguished veterans of World War II.*

39 Deer Forest

3 mi./6 min. North on Friday Rd.; follow signs. Deer, goats, llamas, donkeys, elk, swans, and peacocks are at home in this 30-acre wooded playland; some animals can be fed and petted, and there are ponies and a camel to ride. There's also a train to take visitors through the park, and a number of kiddie rides. In Story Book Lane, live animals represent favorite characters in children's stories. *Open daily Memorial Day–Labor Day. Admission charged.* 🏕

76B 76C Kalamazoo Nature Center

9.5 mi./15 min. North on S. Westnedge Ave.; continue on Park St. (Rte. 131 business), right on N. Westnedge Ave. Start a visit here at the Interpretive Center, with its circular ramp descending through the glass-roofed Sun-Rain Room, a humid jungle environment, to the Growing Place, filled with cacti, orchids, and houseplants. Live animals are displayed in the ecology laboratory. The grounds include 600 acres with trails, an herb garden, an arboretum, a trout stream, and a farm with animals you can pet. Displays about agriculture and farm life and craft demonstra-

tions are offered at the nearby De Lano Homestead, a restored 1858 Greek revival farmhouse. *Open Mon.–Sat. and P.M. Sun. except Thanksgiving Day, Christmas, and New Year's Day. Admission charged.* 🚶

78 Kalamazoo Aviation History Museum

3 min. South on Portage Rd., left on Milham Rd. This museum is devoted to World War II American planes. All are beautifully restored, and most are in flying condition. Among the highlights are an F7F Grumman Tigercat, a Curtiss P-40 Warhawk with a painted shark's mouth on its nose, and an F6F Grumman Hellcat, an unsurpassed dogfighter. Also on display are the Pratt & Whitney Wasp Major R-4360, the largest mass-produced piston engine, and memorabilia. *Open Mon.–Sat. and P.M. Sun. except holidays. Admission charged.*

100 Binder Park Zoo

4 min. South on Beadle Lake Rd.; follow signs. Set in the woodland of Binder Park, the zoo provides naturalistic environments for many of its animals. A boardwalk through a pinewoods overlooks the exhibit areas, where Formosan sika deer reside; bison, peacocks,

and prairie dogs can also be seen; and llamas, Sicilian donkeys, ponies, and a yak can be fed and petted at the petting zoo. Water birds inhabit a lovely pond, and around its edge are enclosures for eagles, emus, wallabies, and white-handed gibbons. *Open daily late Apr.– late Oct. Admission charged.* 🏕 🚶 ♿

110 Honolulu House, Marshall

5 min. South on Rte. 27; follow signs. This curious home, modeled on the executive mansion in Honolulu, was built in 1860 by Judge Abner Pratt, a former U.S. consul in the Sandwich (Hawaiian) Islands, who strove to create the exotic atmosphere of the Pacific islands here in Michigan. The two-story house has a broad veranda and an observation tower reached from the central hall by a spiral staircase; the rooms have 15-foot ceilings, and the murals—wreaths of tropical plants intermixed with cattails, lilies, and classical cupids— have been restored to their appearance in 1885, when a new owner remodeled the house and had the original murals embellished. The furnishings, fine pieces from the mid- to the late 19th century, include the judge's empire sofa in the formal dining room and a handsome huntboard intricately carved with figures of fish and game. *Open P.M. daily late May–Oct. Admission charged.*

142 Michigan Space Center

7 mi./9 min. South on Rte. 127 to M50 exit, west on McDevitt Rd., left on Hague Rd., right on Emmons Rd., left on Browns Lake Rd. Rockets and rocket engines flank the gold geodesic dome of this museum of objects related to the exploration of space. Included are a Mercury Redstone, the rocket that launched a U.S. astronaut into space in 1961, and a J2 engine of the kind that was used in the Apollo moon program. The museum contains the Apollo 9 command module, collections of various satellites, space suits, lunar rocks, and a moon rover used to explore the lunar surface. *Open Mon.–Sat. and P.M. Sun. Apr.–Aug; Tues.–Sat. and P.M. Sun. Sept.–Mar. except Thanksgiving Day, Christmas, New Year's Day, and Easter. Admission charged.* 🏕 ♿

30   26   10   20   35

See N–S book, sec. 31.

See N–S book, sec. 29.

U.S.A.   CANADA
MI

End I-94

180   **206**   **216**   **236**   **I-69B**

150   Waterloo Area Farm Museum

7 mi./10 min. North on Mt. Hope Rd., right on Waterloo-Munith Rd. The museum commemorates the life of a family of German settlers who came to this southern Michigan area as farmers in 1844. Their original one-room log cabin has been reconstructed, and the brick farmhouse they built later is furnished with period pieces. The barn has an assortment of tools that such a family would have used. The outbuildings include an icehouse, a bakehouse, a blacksmith's shop, a milk cellar, and a windmill with clapboard siding to reduce the noise. *Open P.M. Tues.–Sun. June–Aug.; P.M. Sat.–Sun. in Sept. Admission charged.*

180   Nichols Arboretum, Ann Arbor

7 mi./13 min. North on Rte. 23, left on Geddes Rd.; continue on Fuller Rd., left on E. Medical Center Dr.; follow signs. The arboretum, which is run by the University of Michigan, is situated in an attractive mixture of hills, woods, ravines, and parklike meadows beside the Huron River. It combines the native growth with cultivated plantings of lilac, ash, maple, euonymus, and other decorative and useful shrubs and trees; there are numerous walks for pleasant strolling and quiet corners for secluded reverie. *Open year-round.*

206   Henry Ford Museum and Greenfield Village, Dearborn

2.5 mi./6 min. West on Oakwood Blvd. The scope, variety, and quality of one of the nation's largest museum complexes are extraordinary. The museums occupy 103 acres, and the exhibits represent most of the aspects of America's cultural and technological history. Here you will see George Washington's campaign chest and the rocking chair Abraham Lincoln was sitting in when he was assassinated; steam and internal combustion engines as big as houses; the revolutionary 1938 Massey-Harris Model 20 combine harvester; and an astonishing array of printing presses, telephones, radios, and radiotelegraphy equipment. The domestic and decorative arts are also thoroughly represented here.

Greenfield Village is a world of its own, with wide, tree-lined streets and buildings of historical interest brought here from their original sites—the Wright brothers' cycle shop, Henry Ford's birthplace, and Thomas Edison's laboratory. The village also exhibits a gristmill, a working farm of the 1880's, and a community area with most of the amenities a small 19th-century town might have had. *Museum open daily except Thanksgiving Day and Christmas; village interiors open daily except early Jan.–mid-Mar. Admission charged for museum and village.*

216   Detroit, MI 48226

Convention and Visitors Bureau, 2 E. Jefferson Ave. (313) 567-1170. Although best known for its automobiles, Detroit still keeps an antique electric trolley system in service, along with an ultramodern elevated people mover, which provides an interesting perspective of the city. To tour the auto plants always requires advance planning. But the industry is powerfully represented in Diego Rivera's great frescoes in the Detroit Institute of Arts, which in addition has exceptionally well-rounded collections from every major period.

The city also offers such varied attractions as the bustling open-air Eastern Market, with its vast displays of flowers and vegetables, two zoos, a freshwater aquarium, a children's museum, a family amusement park, and a tour of a Motown recording studio.

236   Metro Beach Metropark

4 min. East on Metropolitan Pkwy. A marshy peninsula jutting into Lake St. Clair is the site of an attractive recreation area with a wide range of facilities: marinas, boat and sailboard launching ramps, a sandy beach, a swimming pool, tennis courts, a golf course, and a dance pavilion. Lessons in sailboarding are available, and visitors can help to paddle a 34-foot, 20-passenger voyageur canoe. A nature trail circles the unspoiled marsh. In winter there are 5 miles of cross-country ski trails and skating and ice-hockey rinks. *Open year-round. Admisson charged.*

I-69B   Museum of Arts and History, Port Huron

5 min. East on I-69 (business), continue on Oak St., left on Military St., left on Wall St. Housed in a stately former public library, this museum has a large variety of collections relating to southeastern Michigan and the Great Lakes. Among the attractions are the archeological remains of an ancient fishing village, exhibits on historic forts, the bones of a 10,000-year-old mammoth, and artifacts related to Great Lakes navigation. Art exhibitions supplement the regional history displays. *Open P.M. Wed.–Sun. except holidays.*

216. *Behind the misty rainbow, Renaissance Center symbolizes the new vigor of Detroit.*

I-5 — Portland, OR 97204

Convention and Visitors Association, 26 SW Salmon St. (503) 222-2223. The favored flowers in the City of Roses are at their best in Washington Park from mid-May to late November. Here, too, is a superb Japanese garden, a forestry center, a museum of science and industry, and inviting picnic areas. The zoo is famous for its Asian elephants. Other attractions include a unique block-wide landscaped water fountain, a magnificent mansion, museums of Oregon's history and art, and a museum of advertising.

I-5. *Snowcapped Mt. Hood, 50 miles away, seems to be right in Portland's backyard.*

28 35 — Multnomah Falls

Exit 28: 3 mi./7 min. East on Rte. 30. Exit 35: 3 mi./7 min. West on Rte. 30. This is the spectacular centerpiece of the magnificent Columbia River Gorge National Scenic Area. The falls, plunging 620 feet into the gorge, are the highest of the dozen or more in the area. A 1-mile trail, part of a network throughout the gorge, starts at the base. You can follow it across a bridge to a platform that affords a breathtaking view 660 feet straight down. The visitor center has exhibits on the area's geologic, natural, and human history. The Columbia River Scenic Highway (Rte. 30) west of here is a pleasant and picturesque alternative to the interstate. *Open year-round.*

40 — Bonneville Lock and Dam

5 min. North on access road; follow signs. Bonneville was the first hydroelectric dam on the Columbia River and is now part of a system that supplies half of the total hydroelectric capacity in the U.S.A. At the visitor center on Bradford Island, look through underwater windows and see the fish ladders and salmon, trout, and other species migrating upstream. From an overlook on the shore, watch boats being raised and lowered in the locks, and visit the powerhouse, where the huge generators can be seen from a viewing platform. Exhibits in the visitor center recount the dramatic history of the Columbia River region and highlight local birds, animals, and fish. *Open daily except Thanksgiving Day, Christmas, and New Year's Day.*

62 — Hood River Vineyards

5 min. Exit south, right on Country Club Rd., right on Post Canyon Rd., right on Westwood Dr. This small winery is perched atop a hill overlooking the picturesque orchards of the Hood River valley and the scenic Columbia River gorge. Despite its size, the family-run vineyard turns out a dozen different types of wines, ranging from dry to semisweet. On a tour through the vineyards, all stages of the art of wine making are personally explained by a vintner. *Open daily Mar.–Dec.*

84 85 — Fort Dalles Museum

Exit 84: 2 mi./15 min. East on 2nd St., right on Union St., right on 10th St., left on Trevitt St., left on 15th St. Exit 85: 2 mi./15 min. West on 2nd St., left on Union St.; proceed as above. A varied collection of 19th- and early 20th-century Americana can be seen in this museum's displays. It was once the surgeon's quarters of Ft. Dalles, which in the mid-1800's was the only army post between Ft. Vancouver, Washington, and Ft. Laramie, Wyoming. One room is devoted to saddles and guns, the tools of the frontier soldier's trade. There's also a bedroom furnished in 1890's style and large collections of hand tools, surveying equipment, cartridge cases, kitchen utensils, and china, much of which was donated by first-generation descendants of pioneers. Another building houses a prairie schooner, a surrey, and other vehicles from the past. *Open Tues.–Sun. May–Sept.; Wed.–Sun. Oct.–Apr. except 2 weeks in Jan. Admission free but donations encouraged.*

28–35. *Each of Multnomah's two stages is the veritable essence of woodland waterfall.*

87. *Lewis and Clark would doubtless be astounded at the taming of the mighty Columbia.*

87 | The Dalles Dam and Lake Celilo

5 min. North on Rte. 197, right on NE Frontage Rd. Scenery, history, and technology are combined in a train ride and guided tour of 1½-mile-long The Dalles Dam, the huge powerhouse and navigation locks, with fish ladders where migrating salmon and steelhead trout can be seen. Indian petroglyphs have been moved here for display, and the visitor center offers exhibits on the Lewis and Clark expedition, the Columbia River and Basin, and the work of the U.S. Corps of Engineers. Allow an hour for the tour. Behind the dam 24-mile-long Lake Celilo attracts sailboarders, water-skiers, boaters, and fishermen. *Open daily mid-June–Labor Day.*

188 | Doll and Toy Museum

8 mi./15 min. North on Rte. 395. The major part of this excellent collection is composed of some 2,000 antique dolls, many dating back to the 1850's, including the first doll patented in America. Dolls representing characters as diverse as King Henry VIII, Winston Churchill, John Wayne, General Custer, and Chief Sitting Bull blend the past with the present. The doll buggy, dollhouse, and furniture displays include pieces dating back to the Civil War. For those whose interests run to guns and transportation, there are vintage cap pistols, BB guns, and toy cars and trains. *Open daily May–Oct. Admission charged.*

210 | Pendleton Woolen Mills

3 min. North on 10th St., right on SE Court Pl. The Pendleton Woolen Mills began making Indian blankets in 1909, and has since become famous for its woolen fabrics. On the factory tour you will see how raw wool is turned into finished blankets and bolts of cloth and watch the ingenious machinery that combs, divides, and works the wool into strands and spins them into yarn. In the weave room the Jacquard looms work the yarn into the colorful patterns that give the Pendleton blankets their distinctive character. *Open Mon.–Fri. except first 2 weeks in July and Christmas–New Year's Day.*

234 | Emigrant Springs State Park

2 min. Follow signs. Although the springs that attracted pioneers on the Oregon Trail to this pleasant site have long since dried up, it's still a worthwhile place to stop. The dangers and hardship encountered by the wagon trains are described in exhibits here, and there's a mile-long nature trail with some 40 signs identifying the trees, shrubs, and flowers that grow in this area near the summit of the Blue Mountains. In the spring the mountain meadows are carpeted with colorful wildflowers, and during the summer the temperature is 10 to 15 degrees cooler than in the lowlands. *Open daily mid-May–Oct., weather permitting.*

304 | Oregon Trail Regional Museum, Baker

5 min. West on Campbell St. This impressive brick structure, listed in *The National Register of Historic Places*, was built in 1920 as a natatorium (indoor swimming pool) and a community center with a ballroom. Today the expanding museum houses an extensive and outstanding collection of minerals, semiprecious stones, gemstones, petrified wood and ferns, ores, coral, and seashells. Notable displays include a half-ton cluster of Arkansas crystals and a blacklight room. There are also Indian artifacts, period clothing, early town memorabilia, and interesting items from the history of lumbering, mining, and farming in eastern Oregon. *Open daily mid-May–Sept. Admission free but donations encouraged.*

353 | Farewell Bend State Park

2 min. North on Rte. 30. Surrounded by dry hills of sagebrush and tumbleweed, this pleasant park is a tree-shaded oasis on a curve of the slow-moving Snake River here. The name harks back to pioneer days, when wagon trains, with the dangerous Indian territory behind them, split up at this bend as families headed for different destinations. The history of the Oregon Trail is highlighted in exhibits in the interpretive center. The geological diversity of this area attracts rockhounds in their quest for mineral varieties. *Open year-round.*

353. *Sturdy iron-bound wheels such as these were instrumental in populating the West.*

35 Lake Lowell Sector, Deer Flat National Wildlife Refuge

8 mi./10 min. West on Rte. 55, left on Lake Rd. From September to April this 9,000-acre lake is one of the major wintering and resting places for waterfowl along the Pacific Flyway. The refuge, established by President Theodore Roosevelt in 1909, attracts some 100,000 ducks and geese as well as bald eagles, red-tailed hawks, American kestrels, and prairie falcons. More than 190 species of birds have been seen here. Fishing, wildlife photography, and observation are permitted at various locations when they do not interfere with visiting birdlife. In the summer, sailboats and motorboats may be used during daylight. *Open daily except holidays.*

53 Boise, ID 83702

Convention & Visitors Bureau, 100 N. 9th St. (208) 344-7777. When French fur trappers first came to the site of modern-day Boise (pronounced *Boy*-see), they welcomed the greenery of the region and called its river *la rivière boisée* ("the wooded river"). When the town was platted in 1873, it was named for the river. A lively introduction to Idaho's capital and largest city is provided in summer by the 1890's-style Boise Tour Train, which leaves from the Idaho State Historical Society Museum (a significant attraction in itself) in Julia Davis Park for an hour-long excursion through the town. The park also accommodates the Boise Gallery of Art, Pioneer Village, a rose garden, tennis courts, boating, an amusement park, picnic grounds, and a zoo. Another attraction in downtown Boise is the impressive domed state capitol, a scaled-down version of the federal Capitol in Washington, D.C.

90 Bruneau Dunes State Park

112

Exit 90: 23 mi./30 min. South on Rtes. 51 and 78. Exit 112: 15 mi./20 min. South on Rte. 78. For some 15,000 to 30,000 years, wind-driven sand has collected here in a natural basin. Two large dunes, covering about 600 acres, are the major features of this park; the largest is 470 feet high. The park, in southern Idaho near the Snake River, also has

90–112. Here in this most unlikely place are superb examples of sculptured sand dunes.

several small lakes, where there's fishing for bass and bluegill. Hiking the sandy dunes is a favorite—and quite strenuous—pastime, and there's also a self-guiding 5-mile walk into the desert, around the lakes, and through the dunes. Eagles, hawks, and falcons are seen, as well as shorebirds and migrating ducks and geese. The visitor center features exhibits related to the flora, fauna, and fossils in this unique environment. *Open year-round. Admission charged.*

147 Malad Gorge State Park

2 min. South on access road. The stark beauty of this narrow gorge is hidden from view until you are almost at the edge of the rim, peering down into it. Complete with a waterfall and striking rock formations, the rugged 2½-mile-long chasm was formed a million years ago by a torrent of glacial meltwater that tore through the rocks. A footbridge that crosses the gorge at Devil's Washbowl provides the most spectacular view. At this spot the Malad River cascades 60 feet into a craggy basin, and the gorge is at its widest (140 feet) and deepest (250 feet). Hiking trails run along the rim, and signs recount the history of the area. *Open year-round.*

168 Jerome Bird Farm

2 mi./10 min. West on S. Lincoln St.; follow signs. The primary purpose of this 40-acre game farm is to improve hunting in Idaho by breeding and releasing pheasants, chukars, and other upland game birds. It also offers a rare opportunity to view at close range species that are at best only briefly glimpsed in the wild. Visitors can see thousands of birds at all stages of development, from eggs to chicks to fledglings to full-grown fowl. The farm stocks an astonishingly varied assortment of pheasants, including silvers, Mongolians, black-necks, ringed-necks, and goldens. In addition, it raises peacocks and numerous varieties of waterfowl. *Open year-round.*

173 Shoshone Falls, Twin Falls

10 mi./20 min. South on Rte. 93, left on Falls Ave., left on access road. Known as the Niagara of the West, this magnificent cascade that drops 212 feet into the Snake River is actually 52 feet higher than Niagara's Horseshoe Falls. It is a breathtaking example of nature's unrivaled ability to combine beauty and grace with power. The park offers excellent overlooks, along with a large picnic area and a boat

ID | UT

76   44   14   3   32

See N–S book, sec. 7.

See E–W book, sec. 18.

15

80

| I-86 | 26 | 360 | 346 | I-15 | 111 |

15

End I-84

ramp, and Dierkes Lake, half a mile from the falls, is popular with sailboarders, swimmers, and hikers. Although the spectacle is best in early spring, these thunderous falls are worth seeing in any season. *Open year-round. Admission charged in summer.*

I-86 Massacre Rocks State Park

28 mi./35 min. East on I-86 to Exit 28. Pioneers on the Oregon Trail called this area Gate of Death and Devil's Gate after a series of Shoshone Indian skirmishes left 10 immigrants dead. The ruts made by wagon trains still mark this 566-acre park, and a rock bears names inscribed by pioneers who passed through. The park's other attractions include a 20-station nature walk, magnificent desert scenery on the hiking trails, boating, and fishing on the Snake River. The arid climate supports a surprising 300 species of plants, and some 200 bird species have been sighted. The visitor center has Oregon Trail artifacts, along with displays related to trappers, Indians, and pioneers who passed through here. *Open year-round.*

26 Golden Spike National Historic Site

23 mi./25 min. South on Rte. 83, right on Promontory Rd., right on access road; follow signs. Laying the track for the first American transcontinental railroad across 1,776 miles of hostile wilderness in some 4 years was an unparalleled achievement. When the final spike was driven here at Promontory Summit on May 10, 1869, it firmly united West with East and marked the beginning of the end of the frontier. Only 400 feet wide in most parts, this 2,200-acre park stretches for 15 miles along the original trackbed. A self-guiding 9-mile auto tour follows the historic railroad grade. At the last spike site, working replicas of the original *Jupiter* and *No. 119* steam locomotives are on display from May through September, and in summer months, the operation of these locomotives is demonstrated every day. A ¾-mile hike at the tour's end passes the impressive remains of the Central Pacific's Big Fill. *Open daily except holidays. Admission charged Apr.–Oct.*

360 Willard Bay State Park

1 min. West from exit. A scant quarter-mile from the interstate, this park bustles with boaters, swimmers, and fishermen taking advantage of the 9,900-acre man-made lake. The freshwater lake, which has marinas and campgrounds at its north and south ends, was reclaimed from the salt marshes of the Great Salt Lake. On land, Russian olive, elm, and poplar trees shade camping areas. The area is a haven for birds, and more than 200 species have been sighted. Many can be spotted in early morning along the lake's dike. The sign at Exit 354 leads to the park's older, less interesting southern section. *North marina open year-round; south marina open Apr.–Oct. Admission charged.*

346 Ogden, UT 84401

Golden Spike Empire, 2501 Wall Ave. (801) 399-8288; (800) 255-8824 outside UT. The towns in which steam trains stopped usually prospered, and Ogden's Mediterranean-style station is an imposing monument to the commercial impact of the iron horse. It is now the centerpiece of the 25th Street Historic District, where commercial buildings of bygone days have been converted to modern use. Among the station's displays are model railroads, classic cars, a gem collection, firearms, and a gunsmith's shop. Fort Buenaventura State Park, a reconstruction of a fort established by pioneer Miles Goodyear, recalls the life and times of the mountain men. Visitors with a scientific bent will enjoy the local planetarium and the Natural Science Museum.

I-15 Lagoon Amusement Park and Pioneer Village

18 mi./20 min. South on I-15 to Exit 327, south on Lagoon Dr.; follow signs. This 100-year-old amusement park has everything from traditional arcade games to a merry-go-round with hand-carved animals, Dracula's Castle, gardens and fountains, and an opera house that features Broadway musicals. Rides include bumper cars, a Tilt-A-Whirl, and an 85-foot-high double-loop roller coaster. Pioneer Village, with century-old buildings, contains a jail, a two-story log cabin, a Pony Express station, and a narrow-gauge railroad. Guns, dolls, carriages, and Ute Indian beadwork are on display. *Open daily Memorial Day–Labor Day; weekends only Apr.–May and Sept. Admission charged.*

111 Devil's Slide

Heading west (only), drive 1 mi. past Devil's Slide exit (111) to roadside overlook. The name is not inappropriate for these two steep parallel rock outcrops about 10 feet apart and 800 feet long, with the sides of the chute projecting about 20 feet above the ground. Devil's Slide is a sedimentary formation of limestone. Although it can only be viewed from the road, it is unique, memorable, and worth photographing. *Open year-round.*

26. Jupiter *came from the west,* No. 119 *from the east on rails that spanned the continent.*

5TH | San Francisco, CA 94101

5th St. exit. Visitor Information Center, Hallidie Plaza, lower level, Powell and Market Sts. (415) 391-2000. The dramatic hills, superb harbor, one of the world's most beautiful bridges, and a local citizenry that obviously loves the place all help to make this one of America's favorite cities. The excellent public transportation system—with its buses, subways, and justly famous cable cars—serves all the major attractions, including Golden Gate Park, Fisherman's Wharf, Pier 39, Ghirardelli Square, Japantown, and Chinatown. For an unforgettable view of the city and the Golden Gate Bridge, drive to Vista Point at the north end of the bridge. Another perspective of the bridge and the city can be enjoyed from the various bay sightseeing cruises that leave from the Fisherman's Wharf area.

5TH. *A masterpiece of engineering worthy of its dramatic setting on the Golden Gate.*

UNIV | Lawrence Hall of Science, Berkeley

University Ave. exit: 5 mi./14 min. East on University Ave., left on Oxford St., right on Hearst St., right on Gayley Rd., left on Rim Way, left on Centennial Dr.; follow signs. High on a hilltop overlooking the campus of the University of California at Berkeley, this science center is a memorial to Ernest O. Lawrence, inventor of the cyclotron and the university's first Nobel laureate. The center, recognized as a leader in the development of hands-on science exhibits, has a biology lab where you can hold gentle animals, and a wizard's lab where you can have fun with physics. There's also a planetarium, a dinosaur that howls at visitors as they enter the lobby, a full-scale replica of the nose section of the space shuttle *Challenger*, and Lawrence's original cyclotron. *Open daily except Thanksgiving Day, Christmas eve and day, and New Year's Day. Admission charged.*

ROUTE 37 | Marine World–Africa U.S.A., Vallejo

3 min. West on Rte. 37. Visitors have an unusual relationship with the animals at this popular 65-acre wildlife park; many are so gentle and affectionate that they are allowed to roam around the grounds with their trainers. Among the attractions are dolphins and killer whales that catapult into the air, chimpanzees that ride bicycles, sea lions that kiss the visitors, and nearly 100 species of birds, many of which are rare or endangered. *Open daily Memorial Day–Labor Day; Wed.–Sun. Labor Day–Memorial Day except Thanksgiving Day and Christmas. Admission charged.*

ROUTE 12 | Western Railway Museum

12 mi./16 min. East on Rte. 12 (Beck Ave.). An open-air English trolley that resembles a boat, an electric locomotive used once to haul President Taft's personal train, and a faithfully restored 1903 "standard" passenger car with etched glass and a hand-carved wood interior are included with some of the more than 60 vintage trolleys on display at this outdoor museum. For the price of admission you can ride the museum's 1¼-mile line as many times as you like, enjoy a picnic beside a pond shaded by willows and inhabited by ducks, and visit one of the country's largest railway bookstores, where you can browse and buy an authentic copy of an engineer's cap. *Open weekends. Admission charged.*

BUS | Sacramento, CA 95814

Business exit: Convention and Visitors Bureau, 1421 K St. (916) 442-5542. The gold rush that made Sacramento a boomtown and the state capital is memorialized in the Old Sacramento Historic District and Sutter's Fort State Historic Park. The fort—the first to be restored in the U.S.A.—contains many original shops and historic artifacts. An Indian museum in the park features the handiwork of those who found their way to this region without the lure of gold. The Crocker Art Museum, with its opulent Victorian gallery, features old masters' drawings, Oriental art objects, contemporary paintings, and photographs. Car and rail buffs will enjoy the California Towe Ford Museum and the California State Historic Railroad Museum.

ROUTE 49 | Marshall Gold Discovery State Historic Park

19 mi./40 min. South on Rte. 49. James Marshall, while building a sawmill for John Sutter on the American River here, discovered gold in 1848. They tried to keep the find secret; but word spread, and the California gold rush was on. Today a 280-acre park surrounds a working replica of the original mill. Exhibits and audiovisual presentations in the small museum illuminate the area's history. Trails lead through the town of Coloma past historic monuments, a winery, and ruins and relics that speak of a time when gold fever gripped the country. A recreational area along the river is a favorite spot for picnicking, swimming, trout fishing, white-water rafting, kayaking, and casual gold panning. *Open daily except Thanksgiving Day, Christmas, and New Year's Day. Admission charged.*

ROUTE 174 | Empire Mine State Historic Park

13 mi./25 min. North on Rte. 174. From its discovery in 1850 until it closed in 1957, the Empire Gold Mine was one of the most efficient in the nation, owing in large part to the importation of experienced hard-rock miners from Cornwall, England. Some of the mine's machinery is on view, and you can enter a short distance into the original tunnel and peer into a shaft that was once nearly a mile deep. Gold samples, interpretive exhibits, films, and slide shows are on view in the visitor center. A 90-minute tour includes the former owner's charming granite and redwood residence (circa 1900) and a scale model of the mine's 367 miles of tunnels. A formal garden with nearly 950 rosebushes, which traces the history of roses from Roman times to the 1920's, is most impressive. A checklist of plants and animals in this 784-acre preserve is available. *Open year-round; tours weekends only Dec.–Feb.; house and scale-model room open weekends only Apr.–Nov. Admission charged.*

267. *Lake Tahoe and the snow-mantled Sierra Nevada as seen from the eastern shore.*

ROUTE 267   Ponderosa Ranch

19 mi./20 min. South on Rte. 267, left on Rte. 28. Here high above Lake Tahoe in the Sierra Nevada, surrounded by fragrant pine forests, nestles a full-scale furnished replica of the famous Cartwright ranch house as depicted on television's *Bonanza* series. The surrounding park contains a museum of Western memorabilia; an extensive and well-documented collection of antique cars, steam-driven tractors, carriages, farm and logging equipment; and a frontier town complete with general store, an 1871 church, shops, and of course a saloon. Children will enjoy the shooting gallery, mystery mine, and petting farm. Scenic hiking and horseback treks through the 600-acre backcountry and breakfast hayrides are available in summer; and the Camera Trail offers spectacular views. *Open daily May–Oct. Admission charged.*

ROUTE 267   Lake Tahoe Nevada State Park

25 mi./30 min. South on Rte. 267, left on Rte. 28. The pristine beauty of Lake Tahoe, more than a mile high in the Sierra wilderness, is the distinguishing feature of this park. Along the three miles of shorefront are sandy beaches, shaded picnic areas, and Cave Rock, where fishermen try for Mackinaw and rainbow trout. Well-marked hiking trails, ranging from 1½ to 17 miles round-trip, lead to magnificent lake vistas, as well as meadows of wildflowers and aspen groves, golden in their

seasons. Mountain lions and bears forage in the 13,000 acres of backcountry but are rarely seen. Check with park rangers about guided nature walks, stargazes, and special activities for children. Primitive campsites are available in the backcountry. *Open year-round. Admission charged.*

13   Reno, NV 89501

Chamber of Commerce, 135 N. Sierra St. (702) 329-3558. Although it's probably best known for slot machines and easy divorces, this city has much more to offer. The Fleischmann Planetarium, located on the University of Nevada at Reno campus, features star shows, sky-viewing sessions, and movies of space and nature-related subjects on a 360° screen. Also on the campus is the Nevada Historical Society, which displays pioneer and mining memorabilia and Indian artifacts, including some exquisite Washo Indian basketwork. Near the university is the Wilbur D. May Museum, where Mr. May's remarkably eclectic collections, including more than 80 mounted animal heads, are shown. The Sierra Nevada Museum of Art, in its impressive neo-Georgian mansion, highlights Indian baskets, regional art, and changing exhibits.

15   Virginia City

25 mi./35 min. South on Rte. 395, left on Rte. 341. Between 1859 and 1878 millions of dollars' worth of silver and gold mined from the

Comstock Lode turned Virginia City into the world's richest boomtown. Today the residue of its colorful past is creating a boom of its own. Among the well-preserved structures on C Street is the Territorial Enterprise Building, where a young journalist named Sam Clemens began writing as Mark Twain. Other highlights in the town include some handsome old churches, an opera house, excellent museums, and a variety of architectural styles. You can take a half-hour narrated excursion on the historic Virginia and Truckee Railroad, tours of mines and mansions, a 20-minute informational trolley ride, or brochure-guided walking and driving tours. *Open year-round; most attractions open Memorial Day–Sept. Admission charged for some attractions.*

46   Lahontan State Recreation Area

25 mi./30 min. South on Alt. Rte. 95, left on Rte. 50. Isolated beaches, secluded coves, and the freedom to camp almost anywhere along 72 miles of shoreline enhance this picturesque park in rolling desert country. Formed by a dam on the Carson River, 17-mile-long Lake Lahontan Reservoir is shared in summer by swimmers, water-skiers, boaters, and anglers who try for walleyed pike, bass, crappie, and catfish. With some 34,000 acres to explore, bird-watching, photography, and backpacking are popular all year long. Campers should know that at night the temperature can drop by 50° F or more. *Open year-round. Admission charged.*

106 Pershing County Courthouse, Lovelock

2 min. West on Main St. In the early 1900's the rivalry of Lovelock and Winnemucca was such that when Winnemucca put up a new courthouse, Lovelock had to go them one better. So in 1919 the town fathers built one with an imposing rotunda and a round courtroom. The courtroom can be seen if court is not in session. The surrounding park has a public swimming pool and picnic tables set among shady trees and flowering shrubs. In the 1840's and 1850's, pioneers on the Humboldt Trail stopped here to feed and water their livestock before heading west across 40 miles of desert. *Open year-round.*

106 Tufa Park

6 mi./20 min. North on Central Ave. (becomes Meridian) left on Pitt Rd. for 2½ mi., right on wide gravel road for 1 mi. These strange formations, standing in the stark desert landscape like the fossilized remains of prehistoric beasts, are rocks, properly called tuffs, formed by the eruption of an ancient volcano. Paths wind around the sculpted forms, whose subtle shades of orange, yellow, and green coloring were created by mineral deposits and colonies of lichens. *Open year-round.*

106. *These weathered volcanic deposits could pass for fossilized giant clamshells.*

129 Rye Patch State Recreation Area

2 min. West from exit. This oasis comes as a welcome relief to travelers weary of desert, sagebrush, and the heat of summer. Boating and waterskiing are popular in the 11,000-acre Rye Patch Reservoir, fed by the Humboldt River. The three picnic areas, a beach for swimming, and campgrounds on both river and reservoir are additional enticements.

The river is not a new attraction; digs have revealed 23,000-year-old bones of bison, elephants, and camels, as well as signs of human visits 8,000 years old. *Open year-round. Admission charged.*

176 178 Humboldt Museum, Winnemucca

Exit 176: 5 min. East on Winnemucca Blvd., left on Malarky St., left on Jungo Rd. Exit 178: 5 min. West on Winnemucca Blvd., right on Malarky St., left on Jungo Rd. This small, eclectic museum focuses on regional history from the 1860's onward. Housed in a former church (circa 1907), the exhibits include musical instruments, Indian arrowheads, a long rifle, and a variety of pioneer, mining, railroad, and cowboy memorabilia. A second building features antique cars, Indian carvings, and a 1920 version of that classic of western transportation, the pickup truck. *Open daily except Sun.*

303 Northeastern Nevada Museum, Elko

2 min. South from exit. In the history section there are exhibits of geology, mining, Indians, ranching, and railroading—all the major elements of pioneer life. Rolling stock includes stagecoaches, fire trucks, wagons, buggies, and such. The Shoshone Indian basket collection is one of Nevada's largest. There's also an exhibit on the Basques, who have a long history of sheepherding in the area. Pioneer days are represented with period rooms and an original Pony Express station. Bighorn sheep, bears, eagles, and other animals in the taxidermy display depict the wildlife of the state. In the art gallery the work of regional artists is shown. *Open daily except Thanksgiving Day, Christmas, and New Year's Day.*

351 Angel Lake Campground

13 mi./25 min. South on Rte. 231; follow signs. Here's a fairly easy way to experience the rugged beauty of this state's high country. Angel Lake Campground, bordering a lovely man-made reservoir, is set in a spectacular mountain amphitheater. Surrounded by towering canyon walls, you can try for three kinds of trout just steps from the camp, or sample steep trails flanked with wildflowers in summer and colorful quaking aspens in fall. On your way to the campground you'll be treated to sweeping views of a picturesque valley, but the last 4 miles are a winding mountain road. *Open daily July–Sept.*

2 Bonneville Speedway Museum, Wendover

2 min. South from exit. Sleek bullet-shaped cars, motorcycles in rocketlike cocoons, jet-powered vehicles, and other mechanical marvels have raced against the clock or other machines on the vast, hard, level expanse of the Bonneville salt flats. This unusual museum contains some of those vehicles, along with photographs and drivers' equipment. The museum has a surprising assortment of other things, including antique cars in mint condition, car-hood ornaments, famous guns, old tools, Pima Indian artifacts, musical instruments, motorcycles, old bottles, and a wooden three-wheel bicycle. The entire collection is well displayed and documented. *Open daily June–mid-Sept. Admission charged.*

104 Saltair Beach

1 min. North from exit. As you approach the Great Salt Lake you'll see, stretching mirage-like into the distance, a large Moorish-temple-shaped building that seems to float on the water. This is Saltair Resort—the third. The first, built in 1893, was a splendid bathing resort complete with dance hall, restaurants, shops, arcades, and bathhouses. It burned in 1925 and was rebuilt the following year. In the 1950's a receding lake beached the resort, and it burned again in 1970. The present Saltair opened in 1983, only to be flooded the following spring, when the lake suddenly rose

I-15. *The purpose is profit, but the surprising by-product is a monumental work of art.*

12 feet. Swimming is popular here, and power- and sailboats can be rented for a closer look at the marooned building or a cruise on the lake. *Open year-round.*

310 Salt Lake City, UT 84101

Convention & Visitors Bureau, 180 S. West Temple. (801) 521-2822; (800) 831-4332 outside UT. No other city in America owes so much to one group of people. Since its founding in 1847 by Brigham Young, who told his hardy band of followers: "This is the place," Salt Lake City has been largely created by the Mormons (members of the Church of Jesus Christ of Latter-day Saints). The city is built around Temple Square, dominated by the Gothic-spired Temple. It is closed to the public, but visitors are welcome at the acoustically superb Tabernacle, where the famous choir can be heard Sunday mornings and Thursday nights. Organ recitals are given weekdays at noon and at 4 P.M. on Saturdays and Sundays. Other attractions include the state capitol, the Pioneer Memorial Museum, the Council Hall, the State Arboretum, and Liberty Park.

I-15 Bingham Canyon Mine

25 mi./30 min. South on I-15 to Exit 301, right on Rte. 48; follow signs. The world's first open-pit copper mine (and America's largest man-made excavation) is an awesome 2½ miles across at the top and half a mile deep; it covers almost 2,000 acres. From the visitor center on the mine's rim you can observe drilling, blasting, and loading, as well as the operation of electric shovels that lift 55 tons at a scoop into trucks as big as houses. Plaques show where explosives are placed, and a pamphlet explains how 12 pounds of copper are produced from 1 ton of ore. An audio program explains the day-to-day operations of the open pit mine. *Open daily mid-Apr.–Oct.*

128 Pioneer Trail State Park, Salt Lake City

5 min. North on Rte. 186, right on Sunnyside Ave. Pioneer Trail is a combination of attractions that make it one of Utah's most popular parks. Located at the mouth of Emigration Canyon, it includes portions of the last 35 miles of the difficult 2,000-mile route that brought the first Mormon settlers to their new home in Utah. The living-history museum, Old Deseret, with a dozen buildings erected between 1847 and 1869, including Brigham Young's farmhouse and furnishings, portrays the daily life of the pioneer farmers, blacksmiths, carpenters, and other craftsmen. Nearby, the "This is the place" monument commemorates the centennial of the arrival of the Mormons here in 1847. At the visitor center you'll find maps and brochures. *Park open year-round; Old Deseret open daily May–Sept. Admission charged.*

156 Rockport State Park

5 min. South on Rte. 189. Rockport Lake, formed by the Wanship Dam, is a prime water recreation area, attracting swimmers, sail- and motorboaters, sailboarders, and water-skiers in summer. The beach and the shoreline in this park on the lake's southern edge also offer pleasant spots to picnic. Fishermen take rainbow, brown, and cutthroat trout and smallmouth bass. The park provides scenic views of the lake and a chance to see the native wildlife. Boats and other sports equipment may be rented. Campers will find 250 sites on nine campgrounds during the summer. During the winter cross-country skiers and ice fishermen enjoy the park. *Open year-round. Admission charged.*

310. *The dominant man-made and natural features are the capitol and the Wasatch Range.*

34 Fort Bridger State Historic Site

5 min. Southeast on I-80 loop. This fascinating site played a variety of roles during the development of the western frontier. Jim Bridger, a famous trapper and mountain man, first built a post here in southwestern Wyoming in 1843 to serve pioneer wagon trains in their push westward. It was later bought by Mormons, who set it aflame before fleeing to the Salt Lake area under pressure from the military. It subsequently served as a military post, a Pony Express and overland stage station, and the Shoshone Indian Agency.

The 40-acre site now features Wyoming's first schoolhouse as well as several military structures dating back to the 1880's, including a guardhouse, a commissary, and a bandstand. Bridger's trading post and the commmanding officer's quarters have been reconstructed. Period furnishings and costumed personnel, who demonstrate crafts associated with the fort, bring the past vividly to life.

Along with the historic buildings and the demonstrations, an excellent museum illuminates four aspects of western history: Indian life, the fur trade, immigration and settlement, and military life. *Open daily mid-Apr.–mid-Oct.; weekends only Nov.–Mar.*

89 Sweetwater County Historical Museum, Green River

3 min. South on Flaming Gorge Way. Located in the county courthouse, this museum features small displays on natural history and the Shoshone and Ute Indians in Wyoming. It stresses the period from 1868 onward, when Green River became a major railroad center, and nearby Rock Springs developed an important coal-mining industry. Some 10,000 historic photos document this period in Sweetwater County's development. The Life in Chinatown exhibit, with items dating from 1875 to the 1920's, represents the sizable Chinese population that worked in the coal mines. You can also see examples of hand-carved furniture, guns, farm implements, Indian artifacts, glassware, and period clothing. *Open Mon.–Fri. and P.M. Sat. July–Aug.; Mon.–Fri. Sept.–June except holidays.*

211 / 215 Wyoming Frontier Prison, Rawlins

Exit 211: 5 min. East on Spruce St., left on 6th St. Exit 215: 5 min. West on Cedar St., right on 3rd St., left on Spruce St., right on 6th St. This maximum security prison was the scene of murders, attempted escapes, and executions. It originally held 70 inmates when it was opened in December 1901 but was filled to capacity with more than 400 prisoners when it was closed 80 years later. You'll hear many gruesome tales about the prison on a guided tour that begins with the turnkey office and search room and winds up with the death house and gas chamber. Along the way you'll see the cell blocks, kitchen, mess hall, library, and shower room. You'll also see items produced by the inmates, including blankets, doormats, and, of course, auto license plates. (Early license plates were made of leather.) *Open daily Memorial Day–Labor Day. Admission charged.*

235 Saratoga Hobo Pool

21 mi./25 min. South on Rte. 130, left on 1st St. Local Indians regarded these Wyoming hot springs as sacred, but when the waters failed to cure smallpox (brought by white men), they were considered bad medicine and shunned. Later, the springs were hailed as beneficial for a full spectrum of ailments, and the town of Warm Springs was born in 1900. (The name was later changed to Saratoga, after the city in New York State that is also famous for its springwater. "Hobo" refers to the fact that anyone can go there at any time, and it's free.) With temperatures ranging from 117° F to 128° F, the springs are popular year-round. Many come to fish and hunt. The North Platte River is one of Wyoming's two blue-ribbon trout streams, and the region abounds with grouse, deer, elk, and antelope. *Open year-round.*

3RD Laramie Plains Museum

3rd St. exit: 5 min. North on 3rd St., right on Ivinson Ave. The collections in this Laramie museum are housed in a classic Victorian mansion—something of a museum piece in

329. *The resistant parts of the granite are revealed by the sculpture it has become.*

itself—built in 1892 by the wealthy merchant and banker Edward Ivinson. After his wife's death he donated the house to the Episcopal Church, and it subsequently became a museum. The mansion is filled with regional artifacts and items that belonged to the Ivinsons. The latter include oyster plates hand-painted in Paris, Ivinson's banker's desk, and the clothes the couple wore on their 50th wedding anniversary. Several bedrooms contain collections representative of the Laramie area, including guns from Ft. Sanders, hats, toys, Indian beadwork, railroad memorabilia, relics of the sheep industry, and crafts created by inmates of the territorial prison. One of the most interesting outbuildings is a carriage house with saddles, harnesses, and old bicycles. *Open Mon.–Sat. June–Aug.; P.M. only Mon.–Sat. Sept.–May. Admission charged.*

3RD Geological Museum, University of Wyoming, Laramie

3rd St. exit: 5 min. North on 3rd St., right on Lewis St. This museum presents in an easily understood manner a graphic record of the wide variety of organisms that have existed over millions of years in the Rocky Mountain area. The centerpiece of the impressive collection of fossils is a complete skeleton of the genus *Apatosaurus* (formerly *Brontosaurus*), 70 feet long and 15 feet high at the shoulder.

The skeleton occupies most of the main floor, and its head extends into the balcony. Other fossils include the skeleton of a mosasaur, a giant marine lizard; the skull of a megaloceros, a primitive elk with antlers spanning 9½ feet; and the fossilized remains of camels, bison, mammoths, and rhinoceroses. *Open Mon.–Fri. except holidays.*

329   Vedauwoo Picnic and Campground

2 min. North on Vedauwoo Rd. An Indian word that means "earthbound spirit," Vedauwoo captures that feeling in the striking pink-streaked granite formations created by the wind and rain. A cool breeze in summer draws climbers and hikers to the ancient formations and trails that are found in this 1-square-mile area. A mile away from them, a 60-foot granite pyramid commemorates the efforts of the Ames brothers—who manufactured shovels—to finance construction of the Union Pacific Railroad in the 1860's. *Open year-round but may be inaccessible during snow. Admission charged.*

362   Cheyenne, WY 82001

Chamber of Commerce, 301 W. 16th St. (307) 638-3388. The phrase "Cheyenne to Deadwood 1876" is still visible on the side of a

362. *The capital and the cowboy are two important symbols of the Equality State.*

weather-beaten stagecoach at the Cheyenne Frontier Days Old West Museum, where more than 30 horse-drawn vehicles colorfully recall the days before the automobile. Also shown are an ambulance, a hearse, and sightseeing coaches, along with fancy saddles, rodeo memorabilia, and exhibits on the advent of the railroad and the decline of the Plains Indian tribes. In Lions Park the solar-heated Cheyenne Botanic Gardens and a lake for swimming, boating, and fishing are especially popular. The Wyoming State Museum focuses on state history and frontier life. The exhibits recall the days of the Shoshone and Arapaho Indians, cowboys, pioneer women, and mountain men. Indian beadwork, guns owned by Buffalo Bill Cody, and a diorama of an 1880's cattle roundup are among the highlights.

55   Fort Sidney Officers' Quarters, Sidney
59

Exit 55: 5 mi./10 min. North on Rte. 19, right on Rte. 30, right on 6th Ave. Exit 59: 4 mi./6 min. North on 17J Link, left on Rte. 30, left on 6th Ave. This white clapboard duplex, which once housed two officers and their families, is now the home of the Cheyenne County Museum in Sidney. Here you'll see memorabilia of Ft. Sidney, as well as the county's evolution from raw frontier territory to a prosperous farming community. Other military displays range in time from the Spanish-American War to Vietnam. One room is outfitted as a gentleman's den, with an antique desk and typewriters, cigar tins, and whiskey bottles. Women of the day are represented by late-Victorian dresses, quilts, baby clothes, fans, and hair combs.

The nearby post commander's home, an elegant two-story structure, is furnished to reflect the period before 1894, when the fort was abandoned. The comfortable home has little sense of military rigor. A 19th-century grand piano occupies the parlor, and the simple kitchen contains a cast-iron cooking stove. The master bedroom displays women's dresses and period furnishings. *Officers' quarters open P.M. daily except Thanksgiving Day, Christmas, and New Year's Day; post commander's home open P.M. daily Memorial Day–Labor Day.*

126   Fantasyland, Ogallala

2 min. North on Rte. 61. Fairy tales and Mother Goose stories are brought to life at this roadside attraction for small children. Teddy bears and raccoons, Mother Goose, Woody Woodpecker, Old King Cole, Little Boy Blue, Pinocchio, Santa Claus, and many more childhood favorites have been animated and are accompanied by music. There's also a gypsy camp and an area called "The Forest of No Return," with demon-faced trees and the rumbling sound of thunder. *Open daily June–Sept. and Dec. except Christmas. Admission charged for those over 5.*

126   Mansion on the Hill, Ogallala

5 min. North on Rte. 61. In 1887 a wealthy Ogallala citizen built this three-story brick house to welcome his bride-to-be (the bride, however, decided not to come). Today the mansion, furnished with the trappings of a bygone era, houses the eclectic collections of the Keith County Historical Society. Displays include fans, gloves, shoes, a sheriff's gun and blackjack, fossilized bones, photographs, posthole diggers, and delicate lacework. The second floor contains a collection of high school yearbooks, toys, and clothing; and the attic is a treasure trove of old radios, sewing machines, electric hair-curling machines, and other examples of earlier technology. *Open P.M. Fri.–Wed., Memorial Day–Labor Day.*

126   Lake Ogallala State Recreation Area

8 mi./13 min. North on Rte. 61. Lake Ogallala, 1½ miles long and a quarter-mile wide, is in fact a barrow pit dug when the North Platte River was dammed to create the adjacent Lake McConaughy reservoir. But its diminutive size and serenity are the essence of its appeal. Absent here are the crowds, the clamor, and the noisy motorboats to be found at "Big Mac," as the 26-mile-long Lake McConaughy reservoir is popularly known in these parts. Lake Ogallala's shoreline is low and reedy and offers plenty of peaceful places for picnics and camping. *Open year-round. Admission charged.*

177   Lincoln County Historical Museum, North Platte

5 mi./12 min. North on Rte. 83, left on Rte. 30, right on N. Buffalo Bill Ave. This town is known both as the home of Buffalo Bill and the site of a World War II railroad station canteen that served as many as 5,000 military personnel daily. Its current claim to fame is this large well-organized museum. Exhibits comprise a country store, a barbershop, a doctor's office, World War I military relics, Indian artifacts, telephones, farm equipment, a wide array of household items, and a remembrance of the popular canteen. *Open daily Memorial Day–Labor Day. Admission free but donations encouraged.*

177   Buffalo Bill Ranch State Historical Park, North Platte

5.5 mi./13 min. North on Rte. 83, left on Rte. 30, right on N. Buffalo Bill Ave. A fine old 1887 horse barn with rafters carved in the

177. *The home of the buffalo hunter and wild West character is unexpectedly stylish.*

shape of rifle stocks and adorned with Annie Oakley's logo (a heart-shaped bull's-eye with a bullet hole) dominates the tree-shaded grounds of the ranch that Buffalo Bill called Scout's Rest. His home, a three-story mansion built in 1886, when Cody's Wild West show was a big success, has large bay windows, a turreted third floor, and gingerbread trim.

Memorabilia include posters, photos, silver spurs, and Sitting Bull's ceremonial saddle blanket. On the grounds is an enclosure where buffalo still roam. *Open daily Memorial Day–Labor Day; Mon.–Fri. Apr.–May and Sept.–Oct. Admission charged.*

211   Pony Express Station, Gothenburg

5 min. North on Rte. 47; follow signs. This one-room log cabin with a shingled roof and a stone fireplace served as a Pony Express station in 1860–61, which represents the entire life span of that romantic form of fast mail delivery. At other times the cabin was a fur-trading post on the Oregon Trail and a stage station on the Overland Trail. A replica of the leather mailbag used by the hardy Pony Express riders is displayed, along with moccasins and stone arrowheads from the Indian territory they crossed. In summer you can take a carriage ride around the park and town. *Open daily May–Sept. Admission charged for rides.*

237   Dawson County Historical Museum, Lexington

3 mi./7 min. North on Rte. 283, right on 6th St., left on Taft St. Life in central Nebraska in the 1800's and early 1900's is recalled here with period rooms, a barbershop stocked with razors and lotions, a one-room schoolhouse, and a newspaper office. Early means of transportation on display include a Union Pacific locomotive and caboose, a 1923 Ford coupe auto, an 1882 penny-farthing bicycle, and the Emmett McCabe biplane, with its curiously bowed wings. The extensive collection also features a model train set, musical instruments, toys, guns, uniforms, antique cameras, and photographs from the Civil War through World War II. *Open Mon.–Sat. and P.M. Sun. Mar.–Nov.; Mon.–Sat. Nov.–Mar. except Easter, Thanksgiving Day, Christmas, and New Year's Day. Admission charged.*

257   Chevyland U.S.A.

3 min. North on Rte. 183, right on first access road; follow signs. Here you'll find one of the best collections of Chevrolets known to exist

in America. Models date from 1914 to 1975, and all are in running order. On display are a 1932 Roadster Deluxe; a 1957 Bel Air, the most expensive Chevy of its day; an assortment of Corvettes that trace the car's evolution since 1954; and a 1969 orange and white Camaro that is a replica of the pace car used at the 53rd Indianapolis 500. You'll also see some items not made by Chevrolet, such as a 1928 Whippet Cabriolet, a 1939 Ford pickup, an Indian Chief motorcycle, and a Harley-Davidson 1200 motorcycle with sidecar. Posters and hubcaps add their own nostalgic flavor to the collection. *Open daily Apr.–Oct. Admission charged.*

272   The Frank House, Kearney

4 mi./7 min. North on Rte. 44, left on Rte. 30, right on College Dr. This handsome mansion was built in 1889 by George Washington Frank, a wealthy New York entrepreneur who played a major role in the construction of the Kearney Canal. As a result of its superb craftsmanship and then-unusual amenities—such as electricity and steam heat—Frank's three-story home soon became the city's favorite showplace and social center. The exterior is enhanced by a full-length pillared veranda, a tile roof, and pinkish Colorado sandstone that was cut on-site. Inside you'll find a Grand Hall with Corinthian columns, a large stained-glass window by Louis Comfort Tiffany, six fireplaces, hand-carved oak woodwork, a master bedroom with unusual curved-glass windows, and 19th-century furnishings. *Open P.M. Tues.–Sun. June–Aug. Admission charged.*

272 / 279   Fort Kearny State Historical Park

Exit 272: 6 mi./8 min. South on Rte. 44, left on Rte. 50A. Exit 279: 6 mi./8 min. South on Rte. 10, right on Rte. 50A. As the first fort built by the U.S. Army on the famous Oregon Trail—the route of the great westward migration from the 1840's to the 1870's—Ft. Kearny was established to help protect travelers, settlers, and prospectors, and later housed troops to provide protection for workers on the Union Pacific Railroad. The fort was finally abandoned in 1871. A reconstruction of an old stockade now stands in a 40-acre park that is walled in by adjacent cornfields during the summer. Also on the grounds are a well-equipped blacksmith's shop and several antique wagons, including a covered wagon. *Fort open Memorial Day–Labor Day; grounds open year-round. Admission charged.* ⏆ ♿

279   Harold Warp Pioneer Village

12 mi./15 min. South on Rte. 10; follow signs. This astounding collection of Americana—more than 50,000 artifacts arranged in chronological order showing the nation's progress since 1830—represents virtually every field of human endeavor. Founded in 1953 by Harold Warp, a Nebraska native who became a Chicago plastics manufacturer, the 20-acre village contains 300 antique cars, including a 1903 Ford and a 1905 Buick, original Audubon prints and Currier and Ives prints, an antique steam-powered carousel (still 5 cents a ride), a Pony Express relay station, seven generations of authentically furnished rooms, an 1889 B & M locomotive, historic aircraft, including an early-model helicopter, and one of America's largest collections of antique farm machinery and horse-drawn vehicles. *Open year-round. Admission charged.*

312   Stuhr Museum of the Prairie Pioneer, Grand Island

4 mi./7 min. North on Rte. 281, right on Rte. 34. The life and times of the sodbusters and town builders who settled the Nebraska prairie are exceptionally well illustrated here. The main museum building was designed by architect Edward Durrell Stone and displays artifacts from 1860 to 1910, including dolls and toys, homemaker's equipment, period rooms, clocks, antique clothing, barbed wire, and Limoges dinnerware. A historical account of the pioneer era is narrated by the late Henry Fonda, a native of Grand Island. The cottage in which the Oscar-winning actor was born is one of the 60 restored structures in Railroad Town, an elaborate re-creation of a prairie community, where you can board the last working turn-of-the-century steam-engine train in Nebraska for a tour of the museum's

200 acres. In the town you can see log cabins, Indian artifacts, Civil War memorabilia, and antique farm machinery. *Museum open year-round; other exhibits and buildings open daily May–Sept. Admission charged.* ⏆.

353   Anna Bemis Palmer Museum, York

4 min. North on Rte. 81; follow signs. Named for a local teacher, author, and musician, this museum provides a glimpse into the collective memory of a small Nebraska town. On display are an old coin sorter once used by the bank, a Civil War drum, an 1880 cavalry supply wagon, a large-horned Edison phonograph, a spinning wheel, a sodbuster plow, and period furnishings and clothing. Also on exhibit are the pump organ and published works of James Asher Parks, a local composer who wrote "Santa Claus and Uncle Sam: A Merry Christmas Cantata." *Open Mon.–Fri. and A.M. Sat. except holidays.* ⏆ ♿

401   Lincoln, NE 68508

Convention & Visitors Bureau, 1221 N Street, Suite 320. (402) 476-7511; (800) 423-8212 outside NE. Regarded by experts as an outstanding example of public architecture, the state capitol has a 400-foot tower crowned with a 32-foot bronze statue called "The Sower." At the University of Nebraska State Museum you

can see remarkable displays on the natural history of the Great Plains, including a reconstruction of a gigantic prehistoric rhinoceros. Also on the campus is the Christlieb Collection of Western Art, which includes works by Frederic Remington and Charles Russell. The William Jennings Bryan home, Fairview, contains furnishings and memorabilia of the great orator. Among Lincoln's other attractions are the city parks, a children's zoo, and the unique National Museum of Roller Skating.

I-480   Omaha, NE 68183

Convention & Visitors Bureau, 1819 Farnam St., Suite 1200. (402) 444-4660. There's much more to Nebraska's largest city than the well-known grain and livestock business. The Joslyn Art Museum, an impressive art deco building clad in pink marble, houses fine regional and international collections. A replica of President Lincoln's funeral car, along with other railroad memorabilia, is on view at the Union Pacific Historical Museum. The Great Plains Black Museum features rare photos and displays on black American history, and the Omaha Children's Museum has hands-on exhibits. Gerald Ford's birth site includes exhibits, gardens, and a model of the original house. The Old Market has interesting shops, pubs, galleries, restaurants, and boutiques. Boys Town offers self-guiding and conducted tours.

40l. *Nebraska's imposing state capitol dominates the city by night as well as day.*

452D Fontenelle Forest Nature Center

4 mi./7 min. South on 13th St., left on Bellevue Blvd. These heavily wooded ravines and ridges (created by vast windblown deposits of silt) occupy 1,300 acres on a bend in the Missouri River. It was named for Logan Fontenelle, whose mother was the daughter of an Omaha chief. An interpretive center provides a view of the area's use by Indians and fur traders. A self-guiding history trail leads to a depression left by a collapsed prehistoric Indian earth lodge; other trails follow the perimeter of the floodplain marshland and offer a chance to spot white-tailed deer, coyotes, and red foxes. For birders there are some 200 species to be on the lookout for. *Open daily except Thanksgiving Day, Christmas, and New Year's Day. Admission charged.*

454 Sarpy County Historical Museum, Bellevue

7mi./15min. South on 13th St.; continue on Rte. 75, left on Galvin Rd., left on 24th Ave. This Nebraska county's development from the days of the Indians to the early 20th century is traced here in a variety of chronological exhibits. There is a model of an Omaha Indian earth lodge; a Jefferson peace medal marking a treaty between Indians and settlers; a model of a prairie schooner and an ox yoke; and plows, scythes, and other tools used by pioneers to farm. Re-created turn-of-the-century rooms contain such antique gadgets as an Aurora Acorn cookstove and a stereopticon. Models of a one-room schoolhouse, a sod house, and a 1918 Case steam tractor bring the exhibits to the 20th century. A fine collection of model trains has a Texas Zephyr streamlined diesel and a Mallet heavy freight locomotive. *Open daily except Thanksgiving Day, Christmas, and New Year's Day. Admission charged.*

3 The Historic General Dodge House, Council Bluffs

3 mi./7 min. North on 6th St., right on 5th Ave., right on 3rd St. This three-story Victorian mansion, built in 1869 by Gen. Grenville Dodge, befits the man who once surveyed some 60,000 miles of track and later presided over 16 railroad companies. The house is ele-

gantly detailed throughout; in the dining room, where two magnificent silver tea services are displayed, Dodge was host to five United States presidents and other luminaries. On the ground floor the front and back parlors are graced by fine lace curtains, Austrian crystal chandeliers, and pier mirrors at each end. On the second floor, Mrs. Dodge's bedroom has marble-topped furniture and Bussel's lace curtains. A child's bedroom houses a fine exhibit of period toys and baby clothes as well as a four-story fully furnished dollhouse. The third-floor ballroom holds a square rosewood grand piano, a pump organ, and a large music box. *Open Tues.–Sat. and P.M. Sun. except Jan. Admission charged.*

3. *Christmas decorations add to the charming clutter typical of the Victorian era.*

46 Prairie Rose State Park

8 mi./10 min. North on Rte. M47. Situated at the edge of loess hills, formed by the wind-blown silt of glacier deposits, this park's varied terrain encompasses a mature stand of bur oak, a new and established prairie, and a trail that follows the marshy and upland ground around a shallow lake. Named for the vanished village of Prairie Rose, the park shelters badgers, white-tailed deer, white pelicans, pheasant, and other wildlife. The large lake is fished for bass, channel catfish, crappie, and bluegill, and reedy inlets along its jagged east-

ern shoreline provide a perfect habitat for numerous waterfowl. *Open year-round. Admission charged.*

57 Pellett Gardens

5 mi./6 min. South on Rte. N16, left on first gravel road after railroad crossing. Several acres of woodland offer a refreshing visual change from the surrounding farm country. A trail winds through the woods, where heavy undergrowth in summer provides cover for opossums, raccoons, deer, quail, and pheasants. Squirrels and a variety of colorful birds build their nests in the trees. *Open year-round but impassable after rain.*

I-35 Walnut Woods State Park

7 mi./10 min. South on I-35 to Exit 68, east on Rte. 5; follow signs. Here along the bank of the Raccoon River is one of the largest surviving natural stands of black walnut trees in North America. These majestic specimens tower over a stone lodge set on manicured lawns, lending the park an impressive manorial character. Picnickers appreciate the tree-shaded grounds beside the river, while fishermen concentrate on catching catfish. Walking and bridle trails invite further exploration. *Open year-round. Admission charged.*

I-235 Des Moines, IA 50309

I-235 *Convention & Visitors Bureau, 309 Court Ave., Suite 300 (800) 451-2625.*
Across from the gold-domed capitol, the Iowa State Historical Building provides an introduction to the history and prehistory of the region. The governor's house, Terrace Hill, is a superb example of a mid-19th-century mansion, now opulently furnished as it was in the 1870's. Salisbury House is a remarkable 42-room replica of King's House in Salisbury, England. The vast interior spaces contain furnishings in the Tudor style and are highlighted by the rich colors of Oriental rugs and stained-glass windows. Modern tastes in art and architecture are displayed in the Des Moines Art Center.

See N–S book, sec. 17.

0		14		18		9		9		47		19	
I-35	I-235		I-235		155		164		173		220		80

See N–S book, sec. 17.

155 Trainland USA

4 min. North on Rte. 117. One of America's largest Lionel train layouts features a cross-country trip through elaborately detailed dioramas of the frontier, steam, and diesel eras. Scenes include an Old West gunfight, a three-ring circus in Arizona, and a moonshine still in Missouri. In the diesel display, visitors can activate a missile launch crane at the Florida Space Center, set a coal loader in motion in Kentucky, operate a ski lift in Colorado, and much more. It took 32 people 4½ years to build. The scope and craftsmanship must be seen to be believed. *Open daily Memorial Day–Labor Day; weekends in Sept.; P.M. Fri.–Sun. after Thanksgiving Day. Admission charged.*

164 Jasper County Historical Museum, Newton

1 min. North on Rte. 14, right on S. 12th Ave. W., right on W. 18th St. S. Life in turn-of-the-century Jasper County is illustrated in a variety of spacious displays in this large museum. The re-created interiors of a Victorian home, a barn, and a one-room schoolhouse are complemented by an exhibit of farm implements and a collection of old wall clocks. Some coal-mining tools represent what was one of the area's major industries until Fred Maytag produced his first washing machine in 1907. The evolution of this labor-saving invention is documented with examples dating back to the old wringer models. *Open P.M. daily May–Sept. Admission charged.*

164 Fred Maytag Park, Newton

3 mi./6 min. North on Rte. 14, right on Rte. 6, right on W. 4th St., left on 5th Ave., right on 3rd St. This small but attractive and well-appointed city park was founded by appliance manufacturer Fred Maytag in 1935. The terrain is hilly, well mown, and set with many mature shade trees and ornamental shrubs. The park has three picnic shelters, one an original log cabin that was moved to this site, and the Fred Maytag Bowl, a clamshell amphitheater with wooden bench seating. The park also has tennis courts, a playground with swings and slides, and a large swimming pool with a 170-foot water slide. *Open year-round. Fee charged for pool.*

173 Rock Creek State Park

9 mi./17 min. North on Rte. 224, right on Rte. F27. The centerpiece of this pastoral 1,700-acre park is a large man-made lake, its irregular shoreline lightly wooded in places. Boats can be rented, and there are pleasant lakeside picnic and camping areas. Some of the surrounding meadow areas are reverting to a scrubby, prairielike state that contrasts with the efficiently farmed rolling hills beyond the park's boundaries. Hiking and snowmobile trails traverse the area. *Open year-round. Admission charged.*

220 Amana Colonies

30-mi. loop tour. North on Rte. V77, right on Rte. 6, left on Rte. 220, right on Rte. 151/6; re-enter I-80 at Exit 225. This group of seven Iowa villages was settled in 1855 by 1,000 members of a pietist group of Lutherans who called themselves the Community of True Inspiration. They came from Germany by way of upstate New York in search of religious freedom. They became farmers, established themselves in the woolen, meat-smoking, and furniture industries, and lived communally until 1932, when the land and the businesses were incorporated. Today a peaceful atmosphere pervades these well-tended villages, which gently echo the past.

South Amana's Barn Museum has on display models of historic houses and barns, a shingle and sawmill complex, and a four-story granary. The Old Fashioned Store in High Amana, its interior unchanged for over a century, sells a large variety of traditional goods. The reconstructions, documents, antique tools, and other artifacts on view in the Museum of Amana History in the town of Amana illustrate life in the old colonies. The Amana Woolen Mill, which supplied fabric for Soviet army coats in World War II, has tours. *Barn Museum open daily Apr.–Oct.; Old Fashioned Store open daily except Christmas, New Year's Day, and Sun. in Jan.–Feb.; Museum of Amana History open daily mid-Apr.–mid-Nov.; Amana Woolen Mill open daily except holidays. Admission charged for Barn and Amana History museums.*

235–235. *Reflecting pool and modern sculpture are featured in the Civic Center's plaza.*

239 Kalona Historical Village

21 mi./25 min. South on Rte. 218, right on Rte. 22. A blend of old and new is immediately apparent in the Kalona region, home of the largest Amish community west of the Mississippi. Automobiles coexist with horse-drawn buggies on the streets of Kalona, where hitching posts are a familiar sight.

Kalona began as a railroad stop, and its historical village was conceived as a fitting site for the town's restored 1879 railroad depot, which now houses railroad memorabilia. Other buildings include the Wahl Museum, with fine collections of antique glassware; the Iowa Mennonite Museum and Archives; and a 19th-century log home. *Open daily except Thanksgiving Day, Christmas, and New Year's Day. Admission charged.*

246 Lake MacBride State Park

14 mi./20 min. North on Rte. 1, left on Rte. 382. Lake MacBride was created as part of a recreation area project completed in 1955. The state park surrounds the lake, while a nature recreation area is located to the south. The park provides a narrow swimming beach as well as facilities for camping and picnicking. In winter, trails are open for snowmobiling and cross-country skiing. The recreation area, administered by the University of Iowa, is more varied, its terrain wilder and less developed. The humane work of the Raptor Center is devoted to the rehabilitation of injured birds of prey. Hawks and owls can be observed in large open-air cages. *Open year-round. Admission charged for state park; admission free but donations encouraged at Raptor Center.*

254 Herbert Hoover National Historic Site, West Branch

1 min. North on Parkside Dr. (Rte. X30). The stock market crash of 1929 and the depression that ensued stigmatized the memory of Herbert Hoover, president from 1929 to 1933. This site serves to illuminate Hoover's long and distinguished career as a mining engineer, humanitarian, and statesman. (He remained a public servant until 1955.)

254. *From one white house to another—the birthplace of our 31st Chief Executive.*

Behind a picket fence on its original site sits the tiny cottage where Hoover was born. It attests to the humble beginnings of a man who became a millionaire as a mining engineer and later would not accept his presidential salary. Other 19th-century buildings include the Friends Meetinghouse (Hoover was a committed Quaker) and a schoolhouse.

The Presidential Library-Museum houses exhibits pertaining to Hoover's distinguished career. *Open daily except Thanksgiving Day, Christmas, and New Year's Day. Admission charged at both places.*

277 Wildcat Den State Park

13 mi./17 min. South on Rte. Y26. Wildcats once lived in dens within this complex and fascinating terrain of woods, ravines, and cliffs. Today the park features about 2 miles of trails rimmed with jewelweed and other varieties of blossoming shrubs, ferns, and wildflowers. Pine Creek, a small stream, follows the valley bottom to an old mill and to Pine Creek Bridge, constructed with wood planks on an iron frame in 1833. *Open year-round. Admission charged.*

I-74 The Children's Museum, Bettendorf

5 mi./6 min. East (south) on I-74 to Exit 4 (last Iowa exit), east on Mississippi Blvd. Despite its name, this museum isn't for children only. The Bettendorf Room, for example, is devoted to the history of a company that flourished here in the 1920's as a manufacturer of railroad-car wheel and axle assemblies. Included is a model of a 1930's Bettendorf boxcar. In another room, graphic exhibits portray developments in local history, including an influx of Armenians around 1913 and the establishment of dairy farming.

In the Time Machine section, young visitors can disassemble and play with a variety of small machines. There are also natural history exhibits, working traffic lights, and a hands-on TV studio for children, where they can practice using video equipment and hone their broadcasting skills. *Open Tues.–Sat. and P.M. Sun. except holidays. Admission free but donations encouraged.*

I-74 I-74 John Deere Administrative Center, Moline

I-74 exit: 12.5 mi./16 min. East (south) on I-74 to Exit 4B, east on John Deere Rd. (Rte. 5). I-74 exit: 14 mi./19 min. West on I-74 to Exit 4B, east on John Deere Rd. (Rte. 5). Visitors to these showcase headquarters, designed by Finnish-American architect Eero Saarinen, can tour the building and its atrium, see a film tracing the company's history from the invention of the steel plow by Vermont blacksmith John Deere in 1837 to the present, and browse in the display building, which includes a striking 180-foot mural by artist Alexander Girard that features actual three-dimensional objects such as pioneer tools and other memorabilia. *Display building open year-round; tours Mon.–Fri. except holidays.*

19 Bishop Hill

21 mi./30 min. South on Rte. 82, left on Rte. 570N, right on Rte. 1670E; follow signs. Swedish immigrants founded Bishop Hill as a religious colony in 1846 and endowed it with the simple elegance it still retains. The Steeple Building is a good place to begin your tour. It displays domestic articles that belonged to the first settlers and provides a detailed picture of their aspirations and lifestyle. The old Colony Church, also a museum, contains a wonderful collection of paintings by Olof Krans, a primitive artist who came to the colony as a boy in 1850. The restored Colony Hotel occasionally offers costumed demonstrations of 19th-century life. *Town open year-round; Steeple Building open daily Apr.–Dec.; Colony Church and Colony Hotel open daily except Thanksgiving Day, Christmas, and New Year's Day.*

33   Johnson Sauk Trail State Park

6 mi./8 min. South on Rte. 78. This 1,360-acre park lies at the southern edge of what was once the Great Willow Swamp. The area was famous for its abundant wildlife, and many Indian tribes, attracted by the wild game and fur-bearing animals, made their homes here. Wild creatures still inhabit the region and can sometimes be seen from the many hiking trails. The man-made lake tempts anglers, who come for the plentiful largemouth bass, bluegill, sunfish, crappie, and northern pike.

The lake is also a resting place for migrating water birds. *Open daily except Christmas and New Year's Day.*

75   "Time Was" Village Museum

8 mi./10 min. North on Rte. 251. Here is an intriguing array of the things our grandparents cherished, aspired to, or took for granted: dolls and Easter cards, Valentine cards and walking sticks, doorknobs and keys, trivets and watches, stuffed birds, chewing gum machines, and 419 potato mashers, each with a different design. Several period rooms contain the artifacts and evoke the atmosphere of their time and function. An extensive collection of antique carriages and automobiles includes an ornately carved Ringling Brothers circus bandwagon and a 1905 rear-engine Orient buckboard steered by a tiller. *Open daily May–Oct. Admission charged.*

81   La Salle County Historical Society Museum

4 min. South on Rte. 178. The museum occupies a long stone building constructed in 1848 as a warehouse on the Illinois and Michigan

Canal. Displays describe the productive years of the canal and help the visitor to browse through the area's earlier history. Models, paintings, and chronicles tell the story of the siege of Starved Rock and the Indian Creek massacre. A curious collection of hickory-nuthead dolls represents the Lincoln-Douglas debate in nearby Ottawa, and there are replicas of casts of Lincoln's face and hands. *Open Mon., Wed.–Fri., and P.M. Sat.–Sun. Apr.–Dec.; Wed.–Fri. and P.M. Sat.–Sun. Jan.–Mar. Admission charged.*

90   William Reddick Mansion, Ottawa

5 min. South on Rte. 23, left on Lafayette St. In the summer of 1858 a local crowd watched from the steps of this unusually handsome Italianate mansion as Abraham Lincoln and Stephen A. Douglas debated the issue of slavery in an adjacent park. The house, built a few years earlier by Ottawa businessman and politician William Reddick, served as the Reddick home for 30 years before becoming a library and then a national landmark. The unusual combination of cream Lemont limestone with red brick, the ornamental cornices and the marble fireplaces, the tin speaking tubes that allowed communication between the various parts of the house, and other features make this one of the most architecturally interesting antebellum homes in the state of Illinois. *Open Mon.–Fri. except holidays. Admission free but donations encouraged.*

112   Gebhard Woods State Park

5 min. South on Rte. 47; follow signs. One of several parks that flank the Illinois and Michigan Canal, where teams of mules once towed cargo-laden barges for miles between La Salle and Channahon, this park encompasses about 1 square mile of gently rolling terrain dignified by many old shade trees. The park's four ponds are stocked with trout. Fishing is also permitted in the canal or in Nettle Creek. Along the canal 1 mile to the west is the largest tree in the state: a 120-foot-tall eastern cottonwood with a trunk 27 feet around. Canoes can enter the canal from the park. *Open year-round.*

75. *All the objects in this farm kitchen are now cherished by collectors of antiques.*

See N–S book, sec. 21.

See N–S book, sec. 25. 14

See E–W book, sec. 13. 9

IL | IN   See N–S book, sec. 26.

See E–W book, sec. 6. 30

46

55   137   57   I-57   94   I-94   4   1   65   90   31   80   77   94

137 | Pilcher Park, Joliet

4 mi./6 min. West on Rte. 30, right on Gougar Rd. Set along Hickory Creek, this extensive wooded park on Joliet's outskirts offers a variety of possibilities, including hikes through upland and lowland woods, ski and bike trails, picnic areas, and an interpretive nature center that has displays of native plants, birds, and mammals. Programs matched to the seasons include maple sugaring, bird-watching, fishing contests, ski races, and pond and woodland study trips. One of the various walks is a quarter-mile self-guiding trail marked with informative story boards. An artesian well here is popular with locals, who take its mineral water away by the bucketful. Also featured are a paved trail for the blind and handicapped and a greenhouse with four rooms that display trees, cacti, and flowers of the season. *Open year-round.*

I-57–I-94. *Imagine the superb view from the 103rd floor of the world's tallest building.*

I-57 | I-94 | Chicago, IL 60611

Tourism Council, 163 E. Pearson St. (312) 280-5740. This great cosmopolitan metropolis, beautifully situated on the southwestern shore of Lake Michigan, boasts a number of world-class attractions. The Art Institute is known for a wide-ranging permanent collection and creative special exhibitions. The Terra Museum, opened in 1987, has a superlative collection of American art; the John G. Shedd Aquarium, the world's largest such indoor facility, with more than 200 tanks, displays some 1,000 wonders of the deep. For an intimate sense of the city, take the El (the elevated railroad) around the Loop; and for a breathtaking overview of both the city and lake, try the observation area on the 103rd floor of the Sears Tower, at this writing the tallest building in the world.

1 | Wolf Lake Park, Hammond

7 mi./25 min. North on Calumet Ave. Despite the unpromising surroundings of highways, high-tension lines, and gas storage tanks, this park, with its large lake, miniature golf course, and other recreational facilities, is an obvious success. Rental paddleboats, canoes, and sailboards are available, as is instruction on the last-named. The annual Augustfest, held during the first week of the month, brings some 300,000 people here for entertainment, food, and carnival attractions. A fishing pier and a boat ramp entice the angler to try for walleye, northern pike, or bass. *Open daily mid-June–mid-Sept. Admission charged.*

31 | Wilbur H. Cummings Museum of Electronics, Valparaiso

15 mi./25 min. South on Rte. 49, right on Rte. 130. Electronics changes so quickly that yesterday's marvel soon becomes today's antique. This museum has electronic devices from the period of Edison and Marconi to the present, knowing that its latest state-of-the-art exhibits will soon be obsolescent. Among the highlights are a 1950's Seeburg jukebox that plays 78-r.p.m. records, Admiral Byrd's transmitter from a South Pole expedition, one of the first pinball machines, and radios by Atwater-Kent,

Crosley, Philco, and other noted manufacturers. First-generation computers and VCR's, studio TV equipment, and other outmoded wonders are displayed and explained. The museum is on the campus of Valparaiso Technical Institute. Apply for free admission at the administration building. *Open year-round.*

31. *Consider the time it took the wind to deliver this pile of sand grain by grain.*

31 | Indiana Dunes National Lakeshore

8.5 mi./13 min. North on Rte. 49, east on Rte. 12. These 1,800 acres of woodland trails and 3 miles of beach dominated by towering lakefront dunes evince an almost lyrical delicacy in an obviously industrial environment. A number of plants are relics of the colder climates that existed here at the end of the Ice Age, leaving a remarkable diversity of vegetation: arctic bearberry, alongside prickly-pear cactus and northern jack pines, share dune slopes with southern dogwood. Although the dunes are large (Mt. Tom rises more than 190 feet) and are anchored against the wind by marram grass, sand cherry, cottonwoods, and other native plants, they are susceptible to erosion. A 2-mile trail leads through red oaks and sugar maples to the restored Bailly Homestead and Chellberg Farm. *Open year-round.*

77 — Fort Joseph Museum, Niles

8.5 mi./15 min. North on Rte. 33 and Rte. 31/33. This Michigan fort, built by the French in 1691, commanded a key trade route between their holdings in Canada and Louisiana. In the French and Indian War it was held by the British, then briefly by Spain.

The documents, pictures, books, implements, and furniture in the 100,000-item museum, located in a Victorian carriage house, bring history to vivid life. Here, too, is a large collection of Sioux and other Indian artifacts, including pictographs of chiefs Sitting Bull and Rain-in-the-Face. *Open Tues.–Sun. Admission free but donations encouraged.*

77 — Studebaker National Museum, South Bend

3 mi./9 min. South on Rte. 33, left on Jefferson Blvd. In the 1850's South Bend was known as the Wheel City, because of the scores of wagonmakers living and working here. Part of that tradition was created by the Studebaker Company, which in time went from building covered wagons to producing some of the most imaginative automobiles of the 20th century. You will see examples of these at Century Center (Jefferson Boulevard and St. Joseph Street). Among the highlights are Studebaker's 1902 electric car, the Dictator Series of the 1930's, and the bullet-nosed models so familiar in the 1950's. Dodge, Oliver, and Flanders are also represented. And not just cars: the 1923 Indestructo cabin trunk, for example, brings vivid reminders of those lost days when a trip abroad was the event of a lifetime. A short walk away, at the Archives Center (South Street and Lafayette Boulevard), more than 60 historic vehicles are on display. *Open daily June–Aug.; Tues.–Sun. Sept.–May. Admission charged.*

77 — Potato Creek State Park

24 mi./30 min. South on Rte. 33 and Rte. 31 (business) through South Bend, right on Rte. 4. Fishermen come to Worster Lake for the bass, bluegill, brown trout, crappie, and channel catfish. The 300-acre reservoir was created in 1977, when Potato Creek was dammed, and

in parts of the lake the ghostly trunks of drowned trees can still be seen. The beach is large and boats are for rent. The landscape, with woodland and scrubby pasture, shows how former farmland reverts to its natural state. You can enjoy several trails, including a 3-mile bicycle trail that goes through many scenic areas. Bikes are rented at the same shop that rents boats. *Open year-round. Admission charged.*

101 — The Old Bag Factory, Goshen

12 mi./19 min. South on Rte. 15, right on Rte. 33, right on Indiana Ave. In 1984, when Larion Swartzendruber moved his custom furniture business into this old factory building, he visualized a workplace and sales center for craftsmen. From an upstairs gallery you can see his Hardwood Creations being made. Here, too, are potters, doll and toy makers, a blacksmith's shop (the restoration of wood-burning stoves is a specialty), and an egg-decorating shop. Nearby is Quilt Design, an 1837 log cabin where quilts, sewn by Amish and Mennonite women in 20 states, are displayed and sold. *Open Mon.–Sat.*

121 — Pigeon River State Fish and Wildlife Area

9 mi./12 min. South on Rte. 9, left on Rte. 120; follow signs. This wildlife area, which covers some 11,500 acres of woods, ponds, streams, and marshland, is home to deer, pheasants, and waterfowl as well as pike, bluegill, perch, and of course trout. The Curtis Creek Trout-Rearing Station, which is located in the wildlife area, successfully grows some 60,000 rainbow and brown trout per year. Although not native to Indiana, fingerlings 3 to 4 inches long are brought here from state hatcheries and raised in six 86-foot-long raceways. When 7 to 10 inches long, they are released in various streams and lakes. *Open year-round.*

156 — Pokagon State Park

4 min. South on I-69 to Exit 154, right on Rte. 727. This park, named for Potawatomi chief Pokagon, has year-round appeal. In winter the thrill seekers head for the 1,780-foot refriger-

ated toboggan slide, where they can streak down and over hills at 45 miles per hour. The slide is open from Thanksgiving to March, and the toboggans, rented by the hour, can hold up to four passengers. Other attractions in this vast area include trails for hikers and cross-country skiers (rentals available), ice fishing, ice skating, sledding, and year-round camping. In summer, visitors come to fish, boat, and swim from Lake James's wide and sandy beaches. *Open year-round. Admission charged.*

2, 3 — Harrison Lake State Park

Exit 2: 20 mi./30 min. North on Rte. 15, right on Rte. 20, right on Rte. 27; follow signs. Exit 3: 20 mi./30 min. North on Rte. 108, left on Rte. 20, left on Rte. 66, right on Rte. M. The soggy black soil that once earned this region the nickname the Great Black Swamp today constitutes some of the most fertile farmland in the state of Ohio. Even amid vast fields of corn, oats, and soybeans, this 350-acre park sparkles with inviting greenery. Harrison Lake—framed by shaded picnic areas, lush meadows, and a hiking trail—provides water activities in every season and yields plenty of bluegill, crappie, and largemouth bass. In springtime vesper sparrows, brown thrashers, and yellowthroats are some of the songbirds to be heard and seen here. *Open year round.*

156. *Idyllic day at the park: out of school with friends, fish, and faithful dog.*

4 Fort Meigs State Memorial

3.5 mi./6 min. South on Rte. 20, right on Rte. 65; follow signs. Built on a bluff above the rapids of the Maumee River, Ft. Meigs played a key role in America's victory in the War of 1812. It was built in February 1813, and in May survived a siege and bombardment by the British; in July the British were repulsed again, paving the way for their defeat in the Battle of Lake Erie. The present fort is a reconstruction of the original; three of the seven blockhouses contain exhibits about the war and about the design and construction of forts. Within the stockade are the earthworks that sheltered the troops from cannon fire. *Open Wed.–Sat. and P.M. Sun. and holidays late May–early Sept.; Sat. and P.M. Sun. early Sept.–late Oct. Admission charged.*

I-280 Toledo, OH 43604

Office of Tourism & Conventions, 218 Huron St. (419) 243-8191. This major Great Lakes port is a city of iron and coal, where bicycle and wagon shops gave way to auto parts makers and a flourishing glass industry. The Toledo Museum of Art has magnificent glass displays and extensive collections in many periods of painting and sculpture. "Mad" Anthony Wayne won the Battle of Fallen Timbers here in 1794, at what is now Fort Industry Square. The Portside Festival Marketplace, on the waterfront, is a likely and lively focus for a visit, which could include a sightseeing cruise on the Maumee River and Lake Erie.

6 East Harbor State Park

15 mi./23 min. North on Rte. 53, right on Rte. 2, left on Rte. 269; follow signs. The park is Ohio's largest on Lake Erie, and one of its most popular. It lies on a limestone peninsula and embraces three sheltered harbors. One of these, Middle Harbor, is a wildlife refuge, and a trail along its southeastern shore leads to an observation blind from which waterfowl and shorebirds can be seen. For most people, though, the sandy beaches, boating, swimming, and fishing are the park's major attractions. *Open year-round.* 🏛 ⛺ 🚐 🚶 🏊 🎣

7 Edison Birthplace, Milan

5 min. South on Rte. 250, left on Rte. 113; follow signs. Thomas Edison was born in this modest but appealing house in 1847 and lived here until he was 7 years old. Some of the family furnishings are original—a high chair, a spinning wheel—and a collection of memorabilia includes several of his inventions: a 1901 mimeograph machine, a stock exchange printer, a 1929 model of his first light bulb (it used a strip of carbonized thread as a filament), a battery-powered miner's lamp, and Edison's first talking doll (1888). Just below the house is a marker for the canal that connected Milan with Lake Erie when Edison was a boy. *Open Tues.–Sat. and P.M. Sun. June–Labor Day; P.M. Tues.–Sun. Feb.–May and Labor Day–Nov. Admission charged.*

7 Firelands Museum, Norwalk

7 mi./10 min. South on Rte. 250, right on W. Main St. (Rte. 61), left on Case Ave. The museum is named for those lands that were given to residents of Connecticut to compensate them for property torched by the British during the Revolutionary War. Early maps of the district and surveyor's equipment are displayed, along with collections of firearms (including a Chinese hand-cannon dating from 1000 B.C.) and memorabilia of the Civil War (including cypress grave markers from the prison camp on Johnson's Island). Other items of interest range from authentic Indian arrowheads to a diorama of the Milan ship canal and a mammoth bass viol. The museum occupies a federal-style town house dating from 1835 and contains furnishings of that period. *Open Mon.–Sat. and P.M. Sun. July–Aug.; P.M. Tues.–Sun. May–June and Sept.–Oct.; P.M. Sat.–Sun. Apr. and Nov. Admission charged.*

7 8 Great Lakes Historical Society Museum, Vermilion

Exit 7: 25 mi./32 min. North on Rte. 250, right on Rte. 2, left on Rte. 60. Exit 8: 15 mi./20 min. North on Rte. 57, left on Rte. 2, right on Rte. 60. This lakeside museum provides a fascinating and colorful account of shipping on the Great Lakes. Excellent photographs of storms and wrecks show how dangerous these waters are, and there are models of the many kinds of ships and boats that ply the lakes. Displays of maritime equipment here include compass binnacles and steering wheels, radar units, an engine room console, and a complete steam engine. A comprehensive exhibit of safety and rescue equipment includes steam whistles and foghorns, shore beacons, and the light from a lighthouse on northern Lake Huron, gleaming like a precious chandelier of white and ruby crystal. *Open daily Apr.–Dec.; weekends only Jan.–Mar. Admission charged.*

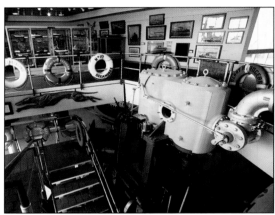

7–8. With yellow steam chest, a steam engine is a key element in a shipshape setting.

10 11 Cleveland, OH 44114

Convention & Visitors Bureau, 1301 E. 6th St. (216) 621-4110. The observation deck in the Terminal Tower gives the best bird's-eye introduction to the city. You can get a more intimate look on a trolley tour; and to see where some of America's great fortunes were founded, take a boat trip down the Cuyahoga River near the steel mills. You can also view the Flats entertainment district, with its waterfront restaurants and boutiques, or stroll through one of Cleveland's many parks and visit the renowned zoo.

The cultural attractions include the Cleveland Museum of Art, the Western Reserve Historical Society, and the Cleveland Museum of Natural History, where dinosaurs, fossils, and many artifacts are on display. An exhibit at the Health Education Museum depicts the workings of the human body.

Not to be missed is the downtown Arcade, where shops and restaurants are housed in a marvelous five-level skylit cast-iron fantasy—one of the largest such structures in the world.

11 12 Hale Farm and Village, Bath

Exit 11: 11 mi./16 min. South on Cleveland-Massillon Rd. (Rte. 21), left on Ira Rd., left on Oak Hill Rd.; follow signs. Exit 12: 15 mi./20 min. South on Rte. 8, right on Rte. 303, left on Riverview Rd., right on Ira Rd.; follow signs. Rural life in the mid-19th century is re-created in this engaging cluster of buildings in what was then the Western Reserve—the land "reserved" for settlers from Connecticut. Many of the buildings were moved to the site from other areas of Ohio. The federal-style farmhouse of Jonathan Hale is surprisingly elegant for an owner who had to hew his farm out of a wilderness. The village comprises a saltbox house, a meetinghouse, a log schoolhouse, a law office, a smithy, and a barn. Demonstrations of spinning and weaving, glassblowing, and smithing evoke life in earlier times. The farm and village are in the 32,000-acre Cuyahoga Valley National Recreation Area. *Open Tues.–Sat. and P.M. Sun. and holidays, mid-May–Oct. and Dec. Admission charged.*

11 12 Stan Hywet Hall and Gardens, Akron

Exit 11: 12 mi./20 min. South on Rte. 21; continue on I-77 to Ghent Rd. exit, east on Ghent Rd.; follow signs. Exit 12: 17 mi./25 min. South on Rte. 8, right on Talmadge Ave., right on Portage Path. This mansion is the largest private home in Ohio, a 65-room Tudor revival structure built in 1912–15 by Frank Seiberling, cofounder of the Goodyear Tire and Rubber Company. The flagstone corridors were artificially worn down to create an impression of age, and there are fan-vaulted ceilings, tapestries, linenfold paneling, and genuine Elizabethan furniture. In some of the rooms there are splendid Chinese wall hangings, Persian rugs, and 2,000-year-old amphorae, while other rooms, like the Great Hall, with its 1-ton chandelier and polar bear rug, suggest a medieval barony. Surpassing authentic Elizabethan mansions, Stan Hywet (from the Anglo-Saxon word for "stone quarry") boasts a 40-foot indoor swimming pool. This vision of opulence is surrounded by gardens with shady walks, velvet lawns, and magnificent flower beds. *Open Tues.–Sat. and P.M. Sun. Admission charged.*

14 Nelson and Kennedy Ledges State Park

16 mi./19 min. Southwest on Rte. 5, right on Rte. 534, left on Rte. 422, left on Rte. 282. In this odd landscape a wooded hillside is crisscrossed by numerous small "canyons" from 10 to 30 feet wide. Trails follow the canyon rims or descend to their floors through crevices and between boulders; a woodland creek tumbles into a deep sinkhole with fern-covered walls. This strange setting seems to belong in an enchanted land. *Open year-round.*

I-76 Mill Creek Recreation Area

15 mi./20 min. West on I-76, left on Rte. 534, right on Rte. 224. This wide 2-mile peninsula jutting into Berlin Lake, a tremendous (3,600-acre) man-made body of water, contains numerous campsites in wooded, grassland, and shoreline areas, as well as picnic spots and boat launch ramps. Created by a dam in a natural river, the lake has developed large fish populations, especially walleye and bass, and is popular with anglers. Water-skiing is also widely enjoyed, but boaters are advised to watch for shallow depths and underwater obstructions. Mill Creek also offers playgrounds, a nature trail, and all facilities, including 47 electricity hookups. *Open mid-May–Sept.*

I-79 McConnells Mill State Park

20 mi./30 min. South on I-79 to Exit 29, west on Rte. 422; follow signs. The handsome board-and-batten gristmill on a foundation of stone was built in 1868 and declared a national landmark in 1974. The full complement of milling machinery in it illustrates the life-giving process of turning grain into flour. One millstone has been restored for grinding. Just downstream from the mill is a covered bridge and the beginning of the Kildoo Trail, a 2-mile hike through a wooded ravine along Slippery Rock Creek. The trail is slippery (and steep) in places; wear appropriate footwear. *Park open year-round; mill open Thurs.–Mon. Memorial Day–Labor Day.*

I-79. *Note the burgeoning fall color, and how the man-made dams complement the rock forms.*

3 Antique Music Museum

13 mi./15 min. North on Rte. 8. In this Pennsylvania building the sound of music—as it used to be—can be heard in remarkable variety. The nickelodeons (which play as many as 13 instruments), band organs used in skating rinks and merry-go-rounds, circus calliopes, and orchestrions are all marvels of mechanical ingenuity and eye-catching design. The monkey organs, music boxes, phonographs, and other melody makers in the collection are less grand in size but no less wondrous and nostalgic. The instruments are all in working order, and many are demonstrated for visitors. In addition to the musical wonders, there are signs, posters, advertisements, and scores of other antiques on display. *Open mid-Apr.– Nov. Admission charged.*

13 Clear Creek State Park

11.5 mi./15 min. North on Rte. 36, right on Rte. 949. Masses of showy rhododendrons, flowering in late June and early July, attract travelers to this lovely woodland park with its rustic bridges, calm lake, and large old trees. Campsites for tents and trailers are prettily situated on the creek or scattered through the woods. Canoeing on the Clarion River is a soothing way to relax, as is fishing for bass and trout. Several trails lead through the park. *Open year-round.*

23 Bald Eagle State Park

9 mi./15 min. North on Rte. 150. Named not for the bird but for an Indian chief, this verdant 6,000-acre park is best known for boating and fishing on Foster Joseph Sayres Dam, which covers more than 600 acres here. The dam, with a pleasant stretch of sandy beach, is nestled in the valley; the impressive Bald Eagle Mountains are to the south. Fishing equipment and boats, including sailboats and canoes, are available for rent at the marina. Some 200 picnic tables, set in a parklike meadowland with stands of shade trees, are conveniently near the playing fields. *Park open year-round; beach open Memorial Day– Labor Day.*

30 Little League Baseball Museum, South Williamsport

16 mi./20 min. North on Rte. 15. This museum is a fascinating destination for young baseball players and fans. A series of well-organized displays illustrates the development of the Little League, shows how equipment is made, and promotes safety. There's a computerized quiz program on rules and regulations. In the Play Ball Lab, kids can pitch, bat, and check out their form on video playback. Major Leaguers' tips on how to play better are displayed, and a 30-minute documentary about Little League baseball is shown in a 100-seat theater. *Open daily except Easter, Thanksgiving Day, Christmas, and New Year's Day. Admission charged.*

34 Bloomsburg National Historic District

5 min. South on Rte. 42, left on Rte. 11. Gracious homes and buildings in the center of this town provide a short course in the architectural history of the 19th century. An introductory tour of the district could begin with Columbia County Courthouse at Market and Second streets. This imposing building, with its high clock tower, was originally designed in the Greek revival style but in the 1890's was completed as Romanesque revival. Proceeding east and west on Second Street and then south on Market Street, you'll see some interesting examples of the Greek, colonial, and Georgian revival styles, among others. *Buildings open year-round.*

39 Eckley Miners' Village

40

Exit 39: 10 mi./15 min. South on Rte. 309, left on Freeland-Drums Hwy. to Freeland, east on Rte. 940; follow signs. Exit 40: 9 mi./20 min. West on Rte. 940; follow signs. Eckley is a living-history museum and hopes to maintain this status. Established in 1854 as a planned company "patch," it became home to generations of immigrant coal miners and their families. Early-Victorian cottages, churches, mine buildings, and the company store stand today much as they were when shovels dug into the hillside and daily life was regulated by the steam whistle. More

39–40. *Stairs, porch, and sloping cellar door add a homey touch to this house of God.*

than 50 people remain, and the 58 buildings on this 100-acre site reveal the disciplined quality of life in a company town. The preserved cottages and a museum in the visitor center have informative displays that tell the story of the mine patches that are found throughout this region of northeastern Pennsylvania, noted for its anthracite coal. *Visitor center open daily May–Sept., daily except holidays Oct.–Apr.; village buildings open Memorial Day–Labor Day and weekends Sept.–Oct. Admission charged.*

48 Quiet Valley Living Historical Farm

4 mi./7 min. South on Rte. 209, left on Hickory Valley Rd., right on Turkey Hill Rd., left on Quiet Valley Rd. Six generations of the Zepper family worked this farm from 1765 until 1913, and fortunately many of the tools and much of the equipment and furnishings have survived intact. As the farm activities are demonstrated by costumed guides, one can only marvel at the self-sufficiency that was attained by early-day farm families. Carding, spinning, weaving, and meat smoking are among the many household chores enacted, and in the mid-19th-century barn are some of the early machines designed to lighten the farmer's load. Everyone worked—including the family dog, which powered the treadmill to run the churn and washing machine. Children

See N–S book,
sec.39.

PA | NJ

See N–S book,
sec.47.

81   31   11   38   30   15   20   2   14   95

39   40   48   30   25   43   56   57   I-95   End I-80

will enjoy the hay jumps in the barn and the animals that can be petted. *Open daily late June–Labor Day. Admission charged.*

25 Village of Waterloo

5 min. North on access road; follow signs. This charming village in a tranquil setting of lawns and shade trees was restored to its 18th- and 19th-century character in 1964. Here you'll find some splendid homes, many open to the public and a few privately owned, along with a working gristmill, a general store and tavern, and a blacksmith's shop.

The Ironmaster's House and the Stagecoach Inn date from the 1760's, when there was a forge. After the Morris Canal was opened in 1831, Waterloo became a major stop; the canal museum contains memorabilia of that era. In the homes and barns, such traditional crafts as candle dipping, broom making, and wheel-thrown pottery are demonstrated. *Open Tues.–Sun. Apr.–Dec. except Thanksgiving Day, Christmas, and New Year's Day. Also open holiday Mondays and closed the following Tuesday. Admission charged.*

43 Jockey Hollow Encampment Area, Morristown

15 mi./20 min. South on I-287 to Exit 26B, north on Rte. 202, left on Tempe Wick Rd.; follow signs. In these pleasant surroundings it requires an act of will to envision the hardship experienced here by some 13,000 soldiers of George Washington's Continental Army in the winter of 1779–80. It was the worst winter of the century. Six-foot snowdrifts blocked supply routes, and the troops had insufficient clothing—many had to wrap themselves in blankets. Illness and frostbite were rampant. General Washington besought the Continental Congress to provide funds for food and supplies—to no avail. Only a mutiny in 1781 forced the lawmakers to fulfill their obligation to the fighting men.

The farmhouse that served as headquarters for Gen. Arthur St. Clair is the main attraction. Much of the red clapboard structure is original, and some of the furnishings are of the period. You can tour the rest of Jockey Hollow on the park roads or on footpaths through the woods. *Open daily except Thanksgiving Day, Christmas, and New Year's Day.*

57 Lambert Castle Museum, Paterson
56

Exit 57 (headed east): 1 min. South on Rte. 20, right on Valley Rd. Exit 56 (headed west): 2 min. Make U-turn on ramps, east on I-80 to Exit 57; proceed as above. On the slope of Garret Mountain, with a panoramic view of the plain below and the Manhattan skyline in the distance, this brown and pink sandstone "castle," complete with crenellated towers, fully justifies its name—Belle Vista. Built by Paterson silk magnate Catholina Lambert in 1892, it now houses a museum run by the Passaic County Historical Society. The magnificent ceilings, inlaid floors, and intricately carved marble and wood fireplaces are beautifully preserved. In the ballroom gallery the museum presents collections that include paintings, furniture, textiles, and decorative art. Very impressive is the Koempel collection of souvenir spoons. About 1,000 of the 5,000-spoon collection are on display, including ones with enameled landscapes, cloisonné spoons from czarist Russia, and mother-of-pearl examples from China. *Open P.M. Wed.–Sun. except holidays. Admission charged.*

I-95 New York, NY 10019

11 mi./20 min. Convention and Visitors Bureau, 2 Columbus Circle. (212) 397-8222. This city's crowded diversity can be overwhelming, but even a short visit will be rewarding if you decide in advance what you want to see.

You might choose the spectacular views from the World Trade Center or Empire State Building; stroll on Fifth Avenue past Rockefeller Center, St. Patrick's Cathedral, and the intriguing shop windows. Central Park might beckon, or Chinatown, Greenwich Village, or the South Street Seaport. For museumgoers the choices are a challenge: will it be the Metropolitan, Guggenheim, Frick, or Whitney (all within walking distance of one another)? And there's also the American Museum of Natural History and the New-York Historical Society to consider. Other temptations are a boat ride in the harbor or to the Statue of Liberty or around the island of Manhattan. Be forewarned, however: the city is a difficult—and expensive—place to park a car.

I-95. *A necklace of beckoning lights on the Brooklyn Bridge leads to the captivating isle of Manhattan, where the skyline is dominated by the twin towers of the World Trade Center.*

17 Castle Rock Campground

5 min. Southeast on access road. Some 15 million years ago, volcanic ash, wind-borne from the nearby Tushar Mountains, settled here and formed rock. Slowly, the rock was carved by the elements into the buttes, pinnacles, and other formations for which the campground is named. A stream whose banks are lined with picturesque cottonwoods flows through the center of the campground. Other campsites are situated among the piñon pines and junipers on higher ground. The campground also serves as a trailhead for hikers bound for the rocky heights of the Tushar Mountains. *Open year-round.*

17 Fremont Indian State Park

5 min. North on access road, right on Park Rd. Mule deer, kit foxes, coyotes, and marmots now roam the red rocks and sage wilderness of Clear Creek Canyon, where Indians of the Fremont culture lived from A.D. 500 to 1400. The visitor center contains interpretive exhibits and some of the rich lode of Indian artifacts unearthed here, but the real adventure lies in exploring the canyon. You'll see petroglyphs along the quarter-mile Art Rock Trail, while the more rugged Discovery and Overlook

17. Indian farmers of the Fremont culture built pit houses like this reconstruction.

trails provide fascinating insights into the Fremonts' use of natural resources. A concessionaire offers horse-and-wagon and horseback-riding trips into the backcountry, and evening activities include cookouts. The creek's sparkling waters are favored by fishermen. *Open year-round. Admission charged.*

22 Big Rock Candy Mountain

7 mi./10 min. South on Rte. 89. This vivid yellow rock formation could well be the inspiration for the hobo song of the same name recorded by Burl Ives, about a fantasyland where "the bulldogs all have rubber teeth, and the hens lay hard-boiled eggs." Although you won't find the "lemonade springs where the whippoorwill sings," you can take the short trail from the mountain's base and get a close view of the interesting geologic confection of weathered volcanic rock tinted by minerals and hot springs. *Open year-round.*

24 Monrovian Park

10 mi./20 min. East on Rte. 118, right on Main St., left on Forest Rd.; follow signs. It comes as a pleasant surprise when the dark and narrow confines of Monroe Canyon suddenly widen, revealing the lush picnic area and a scattering of scrub oaks, narrowleaf cottonwoods, and vine maples. Wildflowers bloom in the shade of great cliff walls, and melodic birdsong mingles with the sound of water flowing over volcanic rocks. Anglers fish Monroe Creek in this delightful hidden park, which also serves as a trailhead for routes leading into Fishlake National Forest. *Open year-round but may be inaccessible due to snow and ice.*

54 Palisade State Park

23 mi./30 min. North on Rte. 89, right on Palisade Park Rd. When Daniel B. Funk settled in central Utah in the mid-1800's, he

---

If You Have Some Extra Time: Arches National Park

180 | 27 mi./40 min. The greatest works of mankind are reduced to insignificance by the arches, spires, columns, fins, cliffs, and buttes that nature created here through erosion on ancient sandstone. This park, which covers nearly 75,000 acres, is named for some 600 natural arches that can be seen in various stages of their timeless development—a process explained in detail near the visitor center. The most dramatic examples are Landscape Arch, believed to be the longest natural arch in the world, and Delicate Arch, a structure of surpassing grace poised at the edge of a great natural amphitheater in a setting of bare red sandstone. The air is marvelously clear, and there are spectacular views across the Colorado River gorge to the snow-capped La Sal Mountains on the horizon.

The relatively few trees that do well here, such as piñon pine and juniper, are those that have become efficient at taking up any available water and releasing it slowly. The desert is dotted with blackbrush, a plant that has both small leathery leaves and sharp spines on its branches. The wildflowers that brighten the landscape—evening primroses and the scarlet monkey flower—have short life cycles. Other wildflowers such as columbines and orchids as well as ferns, cattails, marsh grasses, tree frogs, and toads are found in the few places where water collects. Most of the animals, such as foxes, bobcats, and ringtails, come out primarily at night. During the day you may see jewellike hummingbirds as well as rabbits and scurrying chipmunks. Look also for eagles and hawks, who prey on the small animals.

Time spent among the sculptural forms of colorful sandstone in this unique landscape is not likely to be forgotten. *How to get there: south on Rte. 191; follow signs. Admission charged.*

found so few recreational facilities that he vowed to create a leisure-time area for everyone to enjoy. Mostly through his own efforts, he created a lake, built a dance hall, and planted shade and fruit trees; and in the mid-1870's Palisade State Park was opened.

The site Funk chose for the lake belonged to the Sanpitch Indians. Hoping to avoid trouble, he appealed to Brigham Young, the territorial governor, who helped him get a deed to the property. Today the park is popular for swimming, boating (canoes can be rented), fishing in the trout-stocked waters, and golfing. The annual Winterfest offers skating on the lower pond, sledding, cross-country skiing, and ice fishing. *Open year-round. Admission charged.*

129 | 147 — San Rafael Reef

Headed east: drive past Exit 129 (Ranch exit) 10 mi. to roadside overlook. Headed west: drive past Exit 147 (Rte. 24 exit) 3 mi. to roadside overlook. Where the interstate penetrates the San Rafael Swell through Spotted Wolf Canyon, the scenery on both sides of this road is awesome. The San Rafael Reef is a sawtooth ridge along the eastern edge of the swell, a remnant of a 2,000-square-mile rock dome that bulged forth from the earth's surface 50 to 60 million years ago. The action of the elements over eons has eroded the sedimentary rock into a vast sea of frozen turbulence. The view area reveals spectacular panoramas of Mesozoic-era formations—towering pinnacles, winding canyons, and castlelike mesas. *Open year-round.*

160 | 165 — Green River State Park

Exit 160: 5 min. East on Main St., right on River Blvd. Exit 165: 5 min. West on Main St., left on River Blvd. Located on the banks of the Green River and within the town of the same name, this campground and day-use area, nicely shaded by cottonwoods, is a pleasant oasis for a picnic or as a base for exploring the surrounding territory. The boat launch is a popular access point to the Green River, with its white-water rapids, serene stretches, and spectacular canyons.

Rock collectors will find jasper, agate, and petrified wood, and bird-watchers may spot an egret, a heron, or an ibis. *Open year-round. Admission charged.*

185 — Sego Canyon Indian Rock Art

3 mi./30 min. North on Rte. 94 to a dry-wash crossing; walk 75 yd. to cliffs. The Archaic people, and later the Fremont people and the Ute Indians, who over the centuries have inhabited much of what is now Utah, were all hunters, farmers, and artists. Their enduring artistic creations, incised petroglyphs and painted pictographs, can be seen on the sandstone canyon walls. Some of the images represent desert bighorns and other indigenous wildlife, while the abstract shapes defy definition but stimulate the imagination. Unfortunately, some of the art has been marred by vandals who deface what they cannot comprehend, but the graffiti have not detracted from the significance of the site. *Open year-round but road may be flooded during rain.*

19 — Colorado National Monument

4 min. South on Rte. 340. Stone monoliths rise from sheer-walled canyons 1,000 feet deep, while junipers and piñon pines cover lesser inclines in this 20,400-acre park. Rim Rock Drive twists through 23 miles of spectacular natural sculptures created by wind and water. Grand View, Redlands, and Cold Shivers Point are some of the aptly named scenic turnouts along the way. For hikers, easy trails along the rim afford many fine views, while longer trails with numerous switchbacks descend the canyon walls and link up with trails at the bottom. Bring water with you on all but the shortest trails. Indigenous animals include bighorn sheep, mountain lions, elk, and mule deer. *Open year-round. Admission charged.*

31 — Museum of Western Colorado, Grand Junction

4 mi./12 min. Southwest on Horizon Dr., left on 12th St., right on Ute Ave. Mineral samples, Indian artifacts, and early settlers' tools displayed in this remodeled school building

19. *Juniper foliage and berries contrast beautifully with the sandstone monoliths.*

are among the items that illuminate the social and natural history of the region. Two blocks away, at the Dinosaur Valley branch of the museum, the exhibits focus on a much earlier time; there are fossils, a dinosaur skeleton, half-size animated models of dinosaurs, and photographs of historic paleontological digs in the area. In addition, the museum also operates the Cross Orchards Living History Farm, where costumed guides explain the development of fruit growing in the area. Directions to and hours of the dinosaur exhibit and the farm are available at the main museum. *Museum open Tues–Sat. except holidays; Dinosaur Valley open daily Memorial Day–Sept., Tues.–Sun. Nov.–Memorial Day; farm open Wed.–Sat. mid-May–Oct. Admission charged for dinosaur exhibit and farm.*

| 47 | **Island Acres State Recreation Area** |

2 min. Follow signs. Picnicking on the lush lawn, camping, and winter eagle-watching are popular here, where the Colorado River is surrounded by the towering shale and sandstone walls of De Beque Canyon. A band of well-watered shoreline vegetation contrasts sharply with the bare rock above, and the riverside plants support a wide variety of wildlife, including two bison in a fenced pasture. Four ponds, one for swimming and three for fishing and nonmotorized boats, have recently been added. Skunks are frequently encountered, and visitors should admire them from a respectful distance. *Open year-round. Admission charged.*

| 90 | **Rifle Gap and Rifle Falls State Recreation Areas** |

14 mi./20 min. North on Rte. 13, right on Rte. 325; follow signs. This reservoir in western Colorado provides much-needed water for the surrounding country and also offers excellent boating, swimming (scuba diving is especially fine in the crystal-clear waters), and fishing. The shaded banks of East Rifle Creek support stands of cottonwoods and small growths of ferns and mosses. At Rifle Falls, 5 miles up Route 325, the creek drops over a wide natural cliff of travertine deposits that may have formed when a beaver dam slowed the creek enough for limestone deposits to create the outcrop and plateau. Rifle Box Canyon, located a mile from the falls, has steep, high walls overhung by limestone ledges. The nearby limestone caves are safe and easy to explore with the aid of a flashlight. *Open year-round. Admission charged.*

| 116 | **Hot Springs Pool** |

1 min. East from exit. This spa, surrounded by mountains, has one of the world's largest outdoor pools filled by mineral hot springs. The 400-foot-long outdoor pool, which can be visited even when there's snow on the mountain, is kept at a comfortable 90° F all year; temperatures in a smaller therapy pool climb to 104° F. Flowing at a rate of 2,500 gallons per minute, the springs completely replenish the pools every 8 hours. Called Yampa ("Big Medicine") Springs by the Ute Indians, the heated waters are still reputed to be therapeutic. *Open year-round except 2nd Wed. Sept.–May. Admission charged.*

203–205. *The waning light at dusk brings a subtle blend of colors to the reservoir.*

| 176 | **Colorado Ski Museum and Ski Hall of Fame, Vail** |

1 min. East on S. Frontage Rd. From "snowshoes" used more than 6,000 years ago for hunting and transportation to the sophisticated sports of today, the history of skiing is presented at the Colorado Ski Museum with films, videos, and displays. There are photographs of mailmen making their appointed rounds on long boards in the 1800's, Coloradoans' first ski races, and soldiers of the 10th Mountain Division with skis at the ready. The Hall of Fame displays photos of people who advanced the sport of skiing in the state. The museum is in a pedestrian mall. To reach it, park at the parking structure on the right, take the inner village bus, or walk two blocks west on East Meadow Drive. *Open P.M. Tues.–Sun. June–mid-Oct. and late Nov.–mid-Apr. except Christmas and New Year's Day.*

| 203 | **Scenic Overlook of Dillon Reservoir** |
| 205 | |

Exit 203: 1 min. East from exit. Exit 205: 1 min. West from exit. From this heavily wooded site there is a magnificent alpine view of 3,300-acre Dillon Reservoir, with Grays and Torreys peaks towering in the distance. The water, stored here for the city of Denver, flows through a 23-mile tunnel bored through hard rock beneath the Continental Divide. The reservoir and its 25-mile shoreline and wooded areas provide inviting opportunities for fishing, boating, and water-skiing in summer and cross-country skiing and dogsledding in winter. *Open year-round.*

| 228 | **Georgetown—Silver Plume Historic Landmark District** |

3 min. South on Argentine St. More than 200 original buildings, many restored to their Victorian elegance, confirm picturesque Georgetown's early days as a booming mid-1800's Colorado silver-mining camp. Hamill House Museum, a silver baron's home, displays such luxuries as gaslight, a bathtub, and an outhouse topped with a cupola.

The Georgetown Loop Railroad was built in 1884 on narrow-gauge tracks, which enabled the steam train to maneuver the curves and trestles as it climbed the 700-foot grade from Georgetown to the Silver Plume mines. The train now carries passengers over this breathtaking reconstructed route. *Buildings open year-round; railroad operates daily Memorial Day–Labor Day, weekends only Labor Day–early Oct. Admission charged for train ride and mine tour.*

| 244 | **Central City Blackhawk National Historic District** |

12 mi./30 min. East on Rte. 6, left on Rte. 119. The diamond-dust-backed mirrors of the Teller House Hotel, now a museum, symbolize the luxury of what in its 1870's heyday was Colorado's largest and most famous mining boomtown. The Central City Gold Mine and Museum (in an aboveground building) shows the tools and explains the backbreaking labor that supported the splendor. There is still some gold in the piles of mine waste rock that line Gregory Gulch, and gold seekers still pan

Clear Creek, seeking the glint that dominated early Colorado history. A pleasant half-mile ride on the old Colorado & Southern Railroad affords a view of Central City from the mountains. *Central City Gold Mine and Museum open daily June–Aug.; Teller House open daily June–Sept., weekends only Oct.–May. Admission charged.*

252   Hiwan Homestead Museum, Evergreen

8 mi./15 min. West on Rte. 74, left on Douglas Park Rd., left on Meadow Dr. Begun as a summer retreat in the 1880's, this 17-room log structure evolved into a comfortable year-round house with twin octagonal towers and its own chapel. The last owners, who raised prize Herefords, gave it the name Hiwan, an Anglo-Saxon word meaning "a high, secluded place with enough for one ox to plow." Many rooms are restored to their 1915–30 style with a western motif. Displays involving local history and an extensive doll collection add to the charm of the house. The building is listed in *The National Register of Historic Places. Open P.M. Tues.–Sun. except holidays.*

228. *For this steep, twisting route the track is narrow-gauge and the engine powerful.*

I-25   Denver, CO 80202

Convention & Visitors Bureau, 225 W. Colfax Ave. (303) 892-1112. There is a wealth of museums, parks, and shopping areas in the Mile-High City. The Denver Art Museum, covered with a million reflecting tiles, houses a superb American Indian collection, with many Mesoamerican pieces. Nearby is the U.S. Mint, where you can watch money being stamped. Among the old mansions on Capitol Hill is the popular Molly Brown House, former home of the "unsinkable" heroine of the *Titanic.* The flavor of Denver's past is preserved in Larimer Square, with its restored shops, arcades, and gaslights. The Denver Museum of Natural History has a state-of-the-art planetarium, and the Denver Zoo displays the animals in natural-habitat settings.

310   Comanche Crossing Historical Society Museum, Strasburg

1 min. North on Strasburg Mile Dr., left on Rte. 36. Locals claim that it was here, a year after the driving of the golden spike at Promontory Point in northern Utah, that the first U.S. transcontinental railroad was really completed. Many of the museum's displays focus on rooms from homes and businesses of the late 19th and early 20th centuries. Details catch the eye: the barbershop's handsome assortment of razors, the beauty parlor's electric curling machine, the post office's boxes, and an organ and wicker furniture in the parlor. An annex houses farm vehicles and fire trucks. Also part of the museum complex are a homesteader's cottage, two one-room schoolhouses, and a railroad depot with the stationmaster's living quarters. All are furnished in period style. *Open P.M. daily June–Aug.*

371   Genoa Tower, Genoa

2 min. North on Rte. 109, left on Frontage Rd. This sprawling 20-room complex topped by a brightly painted tower was begun by C. W. Gregory, known as Colorado's P. T. Barnum. There's a touch of the circus carnival to it, with two-headed calves, an eight-legged pig, and a 75,000-year-old skeleton of a mammoth among its attractions. Other exhibits are an extraordinary hodgepodge of old bottles, bullets, Bibles, fiddles, and such. Many rooms are built of rocks with bottles embedded in the ceilings. A steep flight leads to the tower's deck, where you can see parts of six states. *Open year-round. Admission charged.*

17   High Plains Museum, Goodland

2 min. North on Rte. 27, right on 16th St., right on Cherry St. This museum's pride and joy is a full-scale replica of what is claimed to be America's first patented helicopter—the circa 1910 Purvis-Wilson Flying Machine, the work of two Rock Island, Illinois, machinists. Press a button, and the blades will rotate. Another exhibit concentrates on the prairie rainmakers—companies such as the Interstate Artificial Rain Co. and solo operator Frank Melbourne ("The Rain Wizard"). Dioramas and displays, including musical instruments and a 1902 Holsman automobile, also capture the flavor of the region's past. *Open daily Memorial Day–Labor Day; Tues.–Sun. Labor Day–Memorial Day. Admission free but donations encouraged.*

70 | Fick Fossil and History Museum, Oakley

5 mi./10 min. South on Rte. 83, left on 2nd St., left on Center St., left on 3rd St. It is not easy to visualize the dry Kansas plains as a watery realm of sharks, oysters, and prehistoric fish, but the evidence is here. The fossils, impressively displayed, were gathered locally by Mr. and Mrs. Earnest Fick and by Charles and George Sternberg. The sharks' teeth, some 11,000 in all, were arranged by Mrs. Fick in a remarkable variety of patterns and designs. The later history of the area is represented by historical exhibits, including a replica of a sod house, a railroad depot, a general store, an old horse-drawn farm wagon, a century-old Chandler Price printing press, and various local artifacts. *Open daily except Christmas and New Year's Day.*

135 | Cedar Bluff State Park

13 mi./15 min. South on Rte. 147. This park is divided into two parts, one on the north and the other on the south shore of man-made Cedar Bluff Lake. In the northern area—the smaller of the two—there are inviting places to swim or picnic along the lakefront, where pink-blossomed tamarisks and cottonwoods grow at the water's edge. South of the dam the terrain changes dramatically to a desertlike environment with yucca and prickly poppy amid limestone bluffs. Park facilities include a marina and boat ramps. The quality of fishing depends largely on the water level. White bass, walleye, crappie, and catfish are most plentiful; bluegills, rainbow trout, and smallmouth, largemouth, and spotted bass are sparser. *Open daily mid-Apr.–mid-Oct. Admission charged.*

157 | Fort Hays Frontier Historical Park

4 min. South on Rte. 183. Ft. Hays was built on the Smoky Hill stagecoach route in 1867 to protect settlers and railroad workers from Indian attack. As the white population in the area grew, the Plains Indians were forced to migrate, and in 1889 the fort was abandoned. Only 3 buildings of the original 45 still stand: the stone blockhouse, which doubled as a defensive outpost and camp headquarters; a guardhouse where prisoners were confined and guards quartered; and one officer's house. Exhibits include period furnishings, Indian and railroad memorabilia, frontier artillery, and a library with antique jigsaw puzzles. Mannequins add a sense of reality: a cell in the guardhouse holds one mournful-looking mannequin in period underwear while nearby hangs a 20-pound ball and chain. The visitor center displays models of the fort in its prime. *Open year-round.*

168 | Cathedral of the Plains, Victoria

3 min. South on Rte. 255. The twin 141-foot rock spires of this beautifully crafted Roman Catholic church soar above the plains of Kansas. Officially named St. Fidelis Church but rechristened by William Jennings Bryan, this 220-foot-long, 110-foot-wide cruciform structure was built in 1911 of native Kansas stone, hand-quarried and carted in 50- to 100-pound slabs by devout Volga German parishioners. The Romanesque interior features an altarpiece portraying the martyrdom of St. Fidelis, stained glass windows, wood carvings depicting the stations of the cross, and 14 granite pillars topped by hand-carved capitals of Bedford limestone. A reproduction of the original dedication booklet includes such injunctions as "The bells are rung to get the people into the church on time, not to make work for the sacristan." *Open year-round.*

206 | Wilson State Park

7 mi./11 min. North on Rte. 232. Hidden coves and inlets and miniature cliffs along the water's edge are among the enticements of this delightful park on Wilson Lake, where the water has exposed the sandstone underlying the surrounding prairie. The 927-acre park boasts a surprising variety of landscapes, with shiny-leaved cottonwoods along the shore giving way to prairie grass and wildflowers on the upland stretches. There are charming places for picnicking, and each of the six campgrounds has its own distinctive character. *Open year-round. Admission charged.*

206 | Garden of Eden, Lucas

17 mi./22 min. North on Rte. 232, right on Rte. 18; follow signs. A monument to vigorous individuality if not outright eccentricity, this house and garden were created by a Civil War veteran named S.P. Dinsmoor. Among its attractions are what could be the only "log" cabin (circa 1907) built entirely of limestone; a sculpture garden whose various all-concrete pieces are a wondrous mix of biblical, socialist, and personal imagery; and a 40-foot-high mausoleum in which Dinsmoor's body lies, guarded by rather alarming concrete angels. Visitors to the house will see such curios as a weeping willow rocker, a handmade checkerboard table, and a painting of the horse upon which he and his first wife were married. Widowed, he was remarried at the age of 81 to his 20-year-old housekeeper. *Open year-round. Admission charged.*

225 / 238 | Mushroom Rock State Park

Exit 225: 15 mi./24 min. South on Rte. 156, left on Rte. 111, left on Rte. 140, right on Rte. 141, right at sign. Exit 238: 18 mi./23 min. South toward Brookville, right on Rte. 140, left on Rte. 141, right at sign. This 5½-acre park is worth a stop just to marvel at the fascinating and awesome power of nature.

225–238. *It rather boggles the mind, but this is indeed nature's own creation.*

The curious rock formations are the remains of sandstone outcroppings worn away by the persistent winds sweeping across the prairie. The mushroom shapes were developed as soft lower layers eroded more quickly than harder ones above them. Some rocks are 25 feet tall, with caps 15 feet wide. Another interesting oddity is a 15-stripe American flag carved in rock, probably by westbound pioneers. *Open year-round.*

260 Indian Burial Pit

6 mi./9 min. South on Niles Rd., right on Rte. 140; follow signs. An unexpected benefit of the farmland erosion in the dust bowl years of the 1930's was the exposure of this resting place for prehistoric Indians. The 146 skeletal remains of men, women, and children lie as they were found, in layers, many with knees drawn up almost to their chests. Most are on their right sides and face east, probably oriented toward the rising sun. Such artifacts as flint knives, arrowheads, clamshell necklaces, and pendants abound at the site. Particularly poignant are the earrings and necklace placed near the remains of a small child. *Open year-round. Admission charged.*

275 Dwight D. Eisenhower Library, Abilene

2 mi./6 min. South on Rte. 15. Centered around the simple clapboard house that was his boyhood home, this museum-library complex celebrates the achievements of Dwight D. Eisenhower as supreme allied commander in Europe during World War II and as 34th president in the 1950's. The library houses papers, books, and other materials related to his career. In the museum guns, uniforms, and other military memorabilia trace Ike's rise from cadet to five-star general. Cartoons, posters, and buttons bring to life his presidential campaigns, and historic documents illuminate the White House years. Murals in the museum's lobby depict events in his life. The president, first lady, and a son are buried beneath plain marble slabs in the chapellike Place of Meditation. *Open daily except Thanksgiving Day, Christmas, and New Year's Day. Admission charged for museum.*

275. Behind the severe facade is the human story of a president and great general.

301 Fort Riley

3 min. North on Holbrook Ave.; follow signs. The U.S. cavalry played a key role in winning the West, and some of the buildings in this fort memorialize that achievement. At the museum in the former headquarters building, the story of these mounted troops is illustrated by uniforms, weapons, statues, and paintings (including originals by Frederic Remington). Nearby Custer House, named in honor of Gen. George Armstrong Custer, who lived at the fort, is fully furnished in 1880's style. You can take a self-guiding walking tour of the fort, which is the size of a small town and has many handsome structures built of native limestone. *Open daily except Easter, Thanksgiving Day, Christmas, and New Year's Day.*

362B Topeka, KS 66603

Chamber of Commerce, 120 East 6th St. (913) 234-2644. Topeka's 160-acre Gage Park is the home of one of the world's finest zoos, which includes an exhibit of apes and a reconstructed Amazon rain forest complete with exotic vegetation, waterfalls, and free-flying birds. A swimming pool, picnic areas, and a botanical garden add to the attractive amenities of this city park. Topeka's impressive statehouse, in the French Renaissance revival style, is famous for its murals by John Steuart Curry; and the Kansas Museum of History features many period rooms and exhibits, including a 1912 airplane made in Topeka. Other points of interest are the Ward-Meade Historical Park and Botanical Gardens and Lake Shawnee.

202 Clinton State Park

7 mi./12 min. South on Rte. 59, right on Rte. 40, left on Rte. 13. Clinton Lake, an impressive body of water stretching for some 8 miles up the Wakarusa Valley, was built to control flooding and supply water to nearby Lawrence. It also offers many recreational possibilities, and this state park on its north shore takes full advantage of the site, with facilities for camping, boating, and swimming. Five other parks, run by the U.S. Army Corps of Engineers, also provide access to the lake. On the lake's east side a drive across the top of the embankment of the imposing 940-foot-long Clinton Dam affords fine views of the lake. *Open year-round. Admission charged.*

203 Perry State Park

21 mi./25 min. North on Rte. 59, left on Rte. 24, right on Rte. 237. Lovers of wide-open spaces will enjoy this pleasant park on the shore of Perry Lake. Formed in 1969 when the U.S. Army Corps of Engineers dammed the Delaware River as part of a flood control project, the lake has 160 miles of shoreline. A broad, sandy swimming beach backed by a meadow, lakeside camping and picnic facilities, and two boat ramps are the major attractions. Fishermen try for crappie, catfish, and bass. A public-use marina is located next to the park's Delaware Area. *Open year-round. Admission charged.*

203. Catamarans are a popular mode of transportation on man-made Perry Lake.

KS | MO — 29 35 — See N–S book, sec. 15 for I-29; sec. 18 for I-35.

70

224 | 2C | 2D | NOL | 20 | 98 | 148

17 | 11 | 8 | 78 | 50 | 22

224 Agricultural Hall of Fame and National Center

4 min. North on Rte. 7; follow signs. An important aspect of Americana is recalled here in this major national institution dedicated to American farmers. In the Hall of Rural Living, quaint displays re-create the parlor, sewing room, kitchen, and other elements of the country home of an imaginary grandmother. Her washing room has manual and early electric washers, and her "back-porch yard" overflows with canning equipment and glassware. In Ye Ol' Town, scenes of rural life include a general store, a telephone exchange, a dentist's office, and a wheelwright's shop. Also noteworthy are the Museum of Farming, an enormous warehouse filled with farm equipment; the National Farmers Memorial, with massive bronze-relief panels depicting farmers past, present, and future; and Farm Town U.S.A., with a 100-year-old railroad station, a blacksmith's shop, and a restored one-room schoolhouse. *Open daily Apr.–Nov. Admission charged.* ♿

224 Wyandotte County Historical Society and Museum

4 min. North on Rte. 7, right on access road; follow signs. History here in the heart of the Central Plains starts with the Indians, most notably the Wyandot, an educated people who emigrated from Ohio in 1843 and built a town complete with church, school, and council house. The exhibits in this museum trace life in the region from those days until well into this century. Other displays concentrate on local industries. Transportation is a popular theme, with memorabilia from the railroads and riverboats, which caused this strategic crossroads to boom, and from the trolley cars that once plied Kansas City's streets. A 1903 steam-driven fire truck is also on display. *Open Tues.–Sun. late Feb.–late Dec. except Thanksgiving Day.*

2C Kansas City, MO 64107

2D *Convention & Visitors Bureau, 1100 Main St., Suite 2550. (816) 221-5242; (800) 523-5953 outside MO.* It may come as a surprise, but this beautifully planned city has more miles of boulevards than Paris, and, like Rome, has many handsome fountains. Its shopping centers, too, are noted for their appealing ambience. The Country Club Plaza has architectural echoes of Seville, Spain; Crown Center is an 85-acre city within a city; and at Westport Square some handsome Victorian structures have been converted into shops and restaurants. Among the museums here are the unique Miniature Museum and the Nelson-Atkins Museum of Art, known for the wide range of its holdings and its special emphasis on works from China and India. Swope Park, which contains the Kansas City Zoo and other attractions, is one of the nation's largest municipal parks.

NOL Independence, MO 64050

Nolan Rd. N. exit: Truman Home Ticket and Information Center, 223 N. Main St. (816) 254-9929. As might be expected, the man from Independence, our 33rd president, is well remembered here. There is in fact a Harry S Truman Historic District, a walking tour of which begins at the Truman home (the summer White House) and winds through a well-preserved neighborhood of brick sidewalks and stately homes. Elsewhere in the city is the Truman Library and Museum, which has a reproduction of his White House office among other exhibits. The restored office and courtroom where President Truman began his career is located in the Independence Square Courthouse. You can also see a 35-minute audiovisual presentation.

20 Fort Osage

17 mi./24 min. North on Rte. 7, right on Rte. 24, left on Rte. BB; follow signs. The fort built here in 1808 was the first outpost established in the lands acquired by the Louisiana Purchase. It served to protect the territory from intrusions by the Spanish and British, to enforce government licensing of white traders, and to establish friendly relations with 5,000 or so Osage Indians in the area. The present fort is a replica of the original, built on a promontory overlooking the Missouri River. Within a sturdy palisade are the blockhouses,

20. *They seem vulnerable today, but such fortifications were sufficient in their time.*

officers' and enlisted men's quarters, and the trading post. The museum's exhibits focus primarily on Indian culture and artifacts. *Open daily mid-Apr.–mid-Nov.; weekends only mid-Nov.–mid-Apr. Admission charged.* ⛱

98 Arrow Rock State Historic Site

13 mi./15 min. North on Rte. 41. A ferry across the Missouri River and steamboat traffic on the river helped establish this town as a trading center in the early 1800's. It was bypassed, however, by the railroad and fell into decline. In recent years local interest in restoration and preservation has made Arrow Rock something of a museum town. On a guided walking tour you will visit the small brick house of artist George Caleb Bingham, the Dr. John Sappington Memorial Building, where the medical concerns of the community are recalled by exhibits, and the Doctors' Museum, which houses a collection of medical instruments. The small clapboard courthouse and a printshop are also on the tour. There are a number of other historic structures to be seen, many of which are stores and gift shops. *Open year-round; tours daily June–Aug.; weekends only Sept.–Oct. and Apr.–May. Admission charged for tours.* ⛱ ⛺ 🚐

148 Audrain Historical and American Saddle Horse Museum, Mexico

17 mi./23 min. North on Rte. 54; follow signs. This distinguished clapboard mansion with its two-story porch and pediment is home to a museum dedicated to the American saddle horse, and features a number of rooms furnished and maintained by the local historical society in the style of the 1870–1900 period. The beautifully preserved rooms include the Ross Parlor, with its Aubusson carpet and a suite of fine rosewood furniture; the Period Bedroom, with a spool bed, cradle, and other accessories; and the Bride's Room, containing a display of antique wedding gowns. The Children's Room features a large collection of toys, dolls, and dollhouse furniture. Many original Currier and Ives prints grace the walls of the house. *Open P.M. Tues.–Sun., Feb.–Dec. Admission charged.*

148 Winston Churchill Memorial and Library, Fulton

8 mi./14 min. West on Rte. 54, left on Rte. F, left on Westminster Ave. One doesn't expect to see a 17th-century church built in London by Sir Christopher Wren sitting in a small town in Missouri—but here it is. The church, severely damaged by bombs in World War II, was slated for demolition. But it was brought here and rebuilt as a tribute to Sir Winston Churchill, who in 1946 had given his famous Iron Curtain speech at Westminster College in Fulton. The college raised funds by public subscription, and the building, renewed to past beauty, was dedicated in 1969. The Churchill Museum and Library are housed in the undercroft of the church. *Open daily except Thanksgiving Day, Christmas, and New Year's Day. Admission charged.* &

170 Graham Cave State Park

4 mi./6 min. North on Rte. 161, left on Rte. TT. Although this is a pleasant 365-acre recreational park, it is also gaining renown as an archeological dig. Excavations indicate that hunters and fishers lived in this area during the Dalton and Archaic periods from 8000 to 1000 B.C.—much earlier than had formerly been assumed. The early Indians were spear throwers; then, after a long time lapse, bow hunters and pottery makers inhabited this shelter. The cave is still undergoing excavation and cannot be entered, but there are signs and displays to identify notable discoveries. *Open year-round.*   ⛲ ▲ ⛺ 🚶

210 228 Augusta A. Busch Memorial Wildlife Area

Exit 210: 11 mi./20 min. South on Rte. 40/61, right on Rte. 94, right on Rte. D. Exit 228: 14 mi./22 min. South on Rte. 94; right on Rte. D. The most striking features of this 7,000-acre preserve are the 32 man-made lakes with a surface area of 500 acres. Hunting and fishing are popular here. The lakes are stocked with bass, catfish, crappie, and pike, and boats may be rented for fishing. Private boats are not allowed. One lake is reserved as a refuge for waterfowl.

The area is mainly prairie and meadowland, with some forest land of predominantly oak and hickory. Where the land is cultivated, the farmers leave part of their crops unharvested to provide food for the wildlife. In addition to the waterfowl and other birds, the resident mammals are rabbits, coyotes, deer, raccoons, skunks, opossums, squirrels, and groundhogs. A 7.7-mile auto tour leads through the refuge, and a guidebook describes features along the way. *Open daily except Christmas.*   ⛲ 🐟

210–228. *Remarkably elegant digs for one so identified with the rigors of wilderness.*

210 228 Daniel Boone Home

Exit 210: 18 mi./30 min. South on Rte. 40/61, right on Rte. 94, right on Rte. F. Exit 228: 24 mi./36 min. South on Rte. 94, right on Rte. F. For those expecting to find that one of America's most famous frontiersmen lived in a log cabin or humble shack, this handsome four-story Georgian-style house, filled with attractive furnishings, will come as quite a surprise. One reminder of Boone's

vocation is the powder horn he carved himself. Many of the furnishings were used by the Boone family; others are period pieces. As a trailblazer, scout, and Indian fighter, Boone lived by being well prepared. He was equally prepared for the other alternative and stored his coffin under the handsome four-poster bed in which he died. *Open daily mid-March–mid-Dec. Admission charged.*   ⛲

ARCH St. Louis, MO 63102

Arch/Downtown exit: Convention and Visitors Commission, 10 S. Broadway. (314) 421-1023; (800) 247-9791 outside MO. The three spans across the Mississippi here dramatize the role of St. Louis as a jumping-off place to the West, and the magnificent 630-foot Gateway Arch commemorates the days of the wagon trains, when the only river crossings were by water. From the top of the arch one can contemplate the vast reaches so full of promise and danger in the days of the pioneers, an era graphically interpreted in the Museum of Westward Expansion located beneath the arch. St. Louis's excellent zoo has more than 2,500 animals and a miniature railroad to provide an easy introduction. Featured in the 79-acre botanical garden is the domed Climatron greenhouse and the largest Japanese garden in the United States.

63 Vandalia Statehouse State Historic Site

5 min. South on Rte. 51. Abraham Lincoln is not quite the hero in Vandalia that he is in the other parts of his adopted state. He led the effort to move the state capital from here, where it had been since 1820, to the more central location of Springfield. It was moved in 1839 after the local citizens had put up some $23,000 to erect a federal-style building that would serve as a capitol. Their efforts were in vain, and the building was demoted to the status of county courthouse. Now refurbished, it provides a fascinating reminder that in 1839 the corridors of power were heated with a battery of stoves, candles were used for light, and writing was done with quill pens. *Open daily except Thanksgiving Day, Christmas, and New Year's Day.*   &

119. *Hand-hewn logs, dovetailed corners, and shake roof are true to the originals.*

119 | Lincoln Log Cabin State Historic Site

10 mi./20 min. North on Rte. 130; follow signs. The volunteers in the living-history program, dressed in period costumes, plow, plant, and harvest, care for livestock, spin wool, and do the other chores that were required here at Goosenest Prairie in the mid-19th century. There are also first-person role players you can talk to about farm life and events of the era. They must feign ignorance of the world beyond their time and place. Abraham Lincoln's father and stepmother lived here during the mid-1800's in a cabin identical to this reproduction. The future president, then a young lawyer from Springfield, visited them at Goosenest Prairie on occasion. *Open daily except Thanksgiving Day, Christmas, and New Year's Day; interpretive programs daily June–Aug., weekends only May and Sept.*

119 | Fox Ridge State Park

11 mi./22 min. North on Rte. 130. Hills, valleys, and woods come as a welcome surprise here on a plain that seems boundless. This oasis was not made accessible without the obvious labor of building boardwalks, bridges across steep little gorges, and steps up the hillsides for fine views of the forest canopy and the Embarras (pronounced *Am*-braw) River below. Be advised that the trails are on the arduous side, although there is one short trail for the handicapped. Free fishing boats suggest an outing on secluded 18-acre Ridge Lake. *Open daily except Christmas and New Year's Day.*

147 | Lincoln Trail State Park

5 mi./10 min. South on Rte. 1. Part of the Lincoln Heritage Trail, which marks the nearly 1,000-mile route the Lincoln family took from Kentucky to Illinois, this beautiful park centers on a 146-acre lake with many coves and inlets. Photographs of triumphant anglers pinned to the wall of the store at the boat dock indicate that it's a good place to fish for stocked largemouth bass and channel catfish. In season the park is richly bedecked with wildflowers, honeysuckle, and other plants. Maple and American beech trees shade the many inviting ravines in Lincoln Trail. *Open daily except Christmas and New Year's Day.*

147 | Twin Lakes Parks

16.5 mi./30 min. North on Rte. 1 through Paris. On the outskirts of the charming and grand-looking town of Paris, this pair of enjoyable community parks, which share a common main entrance, take their name from two lakes so elongated in shape that they might at first be mistaken for rivers. The shores of the lakes, which are partially edged by private homes, have tables nicely shaded by trees, a pleasant setting for a Sunday outing or picnic—despite the mystifying sign: "No beer, no liquor, no melons." *Open year-round.*

7 | Early Wheels Museum, Terre Haute

3 mi./7 min. North on Rte. 41, right on Rte. 40. A superlative selection of vehicles is displayed in this fascinating museum. A prairie schooner represents the early days, followed by an 1898 Locomobile Steamer and an electric horseless buggy built in Indiana. There are many automobiles made between the turn of the century and World War II, including sleek European models, such as the 1921 Hispano Suiza and the 1921 Isotta Fraschini. Rounding out the collection are race cars and bicycles ranging from penny-farthing high-wheelers to modern lightweight racers. *Open Mon.–Fri. except holidays.*

11 | Dobbs Park and Nature Center, Terre Haute

4 mi./7 min. North on Rte. 46, left on Rte. 42. The emphasis is on nature at this small, enticing park, which encompasses a surprising variety of habitats. Well-charted trails lead from plantations of pine and deciduous trees that harbor owls and deer through a mature forest of white oaks, tulip trees, sycamores, and beeches. In the nature center small animal exhibits and a tell-by-touch quiz attract children. A window looks out onto a bird-feeding station that flashes with the colors of cardinals, purple finches, and jays. Next to the center is a 3-acre lake where you can try for channel catfish, bluegill, and largemouth bass. *Park open year-round; nature center open Mon.–Sat. and P.M. Sun.*

37 | Lieber State Recreation Area

3 mi./8 min. South on Rte. 243. This recreation area boasts hundreds of acres of lake and miles of inviting shoreline created by flood control projects on the Mississippi and Ohio rivers. A long sandy beach and a bathhouse invite swimmers to deep blue Cagles Mill Lake, and a marina with rental boats nestled

69 See N–S book, sec. 29.
To reach I-69,
go north on I-465.   43

15   19

IN | OH

See N–S book,
sec. 31.   75   8

122   137   156   I-75   70

in a quiet bay draws anglers for largemouth bass and bluegill. Exercise enthusiasts will appreciate the elaborate fitness trail; and the meadows and woodlands offer hiking, bird-watching, and berry and nut picking. The campground has more than 400 sites in all. Another popular attraction in this recreation area is Cataract Falls, which is the largest waterfall in Indiana. *Open year-round. Admission charged.*

79B Indianapolis, IN 46225

Convention & Visitors Association, 1 Hoosier Dome, Suite 100. (317) 639-4282. Almost everyone knows that every May, Indianapolis boasts one of the world's largest sports events, the "Indy 500." But there are other attractions worthy of note. Consider, for example, the Indianapolis Museum of Art, the Indiana State Museum, and the Children's Museum, one of the largest and most varied of its kind. You can visit the home of poet James Whitcomb Riley and President Benjamin Harrison's 16-room Victorian mansion. There's a new zoo and three large parks. In the heart of downtown, Festival Market Place in old Union Station, with its many shops and res-

79B. *Indiana's imposing war memorial bears the sculpture "Pro Patria" ("For Country").*

taurants, attracts crowds. And even if it isn't May, the Speedway is worth a visit. The Hall of Fame Museum displays antique and classic cars and more than 32 speedsters that have won the race since it was established in 1911; and you can get the feel of "the Brickyard" on a minibus ride around the circuit.

122 The Henry County Historical Museum, New Castle

5 mi./12 min. North on Rte. 3, right on Indiana Ave., right on S. 14th St. Dignified rather than opulent, this 1870 Victorian Italianate house still reflects the moderate tastes of its former owner, Maj. Gen. William Grose, one of Indiana's most notable Civil War military leaders. The impression of a family home is preserved by Grose family portraits, the general's intact master bedroom, a well-stocked summer kitchen, and 19th-century furnishings throughout the house. Besides Grose family and Henry County memorabilia, the museum has interesting collections of Victorian toys and playthings, day and evening attire, pocket watches, music boxes, and cooking, sewing, and farming implements. *Open P.M. Mon.– Sat. except holidays. Admission free but donations encouraged.*

137 Huddleston Farmhouse Inn Museum, Mt. Auburn

4 mi./15 min. South on Rte. 1, right on Rte. 40. Built between 1839 and 1841 by John Huddleston, this substantial three-story federal-style building with a barn and a smokehouse was not exactly an inn. It was in fact a private farmhouse that offered shelter to travelers on the National Road. For a fee a weary pioneer family could feed and water their horses, buy produce, then cook and bed down for the night in two ground-floor kitchens. This floor and another in the family's quarters upstairs have been restored with period furnishings, including a formal American empire-style parlor set, some fine examples of local chair-making, and a family kitchen with the luxuries of an adjoining springhouse and herb garden. *Open Tues.–Fri. and P.M. Sun. May–Aug; Tues.–Fri. Sept.–Apr. Admission free but donations encouraged.*

156 Wayne County Historical Museum, Richmond

4 mi./10 min. West on Rte. 40; follow signs. Thanks to Julia Meek Gaar, its globe-trotting founder, this museum has a charmingly eclectic collection. A totem pole stands next to an ornate Italian cabinet; Victorian fans flank samurai armor; and the museum's showpiece

is a 3,500-year-old Egyptian mummy. Such delights as Lenci dolls, a perfect 1880's dollhouse, and Meissen china vie for attention with antique cars and re-creations of a pioneer kitchen and a general store. Outside, half a dozen preserved structures form a village square with displays related to local history. *Open Tues.–Fri. and P.M. weekends Feb.– Dec. Admission charged.*

I-75 Dayton, OH 45402

10 mi./18 min. Convention & Visitors Bureau, Chamber Plaza, 5th and Main Sts. (513) 226-8248 or (800) 221-8234; (800) 221-8235 outside OH. This river city seems to have invention in the air. The cash register, the electric starter, and the pull-tab tin-can top were devised by Daytonians. But the best-known local wizards were Orville and Wilbur Wright (see Carillon Park below). Arcade Square, a completely restored turn-of-the-century indoor farmers' market canopied by an enormous glass dome, contains some 50 specialty shops, restaurants, and boutiques. Other highlights in the city are the United States Air Force Museum, the home of black poet Paul Laurence Dunbar, and the baroque collections in the Dayton Art Institute.

I-75 Carillon Park, Dayton

11 mi./20 min. South on I-75 to Exit 51, east on Edwin Moses Blvd., right on the Stewart St. cross bridge, right on Patterson Blvd. Neatly fitted into this lovely park is a little town from yesteryear, re-created with a mixture of relocated original structures and exact replicas. Among others there's a 1796 log tavern, a blacksmith's shop, and a turn-of-the-century brick schoolhouse. But the emphasis is on transportation and Dayton's contributions to it, with a Wright *Flyer*, a railway station, the Wright brothers' cycle shop, a canal lock, and a fine collection of wagons, locomotives, trolleys, and antique cars. The bell tower that gives the park its name is a 150-foot limestone needle with a cascade of 40 bells that ring out in concert on Sundays during the months when the park is open. *Open Tues.– Sun. and Mon. holidays May–Oct.*

41 United States Air Force Museum, Dayton

8 mi./15 min. South on Rte. 4, left on Harshman Rd., right on Springfield Pike. "Where eagles rest" is the motto of this museum with an impressive array of military aircraft and related displays. Fighter biplanes from World War I still look sleek and deadly. World War II Messerschmitts, Spitfires, and Mustangs nestle under the wings of Flying Fortresses and Liberators. In the main hangar and nearby annex almost 200 planes and missiles are on display. They span the history of aviation from a reproduction of the Wright brothers' kitelike 1909 Military Flyer to a charred *Apollo 15* capsule that circled the moon. *Open daily except Christmas.*

62 Buck Creek State Park

4 mi./12 min. West on Rte. 40, right on Bird Rd. (becomes Buck Creek Ln.). In the midst of flat, rich farmlands, the large reservoir here is so unexpected that it seems at first to be a mirage. But it is a dream come true for anyone interested in water sports. For swimmers it offers a bathhouse and a half-mile-long sand beach that is raked daily. Boaters can launch their own or can rent row, sail, paddle, and power boats. Water-skiing, scuba diving, and fishing are also popular. The Corps of Engineers' visitor center has a nature display, and a nearby overlook affords a fine view over the reservoir. A restored federal-style homestead recalls the lifestyle of the early settlers. *Park open year-round; homestead open P.M. Sat. late May–Sept.*

97 Columbus, OH 43215

Convention & Visitors Bureau, 1 Columbus Building, 10 W. Broad St., Suite 1300. (614) 221-6623. The Ohio capitol (mid-1800's) is a noted Greek revival structure. Other architectural styles popular in the 19th century can be seen in Ohio Village at the Ohio Historical Center, which also features displays related to the area's prehistory and paleontology. A former German settlement has been re-created at German Village. Fans of the cartoonist and writer James Thurber can visit his boyhood home. At the Center of Science and Industry (COSI), children and adults can put their hands on displays pertaining to the technology and science in their daily lives. The Columbus Museum of Art has extensive holdings of European and American art, and Ohio State University offers regular tours of the galleries and gardens on the campus.

129 Mound Builders State Memorial

8 mi./15 min. North on Rte. 79. The Great Circle Earthworks is one of the most impressive of the huge geometric mounds that the Hopewell people built in this region close to 2,000 years ago. Now topped by stately trees and a sandy path for visitors, this great circular embankment measures some 1,200 feet in diameter and rises to 14 feet at its highest point. Exquisite pottery, figurines, and body ornaments of copper and mica in the visitor center leave one even more in awe of the complex and sophisticated civilization that mysteriously disappeared some 1,500 years ago. *Open daily Memorial Day–Labor Day; weekends Sept.–Oct. Admission charged.*

164 National Road–Zane Grey Museum

3 min. East on Rte. 22/40. The varied displays in this museum tell two tales. One concerns the great road that connected the new American nation to its western frontier. The other commemorates the noted Western novelist Zane Grey, who was born in Ohio and also wrote about this area's settlement. His great-grandfather, Ebenezer Zane, blazed the trail called Zane's Trace. Dioramas depict the development of the road, and lifelike tableaux re-create a tavern, a wheelwright's shop, and a blacksmith's forge. Historic vehicles on display include a Conestoga wagon and antique autos. *Open daily May–Sept.; Wed.–Sun. Mar.–Apr. and Oct.–Nov. except Thanksgiving Day. Admission charged.*

I-77 Salt Fork State Park

12.5 mi./20 min. North on I-77 to Exit 47, east on Rte. 22. In this 21,000-acre park the extensive lake is the centerpiece, with its many arms that provide sections for boats with unlimited power, no-wave zones for sailboats

97. *Bicentennial Park, overlooking the Scioto River, is a favorite gathering place in Columbus.*

and other quiet craft, and sandy beaches for swimmers. You'll also find an 18-hole golf course, two marinas, boat rentals, and 26 miles of bridle paths through wooded rolling hills. *Open year-round.*

208   Barkcamp State Park

4 min. South on Rte. 149; follow signs. Set in rolling farmlands and wooded hills, this park has an atmosphere of spaciousness and seclusion. Numerous hiking trails meander through the countryside, where a variety of trees, shrubs, and wildflowers provide cover and food for the area's wildlife. Belmont Lake has facilities for swimmers and anglers, with a fishing pier for the handicapped. An antique barn contains an assortment of exhibits, including a boulder inscribed by frontiersman and sharpshooter Lewis Wetzel, that recall Ohio's rural past. *Open year-round. Admission charged.*

1B   Grave Creek Mound State Park, Moundsville

12 mi./17 min. South on Rte. 2; follow signs. The Adena people, first of the prehistoric Mound Builders, constructed this 69-foot-high conical hill as a burial site between 250 and 150 B.C. A path spirals to the top of the mound. In the Delf Norona Museum, dioramas and life-size models portray tribal life as it may have existed 2,000 years ago, and there are exhibits of tools, weapons, and other artifacts. Completely unauthenticated but intriguing is a replica of a small sandstone tablet written in "Iberic-Celtic" script. Where it came from is a mystery, but it is kept on display by popular demand. *Open Mon.–Sat. and P.M. Sun. except holidays. Admission charged.*

2A   Oglebay Park, Wheeling

5 min. Northeast on Rte. 88. This beautifully manicured 1,500-acre estate was given to the town by a Cleveland industrialist. Among the cultural and recreational facilities in the park, the Mansion Museum houses 18th- and 19th-century period rooms and outstanding examples of Wheeling's china and glass industries. Other attractions include a children's zoo, formal gardens and an arboretum, three golf courses on rolling hills, tennis courts, and ski trails. *Grounds open year-round; museum open Mon.–Sat. and P.M. Sun. and holidays except Thanksgiving Day, Christmas, and New Year's Day.*

2A. *The Mansion Museum clearly defines the character of the Greek revival style.*

I-79   Arden Trolley Museum, Washington

5 mi./10 min. North on I-79 to Exit 8E, east on Pike St.; follow signs. Trolley buffs and children of all ages can savor the pleasure of a trolley ride on a 1920's car, smartly fitted with polished woodwork, chrome, and brass, along a 1-mile route in this indoor-outdoor museum. Twenty-five or more trolley cars, some in working order, others undergoing restoration, are exhibited in a large carbarn. The cars come from several towns in Pennsylvania and Boston, with one veteran of New Orleans' Desire line. *Open P.M. daily July 4–Labor Day; P.M. weekends only May–June and Sept.*

I-76   Bushy Run Battlefield, Jeannette

14 mi./25 min. West on I-76 to Exit 7, west on Rte. 30, right on Ash St., right on Pennsylvania Ave., left on Brush Hill Rd., right on Rte. 993. In August 1763 these tranquil woods and meadows on the Pennsylvania frontier were the scene of a desperate and crucial battle fought by the British to rescue Ft. Pitt from siege by the Indians, whose combined forces were under the command of the great chief Pontiac. Guided and self-guiding tours from the visitor center lead to the sites of important episodes in this battle, which established the British on Indian territory after the French and Indian War. *Open Tues.–Sat., P.M. Sun., and July 4, Memorial Day, and Labor Day, but not other holidays. Admission charged.*

9   Fort Ligonier

12 mi./15 min. North on Rte. 711. Built in 1758 and now reconstructed, the fort still guards the frontier crossroads it defended when the British and Americans (including a militia unit commanded by young George Washington, then a colonel in King George's army) successfully held it against the French and the Indians in the mid-1700's. The stockade, which encircles the garrison's sparsely furnished log dwellings, is fiercely protected at the corners by an array of sharply pointed stakes. The visitor center and museum exhibits dioramas, weapons, utensils, and other 18th-century artifacts, as well as period rooms and objects from Ligonier's historic past. Colorful reenactments of battles and demonstrations of traditional handicrafts are featured during the summer months. *Open Apr.–Oct. Admission charged.*

10   Somerset Historical Center

4.5 mi./10 min. North on Rte. 601, left at fork on Rte. 985. A trim restored log house and several outbuildings evoke life in Pennsylvania's pioneer days. The well-furnished main house contains spinning wheels, quaint kitchen equipment, quilts, and other domestic necessities of the period. The visitor center has informative exhibits that explain skills such as preparing and spinning flax, woodworking, and fashioning utensils and tools that were once indispensable. In marked contrast, the technology of modern farming is illustrated by mid-20th-century machinery and implements. *Open Tues.–Sat. and P.M. Sun. and Memorial Day, July 4, and Labor Day, but not other holidays. Admission charged.*

11 Old Bedford Village

5 min. South on Rte. 220 (business); follow signs. In the 18th century, Ft. Bedford saw action in two wars and was the focus of a whiskey tax uprising that was suppressed by President George Washington and 13,000 federal soldiers. Today the village comprises more than 40 restored houses and shops that re-create rural Pennsylvania life around 1795. Authentically costumed staff members use antique tools and utensils to demonstrate the trades of baker, broom maker, blacksmith, bookbinder, and candlestick maker. *Open daily mid-Apr.–Oct. Admission charged.* ⛱ ♿

12 Crawford's Wildlife Exhibit, Breezewood

3 min. South on Rte. 30. Mr. and Mrs. Fred Crawford, natives of Breezewood, traveled extensively throughout the world and on their various safaris bagged some 300 species of wildlife. This collection is now in the museum, with several of the species portrayed in tableaux that re-create their natural habitats. Some of the animals in the exhibit—such as the snow leopard and black-spotted panther—are rare and seldom seen. Others are now extinct. *Open Mon.–Sat. and P.M. Sun. May–Oct. Admission charged.*

13 14 East Broad Top Railroad, Rockhill Furnace

Exit 13: 14 mi./22 min. North on Rte. 522. Exit 14: 18 mi./25 min. North on Rte. 75, left on Rte. 641, right on Rte. 522. Boarding at the charmingly detailed Orbisonia railroad depot, you can take a fascinating 10-mile round-trip on one of the oldest narrow-gauge railways in the U.S.A., through the scenic Aughwick Valley to the Colgate Grove picnic area. At the eight-stall roundhouse, visitors can inspect a steam engine, a gas-electric car, and the Armstrong turntable that rotates the engines. The Trolley Museum and trolley rides on the Shade Gap Electric Railway across the street offer other excursions into the past. *Train rides daily July–Labor Day, weekends only June and Sept.–Oct.; trolley rides weekends and holidays Memorial Day–Oct. Admission charged.* ⛱

22. *Across this rustic bridge is a foundry village little changed since the 19th century.*

14 Big Spring State Park

17 mi./24 min. North on Rte. 75, right on Rte. 274. This small park serves as a base for campers, hikers, hunters, and cross-country skiers who wish to explore and use the adjacent Tuscarora State Forest, which encompasses several mountain ranges typical of this part of the country. The forest can be explored on trails that lead over the great game-filled wooded ridges. One inviting hike traces the course of a stream in the Hemlock State Natural Area as it flows briskly from the ridge to the valley below. Pine trees tower over the picnic grounds. *Open year-round.* ⛱ 🚶

16 Cumberland County Historical Society, Carlisle

4 mi./7 min. North on Rte. 11 (becomes Hanover St.), right on High St., right on Pitt St. An unpretentious brick building houses a surprising wealth of treasures and curiosities, from a 17th-century Jacobean settee to Schimmel and Mountz rooster carvings. The collection captures the very essence of Pennsylvania history with hand-illustrated texts, painted plank-bottom chairs, cast-iron mechanical banks, bookbinding presses, redware pottery, Revolutionary War weapons, samplers, a rich profusion of furniture, silverware, a "Grand Harmonicum," which is played by rubbing the edges of glass goblets, and local artifacts. *Open P.M. Tues.–Fri. and evenings Mon. except holidays.* ♿

17 Harrisburg, PA 17108

Chamber of Commerce, 114 Walnut St. (717) 232-4121. This capital city has a most impressive statehouse, with a dome based on St. Peter's in Rome and a grand interior staircase copied from the Paris Opéra. The nearby State Museum contains a wealth of regional artifacts from every era. The Museum of Scientific Discovery very successfully delivers on its name. The Susquehanna River's beauty can be enjoyed at Riverfront Park, a 5-mile esplanade. Also in the Riverfront District are handsome 18th- and 19th-century mansions.

19 Indian Echo Caverns, Hummelstown

10 mi./15 min. East on Rte. 283, left on Vine St. Over the course of 3 million to 5 million years, the constant dripping of mineral-laden water has shaped a large network of chambers and winding passageways, embellished by countless stalagmites and stalactites, all set against a backdrop of shimmering flowstone. Some formations look like humans, animals, and different kinds of plants. You'll also find a crystal-clear lake and a corallike mass of calcite. The temperature holds at 52° F. *Open daily Apr.–Oct.; weekends only Mar. and Nov. Admission charged.* ⛩

22 Hopewell Furnace National Historic Site

10 mi./16 min. South on Rte. 10, left on Rte. 23, left on Rte. 345. Hopewell was one of the pre-Revolution foundries that defied Britain's decree against producing finished products. It cast iron into cookware, stoves, and other essential products for a growing America and later provided armaments for the Revolution. In a walking tour of the historic village you'll learn about the process of smelting and casting iron. A film and demonstrations of sand casting and forging are scheduled regularly. *Open daily except Christmas and New Year's Day. Admission charged.* 🚶 ♿

24 Valley Forge National Historical Park

2 mi./6 min. North on Rte. 363. Valley Forge is an inspiring reminder of the American spirit during the Revolution. When the British captured Philadelphia in 1777, George Washington chose Valley Forge for his army's winter quarters. Owing to the crude housing, inadequate clothing, and poor rations, some 2,000 of the 12,000 men died here. But Washington's presence and the drill instruction volunteered by the Prussian officer Baron Friedrich von Steuben held the army together. The spring brought the offer of French assistance, and although five more years of conflict lay ahead, a critical turning point had been reached. These events are dramatically explained and exhibited at the visitor center and throughout the park. *Open daily except Christmas. Admission charged.* ⛩ 🚶 ♿

24 Fort Washington State Park

11.5 mi./15 min. East on I-276 to Exit 26, west on Pennsylvania Ave., left on Bethlehem Pike. George Washington's army built a fort here shortly before moving to Valley Forge in the winter of 1777. The fort is long gone, leaving behind its name for this area, but a replica of the original may be visited on the same site on Fort Hill. The 483-acre park's unspoiled meadows and woods along the Wissahickon Creek are popular with visitors. A pamphlet for children describes plants and wildlife on a nature trail. Dogwoods lace the hills in spring. *Open year-round.* ⛩ 🚶 🎣 ♿

24 The Mercer Museum, Doylestown

25 mi./35 min. East on I-276 to Exit 27, north on Rte. 611 to Doylestown exit; continue on S. Main St., right on E. Ashland St., right on Green St. Walk in through the heavy wooden doors, wander down the stone passageways and stairways and into the workshops—you might think you are in a medieval castle. This extensive museum, built from 1913 to 1916 by archeologist Henry Chapman Mercer, houses his fantastic collection of more than 40,000 preindustrial American artifacts. Old fishing boats, carriages, and even a Conestoga wagon hang from the walls and ceiling of a central gallery that soars to a height of six stories. Lighting devices of various kinds, musical instruments, and whaling, barrel-making, and blacksmithing tools are just the beginning. *Open Mon.–Sat. and P.M. Sun. Mar.–Dec. Admission charged.* ♿

39 Philadelphia, PA 19102

Visitors Center, 1625 JFK Blvd. (215) 636-1666. If you plan to stop in Philadelphia, it is advisable not to be in a rush. It takes time to do justice to Independence National Historical Park, which includes Independence Hall and other historic structures on Independence Square. In the park, which covers 42 acres, you'll see the Liberty Bell, Franklin Court, Carpenters' Hall, and several handsomely restored and furnished 18th-century houses.

The Philadelphia Museum of Art and the Franklin Institute Science Museum are justly renowned. The city's other museums are dedicated to such diverse subjects as Afro-American culture, antique toys, Jewish history, and the art of Norman Rockwell. There's also the American Swedish Museum, and the Please Touch Museum for Children.

24. *A winter like this and a supply shortage tested the spirit of America at Valley Forge in 1777.*

See N–S book, sec. 22 for I-55. 55 70
See E–W book, sec. 29 for I-70. 3
55
See N–S book, sec. 25. 12
57 2 3
66
IL : IN

64

I-55 6
61 73 95 78
57

I-55 St. Louis, MO 63102

Convention and Visitors Commission, 10 S. Broadway. (314) 421-1023; (800) 247-9791 outside MO. The three spans crossing the Mississippi here dramatize the role of St. Louis as a jumping-off place to the West, and the magnificent 630-foot Gateway Arch commemorates the days of the wagon trains, when the only river crossings were by water. From the top of the arch you can contemplate the vast reaches offering such promise and danger in the days of the pioneers, an era graphically interpreted in the Museum of Westward Expansion. An excellent zoo has more than 2,500 animals and a miniature railroad to provide an easy introduction. Featured in the 79-acre botanical garden is the domed Climatron and the largest Japanese garden in the United States.

6 Cahokia Mounds State Historic Site, Collinsville

5 min. North on Rte. 111, right on Collinsville Rd. From A.D. 900 to 1250 a mighty society flourished on the Mississippi River. Cahokia, a major town built by the people of the Mississippian Indian culture, had 20,000 to 40,000 inhabitants, who farmed the surrounding land and traded with peoples as far away as the Atlantic and Gulf coasts. They also labored for centuries to build these impressive earthworks a basketful at a time. A few of the mounds were burial sites, but most were used for housing the elite or for ceremonial buildings. Woodhenge, a giant circle of cedar posts, was a sun calendar that determined the changing seasons. *Open daily except Thanksgiving Day, Christmas, and New Year's Day.*

61 Fairview Park, Centralia

12 mi./20 min. North on Rte. 51. This is a modest but pleasant stopping place for a swim in an Olympic-size pool, a picnic, or a game of catch or Frisbee. It also offers an opportunity to inspect two marvels of transportation: the steam locomotive (this one with stylish white wheels) and a jet plane of Korean War vintage. A 65-bell carillon, on which an occasional concert is given, stands in downtown Centralia. *Open year-round.*

73 William Jennings Bryan Museum, Salem

22 mi./30 min. North on I-57 to Exit 116, east on Rte. 50, right on Rte. 37 (S. Broadway). Bryan, a former congressman, secretary of state, and three-time presidential nominee, was born in this simple frame house, where he lived for the first seven years of his life. He was a renowned orator, and his style is demonstrated in a recording of his celebrated cross of gold speech. Here, too, are his baby clothes, his Spanish-American War uniform, and political buttons and ribbons. The modest objects by which Bryan is remembered here are in poignant contrast with his accomplishments. *Open Fri.–Wed. except Thanksgiving Day, Christmas, and New Year's Day.*

95 Mitchell Museum, Mount Vernon

2 mi./10 min. East on Rte. 15 (becomes Broadway), left on 27th St., right on Richview Rd. The striking, windowless museum, surrounded by an elegantly proportioned colonnade, is on the parklike grounds of Cedarhurst, the 80-acre estate of the late John and Eleanor Mitchell. The structure embodies their dream of providing an art center for this part of Illinois. Exhibits include works by local residents as well as nationally touring shows that make stops here. The eclectic Mitchell collection of paintings, drawings, and sculpture, displayed in a nearby building, includes works by John Singer Sargent, Andrew Wyeth, Thomas Eakins, and other 19th- and 20th-century masters. The attractive wooded grounds contain a lake and two nature trails. *Open P.M. Tues.–Sun. except holidays.*

78 Wayne Fitzgerell State Park

15 mi./25 min. South on I-57 to Exit 77, west on Rte. 154 across first part of causeway over Rend Lake. As many as 2 million people per year seek recreation here, but the 19,000-acre Rend Lake and 21,000 adjacent acres of public land can easily accommodate them. (Stop at the visitor center for orientation.) Boating, hiking, swimming, and fishing are all popular, and there's a wildlife refuge with a viewing platform. During the tourist season interpretive programs are sponsored. *Park open year-round; visitor center open Apr.–Oct.*

12 New Harmony Historic District

10 mi./20 min. South on Rte. 165, right on Rte. 66. From the visitor center in the starkly modern Atheneum, walking and buggy tours take

57. *Reconstructed cabin shows the extensive hand-hewing required to build in pioneer times.*

you through this remarkably well-preserved town, which was founded by George Rapp and his followers as a utopian religious colony in 1814. Log houses, red brick dwellings, and community houses were once home to the first Harmonists, while the Workingmen's Institute reflects the intellectual bent of the next inhabitants, who were under the leadership of the Welsh social reformer Robert Owen. That 19th-century community was one of the first in the nation to establish a kindergarten, a free library, and a free public school. Near the so-called Roofless Church, the theologian Paul Tillich is buried. *Visitor center open daily Apr.–Oct., weekends only Nov.–Dec. and Mar. Admission charged for tours.*

25   Mesker Park Zoo, Evansville

18 mi./35 min. South on Rte. 41, right on Rte. 66, left on St. Joseph Ave.; follow signs. Giraffes and cranes in the same enclosure, a galleon crewed by squirrel monkeys, and peacocks residing with elephants give an aura of the wild to this appealing zoo. Lions, tapirs, arctic wolves, and other exotic animals live side by side with such natives as wild turkeys, otters, and geese. Visitors can ride a safari train around the park, maneuver paddle boats among the ducks and swans in the pond, and watch an elephant show. A special section contains goats, ducks, chickens, and rabbits for children to pet. The zoo also has two exhibits of free-flying tropical birds and one devoted to nocturnal animals. *Open daily except Christmas and New Year's Day. Admission charged.*

57   Lincoln Boyhood National Memorial, Lincoln City

9 mi./15 min. South on Rte. 231, left on Rte. 162. This simple working farm, situated within the Lincoln Boyhood National Memorial, commemorates the Lincoln family's 14-year sojourn in Indiana before they moved to their final home in Illinois. In the reconstructed log cabin, domestic items—such as a battling board, used to beat clothes on washdays, and long poles used to tear down the mud-and-wattle chimney when it caught fire—suggest some of the domestic challenges in pioneer

days. A film at the visitor center portrays the life of America's 16th president while he lived in Indiana, and a nearby cemetery contains the grave of his mother. The adjacent Lincoln State Park has an 85-acre lake, pleasant woods and meadows, and an open-air theater where a dramatic presentation based on President Lincoln's boyhood is performed during summer months. *Memorial open daily except Thanksgiving Day, Christmas, and New Year's Day; park open year-round. Admission charged.*

105   Governor Hendricks' Headquarters, Corydon

3 mi./7 min. South on Rte. 135, left on Rte. 62 (becomes Walnut St.). The past is fondly remembered in this handsome federal house, which served as the home and headquarters of Governor William Hendricks from 1822 until 1825, when Indiana's state capital was moved to Indianapolis. The furnishings illustrate Indiana domestic life during three distinct periods from the 1820's to the 1880's. *Open Wed.–Sat. and P.M. Sun. and Tues. May–Sept.; Oct.–Apr. same as above except holidays. Admission free but donations encouraged.*

4   Louisville, KY 40202

5C   *Visitors Information Center, 400 S. 1st St. (502) 584-2121.* Since Churchill Downs is a primary attraction here, the grounds are open even when it's not racing season; and at the Kentucky Derby Museum at the Downs, various media are employed to give the feel of Derby Week. For visitors who have a little time to spend, the *Belle of Louisville,* an honest-to-goodness stern-wheeler, cruises the Ohio River in the leisurely style travelers were once accustomed to.

The J.B. Speed Art Museum adjacent to the University of Louisville comprises both contemporary and traditional art in a handsome neoclassical building; and the Museum of History and Science features natural history and aerospace exhibits, with emphasis on hands-on learning. Old Louisville (Victorian houses), Butchertown (a German neighborhood), and Portland (French and Irish) are among the lovingly restored city districts.

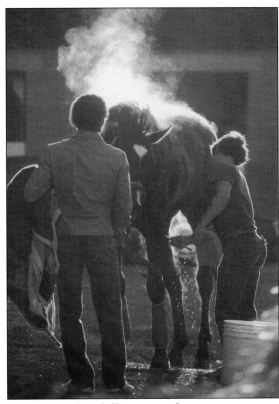

4–5C. At Churchill Downs a horse creates a cloud of steam after a morning workout.

5A 5B   Howard Steamboat Museum, Jeffersonville

3 mi./10 min. Exit 5A: north on I-65, east on Rte. 62, right on Spring St., left on Market St. Exit 5B: proceed as above. Overlooking the Ohio River, this 22-room mansion was built in the early 1890's by Edmunds Howard, whose shipyard produced some of the world's most elegant steamboats. The same superb craftsmanship lavished on the Howard vessels is evident in this luxurious Victorian home. Its hand-carved wooden archways, 36 chandeliers, and grand staircase are all modeled after those originally designed for steamboats. Also on display are scale models of famous boats, the mansion's original furniture in neo-Louis XV style, a $35,000 brass bed, and a steamboat pilot's wheel that's 9 feet wide. *Open Tues.–Sun. except holidays. Admission charged.*

53 58 Liberty Hall, Frankfort

Exit 53: 7 mi./10 min. North on Rte. 127, right on Rte. 60, left on Bridge St., left on Wapping St., right on Wilkinson Blvd. Exit 58: 6 mi./20 min. North on Rte. 60 (becomes E. Main St.) This historic mansion with soft rose-colored hand-made bricks and blue trim is graced by an elegant Palladian window. It was built by U.S. Senator John Brown in the late 1700's in a style that recalls an even earlier period and is named for his father's school. Impeccable antique Georgian furnishings and portraits fill the stately rooms once visited by such notables as James Monroe, Andrew Jackson, and the Marquis de Lafayette. Behind the house a formal garden with many of the ornamental trees and flowers of the period slopes down to the banks of the Kentucky River. Also here is the refurbished Orlando Brown House, built in the 1830's by the senator's son. *Open Tues.–Sat. and P.M. Sun. Mar.–Dec. except Thanksgiving Day and Christmas. Admission charged.*

NWT PAR Lexington, KY 40507

Newtown Pike exit; Paris Pike exit: Convention & Visitors Bureau, 430 W. Vine St. (606) 233-1221. For all the publicity about horses here in the bluegrass country, you don't have to be an equestrian to enjoy a visit. There are historic houses of note, two inviting university campuses, and some interesting renovated shopping areas.

In the Georgian-style Mary Todd Lincoln House, you can see furnishings that are similar to the originals the future First Lady lived with here as a girl. While the Todd House has an engaging charm, the Hunt-Morgan House, with its handsome 19th-century furnishings and woodwork, is a study in the restrained elegance of the federal style. Ashland, the handsome estate of the famous statesman Henry Clay, lies on the outskirts of town. The beautifully furnished Italianate house is surrounded by lawns and woodlands and also has an attractive formal garden.

The University of Kentucky campus offers an art museum, an anthropology museum, and a mile-long Tree Trail through the area.

53–58. *As exemplified here, beautiful proportions and materials are timeless in their appeal.*

94 Fort Boonesborough State Park

15 mi./25 min. South on Rte. 1958, right on Rte. 627, left on Rte. 388. In 1775 Daniel Boone had just established this vital frontier post on the banks of the Kentucky River when his young daughter was captured by Indians. With a few companions Boone set off after the marauders and, against all odds, recovered the girl. On a hill close to the original site, the log walls and blockhouses of Boone's fort have been lovingly reconstructed, as has the pioneer lifestyle itself. You'll see blacksmiths, spinners, toymakers, weavers, and candlemakers at their daily work. Elsewhere in the park you can swim in the river, fish for perch, catfish, and bass, launch a boat, picnic, and camp. Detailed information on the facilities is available at the visitor center. *Park open year-round; fort open daily Apr.–Sept.; Wed.–Sun. Sept.–Oct. Admission charged to fort.*

137 Rodburn Hollow Recreation Area

5 mi./12 min. East on Rte. 32, left on Rte. 60, left on Rodburn Hollow Rd. This wooded valley and the stream that traverses it provide a rest stop for hikers on the Sheltowee Trace, a 254-mile trail that passes through the land explored by Daniel Boone between 1769 and 1771. Sheltowee ("Big Turtle") was the name given to Boone by the Shawnee tribe. The Martin Brand Trail, starting at the ranger station, joins the Sheltowee Trace briefly. Picnic tables and grills are scattered throughout the recreation area, which also has a playing field and some primitive campsites. *Open daily late Apr.–mid-Oct.*

161 Carter Caves State Resort Park

5 mi./10 min. North on Rte. 60, left on Rte. 182. The craggy terrain here is endlessly varied. Cave tours range in difficulty from an easy walk past a 30-foot underground waterfall in magnificent Cascade Cave to a strenuous crawl through the tight passages of Bat Cave with your own flashlight and gear. Hiking trails aboveground wind over hills and into valleys past a huge natural bridge, a "wind tunnel," a box canyon, and carpets of wildflowers in spring. Saltpeter (used to make explosives) was mined here from 1812 to the Civil War. The park's modern amenities include a golf course, tennis courts, and riding stables. *Open year-round. Admission charged for sports.*

185 191   The Kentucky Highlands Museum, Ashland

Exit 185: 7 mi./12 min. Northeast on Rte. 60, right on Bath Ave. Exit 191: 8 mi./15 min. North on Rte. 23, left on 16th St. Built in 1917, this imposing limestone mansion with Renaissance-style porticoes houses a wide variety of items relating to eastern Kentucky's history. There are prehistoric Indian artifacts, models of blast furnaces, and a nostalgic collection of old-fashioned radios. The elegant staircase curves up from the first floor to the third-floor ballroom, which contains a stained-glass skylight that may evoke formally attired ghosts from a bygone era. *Open Tues.–Sat. and P.M. Sun. except holidays. Admission charged.* ♿

6   Camden Park, Huntington

5 min. North on 17th St., left on Rte. 60. All the familiar attractions can be found at this homey amusement park: two roller coasters, bumper cars, a haunted house, a carousel, a wet ride down a log chute, and a variety of sideshows. Roller skating, miniature golf, and an outdoor amphitheater with some famous names on the bill add to the festive atmosphere. A cruise along the Ohio River on the *Camden Queen,* a reproduction of an 1890 stern-wheeler, lets you experience the unique charm of the steamboat era. *Park open daily mid-Apr.–Labor Day; weekends only Apr. and Sept. Boat rides P.M. daily May–Labor Day. Admission charged.* ⛺

8   Huntington Museum of Art

3 mi./8 min. North on Rte. 527, right on Miller Rd.; follow signs. Special exhibitions at this museum have ranged from an extensive display about the Ohio River to a close look at a traditional Japanese house. The permanent collection includes paintings by Andrew Wyeth and John Singer Sargent, works by Millet and Boudin, and a particularly fine Dean gun collection. There's also a sculpture garden and nature trails flanked by oaks, beeches, ferns, and other wildlings. *Open Tues.–Sat. and P.M. Sun. except Christmas and New Year's Day. Admission charged.* 🚶♿

11   Beech Fork State Park, Barboursville

10 mi./20 min. East on Rte. 10, right on Green Valley Rd. After winding down the tortuous approach road and coming upon this serene and spacious area framed by wooded hills, you may feel like an explorer discovering a lost valley. The highlight of this 3,700-acre park, which is still under development, is its 760-acre lake, where canoes, paddleboats, and rowboats may be rented. Anglers can try for crappie, bass, pike, and channel catfish.

At the enticing little coves at the water's edge are 275 modern campsites with bathhouses and laundry facilities. Trails include a long nature trail and a physical fitness trail. There's also a camp store and a visitor center. *Open year-round.* ⛺ 🏕️ 🚐 🚶 🎣 ♿

28   Blenko Glass Company, Milton

2 mi./8 min. South off exit, right on Rte. 60, left on Fairground Rd. Blenko stained glass graces such famous buildings as the Air Force Academy Chapel in Colorado, and Grant's Tomb, St. John the Divine, and St. Patrick's in New York City. The company's decorative glassware has been cherished by a number of First Ladies. The display area comprises an exhibit on the company's history and its current line of glassware. A museum contains historical glass along with the Designer's Corner, where state-of-the-art designs are exhibited by leading stained-glass studios.

Along the walkway to the factory itself, piles of jewellike broken glass await recycling. Inside the plant, you can watch from an observation deck as craftsmen fire and blow molten glass. Nearby, on the Mud River, you might see some of the 200 or so ducks and geese that make their home there. *Visitor center open Mon.–Sat. and P.M. Sun. except holidays; plant open Mon.–Fri. except July 1–15, Dec. 25–Jan. 1, and holidays.*

58A   Sunrise Museums, Charleston

5 min. East on Oakwood Rd., right on MacCorkle Ave. (Rte. 61); bear right and go up C & O ramp, right on Bridge Rd., right on Myrtle Rd. The Children's Museum, housed in a former governor's mansion, captivates youngsters with "open us" discovery boxes of seashells and fossils, an exhibit that explains myths and legends of natural phenomena, a ray table that bends and bounces the light, a dollhouse, models of coaches and a circus wagon, and a 60-seat planetarium. The Art Museum has a fine collection of 17th- to 20th-century American art, along with etchings by Rembrandt and Picasso and engravings by Matisse and Dürer. *Open Tues.–Sat. and P.M. Sun. except holidays. Admission charged.* ♿

11. *In this forested realm, the only openings, such as this park, are man-made.*

58A   Kanawha State Forest

8 mi./15 min. South on Rte. 119, left on Oakwood Rd.; follow signs. There are 17 trails to choose from amid these 9,250 forested acres in West Virginia—ranging from a steep climb over Overlook Rock Trail to a gentle stroll along Spotted Salamander Trail (designed for the handicapped). Joggers and bikers enjoy the paved road through this wilderness of pines, hemlocks, sycamores, and dogwoods. Beside the quiet lake there are wooden seats from which to view the scenic mountain backdrop; anglers try for bass, catfish, and bluegill. Deer, black bears, and raccoons inhabit the forest. *Open year-round. Fee charged for swimming.* ⛺ 🏕️ 🚐 🚶 🎣 ♿

64 **129** 40 **169** 40 **8** 30 **I-81** 30 **I-81** 31 **22** 3 **24**

81 See N–S book, sec. 41.

81 See N–S book, sec. 41.

129 Grandview State Park

5 mi./8 min. Follow signs to park. Breathtaking views of the New River are a prime attraction here. At North Overlook you'll see the horseshoe bend in the river where hawks nest in a rocky gorge; and from Main Overlook the river and trains that run beside it are some 1,500 feet below. The steep hillsides, covered with mountain laurel, hemlock, dogwood, pink lady's slipper, and rhododendron, come alive with color in the spring and summer. On a self-guiding nature trail, you may see some of the turkey vultures, grouse, and wild turkeys that inhabit the park. *Open year-round.*

169 Organ Cave

8 mi./12 min. South on Rte. 219, left on Rte. 63. This gigantic West Virginia cavern stretches for 42 subterranean miles, making it one of the largest in America. Inside you'll find the million-year-old rock formation that gives the cave its name: a 40-foot-high limestone wall that looks like a church organ and has "pipes" that produce sounds when tapped with a wooden mallet. All trails in the cave afford fine views of frozen waterfalls and natural sculptures—including one bearing an eerie resemblance to Gen. Robert E. Lee. It is said that Thomas Jefferson discovered a dinosaur skeleton in the cavern in 1791. *Open daily Apr.–Oct.; by appointment rest of year: (304) 647-5551. Admission charged.*

8 Douthat State Park

6 mi./10 min. North on Rte. 629. Surrounded by George Washington National Forest, this 4,493-acre park is the habitat of a variety of wildlife. Deer amble through the deciduous forest, and industrious beavers build their dams nearby. Fishermen will enjoy 50-acre Douthat Lake, which is the home of bass and bluegill and is stocked weekly with rainbow trout. Rowboats and paddleboats are available for rent. Bird lovers may spot pileated woodpeckers, yellow warblers, screech owls, redtailed hawks, and during migrations, a variety of waterfowl. The half-mile Buck Lick Trail is the shortest in a network of 24 hiking trails. Adjoining the office is a small museum featuring a topographical map of Virginia, local rocks and minerals, and a push-button nature quiz for children. *Open year-round. Admission charged.*

I-81 Natural Bridge

15 mi./20 min. South on I-81 to Exit 50, south on Rte. 11. Natural Bridge is a single block of solid limestone—90 feet long, up to 150 feet wide, and 215 feet high—that straddles Cedar Creek and joins two mountains in the Blue Ridge country. The Monacan Indians named this natural phenomenon the Bridge of God, but geologists credit millions of years of erosion by the creek as its sculptor. Look along the southeast wall of the bridge for the initials G. W., whittled by George Washington when he surveyed the site in 1750. It was once owned by Thomas Jefferson, who purchased it and 157 acres from King George III for 20 shillings. A sound-and-light show, "Drama of Creation," is presented at night. *Open year-round. Admission charged.*

I-81 Woodrow Wilson Birthplace, Staunton

4 mi./8 min. North on I-81 to Exit 57, west on Rte. 250, right on Coalter St. America's 28th president was born in this Greek revival Virginia town house on December 28, 1856. Today, 12 beautifully restored rooms display many of the original furnishings and family memorabilia. You'll see the Bible in which Reverend Joseph Ruggles Wilson, a Presbyterian minister, recorded his son's birth; a period quilt; antique dolls; a rolltop desk and a typewriter desk from Wilson's study at Princeton University, where he was president from 1902 to 1910; and two ornate brass oil lamps that he bought while he was a student at the University of Virginia. A Victorian garden and a carriage house containing Wilson's restored 1920 Pierce-Arrow presidential limousine add to the period atmosphere. A film about Wilson is shown at the reception center. *Open daily Mar.–Dec.; Mon.–Sat. Jan.–Feb. except Thanksgiving Day, Christmas, and New Year's Day. Admission charged.*

22 The University of Virginia, Charlottesville

5 mi./20 min. North on Rte. 29, right on Rte. 250 (business; becomes Ivy Blvd., then University Ave.). Located 20 miles east of the Blue Ridge Mountains, this 1,050-acre campus is a monument to the vision of Thomas Jefferson, who planned the university, designed its buildings, set the curriculum, recruited its first faculty, and served as its first rector. The original complex—with its academic and residential buildings, called pavilions, and hotels representing different European styles—was designated by the American Institute of Architects as an outstanding achievement of American architecture. The dominant structure is the 1826 rotunda, a scaled-down replica of the Roman Pantheon. *Grounds open year-round; rotunda open daily except Thanksgiving Day and mid-Dec.–early Jan.*

24 Monticello, Charlottesville

5 min. South on Rte. 20, left on Rte. 53. On his "little mountain," nestled between rolling farmland and the Blue Ridge Mountains, Thomas Jefferson began to build his dream house, Monticello, in 1768. For the next 40 years this versatile innovator supervised nearly every detail of its design and construction, drawing on his imagination to create one of America's architectural masterpieces. The gracious 21-room Palladian-style mansion—

24. *Thomas Jefferson's masterpiece is an important example of neoclassic architecture.*

crowned with the first dome ever built on an American house—reflects Jefferson's inventiveness and his lifelong love of collecting. It contains original domestic objects and a library with a nucleus of books that launched the Library of Congress. The gardens reflect his interest and skill in horticulture and landscape design. *Open year-round except Christmas. Admission charged.*

34 | 48 | Kings Dominion

Exit 34: 24 mi./25 min. East on I-295, north on I-95 to Exit 40, right on Rte. 30. Exit 48: 29 mi./35 min. West on I-295, north on I-95; proceed as above. It's five theme parks in one. Shock-Wave, the stand-up roller coaster, begins with a 95-foot drop, races in a 360° loop, and ends with a triple corkscrew—just one of the more than 40 rides here. The less intrepid can get their feet wet on one of several spectacular water rides; stroll, snack, and shop along International Street; mingle with Yogi Bear and his pals; chime in for a sing-along; see some 50 species of wild animals from the Safari monorail; or look down on all the bustle from atop a replica of the Eiffel Tower. *Open daily June–Labor Day; weekends late Mar.–May, mid-Sept.–mid-Oct. Admission charged.*

I-95S | Richmond, VA 23219

Convention and Visitors Bureau, 300 E. Main St. (804) 782-2777. Although the imperatives of the present day are stylishly acknowledged at Shockoe Slip and the Sixth Street Marketplace, proud memories of the Old South are found throughout this capital city, which was also the capital of the Confederacy. The handsome state capitol is a classic design selected by Thomas Jefferson. On Monument Avenue, paved with hand-laid brick, the statues of Confederate heroes vie for attention with the stately houses. Other historic highlights are St. John's Church, the John Marshall House, and the Wickham-Valentine House.

Among the attractions of more recent vintage are the Virginia Museum of Fine Arts, the Richmond Children's Museum, and the Science Museum of Virginia.

56. *The original inhabitants would still feel at home on Duke of Gloucester Street.*

56 | Colonial Williamsburg

5 min. South on Rte. 132; follow signs. In this first and finest restoration of an early American town, one can come as close as is possible in the 20th century to experiencing the scope and character of colonial life in the 1700's. The main thoroughfare is the mile-long Duke of Gloucester Street, which runs from the Capitol to the College of William and Mary. Such artisans as weavers, cabinetmakers, gunsmiths, and many others explain their trades as they work. Sheep graze on the village green. The rhythmic clip-clop of carriage horses reinforces the illusion of a less complex and crowded time. *Open year-round. Admission charged.*

57A | Busch Gardens, The Old Country, Williamsburg

4 min. Southwest on Rte. 199; follow signs. This enormous theme park—featuring reproductions of French, Italian, German, and English villages—brings the flavor of the Old World to America. You can enjoy a Renaissance fair, drive a replica of a Le Mans race car, and feast at one of the country's largest restaurants. Rides range from thrilling roller coasters to sedate river cruises, and craftsmen demonstrate everything from making fudge to carving a cuckoo clock. *Open daily mid-May–Labor Day; weekends only Apr.–mid-May, Sept.–Oct. Admission charged.*

62A | The Mariners' Museum, Newport News

3 mi./7 min. South on J. Clyde Morris Blvd.; follow signs. The adventures, romance, and perils of the sea are dramatized in this outstanding collection of marine artifacts and vessels. Hundreds of items are on display: parts from the *Monitor* and the *Merrimack*, whose Civil War clash ushered in the era of ironclad warships; marine paintings dating back to the 17th century; replicas of Columbus's *Santa Maria*; full-size examples of a four-oar Norwegian rowboat and a Venetian gondola; and hand-carved figureheads, including a gilded eagle with a wingspan of 18½ feet that once adorned a U.S. Navy frigate. You'll also see the Crabtree Collection of miniature ships, carved with painstaking attention to detail. *Open Mon.–Sat. and P.M. Sun. except Christmas. Admission charged.*

BAR California Desert Information Center

Barstow Rd. exit: 2 min. North on Barstow Rd.; follow signs. Whether you are about to cross the great Mojave Desert or have already done so, a stop here will enhance your appreciation of the region and its plant and animal life. Noteworthy among the displays are preserved specimens of desert rattlers (surprisingly small in size) and other creatures to watch out for when exploring on foot. Should you plan to venture onto desert roads in a four-wheel-drive vehicle, the center will provide you with a detailed map of the Mojave. On view part of the year is the Old Woman meteorite, the second largest ever found in the United States (the remainder of the year the Smithsonian has the real meteorite, while the center displays a replica). Weighing over 6,000 pounds, it was discovered in 1975 in the Old Woman Mountains in the eastern Mojave. Across the street from the information center you'll find a small, pleasant park with sheltered picnic tables. *Open daily except Christmas and New Year's Day.*

ESS Providence Mountains State Recreation Area

Essex Rd. exit: 16 mi./20 min. North on Essex Rd.; follow signs. This 6,000-acre recreation area, with sunbaked slopes ideally seen in spring, is a good place to explore the Mojave Desert. The visitor center at Mitchell Caverns is reached by a road that climbs imperceptibly over miles of rangeland before making an abrupt ascent into the mountains. On arrival, you'll find a spectacular vista encompassing more than 300 square miles of desert scenery, with the Providence Mountains to the west. The visitor center will provide you with trail maps and lists of the area's wildlife, including bighorn sheep and golden eagles. It is a half-mile walk to the refreshingly cool caverns, which are filled with unusual limestone structures. Also nearby is the Mary Beal Nature Study Trail. Miss Beal spent some 50 years in the Mojave collecting and identifying more than 1,000 specimens of desert flowers. *Recreation area open year-round; caverns and visitor center open mid-Sept.–mid-June. Admission charged for caverns.*

9 London Bridge, Lake Havasu City

20 mi./25 min. South on Rte. 95, right on McCulloch Blvd.; follow signs. A bona fide old stone bridge from foggy London, England, relocated in a raw new city in the sunny Southwest? Incredible as it seems, the 140-year-old bridge was shipped stone by stone to Lake Havasu City, Arizona, in the 1960's. Purchased for about $2.5 million, it was brought here by an American real estate developer to attract visitors. The handsome arched bridge connects the city with Pittsburg Point, a large island in Lake Havasu. State-owned Pittsburg Point is devoted to recreation, and it offers parks, a swimming beach, and other facilities. Around the bridge on the mainland side there is a Tudor-style English village with pavilions, shops, and pubs flanking the water's edge. With pennants flying from the bridge, and sailboats and sightseeing steamers gliding under it, the scene is indeed festive. *Open year-round.*

48 Mohave Museum of History and Arts, Kingman

3 min. East onto W. Beale St. This excellent museum commemorates different periods of Kingman's past with a lively use of local color. Dioramas, artifacts, and a mural by Roy Purcell, a painter of the Southwest, vividly depict the everyday life of the Mohave and Hualapai Indians before and after the advent of the white man in the area. One room honors a favorite citizen, the late Hollywood star Andy Devine, who died in 1977. An early Shell gas pump is a reminder of old Route 66, a nearby section of which has been restored. Another attraction is a complete set of portraits of U.S. presidents and their wives. *Open Mon.–Fri. and P.M. weekends except Thanksgiving Day, Christmas, and New Year's Day. Admission free but donations encouraged.*

51 Hualapai Mountain Park

11.5 mi./15 min. South on Stockton Hill Rd. (becomes Hualapai Mountain Rd.). Beautiful scenery and the pine-scented mountain air make this an ideal destination for a summer picnic. The park also has a number of stone and wood cabins for rent with wood-burning stoves or fireplaces. On weekends people congregate at the large rustic stone lodge, where there's a roaring blaze in the fireplace. Several miles of hiking trails cross the slopes to overlook points ranging in elevation from 6,000 to 8,000 feet or more, and eagles and hawks may be seen soaring overhead. *Open year-round.*

171 Grand Canyon Deer Farm

2 min. Exit north, left on Deer Farm Rd.; follow signs. The deer farm's bright red barn with white trim is a friendly sight reminiscent of a child's picture book. And when you walk into the large fenced yard behind the barn, pet deer, goats, llamas, monkeys, shaggy miniature donkeys, and other small, friendly animals are ready to nuzzle you and take food from your hands. The farm usually has more than 100 deer and other creatures, many of which may be petted by children. Depending upon the time of year, fawns or other baby animals may be seen. *Open daily May–Sept.; Tues.–Sat. Oct.–Dec.; Wed.–Sat. Jan.–Mar. except Thanksgiving Day, Christmas Eve, and Christmas, weather permitting. Admission charged.*

195 Slide Rock State Park

23 mi./30 min. South on I-17 to Exit 337, south on Rte. 89A. The park is in Oak Creek Canyon, one of the most beautiful spots in the Southwest and said to be the setting for Zane Grey's novel *Call of the Canyon*. About 13 miles south of Flagstaff the road suddenly enters the canyon, and for the next 16 miles it zigzags down between dramatic, pine-accented red rock cliffs and spires until you reach Sedona. Although the canyon is a recreation area, parking is difficult until you reach Slide Rock State Park. From the parking lot there, it's a short walk to Slide Rock itself, where the creek has worn a natural water slide over smooth red rocks made slick by moss. Children and adults alike enjoy slipping down the slide into a natural pool. Hiking and casting for rainbow trout are the other attractions. *Open daily. Admission charged.*

195   Lowell Observatory, Flagstaff

3 mi./10 min. North on S. Milton Rd., left on Santa Fe Ave.; follow signs. With a certain old-fashioned charm, this observatory may strike you as too quaint to be involved in serious astronomical research. But ever since its founding by Percival Lowell in 1894, some important observations have been recorded here, including those that led to the discovery by Clyde Tombaugh of the planet Pluto in 1930—a discovery that was predicted by Lowell himself—and to the formulation of the theory of an expanding universe. The observatory has eight telescopes, among them the historic 24-inch Alvan Clark telescope, which is still in use. The telescopes are involved in gathering new data on everything from comets and nearby stars to distant galaxies and quasars. Near the dome is the mausoleum of Percival Lowell, perhaps best known for his studies of the planet Mars. The attractive

204. *No one knows why the Sinaguas chose to live in these cliffs—or why they left.*

grounds provide scenic views of the Flagstaff area. *Open Tues.–Sat. June–Aug.; open for 1:30 P.M. tour only, Sept.–May except holidays. For evening viewing call (602) 774-2096. Admission free but donations encouraged.*

195   Museum of Northern Arizona, Flagstaff

5 mi./20 min. North on S. Milton Rd., right on Santa Fe Ave., left on Humphreys St., left on Rte. 180. This museum has thousands of fascinating specimens and artifacts relating to the cultural and natural history of the region. The intriguing collection of Hopi kachina dolls, carved representations of deified ancestral spirits, is grouped according to the ceremonies with which they are associated. Examples of prehistoric baskets are shown along with exhibits of tools and the methods used to make them. Other crafts include Kayenta pottery and Navajo and Hopi weaving. One wing of the museum depicts the geologic history of the Colorado Plateau, featuring the skeleton of a huge 20,000-year-old sloth. The museum also boasts a lovely cloistered garden. *Open daily except Thanksgiving Day, Christmas, and New Year's Day. Admission charged.*   ♿

204   Walnut Canyon National Monument

5 min. South on Walnut Canyon Rd.; follow signs. The entry road to this national monument whisks you away from the desert and into a forest scented by ponderosa pines and Douglas firs. The banana yuccas flourishing here open their large pale yellow blooms in the spring. Named for the black walnuts that grow within it, the deep canyon has walls of sandstone and limestone, where the Sinagua Indians made their home until about A.D. 1250. The Sinaguas were early hunters and gatherers until they finally turned to farming for survival. You can hike down a steep 240-step trail into the canyon and enter their cliffside homes or follow an easier trail along the rim that provides good views of the dwellings. Mule deer, pronghorns, elk, and other wildlife may be seen nearby, and bald eagles in winter. *Open daily except Thanksgiving Day and Christmas. Admission charged.*   ⛲ 🚶 ♿

If You Have Some Extra Time:

Grand Canyon National Park

165   *60 mi./70 min.* We've all seen the dazzling photographs and read the glowing descriptions of its magnificence and unique evolution. But to stand on the South Rim is to be awed by the panorama of shapes and colors and challenged by the undeniable evidence of time that can only be counted in thousands of millions of years.

About 6 million years ago, the Colorado River began to carve the canyon in an area of land that had been slowly uplifted by movements in the earth's crust. Wind, ice, floods, and gravity also shaped the canyon's rock formations, creating this phenomenal conjunction of infinitely varied towers and walls with layers of limestone, shale, and sandstone left by ancient rivers, seas, and deserts.

It's about 10 miles across to the canyon's North Rim, and about 1 mile down to the Colorado River and the Vishnu schist, a 2-billion-year-old rock. Going from one canyon end to the other, the river twists so much that it is some 277 miles long. The 9-mile trail down to the river passes through four botanical zones; to see a comparable range of plant and animal life you would have to drive from the Mexican desert to northern forests. The canyon is like no other place on earth. If you have time, it's an experience that you'll never forget. *How to get there: Exit 165, north on Rte. 64 to park entrance. South Rim open year-round. Admission charged.*

285–311. *Former giants of the forest have been transformed to colorful solid stone.*

233   Meteor Crater Natural Landmark

5 mi./8 min. South on Meteor Crater Rd. Anyone intrigued by space travel, science fiction, or astrogeology will be fascinated by this amazing site. Some 50,000 years ago a solid nickel-iron meteorite hurtled to Earth at the speed of about 45,000 miles per hour and slammed into the ground here. The result of the impact is a hole 570 feet deep, 4,100 feet wide, and over 3 miles in circumference. Almost nothing has been found of the meteorite—it is thought that most of it vaporized on impact—but the crater is the best preserved on our planet. Apollo astronauts trained here in the late 1960's because the moon is also pitted with meteoritic craters. In fact, from a platform below the rim, it is easy to imagine yourself on the moon. The museum offers exhibits on the history of the site and the study of earth and space sciences. *Open year-round. Admission charged.*

285 311   Petrified Forest National Park

Exit 285: 21 mi./30 min. South on Rte. 180 to South Gate. Exit 311: 1 min. Exit north to North Gate. The park is famous for the Painted Desert (at the North Gate) and the Rainbow Forest (at the South Gate). A scenic 28-mile road connects the two. There are several stopping places, and an excellent park map explains the highlights along the way. In the Painted Desert Visitor Center, a film shows how wood becomes petrified. The Rainbow Forest Museum features exhibits on ancient reptiles and the region's human and geological history. A nearby trail leads past a jumble of 225-million-year-old fallen petrified trees. Some of the most magnificent vistas are at Blue Mesa, reached by a 3-mile loop road. Here the landscape is striated with smoky lavenders and rich blues. *Open daily except Christmas. Admission charged.*

26   Red Rock State Park and Museum

4 mi./7 min. East on Rte. 66, left on Rte. 566; follow signs. Just east of Gallup, which is known as the Indian jewelry capital of the world, this park is an active Indian cultural center. In August the famous Intertribal Indian Ceremonial brings visitors here. But the year-round highlight of the park is the museum, whose modern terra-cotta building stands at the base of spectacular red-hued sandstone monoliths. In it you'll see outstanding examples of Pueblo pottery, Plains Indians beadwork, textiles, basketry, jewelry, and sand paintings. A garden displays some splendid sculptures of Indians carved from tree trunks. Nature trails are being developed that will lead visitors to petroglyph sites. *Park open year-round; museum open daily Memorial Day–Labor Day; Mon.–Fri. Labor Day–Memorial Day except Thanksgiving Day, Christmas, and New Year's Day. Admission free but donations encouraged.*

63   Bluewater Lake State Park

7 mi./15 min. South on Rte. 412. The dazzling blue of the lake, a 7-mile-long reservoir in a deep valley, is a refreshing sight at the end of a drive through the piñon forest of the Zuni Mountains east of the Continental Divide. The chief attraction is the chance to fish for enormous, feisty rainbow trout and channel catfish. The record for both is 16 pounds. Ice fishing is popular in winter. In summer, the elevation (7,400 feet) and the breezes off the water provide relief from the searing heat of the valley below. *Open year-round. Admission charged.*

102   Pueblo of Acoma

16 mi./20 min. South on Rte. 30, left on Rte. 32; follow signs. On its splendid sandstone mesa rising dramatically from the valley floor, Acoma, dating to about A.D. 1150, is called the oldest continuously inhabited community in the nation. In 1540, the first white visitor was the Spanish conquistador Francisco Vásquez de Coronado, who found ascending the mesa on foot so taxing that "we repented climbing to the top." Today visitors are taken to the village by bus. On the guided walking tour you can see the ancient houses, visit a mission chapel dating back to the 1600's, and enjoy the sweeping vistas. The visitor center has exhibits of pottery and jewelry and the history of Acoma. *Open daily except Easter weekend, July 10–13, and first weekend in Oct. Admission charged for tours.*

157A   Albuquerque, NM 87103

Convention & Visitors Bureau, 305 Romero St. NW. (505) 243-3696; (800) 284-2282 outside NM. The Spanish influence is pleasantly recalled in the Old Town area, with its plaza and the San Felipe de Neri Church (1706). The architecture on the University of New Mexico campus has been influenced by the Indian pueblos. Anthropology, geology, and the arts are featured in the city's museums. At the New Mexico Museum of Natural History you can step into a volcano or an Ice Age cave and admire a model of a flying quetzalcoatlus with its wingspan of 40 feet. World War II correspondent Ernie Pyle's home is open to the public. The Indian Pueblo Cultural Center details the culture and history of the Indian peoples of New Mexico.

I-25 Isleta Pueblo

16 mi./20 min. South on I-25 to Exit 213, south on Isleta Blvd., left on Rte. 147. One of the oldest communities in the U.S.A., Isleta was already a settled pueblo when Francisco Vásquez de Coronado passed by in 1540, looking for gold. Isleta's first mission church, begun in 1613, was abandoned during the Pueblo Indian revolt of 1680; it was restored in 1710 and the name changed to St. Augustine in 1720. Two stained-glass windows depict Pueblo Indians receiving the sacraments. The crosses on the church towers serve as landmarks for visitors trying to find their way through a maze of narrow streets to the plaza in the center of town, where pottery is fired and bread baked in beehive-shaped outdoor ovens. *Open year-round.*

I-25 Coronado State Park and State Monument

18 mi./20 min. North on I-25 to Exit 242B, west on Rte. 44. In 1540, Spanish explorers led by Francisco Vásquez de Coronado, in a futile search for gold, camped among Pueblo farmers at this oasis, still used by campers today, along the Rio Grande. Excavations of the Kuaua pueblo ruins revealed a subterranean room, or kiva, the walls of which were covered with murals that are outstanding examples of prehistoric art. Today these and other artifacts from the site are displayed in the monument's museum, and the partially restored village of 1,200 rooms is open for viewing. *Open daily except Thanksgiving Day, Christmas, and New Year's Day. Admission charged.*

164A 167 National Atomic Museum, Albuquerque

Exit 164A: 5 min. South on Wyoming Blvd. Exit 167: 6 mi./9 min. West on Central Ave. (Rte. 66), left on Wyoming Blvd. A B-52 bomber used in the last atmospheric nuclear tests, a 280-mm. atomic cannon, and futuristic-looking surface-to-air missiles occupy the grounds outside this museum, which focuses on nuclear weaponry. Exhibits and films illustrate the history of the first atom bomb and include full-size models of its first two designs. Also featured at the museum are planes and missiles created to carry atomic weapons, the development of the hydrogen bomb, advances in weapons technology, safety and testing, and demonstrations of peaceful uses of nuclear technology. *Open daily except Thanksgiving Day, Christmas, New Year's Day, and Easter.*

167 Sandia Peak Aerial Tramway, Albuquerque

11 mi./15 min. North on Tramway Blvd.; follow signs. One of the world's longest aerial tramways carries riders on a breathtaking trip of 2.7 miles, from Sandia Peak's desert base, over canyons and dense forests, to its verdant top. During the 15-minute ride, which covers a vertical rise of 3,800 feet, visitors may spot mule deer below and golden eagles circling overhead. From Sandia Peak, which is part of the Cibola National Forest, you can enjoy a spectacular view of more than 11,000 square miles. You'll also find hiking trails and areas for rock climbing and hang gliding. In winter the tram is a ski lift, giving access to 25 miles of trails. *Open daily Memorial Day–Labor Day; Thurs.–Tues. and P.M. Wed. Labor Day–Memorial Day. Admission charged.*

If You Have Some Extra Time: Canyon de Chelly National Monument

333 **65 mi./90 min.** Rising 30 to 1,000 feet above the valley floor, the vertical sandstone walls of this Arizona canyon are breathtaking, and the ruined cliff dwellings have varied cultural implications. The Anasazis ("Enemy Ancestors") lived here almost 1,000 years ago. They were primarily farmers dwelling in the valley near the Rio de Chelly, where they planted crops as the Navajo Indians do to this day. The early Pueblo people built shelters in the high ledges of the valley walls. Today the ruins of these cliff dwellings evoke the spirit of an industrious and ingenious people.

This land now belongs to the Navajo Indians, and travel into Canyon de Chelly (pronounced "Shay") and its tributaries is allowed only with a park-ranger escort or in authorized groups. The only unguided walk is a trail (2½ miles round-trip) from an overlook on the South Rim Drive down to the ruins of the Whitehouse, a dwelling constructed in two sections, one on the canyon floor and the other in a cave directly over it.

The archeological museum at the visitor center presents the different Indian cultures that brought life to this dramatically forbidding landscape. *How to get there: Exit 333, north on Rte. 191 to Chinle, right on Indian Rte. 7; follow signs. Monument open year-round; visitor center open daily except Thanksgiving Day, Christmas, and New Year's Day. Admission charged.*

275 Rock Lake Trout Rearing Unit, Santa Rosa

4 mi./9 min. West on Will Rogers Dr. (becomes Parker Ave., then Coronado W.); cross bridge, left on River Rd. This state-run fish hatchery produces an estimated 33 million walleyed pike hatchlings each year for immediate release into lakes in New Mexico and other states. (If the pike are not released within a few days, they will eat each other.) It also raises 305,000 rainbow trout from fingerlings to lengths of 8–10 inches. Highly oxygenated water allows for considerable density of trout (which, unlike pike, are not cannibalistic) in the concrete ponds, where they feed from automatic food dispensers. *Open year-round.*

332. *An engaging array of artifacts, mostly related to the early days of railroading.*

275 Santa Rosa Dam, Lake and State Park

9 mi./15 min. West on Will Rogers Dr. (becomes Parker Ave.), right on 2nd St.; follow signs. Swimmers, water-skiers, and fishermen share Santa Rosa Lake with an abundance of migrating waterfowl. Hiking trails lead through the piñon and juniper trees and cacti that dot the surrounding wild high desert. The information center that overlooks the dam here on the Pecos River has exhibits on more than 250 archeological sites that reveal former habitation by early pueblo-dwelling Indian farmers, nomadic hunters, and the Comanche and Apache tribes. *Open year-round. Admission charged.*

329 356 Ute Lake State Park, Logan

Exit 329: 27 mi./30 min. Northeast on Rte. 54, left on Rte. 540. Exit 356: 25 mi./30 min. North on Rte. 39, left on Rte. 540. One of the largest lakes in New Mexico, Ute Lake is favored by fishermen, who flock from surrounding states to try for walleye, bass, crappie, and channel catfish. Scuba divers swim beneath the surface in pursuit of the biggest fish. Water-skiing, sailboarding, and swimming are other popular activities on this long, narrow lake, which was created by a dam on the Canadian River. *Open year-round. Admission charged.*

332 Tucumcari Historical Museum

5 min. North on Rte. 18, right on Tucumcari Blvd., left on Adams St. An early sheriff's office in this museum recalls the town's wild beginnings as a railroad construction camp called Six Shooter Siding. Other exhibits include Indian artifacts dating to 12,000 B.C., cowboy memorabilia, pioneer kitchens, and an early hospital. Outside there's a turn-of-the-century windmill, a chuck wagon, a Southern Pacific caboose, fossils, and farming and ranching implements. *Open Mon.–Sat. and P.M. Sun. Memorial Day–Labor Day; Tues.–Sat. and P.M. Sun. Labor Day–Memorial Day except Thanksgiving Day, Christmas, and New Year's Day. Admission charged.*

36 Cal Farley's Boys Ranch

21 mi./30 min. North on Rte. 385, right at sign north of Canadian River. This 10,000-acre ranch, founded by an Amarillo businessman in 1939 to help troubled boys, is now a community of nearly 400 students, complete with homelike dormitories, a chapel, and facilities for academic and vocational education through high school. The Old Tascosa Courthouse building, which housed the ranch's first six inhabitants, is now a museum of Panhandle culture and displays Indian artifacts, cowboy and pioneer memorabilia, and photos and documents that relate to Boys Ranch. Near the museum is a small zoo with local wildlife. *Open year-round.*

65 Don Harrington Discovery Center, Amarillo

3 min. North on Coulter Dr.; follow signs. This innovative center aims to generate a sense of wonder about science and the natural world. There are planetarium shows, an aquarium filled with piranhas and other exotic fish, displays that demonstrate the workings of the human body, and an ambitious schedule of special programs. The Black Hole exhibit demonstrates centrifugal force; a giant kaleidoscope and movie screens in the round deliver spectacular visual effects. *Open Tues.– Sat. and P.M. Sun. except holidays. Admission charged for planetarium shows.*

70 Wonderland Park, Amarillo

5 min. North on Buchanan St. (Rte. 287), left on NE 24th Ave. This family amusement park has 21 rides, including such thrillers as the Texas Tornado double-loop roller coaster, the Cyclone, the H_2O Raging Riptide water slide, the Scrambler, and the Big Splash log flume. Those who prefer gentler pursuits may try the carousel, miniature golf, or remote-controlled boats. In spacious Thompson Park, which surrounds Wonderland Park, picnic areas, a swimming pool, and a zoo add diversity. *Wonderland Park open P.M. daily late Apr.–Labor Day; P.M. weekends mid.-Mar.–late Apr. and Sept. Admission charged. Thompson Park open year-round.*

70. *Henry Ford's masterpiece, the Model T, in the Panhandle-Plains Museum.*

163. *The homey charm of the pioneers' kitchen was sacrificed for modern efficiency.*

70   Panhandle–Plains Historical Museum, Canyon

20 mi./23 min. South on I-27 to Exit 106, west on Rte. 217. The ancient past of northwest Texas is imaginatively illustrated with marine fossils and dinosaur skeletons in this regional museum. Human settlement in the area is represented by artifacts from Southern Plains Indian tribes, a full-size 1925 oil drilling rig, and a ranching exhibit with guns, saddles, a chuck wagon, and vintage photographs. *Open Mon.–Sat. and P.M. Sun. except holidays. Admission free but donations encouraged.* ♿

96   Carson County Square House Museum

9 mi./15 min. North on Rte. 207. Exhibits on the history of the Texas Panhandle, from prehistoric Indian culture to space exploration, are presented in and around an 1880's square wood-frame house that, when built, was considered the embodiment of luxury on these treeless plains. Nearby, a dark, cramped dugout illustrates how less affluent settlers lived. (Not only was there no wood, but there were also no stoves and not enough water to make adobe bricks.) Other aspects of pioneer life are exemplified by a blacksmith's shop, a Santa Fe Railroad caboose, and a bank exhibit with a collection of cattle brands. There are

dioramas with aoudad sheep and other wildlife of the area, as well as one of the largest collections of paintings by Southwest Indians in the country. *Open Mon.–Sat. and P.M. Sun. except Thanksgiving Day, Christmas, and New Year's Day.* ♿

163   Pioneer West Museum, Shamrock

4 min. South on Rte. 83, left on 3rd St., right on Madden St. A favorite stop for traveling salesmen since its completion in 1928, the Reynolds Hotel has now become a museum, housing a wide variety of items that reflect Shamrock history. Plains Indian artifacts, cowboy memorabilia, and old weapons line several rooms. Carefully restored and re-created rooms—a doctor's office, a general store, a schoolroom, and a pioneer kitchen—evoke the past. *Open Mon.–Fri. except Thanksgiving Day, Christmas, and New Year's Day.* ♿

38   Old Town Museum Complex, Elk City

5 min. North on Rte. 6 (Main St.), left on Rte. 40 (business; becomes Van Buren Ave., then 3rd St.). Housed in a turn-of-the-century home with gingerbread trim, the museum fea-

tures a mercantile display about original owner O. H. Young's business activities, rooms restored with late-Victorian period furnishings, a pioneer doctor's office, an antique wagon, and old photos and memorabilia from local rodeo impresarios. On the grounds a carefully restored one-room stone schoolhouse, built in 1894, and the Pioneer Chapel represent two formative influences on the lives of town homesteaders. *Open Tues.–Sat. and P.M. Sun. except holidays. Admission charged.* ♿

53   Foss Lake

7 mi./10 min. North on Rte. 44. At the south end of this 8,800-acre reservoir is Foss State Park, where swimmers and sunbathers enjoy the sandy beach, boaters and water-skiers cruise the water, and fishermen try for catfish, bass, walleyed pike, crappie, and bluegill. At the lake's northern end, the Washita National Wildlife Refuge accommodates thousands of migrating waterfowl and sandhill cranes. The birds and other wildlife are easily seen from roads, trails, and an observation platform. During the warm months scissor-tailed flycatchers perform their aerial acrobatics. *Open year-round.*

38. *Generous porches and a handsome gazebo provide welcome shade from the midday sun.*

212. *Traditional Seminole clothing is noted for its color and meticulous handwork.*

ROB Oklahoma City, OK 73102

Robinson Ave. exit: Convention and Tourism Bureau, 4 Santa Fe Plaza. (405) 278-8912. The highlights in this large city—more than 600 square miles in area and named from two Indian words meaning "Land of the Red People"—are widespread and varied. The National Cowboy Hall of Fame and Western Heritage Center attracts those interested in the lore and artifacts of the West, while the National Softball Hall of Fame appeals to sandlot ballplayers of all ages.

The state capitol is unique in that there are working oil wells on its grounds. Nearby, the State Museum presents the major events in the colorful history of the Indian Territory and Oklahoma. Kirkpatrick Center is a large museum complex featuring African, Oriental, and American Indian art, as well as photography and science displays, a planetarium, a greenhouse, and gardens. Oklahoma City's enormous zoo has some 4,000 animals as well as the Aquaticus, which features dolphin and sea lion shows and varied displays of aquatic life.

212 Seminole Nation Museum, Wewoka

17 mi./26 min. South on Rte. 56, left on 6th St. The museum effectively chronicles the Seminole Indians' way of life and their continuing struggle to adapt after forced relocation from the humid shores of Florida and the Gulf Coast to these dry, windy plains. Displays include 19th-century photos, an impressive collection of western sculpture and paintings, and a replica of an early Seminole chikee, a dwelling built on stilts and made of palmetto leaves, tree branches, and leather. The re-created Wewoka Trading Post recalls Oklahoma's pioneer days. *Open P.M. Tues.–Sun. Feb.–Dec. except Thanksgiving Day, Christmas Eve, and Christmas.*

240B Creek Council House Museum, Okmulgee

15 mi./25 min. North on Rte. 75/62, left on 6th St. This museum is housed in the former Creek national capitol, a handsome two-story stone building dating to 1878. It contains an interesting collection of Muskogee Creek and Yuchi Indian paintings, old photographs, historical maps, re-created rooms from territorial days, and tools, beadwork, hunting points, and other artifacts from the aboriginal period.

Until 1907 the Creek tribal council met in three rooms on the second floor, one of which has 48 chairs for the delegates from the 48 tribal towns. Another room displays Creek-made hanging rugs and tapestries along with historical costumes and clothing. *Open Tues.–Sat. except holidays.*

259 Fountainhead State Park

5 mi./8 min. South on Rte. 150. An oak and hickory forest contrasts with the prairies in this 2,800-acre park, which is actually a peninsula extending into Lake Eufaula (pronounced "you-*fall*-uh"). The huge man-made lake is famous for its largemouth and white bass fishing. The Nature Center features displays on the region's varied animals and plants, including bobcats, white-tailed deer, gray foxes, eagles, and owls, as well as the flowering dogwood and persimmon trees, blackberry bushes, and wild grapevines that

provide both logs and food. Longhorn cattle and grazing elk can be viewed from an observation area, horses are available for guided scenic rides, and there are courses for full-scale and miniature golf. *Open year-round. Admission charged for sports activities.*

287 291 Greenleaf State Park

Exit 287: 13.5 mi./22 min. North on Rte. 100, left on Rte. 10. Exit 291: 14 mi./22 min. North on Rte. 10. This aptly named 565-acre park is situated in the beautiful oak-covered Cookson Hills. A 20-mile backpacking trail that circles 930-acre Greenleaf Lake provides striking views of the surrounding blue hills and the green Arkansas River valley. Boats are for rent at the lake, which has a swimming beach and offers excellent fishing for bass and catfish. Nearby Ft. Gibson Military Park, which was once a sprawling outpost at the edge of American civilization, has been rebuilt by the state of Oklahoma and is now open to visitors. *Open year-round.*

307 Spiro Mounds Archeological State Park, Spiro

29 mi./35 min. South on Rte. 59, left on Rte. 9, left on Lock and Dam Rd. No. 14. This small park encompasses 12 earthen mounds, dating from approximately A.D. 600 to 1600, which were used for Indian burial and religious ceremonies; a self-guiding walking tour leads to the largest. An audiovisual presentation at the Interpretive Center explains the sophisticated Spiro Indian culture and the area's importance as a trade center. "Grave goods" (possessions buried with their owners) and other artifacts excavated from the mounds are on display. *Open Tues.–Sat. and P.M. Sun. Apr.–Nov.; Wed.–Sat. and P.M. Sun. Dec.–Mar. except Christmas.*

7 Fort Smith National Historic Site and Old Fort Museum

13 mi./18 min. South on I-540 to Exit 8A, right on Rogers Ave. (Rte. 22). The main attraction here is the national historic site, and most notably the restored courtroom building

7. *Vintage pharmacy in Old Fort Museum has a fountain and the classic furniture.*

where, between 1875 and 1890, the "hanging judge," Isaac C. Parker, sentenced 160 Indian Territory outlaws to death. At the restored gallows nearby, as many as six men could be executed at one time. Although the site is surrounded by the Ft. Smith business district, its tree-lined grounds are evocative of the 19th-century frontier. Reservations for guided group tours must be made in advance by writing or calling the fort.

The Old Fort Museum, one block away, houses artifacts relating to Ft. Smith's military history. Ozarks craftspeople are occasionally on hand to demonstrate pioneer skills. *Historic site open daily except Christmas; museum open daily June–Aug.; Tues.–Sat. and P.M. Sun. Sept.–May except Thanksgiving Day, Christmas Eve, Christmas, and New Year's Day. Admission charged.*   ♿

13   Lake Fort Smith State Park

13 mi./20 min. North on Rte. 71; follow signs. Surrounded by the grand peaks of the Boston Mountains, this wooded park is situated at the edge of a 650-acre lake known to fishermen for its bass, bream, crappie, and catfish. Skirting the lake, a 3½-mile stretch of the 140-mile Ozark Highlands Trail provides scenic views for hikers. An Olympic-size swimming pool, tennis courts, assorted playground equipment, and tree-shaded picnic sites combine to make the park a popular weekend retreat. Boats and canoes are available for rent. *Open year-round.*

81   Mount Nebo State Park, Dardanelle

15 mi./30 min. South on Rte. 7, right on Rte. 22, left on Rte. 155. From its elevation of 1,800 feet, the park affords dramatic views of the Arkansas River, Lake Dardanelle, and nearby peaks. The steep mountain road with its hairpin turns is especially scenic in the fall; in summer, picnickers in the park find a refuge from the heat below. Trails allow hikers to explore a cave, see several natural springs, and cross a natural stone bridge. Amenities include a swimming pool, tennis courts, a ballfield, playgrounds, and bicycles for rent. *Open year-round.*

108   Petit Jean Park and Museum of Automobiles

21 mi./30 min. South on Rte. 9, right on Rte. 154. A drive through this large park on Petit Jean Mountain offers majestic views of the Arkansas River valley. Scenic walking trails lead past waterfalls and along the rims of box canyons inscribed with Indian pictographs.

108. *Ledges tinged with lichen contrast with the deep green pines in Petit Jean Park.*

The many recreational opportunities include tennis courts and rental boats. The rotating collection of classic and antique automobiles at the museum, adjacent to the park, features a rare Arkansas-built Climber, Liberace's "solid gold" Cadillac, a 1914 popcorn wagon with a one-cylinder steam engine, a pink-and-pearl 1937 Packard Towncar that once belonged to Mae West, and several cars owned by Winthrop Rockefeller (former Arkansas governor), including his personal limousine: a seven-passenger 1967 Cadillac Fleetwood. *Park open year-round; museum open daily except Christmas. Admission charged for museum.*

125   Woolly Hollow State Park

18 mi./20 min. North on Rte. 65, right on Rte. 285. Lake Bennett is the focus of this picturesque 400-acre park in the Ozark foothills. The sandy beach is popular with swimmers, and the boat ramp and dock are used by sailboaters and those fishing for catfish, bass, bream, and crappie. Rental flat-bottomed fishing boats, pedal boats, and canoes are well suited to the quiet waters of the lake. A tree-shaded picnic area and a playground overlook the lake, and nearby is a restored 1882 one-room log house. A nature trail that skirts the lake offers colorful views in the fall. *Open year-round.*

129   Toad Suck Ferry Lock and Dam Park

7 mi./14 min. West on Rte. 286. The origin of the name Toad Suck is uncertain, but one theory involves an antebellum tavern frequented by hard-drinking steamboat passengers who sucked down whiskey until they swelled up like toads.

A ferry operated here until 1970, when a lock and a dam were completed as part of an Arkansas River navigation project. The park straddles the river, which is primarily used for boating and fishing for bass and catfish. There are picnic areas and campgrounds, along with a ballfield and a playground. On the east bank one of the old ferryboats is on view. *Park open year-round; park office open Mon.–Fri.*

147 | Pinnacle Mountain State Park

10 mi./20 min. South on I-430 to Exit 9, west on Rte. 10, right on Pinnacle Valley Rd. Thousand-foot-high Pinnacle Mountain, surrounded by the forested lowlands of this 1,770-acre park, is the first elevation of consequence encountered along this interstate (driving west from the Mississippi River), and as such affords some fine scenic vistas of the area.

147. *Cypress knees, part of the root system, create a surreal scene in the water.*

The park is a favorite of bird-watchers and is known for its abundance of flora and fauna, as well as its fine natural history exhibits and interpretive programs. A number of well-marked hiking trails explore the terrain, including one for the handicapped and a rugged one that's of mountaineering caliber.

Several shaded picnic grounds, fishing and boating on the Big and Little Maumelle rivers, and a playground round out the park's recreational facilities. *Open Mon.–Sat. and P.M. Sun.*

I-30 | Little Rock, AR 72201

Convention & Visitors Bureau, Markham St. and Broadway. (501) 376-4781. The very rock that gave the city its name can be seen in Riverfront Park. And if this park doesn't suit your fancy, there are more than 50 others in Little Rock and in North Little Rock, just across the Arkansas River. The city grew rapidly at the turn of the century, which accounts for the Victorian and related styles of many homes to be seen in the Quapaw Quarter and other historic areas. Some 14 restored buildings dating from the early 1800's to the 1850's still stand in the Arkansas Territorial Restoration, and self-guiding auto and walking tours of the historic areas are available. The Old State House, which currently serves as a museum of Arkansas history, has an intriguing touch-and-see display in Granny's Attic. The grounds of the present state capitol feature an extensive rose garden. Other popular attractions are the Arkansas Arts Center, the Decorative Arts Museum, the Arkansas Museum of Science and History, and the excellent zoo.

242 | Village Creek State Park

13 mi./20 min. North on Rte. 284. This huge (7,000-acre) nature park was created to preserve and make available to visitors some of the natural features peculiar to Crowley's Ridge. The ridge is a mantle of windblown silt, up to 10 miles wide and 500 feet high in parts, that wanders for 150 miles through the otherwise flat Mississippi River valley in eastern Arkansas. Its unspoiled upland forests stand in relief against miles of cultivated fields. And most of what you'll see—from the soil and trees to the fish and other varieties of wildlife—is not found elsewhere in the state. Resident naturalists are happy to expound upon this phenomenon. Nature trails meander through the forest and alongside the park's creeks and small lakes. Lakeside picnics, swimming, fishing in stocked waters, and camping are favorite activities. The park is noted for its flowers in spring and foliage color in fall. Flocks of migratory birds punctuate the autumn landscape. *Open year-round.*

1 | Memphis, TN 38103

1D | *Visitors Information Center, 207 Beale St. (901) 526-4880.* King Cotton

still plays a major role in the city's economy, Beale Street and W.C. Handy are appropriately memorialized, and a riverboat still plies the mighty Mississippi; but the best-known attraction is Graceland, home of Elvis Presley, the King of Rock and Roll. Tours are so popular that reservations are suggested. Call (901) 332-3322, or (800) 238-2000 from out of state.

The river that brought life to Memphis is honored at Mud Island by a scale model of the Mississippi from Cairo, Illinois, to New Orleans and the Gulf of Mexico. The Memphis Pink Palace Museum and Planetarium features exhibits on natural history, pioneer life, and the Civil War. The National Ornamental Metal Museum has a working blacksmith on the premises, and for nature lovers there is a zoo with an aquarium and a botanic garden.

56 | Hatchie National Wildlife Refuge

1 min. South on Rte. 76. Preserved as a feeding and resting area for migrating and wintering waterfowl, these 11,556 acres are a prime example of this region's natural terrain. A bottomland periodically flooded by the meandering Hatchie River, it is densely forested with water-tolerant oak. But the woods regularly give way to airy stretches of open water, which are now dotted with nesting boxes for wood ducks. A wide variety of songbirds also breed here, while mallards and black ducks are winter visitors. Red-shouldered hawks, barred owls, and wild turkeys thrive in the refuge. *Open year-round.*

80A | Casey Jones Home and Railroad Museum, Jackson

2 min. South on Bypass 45; follow signs. Down to the shaving mug and straight razor in the bathroom and the green mason jars in the kitchen, the furnishings in this simple white clapboard house give the impression that it was only yesterday that Casey Jones left for his fateful journey on the *Cannonball Express.* The glories of the railroad age are commemorated in displays of lanterns, switch

1–1D. *A Mud Island model of the Mississippi includes the meanders and oxbow lakes.*

keys, uniforms, and other memorabilia, including copies of the music for the 1909 hit that immortalized Jones. Near the house is a sister engine to the one in which Jones met his end. *Open daily except Thanksgiving Day, Christmas, and Easter. Admission charged.*

116 Natchez Trace State Park

5 min. South on Rte. 114. In the 1930's, after a century of farming and erosion, the terrain here was a wasteland of washed-out gullies and bare ridges. But thanks to a government reclamation project, the area today is as well forested and supportive of wildlife as it was when early 19th-century travelers passed through on the trail (then called a trace) that gave the park its name. It is also a spacious, full-scale state park with hiking trails and lakes for swimming, fishing, and boating. There's a self-guiding car tour on several

miles of winding, well-paved roads; a highlight is an ancient 106-foot-high pecan tree, reputedly grown from a nut left by one of Andrew Jackson's men on his way home from the Battle of New Orleans. *Open year-round.*

143 Loretta Lynn's Ranch

6 mi./12 min. North on Rte. 13. Touring the ground floor of the columned white plantation house where the legendary singer lives is a major attraction; but this pleasant, 7,000-acre ranch offers a number of other diversions. For campers there's a swimming pool, a miniature golf course, tennis courts, and a creek with rainbow trout. Day visitors will be interested in the 100-year-old gristmill that has been turned into a museum commemorating Loretta Lynn's career. On display are an impressive number of gold records, some of her early costumes, plaques, citations, and commendations. Photographs of her parents and old mining artifacts prove that she is indeed a coal miner's daughter. *Open Apr.–Oct. Admission charged for museum.*

172 Montgomery Bell State Resort Park

12 mi./25 min. North on Rte. 46, right on Rte. 70. When America was young, rich deposits of iron ore drew settlers to these rolling hills. One of the early ironmasters to come to the South was Montgomery Bell, who forged cannonballs for the Battle of New Orleans. Along the hiking trails of this extensive 3,800-acre park, you can still see the remains of ore pits and smelting furnaces. Lakes nestled in the woods offer swimming, boating, and fishing. *Open year-round.*

192 Warner Parks, Nashville

5 mi./10 min. South on McCrory Ln., left on Rte. 100; follow signs. Establishing an elaborate city park in the midst of open country may have seemed the height of folly in the 1930's. But Percy Warner, his brother Edwin, and his son-in-law Luke Lea revealed remarkable foresight in preserving these 2,600 acres of meadows and wooded hills that are now sur-

rounded by suburban Nashville. The Percy Warner Park has 28 miles of scenic roads with stone bridges and drywalls. The smaller Edwin Warner Park has a nature center with a wildflower garden. *Open year-round.*

I-265 Nashville, TN 37213

I-65 *Tourist Information Center, James Robertson Pkwy. (615) 242-5606.* The city's renown as the headquarters of country music tends to obscure the many other rewarding aspects of this gracious state capital. Tribute is paid to antiquity in the splendid Greek revival capitol and in the Parthenon, an exact-size replica of the ancient temple in Athens containing a museum and an art gallery. Exhibits in the Tennessee State Museum depict life in the area from prehistoric times through the Civil War, and at Ft. Nashborough, a replica of a 1779 frontier fort, the cabins, stockaded walls, and artifacts recall the days of the pioneers. There's a Country Music Hall of Fame and other music-related museums. The Grand Ole Opry and the extensive Opryland Showpark further celebrate Nashville's musical heritage.

I-65 The Carter House, Franklin

20 mi./27 min. South on I-65 to Exit 65, west on Rte. 96; follow signs. The pockmarks and bullet holes on the house and smokehouse here recall the Battle of Franklin, one of the bloodiest engagements of the Civil War. On November 30, 1864, Confederate general John B. Hood launched a desperate attack against the Union forces that were entrenched around the house and its outbuildings. Among the more than 1,700 Confederate fatalities was Capt. Theodrick "Tod" Carter, whose father and sisters found him mortally wounded less than 200 yards from the family home.

The visitor center houses a small museum; there's a slide show and an elaborate model of the battlefield. The modest but handsome house, its doorway flanked by hand-poured glass windows and Doric columns, is furnished with original family possessions and other antiques. *Open Mon.–Sat. and P.M. Sun. except holidays. Admission charged.*

215 Opryland U.S.A., Nashville

7 mi./12 min. North on Rte. 155 (Briley Pkwy.); follow signs. This 120-acre stage show and park complex combines the Grand Ole Opry, the legendary country music showcase, with numerous other attractions. Amusement park rides, some with names based upon musical themes, such as "The Old Mill Scream," appeal to both adults and children; and the stage shows reflect a variety of musical tastes.

Also part of Opryland are the Roy Acuff Museum, which houses a fine collection of memorabilia from the early days of country music, and the *General Jackson*, a paddle-wheel showboat that offers cruises on the Cumberland River during the day and in the evening. *Open daily Memorial Day–Labor Day; weekends Mar.–May and Sept.–Oct. Admission charged.*

221 The Hermitage

4 mi./8 min. North on Rte. 45; follow signs. Andrew Jackson—war hero, Tennessee gentleman, and seventh president of the United States—is fittingly remembered at this 625-acre historic site, where two of his homes have been faithfully restored. The "early Hermitage" is a simple log cabin in which Jackson lived happily with his wife, Rachel, from 1804 to 1819; the Hermitage, their second home, is a gracious mansion with wide verandas and Doric columns. Most of the furnishings belonged to the Jackson family, including the crystal, the fine banquet table, mirrors, and a number of impressive family portraits. The garden, landscaped for Rachel in 1819, contains more than 50 varieties of herbs and flowers, as well as the hickory-shaded Palladian tomb of the president and his wife. *Open daily except Thanksgiving Day and Christmas. Admission charged.*

238 Cedars of Lebanon State Park

6 mi./10 min. South on Rte. 231. More than 20 miles of hiking and bridle paths wind through the cedars in this 9,000-acre facility. (The cedars are not actually cedars of Lebanon, but eastern red cedars.) Along the trails you'll find limestone glades, caves, sinkholes, prickly-pear cacti, and the rare Tennessee purple coneflowers. Park facilities include campsites, cabins, a large swimming pool, and acres of picnic tables. During the summer, programs and guided tours are conducted by the park staff. *Open year-round.*

268 Edgar Evins State Park

5 min. South on Rte. 96. This 6,000-acre park, established in 1975, takes full advantage of one of the loveliest places in Tennessee: Center Hill Lake. Created by the U.S. Army Corps of Engineers in 1948, the lake is surrounded by the hills of the Cumberland Plateau; its miles of indented shoreline, accessible from the park's marina, are edged with rocky bluffs. The lake attracts water-skiers as well as fishermen in search of record-breaking bass.

Campsites here overlook the water, and a village of cabins has its own swimming pool. There are also abundant picnic shelters and tables by the lake. Meandering along the bluffs is the Highland Rim Trail, a favorite of hikers. *Open daily except Christmas Eve–New Year's Day.*

273 Joe L. Evins Appalachian Center for Crafts

6 mi./10 min. South on Rte. 56; cross Hurricane Bridge, left on Center Dr. The scenic road winding its way through the mountainous woodlands of Tennessee's Center Hill Lake region to this Appalachian crafts center is in itself worth the trip. The center, set on a promontory overlooking the lake, is a division of Tennessee Tech University, a school where the students learn a number of traditional and nontraditional techniques in various crafts, including woodworking, sculpture, ceramics, glassblowing, and silver and steel jewelry. A gallery, featuring changing exhibits, serves as a showcase for the handiwork of students, faculty, and area artisans. Attached to the gallery is a shop that sells some of the creations of the students. *Open daily except Thanksgiving Day, Christmas–New Year's week, and last 2 days in June.*

317 Cumberland Mountain State Park

8.5 mi./20 min. South on Rte. 127. This 1,720-acre park, the legacy of 1930's federal government projects, is located around pleasant

407. *Falling water defines the power that drives the mill's wheels and machinery.*

75	See N–S book, sec. 32.	11	20	14	81	See N–S book, sec. 41.	TN : NC	88	0 3 20	40

376A   **387**   **407**   **I-81**   **50** **50B** **53A**

75   See N–S book, sec. 32.

Cumberland Mountain Lake in the wooded hills of the Cumberland Plateau. A lodge and other rough-hewn buildings are made of Crab Orchard stone, an attractive rose-colored sandstone that is quarried in this region. *Open year-round.*

356 / 376A — American Museum of Science and Energy, Oak Ridge

13 mi./ 25 min. Exit 356: northeast on Rte. 58; continue on Rte. 95. Exit 376A: northwest on Rte. 162, left on Rte. 62; follow signs. The secret life of Oak Ridge, Tennessee, changed the course of world history. It was an important part of the World War II Manhattan Project and produced the uranium required for the first atom bomb in 1945. Oak Ridge has remained in the forefront of nuclear research and production ever since.

The purpose of the museum is to inform the visitor of contemporary energy requirements and methods of generation, as well as the history of energy use in the United States and alternatives for the future. The exhibits are dynamic, inviting participation wherever possible. Models demonstrate the principles of gravity, thermodynamics, aerodynamics, and magnetism, and a small area is devoted to Oak Ridge's role in the development of the atom bomb. *Open daily except Thanksgiving Day, Christmas, and New Year's Day.*

387 — Knoxville, TN 37902

Convention and Visitors Bureau, 500 Henley St. (615) 523-2316. Mid-April, when the dogwoods are in bloom, is the most colorful time of the year in Knoxville; but the historic houses, the museums, and the excellent zoo are of interest year-round. Early colonial days are recalled at the Gen. James White Fort with stockade. The territorial era (1790–96) is represented by the handsome two-story clapboard home of the then governor, William Blount. At the Armstrong-Lockett House, built in 1834, there are notable collections of old silver and furniture, and the Civil War era is recalled at Confederate Memorial Hall. The Knoxville Museum of Art, located on the 1982 World's Fair site, features a popular display of period rooms in miniature.

407 — The Old Mill of Pigeon Forge

16 mi./35 min. South on Rte. 66, right on Rte. 441, left at first light. Since its construction in 1830, the charming Old Mill of Pigeon Forge has been working continuously. Powered by the Little Pigeon River, the mill's rumbling 24-foot water wheel and two tub wheels drive the original 2-ton millstones cut from buhrstone. During the Civil War water-powered looms on the second floor helped clothe Confederate soldiers. A gift shop features stone-ground grains, and guided tours are frequent. *Open Mon.–Sat. except Thanksgiving Day and Christmas. Admission charged.*

I-81 — The Crockett Tavern Museum, Morristown

8 mi./15 min. North on I-81 to Exit 8, north on Rte. 25, west on Rte. 11E; follow signs. Davy Crockett was a boy of 10 when his parents built and ran a four-room log tavern and hostelry here along one of the first roads that led west. The tavern was burned after being used as a smallpox hospital after the Civil War, but this reconstruction conveys the atmosphere of the original. All the furniture and the pots and kettles are authentic relics from the days when America was slowly pushing west. *Open Mon.–Sat. and P.M. Sun. May–Oct. Admission charged.*

50 / 50B — Biltmore Estate, Asheville

2 min. North on Rte. 25; follow signs. A thousand men spent 5 years building this majestic mansion with 250 rooms for George Vanderbilt, grandson of the prominent 19th-century New York shipping and railroad magnate Cornelius Vanderbilt. When the mansion was completed on Christmas Eve, 1895, it became one of America's largest privately owned houses—a distinction it still holds. Overlooking the French Broad River valley and the Blue Ridge Mountains, this French Renaissance-style château contains a 20,000-volume library, an ivory chess table once owned by Napoleon, 16th-century Flemish tapestries, paintings by Whistler and Renoir, one of the first heated indoor swimming pools, and one of the oldest existing bowling

50–50B. *The detailing of just one section implies the grandeur of the whole.*

alleys. The beautifully landscaped grounds—highlighted by a 4-acre English garden considered the finest of its kind in America—are the work of Frederick Law Olmsted, the 19th-century architect famous for his design of New York City's Central Park. *Open daily except Thanksgiving Day, Christmas, and New Year's Day. Admission charged.*

53A — Folk Art Center, Asheville

3.5 mi./6 min. East on Rte. 74, left on Blue Ridge Pkwy. Fine craftsmanship is a tradition hereabouts, as a walk through the center's spacious Folk Art Museum quickly reveals. Isolation in the early days demanded that mountain folk create their own tools, pottery, woodwork, woven and leather goods, jewelry, and musical instruments. The tradition still lives, and visitors here can usually see a potter, a wood-carver, or a weaver in action, offering step-by-step demonstrations as the work progresses. *Open daily except Thanksgiving Day, Christmas, and New Year's Day.*

73 Mountain Gateway Museum, Old Fort

1 min. North on Catawba Ave.; follow signs. During the summer of 1776, Gen. Griffith Rutherford stationed some 500 men at the Old Fort Plantation, which was once located here, to protect the frontier while he led a campaign against the Cherokees, who were suspected of being allies of the British. As settlers traveled westward after the Revolution, the area surrounding the Old Fort became a gateway to the Blue Ridge Mountains. The history of the region in general and the fort in particular is preserved in this handsome stone building, constructed by the Works Progress Administration (WPA) during the 1930's. The items on display—each one a reminder that pioneer life called for determination, hard work, and ingenuity—include tin candle holders, photos of moonshine stills, homemade axes, and several musical instruments, including a so-called ukelin, a cross between a ukelele and a violin. *Open daily except Thanksgiving Day, Christmas, and Easter.*

CHR Historic Bethabara Park, Winston-Salem

Cherry St. exit: 5.5 mi./11 min. North on Cherry St., left on University Pkwy., left on Bethabara Rd. A group of immigrant Germans from Saxony, who were members of an evangelical Protestant denomination called the United Brethren (or the Moravians), settled here in 1753, founding Bethabara, the community that today is called Winston-Salem. At this park you will find an archeological site of the original community in addition to three restored buildings and a reconstructed fort. In the 1788 parish house, which contains the minister's quarters, you'll see period furnishings and unusual tile stoves. The 1782 potter's house displays samples of bowls, plates, and other ceramic objects found at this important site of colonial craftsmanship. On view at the 1803 brewer's house are 18th-century German books. The new visitor center contains a slide show and exhibits on the history of the Moravians, the early Bethabara settlement and its trades, and the archeology of the site. *Grounds open year-round; buildings open daily Apr.–mid-Dec.*

270. *A flowering cherry tree and beds of tulips—the very essence of springtime.*

210 217B High Point Museum

Exit 210: 12 mi./19 min. South on Rte. 68, left on Centennial St., left on Rte. 70A (Lexington Ave). Exit 217B: 10.5 mi./17 min. West on Rte. 70A (Lexington Ave). The city of High Point, named for the distinction of being the highest point along the railroad line between Goldsboro and Charlotte, is now noted as one of America's leading producers of furniture and hosiery. This museum traces the Piedmont area's history over three centuries, with changing displays of toys, telephones, firearms, textiles, and an exhibit on the community's black heritage. On the grounds are two log buildings where costumed guides demonstrate candlemaking, spinning, weaving, and open-hearth cooking on weekends. *Open Tues.–Sat. and P.M. Sun.*

126 Hagan-Stone Park

8 mi./12 min. South on Rte. 421, right on Hagan-Stone Park Rd. The crucial role of tobacco farming in the development of the region is always in evidence as you explore this 409-acre park, named for two well-known local citizens. At the Lorillard tobacco exhibit, photos and periodicals explain the planting, picking, and curing processes. Even the park's office, a log cabin from the Civil War era, once served as a storage barn for tobacco leaves. Nature lovers will find several inviting trails, including one that leads to a reconstructed 1846 wood-frame schoolhouse. A 23-acre lake offers paddleboating, rowboating, and fishing. *Open year-round.*

266 270 North Carolina Botanical Garden, Chapel Hill

Exit 266: 7 mi./12 min. South on Rte. 86, north on Rte. 15/501, right on Laurel Hill Rd. Exit 270: 10 mi./16 min. South on Rte. 15/501, left on Laurel Hill Rd. The white ash tree, which furnishes the wood for most baseball bats, and the hardy witch hazel shrub, with a bark, twigs, and leaves that supply the essentials for a classic American skin lotion and flowers that appear in autumn after its leaves have fallen, are only two of the numerous species you'll find at this orderly 500-acre complex of trees, shrubs, and small plants. There are also sections devoted to herb gardens and poisonous plants, as well as one of the best collections of carnivorous plants in the country. Two miles of informative, well-marked trails show the way. *Open daily except Thanksgiving Day, Christmas, and New Year's Day.*

270 Sarah P. Duke Gardens, Durham

5 mi./9 min. North on Rte. 15/501 and Bypass 15/501, south on Rte. 751; follow signs. Nearly every part of these serene gardens, located on Duke University's west campus, is a minor masterpiece of design. You can follow one of three descending paths past a riot of chrysanthemums to a rose garden of formal elegance. In the H.L. Blomquist Garden, step carefully across the native-plants pool on a series of old millstones and enjoy the bleeding hearts, rhododendrons, and hundreds of other rare and native plants shaded by vines and magnolias. The view from the wisteria-covered pergola will further delight the eye and soothe the spirit. *Open year-round.*

408 Moores Creek National Battlefield

14 mi./20 min. West on Rte. 210; follow signs. In February 1776 the quiet of this stretch of woods and rolling meadows was dramatically shattered when a band of patriots successfully ambushed 1,600 kilted Highlanders and area Loyalists who had been recruited by the royal governor. This small victory resulted in North Carolina's vote for independence in Philadelphia a few months later.

Today the informative visitor center illustrates the skirmish with original weapons and an audiovisual program. The History Trail leads through the battleground and along the creek, and a nature trail features plants that were important to the economy of the 18th century. *Open daily except Christmas and New Year's Day.*

408 U.S.S. North Carolina Battleship Memorial

16 mi./20 min. West on Rte. 210, left on Rte. 421; follow signs. This impressive memorial to the 10,000 North Carolinians who died in

408. *Although outmoded, this World War II battlewagon is still an impressive sight.*

World War II faithfully re-creates what military life was like on one of the most powerful battleships of its time. A self-guiding tour lets visitors explore the pilothouse and engine rooms, see how meals were prepared, inspect the quarters of the 2,000-man crew, climb up and down ladders and into a gun turret, examine a Kingfisher floatplane, and aim antiaircraft guns. A summertime sound-and-light show with simulated battle effects illustrates the ship's proud history. *Open year-round. Admission charged.*

ROUTE 132 New Hanover County Museum of Lower Cape Fear, Wilmington

5 mi./15 min. Continue on Rte. 132, right on Rte. 17 (becomes Market St.). A beautifully crafted model of Wilmington's busy harbor in 1863 serves as a centerpiece in this museum, which focuses on the city as a major southern port in the 19th century. The collection also includes artifacts from the Lower Cape Fear Indians, Civil War weapons, samples of early exports and imports, historic photos, antique clothing and furnishings, and a variety of domestic items and tools. Such historical displays, along with the knowledgeable staff, make the museum an especially fine place to begin a visit to Wilmington, where you will find many other historic houses, museums, and gardens. *Open Tues.–Sat. and P.M. Sun. except holidays.*

ROUTE 132 Carolina Beach State Park

14 mi./25 min. Continue on Rte. 132 and Rte. 421. Essentially a large sand dune topped with live oaks, this small park on the Cape Fear River also comprises grasslands and thick, swampy vegetation in its remarkably varied terrain. Ferns, mosses, pines, grasses, even insect-digesting plants such as the sundew, bladderwort, and Venus's-flytrap (found only within a 60-mile radius)—all these grow along the well-marked nature trails. Songbirds as well as ospreys and laughing gulls swoop overhead, and white-tailed deer, marsh rabbits, and raccoons may occasionally be seen. A marina on the river provides launching ramps and boating supplies. *Open daily except Christmas.*

132. *Open and closed leaves attest to the deadly efficiency of the Venus's-flytrap.*

ROUTE 132 Fort Fisher State Historic Site

22 mi./30 min. Continue on Rte. 132 and on Rte. 421. The massive earthworks erected here at the outset of the Civil War gave Confederate forces control of the Cape Fear River and kept Wilmington's port open to supplies for General Lee's army. Visitors today can stroll through the remains of the mounds and fortifications and a restored palisade. The museum uses old photos, drawings, and supplies recovered from sunken blockade-running ships to explain the fortifications and the battles that took place. *Open Mon.–Sat. and P.M. Sun. Apr.–Oct.; Tues.–Sat. and P.M. Sun. Nov.–Mar.*

ROUTE 132 North Carolina Aquarium at Fort Fisher

22.5 mi./30 min. Continue on Rte. 132 and Rte. 421. Nestled in dunes and surrounded by nature trails, this aquarium complex features intriguing exhibits and films about marine life and coastal ecology. More than 15 aquariums hold sharks, lobsters, endangered sea turtles, tropical reef fishes, and other local sea life. One tank has clams, crabs, and whelks that visitors may handle. The humpback whale is thoroughly analyzed in exhibits on whale behavior, and you can view a 49-foot replica of this marine mammal. *Open Mon.–Sat. and P.M. Sun. except Thanksgiving Day, Christmas, and New Year's Day. Admission free but donations encouraged.*

86. *The few plants that have gained a foothold here stand out in the vastness of the dunes.*

42 | West of the Pecos Museum

5 min. North on Rte. 285. In the late 19th century, law "west of the Pecos" meant almost no law at all; and this museum, which is set in and around a turn-of-the-century hotel, tells the story of the Old West at its wildest. In the saloon of the Orient Hotel you can see the spot where a local man dispatched two outlaws. Step outside the museum proper and you'll see the grave of gunfighter Clay Allison, a hanging tree, a jail, and a reproduction of the famous Jersey Lilly Saloon, where Judge Roy Bean dispensed frontier justice. The less violent side of cowboy life is illustrated with displays about ranching and rodeos, reconstructed rooms from a school and a church, and the restored hotel bridal suite. *Open Mon.–Sat. and P.M. Sun. Admission charged.*

86 | Monahans Sandhills State Park

1 min. North on Park Rd. 41. Sand dunes, some 70 feet high, cover this 3,840-acre park. Some dunes shift when blown by the wind, but others are secured by scrubby growths of Harvard shin oak and sagebrush. An interpretive center provides information on the park's animals, plants, history, and geology; the center's large windows look out on the feeding and watering stations that attract wildlife. The past is evoked by an 1880's windmill and a railroad section house from the days when the Texas & Pacific Railroad made a water stop here. A working oil well demonstrates a modern industry in operation. *Open year-round. Admission charged.*

116 | The Presidential Museum, Odessa

2 mi./6 min. Northwest on Rte. 385 (Grant Ave.), left on 7th St. Created after the assassination of President John F. Kennedy, this sophisticated museum honors the office of the presidency and the men who have occupied it. The collection includes portraits and autographs of former presidents, campaign buttons and other memorabilia, excellent reproductions of the Inauguration gowns worn by First Ladies, and an exhibit on the changes in political campaigning brought about by radio and television. Broader topics of American history are presented in changing exhibits. *Open Tues.–Sat. except holidays.*

126 | Water Wonderland, Odessa

5 min. North on Rte. 1788, left on Rte. 80. More than 20 rides and attractions entice the adventurous to hurl down steep water slides, negotiate simulated mountain rapids in a tube, and ride a 30-mile-an-hour water toboggan. A wave pool with 4-foot swells, a beach for sunbathing, and coves for small children are especially popular. A miniature golf course and electronic video games are among the non-aquatic attractions. *Open Memorial Day–Labor Day. Admission charged.*

136 | Petroleum Museum, Library, and Hall of Fame, Midland

2 min. North on Rte. 349, left on N. Frontage Rd. The dramatic history of the oil industry is presented in this well-endowed museum. An immense diorama of the floor of the Permian sea that once covered the area shows replicas of the thousands of underwater creatures whose remains formed the organic substance we call oil. Among the other excellent displays you can see are a re-created street corner of a 1920's West Texas boomtown, polished rock cores that were taken from oil wells, a simulated view of an oil pipeline from a patrol plane, and the fiery spectacle of an oil well blowout. On the grounds outside the museum, the collection of oil rigs ranges from a 1910 cable tool model to modern pumping units. *Open Mon.–Sat. and P.M. Sun. except Thanksgiving Day, Christmas Eve, and Christmas. Admission charged.*

136 | The Museum of the Southwest, Midland

5 min. North on Rte. 349, left on Missouri St. Housed in an elegant brick mansion built in 1934, this fine collection includes paintings by the Taos Society of Artists, a bronze sculpture by western artist Frederic Remington, and a mural-size sand painting. The cultural history of the Southwest is represented by wood carvings, pottery, textiles, tools, Indian baskets, and a tepee. Sharing the grounds with this museum is a children's museum with hands-on exhibits and a planetarium, and there's a research center. *Open Tues.–Sat. and P.M. Sun. except holidays.*

177 | Heritage Museum, Big Spring

3 min. South on Rte. 87, left on 6th St. For some 12,000 years Indians, pioneers, travelers, cattle ranchers, and a variety of animals have been attracted to the watering hole for which the town is named—a colorful history that is recalled here with artifacts and mural-size pictures. The arrival of the Texas & Pacific Railroad in 1881 is represented by the Iron Horse steam whistle in the transportation room, which sounds at the press of a button. Ranching is illustrated by guns, saddles, branding irons, and 54 pairs of horns (some spanning as much as 10 feet) that were once proudly carried by the famous Texas longhorn cattle. Re-created period rooms and a collection of old photographs recall pioneer days. *Open Tues.–Sat. except holidays.* ♿

177 | Big Spring State Recreation Area

4 mi./8 min. South on Rte. 87, right on Rte. FM700. Scenic Mountain, a limestone-capped mesa 200 feet high, is the setting for this urban park. A 2½-mile road carved from its steep sides provides panoramic views of the city of Big Spring and the Texas plains. On the informative nature trail, markers identify the native vegetation, and hikers are likely to see jackrabbits, cottontails, ground squirrels, and many species of birds. Highlights include a

136. *These mechanical monsters were created to bring forth the riches of oil.*

prairie-dog town and bluffs marked with graffiti done by travelers who have stopped here from the 1870's to the present. *Open year-round. Admission charged.* 🏕🚶♿

210 | Lake Colorado City State Recreation Area

6 mi./10 min. South on Rte. FM2836. Since Lake Colorado City is warmer than other area lakes (its water circulates through Colorado City's electric power plant), it offers a longer season for water-skiing and swimming, and anglers catch bigger catfish and bass because the warmer water gives the fish an extended growing season. Mesquite, short grasses, and shrubs provide a habitat for many varieties of songbirds. In winter the lake attracts flocks of migratory waterfowl. *Open year-round. Admission charged.* 🏕⛺🚐🏊🎣♿

244 | Pioneer City-County Museum, Sweetwater

4 min. North on Rte. 70, right on Rte. 80, left on Ragland St. This spacious house, built in 1906, contains Indian artifacts, early ranching and farming implements, photos of pioneers, and other items that have figured in the area's past. History is brought to life by re-creations of an old courtroom, a pioneer schoolroom, and a leather and saddle shop. There are displays of antique toys and dolls and late 19th-century women's fashions. A unique exhibit focuses on the Women Airforce Service Pilots, who trained at nearby Avenger Airfield to ferry aircraft to World War II battle zones. *Open P.M. Tues.–Sat. except holidays.*

283A | Buffalo Gap Historic Village

16 mi./25 min. South on Rte. 83/277; continue on Rte. 89, right on Elm St. This charmingly restored frontier village has an interesting history. Underground water produced unusually lush vegetation, which in turn attracted herds of buffalo; they were followed by buffalo hunters, and in 1874 the area's first permanent residents settled here. The sandstone courthouse and jail, constructed in 1878 when Buffalo Gap was the county seat, has gunports and fortresslike walls designed to withstand possible Comanche attacks. It is surrounded

by 15 original and re-created buildings of the period. A railroad station, physician's office, barbershop, wagon barn, cabinet mill, blacksmith's shop, and other structures are furnished with items in daily use in the late 1800's. *Open daily mid-Mar.–mid-Nov.; weekends in winter except Thanksgiving Day and Christmas. Admission charged.* 🏕

290. *The photographer seems to be as interesting to the giraffes as they to him.*

290 | Abilene Zoological Gardens

5 min. South on Rte. 322; follow signs. This excellent zoo enables visitors to compare the wild turkeys, pronghorns, bison, javelinas, and coyotes of the Texas plains with animals that share a similar environment in the African veld: gnus, zebras, elephants, lions, ostriches, hyenas, and antelopes. A bridge over the giraffe area offers the viewer the unusual experience of seeing these towering animals from above. Other creatures here include sea lions, bears, primates, and alligators, as well as unusual birds and snakes. Native plants and wildflowers help to make the zoo resemble a natural environment. *Open daily except Thanksgiving Day, Christmas, and New Year's Day. Admission charged.* 🏕♿

370 Stephenville Historical House Museum

25 mi./30 min. South on Rte. 108, left on Washington St. A steep-roofed limestone cottage built for a former Confederate colonel in 1869 is surrounded by a collection of 19th-century structures. They include log cabins, houses, a barn, and a schoolhouse, all carefully restored and outfitted with furnishings of the time. Indian artifacts, minerals, and tools are displayed in the Carriage House. The Chapel on the Bosque, a Presbyterian church with Gothic windows and a spire adorned with fish-scale shingles, contains an exhibit that illustrates spiritual growth in the region. *Open P.M. Fri.–Sun. Apply at Chamber of Commerce for admission.*

370. *Gothic architecture with gingerbread trim reveals the colonel's eclectic taste.*

386 Lake Mineral Wells State Park

19 mi./28 min. North on Rte. 281, right on Rte. 180. Small oaks and mesquite cover the rolling hills of this park and frame the 646-acre lake, which attracts boaters, swimmers, and fishermen. Steep-walled gulches in the sandstone and shale are a challenge to rock climbers. Hikers enjoy the 5 miles of trails through bottomland groves of pecan, cottonwood, cedar elm, and red oak. The park provides an excellent habitat for many animals, including white-tailed deer, wild turkeys, opossums, armadillos, and coyotes. *Open year-round. Admission charged.*

409 Holland Lake Park, Weatherford

1 min. North on Santa Fe Dr., right on Holland Lake Dr. The graceful woods and cattails reflected in tranquil Holland Lake serve as a contrast to a garden of cacti and other plants native to the arid Texas plains. The park is a pleasant place for a picnic and a walk on a nature trail. Local history is evoked by two restored 19th-century log cabins, which are connected by a single roof and contain pioneer furnishings and tools. The bullet-scarred walls of one cabin attest to the killing of George McClesky by Indians in 1873. *Open year-round.*

437B Fort Worth, TX 76109

Convention and Visitors Bureau, 123 E. Exchange Ave. (817) 624-4741. Although a large modern city, Fort Worth has not forgotten the Texas of song and story. Activities at the Stockyards Historical District on the north side include cattle trading and shopping for rodeo gear and western wear. But the city also boasts three world-famous art museums: the Kimbell, which displays works dating from pre-Columbian times to the present day; the Amon Carter, which has a fine collection of sculpture, photographs, and paintings featuring, but not limited to, the American West; and the Modern Art Museum of Fort Worth, noted for its 20th-century art. The Museum of Science and History offers imaginative exhibits for children and adults. The terraced Water Gardens enhance the city center.

467A Dallas, TX 75202

Convention & Visitors Bureau, 400 S. Houston St. (lobby of Union Station). (214) 746-6700. Highlights of life in Dallas include the Cotton Bowl, Neiman-Marcus, banking, business, glass-walled skyscrapers, and the $50 million Dallas Museum of Art. At Fair Park the old and the new are combined with a steam train museum, a science museum, gardens, and an aquarium. In Old City Park a bit of 19th-century Dallas is preserved. There's a justly famous zoo and some unusual theme museums, such as the Biblical Arts Center and the Telephone Pioneer Museum. Although they recall a time of trauma, the John F. Kennedy Memorial Plaza and the Texas School Book Depository attract many visitors.

556 Tyler Municipal Rose Garden

12 mi./24 min. South on Rte. 69, right on Front St. W. Hundreds of varieties of roses grow among archways, camellia bushes, fountains, pavilions, and around an ornamental pond, creating an ambience of beauty and fragrance. More than 38,000 rosebushes, a tribute to the region that produces one-third of the commercially grown rosebushes in America, bloom in this 22-acre garden from May through October. A large greenhouse is filled year-round with such tropical plants as the red passion vine, lavender bougainvillea, Amazon lily, hibiscus, and bird-of-paradise. *Garden open year-round; greenhouse open daily except holidays.*

617 Franks Antique Doll Museum, Marshall

5 mi./12 min. North on Rte. 59, left on Grand Ave. This delightful collection of 1,600 antique and unusual dolls includes exquisite French and German bisque dolls, milliner's models, Shirley Temple dolls, dolls made by Limoges and Dresden china companies, Gibson girls, Kewpie dolls, mechanical dolls, and character babies, all outfitted in costumes authentic in their periods. The museum is located behind the grand late-Victorian house of Clara and Francis Franks; it also features buggies, miniature furniture, iron and tin toys, dishes, trunks, and of course dollhouses. *Open by chance, or for appointment call (214) 935-3065. Admission charged.*

633 T. C. Lindsey & Co., Jonesville

3 min. North on Rte. 134. This tin-roofed old-time country general store and post office has been in business since 1847. Veteran clerks boast that the emporium is second to none in its stock of one- and two-gallus overalls, sunbonnets, walking sticks, mint-condition wood cookstoves, bullwhips, wringer washing machines, mule collars, and jawbreakers. The

467A. *As the oil wells went deeper, the Dallas skyline they helped to finance went higher.*

goods for sale are displayed among mounted sets of longhorns, deer heads, butter churns, and thousands of antiques. The store has been used as a set for several movies. *Open Mon.– Sat. except holidays.*

18A R. W. Norton Art Gallery, Shreveport

3 mi./15 min. South on Line Ave., left on Thora Blvd. This outstanding collection is best known for its works by Old West artists Charles M. Russell and Frederic Remington. However, the nearly four centuries of sculpture, painting, and decorative European and American art represented here include such diverse works as 16th-century Flemish tapestries, sculptures by Rodin, and the work of silversmith and patriot Paul Revere. Each spring visitors come to see a different kind of artistic display: a rainbow of azaleas blooming beneath the stately pines. *Open P.M. Tues.– Sun. except holidays.*   ♿

19A Hamel's Amusement Park, Shreveport

6 mi./12 min. Northwest on Spring St., right on Lake St., right on Clyde Fant Pkwy., right on E. 70th St. North Louisiana's largest roller coaster and such other favorites as the Tilt-A-Whirl, Scrambler, bumper cars, and a water-splashed log ride delight visitors of all ages. For small children, a merry-go-round and additional rides are housed in the Kiddie Barn. A train that travels the 15-acre park's perimeter reveals the various attractions and manicured grounds, and from the top of the Ferris wheel you can see the Red River and beyond. *Open Wed.–Fri. evenings and P.M. weekends June–Aug.; P.M. weekends Sept.–Oct. and Mar.–May. Admission charged.*

19A Barnwell Garden and Art Center, Shreveport

3 min. Northwest on Spring St., right on Crockett St. A large glassed-in botanical conservatory is filled with tropical and exotic trees, native shrubs, and seasonal flowers, while another wing that is part of the same building displays visiting and permanent exhibits of works by local artists. Barnwell's beautiful grounds contain a sculpture garden as well as a reflecting pool. Interspersed among towering sycamore and cottonwood trees are scenic overlooks from which visitors can enjoy a panoramic view of the Red River. *Open Mon.–Fri. and P.M. weekends.*   🚶 ♿

33 / 47 Lake Bistineau State Park

Exit 33: 13 mi./27 min. South on Rte. 157, left on Rte. 3227, right on Rte. 164, right on Rte. 163. Exit 47: 13 mi./25 min. South on Rte. 7, right on Rte. 164, left on Rte. 163. A hint of wilderness pervades Lake Bistineau, which was formed by the damming of a serpentine Louisiana bayou. There's a boat ramp and rental boats for fishermen, who try for largemouth and yellow bass, black crappie, bluegill, bullheads, and sunfish. The large beach is popular with swimmers. The picnic grounds and a play area are set among venerable pines. Visitors come to see the hardwood trees draped with Spanish moss, for which the 750-acre park is known. *Open year-round. Admission charged.*   ⛽ ⛺ 🚐 🏊 🎣 ♿

47 Germantown Colony Museum, Minden

10 mi./25 min. North on Lee St., right on Broadway, left on Elm St., right on Germantown Rd.; follow signs. Small clusters of original and restored pioneer log houses and their outbuildings form the remnants of a communal colony of German settlers established here in 1835. Tools and other items displayed in the blacksmith's shop and smokehouse testify to the labors of the settlers, while the tombstones in the hillside graveyard tell of many lives cut short. Ancient mulberry, persimmon, and pear trees on the grounds attract a colorful assortment of birds. *Open Wed.–Sat. and P.M. Sun. Admission charged.*   ⛽

67 Lake Claiborne State Park, Homer

16 mi./30 min. North on Rte. 9, right on Rte. 518, right on Rte. 146. This 6,400-acre lake surrounded by rolling pine-covered hills is a favorite with water-skiers. In the quieter stretches of the lake, fishermen try for channel catfish, largemouth and striped bass, black crappie, and bream. Clear water attracts swimmers to the park's sandy beach; nearby there are boats for rent. More than a hundred picnic sites are scattered throughout the countryside and along the lakeshore under fine old hardwood trees. *Open year-round. Admission charged.*   ⛽ ⛺ 🚐 🚶 🏊 🎣 ♿

84 Louisiana Tech Horticultural and Equine Centers, Ruston

5 min. South on Tech Dr., right on Rte. 80, left on Tech Farm Rd. Visitors to this university are free to browse through the spacious greenhouses filled with fig, banana, and pencil trees, night-blooming cereus, poinsettias, orchids, and tropical ferns. Seasonal shows include a candlelight Christmas walk (the first two weeks of December) that features thousands of poinsettias. The stables, barns, and paddocks of the equine center can also be toured. Owners bring their horses here for breeding, training, and other activities. *Horticultural center open Mon.–Fri. except holidays and last two weeks in Dec.; equine center open daily except holidays.*

118 Louisiana Purchase Gardens and Zoo, Monroe

7 min. South on Rte. 165 Bypass, right on Tichelli Rd. The zoo, built on a swamp with the waterways incorporated in the design, contains a large collection of rare African and Asian animals and is known for its Old World primates, particularly its lemurs. Many of the exhibits can be seen from a tour boat, which winds lazily through the gardens, shaded by Spanish moss-draped cypresses and oaks. A train with a coal-fired steam engine also carries passengers through the park and sometimes has to wait for a free-ranging antelope or bison to move off the tracks. Pelicans, flamingos, ducks, deer, and other native creatures find refuge here. Flowering plants are scattered throughout the park, named for the U.S's great 1803 real estate bargain. *Open daily except Thanksgiving Day, Christmas, and New Year's Day. Admission charged.*

153 Poverty Point State Commemorative Area

18 mi./30 min. North on Rte. 17, right on Rte. 134, left on Rte. 577. Archeologists can only guess at the purpose of these mounds and ridges created along Bayou Macon about 3,000 years ago through long and arduous labor by the inhabitants of Poverty Point. Excavations have turned up thousands of artifacts, including beads, stone tools, spears, and numerous baked-clay objects that were used for cooking. The 400-acre site can be toured by car, but for a closer look visitors can take a tram to the largest mound, where many climb to the top. If an archeological dig is in progress, this too may be seen. Audiovisual programs and artifacts are displayed at the visitor center, where an observation tower provides an overall view of the mounds. *Open daily except holidays. Admission charged.*

4B Vicksburg National Military Park

2 min. West on Clay St. As a major Confederate strongpoint on the Mississippi, Vicksburg resisted a number of attacks, but a 47-day siege in 1863 finally forced the city to surrender, thus opening the river to Union forces and northern shipping. Markers and monuments in a profusion of kinds and sizes line the paved 16-mile drive through the park and the cemetery. The 17,000 Union graves are mute reminders of the human cost of war. At one end of the park the U.S.S. *Cairo* Museum displays artifacts and the recovered remains of the ironclad Union gunboat *Cairo*, the first ship to be sunk by mines detonated by electricity. At the other end the visitor center offers artifacts, life-size exhibits, and an 18-minute film on the Vicksburg siege. Civil War books, maps, and other materials can be purchased at the center. *Park open year-round; visitor center and museum open daily except Christmas. Admission charged.*

46 The Mississippi Agriculture and Forestry Museum, Jackson

5 mi./10 min. North on I-55 to Exit 98B (Lakeland Dr.), east on Lakeland Dr. Life-size tableaux, complete with sound effects and voices, show vivid re-creations of loggers in action, workers hauling bales of cotton, and life in a sharecropper's cottage. Themes include logging days, "the rail age" (including early steam-driven farm machinery), and "the era of roads." Individual exhibits explain cotton processing (there is an authentic Bisland cotton gin), the impact of electricity, and the economics of farm life.

Also here is the National Agricultural Aviation Museum, which focuses on the 20th-century fight against the boll weevil, featuring crop-dusting planes from the 1930's to the present. Some strange boll-weevil catchers of pre-spraying days are also on display.

If you cross the road to the Fortenberry-Parkman Farm, you can see workers in 1920-period dress and talk to them about rural life in the South during the early 20th century. *Open Tues.–Sat. and P.M. Sun. except Thanksgiving Day, Christmas, and New Year's Day. Admission charged.*

118. *Azaleas brighten the winding route of the tour boat through the gardens and the zoo.*

4B. *Monument commemorates the role of the Union navy in taking Vicksburg in 1863.*

46   Jackson, MS 39216

Visitor Information Center, 1180 Lakeland Dr. (601) 960-1800. Jackson's importance as a state capital and rail center brought destruction during the Civil War, but it has also helped to make this the state's leading city today; and the sense of history here is still strong. The mansion where 40 state governors have lived, which briefly served as headquarters for Union general Ulysses S. Grant, is open to the public and furnished with excellent period pieces. The State Historical Museum in the 1839 Greek revival Old State Capitol features dioramas illustrating the history of the state; the Museum of Natural Science also uses dioramas to good effect. The homes of two former Jackson mayors are of interest: The Oaks, an antebellum wood-frame cottage hand-hewn in 1846, and the Manship House, a charming Gothic revival structure built about 10 years later. The history and culture of blacks in Mississippi is featured in the Smith-Robertson Museum and Cultural Center.

77   Roosevelt State Park

5 min. North on Rte. 13; follow signs. Built around Shadow Lake in the 1930's and named for the president at the time, Franklin Roosevelt, this pleasant, well-planned park is deservedly popular. The swimming area boasts a tall wooden diving tower and wide docks for sunbathing. Other attractions include boating, tennis, miniature golf, and softball.

Some exceptional hiking trails with views of the lake meander through a dense oak forest and past magnolias, kudzu vines, and a wide variety of wildflowers. Flocks of geese can at times be seen roaming the roads in the park. *Open year-round. Admission charged.*

150   Okatibbee Lake

8 mi./15 min. North on Rte. 11, left on Rte. 19; follow signs. Created as part of a flood control project for the upper Chickasawhay River in 1962, Okatibbee Lake has developed into an extensive recreational area. There are miles of access to the lake's irregular shoreline, six swimming beaches, picnic grounds sheltered by tall pines, boat launches, campgrounds, basketball courts, softball fields, and a water park with swimming pool and elaborate water slides. The Lake Resource Center at Damsite West provides information about the best places for fishing and bird-watching. An island (visible from atop Okatibbee Dam) is home to the largest egret rookery in Mississippi. *Open year-round.*

150   Jimmie Rodgers Museum, Meridian
153

Exit 150: 3 mi./10 min. North on Rte. 11, right on 8th St., left on 39th Ave., left on Jimmie Rodgers Dr. Exit 153: 6 mi./25 min. North on 22nd Ave., left on 8th St., right on 39th Ave.; left on Jimmie Rodgers Dr. In the 1920's, fans knew him as "the singing brakeman" and "the blue yodeler," and he became the first country music superstar. Born in Meridian in 1897, Jimmie Rodgers really did become a railroad man, and this small museum tells his story. It has records, sheet music, family photos, railroad memorabilia, his boots, and his guitar. He was the first artist in Nashville's Country Music Hall of Fame. Each May, country music stars from all over the nation gather for a week-long Jimmie Rodgers Memorial Festival. The museum is located in an authentic turn-of-the-century park. *Open Mon.–Sat. and P.M. Sun. except Thanksgiving Day, Christmas, and New Year's Day. Admission charged.*

150   Merrehope Mansion, Meridian
153

Exit 150: 3 mi./10 min. North on Rte. 11, right on 8th St., left on Martin Luther King, Jr. Dr.; follow signs. Exit 153: 3 mi./12 min. North on 22nd Ave., left on 8th St., right on Martin Luther King, Jr. Dr.; follow signs. This 20-room modified Greek revival mansion, with a 1968 name formed from the words *Meridian, restoration,* and *hope,* started out as a small cottage. That original structure was one of the few buildings left standing when Gen. William T. Sherman's Union troops set fire to the town in February 1864. Elegant details abound: the deep ruby glass framing the front door, crystal chandeliers, elaborately carved moldings, high canopy beds, even the small mirrors set between table legs that gave ladies a chance to check their petticoat hems. The "Trees of Christmas" exhibit (early December) affords visitors a look at the seasonal decorations of different cultures and various periods. *Open Mon.–Sat. and P.M. Sun. except July 4, Thanksgiving Day, Christmas Eve and Day, and New Year's Eve and Day. Admission charged.*

153   Clarkco State Park

20 mi./25 min. South on Rte. 45; follow signs. The calm, warm waters of Clarkco Lake make this park a favorite of water-skiers and fishermen. There are boats and canoes for rent, and a sun deck and sandy beach attract swimmers. The short nature trail or the longer backpacking trail passes through the lovely woods of oak, pine, and holly. Look for the "double tree," which is a natural combination of a pine and a sweet gum—an amazing amalgam of needles and leaves. *Open year-round. Admission charged.*

71A Mound State Monument

14 mi./16 min. South on Rte. 69 to Mound-ville; follow signs. Scattered across a meadow on the Black Warrior River are 20 remarkably intact earthen mounds, dating from a time when as many as 3,000 Mississippian Indians lived in the area (A.D.1000–1500). A museum, built over two burial sites, provides a memorable perspective of an ancient culture. Here in their burial position are skeletons and objects intended for the afterlife, undiscovered for more than 500 years. Other displays interpret the findings; and outdoors, the main ceremonial mound, topped with a re-creation of a temple, can be climbed for an overview of the site. There is also a reconstructed Indian village, with life-size (and lifelike) figures engaged in everyday tasks. *Open year-round. Admission charged.*

71B Tuscaloosa, AL 35402

Convention and Visitors Bureau, 2200 University Blvd. (205) 758-3072. From 1826 to 1846 this was the capital of Alabama. Cotton was king, and Greek revival was the prevailing architectural style. Economic conditions declined and the capital moved to Montgomery, but reminders of ancient Greece can still be seen in the many attractive columned houses here. In the historic district on the University of Alabama campus, the Gorgas House is open to the public, and the President's Mansion is a stately example of Greek revival. Also on the campus are the Alabama Museum of Natural History and the Children's Hands-On Museum, good architectural examples of their kind. Open elsewhere in town are the Battle-Friedman House, with its elegant chandeliers and family silver, and the Moody-Warner House, which features excellent period furnishings and a superb collection of American art.

73 Lake Lurleen State Park

16 mi./30 min. West on Rte. 82, right on Rte. 21; follow signs. Named after Lurleen Burns Wallace (Alabama's first woman governor and a native of the area), Lake Lurleen is a mean-dering body of green water in a wooded setting. Hiking trails follow the edge of the lake and lead into the surrounding pine forests. Fishermen try for largemouth bass, crappie, and catfish. Boats, canoes, and paddleboats are for rent, and swimmers enjoy the spacious white sand beach. *Open year-round. Admission charged.*

100 Tannehill Historical State Park

3 mi./8 min. East on Tannehill Pkwy.; follow signs. This rustic, densely wooded park pays tribute to Alabama's iron industry and to mid-19th-century life in the region. Tannehill, a major source of armament for the South in the Civil War, was the precursor of the once-mighty steel industry that helped create the nearby city of Birmingham; and in the Iron and Steel Museum all aspects of production are explained. Close by is a reconstruction of the furnaces, where you can climb atop the 50-foot chimney for an overview of the area. The park has a working gristmill, and more

100. *In its wooded setting, the rustic mill is powered by the overshot water wheel.*

than 40 other restored homes and commercial buildings moved from other parts of the state create the ambience of a 19th-century village, complete with a church, a blacksmith's shop, and farm buildings. *Open year-round. Admission charged.*

106 Oak Mountain State Park
136

Exit 106: 10 mi./15 min. East on I-459, right on I-65 to Exit 246; follow signs. Exit 136: 10 mi./15 min. West on I-459, left on I-65 to Exit 246; follow signs. Opportunities for recreation here in Alabama's largest state park—nearly 10,000 acres set in a deep, wooded Appalachian valley—range from canoeing, fishing, swimming, and tennis to bike racing on a track and rugged mountain hiking. Those interested in waterside pursuits have three lakes to choose from, and there are some 30 miles of hiking trails. For the adventurous there's the rough, twisting mountain road to a parking lot and the half-mile walk to scenic Peavine Falls. *Open year-round. Admission charged.*

112 Bessemer Hall of History

2 mi./8 min. East on 18th St., left on Carolina Ave. Built in 1916, this light brown brick railway station, once a stop between New York and New Orleans (circa 1917 schedules are still posted), is now a museum. The recent past is represented by tools and photographs related to the town's beginnings as a producer of iron. Other displays include Civil War memorabilia, old telephones, an ensemble of gowns worn by turn-of-the-century belles, and a large quilt collection. One exhibit portrays every American president, and another depicts all the states. Artifacts created by the Indian residents in the area almost 1,000 years ago are also on display. *Open Tues.–Sat. Admission free but donations encouraged.*

125B Birmingham, AL 35203
126A

Convention & Visitors Bureau, 2027 1st Ave. N. (205) 252-9825. The character of the city as viewed from the base of Vulcan's statue on Red Mountain is vastly different from the smokestack industry image that originally inspired the 55-foot cast-iron monument. Alabama's largest city now boasts an excellent museum of fine arts, a children's museum, the Southern Museum of Flight, and the unique Red Mountain Museum, where walkways along a deep road cut allow you to study some 150 million years of layers of sedimentation and fossils from ancient seas.

You'll find a conservatory of rare plants and a charming Japanese garden at the Birmingham Botanical Gardens; the excellent zoo is nearby. Arlington Antebellum Home, a handsome Greek revival house, has extensive gardens and interesting collections of furniture and decorative art. The early days of the iron industry are recalled in the reconstructed Sloss Furnaces, now a walk-through museum.

185 Women's Army Corps Museum, Fort McClellan

10 mi./20 min. North on Rte. 21; enter Ft. McClellan at fourth entrance, Galloway Gate. Founded during World War II, the Women's Army Corps served the nation until 1978, when women were integrated into the regular service. Ft. McClellan, on the outskirts of Anniston, was the corps's last training center, and the museum traces the WAC's proud history, showing the women's evolution from neatly uniformed army auxiliaries at Teletypes to armed soldiers in camouflage fatigues. Exhibits include photos, recruiting posters, medals, re-created rooms, and changing uniform styles. Drums and other musical instruments and photos recall the corps's widely admired band, which was stationed here. *Open Mon.–Fri. except holidays.*

1 / 3 John Tanner State Park

Exit 1: 7 mi./15 min. South on Rte. 100, left on Rte. 16. Exit 3: 7 mi./15 min. South on Rte. 27, right on Rte. 16. With its ample sandy beach—the largest in a Georgia state park—this secluded 136-acre park is a summer favorite with locals, who come not only to swim but also to fish and boat in its two lakes. Canoes, pedal boats, and bicycles can be rented, and there is a miniature golf course, a nature trail, and a well-used exercise

23. *The architecture of Georgia's state capitol makes a classic statement of pride and power.*

trail as well. Tall pines towering over the campgrounds provide welcome shade in this part of the country where summer can be torrid. *Open year-round, weather permitting.*

13 Six Flags Over Georgia

2 min. South on Six Flags Dr. At this attractive, well-landscaped theme park just outside Atlanta, the first thing you are likely to hear is the screams of anguished delight coming from patrons of such aptly named attractions as Mindbender (a loop-the-loop), Free Fall (a 10-story drop), and Great Gasp (a parachute drop). Water rides take visitors over rapids and falls and down log chutes, but for those who prefer tamer excitements there are plenty of gentler options, such as an 1820's-style train that circles the park. Other attractions include a cartoon characters theater for youngsters, game arcades, and performances by divers, acrobats, and musicians. *Open daily June–Aug.; weekends only mid-Mar.–May, Sept.–Oct. Admission charged.*

23 Atlanta, GA 30303

Convention & Visitors Bureau, 233 Peachtree St., Suite 2000. (404) 521-6600. As this bustling modern metropolis continues to grow, the essence of the Old South becomes more difficult to find. One place to look for it is the Tullie Smith House Restoration, an 1840's farmhouse with typical outbuildings, herb gardens, and craft demonstrations. On the same site is the Swan House, a 20th-century Palladian-style structure with a formal boxwood garden. The Civil War Battle of Atlanta, depicted in the circular painted cyclorama at Grant Park, has sound and light effects and is viewed from a revolving platform. The High Museum of Art, in its handsome modern building on Peachtree Street, has an excellent reputation for its collections of European and American art. The birthplace and tomb of Nobel Prize winner Martin Luther King, Jr., are honored in a two-block national historic site. Other famous Georgians are commemorated in the Hall of Fame in the capitol, also home to the State Museum of Science and Industry.

35B / 35 · Georgia's Stone Mountain Park

25 mi./30 min. Exit 35B (headed east): north on I-285, right on Rte. 78. Exit 35 (headed west): proceed as above. Confederate heroes Jefferson Davis, Robert E. Lee, and Stonewall Jackson are the subjects of the world's largest bas-relief sculpture, carved on the face of Stone Mountain, a large mass of exposed granite. In spring and summer a nightly show of laser fireworks and music dramatizes the carving. Rides can be taken by cable-car, railroad, or riverboat. Other diversions include an antique car museum, a year-round ice skating rink, a golf course, miniature golf, and the 19-building Antebellum Plantation. *Open daily except Christmas. Admission charged.*

35B–35. *A memorial to Confederate heroes Davis, Lee, and Jackson is carved in stone.*

49 · Hard Labor Creek State Park

6 mi./8 min. East on Newborn Rd., left on E. Dixie Hwy., right on Fairplay St. Out of the depths of the Great Depression in the 1930's came this lovely 5,805-acre park created on marginal cropland by the Civilian Conservation Corps. The young men employed in this public works program planted forests, reshaped the land, built roads and picnic and camping facilities. This is the largest state park in Georgia, with two lakes that offer boating, swimming, and fishing. Many varieties of wildlife abound in the mixed pine and hardwood forest. There are hiking and riding trails, and the public golf course is one of the finest in the Southeast. *Park open year-round; golf course and beach open Tues.–Sun. Admission charged.*

51 · Madison-Morgan Cultural Center

4 min. North on Rte. 129/441. This cultural center in Madison is housed in an impressive brick structure, a former schoolhouse built in the Romanesque revival style in 1895. The past is recalled by the building itself, a history museum, and a restored classroom; the present is celebrated in changing exhibitions in four art galleries, as well as the musical and theatrical programs in the restored auditorium, which is noted for its excellent acoustics.

The museum features antique furnishings, tools, Civil War memorabilia, and a reconstructed log house. The classroom is frequently used as a learning laboratory where modern teaching methods are practiced in a setting with turn-of-the-century desks, blackboards, and accoutrements. At the center you can also get directions for seeing more of Madison, the town that Gen. William T. Sherman decreed was too beautiful to destroy on his devastating march to the sea in 1864. *Open daily except holidays. Admission charged.*

51 · Uncle Remus Museum, Eatonton

20 mi./25 min. South on Rte. 129/441. Joel Chandler Harris, creator and author of the Uncle Remus stories, was born in Eatonton in 1848. As a boy he was apprenticed to Joseph Addison Turner, who published a newspaper, *The Countryman*, on his Turnwold plantation. There Harris got a solid writer's education and, through stories told by plantation slaves, the inspiration for his later literary success. Shadow boxes containing wood carvings of Br'er Rabbit, Br'er Bear, Br'er Fox, and other "critters" from Harris's writings, first editions of his works, and memorabilia are displayed in a slave cabin, authentically restored and furnished to look just as young Harris might have known it. *Open Wed.– Mon. Sept.–May. Admission charged.*

55 · A. H. Stephens State Park

3 mi./6 min. North on Rte. 22, right on Rte. 278; follow signs. Although dependent on crutches and a wheelchair, farmer and lawyer Alexander H. Stephens served the South as a member of the state legislature, U.S. congressman, governor of Georgia, and vice president of the Confederacy. His home, Liberty Hall, preserved in the park, includes original furnishings; the adjacent Confederate Museum recalls the Civil War era with weapons, objects from the home front, and several of Stephens's personal belongings. The park also has a swimming pool, a bathhouse, and two lakes. There's a beaver trail and an informative pamphlet describing the life cycle of this busy rodent. *Park open year-round; historic site open Tues.–Sun. except Thanksgiving Day and Christmas. Admission charged for historic site.*

65 · Augusta, GA 30913

Convention & Visitors Bureau, 1301 Greene St. (404) 826-4722. Known to golfers primarily as the home of the Masters Tournament (held during the first full week in April), Augusta also has a rich historic and architectural heritage. Perhaps the best way to appreciate the many old homes, churches, and civic buildings in Augusta is to take a walking or trolley tour of the downtown area, using the easy-to-follow map provided by the Convention & Visitors Bureau. The tour includes such notable sites as St. Paul's Episcopal Church, the Old Government House, the Victorian houses of Olde Town, the Augusta–Richmond County Museum, and Meadow Garden (home of a signer of the Declaration of Independence). The Gertrude Herbert Memorial Art Institute, built as a residence in 1818, has a striking spiral staircase as well as art exhibits.

18 Hopeland Gardens, Aiken

7 mi./14 min. South on Rte. 19, right on Dupree Pl. Live oaks tower over a carpet of English ivy, accented by wax myrtle and camellias, at the entrance to this quiet city park in Aiken. Willows and obelia grace the banks of the duck pond. Elsewhere in this charming setting, seldom disturbed by street noises, evergreens provide the shade for a pleasant landscape of water-lily ponds, brick walks, and plank terraces. A tiny rose garden grows beside a small frame house called the Dollhouse, which serves as the local garden club's headquarters and also as a library. A touch-and-scent trail for the blind (which has plaques written in braille and connected by ropes) is provided. Every Monday evening from May through August visitors can enjoy free concerts here. *Open year-round.*

55 Lexington County Museum

5 min. North on Rte. 6. This 18-building complex is rightly called a gateway to yesterday. History comes alive here—in the Oak Grove Schoolhouse; in the 1772 Corley Log House, with its single open hearth used for cooking, light, and heat; and in the eight-room Hazelius House, where an 1891 revival meeting inspired evangelist Charlie Tillman to write the spiritual, "Give Me That Old-Time Religion." Antique lovers will savor the federal-style Fox House, with furniture locally made in the style of Sheraton and Hepplewhite and a large collection of quilts. On the grounds are dairy sheds, smokehouses, ovens, beehives, rabbit hutches, herb gardens, and a cotton gin. *Open Tues.–Sun. except July 4, Thanksgiving Day, Christmas, and New Year's Day. Admission charged.*

74 Sesquicentennial State Park

5 min. North on Rte. 1. The trails here—a 3½-mile exercise course, an easy 2-mile hiking loop, and an informative quarter-mile nature trail—and the pedal boats on the 30-acre lake make this a good place to stretch your legs. This area, the Carolina Sandhills, once covered by a primeval sea, now supports a cedar bog, hardwoods, and a forest of scrub oak and pine. Evidence of an early-day turpentine plantation can be seen in the slash marks on several of the old longleaf pines. A restored two-story log cabin, built in 1756, was moved to the park and is now an artist's studio. The name of the park is derived from the 150th anniversary of the city of Columbia, when souvenir coins were sold and the proceeds used to purchase the 1,455 acres here. *Open year-round.*

98 Historic Camden

2 min. North on Rte. 521. Built in 1733–34 by royal decree, Camden, the first inland community in South Carolina, was named for Lord Camden, a member of Parliament who opposed taxation of the colonies in America. During the Revolutionary War, British troops under General Cornwallis captured the powder magazine here and occupied the town. The restored historic district is keyed primarily to the 1780–81 occupation and two battles between American and British forces. You can visit a replica of the Kershaw house, where Cornwallis had his headquarters (the original burned in 1865). Other historic buildings have been moved here, re-creating the flavor of an 18th-century village. An audiovisual presentation recounts the history of the area, and dioramas and exhibits further help to bring the past to life. *Open Tues.–Sun. and holidays. Admission charged.*

131 / 141A NMPA Stock Car Hall of Fame, Darlington

Exit 131: 11 mi./20 min. North on Rte. 401, left on Rte. 34/151. Exit 141A: 12 mi./15 min. North on I-95 to Exit 164, left on Rte. 52, left on Rte. 34/151. Located at the Darlington Raceway, this collection of stock cars and trophies won by the men who drove them provides an overview of life on the racetrack and glory at the finish line. In the museum—the dream of a famous driver, Little Joe Weatherly—you'll see record-breaking engines as well as a display of illegal parts that were found to be not "stock." Of all the displays, the most thrilling is a race simulator, where you sit in the driver's seat of a stock car and screech through two filmed laps of an actual race flashing on a screen just beyond your hood. *Open daily except Thanksgiving Day and Christmas. Admission charged.*

141A Florence Museum of Art, Science, History

8 mi./15 min. North on I-95 to Exit 164, right on Rte. 52, right on Rte. 76 (W. Palmetto St.), left on Graham St. to Spruce St. A 26-room former residence in the international style houses an unusual collection of artifacts started in the 1920's with 78 pieces of Hopi Indian pottery. Over the years the museum has added ceramic, textile, and bronze items from Chinese dynasties, Greek and Roman antiquities, African folk art, and American works of art. The South Carolina Hall of History and the museum grounds feature items related to local history, including the old town bell and a Confederate cruiser's propellers. *Open Tues.–Sat. and P.M. Sun. except Aug. and holidays.*

I-20. *Creations once on the cutting edge of science are now forever grounded.*

I-20 Florence Air and Missile Museum

4 mi./6 min. Continue on I-20 spur, left on Rte. 76; follow signs. A World War II V-2 rocket, a B-26 flown by U.S. airmen in three wars, and an F-11F retired from service with the Blue Angels (the navy's top precision flying team) are among the more than three dozen combat aircraft and missiles to be seen here. Exhibits trace aviation and space developments from the beginning of U.S. air warfare in France in 1918 to the space voyages of the Apollo project and the *Challenger* tragedy. *Open year-round. Admission charged.*

See N–S book, sec. 4.

See N–S book, sec. 9.

ROUTE 1 — Will Rogers State Beach, Los Angeles

5 mi./10 min. North on Rte. 1 (Pacific Coast Hwy.). This is a classic southern California beach, with glistening white sand, rolling breakers, and sailboats dotting the horizon. Mansions line the white cliffs above. The beach offers all the pleasures of the Pacific: sunbathing, swimming, volleyball, picnicking, jogging, sailboarding, surfboarding, and bodysurfing (3- to 4-foot waves are common). The water is usually tolerable from April through September. Just south of here you'll find Santa Monica State Beach and its famous pier, and south of that the equally famous Muscle Beach and Venice Beach. *Open year-round. Fee for parking.*

HAR — Los Angeles, CA 90071

Harbor Frwy. exit. Visitor Information Center, 505 S. Flower St., Level B. (213) 689-8822. The maze of freeways in and around L.A. can frustrate even the most unflappable driver, but a little aggravation is a small price to pay for this vast city's many charms. Mulholland Drive in the Hollywood Hills or the 27-story City Hall Tower downtown provides spectacular views of the city. Hollywood Boulevard has changed since the old days, but Mann's Chinese Theater is a plush reminder of the glamour that was. To see moviemaking today, take the Universal Studios tour. Those who prefer still pictures can sample the outstanding collections at the Los Angeles County Museum of Art. Griffith Park, the largest city park in the country, has over 4,000 hilly acres to explore, and the Los Angeles Zoo boasts some 2,500 animals. Among L.A.'s innumerable other attractions is an astonishing variety of plants at the 165-acre Descanso Gardens.

HAR — Norton Simon Museum of Art, Pasadena

Harbor Frwy. exit. 9 mi./15 min. North on Harbor Frwy. (becomes Pasadena Frwy.), left on N. Orange Grove Blvd., right on W. Colorado Blvd. One of the lesser-known treasures of southern California, this first-rate art collection ranges from ancient Indian and Asian religious sculpture to contemporary American works. Rodin's heroic bronze, "The Burghers of Calais," graces the entrance, and galleries are devoted to Dutch and Flemish masters, including a number of Rembrandt portraits. European paintings from the 15th to the 19th centuries are represented by Botticelli, Raphael, and others. Among the impressionists

HAR. *This masterpiece by Auguste Rodin sets the stage for treasures within.*

are Bonnard, Monet, Renoir, Cézanne, and Van Gogh. Degas's dancers fill one entire gallery, and modernists Klee, Braque, and Picasso, as well as Americans Frank Stella and Richard Diebenkorn, are also featured. *Open Thurs.–Sun. Admission charged.*

HAR — Pasadena Historical Society

Harbor Frwy. exit. 10 mi./20 min. North on Harbor Frwy. (becomes Pasadena Frwy.), left on N. Orange Grove Blvd., right on W. Walnut St. A stately beaux arts–style mansion, built in 1905 and used for many Hollywood films, houses antiques, paintings, Oriental rugs, and memorabilia that reflect the lifestyle of Pasadena's affluent families at the turn of the century. The lush Finlandia Gardens are a vivid reminder that you are in the City of Roses. On the grounds is the Finnish Folk Art Museum, featuring a quaint reproduction of a 19th-century rural Finnish home complete with an open hearth, a spinning wheel, chests, a hand-carved rocking chair, and a tall clock by the famous Könni family of clock makers. *Open P.M. Tues. and Thurs. and first, second, and the last Sun. of the month except Aug. Admission charged.*

GAR / TWN — Adobe de Palomares, Pomona

Garey Ave. exit: 3 min. North on Garey Ave., right on E. Arrow Hwy.; follow signs. Towne Ave. exit: 3 min. North on Towne Ave., left on E. Arrow Hwy.; follow signs. When Don Ygnacio Palomares built the *casa* of his dreams in 1854, the wealthy rancher established a lasting architectural style. This is unmistakably a ranch-style house. Its 13 rooms are all on one level, and the shingled roof overhangs a long porch around most of the outside. In its time it was known as the house of hospitality, for both its welcoming aspect and the fiestas, barbecues, and dances given by Don Ygnacio and his wife. Stagecoaches stopped here, as did the 20-mule-team freight wagons bringing supplies from the East. The current restoration, which includes authentic farm implements, clothing, furniture, tools, and kitchen utensils, vividly evokes southern California life in the golden days of its early Mexican rancho period. *Open P.M. Tues.–Sun. except Thanksgiving Day, Christmas, and New Year's Day.*

I-215 — Glen Helen Regional Park

15 mi./20 min. North on I-215, left on Devore Rd. With its sparkling blue lakes framed by mountain peaks and its grassy banks shaded by lovely sycamore and ash trees, this sheltered alpine glen looks like a picture postcard that has come to life. Follow the log-and-plank ecology trail through the natural marsh area. You'll find wild grapes growing free, a clear stream edged with watercress, and descriptive signs that are both informative and amusing. Two famous ski areas, Mt. Baldy and Big Bear Lake, are only a short drive away from this park. *Open daily except Christmas. Admission charged.*

I-215 — Riverside, CA 92501

7 mi./12 min. Visitors & Convention Bureau, 3443 Orange St. (714) 787-7950. Once a center of California's orange industry, Riverside is now the home of a number of museums, parks, and historical landmarks. Mission Inn, an architectural gem in the Spanish style, contains artifacts, bells, and a wedding chapel with a 300-year-old altar. The Sherman Indian Museum has dioramas on Indian culture, and in the Riverside Municipal Museum you can see exhibits on regional and natural history. Heritage House, built in 1891, is a lavishly furnished late-Victorian mansion. An excellent photography museum is located in the downtown area. At the University of California at Riverside, there's a botanic garden with 2,000 species of plants from all over the world.

ROUTE 243 Idyllwild County Park

26 mi./45 min. South on Rte. 243. Although this site is farther from the interstate than most others, it's worth a visit if you have time. As the road climbs 5,400 feet from the Colorado Desert to the forested San Jacinto Mountains, each turn unveils a different view of the same breathtaking sight: deep green valleys and bald granite peaks set against a cobalt blue sky. At the visitor center pick up a map of the self-guiding nature trail, meandering through fragrant ponderosa pines and graceful cedars. Hikers can take Deer Spring Trail up 10,805-foot Mt. San Jacinto. In a forested valley a short walk from the park lies Idyllwild Village, with its charming shops and restaurants. *Open year-round.*

ROUTE 111 Palm Springs Aerial Tramway

IND *Rte. 111 exit: 12 mi./20 min. Southeast on Rte. 111, right on Tramway Rd. Indian Ave. exit: 8 mi./15 min. South on Indian Ave., right on San Rafael Rd. (becomes Tramway Rd.).* Take a good deep breath before you start this 5,873-foot ascent from desert to alpine forest, because you may not take another one until this thrilling ride is over. The unforgettable 14-minute adventure in a glass-sided tram provides a bird's-eye view that encompasses 75 miles and a glimpse of vegetation from five different life zones. At the top you'll find 14,000-acre Mt. San Jacinto State Park, with 54 miles of hiking trails, mule-train rides, and campsites. The seasonal events are as varied as dogsled races in January to a spring Easter-egg hunt. *Open daily except Aug. Admission charged.*

YV PALM Desert Hot Springs

Yucca Valley exit: 9 mi./16 min. North on Rte. 62, right on Pierson Blvd. Palm Dr. exit: 5 mi./9 min. North on Palm Dr., right on Pierson Blvd. The remains of adobe buildings testify to a simpler time before the discovery of subterranean hot springs brought rapid development to this area. Some 65 motels and resorts, ranging from simple to luxurious, attract the health-conscious with pools and spas that are nourished by natural 95° F–170° F mineral water—warm enough to counter the chill of the coolest desert air. Nonresidents can often use these facilities for a small fee. *Open year-round.*

YV PALM Cabot's Old Indian Pueblo, Desert Hot Springs

Yucca Valley exit: 11 mi./20 min. North on Rte. 62, right on Pierson Blvd., right on Miracle Hill Rd. Palm Dr. exit: 7 mi./15 min. North on Palm Dr, right on Pierson Blvd., right on Miracle Hill Rd. In 1913 Cabot Yerxa, a confirmed eccentric, staked a claim in this then-uninhabited desert and, working with his faithful burro, Merry Xmas, built his first cabin. By 1941 he had

111–IND. *From inside the aerial tram, the unimpeded view is a thrilling spectacle.*

nestled a Hopi-style pueblo into the mountainside, using hand-mixed adobe, old railroad ties, and rusty nails. After some 20 years of painstaking labor he completed the present structure—a four-story warren with 35 rooms, 150 windows, 65 doors, and an entrance for mice-eating snakes. The building contains rough wooden furniture, an astronomical observation tower, and a long gallery of Indian artifacts, featuring Navajo blankets, a full Sioux warrior costume, and a tomahawk from the Battle of the Little Bighorn. *Open Wed.–Sun. Admission charged.*

WASH Jensen's and Shields' Date Gardens

Washington St. exit: 5 mi./10 min. South on Washington St., left on Rte. 111. Located in the heart of the Coachella Valley, which produces over 90 percent of the dates grown in America, these family-owned farms are two of the oldest establishments in the area. Jensen's has 60-foot-tall date trees and exotic citrus trees, including one that bears nine varieties of fruit. A series of plaques details the history of the date and citrus industries. The Shields farm has a long soda fountain that features black date ice cream and date shakes. Dates of many kinds are sold at both farms. *Jensen's open daily except Thanksgiving Day, Christmas, and Easter; Shields' open daily except Christmas.*

JTM Cottonwood Visitor Center, Joshua Tree National Monument

Joshua Tree Monument exit: 10 mi./15 min. North on Monument Rd.; follow signs. Parched golden valleys with stands of creosote bush, cholla cactus, and ocotillo delineate the Colorado Desert section of this monument. Here, too, is a man-made fan-palm oasis that supports a variety of plants and attracts a large number of birds. The odd-looking trees for which the monument is named grow in the western section of the park. Massive rock formations and dense vegetation make this the most scenic portion. If you have time, consider a drive through that area and back to I-10 via Route 62. Maps available at the visitor center show the roads, hiking trails, and other highlights. *Open year-round.*

Hi Jolly Camel Driver's Tomb, Quartzsite

1 min. North on Quartzsite business loop; follow signs. In the old cemetery at Quartzsite a pyramid-shaped monument of native stone topped with a metal camel marks the grave of Hadji Ali, an Arab camel driver dubbed Hi Jolly by his American companions. He came to this country from the Near East in 1856, with camels imported by the U. S. Army for its short-lived Camel Corps, and served as one of the camel drivers for the expedition that laid out the western portion of U. S. Route 66. A plaque next to the monument pays tribute to the pioneering accomplishments of Hi Jolly, who is said to have died near Quartzsite. *Open year-round.*

124 **Wildlife World Zoo, Glendale**

7.5 mi./15 min. North on Cotton Lane Rd., right on Northern Ave. This unusual 45-acre zoo is largely devoted to breeding and raising rare and endangered species for other institutions. The excellent bird collection includes pheasants, ostriches and other flightless birds, black curassows from South America, and a rainbow flock of lories (Australasian parrots) that eat apples from visitors' hands. Kangaroos may be seen carrying their young in their pouches. A black jaguar graces a bare branch, and there are tigers, apes, monkeys, porcupines, giraffes, and families of dromedaries and rare oryxes. Goats, llamas, baby deer, and ducklings may be found in the petting area. *Open year-round. Admission charged.* &

142 **Phoenix, AZ 85004**

Convention & Visitors Bureau, 505 N. 2nd St. (602) 254-6500. The brilliant sunshine that accounts for the city's rapid growth also supports a surprising variety of native plants, many of which can be seen on the grounds of the state capitol. Although Phoenix is considered a mecca for retirees, many attractions here appeal to children as well. The Phoenix Art Museum has a junior gallery and some appealing miniature rooms, as well as fine collections of sculpture and Asian art. The Arizona Historical Society includes toys, an

7TH–150. *Stone shelters—built to last—frame views of the valley and distant mountains.*

early drugstore, and a children's room. The Arizona Museum of Science and Technology features a young people's discovery area. And children as well as adults will be intrigued by the extensive collection of colorful kachina dolls at the excellent Heard Museum of Anthropology and Primitive Art.

7TH **South Mountain Park, Phoenix**

150

7th Ave. exit: 6 mi./12 min. South on 7th Ave., left on Baseline Rd., then right on Central Ave. Exit 150: 7 mi./20 min. South on 24th St., right on Baseline Rd., left on Central Ave. Extensive hiking and saddle trails crisscross this 16,000-acre former Indian hunting ground, which is now a large municipal park in Phoenix. From Dobbins Lookout high in the park's jagged Salt River Mountains, the sprawling outlines of Phoenix are visible. Hieroglyphics, a natural bridge and tunnel, and views that include the Superstition, White Tank, and Estrella mountains can also be enjoyed. Horses are available for rent. *Open year-round.*

153A **McCormick Railroad Park, Scottsdale**

8 mi./25 min. North on 48th St., right on Camelback Rd., left on Scottsdale Rd. A good introduction to this 30-acre park devoted to

trains is to board a diesel train. The train takes passengers through the McCormick Railroad Arboretum (a part of this park), where more than 100 desert plants and shrubs form a panorama of color and texture. On weekends a Paradise & Pacific $5/_{12}$"-scale steam locomotive follows the same route. Visitors will also enjoy a ride on the 1929 antique carousel. Near the brick railroad station several refurbished full-size cars from the Santa Fe line are displayed. And a model train runs through a Disneyland-like setting, with gnomes, cartoon characters, piles of candy, and alpine scenery. *Open year-round. Fee charged for rides.*

153A **Papago Park, Phoenix**

5 mi./18 min. North on 48th St., right on Van Buren St., left on Galvin Pkwy. In one of the busiest parts of the city, among an outcropping of red sculpted boulders, are the Desert Botanical Garden, Phoenix Zoo, riding stables, and a golf course. The Desert Botanical Garden boasts an in-depth collection of plants from deserts worldwide, including organ-pipe cactus, teddy bear cholla, living rocks, and the exotic upside-down boojum tree. The zoo specializes in birds and animals from the warmer regions of the world, many of them endangered species. *Open year-round. Admission charged for zoo and garden.*

| 5 | | 3 | | 3 | 0 | 1 | | | 40 | | | 25 | | | 39 | |
| 142 | 7TH | 150 | | 153A | 153B | 154 | | | | 194 | | | | | 219 | 10 |

8 See E–W book, sec. 56.

153B Big Surf, Tempe

6 mi./25 min. East on Broadway Rd., left on McClintock Rd. (becomes Hayden Rd.). This surprising attraction brings the ocean to the Arizona desert. Palm trees sway over a wide, sandy beach while a huge man-made lagoon resounds with 3- to 5-foot breakers that are generated by a wave machine. There are scheduled times for swimming and rafting, and shallow areas for children. A long winding water slide passes through the belly of a whale, and for the more adventurous there's a steep slide from a 3½-story tower into a 100-foot-long pool. Boogie boards to ride the waves can be rented. *Open daily Mar.–Sept. Admission charged.*

154 Mesa Southwest Museum

8 mi./30 min. East on Rte. 360, left on Country Club Dr., right on 1st St. Displays of Pima and Apache artifacts, Spanish armor, and a reconstructed Hohokam pit house are imaginatively presented to portray the early history of this area. Sparkling geodes and minerals set the stage for the story of the Lost Dutchman's Mine. A re-creation of a Mesa street scene evokes the 1920's, and visitors can pan for gold in a small stream. Murals and a life-size automated model of a triceratops dramatize prehistoric times, while models and illustrations of space explorations suggest what the future may hold in store. *Open year-round. Admission charged.*

154 Champlin Fighter Museum, Mesa

7 mi./23 min. East on Superstition Frwy. (Rte. 360), left on Greenfield Rd., right on McKellips Rd.; follow signs to Falcon Field Airport. Two large hangars house a collection of more than 30 fighter aircraft dating from World War I to the Korean War. All are beautifully refurbished or reproduced and in flying condition. The visitor can get a close-up view of such famous planes as the French Nieuport, the German Fokker and Messerschmitt, the English Sopwith Camel and Spitfire, and the American P-47 Thunderbolt and P-40 Warhawk. Separate exhibits feature a large collection of machine guns and other weapons, and numerous autographed photos of flying aces from various countries, the aviators dashingly attired in goggles and silk scarves. *Open year-round. Admission charged.*

194 Casa Grande Valley Historical Society Museum

6 mi./10 min. West on Rte. 287. A former church, this unusual rough stone building recalls the colorful history of the Casa Grande area from the time of the Hohokam Indians, through the silver and copper booms, to the rich farming economy of today. Displays include three "pioneer rooms" furnished in turn-of-the-century style, collections of Indian artifacts, early mining tools, dolls and tin toys, a 1900's storefront, a 1929 fire engine, and an elaborate map system detailing the flow of precious water here. Clippings and photographs recall the con man James Reavis, "Baron of Arizona," who used fake royal Spanish deeds to lay claim to more than 1 million acres of the state and live lavishly off rents he demanded from ranchers. *Open Tues.–Sun. mid-Sept.–mid-June. Admission free but donations encouraged.*

219 Picacho Peak State Park

5 min. South on Picacho Peak Rd. Picacho Peak's distinctive horn-shaped summit has long been a landmark for travelers, and the pass it guards was the site of Arizona's only Civil War battle. Tucked against the steep slope of the mountain, the park offers lovely vistas of the desert valley below, where forests of saguaro cactus grow amid dark red rock. A 2-mile trail climbs some 1,500 feet to the top, and it's so steep in one part that cables are provided. Going up and back takes 4 to 5 hours. You can also drive along the base of the mountain on a scenic route where there are cliffside picnic shelters and short hiking trails. *Open year-round. Admission charged.*

219. *The harsh, forbidding landscape is lightened by a bright drift of Mexican gold poppies.*

260. *The fired adobe facade of the mission fairly glows in the warm light of late afternoon.*

small cats, through-the-glass views of underwater and burrowing creatures, a grove of towering saguaro cacti, and a man-made "cavern" so real that it fools a flock of bats. *Open year-round. Admission charged.*

258   Tucson, AZ 85701

Convention & Visitors Bureau, 130 S. Scott Ave. (602) 624-1817. The life and architecture of this sunshine-filled city reflect the four cultures that built it: Indian, Spanish, Mexican, and frontier American. Among the desert-style buildings that still exist is La Casa Cordova, dating from the 1850's. Nearby is the John C. Frémont House, a restored mid-19th-century dwelling where walking tours begin. One of the sites on the tour is the Wishing Shrine, where according to local lore your wish will come true if a candle placed at the shrine's base continues to burn until daylight.

One of the highlights of Tucson is the University of Arizona, founded in 1885 on 300 acres that are now part of the city center. Attractions to be seen on the university's campus include the Arizona State Museum, which has an unusual archeological collection, and the University Art Gallery, where the Kress Collection of Renaissance Art is housed.

260   Old Tucson

12 mi./18 min. South on I-19 to Exit 99, right on Rte. 86, right on Kinney Rd. The small whitewashed church, a yellow clapboard depot, a ramshackle post office, and dusty Front Street in this sprawling Old West town may well look familiar. Since it was built in 1939 for the movie *Arizona*, the remarkably authentic-looking town has served as a setting for more than a hundred films, as well as innumerable television shows and commercials; an 8-minute movie has clips from several. Attractions include action-packed gunfights and stunt shows, country music performances, and costumed dancing girls in the saloons. For rides, there's a stagecoach, a carousel, a narrow-gauge railroad, and miniature cars. *Open year-round. Admission charged.*

260   The Arizona–Sonora Desert Museum

14 mi./22 min. South on I-19 to Exit 99, right on Rte. 86, right on Kinney Rd. Celebrating the desert and the surprising number of plants and animals that survive in it, this renowned and innovative complex is a combination of zoo, botanical garden, natural history museum, and mountain park. An extensive series of exhibits presents more than 500 species of desert animals and plants in settings that are extraordinarily realistic and very instructive. Among the exhibits are a huge walk-through aviary, an earth sciences center, a grotto for

260   Saguaro National Monument, Tucson Mountain Unit

16 mi./26 min. South on I-19 to Exit 99, right on Rte. 86, right on Kinney Rd. The gentle slopes covered with tall cacti and the ever-changing magenta and orange light on the desert horizon make this one of the most beautiful spots in Arizona. A 6-mile drive loops through the luxuriant stands of ironwood trees and a saguaro forest that is one of the densest in the country. For those who want to experience the beauty of the desert more closely, there are about 8 miles of trails, ranging from an easy, well-marked half-mile nature walk near the visitor center to one that follows a mountain ridge and passes the ruins of several copper mines. Water as well as maps of the monument are available at the visitor center. *Open year-round.*

260   Mission San Xavier del Bac

7 mi./10 min. South on I-19 to Exit 92; follow signs. The pristine beauty of this Franciscan church, on the Papago Indian Reservation near the Santa Cruz River, stands out against the desert landscape. Built between 1783 and 1797 near the site of a mission founded a century earlier, it is an intriguing blend of Spanish, Moorish, Byzantine, and Mexican styles of architecture. The church is adorned with many statues, paintings, wood carvings, and plaster moldings. The intricately carved wooden altar is watched over by several brightly colored religious figures. According to legend, when the cat perched on one side of the altarpiece behind the altar catches the mouse on the other side, the end of the world will have arrived. *Open year-round.*

275   Saguaro National Monument, Rincon Mountain Unit

13 mi./25 min. North on Houghton Rd., right on Escalante Rd.; follow signs. In this 57,000-acre preserve, where saguaro cacti flourish, is a forest of 150- to 200-year-old specimens, some more than 30 feet tall. This vast grove can be seen from the 8-mile Cactus Forest Drive. The monument includes more than 75 miles of hiking and horseback trails, crossing the desert scrubland and going up into the pine and fir forests of the higher elevations. A hike along the quarter-mile Desert Ecology Trail takes about 40 minutes. The saguaros, which provide nesting places for many species of birds, bloom in spring and summer, along with other desert plants. Camping is by permit only. *Open year-round.*

279 Colossal Cave

7 mi./16 min. North on Vail–Colossal Cave Rd. The water that formed the stalactites, stalagmites, and smooth, folded stone draperies has long since stopped dripping, making this one of the largest dry caverns in the world. Going through the spacious chambers that yawn into darkness overhead may seem more like touring an ancient castle than a cave. Bones, artifacts, and soot marks indicate that from ancient times Indians used the site—as did fleeing train robbers in the 1880's. Spelunkers still explore the cave's unmapped reaches and dream of stumbling onto aban-

275. *It took a very large cactus to produce this bouquet of a dozen saguaro flowers.*

doned loot. The cave entrance is on a high mountain slope, and the park there offers a memorable view of the desert highlands. The road to the cave is narrow and winding. *Open year-round. Admission charged.*

318 Amerind Foundation

3 min. East on Triangle T Rd.; follow signs. Amerind is a scholar's contraction of American Indian, and this foundation, started in 1937 by amateur archeologist William S. Fulton, is devoted to the study of Native American history and culture. Exhibits in the Spanish-style museum run by the foundation include artifacts from archeological digs in the Southwest and Mexico, as well as fine examples of Indian clothing, beadwork, pottery, basketry, and other handiwork. The Hopi ceremonial dance costumes are of special interest. A separate art gallery displays works with western themes. Unusual massive rock formations in the surrounding canyon are another attraction. *Open daily Sept.–May; Wed.–Sun. June and Aug. except holidays. Admission charged.*

331 Pearce Ghost Town

23 mi./35 min. South on Rte. 666; follow signs. Pearce is one of many Arizona ghost towns—such as Goldfield, Goldroad, Paradise, and Tombstone—that are forlorn reminders of the boom days when gold and silver fever gripped the West and the railroads came pushing through. The town was named for Johnny Pearce, whose 1894 gold strike became the Commonwealth Mine, the richest in southern Arizona. The deserted buildings here include a post office, a mill, and adobe houses. A window in an adobe general store still carries a faded sign: "This store is protected by a loaded shotgun three days a week. You guess which days." *Open year-round.*

340 Museum of the Southwest, Wilcox

3 min. Exit west, right on Circle I Rd. Brightly painted tepees frame the entrance of the tourist information center and set the tone for the museum it houses. The extensive exhibits concentrate on the history of Cochise County,

especially on the Chiricahuas, a formidable Apache tribe that used this rugged terrain to outmaneuver the Spaniards, Mexicans, and Americans for some 300 years. There are fascinating pictures of the great chiefs Cochise and Geronimo, along with weapons used by their braves and a full-scale wickiup, a hut that these nomads used for shelter. Exhibits also display memorabilia related to other tribes, and to ranching and railroading. *Open Mon.–Sat. and P.M. Sun.*

340 366 Fort Bowie National Historic Site

Exit 340: 22 mi./36 min. Southeast on Rte. 186, left on Apache Pass Rd.; follow signs. Exit 366: 18 mi./30 min. West into Bowie, left on Apache Pass Rd.; follow signs. Ft. Bowie is a rich source of frontier lore: Chiricahua Apache chief Cochise and his 10-year wars against white settlers; Geronimo, fighting vainly to retain Indian lands. The fort, established in 1862 to guard Apache Pass, the route of the vital Butterfield stagecoach line, was the army's headquarters for its campaigns against the Indians. Ringed by lofty mountains, the ruins of the fort and the old stagecoach station can only be reached by foot, along a 1½-mile path that starts in the parking area and winds through a valley of mesquite with eagles and hawks soaring overhead. A park ranger is on duty at this historic site most of the time. *Open year-round.*

82A Rock Hound State Park

13 mi./25 min. South on Rte. 11, left on Rock Hound Rd. Perched at the foot of the Little Florida Mountains, this ruggedly beautiful desert park lives up to its reputation as a paradise for rock enthusiasts. A display near the entrance shows the types of rocks commonly found along the steep mountain trails, which are flanked by barrel cacti and prickly pear and studded with boulders and rough outcroppings. Likely mineral finds include blue agate, common opals, jasper, quartz crystals, and perlite. One ridge is noted for variegated jasper, geodes, and thunder eggs. Each visitor can take up 20 pounds of rocks. *Open year-round. Admission charged.*

85   Deming Luna Mimbres Museum

1.5 mi./8 min. Exit south across overpass; continue on Spruce St., left on Silver St. Housed in an imposing old brick armory building, this large, rambling museum includes a very fine collection of Indian pottery and extensive exhibits of western and local memorabilia. The delicate white Indian pottery is decorated with remarkably sophisticated black and red geometric designs, animal figures, and scenes from daily life. It was found in the burial grounds of the Mimbres Indians, who mysteriously left this region some 800 years ago.

85. *The elegance of Mimbres pottery is typified by this bowl's lightning motif.*

Other exhibits include saddles and tack, a restored chuck wagon, a jail cell, a beauty salon, and household furnishings used by local settlers. Impressive collections of dolls, quilts and lace, polished and raw minerals, and Stetson hats are on view. *Open Mon.–Sat. and P.M. Sun. except Thanksgiving Day, Christmas, and New Year's Day. Admission free but donations encouraged.*

102   Bowlin's Akela Flats Trading Post

1 min. North from exit. This trading post is modeled on the one Claude Bowlin established in northwestern New Mexico at the turn of the century. He encouraged Indians to trade with him by offering them free coffee and tobacco. Free coffee is still offered to passersby who stop here to investigate the brightly colored buildings. A store sells Western souvenirs, jewelry, Indian pottery, and fresh pecans that are grown on a 105-acre farm behind the store. The post has a museum featuring a life-size diorama of Pueblo Indians in a cliff dwelling, along with examples of Zuni prayer sticks, antique kachina dolls, and traditional pottery, including many examples of the deep black vessels made by the Santa Clara Indians. *Open daily except Thanksgiving Day and Christmas.*

140   La Mesilla Historic Village

2 mi./15 min. South on Rte. 28; follow signs. This quaint Spanish-style village was Mexican until 1854, when the Gadsden Purchase was signed and the American flag was raised in its plaza. The area's largest settlement and a natural crossroads, it thrived as a major stop on the Butterfield overland stagecoach route. The town's colorful history includes capture by Confederates for a short period, bloody political shoot-outs during the cattle wars, a trial of Billy the Kid, and harassment by the Apache war chief Geronimo. Today La Mesilla, which was bypassed by the railroad, looks much as it did in the 19th century. The mission-style church of San Albino dominates the plaza, and many restored adobe buildings house restaurants, gift shops, and galleries. The Gadsden Museum has many fascinating items related to local history, including a chapel filled with the charming religious figures known as *santos*, which are carved from wood and colorfully painted. *Museum open daily except Thanksgiving Day, Christmas, and Easter. Admission charged for museum.*

I-25   Fort Selden State Monument

19 mi./28 min. North on I-25 to Exit 19, left on access road. Set on the banks of the Rio Grande, this fort was established in 1865 to protect settlers in the Las Cruces area from Apaches. The troops were also responsible for escorting travelers along the dangerously dry Jornada del Muerto ("Journey of Death") desert trail

140. *The stone gate's arch echoes the rounded form of the prickly pear cactus.*

to the north. To re-create life in the remote outpost in the 19th century, exhibits in the visitor center make use of models, photographs, weapons, and uniforms, including the Prussian-style coats and plumed hats of the Buffalo soldiers, a famed black cavalry unit. The remains of the extensive fort's adobe walls are well marked with signs explaining how the rooms were used. *Open daily except holidays. Admission charged.*

I-25   Leasburg Dam State Park

20 mi./30 min. North on I-25 to Exit 19, left on access road. This rugged park extends from a bluff overlooking the Rio Grande down to the river shore. From the hiking trail there are extensive views of the river as it makes its way through the surrounding desert and backs up against the dam here. A sandy area for swimmers near the dam, fishing below the dam, and a shaded trail along the grassy shoreline offer pleasant diversions. *Open year-round. Admission charged.*

DNTN   El Paso, TX 79901 and Ciudad Juárez, Mexico

Downtown exit: Tourist Information Center, 5 Civic Center Plaza. (915) 534-0686. Shopping seems to be in order on both sides of the border: at flea markets, farmers' markets, and factory outlets in El Paso and in nearby Juárez at the government-sponsored ProNaF Center, where prices are fixed, and the Central Market, where bargaining is expected. To cross the border and return, you need two proofs of

U.S. citizenship or residence (a birth certificate and a driver's license, for example). El Paso has the skyline of a modern city, but it dates back to the late 16th century, and its long and colorful history is recalled at the Fort Bliss Museum and the Magoffin Home State Historical Site. The El Paso Museum of Art is noted for its fine collection of European old masters. On the Mexican side of the border you can visit the excellent Museum of History and Art and the Museum of Archeology.

32　Tigua Indian Reservation, El Paso

5 min. South on Zaragosa Rd., left on Alameda St., right on Old Pueblo Rd. The Tiguas settled here in 1681 after being forced to move south with retreating Spaniards during the great Pueblo uprising. A museum building made of adobe is devoted to Pueblo Indian culture. In the adjacent courtyard, restored pueblo buildings have displays and shops devoted to weaving, pottery making, and other crafts. There is a round ceremonial kiva and an open-air clay stage where young Tiguas perform traditional dances every weekend and on weekdays during the summer. *Open daily except Thanksgiving Day, Christmas, and New Year's Day. Admission charged for dance performances.*

206　Balmorhea State
209　Recreation Area

Exit 206: 5 min. South on Rte. 2903, right on Rte. 290. Exit 209: 7 mi./12 min. West on Rte. 290. With wide lawns, white stucco buildings, and an enormous spring-fed swimming pool edged with cottonwoods and willows, this park provides a welcome relief from the surrounding desert plains. The 1¾-acre pool, with stone grottoes and ledges along its sides, looks more like a lake than a pool. Fish and other aquatic creatures live in the clear, fresh waters around the mouth of the spring, and scuba divers love to explore its depths. In canals meandering through the park, two rare and endangered species, the Comanche Springs pupfish and the Pecos gambusia, can be seen. *Park open year-round; pool open late May–Labor Day. Admission charged.*

261　Old Fort Stockton

2 mi./10 min. West on Rte. 290 to Main St.; follow signs. With its abundant water, Comanche Springs became a stopping place for the stagecoaches and wagon trains that brought immigrants to the West in frontier days. In 1858 the U.S. Army established a fort to provide protection from hostile Indians. It was abandoned to the Confederates during the Civil War, but the army returned in 1867 and stayed on until 1886. Today the remains of the fort are surrounded by the town that bears its name. The old compound can be traced by following an interpretive trail that goes past the parade ground. The stone guardhouse, with barred windows and shackles on the floor, still stands, as do three houses on officers' row. *Open year-round.*

392　Caverns of Sonora

8 mi./11 min. South on Caverns of Sonora Rd.; follow signs. Discovered about 1900 when a rancher's dog chased a raccoon down a hole,

392. *A close look will reveal a great variety of calcite shapes in just one place.*

these remarkably varied and beautiful caverns have become a major attraction. The 1½-mile subterranean tour reveals a long passage with calcite formations resembling popcorn or miniature mushrooms. There are clusters of crystals that resemble chandeliers, translucent columns of stone, and colorful crystal shapes as varied as ocean waves, burning candles, firecrackers, and cauliflower. The evolution of this amazing netherworld of stalagmites, stalactites, flowstone, and helictites is described by well-informed guides. *Open daily except Christmas. Admission charged.*

508　Cowboy Artists of America Museum

5 mi./10 min. South on Rte. 16, left on Bandera Hwy. This museum, opened in 1983, features the work of more than 30 artists, many of whom were part-time cowpunchers with a passion for realistic paintings of western scenes. To present the Old West as it really was, the museum acquires only historically authentic art works. The building has mesquite hardwood floors and an area with 23 brick domes, constructed by a method derived from the Moors and now practiced by only a few Mexican craftsmen. There's a shop that sells reproductions. *Open Mon.–Sat. and P.M. Sun. Memorial Day–Labor Day; Tues.–Sat. and P.M. Sun. rest of year except Thanksgiving Day, Christmas, New Year's Day, and Easter. Admission charged.*

508　Kerrville State Recreation Area

7 mi./13 min. South on Rte. 16, left on Rte. 173. This 500-acre park on the shores of Flatrock Lake and the Guadalupe River is divided into two areas. The Lake Unit has a walk along the river, with picnic tables shaded by oaks and willows. Swimming and tubing are allowed in the lake area; and there's fishing for crappie, catfish, and bass. The Hill Country Unit offers miles of trails through terrain ranging from wooded hills to rocky arroyos. Mesquite, sumac, buckeye, and bluebonnets are abundant, as are birds, jackrabbits, and white-tailed deer. It's the kind of country seen in cowboy movies. *Open year-round. Admission charged.*

570 574   San Antonio, TX 78205

Visitor Information Center, 317 Alamo Plaza. (512) 299-8155. The Alamo, of course, is the major historical treasure here. The second best-known attraction is the Paseo del Rio, a below-street-level string of sidewalk cafés, clubs, hotels, and artisans' shops that line the banks of the meandering San Antonio River. A good spot for an overview is the top of the 750-foot-high Tower of the Americas. Be sure to visit the San Antonio Museum of Art and the Witte Museum's displays of anthropology, history, and natural science. The 1749 Spanish Governor's Palace and the Alamo's four sister missions further reveal the city's heritage.

609   Max Starckey Park, Seguin

3 mi./6 min. South on Rte. 123 (business). The open green fields and flowering trees of this well-equipped municipal park offer a welcome respite from the surrounding plains. An 18-hole golf course, a swimming pool, a baseball field, volleyball courts, and secluded picnic spots overlooking the Guadalupe River are among the park's amenities. The spacious stone picnic shelters with long pits for Texas-style barbecues and the stone terraces with tables are all set on the steep riverbank. A scenic drive shaded by pecan trees runs along the river, with views of the Victorian houses and gardens on the opposite shore. *Open year-round.* 🏕️ 🚶 🎣 ♿

ROUTE 183   Palmetto State Park

4 mi./6 min. South on Rte. 183, right on Park Rd. 11. Spread along the winding shores of the San Marcos River, these 263 acres of swampy woodlands offer a remarkable contrast to the open terrain surrounding them. Lush hedgerows of dwarf palmettos and other subtropical plants grow along the main road, and willow forests line the river's edge. All told, more than 500 eastern and western plant species grow in the area. Many are marked along 1½ miles of trails. Chameleons, armadillos, and rabbits are among the animals commonly seen, and some 240 bird species have

183. Reflections in Ottine Swamp double the impact of its mysterious beauty.

been spotted. Swimming, tubing, and fishing are popular. After a rainstorm, watch your step as you walk along the river. The banks turn into a slippery, impassable slime that locals like to call gumbo mud. *Open year-round. Admission charged.* 🏕️ ⛺ 🚐 🚶 🏊 🎣

ROUTE 183   Gonzales County Jail

13 mi./15 min. South on Rte. 183, left on St. Lawrence St. The Old West comes to life (and death) in this three-story yellow limestone jailhouse built in 1887 and used as the county's lockup until 1975. Six-shooters, gun belts, ten-gallon hats, and saddles used by 19th-century lawmen are displayed in the lobby along with vintage photographs, handcuffs, and weapons ingeniously crafted by inmates. Here, too, is the story of the notorious gunman John Wesley Hardin, who opened a law office in town after studying for the bar while in prison. In the cells crisscrossed bars cover windows and doors, and inmates' names are scratched on the black steel walls. There's also a grim, lightless dungeon and, on the second floor, cagelike cells surrounding a worn gallows with a hangman's noose. *Open daily except holidays.*

ROUTE 183   Gonzales Memorial Museum

13 mi./15 min. South on Rte. 183, left on St. Lawrence St. Texas's war for independence began in 1835 when the American settlers in Gonzales refused to surrender a small cannon to Mexican troops. Instead, they unfurled a crude banner with the motto "Come and Take It" stitched on it and used the cannon to help rout the Mexicans. The cannon, the flag, and other items from the revolution can be seen in this impressive structure with art deco touches built in 1937 to commemorate Texas's centennial. In another wing, books, clothing, and household items recall the lives of early settlers. A pleasant park surrounds the building, and a memorial by a reflecting pool pays tribute to 32 Gonzales men who fought their way into the Alamo and died there. *Open Tues.– Sun. except holidays. Admission charged.*

674   Monument Hill State Historic Site

16 mi./18 min. North on Rte. 77, left on Spur 92. Hostilities with Mexico continued for years after Texas won independence. In 1842 36 Texans died at the Battle of Salado Creek. The next year, in the Black Bean Episode, their Mexican captors shot 17 others, forced to draw beans from a pot to see who would be executed. Here on a high bluff overlooking the Colorado River, their remains are entombed, and the site is marked with a 48-foot tower of shellstone on which brightly colored friezes illustrate some of the events. The design, ironically, has a Mexican influence. Also here you'll find the ruins of a three-story stone brewery built in the early 1870's and, still standing, the home of the Kriesche family, who ran it. The visitor center has memorabilia related to the brewery. *Open year-round. Admission charged.* 🏕️ 🚶 ♿

674   N. W. Faison Home, La Grange

17 mi./19 min. North on Rte. 77. N. W. Faison is a Texas hero who spent 2 hard years in a Mexican prison after being captured at the Battle of Salado Creek, in September 1842, during the struggle to keep the republic's hard-won independence. Faison, who was a surveyor and county clerk, worked tirelessly after his release to have the remains of the men who fought by his side removed from their shallow battlefield graves and reburied at nearby Monument Hill. Faison's home, a modest one-story clapboard house with gingerbread trim, stands shaded by old oaks on one of La Grange's main streets. Iron hitching posts on the front lawn recall earlier days, and flowering plants form a Texas star on the back terrace. Inside, the furnishings reveal the lifestyle of Texans during the formative years of the Lone Star State. *Open P.M. Sun. Apr.–May and Sept.–Oct. Admission charged.*

723 Stephen F. Austin State Historical Museum

5 min. North on Rte. FM 1458. It's no wonder that Stephen Austin selected this site for Texas's first American colony in 1824. These woodlands and fields where cattle now graze at roadside are some of the most pleasant in Texas. The 664-acre park is devoted entirely to recreation, with an 18-hole golf course and a large swimming pool among the facilities. Some artifacts from the original town of Austin and an imposing bronze statue of the Father of Texas are at the J. J. Josey General Store Museum on Route FM 1458 just north of the park entrance. *Open year-round. Admission charged.*

763 Astroworld, Houston

775A

Exit 763: 10 mi./20 min. South on I-610 Loop. Exit 775A: 15 mi./25 min. South on I-610 Loop. A bright high-tech atmosphere prevails at this enormous theme park across from the Houston Astrodome. The state-of-the-art rides include a sleek roller coaster that plunges downward at 50 feet per second. The park has Japanese, Mexican, German, and Italian sections as well as Gay Nineties and Wild West areas. Each has activities, restaurants, and shops related to the theme. The entertainment includes performances by magicians, dolphins, and divers. For children the Enchanted Kingdom offers elaborate play equipment and a cartoon theater. The admission price is relatively high but includes all rides and shows. Waterworld, with a body

slide, surfing, and rapids to shoot, has a separate admission. *Open Tues.–Sun. Memorial Day–Labor Day; weekends Apr.–May and Sept.–Oct. Admission charged.*

769A. *The Pillot House in Sam Houston Park is a refreshing evocation of times gone by.*

769A Houston, TX 77002

Convention and Visitors Bureau, 3300 Main St. (713) 523-5050. Houston's dramatic modern skyline suggests that the present and the future are of primary interest in this city. The past, however, is recalled right in the heart of downtown in Sam Houston Park, where you can tour seven historic buildings dating from the early 19th century to the early 20th century. And the Museum of Texas History displays artifacts going back to the early 16th century. The Museum of Fine Arts presents an extensive collection, from pre-Columbian pieces to contemporary sculpture. The 15 halls of the Museum of Natural Science in Hermann Park house exhibits ranging from gems and minerals to the petroleum sciences and space exploration. A zoo, a garden center, and a miniature train ride complete this park's attractions.

787 San Jacinto Battleground State Historical Park, La Porte

4 mi./10 min. South on Rte. 134; take free ferry leaving every 10 min. It took only 18 minutes for Sam Houston and his men to avenge the Alamo and win Texas independence in the bloody battle fought here in 1836. A sleek 570-foot limestone tower topped by a lone star marks the site. Displays in the museum relate not only to the battle but to the history of Texas from the days of Indians and

conquistadors until it achieved statehood. The tower's observation deck, accessible by elevator, offers a sweeping view of Houston's skyline. Visitors can board the 573-foot U.S.S. *Texas,* the only surviving battleship that saw duty in both world wars. *Park open daily except Christmas; museum and tower open daily except Christmas Eve and Christmas. Admission charged for tower.*

787. *A proud and elegant symbol of independence dominates the battleground and park.*

851 Art Museum of Southeast Texas, Beaumont

5 min. South on Pearl St., left on Bowie St., right on Main St. Capped with an imposing glass pyramid, this striking postmodern–art deco structure stands out in the center of downtown Beaumont. The interior, too, is Texas-scale, with 20-foot ceilings, polished stone floors, glass walls, and gleaming metal trim. The permanant collection is not large, and some of the extensive space will be used for concerts, lectures, multimedia shows, and changing exhibits. The emphasis is usually on local, ethnic, and folk art. *Open Tues.–Sun. Admission charged.*

<table>
</table>

29 30 Imperial Calcasieu Museum, Lake Charles

Exit 29: 5 mi./10 min. South on N. Lakeshore Dr., left on Watkins St.; follow signs. Exit 30: 4 mi./9 min. South on Ryan St., right on Mill St., left on Lakeshore Dr.; proceed as above. The museum is on the site of a homestead established in the late 1700's by Charles Sallier, for whom the city of Lake Charles was named. The facade, in Louisiana colonial style, incorporates bricks, columns, and balustrades salvaged from historic buildings in the area. The past is also recalled in the interior, with a richly decorated turn-of-the-century parlor, a country kitchen, and a bedroom with a massive rosewood bedstead. There's a pharmacy display, with colorful bottles in glass cases, and a barbershop with antique fixtures and personalized shaving mugs. The Gibson Library houses a fine collection of Audubon prints and excerpts from the diary the artist kept while he lived in Louisiana. A fine arts gallery, opened in 1984, features changing exhibits. On the grounds is the magnificent 300-year-old Sallier live oak. *Open year-round.*

33 Sam Houston Jones State Park

7 mi./12 min. North on Rte. 171, left on Rte. 378, right on Rte. 378 spur; follow signs. This is a refreshing watery domain between the Calcasieu River and a cypress lagoon. Picnic tables are set on raised decks and shelters are located near the river, with adjacent lawns for impromptu games. The park features a pen of white-tailed deer and a pond where beavers and nutrias can be seen. Ducks, geese, and other waterfowl enliven the surface of the deep-green cypress swamp. There are canoes for rent and a boat launch area. *Open year-round. Admission charged.*

64 Zigler Museum, Jennings

5 min. South on Rte. 26, left on Clara St.; follow signs. This former home of a prominent local family now houses an impressive collection of art from medieval times to the 20th century, including works by Rembrandt, Van Dyck, and Whistler, and landscape paintings by artists of the Hudson River school. Events in the history of painting that affected each work are described, providing an interesting walking tour of art history. In the gallery of wildlife art, recorded birdcalls follow your tour through a gallery of prints by Audubon and other wildlife painters, as well as a selection of lifelike waterfowl wood carvings. *Open Tues.–Sun. except holidays. Admission free but donations encouraged.*

100. *As the church was central to the Acadian way of life, so it is in this village.*

100 Acadian Village, Lafayette

8 mi./18 min. South on Ambassador Caffery Rd., right on Ridge Rd., left on W. Broussard Rd. Original cabins with whitewashed fronts and steeply sloping roofs evoke the way of life of the 19th-century Acadians, popularly called Cajuns. Their French Catholic ancestors settled in southern Louisiana after they were exiled from Nova Scotia and New Brunswick by the British in 1755. The village, with its schoolhouse, chapel, and general store, sits on a bayou amid 10 acres of gardens and woodlands. The cabins contain the simple wooden furniture, moss-filled mattresses, and homespun coverlets of the period. Songbooks, records, and photographs of musicians document the importance of music and dance in the Cajun culture. *Open daily except holidays; open evenings only, first 2 weeks in Dec. Admission charged.*

101 Lafayette Natural History Museum and Planetarium

5 mi./15 min. South on University Ave., right on Taft St. (becomes Girard Park Dr.). A glittering room with distorted mirrors and unusual lenses illustrates the imaginative approach of this museum. Butterflies, minerals, skulls, an alligator skin, a turtle shell, tree branches, and fossils make up the permanent collection. The museum also features changing exhibits pertaining to natural history and Louisiana culture. At the planetarium you might see special programs devoted to astronomy and space. *Museum open year-round; planetarium open P.M. Sun.–Tues. Admission free but donations encouraged.*

103 Acadiana Park Nature Station, Lafayette

3 mi./8 min. South on Rte. 167, left on Willow St., left on Louisiana Ave., right on E. Alexander St. The Acadiana Nature Trail leads through dense oak woods along a small creek, passing an environment typical of these southern prairies and floodplain forests. From observation decks up among the treetops at the three-story Nature Station, you can view the park with the help of enthusiastic naturalists and available binoculars. There are exhibits of the animals and plants that inhabit the park today, and tool fragments and spearpoints from the Indians whose land this was before the 18th century. *Open year-round.*

155B Baton Rouge, LA 70801

Convention and Visitors Bureau, New State Capitol, State Capitol Dr. (504) 342-7317. The 34-story state capitol building dominates the skyline, and from the observation tower there's a panoramic view of the surrounding countryside and the mighty Mississippi River. In contrast, the Old State Capitol has the eccentric charm of the 19th century, when architects reached deep into the past for symbols to express the power of government.

The Louisiana Arts and Science Center offers a more intimate view of the river and port, along with paintings, sculpture, a country store, a 1918 steam engine, and an Egyptian

See N–S book,
sec. 24

55

24　　　　3　　　　52　　　　　　0　　0　　1　　　12　　　22

155B　　　　179　182　　　　234A
234C　235A　ROUTE
90B　235B　　247

10

mummy. One can also wander the riverfront in Catfish Town, where old warehouses have been converted into shops and restaurants.

179　Houmas House Plantation

4 mi./10 min. South on Rte. 44, right on Rte. 942; follow signs. This classic plantation home, with its 14 stately columns and its formal gardens enhanced by classical Greek sculpture, was built in 1840 in the Greek revival style. The mansion was restored a century later and has been the backdrop for many Hollywood epics. Here the atmosphere and elegance of the Old South live on within view of the Mississippi, the lifeline of the plantation system. Guides in period dress conduct tours of the house. *Open daily except Thanksgiving Day, Christmas, and New Year's Day. Admission charged.*

182　Oak Alley Plantation, Vacherie

18 mi./24 min. West on Rte. 70 over Sunshine Bridge, left at bottom of bridge onto service road, right on Rte. 18. Twenty-eight magnificent live oaks spread their branches to form a spectacular quarter-mile *allée* leading to a Greek revival-style mansion with two-story pillars and wide verandas, built in 1837–39 for a French sugar planter. The 250-year-old trees and the opulence of the mansion have made this the setting for movies and television shows. House tours are conducted by former servants of the last family to live here, and a bygone era comes to life with their anecdotes. *Open daily except Thanksgiving Day, Christmas, and New Year's Day. Admission charged.*

234A
234C　New Orleans, LA 70112
235A

Tourist & Convention Commission, 1520 Sugar Bowl Dr. (504) 566-5011. The music, food, architecture, history, and ambience make this one of America's most celebrated cities. Jackson Square in the heart of the French Quarter, the city's best-known area, is a good place to start a walking tour. On the square you'll see the beautiful St. Louis Cathedral and the superb wrought-iron balco-

234A/C–235A. *The stately symmetry of St. Louis Cathedral as seen from Jackson Square.*

nies of the Pontalba Apartments. The nearby French Market features outdoor cafés and eye-catching displays of produce. At night the sound of music—blues, ragtime, Cajun zydeco, country, and of course New Orleans jazz—emanates from clubs and bars that line the length of Bourbon Street. The St. Charles streetcar still clangs and rattles through the Garden District, an area of large live oaks and handsome antebellum houses that also rewards strolling. To get the feel of the Mississippi River, which loops dramatically around the city, try the free ferry or one of the cruises.

ROUTE
90B　Jean Lafitte National
　　　Historical Park, Barataria Unit
235B

17 mi./30 min. Rte. 90B exit (headed east): east across Greater New Orleans Bridge, southwest on Rte. 90 (business; West Bank Expy.), left on Rte. 45 (Barataria Blvd.). Exit 235B (headed west): proceed as above. Named for the noted Louisiana resident—and sometime pirate—who helped the American forces defeat the British at the battle of New

Orleans, this park preserves the Mississippi Delta's rich blend of early American history, French culture, and magnificent wildlife. The Barataria Unit, with some 8,600 acres of coastal wetlands, was settled by the first Native Americans around 300 B.C. Three different trails wind through this dense, misty jungle of hardwood forest, cypress swamp, and freshwater marsh that is shared by white-tailed deer, alligators, giant spiderwebs, and some 200 species of birds. The visitor center offers exhibits on hunting, trapping, and fishing. *Open daily except Christmas.*　🛆🚶♿

247　Jean Lafitte National Historical
　　　Park, Chalmette Unit

10 mi./20 min. South on Rte. 47, right on St. Bernard Hwy. (Rte. 46); follow signs. The battle of New Orleans, famed in song and story, erupted along this narrow Mississippi riverbank on a foggy Christmas Eve morning in 1814 and raged for 2 weeks. The 1½-mile driving tour along the battlefield follows the progress of the conflict in which Gen. Andrew Jackson's American forces fought to keep New Orleans from falling into British hands.

At the visitor center, exhibits, paintings, and a slide show depict scenes from the War of 1812, and in summer a guide in an 1812-style soldier's uniform tells about the action and demonstrates the use of a musket. A tall granite monument commemorates those who fell in battle. *Open year-round.*　🛆♿

247. *The lack of firepower in 1814 was compensated for in sartorial splendor.*

57. *Although they seem a world apart, the Gulf islands' fascinating vistas of sand and slash pines (and the occasional full moon) are but a short boat ride from the Mississippi mainland.*

267 / 1 Fontainebleau State Park

20 mi./30 min. Exit 267 (headed east): west on I-12 to Exit 74, left on Rte. 434, right on Rte. 190. Exit 1 (headed west): proceed as above. The open areas around Lake Pontchartrain combine with dense forest to give this area its unique character. In the park, once part of Bernard de Marigny de Mandeville's estate, Fontainebleau, are the crumbling brick ruins of a sugar mill, on which at least one of his many reputed fortunes was founded. The swimming pool and picnic shelters invite you to linger, and a nature trail through the oak forests introduces the area's local plant and animal life. *Open year-round.*

2 / 13 Buccaneer State Park

Exit 2: 15 mi./25 min. East on Rte. 607, right on Rte. 90; follow signs. Exit 13: 11 mi./20 min. South on Rte. 603, right on Beach Blvd. The park's name acknowledges the profession of Jean Lafitte and others who once terrorized this stretch of coast. Violence in another context is recalled by the Old Hickory Nature Trail, named for Andrew Jackson, who camped here and used it as a base during the battle of New Orleans. All is peace and quiet now on the wooded ridge and swampy lowlands where muskrats, rabbits, and aquatic birds play the leading roles. In another section of the park you'll find a wave pool, tennis courts, and another nature trail. Crowded on weekends in summer. *Open year-round. Admission charged.*

44 Beauvoir

8 mi./15 min. South on Rte. 15, right on Rte. 90. The gracious, magnolia-shaded home of Confederate President Jefferson Davis is one of a row of antebellum mansions on the Gulf Coast in Biloxi. It is a stately white Greek revival house flanked by two square pavilions. Davis moved into the house at the age of 69, and it was here that he wrote his famous treatise, *The Rise and Fall of the Confederate Government.* You will see his writing desk and pen in the library pavilion. The airy rooms are filled with rich tapestries, lace, and fine Mallard furniture from New Orleans; many pieces belonged to the Davis family. A museum of the family's personal effects is on the ground floor, and there's a Confederate Museum on the grounds. *Open year-round. Admission charged.*

57 Gulf Islands National Seashore, Mississippi District

5 mi./10 min. South on Rte. 57, right on Rte. 90. At the headquarters in Ocean Springs on Davis Bayou on the mainland, you'll get an informative introduction to the barrier islands that lie offshore here. Exhibits trace the region's history and display its flora and fauna. A 28-minute film provides a colorful view of the islands in a whirlwind tour, and the satellite and aerial photographs provide added perspective. The bayou winds through pinewood flats, which can be investigated on two short nature trails. Boat trips to West Ship Island are available in both Gulfport and Biloxi. *Open year-round.*

15A Bellingrath Gardens and Home

12 mi./15 min. West on Rte. 90, left on Bellingrath Rd. Floral exuberance and abundance characterize these 65 acres of gardens, created in the midst of a semitropical riverfront jungle. One of the first delights along the walking tour is the Oriental-American garden. Here a wooden teahouse sits between a carp stream and a placid lake, where swans glide against a backdrop of weeping Yoshima cherry trees. Near the imposing brick house are brilliant beds of perennials. The wheel-shaped rose garden is an inviting source of color and fragrance for 9 months of the year. In the fall the landscape here is brightened by one of the world's largest outdoor displays of chrysanthemums—some 80,000 plants. A conservatory houses orchids and other exotics.

Antique furnishings and objets d'art are displayed in the Walter D. Bellingrath home, and the nearby Boehm Gallery houses more than 230 of the famed Edward Marshall Boehm porcelain sculptures. *Open year-round. Admission charged for garden and home.*

26A Mobile, AL 36602

Chamber of Commerce, 451 Government St. (205) 433-6951. In this charming city one feels the essence of the Old South: the magnolias, live oaks, crape myrtles, camellias, and azaleas in abundance and scores of gracious antebellum houses. The five historic districts and adjacent neighborhoods constitute a veritable museum of architectural styles, from federal to late Victorian, including the Richards-D.A.R. House, embellished with ornate lace ironwork, and Oakleigh, a classic of southern Greek revival design. Other highlights are the City Museum and a reconstructed French fort. In Battleship U.S.S. *Alabama* Memorial Park, you can board the World War II battleship as well as a submarine and see a B-52 bomber and other aircraft of the era.

35 | Historic Blakeley State Park

6 mi./12 min. North on Rte. 98, right on Rte. 31, left on Rte. 225. Set on the Tensaw River, this wooded 3,800-acre park memorializes the last great battle of the Civil War, where fighting continued for hours on April 9, 1865, after General Lee had surrendered in Virginia. Self-guiding maps of the Blakeley park and battleground are available from the park ranger. One trail traverses woodlands atop well-preserved Confederate breastworks; near the beaver pond, a bucolic picnic and cane pole fishing spot, you can see the incongruously peaceful remains of a gun emplacement. In early April the park sponsors an annual reenactment of the South's bold last stand.

Another trail leads to the 1,000-year-old Jury Oak, which early 19th-century settlers from the now vanished town of Blakeley reportedly used as a courthouse. The judge sat in a fork among the lower branches, the defendant stood below, and if the verdict was guilty, the Hanging Tree was just a few steps away. Be warned: the dirt roads into and through the park can be quite rough. *Open daily except Christmas. Admission charged.*

53 | Styx River Water World

2 min. North on Wilcox Rd. It would be difficult for any child —and most adults—to resist the charms of this delightful aquatic playground. The park features a swinging rope bridge that leads to the Tarzan ride, where would-be ape-men can swing from a rope and drop into the pool below. There are high-speed water slides, an inner-tube rapids ride,

and a small lake with separate areas for bumper boats, paddleboats, and miniature speedboats. For quieter enjoyment, try a 2-hour trip down the sandy Styx River on an inner tube; a bus takes tubers upstream to float back to the park. Tots will enjoy the kiddies' pool, a dinosaur trampoline, climbing equipment, and every hour two animated shows: one of a rock band and the other of a western band. A frog and a pelican wander through the park and greet visitors. *Open daily June–Labor Day; weekends Apr.–May. Admission charged.*

4 | Gulf Islands National Seashore, Florida Section

22 mi./30 min. South on Rte. 110, left on Rte. 98, right on Rte. 399; follow signs. The two most popular areas, both on Santa Rosa Island, are Ft. Pickens, built between 1829 and 1834 to protect the Gulf Coast from invaders, and

4. *A great blue heron strides confidently into the surf in search of a meal of fresh fish.*

the Santa Rosa Area, where the warm, clear waters of the Gulf are bordered by an idyllic sandy beach that stretches for miles.

During the Civil War Ft. Pickens was occupied by Union forces, and from 1886 to 1888 a group of Chiricahua Apaches, including the famous Geronimo, was imprisoned here.

Visitors can enjoy swimming and picnicking at both areas. Lifeguards are on duty in the summer. Scuba diving is popular in the mild waters, and schools of brightly colored fish are visible even to the cautious wader. *Open year-round.*

10 11 | Blackwater River State Park

Exit 10: 7 mi./10 min. North on Rte. 87, left on Rte. 90; follow signs. Exit 11: 12 mi./15 min. North on Rte. 189, right on Rte. 90; follow signs. This rustic park has the ambience of a Huck Finn adventure, with schoolboys practicing daredevil dives from an old bridge, fishermen dropping lines from another, and troops of raccoons, sheltered by the sandy woodlands, cautiously creeping to the edge of the river to catch fish.

The slow-moving waters and wide sandy banks, with picnic tables nearby, entice both sunbathers and swimmers. A nature trail rambles along the swamps to a chain of small lakes. One of several bridges in the park leads to the campground. *Open year-round. Admission charged.*

12 | Sasquatch Canoe Rentals

7 mi./10 min. North on Rte. 85, left on Rte. 90. Canoeing here on the Shoal River, a shallow stream with many wide sandbars that invite swimmers and picnickers, offers a quiet, relaxing outing past chalky cliffs and dense stands of oaks and cypresses. Trips vary from 4 hours to a full day or even overnight. In addition to canoes, other related equipment is available.

Although named for the elusive manlike creature whose wanderings have been reported in this area, Sasquatch Canoe Rentals has heard of no such sightings by any of their customers. *Open Apr.–Nov., river level permitting. For reservations call (904) 682-3949.*

13 Fred Gannon Rocky Bayou State Recreation Area

20 mi./30 min. South on Rte. 285, left on Rte. 20; follow signs. Tall pines shelter the sandy shore along the southern edge of Rocky Bayou, a narrow finger of salt water stretching up from the Choctawhatchee Bay of the Gulf of Mexico. Boating is especially popular here, and there are several nature trails, including one through the sand pine forest, a wooded area for which the park is noted. At man-made Puddin Head Lake you may be able to see alligators seeking their prey in the brackish water. The campsites are set along the bayou, where the sunsets are truly spectacular. *Open year-round.*

15 Ponce de Leon Springs State Recreation Area

3 mi./10 min. North on Rte. 81, right on Rte. 90, right on Rte. 181A; follow signs. Although they are not the Fountain of Youth, legend suggests the springs' name stems from the refreshing quality of their clear, cool waters. These springs have two boils whose flow keeps the water at 68° F year-round. First enjoyed by the Smithgall family, who bought the property in 1925 and created a parklike setting here, the springs today have Spanish-style bathhouses and sunning platforms. Their waters flow into Sandy Creek, where fishermen cast for chain pickerel and largemouth bass. *Open year-round.*

18 Falling Waters State Recreation Area

10 mi./15 min. South on Rte. 77; follow signs. Sheltered by a forest of white oaks, American beeches, and southern magnolias, the park contains several geological sinks. Over the years acids in rainwater slowly dissolve the underlying limestone and create these interesting depressions on the surface. Falling Waters Sink, the most unusual of those found here, is named for the gentle, sparkling waterfall that drops for 100 feet down straight, smooth, fern-fringed walls. Timbers from a gristmill that once stood here can be seen at the bottom. Campsites and a man-made lake round out the attractions. *Open year-round.*

20–21. *An unpredictable flow of mineral-laden waters produced these amazing shapes.*

20 21 Florida Caverns State Park

Exit 20: 10.5 mi./12 min. North on Rte. 167 through Marianna; follow signs. Exit 21: 7.5 mi./10 min. North on Rte. 71, left on Rte. 90 to Marianna, right on Rte. 167; follow signs. A long stairway here leads you to an extraordinary underground world where stalactites, stalagmites, sodastraws, rimstone, columns, flowstone, and draperies are commonplace. The last-named, stone stretched as thin as fabric and beautifully translucent, are the most amazing. The mineral-laden water that over the ages formed the limestone caves is still oozing and dripping, slowly and imperceptibly changing the intricate structure. Water that collects in pools clearly reflects the surroundings. At 65 feet underground, you will feel the impact of total darkness when the guide turns off the light. Aboveground you can enjoy the nature trails and a spring-fed swimming hole. *Open year-round. Admission charged.*

24 Torreya State Park

16 mi./20 min. North on Rte. 270 toward Chattahoochee, left on Rte. 269; follow signs. Taking its name from the rare and endangered torreya tree, which originally grew only along the Apalachicola River, the park combines the charm of a southern plantation house with a wooded setting laced with inviting hiking trails through the steep and wooded ravines.

Gregory House, a typical planter's home in the Greek revival style, sits on the high bluffs overlooking the Apalachicola. In the 1930's it was moved to this site from an old cotton plantation across the river. *Open year-round. Admission charged.*

29 Tallahassee, FL 32302

Chamber of Commerce, 100 N. Duval St. (904) 224-8116. The historic Old Capitol, built in the 1840's, is now a museum furnished in late 19th-century style. It houses an extensive collection of Florida artifacts. The new capitol, dedicated in 1978, stands nearby. The Museum of Florida History contains wide-ranging exhibits related to the era when mastodons roamed through this area, the days of the Spanish explorers, the Civil War, and the 20th century. Of particular interest to children is the Tallahassee Junior Museum, a 52-acre attraction featuring historic buildings, several trails, and native wildlife in natural habitats.

30 Alfred B. Maclay State Gardens, Tallahassee

5 min. North on Rte. 319. Wide brick pathways flanked by magnolias, dogwoods, crape myrtles, and torreya trees lead through a stunning world of dazzling color and richly textured foliage. Formal flower beds, reflecting pools, and sparkling fountains enhance the lavishly furnished former residence of the Alfred B. Maclay family. Few flowers bloom here year-round, but the colorful azaleas in February and March and the lovely camellias from November through April are the real glory of the gardens. *Open year-round. Admission charged.*

30 Pebble Hill Plantation

24 mi./30 min. North on Rte. 319. The elegant mansion—with its spacious lawns, gardens, tennis court, swimming pool, stables, carriage house, cow barn, and dairy—bespeaks a way of life enjoyed by a privileged few. It was the winter home of a wealthy Cleveland family and was bequeathed to a private trust.

The owner's interest in the hunt is apparent in paintings, carvings, and sculptures of hors-

es and hounds. Collections of silver, crystal, shells, and Indian relics, along with antiques, reflect the family's discerning taste. *Open Tues.–Sun. Oct.–Aug. Admission charged. Children under 12 not admitted.* 🛉

38 39 Suwannee River State Park

Exit 38: 10 mi./13 min. North on Rte. 255 to Lee, right on Rte. 90. Exit 39: 5 min. West on Rte. 90. The haunting echoes of steamboat whistles resounding from the banks of the Suwannee and the Withlacoochee have long since faded. But the rivers, as seen from the rustic overlook in this park, can still stir the imagination. Here, too, are some Civil War earthworks, grim reminders of that tragic conflict. Interesting plants and landforms can be seen on two trails, one going through the hardwood hammock and the other traversing a sparse pine forest. *Open year-round. Admission charged.* 🛉 ⛺ 🚐 🚶 🎣 ♿

43 Stephen Foster State Folk Culture Center

12 mi./15 min. North on Rte. 41 through White Springs; follow signs. The familiar strains of "Old Folks at Home," "Oh, Susanna," and other Stephen Foster melodies ring out from the carillon tower. While listening, the visitor can peruse the composer's handwritten manuscripts and scores, see a piano he composed on, and admire the instruments and costumes of the minstrel bands that played such an important role in popularizing his music—all on display on the mezzanine of the carillon tower.

In the visitor center elaborately ingenious mechanized dioramas depict the themes of his most famous songs: horses run in the "Camptown Races," steamboats ply the Suwannee River, and cowboys gather around to hear "Oh, Susanna." Traditional crafts are represented by Seminole Indian baskets, Cuban cigars, and artifacts from local turpentine camps. Headphones bring you the music of the region, played on banjos and by steel bands and a Latin dance band. *Open year-round. Admission charged.* 🛉 ♿

45 Olustee Battlefield State Historic Site

8 mi./10 min. West on Rte. 90. In these flat pinewoods Confederate and Union soldiers met on February 20, 1864, in one of the bloodiest battles of the the Civil War. The fierce struggle for an important communications link and supply route raged relentlessly for some 5 hours. When the Union soldiers finally retreated into the woods, they left behind 1,861 dead; the Confederates lost 946 men in the battle. At the interpretive center you can observe a fascinating exposition of this historic and deadly confrontation, and from an observation platform you can look out over the battlefield as you listen to a poignant taped account read by an "eyewitness." *Open year-round. Admission charged.* 🛉

I-95 Jacksonville, FL 32202

Convention & Visitors Bureau, 33 S. Hogan St. (904) 353-9736. The bend in the St. John's River here has been a crossing place and focal point since prehistoric times. Today you can enjoy the river from either side: Jacksonville Landing, on the north side, offers stores, markets, and restaurants, Riverwalk, on the opposite side, features restaurants, entertainment, and a boardwalk more than a mile long. Elephant rides and a Safari train are attractions at the Jacksonville Zoological Park. The Cummer Gallery of Art, the Jacksonville Museum of Arts and Sciences, the Jacksonville Art Museum, the Jacksonville Fire Museum, and the Lightner Museum provide an abundance of artistic, scientific, and historical riches.

38–39. *Lush growth along the banks, the mysterious play of light and shadow, and the sound of its name all contribute to the charm of the Suwannee River, famed in song and story.*

I-95. *The waterscape here at Riverwalk is as attractive by day as it is by night.*

ROUTE 209 — Cabrillo National Monument

10 mi./20 min. South on Rte. 209; follow signs. Juan Rodríguez Cabrillo was the first European to explore this section of the Pacific Coast, and it was this windswept finger of land that greeted him when he sailed into the harbor here. Today, at this park named in his honor, he wouldn't recognize the view to the east: a panorama of ocean freighters against a backdrop of San Diego's white skyscrapers. But to the west is the vast unchanged Pacific, where whale watching is now popular from late December to mid-March. Exhibits in the visitor center concentrate on the peninsula's history and natural features, local Indian artifacts, and Spanish explorers. There is also a restored lighthouse; and a 2-mile round-trip nature trail, edged by chaparral, runs alongside the harbor. *Open year-round.*

ROUTE 163 — San Diego Zoo

5 mi./10 min. South on Rte. 163 to Park Blvd. exit; follow signs. With a population of 3,200, representing some 800 species from around the world, this outstanding 100-acre zoo is a veritable United Nations of the animal kingdom. If you have enough time, take the 40-minute guided bus tour for orientation, then return to your favorite exhibits on foot or via outdoor escalators and moving walkways. You will see Australian koalas, highland gorillas, miniature deer, giant anteaters, Mongolian wild horses, and the world's largest collection of parrots and parrotlike birds. The children's zoo is scaled to four-year-olds and features a nursery where baby mammals are bottle-fed, bathed, and diapered. There are elephant and camel rides, animal shows, an overhead Skyfari, "behind the scenes" group tours, and special facilities for the disabled. *Open year-round. Admission charged.*

MG — Mission Basilica San Diego de Alcala

Mission Gorge Rd. exit: 4 mi./12 min. North on Mission Gorge Rd., left on Twain Ave. Known as the Mother of Missions, this was the first of the early California missions and was built by Father Junípero Serra in 1769. The mission's tall white walls enclose an inner sanctuary of gardens and candle-lit shrines. A *campanario* with bells in its arches stands guard at the church's main entrance. Inside, the decor is surprisingly simple: a red tile floor, a flat ceiling, and a rough-hewn wooden altar. The cavelike rooms where the friars lived are equally stark, but the religious vestments and vessels on display are richly ornate. Other exhibits detail the mission's history and, amid the hibiscus and other tropical plants, give color to the main courtyard. In the mission garden there is a wishing well reputed to bring answers to prayers. *Open year-round. Admission charged.*

MG. *These were the humble quarters of the Franciscan friar Father Junípero Serra.*

ROUTE 79 — Cuyamaca Rancho State Park

8 mi./15 min. North on Rte. 79. With its rugged oak and evergreen forests, boulder-strewn streams, and stretches of grassy meadows, this spacious mountain park offers a surprising change of pace from the surrounding desert. More than half of the 25,000 acres are a wilderness area that can be explored on trails following the cascading Sweetwater River or leading to the top of Cuyamaca Peak and to other summits. The area's unusual beauty can also be enjoyed from numerous lookouts and roadside picnic areas and two campgrounds. A museum displays artifacts left by Indians and gold miners. Adjacent to the park's north end, Cuyamaca Lake, set in an inviting green basin, has a wooded island, a long white fishing pier, and shoreside trails. *Open year-round. Admission charged.*

ROUTE S2 — Anza-Borrego Desert State Park

18 mi./28 min. North on Rte. S2. In this setting of arid beauty, striking rock formations and hidden canyons punctuate spacious stretches of open desert land, and the forbidding brown peaks of the Superstition Mountains darken the horizon. Five hundred miles of primitive dirt roads crisscross the 600,000-acre park, and primitive camping is permitted in most areas. At Bow Willow campground there are wooden shelters at campsites and well-marked trails leading into the nearby rocky arroyos. Farther north along Highway S2, Agua Caliente County Park, with its hot springs, is an oasis of trees and flowers. The campground offers an enclosed mineral-water pool as well as an outdoor swimming pool. There are equestrian trails throughout the park. *Open year-round.*

IKP — Desert View Tower

In-Ko-Pah exit. Headed east: 5 mi./7 min. Left on Old Hwy. 80. Headed west: 5 mi./7 min. Right on Old Hwy. 80. This tall round tower of fitted stone, built in 1922 by a local businessman to honor the pioneers, is now a registered historic landmark that houses a museum of desert Americana. Exhibits in the four-story structure include Indian masks, Navajo blankets, and paintings of cowboys. Antique china and beaded dresses are among the items for sale in the first-floor shop. From the observation tower, where you can see for 110 miles on a clear day, there's a spectacular view of the Coyote Mountains. Outside is a garden of rocks from around the world. Don't miss the animal caves, with a bulbous frog, an alligator family, a raven's head, and a buffalo carved from the stone in the caverns. *Open year-round. Admission charged.*

CA | AZ

See E–W book, sec. 49.

100

76

10

GIS

102

178 End I-8

ROUTE 111   Mexicali, Mexico

10 mi./21 min. South on Rte. 111 and cross border by car. Or south on Rte. 111, left on 1st St. to parking lot in Calexico and cross border on foot. The Mexican border towns offer the most immediate contrast between one culture and another, and this one is no exception. Avoid a long wait at customs by parking in Calexico and crossing the border on foot. The arcades are lined with shops selling sombreros, woven wool blankets and rugs, huaraches, embroidered clothing, pottery, and all manner of souvenirs and trinkets. In the open-air produce market 7 blocks south on Calle Mexico, you can get a step closer to the real Mexico and see colorful mounds of fresh fruit, peppers, and other vegetables invitingly displayed for the local populace.

GIS   Quechan Indian Reservation, Yuma

Giss Pkwy. exit: 5 min. West on Giss Pkwy., right on Gila St., right on 1st St., right on Indian Hill Rd. This cluster of tile-roofed buildings overlooking an ancient Colorado River crossing is one of the area's oldest settlements. And it is a study in contrasts. A white Spanish mission church with a single-scalloped bell tower has a flower-filled garden with palm-shaded benches and tile birdbaths. Next door is an Indian cultural center made of rough-hewn logs and painted with bright animal designs. A former frontier military post, Ft. Yuma, houses an Indian museum, with exhibits of Quechan baskets and pottery as well as displays on the fort and the missionary era. A reconstructed Quechan adobe house is in the yard. *Open Mon.–Fri. except holidays. Admission charged.*

GIS   Yuma Territorial Prison State Historic Park

Giss Pkwy. exit: 5 min. Headed east: east on Giss Pkwy., left on Prison Hill Rd. Headed west: west on Giss Pkwy., right on Prison Hill Rd. Photographs and case histories of 15-year-old thieves, female murderers, Indians victimized by the white man's whiskey, and others imprisoned here between 1876 and 1909 reveal the scope of crime in the Arizona Territory. Despite its thick caliche walls, iron bars, and 6- by 10-foot cells, the prison was not a hellhole. It was a model institution for its time, where prisoners learned to read and write (one of the area's first public libraries was built here) and produced crafts, such as the delicate lacework, leather goods, and horsehair ropes on display. *Open daily except Christmas. Admission charged.*

GIS   Yuma, AZ 85364

Giss Pkwy. exit. Chamber of Commerce, 377 S. Main St. (602) 782-2567. Chances are you won't be caught in a rainstorm in Yuma, one of the sunniest and least humid places in the country. When you have had all the sun you need, there are a number of inviting indoor places to visit. The Century House Museum, the former home of a pioneer businessman, has exhibits on the early Arizona Territory as well as gardens and exotic birds. Both traditional and present-day art can be seen at the Yuma Art Center, located in a restored railroad depot. You can enjoy the historic Colorado River by taking a boat tour (2 hours) or a train ride (2½ hours) along the river.

102   Painted Rock State Historical Park

15 mi./30 min. North on Painted Rock Rd. Arid stretches of white sand desert surround a mound of black basalt boulders carved with 1,000-year-old petroglyphs of animals, birds, people, and geometric designs. You can climb to the top, where the workings can be seen close up. In pioneer times the rocks were important as a landmark for travelers through the desert, including those who followed the Mormon Battalion Trail, which went by here around 1846. *Open year-round. Admission charged.*

178   Casa Grande Ruins National Monument

24 mi./30 min. West on I-10 to Exit 185, east on Rte. 387, right on Rte. 87. The purpose of this towering, symmetrical, ocher-colored building is as mysterious as the fate of pre-Columbian Hohokam Indians who built it some 650 years ago. Named by a Spanish explorer in the 17th century, it is distinguished by inwardly sloping earth walls. They dominate the remains of a 2-acre compound that once contained more than 60 rooms, a ball court, and segments of a 600-mile network of irrigation canals. Fragments of pottery, cloth, and copper bells in the visitor center provide tantalizing glimpses into the lives of the vanished Hohokams. *Open year-round. Admission charged.*

S2. *Surrealistic scene of cholla and rocks beautifully backlit on a morning in May.*

Picture credits

The numbers in **bold type** below refer to the section numbers at the bottom of each page. The positions of the photographs for each section are indicated thus: (l) left, (m) middle, (r) right, (t) top, (b) bottom.

Cover Robert Frerck/Odyssey Productions, Chicago. **Back cover** (tl) Clayton Wolt; (tr) J. Nettis/H. Armstrong Roberts; (bl) Arnout Hyde, Jr.; (bm) Eric Carle/Shostal Associates; (br) © David Muench Photography 1988.

North–South Book

Introduction Jay Maisel. **1** (l) © Pat O'Hara; (m) Randy Wells; (r) © David Muench Photography 1988. **2** (l) Ron Kimball/Wildlife Safari; (m) Michael Dunn; (r) R. Krubner/H. Armstrong Roberts. **3** (l) John F. Reginato/Shasta-Cascade Wonderland Association; (m) Audrey Gibson; (r) E. Cooper/H. Armstrong Roberts. **4** (l) Alan Pitcairn/Grant Heilman Photography; (m) W. Talarowski/H. Armstrong Roberts; (r) © David Muench Photography 1988. **5** (l) © David Muench Photography 1988; (r) David Hiser/Photographers Aspen. **6** (tl) Tom and Pat Leeson; (bl) Jeff Gnass; (r) Rickers Film Productions. **7** (l) E. Cooper/H. Armstrong Roberts; (tr) © David Muench Photography 1988; (br) Royce L. Bair/The Stock Solution. **8** (l) © David Muench Photography 1988; (r) Manley Photo/Shostal Associates. **9** (l) Kent and Donna Dannen; (r) Lee Foster. **10** (l) Wyoming Travel Commission; (r) Jeff Gnass. **11** (tl) A. Bilsten/H. Armstrong Roberts; (bl) © David Muench Photography 1988; (tr) R. Krubner/H. Armstrong Roberts; (br) Eduardo Fuss. **12** (l) Eduardo Fuss; (r) Willard Clay. **13** (l) Clayton Wolt; (r) South Dakota Tourism. **14** Paul Horsted/South Dakota Tourism. **15** (l) Audrey Gibson; (r) Bob Glander/Shostal Associates. **16** (l) R. Hamilton Smith; (r) Positive Reflections. **17** (l) Iowa Department of Natural Resources; (r) Mike Whye. **18** (l) Mark E. Gibson; (m) Positive Reflections; (r) Bob Taylor. **19** (l) Positive Reflections; (r) Richard Stockton/The Stockhouse. **20** (l) Bob Daemmrich/Light Images; (tr) Kent and Donna Dannen; (br) Lee Foster. **21** (tl) Ken Dequaine; (m) George R. Cassidy/Third Coast; (br) Willard Clay; (tr) Ray F. Hillstrom/Hillstrom Stock Photo. **22** (l) James P. Rowan/Hillstrom Stock Photo; (m) Mark E. Gibson; (r) Frank Oberle/Six Flags Over Mid-America. **23** (l) Ken Dequaine; (r) Robert Jordan/The University of Mississippi. **24** (l) Florewood River Plantation; (tr) Don Warren; (br) Garry D. McMichael/Southern Images. **25** Greg Laun/Hillstrom Stock Photo. **26** (l) Charles Westerfield; (tr) William Strode; (br) Charles Westerfield. **27** (l) Ed Malles/Photo Options; (r) Raymond G. Barnes:Click/Chicago. **28** (t) Mark E. Gibson; (b) Grant Heilman/Grant Heilman Photography. **29** Positive Reflections. **30** (l) Ken Dequaine; (r) Larry West. **31** (l) Positive Reflections; (r) Joseph P. Messana. **32** (l) © David Muench Photography 1988; (r) Thomas Peters Lake. **33** Tourist Division, Georgia Department of Industry and Trade. **34** (l) Florida Division of Tourism; (m) Jungle Larry's Safari Park, Naples, FL; (r) M. Landre/H. Armstrong Roberts. **35** (tl) Elsie Ziegler; (bl) Mark E. Gibson; (r) Wolfgang Weber. **36** (tl) B. Cory Kilvert, Jr.; (bl, r) Arnout Hyde, Jr. **37** (l) Bruce Roberts; (r) © David Muench Photography 1988. **38** (l) H. Edelman/View Finder; (r) Arnout Hyde, Jr. **39** (l) The 1890 House Museum and Center for the Arts; (r) Zmiejko Photographics/Hillstrom Stock Photo. **40** (l) © David Muench Photography 1988; (r) M. Woodbridge Williams. **41** (l) © David Muench Photography 1988; (r) Ken Dequaine. **42** (l) Olana State Historic Site/Friends of Olana, Inc.; (r) Guy Gillette. **43** (l) Thomas Ames, Jr.: f/Stop Pictures; (m) James A. McInnis; (r) Fred M. Dole: f/Stop Pictures. **44** (tl, bl) John R. Wells; (r) © 1988 Joseph St. Pierre. **45** (l) John R. Wells; (tr, br) © David Muench Photography 1988. **46** (l) B. Cory Kilvert, Jr.; (tr) Eric Carle/Shostal Associates; (br) Clyde H. Smith. **47** (l) Eric Carle/Shostal Associates; (r) J. Nettis/H. Armstrong Roberts. **48** (l) G. Ahrens/H. Armstrong Roberts; (r) W. Bertsch/H. Armstrong Roberts. **49** (l) B. Cory Kilvert, Jr.; (r) Jack Dermid. **50** (l) Max and Bea Hunn/Shostal Associates; (r) W. Bertsch/H. Armstrong Roberts. **51** (l) Luis Casteñeda/The Image Bank; (r) Dave Forbert/Shostal Associates.

Center Portfolio

Top row: (l to r) © David Muench Photography 1988; Ray F. Hillstrom/Hillstrom Stock Photo; Positive Reflections; © David Muench Photography 1988; W. Bertsch/H. Armstrong Roberts; Mark E. Gibson; Larry Burton; Tourist Division, Georgia Department of Industry and Trade. **Second row:** D. Muench/H. Armstrong Roberts; Mark E. Gibson; Thomas Peters Lake; © David Muench Photography 1988; © David Muench Photography 1988; Ron Kimball/Wildlife Safari; Lee Foster; Arnout Hyde, Jr. **Third row:** Jackson Hill; Kent and Donna Dannen; Positive Reflections; © David Muench Photography 1988; Olana State Historic Site/Friends of Olana, Inc.; Kent and Donna Dannen; Garry D. McMichael/Southern Images; Larry and Jan Aiuppy. **Bottom row:** Jeff Gnass; Eduardo Fuss; Larry West; © David Muench Photography 1988; George R. Cassidy/Third Coast; John R. Wells; Jeff Gnass; Jack Dermid.

East–West Book

Introduction Jay Maisel. **1** Ray Atkeson. **2** (l) Larry and Jan Aiuppy; (r) Jeff Gnass. **3** (l) © David Muench Photography 1988; (r) Mark E. Gibson. **4** (l) © David Muench Photography 1988; (m) Jeff Gnass; (r) Positive Reflections. **5** (l) © David Muench Photography 1988; (r) Ken Dequaine. **6** (l) James P. Rowan: Click/Chicago; (r) Joseph Jacobson/Journalism Services. **7** (l) Indiana State Parks Department of Natural Resources; (tr) Wolfgang Weber; (br) Jim Schafer/View Finder. **8** (l) Zefa/H. Armstrong Roberts; (bl, r) Doris Gehrig Barker. **9** (l) Naoki Okamoto; (r) Mark E. Gibson. **10** (l) Montana Travel Promotion; (r) © David Muench Photography 1988. **11** (l) Clayton Wolt; (r) Wilford L. Miller. **12** Positive Reflections. **13** (l) R. Krubner/H. Armstrong Roberts; (r) William Meyer/Third Coast. **14** (l) Dave Gustafson/Kalamazoo Aviation History Museum; (r) Lee Foster. **15** (l, bl) © David Muench Photography 1988; (tr) D. C. Lowe; (br) Lynda Hatch/Ric Ergenbright Photography. **16** (l) © David Muench Photography 1988; (r) Kent and Donna Dannen. **17** (l) D. C. Lowe/Shostal Associates; (r) Joseph Beckner/Amwest. **18** D. Muench/H. Armstrong Roberts; (tr) Ravell Call/Hillstrom Stock Photo; (br) G. Ahrens/H. Armstrong Roberts. **19** (l) Jeff Gnass; (r) Kent and Donna Dannen. **20** (l) Kent and Donna Dannen; (r) Nebraska Game and Parks Commission. **21** (l) Mike Whye; (r) Tom Bean. **22** Positive Reflections. **23** (l) Ray F. Hillstrom/Hillstrom Stock Photo; (m) Bill Thomas; (r) Ruth Chin. **24** (l) Mark E. Gibson; (r) Carl Lindquist/View Finder. **25** E. R. Degginger. **26** (tl) Kent and Donna Dannen; (bl) © David Muench Photography 1988; (r) Larry Burton. **27** (l) Todd Powell; (r) Kent and Donna Dannen. **28** (l, tr) Dick Herpich; (br) Daniel Dancer. **29** (l) Jack Zehrt; (r) Bets Anderson Bailly/Unicorn Stock Photos. **30** (l) Ken Dequaine/Third Coast; (r) Audrey Gibson. **31** (l) Larry Hamill; (r) Arnout Hyde, Jr. **32** (l) Steve Solum/West Stock; (r) Shostal Associates. **33** (l) Thomas Peters Lake; (r) Patrick L. Pfister. **34** (l) Charles Westerfield; (r) Arnout Hyde, Jr. **35** © David Muench Photography 1988. **36** (l) © David Muench Photography 1988; (r) Eduardo Fuss. **37** (l) Willard Clay; (r) M. Schneiders/H. Armstrong Roberts. **38** Positive Reflections. **39** (l) Positive Reflections; (tr) Mark E. Gibson; (br) E. Cooper/H. Armstrong Roberts. **40** (l) Matt Bradley; (r) R. Krubner/H. Armstrong Roberts. **41** (l) John Netherton; (r) Chip Henderson. **42** (l) James P. Valentine; (br) Don C. Olive; (tr) Jack Dermid. **43** (l) © David Muench Photography 1988; (br) Scott Berner/The Stockhouse, Inc.; (tr) Laurence E. Parent. **44** Kent and Donna Dannen; (r) Mark E. Gibson. **45** (l) Louisiana Purchase Gardens and Zoo; (r) © David Muench Photography 1988. **46** (l) Ed Malles/Photo Options; (r) Aerial Photography Services. **47** (l) Ken Dequaine; (r) Danny C. Booker. **48** (l) Richard B. Spencer/Shostal Associates; (r) Mark E. Gibson. **49** (l) Tom Bean; (r) © David Muench Photography 1988. **50** (l) Willard Clay; (r) © David Muench Photography 1988. **51** (l) Todd Powell; (m) Eduardo Fuss; (r) John Ward/Unicorn Stock Photos. **52** (l) © David Muench Photography 1988; (m) Mark E. Gibson; (r) © David Muench Photography 1988. **53** (l) Thomas Peters Lake; (tr) Philip Gould; (br) Jackson Hill. **54** Connie Toops. **55** (l) Florida Caverns State Park; (m) Don C. Olive; (r) W. Bertsch/H. Armstrong Roberts. **56** (l) Mark E. Gibson; (r) Jeff Gnass.

Credits and acknowledgments

The editors gratefully acknowledge the assistance of the many individuals, chambers of commerce, tourist bureaus, and state and local park, highway, and police departments that helped make this book possible.

Driver-reporters (and the routes they drove)

Gregory Archbald (I-5, I-80), Thomas Barr (I-5, I-15, I-25, I-80, I-84, I-90), Noreen Church (I-5, I-15), Kent and Donna Dannen (I-15, I-25, I-70), Jon and Jane Farber (I-40), Don Earnest (I-25), Cory Kilvert (I-20, I-26, I-40, I-64, I-70, I-75, I-77, I-81, I-87, I-90, I-91, I-93, I-95), Robert Lancaster (I-20, I-35, I-55), Norman Mack (I-35), Susan Macovsky (I-25), George Marsden (I-40, I-57, I-64, I-65, I-69, I-70, I-75, I-77, I-79, I-90), Richard Marshall (I-25, I-29, I-35, I-43, I-55, I-69, I-70, I-75, I-80, I-90, I-94), Barbara Roether (I-5, I-8, I-10, I-20, I-55, I-65).

Library of Congress Cataloging in Publication Data

On the road, U.S.A.

  At head of title: Reader's digest.
  Includes index.
  1. United States—Description and travel—1981–
—Guide-books. I. Calkins, Carroll C. II. Reader's
Digest Association. III. Reader's digest.
E158.044 1989   917.3'04927   88-31763
ISBN 0-89577-323-6

Index

The letter **N** in **bold type** preceding a section number indicates the North–South book at the beginning of this volume; **E** indicates the East–West book, the second half of this volume.